HERITAGE OF MUSIC

VOLUME IV

MUSIC IN THE TWENTIETH CENTURY

HERITAGE OF MUSIC

EDITED BY
MICHAEL RAEBURN AND ALAN KENDALL

VOLUME IV
MUSIC IN THE TWENTIETH CENTURY

CONSULTANT EDITORS
FELIX APRAHAMIAN
AND WILFRID MELLERS

OXFORD NEW YORK
OXFORD UNIVERSITY PRESS
1989

Oxford University Press, Walton Street, Oxford OX2 6DP
Oxford New York Toronto
Delhi Bombay Calcutta Madras Karachi
Petaling Jaya Singapore Hong Kong Tokyo
Nairobi Dar es Salaam Cape Town
Melbourne Auckland
and associated companies in
Berlin Ibadan

Oxford is a trade mark of Oxford University Press

Published in the United States
by Oxford University Press

British Library Cataloguing in Publication Data
Heritage of music.
1. Music—History and criticism I. Raeburn, Michael, 1940- .II. Kendall, Alan, 1939-
780'.903 ML193
ISBN 0–19–520493–X (set)
0–19–505373–7 (vol.4)

Library of Congress Cataloguing in Publication Data
Main entry under title:
Heritage of music.
Includes index.
Contents: 1. Classical music and its origins — 2. Romantic music — 3. Legacy of nineteenth-century music — [etc.]
1. Music—History and criticism. I. Raeburn, Michael, 1940- . II. Kendall, Alan, 1939-
ML160.H527 1988 780'.9 85-21429
ISBN 0–19–520493–X (set)
0–19–505373–7 (vol.4)

Title-page illustration: Natalia Goncharova, Design for Stravinsky's *Les Noces*, 1922.

Produced by Heritage of Music Ltd
Design and art direction: David Warner
Picture research: Julia Engelhardt, Charlotte Mosley
Artwork: Roy Coombs
Color origination: Scala, Florence

Printed in Hong Kong

CONTENTS

PAUL
COLIN

MUSIC OF THE NEW CENTURY

FELIX APRAHAMIAN

Opposite: The violin in *L'Orchestre en liberté.* The ballet, with music by Henri Sauveplaine, had its première at the Paris Opéra on 16 February 1931. This dynamic costume design by Paul Colin was for the character danced by Serge Lifar.

Just as Beethoven's music had a colossal influence on composers of the generation which followed him, so musicians around the turn of the next century were overwhelmed by the example of Wagner. And it was not only musicians who felt this influence. Baudelaire had, at the beginning of the 1860s, been one of the first in France to recognize Wagner's importance; Mallarmé later became an uneasy admirer, and the plays of Maeterlinck are almost Wagnerian operas without the music: Debussy and Dukas were to respond to them as such in their operatic settings of *Pelléas et Mélisande* and *Ariane et Barbebleue* respectively. Debussy and Dukas were among the very many composers who succumbed to the spell of Wagner's music in their twenties, even to the extent that their own styles were momentarily engulfed by his. A visit to Bayreuth became part of a young composer's education: Chausson went there in 1882, the year of the first *Parsifal*, followed by Debussy in 1888 and 1889, Sibelius in 1894, Bartók in 1904 and Stravinsky, no less, in 1912. Naturally there was some spirit of pilgrimage in these journeyings, but there was practical necessity too, for the *Ring* was rarely staged anywhere else at this period, and Bayreuth guarded a monopoly on *Parsifal*, broken only by a couple of American productions, until 1913.

The reasons why Wagner was regarded so highly are complex. In part, as Baudelaire realized, the peculiar fascination of the music dramas lay in their presentation of mythological situations, carrying implicitly the suggestion that they are universal models of human behavior and emotion, not studies of particular cases. Then again, Wagner's conjoining of every artistic resource – music, drama, architecture, scene-painting – had a powerful appeal at the end of a century, when artists' visions had become increasingly grandiose: in this respect the ultimate Wagnerian ambition would be represented by Skriabin's 'mystery,' a mercifully unaccomplished ceremony of music, poetry, color and perfume that the deranged composer imagined might end with the destruction of the world. On a more restrained level, the influence of Wagner on musicians was obviously quickened by his achievements in orchestration (the brass-heavy, doom-laden sound of Siegfried's funeral music, but also the luminosity of the middle act of *Siegfried* and of *Parsifal*), his use of distinctive themes over a vast time-span and his rich harmony, which makes those vast time-spans possible by forever frustrating and complicating the music's urge to resolve. Length is indeed central to the Wagnerian phenomenon. Simply because the works last so long, they begin to envelop the spectator, to draw him into their world; otherwise they could not be the subject of such adulation. On the other hand, such length not only depends on Wagner's control of motif and harmony but also almost requires his style of drama, with the weight of myth to match the extension of duration.

Only the most ill-advised of Wagnerian adepts, however, attempted to emulate him by creating operas on a similar scale: the forgotten *Fervaal* (1889-93) of d'Indy and unhappy *Le Roi Arthus* (1886-95) of Chausson are among the more noble of such failures. As Debussy was to recognize, Wagner was 'a beautiful sunset mistaken for a dawn'; the need, as he said on another occasion, was to succeed Wagner, not merely to follow him. Thus within Debussy's own output the direct influence of Wagner is small and transitory, just as it is in Bartók's or Mallarmé's works. For them Wagner was a lesson they could learn and assimilate. In the case of Debussy, the heated Bayreuth atmosphere still lingers about the 'Five Baudelaire Poems' he wrote around the time of his visits to the Wagner shrine, but it would be hard to point to a single measure in *Pelléas et Mélisande* that sounds like Wagner, even though the whole opera unfolds in a Wagnerian mythological limbo where people are the embodiments of timeless human impulses, and even though, too, the score could not have been imagined without *Parsifal.*

With some of Debussy's near contemporaries the case is different. In France in the 1880s and 1890s the influence of Wagner had become something of a creative hysteria: if an artist were not to be overcome, as were d'Indy and Chausson in their operas, then he had to behave with Debussy's circumspection. Quite why Paris should have been so much taken with Wagnerolatry is harder to determine: perhaps a mood of national self-immolation, after suffering defeat in the Franco-Prussian War of 1870-1, played some part. But outside France the cult of Wagner was celebrated in a more measured manner, and composers could afford to come nearer without their individualities being extinguished. To take a few outstanding examples from Debussy's generation, the works of Elgar,

Left: Scene from *Jack in the Box* (1926). The public for new music in the first quarter of the century was greatly enlarged by the triumphant tours of Diaghilev's Ballets Russes. The impresario's appreciation of dancers and his taste in painters was as acute as his ear for musicians. This ballet was designed by André Derain and choreographed by Balanchine to Milhaud's orchestration of a piano score by Erik Satie, who had recently died. The photograph was taken by Man Ray.

Mahler, Sibelius and Richard Strauss are all much closer to Wagner in sonority at times, though it is significant that even for these composers, as earlier for Bruckner, the risk of opera was too great. Neither Elgar nor Mahler made more than a stab at an opera; Sibelius's *The Maiden in the Tower* is an early one-acter of no importance, never published by its composer; and Strauss only became successful as a composer of operas with *Salome* in 1905, written after a full two decades during which his main effort had gone into orchestral music.

This was the principal arena too for Elgar, Mahler and Sibelius, the swerve towards orchestral music paralleling, necessarily perhaps, a change in public taste. The last two decades of the nineteenth century saw the foundation of many lasting orchestras and concert organizations: that of the Boston Symphony in 1881, the Berlin Philharmonic in 1882, the Chicago Symphony in 1891 and the Promenade Concerts in London in 1895. At the same time, there began to emerge a new race of conductors as virtuoso musicians, rather than mere showmen. Hans Richter became the prototype for many a later conductor, commuting between Bayreuth and Manchester as he continued his work at the Wagner Festivals while also holding the conductorship of the Hallé Orchestra. In Manchester Richter conducted the first performance of Elgar's First Symphony, the British première of Sibelius's Second and the first foreign performance of Bartók's *Kossuth*, all in the space of a few years (1904-8), while Henry Wood's Promenade Concerts were even more remarkable. There the assiduous concertgoer could acquaint himself not only with much new English music but also with the latest works of Debussy, Mahler, Strauss and even Schoenberg.

During the span of a generation, roughly from 1880 to 1910, public encouragement joined with personal intent to produce a great flowering of orchestral music and a great development of the orchestra. No doubt there were underlying social changes that stimulated the shift from the drawing-room to the public concert, but whatever the cause, chamber music fell into neglect (Mahler, Elgar, Debussy, Sibelius and Strauss all wrote very little in this genre), while orchestral music and the orchestra grew steadily in importance. As far as the orchestra itself was concerned, the standard Brahms ensemble of woodwind and trumpets in pairs, four horns, timpani and strings was rapidly enlarged around the turn of the century, and by 1911, when Schoenberg completed the orchestration of his *Gurrelieder*, it had become possible to write for a gigantic ensemble including eight flutes, seven clarinets, ten horns, much percussion and strings to match.

• Musical language •

While the bounds of the traditional orchestra were thus being breached, so were the bounds of the traditional orchestral form, the symphony. There were, to be sure, composers such as Elgar and Sibelius who continued to write in the four-movement pattern inherited from Brahms, Beethoven and ultimately Haydn, but they were in the minority. For Mahler, the symphony was a concept to be interpreted anew in each work, and his divergences from convention were justified not simply by the eccentricity of his own musical ideas but also by the notion, which he shared with most of his contemporaries, that music is more than notes and sound, that it is rather a language of the emotions and that the symphony, as the highest musical form, can be made a panorama of emotional experience. This notion was already current when Berlioz wrote his *Symphonie fantastique*, but in

Left: Front cover for the piano version of Honegger's symphonic work *Pacific 231*, 1923. After World War I, music too served the optimistic esthetic of the machine age.

the meantime there had been the example of Wagner to indicate how forcefully music could be employed to evoke emotional states, so that Mahler was able to write as if feelings of anxiety, terror, bitterness and love could be summoned in the hearer with exactness.

Other composers were unwilling to stretch the symphony so far and preferred to find new forms of expression, such as the 'symphonic poem,' a title implying nothing more than that the work concerned is a single movement for orchestra. Strauss's symphonic poems, most of them dating from the 1890s, usually have a certain savor of the symphony and its division into four parts of conflict, seriousness, comedy and energy. Debussy's orchestral pieces, though roughly contemporary, generally avoid anything so blatantly symphonic, except in the case of the three-movement *La Mer* (1903-5). Even in the middle of these 'symphonic sketches,' however, there is a movement called 'Jeux des vagues' that moves from one idea to another in a butterfly dance of allusive connection, owing very little to established musical forms.

The rise of the symphonic poem, beginning with Liszt in the 1840s and reaching its culmination with Debussy and Strauss just before the First World War, was one symptom of music's closeness to literature during this period. Baudelaire's doctrine of 'correspondences' between words, sounds and visual images was simply one of the earliest and strictest statements of a view that music and painting were as much languages as language itself, and that therefore music could tell a story, as it is required to do in the symphonies of Mahler and the symphonic poems of Strauss; or paint a picture, as often seems to be the case in Debussy's compositions.

Debussy's own intentions are quite clear from various of his writings. When he composed a piece based on a poem, such as his orchestral *Prélude* to Mallarmé's *L'Après-midi d'un faune* (1894), or stimulated by some work of visual art, such as his piano piece 'Poissons d'or' (1907-8) after an example of oriental lacquerwork, what he attempted to convey was not the original stimulus but his reaction to it, a reaction which, since it came from a musician, was couched in musical terms. Of course, elements of the original can be discerned: the Grecian scene, the afternoon heat and the sensual languor of the Mallarmé eclogue, for instance, or the flash of the fish. But the essence is new, because it is music. The importance of the model, whether literary or visual, is hardly more than facilitatory, helping Debussy to discover within himself new areas of musical expression.

Nor is it hard to understand why he, and the great majority of his contemporaries, should have needed such help. The tradition of writing pure music had become a tradition of academicism, concerned with reworking the principles of form that had been developed by Haydn more than a century before. If alternatives were to be found, then they might more usefully be stimulated by works of art in other media than music, which is one reason why Debussy's personal friendships and artistic allegiances were more with writers and painters than with fellow-musicians. Nevertheless, it is difficult to pursue the Baudelairean 'correspondences' very far. Debussy's music has sometimes been called 'impressionist,' and indeed there are links of technique and feeling with Monet in particular: the lack of thematic definition, the delight in vibrant color, the preference for mottled textures. But as something that changes in time, a piece of music is essentially quite different from a painting; and similarly it can have only the vaguest connection with something as precise in connotation as a poem. As Mallarmé recognized, Debussy's *Prélude* made something quite different of his *L'Après-midi d'un faune*, and even his songs, including settings of Mallarmé, Verlaine and his friend Pierre Louÿs, become primarily musical expressions, like all great songs. In any event, to look for pictorial or literary features in Debussy's music is to look at the question from the wrong end. This was the time when Walter Pater was pronouncing all art to be aspiring to 'the condition of music,' and one should rather look for musical tendencies in the paintings of Monet or the poems

Above: Darius Milhaud (left), Fernand Léger (center) and André Maurois seated in front of Léger's drop-curtain for *La Création du monde*, first produced at the Théâtre des Champs-Elysées on 25 October 1923. Rolf de Maré followed Diaghilev's lead in collecting brilliant collaborators for his Ballet Suédois. Milhaud's music and Léger's sets and costumes were matched by Blaise Cendrar's book and the choreography by Jean Börlin.

of Mallarmé. As far as Debussy is concerned, the important thing to note is his view, coloring his whole approach to his art, that music is not a separate discipline but a mode of expression variously linked with the other arts and even with the technological developments of its time.

This was not a view shared by all composers around the turn of the century. If one can ascribe to Wagner's influence the literary tendency in the music of Debussy and Strauss, then at the same time there was a stream stemming from Brahms, and continuing his implicit regard for music as a thing in itself: the difference was one of symphonic poem versus symphony, harmonic venturesomeness versus harmonic integrity, color versus counterpoint. Among the chief representatives of the more traditional current were Reger and Elgar, both of them much impressed by Brahms, and both writing instrumental music in the standard forms: organ music and chamber works in the case of Reger, symphonies and concertos in the case of Elgar, although, of course, neither could ignore the existence of Wagner.

In reality, though, the period around 1900 was a very special time, and the great burgeoning of the orchestra was only one sign of a hothouse atmosphere that encouraged large statements, rapid developments and an ever widening gulf between conservatives, like Elgar, and progressives, like Debussy. The almost fevered pace of artistic change at this time is documented in the operas of Strauss, the symphonies of Mahler and the chamber music of Reger, and it had as its seemingly inevitable outcome the break into atonality that Schoenberg made in 1908. But it was not only the most radical composers who felt the pressure of the times. Elgar wrote very little of importance after his Cello Concerto of 1919; Sibelius seems virtually to have abandoned composition after his *Tapiola* of 1926. In both cases, no doubt, there were personal reasons for a decline in creativity, but at the same time it is hard to avoid the conclusion that the Romantic era had run its course by the time of the First World War – indeed, that the war itself made it hard to continue with the notion of self-determination central to Romanticism. Whatever else they had been writing about, Schumann, Liszt, Berlioz and Wagner had all been writing essentially about themselves, and Mahler had followed them in the almost embarrassingly frank autobiography that his symphonies outline. But if the self was no longer to be the subject of music, what was?

Various possibilities had been appearing some years before the war. Debussy, though declaring his aim to be that of penetrating to 'the naked flesh of emotion,' is certainly very far from the emotionalism of a Tchaikovsky or a Rachmaninov. Instead his emotions are for the most part esthetic ones, aroused by a poem, a postcard, a natural phenomenon or a pattern of notes, and even in his opera *Pelléas et Mélisande* the concern is much more with fantasy, suspicion and suggestion than with feeling directly confronted. Alternatively, in the music of Reger and Elgar, the traditional superficies serve to disguise whatever emotional confession may be taking place at the

Left: Portrait of Enrique Granados (1867-1916) by Ramon Casas. Granados founded a music school in Barcelona and helped Spain to find its own voice, working to establish a national consciousness of Spanish music by including popular Spanish music in his own work.

Below: Béla Bartók and Zoltán Kodály on a field-trip with Joan Busitia, collecting folksongs in Rumania in 1917. Of all the nationalistic composers interested in folksong, Bartók and Kodály did the most thorough research, Bartók absorbing the essence of folksong into his own music, Kodály using folksong material directly.

same time, while Dvořák and Smetana had already indicated how music might become the expression of a nation rather than of an individual by being based in popular dance and folksong.

In the period around 1900 such musical nationalism developed in intensity and variety. Naturally enough, a national mode of expression seemed particularly apropos in countries struggling for independence from larger empires: Sibelius's Finland, Janáček's Czechoslovakia, Bartók's and Kodály's Hungary. But these were by no means the only regions to sport a new national kind of music, and indeed there were many composers who took to using local traditions without any sort of political motive. Here the outstanding example is again Debussy. His encounter with Javanese music at the Universal Exhibition in Paris in 1889 was one of the experiences which shaped his early musical life, and the appeal of the exotic was something to which he succumbed again and again in his music, exhibiting a taste for oriental delicacy and eroticism that he shared with many of his poet and painter colleagues, not least Louÿs. It was not only the East, however, that served his preference for the exotic. Just across the Pyrenees lay the flamboyant world of Spain, a country he visited only once and very briefly, but whose music, warmth and color he took into a whole series of works.

Left: Musique Barbare by Paul Gauguin, 1892, evocative of the interest of Debussy and his contemporaries in Javanese music, particularly the exotic sound of the gamelan, or East Indian 'orchestra.'

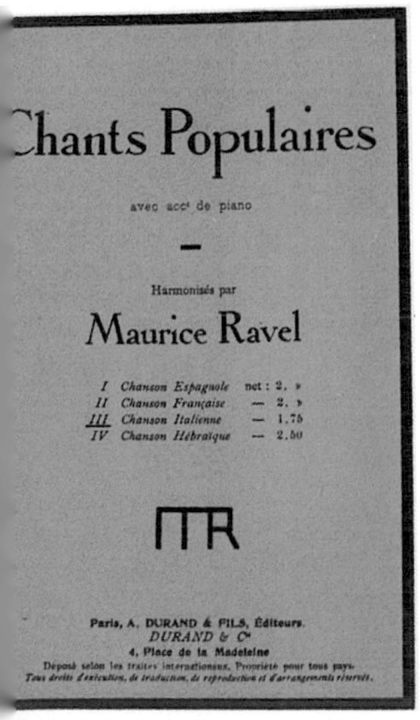

Above: Ravel's popular songs published in 1910 included Spanish, French, Italian and Hebrew songs, and earlier he had set several Greek popular songs.

Ravel was even more drawn towards this fictitious Spain imagined by French and Russian composers from Glinka and Chabrier onwards. Indeed, Debussy's *Ibéria* (1908) was partly influenced by the 'Alborada del gracioso' (1905), the *Rapsodie espagnole* and the opera *L'Heure espagnole* (also 1907) of his younger compatriot, just as Debussy's earlier music had provided an important stimulus for Ravel, especially in the latter's contribution to musical orientalism, the orchestral song-cycle *Shéhérazade* (1903).

Nor was it only French composers who looked to the East for inspiration. The tendency was equally well established in Russian music, particularly among composers influenced by Balakirev and his tone-poem *Thamar* (1867-82): Rimsky-Korsakov, Borodin and Musorgsky all provided examples and, filtered through Rimsky, the same Eastern richness finds its way into Stravinsky's *Firebird* (1910). In some of Rachmaninov's songs and piano pieces, too, there is an oriental color, though now more decorous and picturesque, more in the manner of Tchaikovsky than of Balakirev. But Rachmaninov was in this respect a retrograde artist. More generally, in the first two or three decades of the twentieth century, the tendency was for musical orientalism to become more analytical, more linear, removing the plushness of Rimsky-Korsakov to discover the essential elegance and clarity typical of the Japanese art that was being treasured at the time by artists and intellectuals. Here Stravinsky's *Trois poèmes de la lyrique japonaise* (1912-13) offered an important example, followed by Ravel in his *Chansons madécasses* (1925-7) and by Roussel in his Chinese songs (1927 and 1932), where the spareness of invention is in complete contrast with the flamboyant splendor of his symphonic poem *Evocations* (1910-11) or his opera-ballet of ancient India *Padmâvatî* (1914-18).

This latter work can be regarded as the climax of the Franco-Russian orientalism that had recently been fanned by the Paris seasons of Diaghilev's Russian Ballet, beginning in 1909. With their opulent costumes by Bakst, their spectacular choreography by Fokine and their use of such music as Rimsky-Korsakov's *Sheherazade*, Borodin's *Polovtsian Dances* and Stravinsky's *Firebird*, the Russian Ballet began a sovereignty over French taste that lasted until Diaghilev's death in 1929. That would not have been possible, however, if Diaghilev had been content merely to continue the Eastern magic of his 1909 and 1910 seasons. He was, on the contrary, ever eager for something new,

The 'neoclassical' – or at least anti-Romantic – approach of the group of composers around Jean Cocteau gave rise to a number of religious works, in particular by the Protestant Honegger (Ingrid Bergman is seen, *far left*, in the film version of his 'dramatic oratorio' *Joan of Arc at the Stake*, written in 1935) and the Catholic Poulenc (*left*, in 1954, the year his opera *Dialogues des carmélites* received its first performance), whose fervent faith inspired his important output of church music.

whether that meant the antique luxuriousness of Ravel's *Daphnis et Chloé* (1911), the savagery of Stravinsky's *Rite of Spring* (1913), the sophisticated sensuousness of Poulenc's *Les Biches* (1923) or the aggressive modernism of Prokofiev's *Le Pas d'acier* (1927).

• Neoclassicism •

Daphnis exemplifies a taste for the ancient Greek that was as deep-rooted in French art of the period as was the taste for the oriental: in both cases one may imagine the appeal to have lain in the combination of esthetic fineness and eroticism so near the surface in Louÿs's novels, in Ravel's ballet score and in such pieces by Debussy as his *Chansons de Bilitis* (1892-8, with texts by Louÿs). The musical origin for this style of limpidity and grace is the set of *Trois gymnopédies* (1888) by Satie, whose influence on Debussy around this time was profound. It was Satie, in these *Gymnopédies* and other piano pieces, who displayed an indifference to late Romantic expectations of harmonic weight, textural richness and high rhetoric: his pieces are generally short, utterly simple and severe in their material, and ready to use such straightforward but entirely novel chords as the unadorned fifth. Debussy was evidently impressed by this style when he came to write his own Grecian pieces – not just the *Chansons de Bilitis*, but also such piano pieces as 'Danseuses de Delphes' (1909) – and he repaid his debt to Satie by orchestrating two of the *Gymnopédies*. Later, near the end of his career, Satie himself returned to the antique style in his cantata *Socrate* (1919), which now influenced a new generation of composers working in France: Milhaud in his incidental music for the *Oresteia* (1913-22), Roussel in his ballet *Aeneas* (1930) and Stravinsky in his ballet *Apollo* (1927-8) and his cantata-ballet *Perséphone* (1933-4).

In these post-war works, and especially in those by Stravinsky, the classical theme was united with a revived interest in music of the baroque and classical periods, a development commonly referred to as 'neoclassicism.' In part this can be understood as a rediscovery of musical roots after the catastrophe of the First World War. For, as has already been suggested, the war was as much a watershed in music as it was in the wider world. The years before 1914 had seen the late Romantic tradition brought to a point of rupture in such works as Stravinsky's *Rite of Spring*, Debussy's *Jeux*, the last symphonies of Mahler and the early atonal music of Schoenberg. It was a period of excess, a period of huge orchestras, highly complex harmony and of musical styles reaching towards extreme

Above: Poulenc's last collaboration with Cocteau was his setting of the poet's 1930 monologue *La Voix humaine* as an opera (1959) for Denise Duval – a work which consists of one side of a telephone conversation between a woman and the lover who is rejecting her.

Left: Scene for Albert Roussel's opera-ballet *Padmâvatî*, completed in 1918 and first performed in 1923 at the Paris Opéra. Roussel's extensive travels in the East lent a quite authentic oriental flavor to this tale of a beautiful Hindu princess and a Mongolian Khan, whose music remains always in the French classical mold.

sophistication (in the case of Debussy) or else breaking through to a brutal simplicity (in some elements of *The Rite of Spring*). After 1918 there was a need for new foundations to be established, and for many composers this meant looking again at the clear-cut forms, the open textures and the clean counterpoint of the eighteenth century, forgetting the nineteenth and its cultivation of personal expression. Neoclassicism was, therefore, a part of the common trend towards a more general and objective kind of music.

It was not, though, entirely a post-war phenomenon. Reger had been keenly aware of Bach's potential fruitfulness from before the end of the old century, and Debussy had included eighteenth-century dance forms, the minuet and the passepied, in his *Suite bergamasque* for piano, written in 1890. Nevertheless, these were rather special cases. Reger's reverence for Bach sprang from his work as an organ composer, and in the field of organ music Bach's influence has always been inescapable for composers in the German tradition. Moreover, Reger's neoclassicism in no way involved denying the nineteenth century, for Brahms remained quite as important to him as Bach. In the case of Debussy, the feeling for the eighteenth century is akin to that of Verlaine, whose poetry he was setting around the time of the *Suite bergamasque*: it is a vision of Watteauesque characters at sport in an unfallen world, a poetic image more than the base for a new compositional style. Only at the very end of his life, in the three sonatas he composed during the war, did Debussy become anything like an out-and-out neoclassicist, composing in abstract forms for the first time since his String Quartet of twenty years before. And even here the neoclassicism is motivated as much by patriotic as by structural concerns, for Debussy wanted to affirm his connection with the French taste, the line of Rameau and Couperin, and signed himself in these sonatas 'Claude Debussy, musicien français.'

After the war was over, however, neoclassicism became almost inescapable in Paris. This was partly because of the presence of Stravinsky, whose reworking of eighteenth-century Neapolitan music in his ballet *Pulcinella* (1919-20) led him towards an invoking of classical and baroque principles of form and design in much of his music of the next thirty years. Partly, too, it came about as a reaction against the extravagance of the Romantic style as represented by Wagner and even Debussy. The poet Jean Cocteau played an important part in animating a group of composers with his ideas that music should be straightforward, economical, elegant and alert: everything that the much berated Wagner was not. He found a model for the kind of music he wanted in Satie, who in the period 1913 to 1915 produced an abundance of tiny piano pieces having such absurd titles as 'Dried embryos,' 'Secular and instantaneous hours,' and 'Chapters turned in every direction.' He then got together a band of younger composers, whose label of 'Les Six' stuck much longer than their adherence to Cocteau's brisk esthetic.

The six – Poulenc, Honegger, Milhaud, Tailleferre, Auric and Durey, started giving concerts together in 1917, and in January 1920 Henri Collet, the music critic of *Commœdia*, thought the time was ripe to pay attention to these young people who were creating a stir in 'advanced' circles. His article about them needed a title. Russia had its 'Five;' why should not France boast its 'Six?' It proved an effective headline; within a week Paris became familiar with it, and the new collective title became almost as current colloquially as the old. As a group they were supposed to follow an esthetic which, already propounded by Satie and postulated by Cocteau in his *Le Coq et l'arlequin*, opposed the vagueness of impressionism, or the suggestiveness of symbolism, and preferred bolder and more direct expression, the music of the circus and *café-concert*. Even in its short-lived heyday, Les Six did not reduce all its members to this common denominator, and with its dissolution as a group, begun by Durey's secession, and after the one final collaboration of the remaining five with Jean Cocteau in the entertainment *Les Mariés de la Tour Eiffel* in 1921, its members pursued their individual careers. Auric scored his greatest successes as a film composer, especially for Cocteau's films of the 1930s and 1940s; Tailleferre and Durey lapsed into the moderate obscurity where they might always have lain had it not been for the unwanted exposure of Les Six; while Poulenc, Honegger and Milhaud all became more considerable figures.

However, if Honegger's music is compared with Poulenc's and Milhaud's, or Stravinsky's with Hindemith's, or Prokofiev's with Bartók's, it becomes clear how little is meant in specific terms by 'neoclassicism.' Even so, this list of names proves too how universal the rediscovery of the past was, affecting almost every composer in the 1920s and 1930s, from Elgar in his orchestrations of Bach and Handel to Ravel in his pseudo-baroque suite *Le Tombeau de Couperin* (1917), or from Rachmaninov in his 'Corelli' Variations (1931) to Roussel in his orchestral F major Suite (1926). Sometimes this move-

Above: El Bohemio, 1891 by Ramon Casas: a portrait of Erik Satie in his days as a Montmartre café pianist.

ment has been compared with similar episodes in other arts, with Picasso's glosses on Ingres and Velázquez, for example, or with the reinterpretation of classical subjects in the writings of Valéry, Eliot, Gide and Joyce. Only in music was neoclassicism so very general, possibly because only in music did eighteenth-century style provide such fertile material for reinterpretation. It may also be, in addition, that only in music had the pre-war years brought such a devastating break with the past, producing the conditions for a rediscovery that knows itself to be operating from outside. And it is this irony, this sense of approaching the past as if in ignorance of what has happened in between, that distinguishes the neoclassicism of the inter-war years from that of Reger or Busoni.

• Folksong •

Even though neoclassicism was so very widely practiced, it was not the only means by which composers sought to attain a more measured style and a more objective mode of expression. There was also the lesson of folksong, used not as a source of exoticism as in Debussy and Ravel but taken as the basic substance for a national musical style. The difference, though, may not be so very easy to detect. When a group of outstanding Spanish composers emerged towards the end of the nineteenth century – Albéniz and Granados among them – they found that their national identity had already been assumed by composers in France and Russia: Chabrier's *España* (1883), for instance, antedates the first important works of both Albéniz and Granados. Nevertheless, Albéniz's authentic Spanish music had a powerful influence on the Spanish pieces of Debussy and Ravel (Albéniz lived in Paris from 1893 onwards), and his sumptuous piano style probably had a wider impact among French composers. During the years before the First World War, the direction of influence turned again, and in Paris the young Falla was greatly influenced by Debussy, Ravel and Dukas in such works as his ballet *El Sombrero de tres picos* (1918-19), another piece from the Diaghilev repertory. The connection with the Diaghilev company was important for Falla as it was for many composers, since it brought about an acquaintance with Stravinsky, who had a marked effect on Falla's post-war music. Just as Stravinsky moved from the vast forces of *The Firebird* and *The Rite of Spring* to the efficient small ensembles of *Le Renard* and *Les Noces*, so Falla abandoned the large orchestra of his earlier music and preferred a compact but variegated formation for his puppet opera *El Retablo de Maese Pedro* (1919-22) and a spare sextet for his Harpsichord Concerto (1923-6). In these and other works of the period Falla's Spanishness also became at once more general and more specific: more general in drawing upon Renaissance and baroque art music as well as on the folk music of Andalusia, more specific in sifting out essentials from the more flamboyant Spanish style of Albéniz and Granados and of his own earlier music.

In that respect Falla belonged with the general movement towards greater clarity and concision in the years after the war, a movement in which Stravinsky played a leading part. For while composers in Paris were impressed by Stravinsky's appeal to the eighteenth century, musicians further afield followed him in his more incisive use of folk materials. Bartók too was a great admirer of Stravinsky's economy and folk-mindedness in such works as *Pribautki* (1914) for voice and mixed nonet, though Bartók himself had already been musically immersed in folksong for some years, thanks in large part to a productive friendship with his fellow countryman Kodály. The two of them together took folksong-influenced composition into a new era, for where Dvořák and Brahms had been concerned only with the generalities of folk styles, and where Stravinsky and Falla took their knowledge of folk music from printed sources, Bartók and Kodály went out into the villages of Hungary and neighboring countries to collect the peasants' songs and dances themselves. Inevitably this gave them a closer awareness of folk music: for one thing, the need to classify their collections led them to analyze and compare tunes with great thoroughness. Consequently the peasant material quite naturally took deeper root in their creative personalities.

For Bartók this meant so close an identification with folk music that it is difficult to disentangle what he owed to peasant sources from what he drew from the art tradition: his themes, his rhythms, his sonorities and even his forms are affected by what he heard from the peasants. Kodály was a less analytical artist and, unlike Bartók, he restricted his interests to the music of the Magyars. Often he used their tunes wholesale, as in the sets of dances from Marosszék

(1930) and Galánta (1933), or in his 'Peacock' Variations for orchestra (1938-9). Where he invented his own themes, as in his comic-fantastic opera *Háry János* (1926) or his *Psalmus hungaricus* (1923), he invented in the spirit of Hungarian folk music. As Bartók was always ready to affirm, Kodály was the outstanding Hungarian composer of his time, in the sense that his music embodied most purely and directly the musical culture that from 1906 onwards he and Bartók set out to discover in the Hungarian countryside.

Their initiative was thus almost exactly contemporary with that undertaken in England by Cecil Sharp and Vaughan Williams, who began their collecting activities around 1902-3. Moreover, Sharp and Vaughan Williams seem to have started out with utopian aims similar to those cherished by Bartók and Kodály: they hoped to draw public attention to a neglected national treasure and to use folk music as a tool to improve standards of musical education and taste. Both the Englishmen and the Hungarians were quick to publish volumes of arrangements for chorus or for voice and piano, and to do everything in their power to encourage appreciation of folk music. In one respect this can be seen as another instance of the reaction against the Romantic emphasis on the individual, an attempt to make music again a social pursuit. Even though initial response to their efforts was limited, later both in England and in Hungary folksong gradually became established as

Opposite: Picasso's drop curtain for *Parade*, the ballet devised by Cocteau with music by Satie whose provocative flippancy outraged war-torn Paris when first performed there by the Ballets Russes in 1917.

Left: Francis Picabia's design for the program for the first production of Satie's *Relâche*, another scandalous ballet, first performed at the Théâtre des Champs-Elysées in 1924.

Far left: Fernand Léger's costume design for the King in Milhaud's ballet *La Création du monde*, a work inspired by the spirit of jazz.

Right: The Nordic Music Festival held in Copenhagen in 1919, a celebration of national folk music. Among many musicians here present are Sibelius, Nielsen, Stenhammar, Kajanus, Melartin and Halvorsen.

a part of a child's school life, and music in the wider sense assumed a place in the educational curriculum. In Germany, Hindemith had a part in a similar development through his collections of music for schools.

Meanwhile, for Vaughan Williams, as for Bartók and Kodály, involvement with folk music had an indelible effect on his composing. Indeed, the difference between Vaughan Williams and Kodály is essentially the difference between English music and Hungarian, so completely does each composer enter the particular modal and rhythmic world of his native tradition. Vaughan Williams's music is therefore generally smoother, nearer to traditional tonality, and so in many outer features more conventional. Like Falla, too, Vaughan Williams also paid attention to the art music of his country. He edited the music for the *English Hymnal*, and his feeling for the music of Tudor England (in its essentials not so far from folksong) is evident in such works as his Tallis Fantasia for string orchestra (1910) and Mass in G minor (1920-1).

•Tradition and change•

Vaughan Williams therefore sits uncomfortably astride the distinction often made in this period between composers who looked to the future and those who sought to continue the nineteenth-century tradition. As a pupil of Ravel he may never have achieved the 'French polish' he looked for, but he certainly learned that harmony could go otherwise than by textbook progressions. And yet his music – quite unlike that of Falla, or Kodály, or Ravel, or any of Les Six – behaves as if Stravinsky had never existed. Possibly the most useful comparison is with Sibelius, who, lacking a native tradition in which to ground his music, developed his own in the play of his imagination on the Finnish myths collected in the *Kalevala* and who started out from the area of Tchaikovsky to find, as Vaughan Williams found, a symphonic style that was wholly individual.

The truth is, perhaps, that no artist can be immune to the temper of his times. The half-century from around 1890 to around 1940 was one of creative turmoil, when all the conventions of the Western musical tradition were being overturned. No composer, however conservative his tastes, could ignore what was happening: the alternatives were either silence or some response to the change, usually a thinning of texture, sharpening of harmony and clarifying of form, as was brought about largely through the influence of Stravinsky in the music of Ravel and Roussel. Two further cases can illustrate the point: those of Rachmaninov, possibly the most profoundly conservative composer of this period, and Janáček, who, like Elgar, was fully formed as a composer before the collapse of the old world began, but who, unlike Elgar, found the will and the means to find a new self in the revised order.

Rachmaninov, like Sibelius, took Tchaikovsky as his main starting-point, and so aligned himself with a westernizing, classicizing stream in Russian art opposed to the nationalist school represented in music by Balakirev and Borodin, Musorgsky and Rimsky-Korsakov. The conflict was akin to that being waged in western Europe between the supporters of Brahms and those of Wagner, and the Tolstoy–Dostoyevsky polarity provides another parallel. It took a Stravinsky to effect a bridge within the Russian tradition, just as it took a Schoenberg to do the same in the West, but Rachmaninov, despite some brief flirtation with the nationalist style, never made any such attempt and remained true throughout his composing life to the Tchaikovsky line. Like Elgar, he almost abandoned composition

Left: Vaughan Williams harvesting in the fields, in 1934. Previously, British composers, though aware of their musical heritage, were not absorbed by it; Vaughan Williams was the first to be closely associated with the land and with local tradition – mainly through his collection of English folksong.

around the time of the First World War: in his case there was the reason of exile, since in December 1917 he left Russia never to return. (Stravinsky too was an exile, but the effect on him was to quicken his taste for Russian folk art and stimulate the group of works around *Les Noces.*)

Later, when he returned to regular composition in the 1930s, it was within a style that had not greatly changed. Given the period through which Rachmaninov lived, there is astonishingly little difference in style between his Third Symphony of 1935-6 and his First of 1895, despite the fact that the forty intervening years had seen *The Rite of Spring*, most of Debussy and all of Berg. And yet there is a change. The Third Symphony has the resilience of sonority that appears in a lot of music written around this time for American orchestras: Roussel's Third Symphony of 1929-30 is another example. The first dozen years after the war had not been a propitious time for orchestral composition, for a variety of economic and musical reasons. Then in the 1930s the virtuoso orchestras of the United States – the Philadelphia (for whom Rachmaninov wrote his Third Symphony), the Boston Symphony (for whom Roussel wrote his), the New York Philharmonic and the Chicago Symphony – were liberal with commissions and encouraged a buoyancy that brought a new expressive tone even in music of such backward-looking style as Rachmaninov's. And of course there is nothing morally or esthetically wrong in a style that is backward-looking: for the expression of Rachmaninov's nostalgia it could hardly have been otherwise.

Janáček provides an almost complete contrast. Where Rachmaninov stayed in a stylistic world that was already old-fashioned when he began composing, Janáček suddenly found himself a new frame of reference and a new creative energy when he was over sixty. As so often, the reasons were as much personal as musical. The break came in 1917, when he began a passionate affair by correspondence with a young married woman, and when, too, he would have begun to gain some acquaintance with Stravinsky. As with Falla, Stravinsky was largely responsible for his developing a tauter, sparer style, one based on highly expressive and colorful motifs, on *ostinato* and contrast rather than steady development: this was the style of the four operas, the *Glagolitic Mass*, the two string quartets and the many other works he completed in the dazzling last decade of his life, and so fierce is the power of this style that his numerous earlier works have tended to be forgotten, or valued only for what they foreshadow. For Janáček, therefore, 1917 was a beginning, whereas for Rachmaninov it was very much the end. It was, inescapably, a turning-point for all the other composers active at this time, a moment when the old tradition slipped out of reach and the challenge became that of building the new.

Above: Lithograph of Frederick Delius at an outdoor concert at Wiesbaden in 1922, by Edvard Munch. The two men were friends, and in fact kindred spirits, both sharing a restlessness that prevented either from settling down easily. Munch spent much of his life in Berlin and Paris before eventually returning to his native Norway, while Delius, English by birth but of German parentage, divided his time between Germany, America and France, though he is thought of as a British composer.

GABRIEL FAURÉ

RONALD CRICHTON

Opposite: Gabriel Fauré (1845-1924), in a portrait by John Singer Sargent.

Gabriel Urbain Fauré was born on 12 May 1845 at Pamiers in the Ariège, near the eastern end of the Pyrenees, the sixth child of Toussaint-Honoré Fauré, deputy-inspector of primary education. His mother, also of local extraction, was the daughter of an officer in the imperial army. Fauré was put out to nurse in infancy, and by the time he returned to the family his father was head of a college at Montgauzy near Foix. There was a garden which the boy loved and a chapel with a harmonium on which he discovered an aptitude for music without, it seems, having formal lessons. His father was sensible enough to follow the advice of a local deputy and send Gabriel, with the aid of a grant, to Paris in 1854 to study at the recently founded Ecole Niedermeyer for the training of church musicians.

Life at the school was spartan and the training severe. Schumann and Chopin were 'unsuitable' for young musicians. The staple diet was Gregorian chant, Palestrina and J. S. Bach. The teaching, however, was less hidebound than at the Conservatoire, in particular with regard to the study and use of church modes. When Niedermeyer (Swiss by birth and an opera composer of some note) died in 1861, he was succeeded as professor of piano by Camille Saint-Saëns, ten years Fauré's senior, who became a lifelong friend. The influence of Saint-Saëns went beyond piano classes. He had the knowledge and enthusiasm to introduce the pupils to modern music. Later, Fauré was associated with him in the foundation, in 1871, of the Société Nationale for the performance of chamber and orchestral music by French composers.

Fauré's professional career began in 1866 with an appointment as organist at Rennes in Brittany. He obtained a similar post in Paris just before the outbreak of the Franco-Prussian War. During the Commune he escaped from Paris and briefly rejoined his old school, temporarily established on the Niedermeyer estates near Lausanne, as a teacher. Here he made another enduring friendship, with André Messager, the future composer of *Véronique.* Back in Paris, Fauré was appointed assistant to Widor, organist at Saint-Sulpice, and in 1874 deputy organist to Saint-Saëns at the Madeleine. Three years later he became choirmaster at this, the most fashionable church in Paris. He was to become titular organist there himself, for nine years from 1896.

In the early days of the Third Republic Saint-Saëns introduced Fauré to the Parisian salon of the famous singer Pauline Viardot. He fell passionately in love with her daughter, Marianne, and they became engaged in July 1877, but three months later she broke off the engagement. Fauré frequented other salons during the middle period of his life. The label 'salon composer' has consequently been attached to him, though most of what may reasonably be considered his salon music was composed early in his career, and the idea of Fauré as one of music's butterflies does not bear a moment's serious examination. The Viardot gatherings, where Fauré met Flaubert, George Sand, Turgenev and others under boisterously informal conditions, were anything but worldly in the pejorative sense. On their different levels the salons presided over by Mme de Saint-Marceaux (described by Colette as the place which set the seal on the reputation of composers and virtuoso performers alike) and the Princesse Edmond de Polignac, which Fauré subsequently attended, were useful, indeed essential, foyers for progressive musicians, whose opportunities were cramped by the limitations of Parisian concert life and the minimal interest or understanding of any modern music apart from Wagner's. Nectoux quotes Fauré's reply to an interviewer who remarked on his 'success' in the salons: 'I was very attracted by the material side of life. I had some good friends, and if one is ignored by the general public, one is grateful for the understanding of a few people.'

• Early works •

From his first published work, 'Le Papillon et la fleur' (op.1 no.1, 1861), to the cycle *L'Horizon chimérique* (op.118), written no less than sixty years later, Fauré's hundred-odd songs form a thread through his long list of compositions. Among the songs from the start of his career, the ever-popular 'Après un rêve' (op.7 no.1), written in 1878, shows one side of the early Fauré at his best. The mood is close to that of the equally famous *Elégie* for cello, but the tune, though one might not think so from the way some singers allow it to droop, is a noble one. The singer Croiza related how, when she asked Fauré about the correct speed for 'Après

Right: The composer, aged eighteen, during his years at the Ecole Niedermeyer in Paris.

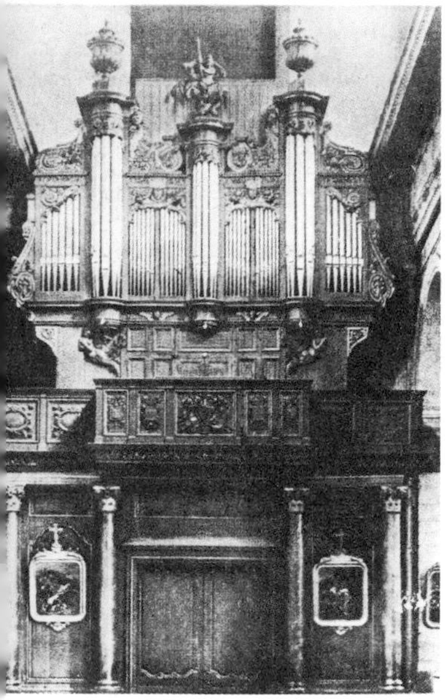

Above: The organ at the church of Saint-Sauveur, Rennes. Fauré was organist there from 1866 to 1870. He found Breton provincial life dull and scandalized the local priest by accompanying scenes from Gounod's *Faust* at the town theater.

un rêve,' he replied 'Without slowing down – without slowing down!' 'Sans ralentir' or 'Keep going' may serve as motto for all performers of Fauré – not only singers. 'Automne' (op.18 no.3 of the same year), a grandly positive statement of somber grief, represents the stormy side of Fauré, often overlooked, more expansively revealed in the chamber music and works for solo piano.

Like the songs, piano works occur throughout Fauré's career. They started slowly. The *Trois Romances sans paroles*, op.17, from the Ecole Niedermeyer period, are believed to have been written in 1863, two years after the first song; the First Nocturne and Barcarolle came respectively about twelve and eighteen years later (the exact dates are not certain), after which the trickle became a stream, flowing at various levels but never drying up until 1921, the date of the Thirteenth Barcarolle and Thirteenth Nocturne, three years before Fauré's death.

Unlike Saint-Saëns, Fauré neither sought nor achieved a career as a virtuoso, but he frequently played his own music, especially song accompaniments, in public as well as private. Descriptions of his playing are important for the implications they carry for interpreters. Philippe Fauré-Fremiet wrote 'His hands were strong and looked heavy: in reality they were supple and light. He barely needed to raise them above the keyboard to do what he wanted. He hated empty virtuosity, rubato and the kind of effects that make listeners swoon. He stuck to the text, in strict time.' Others have emphasized the question of strict time. Croiza described Fauré as 'a living metronome.' The important word is 'living' – metronomic strictness does not necessarily enforce rigidity or exclude expressive phrasing. The samples of Fauré's playing reproduced by means of Welte-Mignon piano rolls are anything but cold.

The earliest and most popular of Fauré's chamber works is the Sonata no.1 for violin and piano in A major, op.13. This was written in 1875/6 and dedicated to Paul Viardot, son of Pauline and brother of Marianne. The sonata appeared so novel that no French publisher could be found to take the risk, though the four movements brim with melody and rhythmic vitality. It is generously planned, and Fauré writes as resonantly for his two instruments as if their combination were the easiest thing in the world. The Quartet no.1 for piano and strings in C minor, op.15, was begun in 1876. There were two premières, the first in 1880, the second, with the finale rewritten, in 1884. The dates betray the composer's difficulties, but one would not suspect them from the confident brilliance of the result – least of all in the finale. Fauré did not think naturally in terms of the orchestra, but the sound of his chamber works proves that he had no difficulty in thinking instrumentally. That sound may be admired in all its richness in the first and third movements of the C minor Quartet, both in full passages and in the quiet closes. The movements are separated by one of the nineteenth century's most ravishing scherzos, light as air, set out on generous lines with Fauré's sure sense of proportion. The last movement, with a joyfully singing second idea, is one of the composer's most buoyant finales, bowling along without a sign of the trouble it caused him.

• Church music •

Even leaving out of account his student years at the Ecole Niedermeyer, Fauré spent half his life in the service of the Church, as organist at Rennes and later in Paris, chiefly at the Madeleine. This was less a matter of faith, conviction or compatibility than of material necessity. Fauré was not a conventional believer. The organ loft did not enter his soul. Though his improvisations were admired, he wrote nothing of importance for the solo instrument. With one exception, the Requiem, he left little of importance either in the way of choral music. One short early work, the *Cantique de Jean Racine*, op.11, won first prize for composition at the Ecole Niedermeyer in 1865. Originally for mixed voices and organ, it was later orchestrated. The choral writing has a grave but graceful fluency: Fauré can already summon cat-like grace to help him avoid over-sweetness.

The *Messe basse* for womens' (or preferably boys') voices and organ, has been identified by Nectoux as a product of holidays at Villerville in Normandy with the hospitable Clerc family, where the Mass was given in 1881 for the benefit of local fishermen. Fauré shared the writing with Messager, the former being responsible for Gloria, Sanctus and Agnus Dei, the latter for Kyrie and the additional 'O salutaris.' When Fauré's contribution was published, much later (1907), his Gloria was dropped except for 'Qui tollis,' refashioned into Benedictus. The present Kyrie, by Fauré, added for the publication, is also believed to date from about 1881. The 'Fishermen's Mass,' considering the small outlay involved, is worth more frequent performance in church or intimate concert. The new Kyrie and Benedictus both have an unmistakably personal touch.

The Requiem, op.48, for soprano and baritone solo, mixed choir and orchestra, has a more complicated history than the unearthly tranquillity of the score as a whole might suggest. This best-known and loved of the composer's major works is usually connected with the deaths of Fauré's father in 1885 and of his mother at the very beginning of 1888, though in its original form for baritone and organ the 'Libera me' dates from 1877, before the *Messe basse*. The first version of the Requiem, given at the Madeleine in 1888, consisted only of Introit and Kyrie, Sanctus, 'Pie Jesu,' Agnus Dei and 'In paradisum,' with an orchestra of strings without violins (except for a solo violin in the Sanctus), harp, timpani and organ. The soloist in 'Pie Jesu' was a boy treble – no baritone was needed at that stage – and the children of Fauré's choir at the Madeleine took the choral soprano line. In 1889 Fauré added the Offertory. This, and the extended 'Libera me,' now with chorus, were included at the first complete performance, again at the Madeleine, in 1893. Horns, trumpets and trombones now made their appearance. Woodwind parts were added and the organ part accordingly reduced, for the third version, first heard at the Trocadéro in 1900. This accords with the published version of 1901.

The instrumental additions were presumably made at the prompting of the publisher, who may have foreseen that the potential popularity of the Requiem could be limited by small forces. Yet unless the conductor is discreet, something is lost. The special sound of the Requiem is heard at its purest not in the radiant directness of 'Pie Jesu' or the ineffable innocence of 'In paradisum' but in the Offertory, where divided lower strings and organ give Fauré's calm acceptance of death a peculiar solemnity – in those strange, expanding and contracting eight-part chords the Sibelian forests of *Tapiola* seem to have moved south. Woodwind and brass are silent here. Elsewhere, though they help to make the Requiem tell in large concert halls, for which it was not intended, their underlinings endanger precisely the qualities of 'purity, mystery and restraint' in the face of which, as Orledge claims, 'criticism pales into insignificance.'

In 1883 Faure had married Marie, daughter of a well-known sculptor, Emmanuel Fremiet. There were two sons of the marriage, Emmanuel and Philippe, born in 1883 and 1889. Marie was a self-effacing, neurotic woman who felt overshadowed between the two celebrated men, husband and father; she stayed at home and took no part in her husband's public life. During his absences for work or holiday (when the greater part of his composition had to be done) Fauré wrote to her regularly and copiously. His letters have the affectionate, concerned but slightly dispassionate tone of correspondence with a younger sister. Fortunately there were musical ladies to provide the kind of companionship Fauré needed and Marie withheld – among them Adela Maddison, wife of a prosperous English solicitor, the gifted amateur singer Emma Bardac, who inspired *La Bonne Chanson* and was later Debussy's second wife; and most of all the pianist Marguerite Hasselmans.

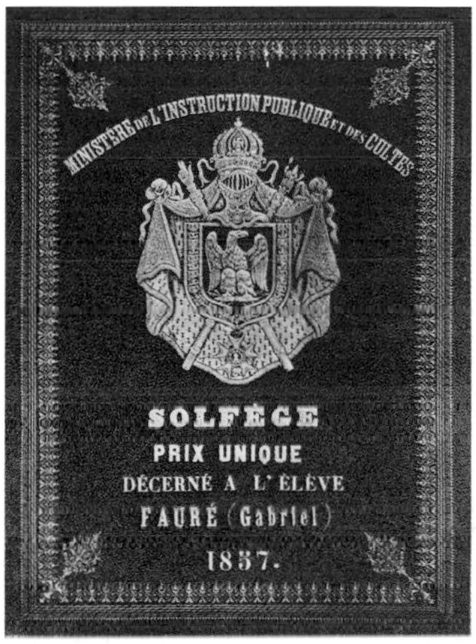

Above: Cover to a prize awarded to the twelve-year-old Fauré during his third year at the Ecole Niedermeyer.

Left: Pauline Viardot's famous Paris musical salon. At her gatherings Fauré met such celebrities as Flaubert and George Sand. He fell in love with Mme Viardot's daughter Marianne, and was deeply hurt when she broke off their engagement.

Above: A 1904 poster by Jules Chéret advertising *Le Figaro*. Fauré was music critic for the famous Paris newspaper from 1903 until 1921.

• Songs and the piano •

Fauré's first setting of Verlaine, and the first undoubted masterpiece among his songs, is 'Clair de lune' (op.46 no.2, 1887). The mood of silvery enchantment is conjured by a kind of severe alchemy. The pianist's right hand unfolds a winding melody in minuet rhythm against broken arpeggio figures in the left hand. The voice enters at the twelfth measure with a counter-melody, occasionally, but only occasionally, coinciding with the piano line, sometimes crossing beneath it. Thus Verlaine's Italian comedy figures flit through their masques and bergamasques, 'Jouant du luth et dansant, et quasi Tristes sous leurs déguisements fantasques.' It is typical of Fauré's classical approach to composition that the potent if ambiguous atmosphere should be built up, not with impressionist dabs and washes but with two extended, implacable lines.

The four songs which make up op.51 of 1888 demonstrate Fauré's wide range. First, 'Larmes' with an insistent, broken figure in the piano as prickly as Britten, one of the 'gentle' Fauré's most aggressive, embittered outbursts. Then 'Au cimetière,' a ternary-form song whose outer verses of slow chords with a more formally melodic vocal line frame a short but passionate middle section. The third, 'Spleen,' is a delicate setting of Verlaine's 'Il pleure dans mon coeur.' The fourth 'La Rose,' is an anacreontic ode full of happiness, with rising phrases in the piano like coils of mist floating upwards in the morning sunshine.

Verlaine returns with the first of Fauré's cycles, the *Cinq mélodies*, op.58, of 1891, to whose title the words 'de Venise' are often added. The dedicatee was the munificent, American-born patron of music who, by the time the songs were published, had become Princesse Edmond de Polignac. In May 1891 Fauré was her guest on his first visit to Venice (he had already written four Barcarolles and the music for *Shylock*): the place made an unforgettable impression. To the peaceful palazzo he preferred the animation of the Café Florian on the Piazza. There he completed 'Mandoline' and began 'En sourdine.' The remainder were finished later on his return, his mind so full of the delights of the aqueous city that the cycle's nickname is justified.

The following year, or to be exact the summers of 1892 and 1893, saw an even more remarkable explosion, the composition of the first eight songs of the second Verlaine cycle, *La Bonne Chanson*, op.61 (the ninth was added in 1894). They were inspired by and composed for Emma Bardac. The poems had been written in a mood of self-induced ecstasy occasioned by Verlaine's disastrous marriage to the sixteen-year-old Mathilde Mauté. Fauré's music astounds with ardent spontaneity, rich writing and symphonic density, with five themes gradually introduced and woven into the texture.

The songs from the decade round the turn of the century coincide with some of Fauré's outstanding works in other genres – the Sixth and Seventh Nocturnes, the Fifth Barcarolle and Theme and Variations for piano, the music for *Pelléas et Mélisande*, *Prométhée*, and the First Piano Quintet. Much of this music is passionate in feeling and somber in tone. So are several of the songs. 'Prison,' a setting of a poem from Verlaine's *Sagesse*, is the bitterest, most unflinching epilogue to the two Verlaine cycles. The song is paired with the justly loved, totally different 'Soir,' in which Fauré bathes Albert Samain's scented conceits in golden, sunset light. The same poet provided the text for 'Arpège,' a volatile nine-eight *sicilienne* with feathery piano trills.

The *Ballade* for piano and orchestra in F sharp, op.19, was originally written for piano solo and published in that form in 1880. Fauré arranged it for piano and orchestra in 1881 and played the solo part at the first performance that year. It was, however, the solo version which Fauré showed to Liszt when he went with Saint-Saëns to see the great man in Zürich in 1882. Liszt's formal experiments had affected Fauré's scheme: two sections in moderate tempo enclosing a faster central one. The dovetailing is close – the second idea of the first section persists through the central allegro, by which time the pastoral six-eight idea that is to become the main theme of the third section has already been introduced in two forms, one of them, in common time, receiving quite extended treatment. The *cantabile* tune with which the *Ballade* opens is a candidate for Proust's 'petite phrase.' Fauré made some vague remarks connecting the *Ballade* with the Forest Murmurs scene in *Siegfried*, but he was too discriminating an admirer of Wagner to descend to imitation. The sensuous charms of the *Ballade* are very much his own.

With the partial exception of the brooding no.1 (written about 1875), the first five Nocturnes for piano (published in 1883 and 1884 as op.33, 36 and 37) still inhabit, more or less, the world of Chopin, though there are hints of Liszt in nos.3 and 4. Ten years passed before the birth of the next Nocturne, no.6 in D flat, op.63 (1894) and with this and with no.7 we are on the heights of Fauré's music and of Romantic piano literature. The Barcarolles are on the whole slighter works, but they have much to offer, including in no.5 in F sharp minor, op.66 (1894), a worthy partner for the Sixth Nocturne of the same year and the only one of Fauré's Barcarolles so far to equal in intensity, and surpass in variety of mood, Chopin's single, splendid example of 1846. Other works of this

Right: Paul Verlaine, a portrait by Eugène Carrière. Fauré became acquainted with Verlaine's poetry around 1887, and from then on he was one of the chief sources of Fauré's inspiration in the field of song. His *Cinq mélodies de Venise* and the group published collectively as *La Bonne Chanson* are among his finest Verlaine settings.

Above: A sketch of Fauré by Sargent (1898). The artist was one of the composer's many loyal London friends. He visited the British capital regularly between 1892 and 1900, sometimes to attend privately organized concerts of his music.

period include the first three Impromptus, some of the *Huit pièces brèves* and the four *Valses caprices*. The latter, written between 1882 and 1894, are extended salon-pieces written in the wake of Chopin, Liszt and Saint-Saëns with Fauré's personal traits of feline grace and opalescent harmony. They form a half-way house between the real thing and the later stylistic evocations of Ravel – no.2 contains hints of the *Valses nobles et sentimentales*. From the end of this period are the four-hand suite *Dolly*, op.56 (1894-7), one of Fauré's most popular works in the original form and in the orchestration by Rabaud (1906), written for the young daughter of Emma Bardac, and the Theme and Variations in C sharp minor, op.73 (1895), Fauré's only essay in variation form. The theme, in his elegiac slow march mood with off-beat accompanying chords, is striking, and of the eleven variations all but the last keep to the minor key and stay close to the theme. Fauré combines strong contrast between individual variations with an overall plan of tension and relaxation.

The Piano Quartet no.2, in G minor (op.45, 1887) came to Fauré more easily than his first quartet, over a period of two years, and although the texture is similar, the mood is darker. The glory of the work is the slow movement, an enchanted *adagio non troppo* whose opening figure (first heard in the lower regions of the piano but equally effective when it is transferred later to the strings) was suggested by childhood memories of distant bells heard in the garden of the headmaster's house at Montgauzy.

If the overshadowing of the G minor Piano Quartet by its predecessor is regrettable, what can one say about the gross neglect of Fauré's two piano quintets – later, riper, with even richer textures? The first of these, in D minor, op.89, was sketched as a piano quartet in 1891 then put away for some years, subsequently resumed, overhauled, and finally finished in 1905. The opening of the first movement, with the unfolding of a long, wondering theme against a shimmer of arpeggio figures on the piano, the second violin stealing in, then joined by the other strings one after the other, is one of the most sensuously beautiful inventions in Fauré's music. The atmosphere is held through pages of close but never clotted contrapuntal weaving – Fauré's mastery of the long paragraph and his

instinct for pouncing at the right moment on a crucial chord are strongly in evidence. The adagio (there is no scherzo) is on the same exalted plane of deep feeling handled with great mastery – there is an especially fine extended coda, 'terminal developments' being a formal device congenial to Fauré in his chamber music. The third and last movement does not please all commentators. It was clearly difficult to find the right scherzo-finale to follow the two previous movements, both amply planned and moderate in speed. The solution begins with a carillon theme on the piano with pizzicato pointings from the strings (the scoring of the theme's many reappearances is varied but always transparent). Fauré worried about a resemblance to the finale of Beethoven's Ninth Symphony, but a modern listener is as likely to think of Franck's Violin Sonata. One may feel less happy about the remaining material, which casts a slight haze over the music without providing sharp contrast. The quintet is dedicated to the Belgian violinist Ysaye, whose quartet (with Fauré at the piano) gave the first performance, in Brussels, in 1906.

Above: Fauré and his wife Marie, pictured about a year after their marriage in March 1883. The composer is playing what seems to be a reconstructed ancient Egyptian or Babylonian harp.

Below: Autograph sketch for the Offertory (1889) of his Requiem.

•Music for the stage•

Fauré was born far enough into the nineteenth century for it not to matter too much that he, a Frenchman, was primarily a non-operatic composer. Nevertheless, to have written no opera at all would have been as odd as for a late-Victorian English composer to avoid oratorio. Fauré approached the problem prudently, from the shallow end, with incidental music for two dramas at the Théâtre de l'Odéon in Paris in consecutive years, 1888 and 1889. *Caligula* was a revival of a tragedy by the elder Dumas; *Shylock* a comedy by Edmond Haraucourt, based on *The Merchant of Venice*. From both, Fauré made suites for normal orchestra. That from *Caligula*, op.52, contains an 'air de danse,' a rare, and successful, excursion into exoticism, and some prettily contrasted choruses for women's voices. The *Shylock* music, op.57, has greater substance and variety, with two songs for tenor (found in volume 3 of the songs as 'Chanson de Shylock' and 'Madrigal'), an impassioned 'Epithalame,' an exquisite 'Nocturne' and a lively aubade-finale. These suites alone refute the idea of Fauré as a dull or incompetent orchestrator. The more familiar music for *Pelléas et Mélisande* was written for a London production in 1898 of Maeterlinck's play in Mackail's English translation with Mrs Patrick Campbell, costumed by Burne-Jones, as the heroine. The spinning-song and the 'Sicilienne' (published earlier as a cello solo) have the full Fauré charm but are outclassed in delicacy and poignancy by the opening prelude and the final 'Death of Mélisande.'

The year 1900 brought something very different. At the open-air amphitheater at Béziers in south-western France not far from Fauré's native Ariège, a local magnate had instituted summer festivals presenting plays with music, treating ancient Greek themes. Fauré was invited to follow Saint-Säens's *Déjanire* with a *Prométhée* on a text by Jean Lorrain and Ferdinand Hérold based on Aeschylus. The saga of preparation was described in great and amusing detail in daily letters to Fauré's wife: he used hundreds of singers, dancers and musicians, including massed strings, thirty trumpets and eighteen harps, but wisely left the scoring to a military band expert from Montpellier, himself preparing the later, indoor version. The music moves easily on the giant scale without betraying

Fauré's habitual restraint – though the result does not sound like Wagner, one can see how much he had learned from Bayreuth. In their simple strength, the themes foreshadow *Pénélope*, and the music for Pandora's cortège and for the Oceanides has a blanched, remote quality not quite like anything else.

• After 1900 •

In 1892 Fauré had been made inspector of music for the provincial conservatoires, enabling him to give up private teaching but involving constant traveling. In 1896, the year of the full Madeleine appointment, there occurred the death at a great age of Ambroise Thomas, composer of *Mignon*, director of the Conservatoire since 1871 (Thomas had regarded Fauré as a dangerous subversive). His disappearance led to a reshuffle, in the course of which Fauré took over Massenet's class for composition, counterpoint and fugue. The foot was in the door. When, in 1905, Théodore Dubois, Thomas's successor, resigned the directorship over the Ravel affair, Fauré – to general consternation, for he was not a Conservatoire product – was appointed director, revealing such firm ideas about the running and staffing of the place that he earned the nickname 'Robespierre.'

He proved an excellent administrator and was beloved as a teacher by a succession of distinguished pupils – Roland-Manuel described Fauré's class as being 'for composers, what Mallarmé's salon was for poets.' Fauré's directorship was marred by increasing deafness: he could hear speech, but pitched sounds were distorted at either end of the compass, a third down at the top, a third up at the bottom. In 1920, with official encouragement, he resigned.

In 1909 Fauré was invited to become president of the new Société Musicale Indépendante representing the young dissidents opposed to d'Indy and the Schola Cantorum faction, which now ruled the Société Nationale – a bold step for the director of the Conservatoire, who had, moreover, just been elected to the Institut. At the opening concert of the new society, Fauré's ten songs of *La Chanson d'Eve* (op.95, written between 1906 and 1910) were performed by Jeanne Raunay, the singer to whom they are dedicated, with Fauré at the piano. The poems are by the Belgian symbolist and mystic, Charles Van Lerberghe. The first song, 'Paradis,' is by far the longest, opening with the first of the work's two cyclical themes – a slow, five-measure chordal progression from E minor to C. This theme was taken from 'Mélisande's Song' of 1898 (part of the music for *Pelléas* but published much later), which has a certain likeness to the 'Twilight fancies' of Delius. The second theme, more sinuous, less definite, is heard when the note-values double at the change from minor to major. 'C'est le premier matin du monde': space, near-silence, the beginning of everything, a Holstian spareness and transparency, but not wintry in Holst's way, a light more blue than white. God bids the 'young and divine Eve' bring the Word to the human race. The following songs are much shorter, but they inhabit the same elevated, rarefied yet not inaccessible plane. In the last song, 'O mort, poussière d'étoiles,' there are slow chords and a vocal line gradually rising and falling – surely the voice parts of Fauré's mature songs are filled with memories, partly subconscious perhaps, of the plainchant absorbed in student days at the Ecole Niedermeyer?

By now Fauré had embarked on *Pénélope*. He had found no congenial subject for an opera until the singer Lucienne Bréval suggested a libretto by the dramatist René Fauchois on the Homeric story of Penelope's long wait for the return of her husband Odysseus. The progress of *Pénélope* during summer (and one Easter) vacations between 1907 and 1912 (1910 was a blank year) is documented in the letters to Mme Fauré. Considering the limited time available to him each year for sustained composition, the progress was not so slow as the lapse of time suggests. *Pénélope* was ready for production at Monte Carlo in March 1913. It was presented in Paris at the new Théâtre des Champs-Elysées two months later, with Hasselmans conducting (Bréval sang the title-role in both productions), and was a much greater success, but the Debussy–Nijinsky ballet *Jeux* stole the limelight at the same theater in a matter of days, while both works were eclipsed there later in the same month by the resounding scandal of *Le Sacre du printemps*. Lovers of Fauré regard his opera with veneration. It stands high among the music dramas of the century, yet it has still to establish itself firmly in the repertory even in France.

Like Debussy in his *Pelléas*, Fauré makes sparing but effective use of *leitmotifs*. Three of them are introduced in the masterly prelude: first, a striking chordal progression for the anxious, waiting Penelope, which at her entrance in Act I assumes an impressive degree of regal anger and grief; second, the theme of Odysseus heard on the trumpet, with leaping seconds and octaves, a Wagnerian triplet and a prominent pair of rising fifths; and third, a serenely ascending love theme in which the sharpened fourth of his early song 'Lydia' is heard again. In due course the brawling suitors are characterized with an angular, nagging, dotted-note phrase. Fauré does unexpected things, insinuating flute-and-harp dances into the outer acts with perfect propriety, finding vivid musical ideas for the unpicking of Penelope's shroud (an ingenious transformation of the theme of Odysseus), for Odysseus's bending of his great bow and his swift revenge on the suitors. No surprise need be caused by the admirable monologues of Penelope, with her great cry 'J'ai tant d'amour à lui donner encore' (I have so much love to give him still), marked by the unsentimental Fauré 'sans ralentir,' or by the mixture of grit, courage and craftiness in the music for Odysseus. Penelope is firmly drawn in her strength and constancy, but her heroic virtues (there is no feminine forgiving in her attitude to the suitors) do not attract protective sympathy like poor,

Above: The Art Nouveau cover design to the first edition of the song 'Le Don silencieux.' This was composed in 1906, relatively late in Fauré's career, when his style became increasingly restrained and economical.

Left: The Dream, painted by Puvis de Chavannes in 1883. Five years earlier, Fauré had composed 'Après un rêve' (After a dream), one of his best-loved songs, also known in its arrangement for cello and piano. Classicism infused with symbolic meaning, which was an inspiration to younger, more revolutionary artists, was a characteristic of both painter and composer.

frightened little Mélisande. The strong lines and clear light of Greece make a less ready appeal than Maeterlinck and Debussy's shadowy, northern never-never-land with its far from heroic, all too human inhabitants. Yet some knowledge of *Pénélope* is essential for a full understanding of Fauré.

After the completion of his opera Fauré returned to Van Lerberghe for the eight poems of *Le Jardin clos*, op.106, first performed by Claire Croiza in 1915. These had no thematic connections, but a unity of mood: the composer was no longer concerned with wide vistas of paradise but with an enclosed garden. Although the warm, human atmosphere is more welcoming than the high air of *La Chanson d'Eve*, the stripping of essentials is taken a stage further. More than one writer has commented on the white appearance of the printed page in *Le Jardin clos*.

It was followed by two further song-cycles, each consisting of four songs, but with little else in common. The poet for *Mirages*, op.113, was the Baronne de Brimont, a great-niece of Lamartine and a bluestocking, to judge from these verses, which suggest parodies of Maeterlinck. Nevertheless, for all their affectations they stimulated Fauré to some remarkable music. Mood and pace in the first three songs are dangerously close, yet the second, 'Reflets dans l'eau,' is interrupted, when the poet toys with the idea of drowning herself in a pool, by discreetly convincing suggestions of eddies and circles on the water. Fauré shunned illustration, and although he could not resist watery subjects, his treatment of them here as elsewhere is more generalized, less pictorial, than Debussy's in the piano piece of the same name. The fourth song, 'Danseuse,' is a complete surprise, with a jagged, dotted-note figure in the piano part, suggesting ragtime (the date was 1919) and rising to a pitch of unusual insistence.

For *L'Horizon chimérique*, op.118 (1921), his last songs, Fauré chose verses by a young poet killed in the war, Jean de la Ville de Mirmont. In spite of the limpid concision, there is a powerful impression of banked fires, of a longing for new departures, spiritual as well as physical, remarkable in an old, sick man. The third song,

Right: Maurice Denis's decorative painting for the interior of the chapel of Sainte-Croix du Vésinet, 1899. Fauré's music corresponds most closely to the symbolist French painting of the turn of the century, and like the painters he was much influenced by both Verlaine and the Belgian writer Maurice Maeterlinck.

'Diane, Séléné,' an invocation to the moon on the waters, is perhaps the most beautiful of Fauré's many chains of slow, shifting chords.

While Fauré was engaged on *Pénélope* he composed his Ninth and Tenth Nocturnes for piano, which share the opera's lean eloquence, and in 1905 he resumed the series of Barcarolles, which also fall under the fertilizing shadow of *Pénélope*. The neglected set of Preludes, op.103, date from 1909-10. There are nine of them, each one vividly characterized.

The *Fantaisie* in G, op.111 (1918) for piano and orchestra, was dedicated to the eminent pianist Alfred Cortot, who gave the first Paris performance – the première had been given a month earlier, at Monte Carlo, by the beloved Marguerite Hasselmans. Fauré sketched the work for two pianos, intending to do the orchestration himself. In the event that was undertaken, under the composer's supervision, by Marcel Samuel-Rousseau. Fauré's music offers many examples of initially evasive works growing on the listener with repeated hearings, but few do this to so unexpected an extent as the *Fantaisie*. The sound has the luminous clarity of Saint-Saëns: harmonically of course Fauré goes a long way beyond anything his revered master would have attempted.

With the last three Nocturnes we are once more on the heights, now bleak and exposed. No.11 in F sharp minor, op.104 no.1 (1913), is a dirge for the deceased wife of the critic Pierre Lalo, a short, concentrated tribute of great poignancy. No.12 in E minor, op.107 (1915), is a big, passionate piece whose first theme has Brahmsian alternating major and minor thirds. Though less Romantically expressed than in no.7, the agony is equally intense. There is a gap of six years before the last Nocturne, no.13 in B minor, op.119 (1922, written at the end of the previous year). This extraordinary production for a composer in his middle seventies opens in the same mood of restrained, Bachian grief and Schubertian loneliness as no.11. There follows a long, energetic, quite ornate middle section, which includes a brief cadenza before sinking back in grand resignation to the mood of the opening.

Fauré made his farewell to the theater with *Masques et bergamasques*, op.112, a one-act *divertissement* with a scenario by Fauchois, commissioned by the Prince of Monaco at the prompting, Fauré believed, of Saint-Saëns. Old and new mingle happily in this return to the world of *fêtes champêtres*. With assistance from Samuel-Rousseau, Fauré orchestrated the songs 'Clair de lune' and 'Le plus doux chemin,' and the *Madrigal* of 1883 for vocal quartet or chorus; he also used the version with quartet or chorus of the delightful, ever-popular *Pavane*, op.50, one of Fauré's works which Debussy admitted to liking. He set these among four orchestral movements, from which he later made the eponymous suite: a delicious miniature overture, a gavotte and a minuet – the first two, and possibly the third as well, dating from some fifty years earlier – crowned with an entirely new 'Pastorale' containing an allusion to the overture but written in the late manner, showing how consistent across the gulf of time and style was his musical personality.

Above: The Chariot of Apollo by Odilon Redon, in which classical myth is given new symbolic meaning. Fauré turned again to classical subject-matter in both *Prométhée* and *Pénélope*.

•The last chamber works•

The Sonata no.2 for violin and piano, in E minor, op.108, written in 1916-17, highlights some procedures typical of Fauré's chamber music: strong basses apparently independent of, yet in reality closely related to, the top line; long paragraphs; long measures (one wonders if Fauré would not have liked to rely on the naturally strong rhythmic pulse of his music to abolish bars altogether); avoidance of outwardly dramatic contrast; a shuffling of conventional sonata form in favor of developments that are also re-expositions (with the themes in the original order) and of recapitulations that are also second developments.

Unlike the violin sonatas the two for cello and piano came fairly close together, the gap between them being not forty years but four.

The Cello Sonata no.1 in D minor, op.109, was written in 1917, hard on the heels of the second for violin. Begun in Paris during the winter, it was completed, at unusual speed for Fauré, during the summer at St Raphaël. The angry cracklings of the first movement might seem to reflect a disquieting phase of the First World War, yet this could hardly apply to the carefree finale. The sonata opens with a softly percussive, syncopated figure on the piano with as many rests as notes. Over this the cello gruffly proposes a spiky theme descended through the opening of Act III of *Pénélope* from the D minor symphony already raided for the second Violin Sonata. Contrast comes with the curving second idea, passed from piano to cello, consoling without being expansive. The piano writing has a hint or two of jazz; the cello writing shows off the instrument in a way hardly to be expected from the composer of the suave *Elégie*. The movement closes, unappeased, in the minor.

In the andante a dotted-note cello theme in saraband rhythm quickly gives way to an ultimately more important successor accompanied by the piano in canonic imitation – a procedure much used in this movement for expressive ends, sometimes pushing the harmony off the expected path. The piano part resembles an anthology of Fauré's late song accompaniment figures, though here extremes of compass are not avoided. The third movement, which, Fauré wrote to his wife, came to him 'in front of a sea of unchanging blue,' is in every sense one of his happiest finales. The sonata is among his finest chamber works.

The Cello Sonata no.2 in G minor, op.117 (1921) owes its existence to the slow movement, a transcription by Fauré of the *Chant funéraire* for wind band, commissioned by the State for the centenary of the death of Napoleon and performed at the Invalides in Paris in May 1921. Here Fauré recaptures the mood of the *Elégie*, but with youthful ardor grown stern and no flamboyant climax. In the sonata, the lament is flanked by two quick movements.

The two Cello Sonatas are separated by a masterpiece, the Piano Quintet no.2 in C minor, op.115 (1921), written over a period of about sixteen months, mostly on holiday during the last year of his directorship of the Conservatoire but finished 'without fatigue,' as he told his wife, after that load had been eased from his shoulders. The composer's son Philippe described the scene at the work's première in the old hall of the Conservatoire: '. . . from the first measures the public was carried away on a single rush of surprise and astonishment . . . as the work unfolded enthusiasm increased, mingled, so it seemed, with remorse that the old man who had so much still to offer had perhaps been unfairly overlooked. By the last chord, everyone was on their feet. The audience shouted, hands stretched towards the large jury box, where Gabriel Fauré, who incidentally had not heard a note, was concealed. He came forward, a solitary figure, shaking his head, to the front of the box. His glance took in the hall where Berlioz and Liszt, Chopin and Wagner, had experienced fiery hours and the crowd, carried away by music alone.'

The C minor Quintet offers a cluster of typical Faurean features: long, arching melodies; short, pregnant figures; chorale-type themes gently syncopated against off-beat chords; a prominent example of the octave-leap figure with a second interval a degree beyond or within the octave, related to the Odysseus theme in *Pénélope*; everything shown in sharp profile with unabating vigor. For the last time Fauré returns to the four-movement scheme, including after the opening allegro moderato, a scherzo of astonishingly youthful, prickling gusto. The noble slow movement shares with the first the exultant sonority that comes, as Orledge suggests, from a general avoidance of the deeper bass registers. In the finale, Fauré juggles with a wealth of material, maintaining constant forward impetus, keeping the texture airy, indulging at the end in a celebration of the tonic major nearly as clamorous as the close of the first movement.

The Trio for piano and strings in D minor, op.120 (1923), shares with the Second Cello Sonata the Mozartian virtues of transparency and economy, together with richer material. It is more emotionally forthcoming and straightforward, more diatonic, less chromatic, than most middle or late Fauré. The first two move-

Below: Photograph, on the June 1910 cover of the magazine *Musica*, of Fauré (seated, closest to the camera) and other members of the committee of the newly founded Société Musicale Indépendante. Ravel is standing third from the left, and next to him is the composer and conductor André Caplet, who worked closely with Debussy.

Right: Caricature of Fauré, composer of the charming *Dolly Suite* (1894-7), dedicted to Dolly Bardac, daughter of Emma Bardac by her first marriage (her second, in 1908, was to Debussy). The work was originally written for four hands at the piano, and it was orchestrated by Henri Rabaud.

ments are as elegiac as wash-drawings by Claude, autumnal but mellow, not misty or wintry. The scherzo-finale is a movement of slim, muscly vigor, transformed at the end into a Faurean tonic-major coda.The trio's neglect must presumably be ascribed to the absence of showy writing or (thinking of Ravel's equally admirable, very different, example) exotic color.

Not long after completing this work Fauré, wrapped in discretion and secrecy, full of humility before the inhibiting example of Beethoven, began his only string quartet, indeed, his only important chamber work without piano. He wrote the slow movement first, at Annecy in the summer of 1923, then the first movement, in Paris, during the autumn. The finale followed in the summer of 1924, at Divonne-les-Bains and then at Annecy again. In September he took to his bed with double pneumonia but was able to reach Paris and home a few weeks before he died. He had left instructions for his pupil Roger-Ducasse to put the finishing touches to the score and for the work to be submitted to the small group of fellow-musicians (including Paul Dukas) whose opinion he liked to hear before having a new work performed. He refused the offer of a run-through at his home because of the distortion the music would undergo in his ears.

So it was not until after the composer's death that the String Quartet in E minor, op.121, was performed, at the Société Nationale in Paris in June 1925, by a quartet led by Jacques Thibaud. More perhaps than any of Fauré's chamber music, the quartet moves on a late-Beethoven plane, beyond everyday joys and sorrows but neither inhuman nor esoteric. At first, because of the lack of strong contrast between movements (quadruple meter is used throughout) and between the themes in the movements, the quartet may sound elusive. Fauré considered a fourth movement but decided against one. Conceivably a short piece in triple time placed between the opening allegro moderato and the andante would have relieved a certain degree of metrical sameness. Be that as it may, the three ample movements that we have well repay attentive and repeated listening. One grows to love the question-and-answer dialogues of the first movement (ancient material again, this time from the unfinished, unpublished Violin Concerto of 1878/9), in which the viola plays the questioning role, and the refined spirituality of the slow movement, which brings, as early as the sixteenth measure, a second idea of great beauty, gently syncopated against rising figures of quietly throbbing, even eighth-notes.

Above: Another caricature of Fauré, this time featuring him as composer of the song-cycle *La Bonne Chanson*, dedicated to Emma Bardac.

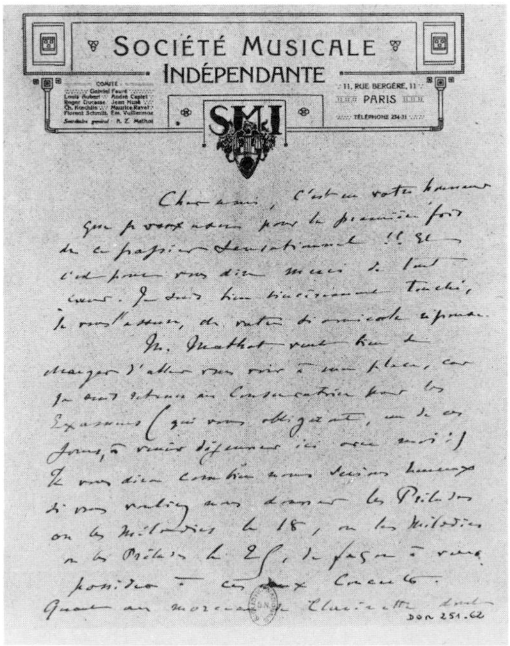
SOCIÉTÉ MUSICALE
INDÉPENDANTE
SMI
11, RUE BERGÈRE, 11
PARIS

Cher ami, c'est en votre honneur que je vous adresse pour la première fois de ce papier sensationnel !! Et c'est pour vous dire merci de tout cœur. Je suis bien sincèrement touché, je vous assure, de votre si amicale réponse.

Right: Part of a letter Fauré wrote to Debussy from the Société Musicale Indépendante in 1910. The previous year he had helped to found the Society – aimed at promoting new music – and became its president.

The composer described the finale as 'a sort of dance of happy souls.' The dance is underpinned by a pizzicato figure which with insistent reiteration shows a touch of the implacability of the opening movement of the first Cello Sonata and of the piano accompaniment to 'Danseuse' (op.113 no.4). There is nothing of a farewell about this unusual finale, and no sign of failing invention. If Fauré's health had not given way there seems no reason why the golden harvest of chamber music should not have continued.

Fauré died on 4 November 1924, in Paris. In French musical life he occupied a paradoxical position. He was at the center, in personal and official contact with Saint-Saëns, d'Indy, Debussy, Ravel and younger composers. Nevertheless he remained independent of the main currents, unobtrusively himself, unsensationally but fundamentally innovating from within, behind a screen of classicism that was also a firm foundation. He remained a tonal composer while pushing tonality to the limit by means both logical and surreptitious: supple modulations, modal harmony, enharmonic change, suspensions. One thing that set him apart was his lack of ambition as regards large forms or (*Prométhée* being a notable exception) large forces. Like Bach and Brahms, he was content to work with what had been handed down to him.

The Conservatoire

The role of the Paris Conservatoire in French musical life during the nineteenth century was similar to that played by the court in earlier centuries: it sponsored an extremely thorough academic musical education, but also dictated the rules of style that composers must follow. Its influence was profound – partly by providing a focus for opposition to its rigid standards – and this persisted well into the twentieth century. It had been founded in 1795 and by 1806 had a staff of forty and over four hundred students. Five years later it moved into a new building with a concert hall that held an audience of over a thousand. Cherubini, who had been on the staff practically from the start, became director in 1822 and established the Conservatoire Concert Society; but the main function was musical education, and there were numerous departments, in each of which annual prizes were awarded.

One of the most influential teachers in the first half of the century was J. F. Halévy (1799-1862) (*below*), whose career typified the Conservatoire's self-perpetuating nature: he first entered at the age of nine, and

at twelve he became a composition pupil of Cherubini's; in 1819 he won the Prix de Rome, but came back to the Conservatoire in 1827 as professor of harmony and accompaniment, eventually becoming professor of composition in 1840; among his pupils were Saint-Saëns, Gounod and Bizet – who married his daughter.

The crowning success of a composition student in Paris was to win the Prix de Rome – awarded for a cantata by the Académie des Beaux Arts, but almost invariably to a Conservatoire student – giving up to four years' study at the French Academy in the Villa Medici in Rome. There was a similar prize for art students, and many friendships between musicians and painters were made there. The director for many years was J. A. D. Ingres, whose portrait of Gounod playing Mozart's *Don Giovanni* (*left*) was painted in Rome in 1841, two years after the composer had won the prize.

On Cherubini's death in 1842 King Louis Philippe appointed as his successor Daniel Auber (1782-1871), seen (*below*) in 1838, who held the post for nearly thirty years. He belonged to the operatic establishment, having written many successful works both for the Opéra and the Opéra Comique, as well as ballet music for Taglioni. However, he was painfully shy, and although he strengthened the teaching of piano at the Conservatoire – with the appointment of J. F. Marmontel as professor in 1848 – and of orchestral instruments, his influence on the students was much less than that of his professors of composition, Halévy and, later, Ambroise Thomas.

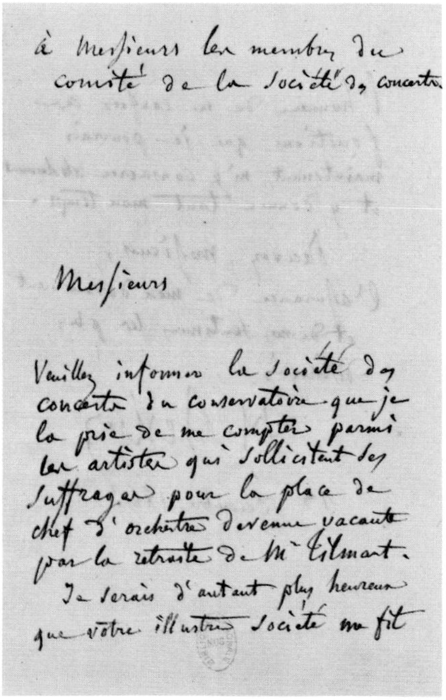
à Messieurs les membres du comité de la Société des concerts

Messieurs

Veuillez informer la Société des concerts du conservatoire que je la prie de me compter parmi les artistes qui sollicitent les suffrages pour la place de chef d'orchestre devenue vacante par la retraite de Mr Tilmant.

Je serais d'autant plus heureux que votre illustre Société me fit

Much of the credit for the foundation in 1828 of the Conservatoire Concert Society should go to F. A. Habeneck (1781-1849). From 1806 to 1815 he had been in charge of the students' orchestra, and he conducted the Conservatoire concerts until 1849, being succeeded by Narcisse Guiraud and then Théophile Tilmant. On Tilmant's resignation in 1864, Berlioz applied (in the letter *above*) for the vacant post, but despite his fame as both composer and conductor, the new chief conductor of the Opéra, François Hainl, was given preference.

Left: Caricature entitled 'Galop chromatique exécuté par le diable de l'harmonie,' showing Habeneck conducting a concert in 1843 in which Liszt is playing the piano; the figure on the left is the celebrated bass Luigi Lablache. Habeneck was first and foremost a violinist – he studied and later taught the violin at the Conservatoire; but it is as trainer and conductor of the orchestras at both the Conservatoire and the Opéra, whose standards were envied throughout Europe, that he is best remembered.

Below: Cartoon celebrating the move of the Conservatoire into new premises in 1911. Thomas had been succeeded as director in 1896 by his own pupil Théodore Dubois (who had been teaching there since 1871), and Dubois in turn was succeeded in 1905 by Gabriel Fauré, whom Thomas had in his time refused to appoint to the teaching staff. Fauré, pushing the wheelbarrow, leads the procession, followed by members of his staff; these include Saint-Saëns with the white beard, who is partly hidden by Massenet (who had taught a composition class at the Conservatoire since 1878) pushing the cart containing a barrel-organ; Debussy behind them is followed by his friend Paul Antonin Vidal (1863-1931), brandishing a baton, a teacher at the Conservatoire since 1894; at the back, is Charles-Maurice Widor (1845-1937), who had succeeded Franck as professor of organ in 1890 and Dubois as professor of composition six years later when Dubois was made director.

Left: Ambroise Thomas (1811-96), Prix de Rome winner in 1832, became professor of composition in 1856 and Auber's successor as director in 1871, introducing important reforms in teaching, though a firm conservative in musical matters. The drawing by Toulouse-Lautrec shows him conducting his opera *Françoise de Rimini* at a concert in 1882.

Jean Béraud's painting (*right*) conjures up the scene outside the Conservatoire at the turn of the century (before the move) as pupils leave after their day's studies. Entry, which was by examination, was always strongly contested, and pupils could begin their studies from the age of ten, while the system of prizes and frequent examinations made for a highly competitive atmosphere. Since the Conservatoire's foundation, the curriculum and examination statutes had been laid down in detail, and there were intermediate examinations twice a year. Students started with *solfège*, the rudiments of musical theory, moved on to the technique of singing and playing their own instruments, and finally took in musical theory and history and the study of accompaniment. It was the most thorough training for professional musicians, and the most advanced pupils might also have a place in the orchestra, which was entirely made up of teachers, pupils and former pupils.

Above: The entrance to the Conservatoire concert hall, which opened in 1811, seen in 1848. It carried on a tradition of public concerts in Paris that had been established with the foundation by A. D. Philidor in 1725 of the *Concert Spirituel*, which continued until 1791. Concerts by the Conservatoire's annual prizewinners had been started in 1797, and there had been pupils' concerts from 1800 to 1824, but it was the founding of the Société des Concerts du Conservatoire by Cherubini and Habeneck in 1828 that began the golden age, ushered in on 8 March 1828 with a performance of the 'Eroica.' At the time there were eighty-six players and seventy-nine singers, and seven concerts were given each season, with soloists who included Chopin and Liszt. Later, despite rival concert series, the popularity of the Conservatoire concerts was such that the number given each season was doubled.

Above: Plate showing the first prizewinners in 1849. The cellist A. J. Tolbèque was later to become an influential teacher.

Above: Interior of the concert hall. Habeneck's championship of Beethoven was brave – he played all the symphonies within the Society's first four years – since even a musical enthusiast like Delacroix had doubts: 'The concert was not very good. I had remembered the 'Eroica' Symphony as being better. Beethoven is definitely terribly uneven. The first movement is beautiful, the andante, which I was looking forward to, was a complete disappointment. Nothing beautiful or sublime in the opening! Suddenly you fall a hundred feet in the middle of the most extraordinary vulgarity. The last movement also lacks unity.'

Below: Caricature statuette of Habeneck by Dantan. For many years he continued to conduct the orchestra with his bow from the violin part.

Above: The public examination for the double-bass in 1886, presided over by the director, Ambroise Thomas, with members of his staff, who include Gounod and Massenet.

Right: The notice-board scanned for the results of the examinations. A prize at the Conservatoire virtually assured a successful musical career, as player or teacher, or both.

Above: A public piano examination around 1907. The new director, Fauré, who presides, had made an important innovation, bringing in distinguished players who did not necessarily teach at the Conservatoire, to sit on his juries. Here they are seated on his right: Moritz Moszkowski (next to him), Isaac Albéniz, Alfred Cortot and Ricardo Viñes.

In an effort to bring new music before the public, Jules-Etienne Pasdeloup (1819-87), a former pupil and now teacher at the Conservatoire, in 1852 founded a new concert society with an orchestra of sixty-two and choir of forty made up of students, the Société des Jeunes Artistes du Conservatoire. The cartoon (*left*) depicts Pasdeloup in triumph later in his career (in 1868), having revived Gluck at the Théâtre Lyrique and brought performances of Wagner to the Cirque Napoléon.

Pasdeloup's concerts were given official backing by Auber in 1856, but the Conservatoire concert hall was far too small and the tickets too expensive. So in 1861 he initiated a new concert series in the huge iron-and-glass Cirque Napoléon, the Concerts Populaires de Musique Classique. His orchestra of eighty-one players included forty-four winners of the first prize at the Conservatoire, and the concerts continued successfully for over twenty years.

The program (*above*) for a concert in their ninety-fourth year is a reminder of the strong tradition of the Conservatoire Concerts, but it dates from the end of an era, the year of Fauré's retirement as director, a time when French music was in the hands of a new generation who rejected all forms of academicism.

CLAUDE DEBUSSY

FELIX APRAHAMIAN

Opposite: Claude Debussy (1862-1918), a pastel portrait by Marcel Baschet, his fellow student in Rome in 1884.

The first conductor of Debussy's opera *Pelléas et Mélisande* once remarked to a friend that when, in the final scene, the dying Mélisande asked for the window to be opened, it let in not only the sunset but all modern music. *Pelléas*, a landmark in operatic history, heralding a new era as surely as it bade farewell to the past, was revealed in 1902. Already, ten years earlier, its composer, inspired by an eclogue by Stéphane Mallarmé, had begun writing an orchestral work unlike any heard before it, and affecting, directly or indirectly, all written after it. Both the *Prélude à l'après-midi d'un faune* and *Pelléas et Mélisande* are key works. They entitle Debussy to pride of place in any discussion of twentieth-century music. Like the great Bach, Debussy looked backward as well as forward in his music, but Bach's musical antecedents were nearer to him, immediate precursors or senior contemporaries, whereas Debussy's included more ancient and exotic elements; they contributed to the formation of a musical voice that remains unique.

Achille-Claude Debussy, born on 22 August 1862 in Saint-Germain-en-Laye, was the eldest of five children. The ancestry of the composer whom D'Annunzio would one day dub 'Claude de France,' and who would more humbly call himself 'musicien français,' was modest. His parents ran a crockery shop on the ground floor of the house in which he was born. They gave it up in 1864, two years after Debussy's birth, and left Saint-Germain-en-Laye, presumably for Paris, where their presence in 1867 is recorded. In 1871, the composer's father joined the Garde Nationale, becoming captain of a battalion. As a result, he suffered imprisonment as a Communard when the revolution was quelled. This must have left its mark on the boy at an impressionable age, and it may explain the silence he always maintained about this period of his life. It may also have contributed to his moody nature: throughout his life he was prone to alternate bouts of elation and depression, though to observers the withdrawn, taciturn and depressed moments outnumbered the more cheerful and sociable. His mother's severity towards her children offers another clue to Debussy's essential loneliness.

Whatever parental deprivation Debussy may have known, his good fortune began with his first important music teacher, Mme Mauté de Fleurville, mother-in-law of Paul Verlaine. Whether or not Debussy was even vaguely aware of the troubles that beset his piano teacher at the time, because of her son-in-law's entanglement with Arthur Rimbaud, his own family background – a father in prison and an impoverished mother – must have been unsettling enough. However, in October 1872, after only one year of piano lessons with Mme Mauté de Fleurville (preceded by some in 1871 from an Italian teacher in Cannes, where Debussy stayed with his paternal aunt), the boy, barely turned ten, was admitted to the Paris Conservatoire. If this points to Debussy's unusual precocity as a pianist, it also testifies to the lady's exceptional gifts as a teacher. All Debussy's music originated at the piano. All his scores were sketched at that instrument. To it he confided his most intimate musical thoughts, some of which later acquired the gorgeous garb of his jeweled orchestration.

From the time of his entry into the *solfège* class of Lavignac and the piano class of Marmontel in 1872 until his departure in 1887, at the age of twenty-five, from the Villa Medici in Rome, Debussy acquired the traditional musical background of the Paris Conservatoire, as student, graduate and, eventually, winner of the coveted Prix de Rome. In 1874, at the age of twelve, Debussy was evidently a sufficiently competent pianist to be allowed to play Chopin's First Piano Concerto with the Conservatoire orchestra. In 1876 he entered the harmony class of Emile Durand; apart from some academic exercises, however, it seems unlikely that any of his now published works were composed as early as this, when he was only fourteen, despite some previous misdatings. In 1879 his second attempt to win a *premier prix* at the annual Concours for piano-playing met with failure, putting paid to any ambition he might have had to become a concert pianist. However, in 1880 he won first prize in a score-reading competition, enabling him to enter a composition class. His true *métier* must have been clear to him about this time. A group of settings of poems by Théodore de Banville and the beautiful 'Beau soir,' a setting of a poem by Paul Bourget, date from about 1880. They leave no doubt of Debussy's creative gifts at the age of eighteen.

His piano-playing continued to serve him well in these early years. Already in the summer of 1879 he had been engaged as house-pianist by the châtelaine of the famous Loire château of Chenonceaux. The following two years brought

Left: Debussy at the age of five, at Saint-Germain-en-Laye, where he spent the first few years of his life. His parents were not well-to-do and were apparently unmusical, but by the time he was ten, and having had piano lessons from Mme Mauté, Debussy was studying at the Paris Conservatoire, his musical talent clearly recognized.

him a wealthy and cultured patroness, Mme von Meck, the 'beloved friend' of Tchaikovsky. As her house-pianist, the young Debussy accompanied her to Interlaken, Arcachon and Fiesole in 1880, and to Moscow in 1881. In her household he must have become acquainted with the music of Tchaikovsky above all other Russian composers. His awareness of 'The Five,' and Musorgsky in particular, was to come later.

The early 1880s were crucial years for the young Debussy, although, at first, his extravagant harmonic improvisations met with criticism and understandable misunderstanding. One of his fellow students testified that one day in the spring of 1884, when Léo Delibes, the blameless composer of *Sylvia*, was absent from his class, Debussy had the audacity to take the master's place, in order, as he put it, 'to feed the little orphaned birds.' He fed them, apparently, 'with a regular debauch of chords, a stream of outlandish arpeggios, a gurgling of triple trills in both hands simultaneously, continuous successions of indescribable harmonies.' The session, according to Léon Vallas, lasted for more than an hour. It was brought to an abrupt end by the unexpected arrival of a superintendent who summarily ejected the impossible 'fanatic.'

•The Prix de Rome•

There are other accounts of academic resistance to the young man's innovations. Wisest and most expedient, perhaps, was the attitude of Ernest Guiraud, the principal of his composition class, when Debussy showed him his setting of de Banville's 'Diane au Bois,' a work in which a musical personality is already established. Guiraud read the work carefully, admired what he thought were its good points, but said with great honesty: 'It's all very interesting. But you must keep that sort of thing for later on, or else you'll never get the Prix de Rome.' The effect of that friendly criticism was that Debussy played the academics' game, won the Second Prix de Rome with his cantata *Le Gladiateur* in 1883, and the First Prix de Rome the following year, 1884, with *L'Enfant prodigue*, a charming cantata in a style more conservative than that which he had already formulated for himself. While performances of the whole cantata are rare, its 'Air de Lia' remains a popular extract. It is to the credit of Gounod, who once referred to César Franck's Symphony as the 'affirmation of impotence pushed to the lengths of dogma,' that, as a member of the Conservatoire jury, he supported Debussy, declaring that posterity would judge them harshly if they did not award him the *Premier Grand Prix de Rome.*

Three years before Debussy took up this scholarship at the Villa Medici in Rome, he had become attached to a Mme Blanche Vasnier, the singer to whom his early songs are dedicated, including the early Verlaine settings. The liaison appears to have been beneficial, for there was a flow of *mélodies* at this period in Debussy's development. There was also a general widening of literary and artistic horizons. A setting of a poem by Mallarmé ('Apparition') antedates by a few months the composition of *L'Enfant prodigue.* Debussy must have read avidly at this period. His acquaintance of English literature in translation was not restricted to Shakespeare and Shelley, but included more recent figures such as Swinburne and Rossetti, and, in Baudelaire's versions, the work of Edgar Allan Poe, who was to become a crucial influence.

From Rome, Debussy made two return journeys to Paris. In 1885 he was dissuaded from cutting short his stay in Rome by the husband of his Egeria. During his Roman sojourn he appears to have been restless and far more active than the ailing Parisian sybarite of later years. The seventy-four-year-old Liszt counseled him to hear the music of Palestrina and Lassus while in Rome, which he did and wrote about with enthusiasm. At the Conservatoire Debussy's training had been traditional; from *solfège* to the Prix de Rome cantata, it had enjoyed none of the special training in the modes offered by the rival institution, the Schola Cantorum, which was geared primarily to the training of church musicians, and where the harmony textbook used was far less conventional than that used by the Conservatoire. And yet, Debussy embraced modality as warmly as chromatic harmony. His experience of ecclesiastical music did not stop with the early masters of polyphony to whom Liszt directed him. He is recorded as having visited the Abbey of Solesmes in 1893, carefully noting the plainsong he heard there at

Matins, Lauds and Nones and the First Vespers of the following day.

But seven years earlier, at the time of his second flight back to Paris from the Villa Medici, other impressions, literary as well as musical, were crowding in on the young man. He was twenty-four when in 1886, his final return to Rome, he composed *Le Printemps*, his second *envoi de Rome*, which was said to have been inspired by Botticelli's *Primavera*. (The first *envoi*, submitted as an *Ode symphonique*, was trounced by the fathers of the Académie: 'Today, M. Debussy seems to be tormented by the desire to produce the bizarre, incomprehensible and unplayable.' The manuscript has not survived, but it might well have contained the germs of his future musical innovations.) In a letter, Debussy wrote of *Le Printemps*: 'My idea was to compose a work in a very special color covering a wide range of feelings. It is to be called *Printemps*, not a descriptive Spring, but a human one. I want to explain the slow and painful genesis of beings and things in nature, their gradual blossoming and the final bursting joy of rebirth into new life.' *Le Printemps*, too, did not altogether please the distinguished examiners, who, that year, consisted of Ambroise Thomas, Gounod, Delibes, Reyer, Massenet and Saint-Saëns. The wordless chorus Debussy had included in the otherwise orchestral score was an innovation which worried them, and, declared Saint-Saëns: 'One doesn't write for orchestra in F sharp major.' Their official report said: 'M. Debussy does not transgress in platitudes or banality. On the contrary, he shows an over-pronounced taste for the unusual. His feeling for musical color is so strong that he is apt to forget the importance of accuracy of line and form. He should be aware of this vague impressionism which is one of the most dangerous enemies of artistic truth.' Amazingly, perhaps, these gentlemen were foreshadowing the kind of criticism leveled at Debussy immediately after his death by the *young* Parisians of the early 1920s. Nothing daunted, Debussy turned in 1887 to a French translation of Rossetti's *The Blessed Damozel* for his third *envoi de Rome*. By then, he had returned finally to Paris and was living with his parents. This was the time at which he became acquainted with the poets of Mallarmé's circle: it had been a short step from the French Symbolists to the English Pre-Raphaelites, then also enjoying Parisian attention.

Another influence, to which all French composers of the time were subject in varying degrees, was that of Wagner. The pilgrimage to Bayreuth was an essential experience, and one already known to many of Debussy's immediate French precursors. In 1887 Debussy heard

Left: With a group of fellow students at the Villa Medici in Rome; Debussy is shown sitting on the balustrade, wearing a pale jacket.

Below left: Debussy playing the piano at the house of the composer Ernest Chausson at Luzancy, 1893, together with Chausson's nieces Yvonne and Christine Lerolle and their parents. Chausson and Debussy had recently become close friends, but their friendship was short-lived, coming to a dramatic end over a love affair.

Below: Debussy, with Chausson and Henri and Mme Bonheur, boating on the River Marne at Luzancy in 1893.

Right: Frontispiece by Maurice Denis for the first edition of *La Damoiselle élue*, which Debussy composed in 1887-8. The piece, based on Rossetti's poem *The Blessed Damozel*, was written as an *envoi* (an obligatory set piece) for the Académie des Beaux Arts. Its first official performance for the Académie was canceled, since Debussy refused to conform to tradition by writing an overture for it, and *La Damoiselle* was not given its première until 1893, at the Société Nationale.

Below: Orpheus, *c.*1894, by Henri Martin, an artist belonging to the symbolist group with whom Debussy was associated in Paris. Symbolist artists, reacting to the naturalism of realist and impressionist painters, sought to express the *essence* of reality rather than its actual appearance, using form and color to express a subjective idea rather than objective truth.

Lohengrin in Paris. In the two following summers he himself became a Bayreuth pilgrim, hearing *Parsifal* and *Die Meistersinger* in 1888, and again in 1889, when he also heard *Tristan und Isolde*. In 1893 he played extracts of *Das Rheingold* at the Paris Opéra in a two-piano version with Raoul Pugno, and heard *Die Walküre* there six days later. Later, in his musical writings, Debussy was to make some caustic remarks about Wagner's music, but it cast its spell, in particular the score of *Parsifal*.

In these formative years Debussy's experience of Wagner must have contributed to his own harmonic richness. The *Cinq poèmes de Baudelaire* (1887-9), which he thought of well enough to publish privately in a limited edition of 150 in 1890, take a leap forward from his earlier *mélodies* in the direction of Wagnerian harmonic sensuousness: the first of them, 'Le Balcon,' in effect a lengthy *scena*, makes almost Wagnerian demands on vocal compass and stamina.

Indeed, the last decade of the nineteenth century found Debussy still absorbing and assimilating musical, literary and visual experiences in the formation of his own artistic personality. Among the works composed at this time are some that reflect the sound training he received as a musical craftsman: pieces like the popular *Petite suite* (1886-9) for piano duet and the *Deux arabesques* (1888-91) for piano solo. On the other hand, there is the curiously neglected *Fantaisie pour piano et orchestre* (1889-90), of which Debussy himself was partly responsible for the belated publication. It was to have been given at an official concert of his music before his academic judges as a fourth *envoi de Rome* in 1890. Because the program proved over-long, Vincent d'Indy, who was conducting, proposed that only the first of its three movements should be performed. Displeased by this, Debussy himself gathered up the orchestral parts after the final rehearsal, effectively barring it from being heard in the evening. He sent d'Indy a well-worded letter of apology in which he pointed out that playing just the first part of the *Fantaisie* would not only be dangerous but would give a false idea of it. When, however, a performance of the *Fantaisie* was announced by the Concerts Lamoureux in the following year, he again withdrew it. One explanation for this withdrawal was put forward by Debussy's one-time teacher Guiraud. It draws attention to yet another influence Debussy absorbed, like that of Wagner, but relinquished perhaps more successfully, that of cyclic form, dear to César Franck and his devoted school. Guiraud recounts that, on his return from Rome, Debussy declared before his most tolerant teachers that the sonata with two themes was well and truly dead. To have issued and approved a work so solidly structured as the *Fantaisie* at that moment must have struck Debussy as inconsistent with views he had expressed.

If the *Fantaisie*, which Debussy later declared he would like to reorchestrate and for which he expressed a kind of devotion as late as 1909, shows his assimilation of principles of

Below: Claude Monet's famous impressionist painting *Rouen Cathedral in Full Snow*, dated 1894. Debussy's involvement with the symbolist movement ran alongside an interest in Impressionism. His often delicate but equally powerful and unconventional harmonies, conjuring rich, undefinable, ever-changing images, are sometimes described as 'impressionist'.

musical form adopted by the Franckistes, so too does his one and only string quartet. He titled it *Premier quatuor*, although it never had a successor, and it remains the only one of his works to bear a published opus number: op.10. Completed in 1893 and first performed by its dedicatees, the Ysaye Quartet, at the Société Nationale in Paris on 19 December of that year, it brought Debussy's name to a much wider public. One basic theme, in the Phrygian mode on G, informs all four movements, though its transformation in the andante is less obvious. Without strictly observing classical procedures, Debussy nevertheless imparts enough classical feeling to the structure of his quartet to link it with those of earlier masters of the string quartet, in whose company Debussy's position is now secure. But in 1893 it must have sounded a new note. In addition to the modality of its motto-theme, it touched the whole-tone scale and the augmented triad it produces. And it juxtaposed common chords in an uncommon manner. This Debussy may have picked up from his friend Erik Satie, four years his junior and undoubtedly a harmonic pioneer. Satie was to become a mascot for the younger generation of French composers after Debussy's death, but his slender gifts were understandably overshadowed by the superior genius of his friend.

•Two landmark works•

That genius, as we have seen, was being nourished from several sources. One dating from 1889 and bearing fruit within the following decade was the sound of the Javanese gamelan, which Debussy heard at the Universal Exhibition in Paris. That same year Debussy became acquainted with the score of Musorgsky's *Boris Godunov*, a marked contrast to Wagner's *Tristan*, which he had just heard at Bayreuth. The musical vocabulary of both works undoubtedly contributed to that which Debussy would establish as his own in his one and only completed opera. But, before that, he was to complete an orchestral work of profound originality and significance. Its inspiration was a poem.

L'Après-midi d'un faune is a eclogue which the poet Stéphane Mallarmé, then a humble teacher in a Lycée in Tournon, began in 1865. At the time, the composer who was to become his friend and the perfect translator of his poem into another medium was only three years old. Debussy's *Prélude à l'après-midi d'un faune* began as incidental music for the reading or dramatic presentation of the poem. It represents his final version of a score announced during its period of composition (1892-4) as *Prélude, interludes et paraphrase finale pour l'après-midi d'un faune*. The first performance was given at a concert of the Société Nationale in Paris under Gustave Doret on 23 December 1894, when the public demanded a repeat.

The score of the *Prélude* defies analysis in a conventional manner. Debussy created a mold within which its contents, iridescent and fluid, are as clearly and tautly held as in any classical procedure, just as Mallarmé's tantalizing poem has its own formal perfection.

In the years immediately preceding the composition of the *Prélude* Debussy had been often drawn to the verse of Paul Verlaine. In all, he set no fewer than twenty of his poems. Between the first, the early setting of 'Fantoches' (1882), and the last 'Colloque sentimental' (1904), which concludes the second set of *Fêtes galantes*, Debussy's art in the setting of words to music had been refined in the process of composing a work which constitutes another landmark in musical history, the opera *Pelléas et Mélisande*.

Pelléas et Mélisande was first performed at the Paris Opéra Comique on 30 April 1902, and given on no other stage until 1907. In the field of opera, succeeding composers profited

Left: A group photograph taken at Eragny the morning after the first performance of *Pelléas et Mélisande*, which took place at the Opéra Comique on 30 April 1902. From left to right: the critic Pierre Lalo, Debussy, the composer Paul Dukas, Mme Debussy and Paul Poujaud, a young lawyer and enthusiastic music-lover.

from the new sensitivity initiated by Debussy, observing speech rhythms in a musical setting, even if they clung to the set pieces of traditional operatic forms. There are no arias or ensembles in *Pelléas et Mélisande*. The orchestral interludes which link the component scenes of the first four acts, although extended by Debussy to their present length during the course of rehearsals for the première to meet the exigencies of scene-changing, are an integral part of the work and constitute its only 'development.' Transcending their original purpose, in conducting the listener from one scene to another, they supply what words are powerless to express. Prolonging one scene and preparing for another, they provide a dramatic commentary as well as a visual thread for the mind's eye. As such, they command the greatest concentration, for elsewhere Debussy's music is intentionally the servant of the text, however vividly it may paint each individual scene.

In *Pelléas et Mélisande* the text must be of paramount importance to the listener, as it was to the composer; he never regarded it merely as a convenient peg on which to hang a succession of arias and ensembles. Long before 1893, the year in which Debussy bought and read Maeterlinck's play, he had, as a student, described the kind of operatic collaborator that he sought: 'one who, saying things by halves, would allow me to graft my dream on to his; who could conceive characters whose story belonged to no time or place, who would not despotically impose on me the scene to be painted, and would leave me free, here and there, to have more art than he and complete his work. But he need have no fear! I will not follow the errant path of opera, where the music insolently predominates, where poetry is relegated to second place, stifled by too heavy a musical clothing. In the opera house they sing too much. One should sing when it is worth the trouble, and hold pathetic accents in reserve. There must be differences in the energy of the expression. In places, it is necessary to paint in monochrome, and to be content with grays. . . . Nothing should impede the progress of the drama: all musical development not called for by the words is a mistake. . . . I dream of texts which will not condemn me to perpetrate long, heavy acts, but will offer me instead changing scenes, varied in place and mood, where the characters of the play do not argue, but submit to life and fate.'

Debussy could hardly have described more accurately the play that would in a very few years' time furnish him with the libretto of his dream, for these words, spoken in October 1889 and noted by Maurice Emmanuel, a fellow student at the Paris Conservatoire, fit Maeterlinck's *Pelléas et Mélisande* like a glove. It is possible, however, that Debussy's declared esthetic had already been influenced by an earlier Maeterlinck play, *La Princesse Maleine*, published in 1889. At least three musicians were attracted to it. D'Indy, Debussy and Satie all approached Maeterlinck, who was more attracted to the idea of having d'Indy, eleven years Debussy's senior and a far more prominent figure at the time, as a musical collaborator. And poor Satie relinquished it utterly, for he knew his limitations. Yet it was Satie who, according to Debussy's own admission to Cocteau, determined the esthetic of *Pelléas* by the following advice: 'There is no need for the orchestra to grimace when a character comes onto the stage. Do the trees in the scenery pull faces? What we have to do is to create a musical scenery, a musical atmosphere in which characters move and talk. No couplets – no *leitmotifs*, but we should aim at creating the kind of atmosphere that suggests Puvis de Chavannes.'

Here, too, Satie proved wise before the event, for Debussy does, in fact, create 'a musical scenery, a musical atmosphere in which characters move and talk.' Of course, where not only Satie was unprophetic but Debussy was less than generous was in the denial of *leitmotifs*. Both Debussy and Satie grew up at a time when the cult of Wagner in France was at its height, and both were probably aggravated by the enslavement to Wagnerism of such senior compatriots as Chabrier and Vincent d'Indy. More than once, Debussy harped on his reaction to Wagner. But in a brilliant essay that summarized Debussy's achievement in his unique opera, Romain Rolland differentiated between the art of Wagner and that of Debussy, but wisely qualified Debussy's obstinate insistence that *Pelléas* contained no *leitmotifs* with the statement that: 'In *Pelléas et Mélisande* one finds no persistent *leitmotifs* running through the work, or themes which pretend to translate into music the life of characters and type; but, instead, we

Right: Scene from the first production of *Pelléas et Mélisande*, showing the death of Pelléas. Golaud was played by Hector Dufranne, Mélisande by Mary Garden, and Pelléas by Jean Périer; the stage design was by Jusseaume. The première had a mixed reception, with much hostile criticism both from its audience and from Maeterlinck, whose wife Georgette Leblanc Debussy had rejected for the title-role.

Right: Debussy's sketch for Act II Scene 3 of *Pelléas*. His use of recognizable themes was intentionally different from the commonly accepted and indeed expected usage of Wagnerian *leitmotifs*; Debussy strove to express an *idea* or feeling, the essence of a situation rather than its obvious character.

Below: Mary Garden, the first Mélisande, photographed in her costume for the first production.

have phrases that express changed feelings – that change with the feelings.'

Rolland's meaning is clearer if the word 'persistent' rather than *leitmotifs* is accented, for later critics – Emmanuel (1933), Golea (1942) and Van Ackere (1952) – have shown how dependent Debussy was on *leitmotifs* and how they supply the very warp and weft of his musical texture. But the motifs – Emmanuel lists thirteen – particularly those representing the three principal characters, are not immutable, but fluid, flexible and variable in the manner in which they are deployed. They change with the mood of the characters instead of serving as a fanfare or identity tag. If Debussy, by subtle means, adapted Wagnerian formulae to his own purpose, he also, perhaps quite unconsciously, followed the advice of an earlier and no less musical French man-of-letters than Rolland. In his *Lettre sur la musique française*, Jean-Jacques Rousseau, after pointing out the disparity between the inflexions of French speech 'whose accents are so harmonious and simple' and 'the shrill and noisy intonations' of the recitatives of French opera of his day, postulated that the kind of recitative best suited to French should 'wander between little intervals, and neither raise nor lower the voice very much; and should have little sustained sound, no noise, and no cries of any description – nothing indeed that resembled singing, and little inequality in the duration or value of the notes, or in their intervals.' This reads almost as if the *Promeneur Solitaire* had dreamed of Geneviève's reading to Arkel of Golaud's letter to his half-brother in the second scene of Debussy's opera. Although in five acts, like the play, Debussy's opera reduces Maeterlinck's nineteen scenes to fifteen. The omitted scenes are either mainly symbolical or superfluous to the understanding of the shadowy figures of the drama and their fate, which is predetermined by an inexorable destiny.

• *Nocturnes* and *La Mer* •

Begun after *Pelléas*, but completed before it, come the three *Nocturnes*, a symphonic triptych with a choir of women's voices in the third. They were originally conceived in a form different from that in which they are known today. As early as September 1894, Debussy wrote to the Belgian violinist Ysaye: 'I am working at three nocturnes for violin and orchestra that are intended for you; the first is scored for strings, the second for three flutes, four horns, three trumpets and two harps; the third combines both these groups. This is, in fact, an experiment in the various arrangements that can be made with a single color – what a study in gray would be in painting.' Two years later, in 1896, the nocturnes still existed in this form, for Debussy wrote to Ysaye that he would prefer to forgo their performance unless Ysaye himself undertook it in Brussels. But nothing came of this project, and the score of this original version has never been seen. The *Trois Nocturnes* – 'Nuages,' 'Fêtes' and 'Sirènes' – were composed between December 1897 and December 1898 and published in 1900. Camille Chevillard conducted the first performance of the first two at a Lamoureux concert on 9 December 1900, and the complete triptych on 27 October 1901.

The composer's reference to the sister art of painting in his letter to Ysaye clearly indicates his attitude to the *Nocturnes*: 'a study in gray' conjures up Whistler, a favorite painter of Debussy's, and it is this artist's *Nocturnes* rather than those of Chopin that are evoked by these marvelously refined pieces. Debussy's comment on the final version of the *Nocturnes* brings the parallel even closer: 'The title *Nocturnes* is to be interpreted here in a general and, more particularly, decorative sense. Therefore, it is not meant to designate the usual form of the nocturne, but rather all the various impressions and the special effects of light that the word suggests.'

Debussy's 'slow, solemn motion of the clouds' begins with a meandering alternation of fifths and thirds – a note-for-note borrowing, undoubtedly unconscious, of the piano accompaniment to one of Musorgsky's *Sunless* songs. He makes this theme his own by coloring it first with clarinets and bassoons, pointed at the third measure by an oboe, and then – after a haunting little cor anglais phrase which recurs – with the ethereal sound of muted violins *divisi*. Later, there is another easily recognized motif, pentatonic this time, for flute and harp against a quiet background of held string chords. These are the elements with which Debussy paints one of the most beautiful and restrained examples of musical impressionism.

If the *divisi* strings of 'Nuages' recall Debussy's original plan for the scoring of the first *Nocturne*, that for the second may be recognized in the scintillating writing for woodwind and brass in 'Fêtes,' where, in fact, trumpets, trombones, tuba and percussion are added to the more modest orchestral requirements of 'Nuages.' Even the two harps have their place, in magnificent glissandi near the beginning, and, later, preparing for the distant, muted trumpet-calls that herald the approach of the festival procession. For the marine nocturne 'Sirènes' Debussy modified his palette by suppressing the trombones, tuba and percussion, but adding a small choir of female voices used instrumentally. Their siren-song is loath to venture beyond the conjunct interval of a second, yet it haunts the ear.

Between the triumph of the *Nocturnes* in 1901 and that of its successor in the orchestral field, *La Mer*, in 1905, Debussy's life became fraught with incident and agitation. In 1888 Mme Vasnier had been succeeded in the affections of the twenty-six-year-old composer by Gabrielle Dupont, with whom his liaison lasted for ten years. In 1899 he married Rosalie (Lily) Texier, a dressmaker, whom he abandoned in 1904 for Emma Bardac (*née* Moyse). Mme Bardac, the wife of a banker, was, like Mme Vasnier, a singer, and as the dedicatee of Gabriel Fauré's *La Bonne Chanson* had already earned herself a place in the annals of French music before she met the younger composer. They met through her son, Raoul Bardac, an aspiring composer who had sought instruction from Debussy. Before long, Mme Bardac was inspiring *mélodies* from Debussy as formerly she had from Fauré, who had also annually marked the birthdays of her daughter Dolly with a piece for piano duet. The first of these was the well-known 'Berceuse' which opens the 'Dolly' Suite. Lily Debussy attempted suicide in 1904. In 1905 Emma Bardac bore Debussy a daughter, Claude-Emma (Chou-Chou). Debussy divorced Lily and married the mother of his daughter.

Left: This Japanese lacquered screen belonged to Debussy and is thought to have inspired 'Poissons d'or,' the third piece in his second set of *Images* for piano, dated 1907.

It was in the midst of this turmoil that Debussy's orchestral masterpiece, *La Mer*, was conceived and completed. His second marriage proved a stable feature in his life. Another was his cordial relationship with his publisher Jacques Durand. Debussy had previously disposed of his music to other publishers, but had issued the Baudelaire songs and *La Damoiselle élue* at his own expense on subscription. A similar arrangement for *Pelléas et Mélisande* with the publisher Fromont had been made without Maeterlinck's blessing, for he had become estranged from Debussy over the casting of the opera. Durand, having meanwhile taken over the two other privately issued works, now negotiated with the two former collaborators, both of whom were happy that he should publish a new edition of *Pelléas*. So began a loyal composer–publisher relationship which, lasting for the rest of Debussy's life, assured a regular income for an increasingly fastidious composer, who, from time to time, perhaps, had to be goaded into greater activity, but whose artistic taste was given full scope in the graphic presentation of his scores.

An example of this is the reproduction of part of Hokusai's famous print *The Great Wave* on the cover of the full score and piano-duet version of *La Mer*, Debussy's work which, more than any other, by reason of its dimensions, approaches the symphony. He first announced the work in two letters written on 12 September 1903, from Bichain, Yonne, where he was spending the summer. One to Jacques Durand reads: 'What do you say to this: *La Mer*, three

Right: A woodblock print in the Japanese manner by the Parisian Henri Rivière, showing the Eiffel Tower under construction in 1898.

Below: The original front cover of *La Mer*, first published in 1905, was based on *The Great Wave*, a print by the very popular nineteenth-century Japanese artist Hokusai.

symphonic sketches for orchestra. (i) "Mer belle aux Îles Sanguinaires," (ii) "Jeux de vagues," (iii) "Le vent fait danser la mer." This is what I am working at, drawing on innumerable memories, and what I hope to finish here.'

The other letter, to his friend André Messager, repeats this information, adding, 'You are perhaps unaware that I was destined for the happy life of a sailor, and that only the hazards of existence led me in another direction. Nevertheless, I have always retained a sincere passion for Her [the sea]. You will say that the ocean does not exactly wash the Burgundian hillsides . . . ! And that this might well resemble landscapes painted in the studio! But I have innumerable memories; to my mind, this is worth more than a reality whose charm generally weighs too heavily on our thought.'

Thus Debussy defined the imaginative quality of his musical impressionism, for few works so completely evoke the sea, except, perhaps, his own 'Sirènes,' of which *La Mer* is a development, or the grotto scene in *Pelléas et Mélisande*.

Debussy worked at *La Mer* until 1905, 'Sunday, 5th March at six o'clock in the evening,' as he inscribed the completed orchestral score. The following day he was able to write to Durand, who was staying in the south of France and was anxious about *La Mer*, that the score was finished and already in the hands of the engravers and copyists. The work received its first performance at the Concerts Lamoureux under Camille Chevillard on 15 October 1905.

La Mer is scored for a large orchestra, including, in the last movement, two cornets as well as three trumpets. Discarding his originally planned title, Debussy called the first part 'De l'aube à midi sur la mer' (From dawn to noon

Right: Nocturne by James McNeill Whistler. It is quite likely that Debussy knew Whistler through visiting the salons of Bailley or Mallarmé. Composer and painter were thought of by their contemporaries as kindred spirits, and certainly Debussy used painterly and descriptive titles for his music. He described the monochromatic nature of his own *Nocturnes* as equivalent to 'a study in gray in painting.'

at sea). So aptly does this describe the music that Erik Satie, complimenting the composer, could not resist expressing particular appreciation of 'that charming bit at about a quarter past eleven.' The miracle of this tonal seascape is that although composed of a succession of different musical elements, these make up a musical whole as melodically compelling and as formally satisfying as any symphonic movement in sonata form, so naturally does one phrase lead into the next.

• Piano music •

In the first decade of the twentieth century, Claude Debussy not only proved a unique genius in the field of opera and orchestral compositions but also endowed the repertory of his own instrument, the piano, with a succession of pieces that have enjoyed the suffrage of pianists and their audiences ever since. Begun in 1894, but not completed until 1901, the suite entitled *Pour le piano* is a transitional work, linking the sometimes derivative early Debussy with the later, when abstractions give way to a kind of impressionistic and poetic descriptiveness.

The initial 'Prélude' is based on a striking, strongly accented theme, reiterated obsessively. It is colored by contrasting common chords with those of the augmented fifth, from which Debussy smoothly approaches the whole-tone scale. He salvaged the central 'Sarabande' from an early set of *Images* for piano, composed in 1894 and unpublished during his lifetime. It provides an early example of Debussy's blending of the old and the new, the archaic and the modern, for there seems to be a modal basis for its grave harmonies, yet they admit a new element in the shape of unresolved sevenths and ninths. For these, Debussy was undoubtedly indebted to his young friend Erik Satie, whose own *Trois sarabandes* included such innovations seven years earlier, in 1887. The final 'Toccata' of *Pour le piano* pursues a brilliant and unflagging course, not without its own subtleties of harmonic coloring and dynamic light and shade.

Composed in July 1903, the set of three *Estampes* were engraved, printed and handsomely presented in a cover of *papier Ingres*, which delighted Debussy. Ricardo Viñes played the set for the first time at a concert of the Société Nationale in the Salle Erard on 9 January 1904. Undoubtedly the inspiration of the first piece, 'Pagodes,' was the Paris Universal Exhibition of 1889 at which Debussy and other French musicians of the time heard the Javanese and Cambodian music played by native performers. The piece uses four modes of the pentatonic scale, which are presented, developed and recapitulated with immense subtlety, so that although 'Pagodes' has a structure as architectonically sound as any of those picturesque and exotic landmarks, it flows like the music of the gamelan and casts a similar spell on the listener through its repeated motifs, all grounded in a pentatonic B major.

'Soirée dans Grenade,' the second *Estampe*, unfolds languidly in a habanera rhythm in F sharp minor, with a more vigorous second strain in A major, a more sensuous third idea in F sharp major, interrupted by two tiny 'guitar' interludes, and a coda based on the first idea. Manuel de Falla, the Spanish composer who best encapsulated the spirit of Spain in the most concise of musical terms, was able to proclaim: 'The descriptive skill which is condensed into the few pages of the "Soirée dans Grenade" seems nothing short of miraculous when one considers that this music was written by a foreigner, guided almost entirely by his own insight and genius. . . . This is indeed Andalusia that he depicts for us: unauthentic truth, we might call it; seeing that not one single measure has been directly borrowed from Spanish folk music and that, notwithstanding, the entire piece, down to its smallest details, is characteristically Spanish.'

After his excursion to the Far East in 'Pagodes' and to a languorous Spain in the 'Soirée,' Debussy returned to France with a Parisian toccata for the third *Estampe*. 'Jardins sous la pluie' is a townscape with children, a revised version of the third of the unpublished *Images* of 1894. Like its companion *Estampes*, the piece is soundly structured. Its two themes are both children's songs: the lullaby 'Do-do, l'enfant do' and 'Nous n'irons plus au bois.'

Debussy published three sets of triptychs under the title of *Images*: two for piano solo, the third for orchestra (although originally conceived for two pianos). The first of these dates from 1905, and the three pieces it comprises were completed, if not actually composed, in England. On 26 July 1905, in a letter to his publisher, Debussy announced his arrival in Eastbourne. 'A peaceful and charming place,' he called it. 'I hope to be able to send you some music next week,' he added.

The first piece of the *Images*, 'Reflets dans l'eau,' is a pianistic rhapsody on the drowsily harmonic three-note figure heard at the outset. The second of the *Images*, 'Hommage à Rameau' stems as much from one of Debussy's personal musical enthusiasms as from one of the editorial chores he undertook for Durand. In 1903 the composer was heard to have cried out after the performance of a Rameau ballet at the Schola Cantorum: 'Vive Rameau! A bas Gluck!' He was undoubtedly in sympathy with the job of preparing Rameau's *Les Fêtes de Polyminie* for the collected edition that Durand was bringing out. Debussy's 'Hommage à Rameau' takes the form of a grave and dignified sarabande with a strongly modal flavor. The third *Image*, 'Mouvement,' is a *moto perpetuo*.

Whereas Debussy contained all the pianistic textures of this first set of *Images* on two staves, the second set, composed two years later in 1907, uses three, a measure of the increased subtlety and refinement of his piano writing, though there is greater economy of thematic material. Debussy's friend Louis Laloy relates that he wrote to the composer about the touching country custom of sounding knells from the Vespers of All Saints' Day until the time of the Mass for the Dead the next morning on All Souls' Day. These would resound from village to village, across yellowing woods in the silence of the night. This apparently gave Debussy the idea for the first of the second set of *Images*, 'Cloches à travers les feuilles' (Bells through the leaves). His gentle carillons, which rise to a central climax, emerge from and recede into a whole-tone landscape.

The second piece, 'Et la lune descend sur le temple qui fût' (And the moonbeams fall on the temple that was), is a nocturnal landscape containing some forty indications of *pianissimo* in its five pages and rising nowhere above a slight *crescendo* from *piano*. All Debussy's now familiar musical fingerprints are here: a grave sequence of organum-like chords moving in parallel, conjuring up an atmosphere of mysterious antiquity, whether oriental or occidental, and

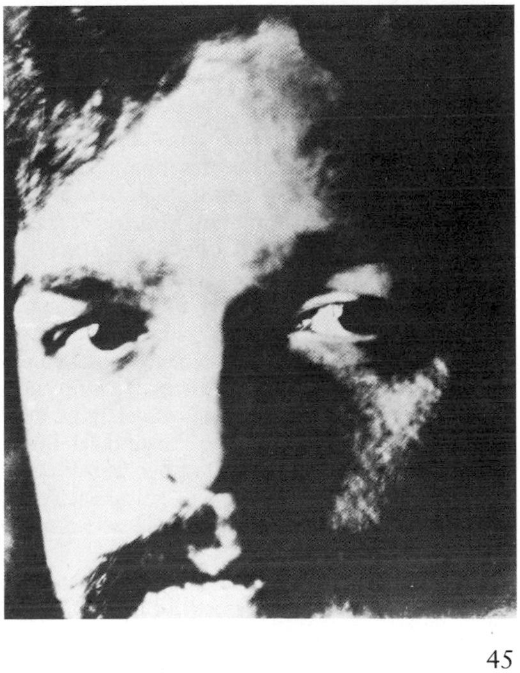

Three photographs of Debussy by Pierre Louÿs (taken at Louÿs's house), with (*bottom left*) their friend Zohra in Moroccan costume. Louÿs, whose poems concentrate on the exotic and erotic, was a close friend of Debussy's and one of the more decadent of the self-indulgent writers who saw themselves as part of the French symbolist movement in literature. His three erotic poems, the *Chansons de Bilitis*, were set by Debussy between 1897 and 1898; their titles were 'La flûte de Pan,' 'La chevelure' and 'Le tombeau des naïades.' Later, in the summer of 1914, Debussy arranged these song settings for piano duet.

ending in a chant-like phrase in octaves; a sequence of chords to which consecutive thirds give a *rondure* as of marble columns, a delicate dialogue of chimes and dulcimers, and, finally, the rapt stillness and distance into which so many of Debussy's musical landscapes dissolve.

For the third piece, 'Poissons d'or,' Debussy's inspiration was a panel of Japanese lacquer showing a goldfish and its reflection in the water. But the music itself is more suggestive of the living thing, those ornamental creatures darting and gliding in the light and shade of a lily pool, for this is perhaps the most mercurial and iridescent of all Debussy's *Images*. Appoggiature, harmonic and melodic, give it its watery instability.

Dating from the same period are two pieces composed in the summer of 1904 and published separately later that year: *Masques* and *L'Isle joyeuse*. Both titles evoke the *Fêtes galantes* of Verlaine. *Masques* is another of Debussy's transitional pieces, combining elements of his earlier and later manners, as much by the composer of the orchestral 'Fêtes' and the last sonatas as of the *Suite bergamasque*. The 'happy island' of the other piece is Cytherea, and its supposed inspiration is the famous painting by Antoine Watteau, *L'Embarquement pour Cythère*, although Debussy himself never declared this except by the title's implication. *L'Isle joyeuse* is his longest piano piece. Its breadth and pianistic scope, as well as its dynamic range, seem to evoke something more substantial than the early eighteenth-century artificiality of Watteau's elegant aristocracy on pleasure bent. To Durand, Debussy wrote from Dieppe, in September 1904: 'But, Lord, how difficult it is to play – this piece seems to me to combine all the ways of attacking a piano if I may say so.'

With pianistic masterpieces like the *Estampes*, *Images* and *L'Isle joyeuse* behind him, Debussy composed his *Children's Corner* (1906-8), a suite of six short pieces. He was one of those composers who have captured the secret of childhood in their music. Here he proved his kinship with such masters as Schumann and Musorgsky, for *Children's Corner* cedes nothing to either the *Kinderszenen* of the one or the *Nursery* of the other, or, for that matter, to Ravel's adorable *Ma Mère l'Oye*, in that sense of charm and innocence that is the prerogative of children, and which all four composers have crystallized in a few pages.

The six piano pieces of *Children's Corner* are easier to play than many of Debussy's other piano pieces, yet it would require an uncommonly gifted and sensitive child to do them full justice. With its picturesque titles and deft pictorialism, the suite might hold the interest of children who heard it: more important is the fact that adults play it and in listening to it recognize in its intimate appeal a touching evocation of the child mind – in boredom, gaiety, tenderness, wistfulness and sheer fun. The album is dedicated to 'my dearest Chou-Chou, with her father's apologies for what follows.' Chou-Chou was to survive her adoring father by only one year, for in 1919, at the early age of fourteen, she fell victim to a diphtheria epidemic.

•The acknowledged master•

In 1903 Claude Debussy was decorated Chevalier of the Légion d'Honneur. Unlike his junior, Maurice Ravel, who became embroiled in the musical politics of the Paris Conservatoire, and, disgusted with the musical establishment, eventually refused that honor, Debussy had no quarrel with his alma mater. In 1905, as a result of the scandal created by the refusal of the Conservatoire authorities to allow Ravel to make a fourth attempt to compete for the Prix de Rome, the director, Théodore Dubois, was obliged to resign and Gabriel Fauré, Ravel's composition teacher, was appointed in his place.

Far left: Another of Louÿs's photographs of Debussy – seated with a bass clarinet.

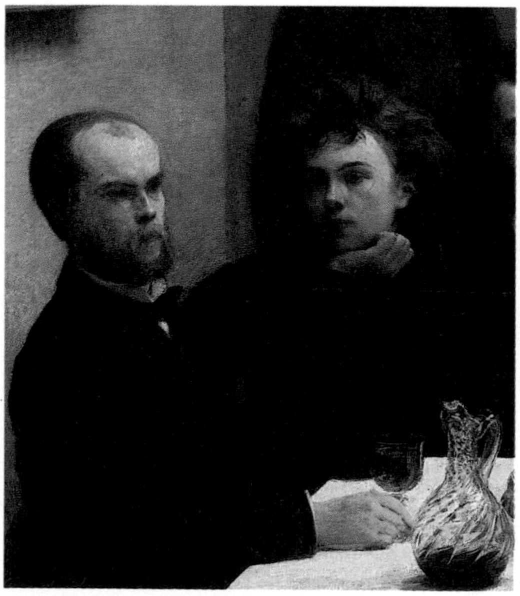

Left: Detail of a painting by Henri Fantin-Latour, showing the poets Verlaine and Rimbaud. Their symbolist – and often outrageous – work exerted considerable influence on Debussy, who used many of Verlaine's poems for song-settings.

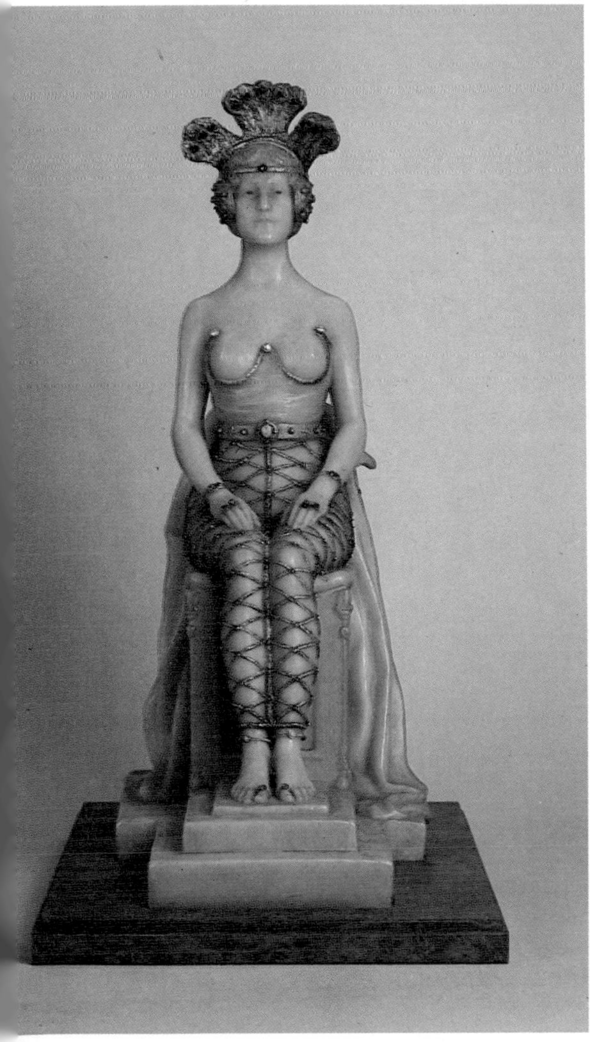

There was little cordiality between Fauré and Debussy, who had supplanted him in the affections of Emma Bardac. Yet, with admirable impartiality, the older composer appointed the younger a member of the Conservatoire's Conseil Supérieur in 1909. That year Debussy was one of the adjudicators for the Concours for ladies' voices and woodwind. The first, he did not look forward to; the other proved very agreeable. It led to his writing the clarinet test pieces for the following year.

The *Première rapsodie* for clarinet (fated, like the *Premier quatuor*, to be without a successor) was the 1910 competition piece. 'On Sunday, pity me, I will hear the Rapsodie for B flat clarinet eleven times,' he wrote to Jacques Durand. 'I will tell you all about it, if I am still alive.' But he survived the Concours, even enjoyed it, writing enthusiastically about the winner a week later. Debussy evidently thought well of the *Rapsodie*, for he gladly acceded to Durand's request that he should orchestrate the piano accompaniment, and in 1911 he referred to it as 'certainly one of the most pleasant pieces I have ever written.'

In 1909, within a year of his second marriage, Debussy displayed the first signs of the cancer which was to kill him within a decade. Almost daily hemorrhages obliged him to take morphine and cocaine. And yet, this was a period in which he was in demand as a conductor of his own orchestral works, both in Paris and abroad. At home he continued to work on *La Chute de la Maison Usher*, the scenario and music for an opera based on Edgar Allan Poe, but it made little progress, and Durand was probably grateful that his ailing composer could

Above: Sappho by Sir Lawrence Alma-Tadema; the sensual atmosphere of the artist's evocations of the classical world (executed from before 1870 up until 1910) is often heightened by the sound of music. Debussy's *Prélude à l'après-midi d'un faune*, *Chansons de Bilitis*, *Syrinx* and other Grecian works share the same *fin-de-siècle* sense of hedonistic indulgence.

Left: A jewel-encrusted wax figure by Etienne Lami of Ida Rubinstein, the dancer, for whom Debussy was commissioned to write *Le Martyre de Saint-Sébastien*. Here she is seen in the role of Cléopâtre in the ballet to music principally by Arensky, in which she made her first sensational entrance carried on stage wrapped in a sumptuously decorated mummy-cloth, which was unwound to reveal her in Bakst's dancing costume.

also turn his hand to more immediately saleable music like the piano Preludes, the first of which were composed in 1909.

Debussy published two books of *Douze préludes*, the first in 1910, the second in 1913. The first occupied him from 7 December 1909 to 5 January 1910, each manuscript bearing the day and month in which it was written. The descriptive titles Debussy attached to the pieces are printed not at the beginning but at the end of each piece. While the Preludes undoubtedly had a practical purpose, they rose far above the general level of intended pot-boilers. With admirable concision, they offer a valid guide to Debussy's musical eclecticism and his integration of elements old and new in an expressive language which bears his personal accent.

The completion, performance and publication of an important orchestral work, the third set of *Images*, divides Debussy's first book of *Douze préludes* from the second. He planned to let his publisher have this orchestral triptych in 1906, a year after the success of *La Mer*, but it was not until 1912 that all three panels of it were ready. The first complete performance of the *Images*, as the composer originally conceived them, took place at a Concert Colonne in Paris on 26 January 1913, with Debussy's disciple André Caplet conducting. The *Images* proved to be Debussy's last orchestral concert-room work, for these three pieces – already enlivened by dance-rhythms, jig, habanera and round – are the precursors only of *Jeux*, written, at Diaghilev's behest, for dancing. The second and third orchestral *Images* were first intended as two-piano pieces, and even 'Gigues' was ready for Durand in a four-hand piano version before Debussy finally released it in orchestral score.

As in his earlier piano triptych, *Estampes*, Debussy sought to evoke in the three orchestral *Images* what were, to him, characteristic aspects of three countries, substituting England ('Gigues') for the Orient ('Pagodes'), but retaining Spain and France for the second and third *Images* ('Soirée dans Grenade' being replaced by 'Ibéria' and 'Jardins sous la pluie' by 'Rondes de printemps'). Although both Spanish pieces are redolent of Spanish folksong without actual quotation, 'Gigues' and 'Rondes de printemps' have recourse to traditional tunes. Perhaps it was his use of these that led Debussy to describe the *Images* as an attempt 'to do something different – to achieve not what some fools call *impressionism*, but *realities*.' But so sketchy is his treatment of the tunes – they are more suggested than heard – that they become brushstrokes among many in musical canvases that are, despite Debussy's claim, highly impressionistic in their effects of light and color in the manner of his contemporary Claude Monet.

This analogy with painting is useful, for it is Debussy's empirical use of orchestral and harmonic colors that constitutes the novelty of his work. He treats chords of the seventh and ninth not as modulatory but as autonomous elements, able to move in parallel as freely as his melodies or his bare fifths, which point to plainsong and organum as his musical ancestry rather than the Beethovenian symphony. Plastic melodies, emancipated harmonies and an equally sensitive attitude to timbre, as an essential element of rather than an imposed adjunct to music, are the chief characteristics of an individuality which shines brighly in the *Images*.

Following the welcome given his first book of *Douze préludes* in 1910, Debussy followed it with a second book. This occupied him between 1910 and 1912, and it was published in 1913. Curiously enough, the second set of twelve Preludes, like the second set of piano *Images*, is printed mostly on three staves, generally clarifying the three planes on which Debussy's wide-ranging piano writing unfolds.

Right: Debussy with his daughter Claude-Emma, always affectionately known as Chou-Chou. She was born on 30 October 1905; Debussy married her mother, Emma Bardac in 1908, after years of criticism from his friends about the way he had treated his first wife Rosalie (Lily) Texier.

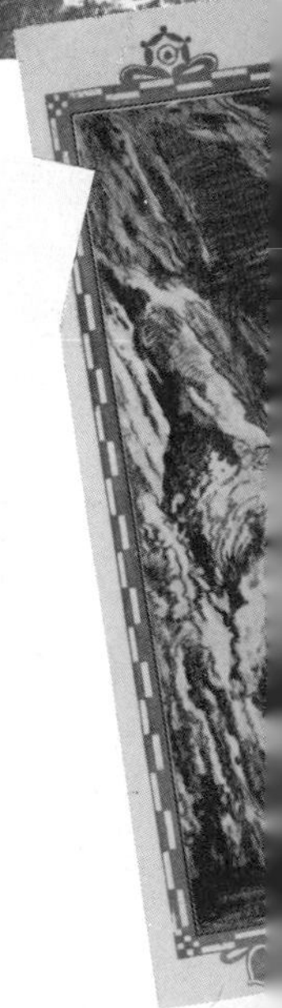

Above left: Front cover of *La Boîte à joujoux*, a ballet designed by André Hellé specifically to amuse children, with music by Debussy. The first performance took place on 10 December 1919, after his death, at the Théâtre Lyrique, and only the beginning was completed by the composer; the rest was orchestrated by Caplet from Debussy's sketches.

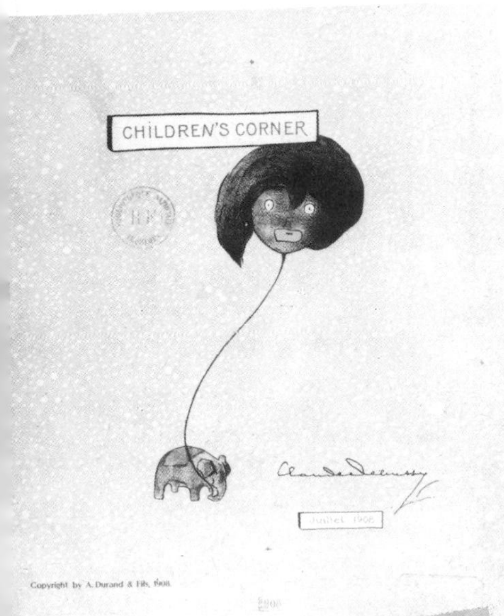

Left: Front cover of the first edition of *Children's Corner*, a series of piano pieces written by Debussy for his daughter and first published in 1908. The series consists of a group of six pieces, some humorous, some serious.

Left: Stage design for Debussy's ballet *Jeux*, by Léon Bakst. *Jeux*, commissioned by Diaghilev and choreographed by Nijinsky, was first performed on 15 May 1913 at the Théâtre des Champs-Elysées, but Debussy was unhappy with the choreography, which did not match the subtlety of his score.

•Works for the theater•

Before the completion of the second book of Preludes in 1912, Debussy had undertaken a few commissions. The first dated from 1910, when the dancer Maud Allan appointed Debussy to compose the music for a ballet for which she had devised the scenario with W. L. Courtney. A contract was signed on 30 September 1910, and Debussy worked on *Khamma* during 1911. A more urgent task, however, was *Le Martyre de Saint-Sébastien*, for which Debussy wrote music at the behest of its author Gabriele D'Annunzio, the mystical Italian poet, and which he described as 'a much more lavish proposition than the wretched Anglo-Egyptian ballet.'

The source of the money for this five-act 'mystery' was the Russian-Jewish dancer Ida Rubinstein, whose liaison with a member of a very wealthy Irish brewing family resulted in more than one remarkable artistic conjunction. It was she for whom D'Annunzio created the role of the Saint, and, later, Gide and Stravinsky collaborated for her in *Perséphone*, and Claudel and Honegger in *Jeanne d'Arc au bûcher*. Formerly a member of the Diaghilev company that took Paris by storm, Mme Rubinstein used her considerable wealth to commission works in which she could take part as both actress and dancer. D'Annunzio's work reached Debussy in sections between 9 January and 2 March 1911. By May the score had to be complete. Working day and night, Debussy would pass on what he had written, page by page, to his disciple André Caplet, who, under Debussy's supervision, established the full score and who also conducted the performance. The players and singers rehearsed the music in fragments, with little idea of what it was all about until the last rehearsal of the music alone. This proved a revelation to everyone. Debussy, after weeks of feverish activity, emerged from his retreat to attend it. Abandoning the slightly sarcastic goodwill he reserved for such occasions, he wept with emotion, for the play with its archaic theatrical French undoubtedly struck a chord in him. But that rehearsal was Debussy's final triumph, for the martyrdom of *Le Martyre* was to begin with the dress rehearsals. The production, despite the sumptuous décor by Bakst and the choreography by Fokine, conflicted with the presentation of Debussy's score. And there were difficulties, too, outside the Théâtre du Châtelet before the première on 22 May 1911. Without having read the play, the Cardinal-Archbishop of Paris forbade Catholics to attend. It was known that D'Annunzio had incorporated a good deal of picturesque paganism into his poem of a Christian martyr. The interdict brought forward a dignified reply from the authors. But the damage was done, and the work never recovered from its bad start. In the concert room, however, Debussy's music occasionally comes into its own, either in its complete form, with a narration which links the music of five *mansions* of the long and wordy *Mystère*, or in the symphonic Suite which is Caplet's work. The Suite, being purely orchestral, does not include the fifth *mansion*, 'Le Paradis,' where Sébastien's soul is received by the celestial choirs of Martyrs, Virgins, Apostles and Angels, ending with a paraphrase of Psalm 150.

After *Le Martyre*, Debussy was able to revert to *Khamma*, which he described to his publisher, in a letter dated 1 February 1912, as 'this curious ballet with its trumpet-calls suggesting a riot or fire and giving you cold in the back.' Durand published Debussy's piano score of *Khamma* in 1912, before its orchestration was completed under Debussy's supervision, by Charles Koechlin. Both Debussy and Maud Allan were dead before the score was first heard (at the Concerts

Colonne in 1924) and the ballet first staged (Opéra Comique, 27 March 1947), so that *Khamma* remains relatively unknown, though even the piano score shows its affinity with *Jeux*, a masterpiece completed and performed before it.

Jeux is Debussy's last major orchestral work. Described as 'a plastic vindication of the man of 1913,' *Jeux* began as a ballet scenario by the dancer Nijinsky. Diaghilev outlined it to Debussy and asked him to compose the music. The very flimsiness of the scenario and its suggestive undertones seem to have attracted Debussy, as he confessed in an article published on the day of the first performance of the ballet (Théâtre des Champs-Elysées, 15 May 1913): '. . . a scenario made of that subtle *rien du tout* of which I think the poem of a ballet should be composed . . . a park, a game of tennis, the chance encounter of two girls and a young man in pursuit of a lost tennis-ball, a mysterious, nocturnal landscape, with that slightly naughty, indefinable something sheltered by the shadows; leaps, turns, capricious steps, all that's necessary to bring rhythm to life in a musical atmosphere.'

If the subject fascinated Debussy, its choreographic realization undoubtedly disappointed him. He had worked hard at the score, for, as he explained to Durand, in a letter dated 12 September 1912: 'There's something rather difficult to accomplish here, for the music has to convey a rather *risqué* situation!' He added, almost prophetically: 'It's true that, where ballet is concerned, immorality passes between the legs of the dancers and ends in pirouetting.'

Unfortunately, *Jeux* was to be eclipsed exactly two weeks after its première by that of Stravinsky's more epoch-making *Rite of Spring*. Nonetheless, *Jeux* marked an important point in Debussy's development – one, alas, that had no future in the brief span of life left to him. Just before putting the finishing touches to *Jeux*, Debussy wrote to Caplet about it: 'I had to find an orchestration "without feet" for this music. Don't think I mean an orchestra composed exclusively of cripples! No! I am thinking of that orchestral coloring which seems to be lit up from behind, and of which there are such marvelous effects in *Parsifal*.' Consciously, Debussy made his last purely orchestral masterpiece diaphanous in texture and fleet of foot.

After *Jeux*, Debussy worked on another balletic work of more modest intent, *La Boîte à joujoux*, on a scenario by the children's-book illustrator André Hellé, in which the puppet inhabitants of a child's toy-box come to life. The subject seems to have appealed to the composer of *Children's Corner*, but illness prevented him from completing its scoring, and this task was undertaken by André Caplet after Debussy's death. The year 1913 was also the one in which Debussy composed his last set of three songs, the *Trois poèmes de Mallarmé*, music of quintessential refinement that is rarely heard. Two of the three poems were also those of Ravel's *Trois poèmes de Mallarmé*, composed in the same year but with the accompaniment of a chamber ensemble.

Right: Design by Léon Bakst showing Ida Rubinstein as Saint-Sébastien.

• 'Musicien français' •

The period leading up to the First World War found Debussy a famous composer sought after as a conductor of his own music, but technically inadequate to do it justice. Depressed by his illness and harassed by creditors, he undertook engagements in Moscow and St Petersburg in December 1913 and in Rome the following February. The year 1914 also took him to The Hague, Amsterdam and Brussels, and, finally, in July, to London, where he had fulfilled the first of his important engagements abroad in 1902.

In July, 1914, just before the outbreak of war, Debussy arranged for piano duet some of the incidental music he had composed at the turn of the century for readings of the *Chansons de Bilitis* of his friend Pierre Louÿs, music which even then was more impersonally decorative than his still earlier song-settings of these poems.

Fifty-two years old when war was declared in August 1914, the ailing composer, more than ever conscious of his patriotic sympathies and physical disability, wrote to his publisher asking for work he could do. Ten days later, he confessed that he found it almost impossible to work. Nevertheless, by November he was able to compose and in the following month, he scored his 'Berceuse héroïque,' first printed in *King Albert's Book*, a tribute to the King of the Belgians and his soldiers, published by the London *Daily Telegraph*. Debussy's homage appropriately quoted 'La Brabançonne,' the Belgian national anthem.

The year of 1915 found Debussy 'editing' Chopin and Bach for his publisher, but towards the end of June 1915 the clouds had lifted

Left: Bakst's cover for the program of the first performance of Diaghilev's ballet (1912) based on the *Prélude à l'après-midi d'un faune*, 1892-4, showing Nijinsky as the Faun.

Right: Portrait drawing of Bakst by Picasso, dated 1 April 1922.

Below: Bakst's stage design for the *Prélude à l'après-midi d'un faune*.

sufficiently for Debussy to ask Durand whether the revision of the Bach sonatas for violin and clavier was urgent, '. . . because, having a few ideas at the moment, don't hurry us to explain – I would like to cultivate them for the benefit of pieces for two pianos . . . Without saying so, I have suffered much from the long drought imposed on my brain by the war.'

At first, Debussy titled the set *Caprices en blanc et noir*. With his many highly colored orchestral scores now behind him, Debussy saw his own instrument, the piano, as monochromatic as the medium of Goya's etched *Caprices* and *Disasters of War*. On 12 July 1915, Debussy went to spend three months at Pourville, near Dieppe, and it was there that *En blanc et noir* was completed. Already on 14 July he was able to write to Durand: 'I must tell you that I have slightly altered No.2 of the *Caprices* (the "Ballade de Villon contre les ennemis de la France"); it tended to be too dark and almost as tragic as a *Caprice* by Goya.' There can be little doubt that Debussy's musical faculty was strongly visual, and that he saw as well as heard *En blanc et noir*, for in the following February he wrote of the set to Godet: 'These pieces seek to take their color and feeling from the ordinary piano, like the "grays" of Velazquez, if you wish.'

The first piece, dedicated to Koussevitzky, who had been responsible for Debussy's visit to Russia in 1913, is a musical commentary on a quotation of four lines from the libretto of Gounod's *Roméo et Juliette*, applied ironically by Debussy to those who, standing aside from the Dance of War, tacitly admit to some physical defect. In a letter written to Godet shortly after his return to Paris, Debussy confessed that at Pourville he had recovered the ability to think in terms of music, and that he had written there like one possessed, or like one who had to die on the morrow. He adds a comment which seems to connect with this first piece: 'Of course, during three months I haven't forgotten the war . . . yet I've seen its horrible necessity better. The futility of adding to the number of "disabled" struck me, and, considering everything, it would have been cowardice to think only of the horrors committed without trying to react against them by re-creating, to the best of my ability, a little of that beauty which is being hounded.' Debussy's musical comment, then, takes the form of a caprice in swift waltz tempo, elegant, fluid and essentially aloof.

The *Caprice* which Debussy felt obliged to lighten from the blacks of Goya to the grays of Velazquez is, nevertheless, a war piece. Debussy dedicated it 'au Lieutenant Jacques Charlot, tué à l'ennemi en 1915, le 3 mars' (Charlot was the cousin and business colleague of Jacques Durand. He is also commemorated by the prelude of Ravel's *Le Tombeau de Couperin*). Sending it to Durand on 12 July 1915, Debussy wrote: 'You will see how Luther's Hymn catches it for having imprudently strayed into a French "Caprice"! Towards the end, a modest carillon rings out a pre-Marseillaise; whilst apologizing for this anachronism, it's permissible at a time when the very pavements and forest trees are vibrating to this ubiquitous song.' And indeed, titled with the *envoi* of Villon's 'Ballade against the enemies of France,' the piece is a grim little microcosm of the war seen through patriotic French eyes. The grave rumblings of artillery and shrill bugle-calls give way to the contemplative peace of the French landscape, which is then torn by war-like agitation and the inexorable tread of 'Ein' feste Burg.'

The third piece, titled with the first line of a poem by Charles d'Orléans ('Yver, vous n'estes qu'un vilain'), which Debussy had set for *a cappella* choir in 1908 as the third of his *Trois chansons de Charles d'Orléans*, was completed before the more troublesome second *Caprice*. Inscribed 'à mon ami Igor Stravinsky,' it unfolds as a winter landscape without any specific allusion to the war. In its chromatic idiom and exquisitely refined keyboard writing, it heralds the masterpieces which were to follow almost immediately – Debussy's *Douze études*.

Debussy hesitated about the dedication of his *Douze études*. 'They will be dedicated,' he wrote to Durand, 'to F. Chopin or to F. Couperin. I've as much respectful gratitude to the one as to the other of these two masters.' Finally he opted for Chopin, to whose memory the set is inscribed. The *Douze études* have a very special place in Debussy's *oeuvre*, as they have in piano literature. Completed in September 1915, they are the last solo pieces Debussy wrote for his own instrument. When sending the printed copy to André Caplet in the following summer of 1916, he described the studies as 'a thousand ways of treating pianists according to their deserts.' The technical problems are presented *seriatim*: the first book of six comprises, in order, studies for the five fingers, thirds, fourths, sixths, octaves and the eight fingers; the second book deals with such pianistic refinements as chromatic intervals, ornaments, repeated notes, contrasted sonorities, compound arpeggios and chords.

Opposite: The Violin Concert, a print of Bella Edwards and the violinist Eva Mudocci (Evangeline Muddock) dated 1903, by the Norwegian painter Edvard Munch, born a year after Debussy and, like him, a source of inspiration for the twentieth-century revolution in artistic form.

Below and opposite: Works by two of the pioneers of modern art, inspired – like many of their musician colleagues – by the stimulating atmosphere of Paris at the turn of the century: Picasso's drawing of himself and friends leaving the World's Fair held in the city in 1900; and Marcel Duchamp's drawing of the great Russian ballerina Tamara Karsavina, dated 1909.

Towards the end of his life Debussy turned again to chamber music. The String Quartet, composed in the last century, had had no successor. Now, in a depressed state, because of his terminal illness, financial worries and the state of war, he sought a kind of introspective refuge in planning a series of six chamber sonatas, of which only three were written: those for cello and piano (1915), for flute, viola and harp (1915) and for piano and violin (1916-17). The order of the instruments – piano before violin – is Debussy's own in this his last completed work.

The three completed sonatas are almost a distillation of Debussy's art, looking backward as well as forward to realms he did not live to conquer. All three have a distinctly modal flavor, as if the composer, self-styled 'musicien français' on the title-pages, was evoking the perfume of the distant musical past of his native land, the *melismas* of plainsong and the songs of the *trouvères*.

Debussy himself confessed of the *Sonate pour violoncelle et piano* that he liked 'its proportions and its form, which is almost classical in the true sense of the word.' Once again, a compatriot precursor, Jean-Marie Leclair, rather than Beethoven, provides the general structural model for this three-movement work. Perhaps the best clue to the Cello Sonata is Debussy's original intention of titling it 'Pierrot fâché avec la lune.' And if he also wished it to evoke characters from the Italian *commedia dell'arte*, he must surely have thought of them in terms of Verlaine's *Fêtes galantes*. Like its companions, the Cello Sonata is dedicated to his wife. Debussy composed it in July and August 1915, joining the cellist Joseph Salmon in its first performance on 24 March 1917.

The *Sonate pour flûte, alto et harpe*, which occupied Debussy from the end of September to October 1915, also has its own subtle Debussyan form, in which elements of the first movement are echoed in the other two. The timbre of the chosen instruments, as well as the fusion of modal and chromatic harmonies, confer a tender sadness on the work.

If the first two Sonatas were composed with comparative ease, the third cost its dying composer a much greater effort. It was to be his swansong. He had begun work on it in October 1916. The first and second movements were finished by February 1917, but the finale, the germ idea of which he had found the previous year, proved recalcitrant. It was not until 5 May that the problems posed by the finale were solved to his satisfaction. On that day he accompanied the violinist Gaston Poulet in the first performance of the *Sonate pour piano et violon* at the Salle Gaveau. In September they repeated the work at Saint-Jean-de-Luz, where Debussy was staying. These were his last public appearances. On 25 January 1918, at a time when the tide of war had not yet turned in favor of the Allies and Paris was being bombarded by the Germans, Debussy died of the cancer which had been slowly killing him for ten years.

The Spanish Renaissance

Music in Spain at the turn of the century was a microcosm of the world of late nineteenth-century music. After the domination by the Italians over opera and the Germans over symphonic music, national feeling began to be voiced both in the revival of old Spanish music and in the rediscovery of popular musical traditions. Catalonia, with its own nationalist aspirations, was the most important center of this musical activity, starting as early as the mid-century with the founding of workers' choral societies by Anselmo Clavé (1824-74). His work was carried on by the ardent Wagnerian Josep Roboreda (1851-1922), while the founder of musicological studies in Spain was Felipe Pedrell (1841-1922), who was also the most influential teacher of the period. Pedrell was the editor of much ancient music, including the complete works of the Renaissance composer Victoria, but he was also the composer of four *zarzuelas* (popular operas) with Catalan texts, and he sought to introduce Hispanic elements, derived from ancient and popular traditions, into both instrumental and dramatic music; his pupils included Granados, de Falla and Gerhard.

The influence of Wagner was also very strong during the 1890s, deriving largely from the French Wagnerians, in particular Vincent d'Indy, who spent some time in Catalonia. Through the work of Enric Morera (1865-1942) these different strands – the choral, nationalist and Wagnerian movements – became associated with the literary and artistic *modernista* movement in Barcelona, while the ancient music of Andalusia proved the most potent influence on Granados, Albéniz and de Falla.

Left: Isaac Albéniz (1860-1909), by the *modernista* painter Ramon Casas. As a pianist Albéniz showed a prodigious talent, and he studied in Barcelona, Paris and Madrid. In his teens he traveled widely in the Americas, then went back to Barcelona, but also spent many years in Paris, where he became a friend of Fauré, d'Indy, Dukas and Debussy. Though now known chiefly for his piano music, he also wrote operas, orchestral works and songs, combining the influence of French music with the inspiration of Spain. Despite his cosmopolitan outlook, the Spanish elements in his compositions derived from genuine national traditions and were not simply local color of the kind made popular by Glinka, Tchaikovsky and Chabrier.

Above: Pau Casals (1876-1973), also from a drawing by Ramon Casas. It was Albéniz who discovered Casals playing in a Barcelona café and introduced him to a patron who enabled him to study abroad. Today Casals is best remembered as a cellist – particularly for his playing of the Bach suites for solo cello. However, he had a much wider role in the musical life of Spain before the Civil War, both as composer and through founding his own orchestra and, in 1926, the workers' concert society.

Above: First page of Albéniz's manuscript of 'Triana' from *Iberia*. In earlier works Albéniz often relied overmuch on post-Romantic keyboard virtuosity, but in *Iberia* he refined his style, while integrating strongly Spanish – and particularly Andalusian – elements into a masterpiece of decorative polyphony. Blanche Selva (1884-1942), the pianist to whom this piece is dedicated, prepared *Iberia* for publication, and the pencil marks on the manuscript are hers; but Albéniz himself also made very precise phrasing and dynamic marks. Debussy wrote of Albéniz: 'Never has music attained such a diversity of impressions and colors: dazzled by a torrent of images, we have to close our eyes . . .'

Left: One of Morera's many arrangements of Catalan folksongs, 'La Mala Nova' (Bad Tidings), published by *L'Avenç*, the *modernista* journal whose heroes included Nietzsche, Wagner, Ibsen, Baudelaire and Maeterlinck. Morera was a prolific composer and also wrote incidental music for several works by Rusiñol, including his drama *L'Alegria que passa* (1898), while his *La Fada*, a Wagnerian fairy opera, was composed in 1897 for the *Festes Modernistes* in Sitges, the festival of the arts organized by Rusiñol.

Above: Interior of the Palau de la Música Catalana, built in 1905-8 for the *Orfeó Català* by Lluís Domènech. The choral society had been founded in 1891 by Lluís Millet and Amadeu Vives, and the style of the building also reflects Catalan *modernisme*.

Below: Enric Morera conducting his Catalunya Nova choir portrayed by the *modernista* poet and painter Santiago Rusiñol. Morera, a pupil of Pedrell and friend of Albéniz, founded his choir in 1895, and their performances of works by Clavé, the founder of the Catalan choral movement, provoked controversy because of the political implications of their strong local patriotism. Morera was also a prolific composer and arranger; among his most interesting works are his choral *sardanas* – traditional Catalan round dances.

Below: Title-page of Granados's *Colección de Tonadillas*, 1914. The *tonadilla* was a traditional solo song, often of a satirical character, and had enjoyed great popularity in the eighteenth century. Granados's pieces reflect the Spanish music of that period.

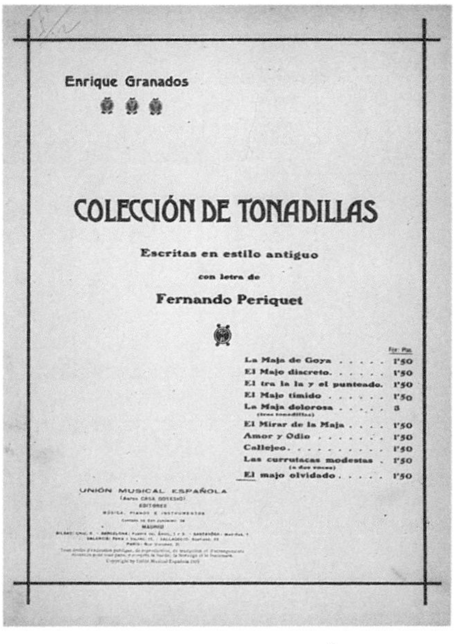

Above: Enrique Granados (1867-1916). Together with Albéniz, Granados was the founder of the modern Spanish piano school. He studied both with Pedrell and in Paris, and his earlier piano music tends to be in a conventional *salon* style with local Spanish color. However, both in the piano parts of his *Tonadillas* and in *Goyescas* (1911), Granados, like Albéniz in *Iberia*, found an individual, authentically Spanish voice. The paintings of Goya fascinated Granados, although the *Goyescas* reflect the artist's less tragic moods, and the music was reworked to form an opera of the same name, first performed at the Metropolitan Opera, New York, in 1916. This was, in fact, the last of five operas by Granados, all derived from the tradition of the *zarzuela*, a local genre of lyric dramatic work, influenced by Italian opera, which was immensely popular throughout the nineteenth century.

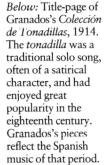

Right: Anna Fitziu as Rosario in *Goyescas*, a photograph inscribed for Mme Granados. In making Granados' piano suite into an opera, the librettist Fernando Periquet, who had to write words to fit existing music, again went to Goya for his settings and characters. At the first performance in January 1916, Fitziu sang with Martinelli in the role of Don Fernando, the captain in love with Rosario, and with de Luca in that of the toreador Paquiro, who fatally wounds Fernando in a duel. The famous aria 'La maja y el ruiseñor' is sung by Rosario at the start of Act III.

Above: El Amor brujo, 1915, was de Falla's first major work. It began as a *gitanería* with dances, songs and spoken passages, but the composer revised the work as a ballet with songs. It was inspired by the singer and dancer Pastora Imperio, for whom it was written, and her mother, Rosario la Mejorana, from whom de Falla learned much of the ancient music and folklore of Andalusia. The work draws on *cante jondo*, not by quotation, but in its rhythms and sonorities.

Left: Manuel de Falla (1876-1946) was an Andalusian, though much of his musical formation came from Barcelona, where he studied with Pedrell, and Paris, where he spent the years from 1907 to 1914 and was in contact with Albéniz, Ravel and Stravinsky. His early works – *La Vida breve* (1913), *El Amor brujo* (1916) and *Noches en los jardines de España* (1916) for piano and orchestra – are the final flowering of impressionistic nationalism, while his later works, like the Chamber Concerto for harpsichord (1926), show an increasing asceticism and simplicity, influenced in part by Stravinsky's 'neo-classical' works.

Above: Massine in a scene from *El Sombrero de tres picos*, de Falla's ballet commissioned by Diaghilev in 1916. The final version was staged in 1919 with set and costumes by Picasso and choreography by Massine; the dancers were trained by the unstable but brilliant *flamenco* dancer Felix Fernandez.

Above: Federico García Lorca (1898-1936). Lorca's fascination with Spanish folklore, with the *cante jondo* and with gypsy *flamenco* music colored much of his poetry, and his association with de Falla played an important role in his life. He had studied the piano as a child and first met de Falla in 1919. Three years later they collaborated with the painter Zuloaga in directing a festival of *cante jondo*. They were keen to promote a revival of this ancient art, as they saw that the effects of city life were destroying the old traditions of Spain, even in the remote south. *Cante jondo* (deep song) is the purest and oldest strain in the *flamenco* tradition that originates from Andalusia, an almost orgiastic lament, whose harmonic basis and melismatic line seem to derive from the music of the Moors. Its tragic nature and its association with the lowest strata of society are reflected in Lorca's *Poema del cante jondo*, which he had written in 1921. De Falla had also explored *cante jondo*, not only in *El Amor brujo*, but more recently in his *Fantasía bética* of 1919 for piano. Another interest shared by Lorca and de Falla was in the old tradition of puppet plays. In 1923 de Falla wrote the puppet opera *El Retablo de Maese Pedro*, and in the same year they collaborated on a puppet play for which Lorca designed the sets and de Falla arranged and performed the music. Later Lorca himself wrote music for La Barraca, the traveling theater he directed, drawing on Spanish folksong and on songs collected earlier by Barbieri and Pedrell. Lorca, as well as de Falla and his predecessors, was instrumental in ensuring the survival of the authentic musical tradition of Spain, which still remains separate from the mainstream of 'classical' music.

Right: Ravel's set of three songs, *Don Quichotte à Dulcinée* (1932-3), was his last work, the only part he completed of a score for a film of Cervantes' epic work starring the Russian bass Chaliapin. The thread of Spain runs through Ravel's work, particularly in his early years, from the youthful 'Habanera' (1895) and that most evocative of piano works, the 'Alborada del Gracioso' from *Miroirs* (1905), to his opera *L'Heure espagnole*, the *Vocalise en forme de Habanera* and the *Rapsodie espagnole*, all written in 1907. Although influenced by the Chabrier of *España*, Ravel penetrated far more deeply into the true character of Spanish music: in the first place, his mother was a Basque, and he was born in that region, and there was also his close friendship since schooldays with the Catalan pianist Ricardo Vines.

Left: Ida Rubinstein in *Boléro*, the work that Ravel wrote in 1928 in response to a request from the dancer to orchestrate a group of pieces from Albéniz's *Iberia* as a ballet for her. In an interview Ravel said of the work: 'It constitutes an experiment in a very special and limited direction, and should not be suspected of aiming at achieving anything different from, or more than what it actually does achieve. Before its first performance I issued a warning to the effect that what I had written was a piece lasting seventeen minutes and consisting wholly of 'orchestral tissue without music' – of one long, very gradual *crescendo*. There are no contrasts, and there is practically no invention except the plan and the manner of the execution. The themes are altogether impersonal – folk-tunes of the usual Spanish-Arabic kind. And (whatever may have been said to the contrary), the orchestral writing is simple and straightforward . . . . It is perhaps because of these peculiarities that no single composer likes the *Boléro* – and from their point of view they are quite right.'

à
M·Ravel
en souvenir amical
Ouvré
1909

RAVEL, ROUSSEL, SATIE AND LES SIX

FELIX APRAHAMIAN

Opposite: Portrait of Maurice Ravel (1875-1937) in his pyjamas, by Achille Ouvré, dated 1909.

Two names dominated French music in the early part of the twentieth century – those of Debussy and Ravel. The two were often linked, and many parallels can be drawn between them: Debussy and Ravel both used a similar harmonic palette, one of remarkable post-Wagnerian richness; both enriched the repertory of the piano, their own instrument, and were consummate masters of the orchestra. But a closer examination of the music of each composer reveals the differences between them, in particular their individual use of the harmonic ingredients. Whereas Debussy, the great original, used chords empirically, often in parallel sequences, Ravel's use of chords tends towards more conventional musical logic, in which they may appear as points of color. Of course, exceptions may be found. Their similarity is one of musical vocabulary rather than one of language, for each speaks in his own very personal manner.

Ravel, the younger by thirteen years, was born on 7 March 1875 in Ciboure, a fishing village close to Saint-Jean-de-Luz, in the Basque region of France. His father, Pierre Joseph Ravel, was a Swiss-born civil engineer of Savoyard French origin; his mother, Marie Delouart, was a Basque. His parents met in Spain, where Joseph Ravel was working on the construction of a railway. They lived first in Ciboure, before moving to Paris a few months after the birth of Maurice, the elder of two sons. Ravel maintained his own links with the region of his birthplace throughout his life, although he was an infant in arms when his parents moved to Paris. The fact that the Basque region remained as much his spiritual home as Paris may be explained by his extraordinary attachment to his mother and to her background. From Joseph Ravel, the more gifted Maurice inherited not only an aptitude for music but also his father's feeling for mechanical contrivances, although since Maurice was essentially a miniaturist, tiny clockwork models probably held more fascination for him than the motors and engines of his father's profession.

It was above all to his mother that Maurice Ravel was drawn. He was a *fils à maman* all his life, and her death in 1917, after a period of declining health, was a blow from which he never really recovered. She was seventy-six; Ravel, already in his forties, had never been separated from her. Maurice acquired friends of both sexes, but there was no hint of a deeper liaison with either. The depth of his affection for his mother may well have accounted for a certain prolongation of his adolescence, even a kind of infantilism and auto-eroticism. As will be seen, Ravel, unmarried and childless, adored children and seemed to be more at home in their company than that of their parents. This trait resulted in some very characteristic works; it is mirrored in his love of miniature things, the bonsai and dwarf conifers in his garden and the *objets d'art* in the tiny house which was to become his home from 1921.

It seems to have been a foregone conclusion from his early childhood that Maurice Ravel would be a musician. There is no evidence that he received any more general education. Piano lessons began in May 1882, when he was seven, with Henri Ghys. Then he took lessons in musical theory with Charles-René. So began a solid grounding in music. Ghys was succeeded by Emile Decombes as Ravel's second piano teacher, whose pupils at the time also included Reynaldo Hahn and Alfred Cortot. In June 1889, twenty-four of these pupils played excerpts from various concerted works in a Salle Erard recital. Thus Ravel made his first known public appearance, in part of Moscheles's Third Concerto, proof that the lad of fourteen was already at least a competent pianist.

The researches of Arbie Orenstein, the most distinguished of recent Ravel scholars, have shed a clear light on Ravel's career at the Conservatoire. It is fascinating to note that, having failed to win a prize in three consecutive years of competition, one of the twentieth century's greatest masters of harmony was dismissed from the harmony course of Emile Pessard, which he had attended from November 1891 to July 1895. At the same time, having failed to obtain the piano prize, he was compelled to relinquish the piano class. So Ravel left the Conservatoire. Two and a half years were to pass before he re-entered the august establishment as a student. The break was crucial in two ways: during the interval Ravel developed his own personality as a composer; but his return to the academic fold at the age of nearly twenty-three made his newly found musical assurance perhaps less acceptable to the conservative hierarchy of the Conservatoire.

There were, however, formative influences on Ravel in his first period at the Conservatoire: an important one was the Paris Universal Exhibition of 1889, where, together with Debussy, Ravel heard the Javanese gamelan. Chabrier and Satie were also known to have heard this instrument, as well as Rimsky-Korsakov, who was in Paris to conduct some concerts of Russian music. The work of all four composers, as well as the exotic timbres and scales of the gamelan, was certainly not lost on the fourteen-year-old Maurice Ravel. In the previous year Ravel had met Ricardo Viñes, his exact contemporary, and like him a pianist in the formative stage. They passed the Conservatoire entrance examination on the same day. Soon they were making music together, while their mothers conversed in Spanish. In 1893 they went to play Chabrier's *Trois valses romantiques* for two pianos to the ailing composer. Ravel always acknowledged his musical debt to Chabrier, as well as to Erik Satie, then pianist at the Café de la Nouvelle Athènes, to whom Joseph Ravel had introduced his young son. Viñes, the ever questing Spanish pianist–interpreter; Chabrier, who had brought a whiff of Spain into his very French music; Satie, an unorthodox harmonic pioneer; the gamelan; the orchestral splendor of the Russian scores introduced by Rimsky-Korsakov; and, above all, the sheer genius of Ravel's great contemporary compatriot, Claude Debussy – these were all elements in the formation of Maurice Ravel, the composer.

In an autobiographical sketch, prized out of Ravel in 1928 by his friend and pupil Roland-Manuel to accompany a set of pianola-rolls of Ravel's music, he wrote: 'My first compositions, which have remained unpublished [they have since been issued, in 1975], date from about 1893. I was then in the harmony class of Pessard. The influence of Emmanuel Chabrier could be seen in the *Sérénade grotesque* for piano; that of Satie in the *Ballade de la reine morte d'aimer*.' Two years later, in 1895, Ravel set Verlaine's 'Un grand sommeil noir,' a *mélodie* not published until 1953, and composed his first published work, the *Menuet antique*, which evokes a different aspect of Verlaine in its title, the Verlaine of the *Fêtes galantes* that had already supplied Debussy with texts. In musical content it derives more specifically from the Chabrier of the *Menuet pompeux*, which Ravel himself was to orchestrate for the Ballets Russes in 1918. Ravel dedicated the *Menuet antique* to Viñes, who was the first to play it. The *Menuet antique* contains traces of the future Ravel: the unresolved sevenths and ninths Satie toyed with are already there. The 'antiquity' of the piece lies in the modal flavor bestowed by a flattened second and seventh; its resemblance to the Chabrier *Menuet* is not merely one of form.

The *Sites auriculaires* for two pianos, composed in 1895-7 (but not published until 1975), also look forward as well as backward. In the first of the two pieces, 'Habanera,' Ravel – following Bizet and Chabrier, but preceding Debussy – uses a characteristic Spanish dance-rhythm for the first time. 'Entre cloches,' the second piece, is an impressionistic essay in bell-sounds. From the same period date Ravel's first Mallarmé setting, 'Sainte,' composed in 1896, when he was already well acquainted with the work of the Symbolists, and his setting of Marot's 'D'Anne jouant de l'espinette,' the second of his *Deux épigrammes de Clément Marot*, which evokes the period of the Pléiade poets.

• Ravel and the Conservatoire •

On returning to the Conservatoire in 1898, Ravel entered Fauré's composition class. He also continued his private studies in counterpoint and orchestration with André Gedalge. In his autobiographical sketch Ravel wrote: 'I am happy to say that I owe the most precious elements of my craft to André Gedalge. As to Fauré, his encouragement and artistic advice were no less profitable.'

Right: Last page of Ravel's signed autograph score of *Jeux d'eau*, dated 11 November 1901. Dedicated to Fauré, with whom he studied at the Conservatoire, it was first performed by Ravel's faithful and untiring disciple Viñes, a brilliant pianist. The 'waves' so evident in the score itself echo the musical sound they produce.

The first fruits of Ravel's return included his orchestral score, the *Ouverture de Shéhérazade*, which dates from 1898. This shares little but its title with the beautiful song-cycle Ravel was later to compose, though some modal melodic comparisons may be drawn. What the work clearly reveals is that at twenty-three Ravel was already an accomplished orchestral colorist, as yet a disciple of Rimsky-Korsakov rather than follower of Debussy, although by 1898 he must have been well aware of the *Prélude à l'après-midi d'un faune* (which he later transcribed). Years later Ravel confessed to Roland-Manuel that he found the Overture '*mal fichue* and full of whole-tone scales. So many as to make me sick of them for life.' It was, nevertheless, an auspicious beginning. The piece was noticed in several critical articles, and Ravel's name was becoming known while he was still a student. His personal reserve did not prevent him from enjoying the company of a few intimates or frequenting certain salons. His teacher Fauré introduced him to that of Mme de Saint-Marceaux, where Debussy, d'Indy and Messager also used to go. Years later, Colette, the librettist of his *L'Enfant et les sortilèges*, recalled having met Ravel there.

Another of Ravel's hostesses was the Princesse Edmond de Polignac, for whom, in 1899, he wrote the *Pavane pour une infante défunte* for piano solo. Here, the Spanish flavor was restricted only to the poetic title. Discouraging the idea that the piece was intended as a lament for a recently deceased Infanta, Ravel preferred that it should evoke the pavane which a young princess might once have danced at the court of Spain. He rejected more fanciful interpretations with the comment that his only thought when choosing the words of the title was the pleasure of alliteration. Always critical of his own work, Ravel declared in 1912 that, while he no longer saw the *Pavane's* qualities, he could see its faults only too well: 'the influence of Chabrier, flagrantly obvious, and rather poor form.' The form Ravel thought 'rather poor' is that of the rondo in which the opening strain twice recurs, slightly varied. In 1910, however, he scored the work for a modest orchestra, and in this version the *Pavane*, even more than the *Menuet antique*, belies its origin as a piano solo. This pattern was repeated often in Ravel's composing career, for several of his best-known orchestral scores began as piano pieces.

The turn of the century found Ravel at twenty-five still *in statu pupillari*, an aspirant for the Prix de Rome during the next five years. Dryly, the autobiography records: 'I competed for the Prix de Rome in 1901 (when I won a *second Grand Prix*), in 1902 and in 1903. In 1905 the jury barred me from the final competition.' By this time Ravel was already famous, and his rejection provoked a justified scandal; how justified may be assessed from his achievements in the period leading up to it.

Jeux d'eau, the earliest of Ravel's important piano pieces, was composed in 1901 and dedicated to Ravel's 'dear master, Gabriel Fauré.' Of it Ravel declared: 'In *Jeux d'eau* is to be found the origin of all the innovations in piano-writing that have been noticed in my work. I found inspiration for it in the sound of water and the music of fountains, cascades and streams. It is based on two themes, in the manner of sonata form, without, however, being subjected to the classical tonal plan.' A line by Henri de Régnier

Below left: Title-page of the piano edition of Ravel's *Pavane pour une infante défunte*.

Below: Ravel at the piano with members of the group 'Les Apaches' – from left to right: Robert Mortier, L'Abbé Léonce Petit, Ricardo Viñes and Jane Mortier.

Left: Costume design by A. Maré for the watchmaker Torquemada in Ravel's one-act opera *L'Heure espagnole*. This particular design was for a production staged at the Paris Opéra in 1921.

Left: Diaghilev with his nanny, a portrait by Léon Bakst dating from 1905, before Diaghilev left Russia.

prefaces the piece 'Dieu fluvial riant de l'eau qui le chatouille' (The river-god laughing as the water tickles him). As a piano piece descriptive of water, Ravel's work is preceded by Liszt's *Jeux d'eau à la Villa d'Este*, but still it has few rivals.

Ravel's String Quartet, his first and only work in this medium, was begun in December 1902 and completed in April 1903. Its model is without doubt Debussy's Quartet; there are too many parallels for the similarities to be fortuitous. Each work is in four movements, with an exotically colored scherzo preceding the slow movement, in each case the first movement is in sonata form. Far more important is that both works adopt the 'cyclic' form, dear to the heart of César Franck and propagated by his disciples. This was an influence resisted by Debussy early in his composing career. Ravel was never exposed to it directly, so that the 'cyclic' transformation of themes and recurrence of motifs in other movements of the Quartet derives from Debussy's example rather than from a more direct tutorial source.

Ravel submitted the first movement of the String Quartet for the Composition Prize at the Conservatoire in January 1903. It was rejected, along with its composer, by the conservative elements controlling the Conservatoire. Ravel was a victim of an institutional hierarchy that regarded the *Jeux d'eau* as cacophony (the opinion of Saint-Saëns), and the first movement of the String Quartet as unacceptable. Soon after Ravel's expulsion from the Conservatoire, he completed the String Quartet. Fauré, its dedicatee, apparently found the final movement 'manqué.' The story goes that the worried Ravel was reassured by Debussy: 'In the name of the gods of Music and in mine, alter nothing that you have written in your Quartet.'

Another important work of this period was *Shéhérazade*, a song-cycle with orchestra. Dating from 1903, the work was written when Ravel was twenty-eight and had attained complete maturity as a composer. In its musical impressionism and in its attitude to the text of the work, it is Ravel's closest approach to the thought of Debussy, for the revelation of *Pelléas et Mélisande* in the previous year could not have escaped the younger composer. The cycle takes its title from a volume of verse by Ravel's friend Tristan Klingsor (a Wagnerian disguise for Léon Leclerc – a painter and composer himself as well as poet). The three poems are colorful, sensual and sensitive evocations of the Orient, rich in possibilities for musical pictorial imagery. Klingsor, who was made to read the poems aloud, so that Ravel would mistake none of his intentions, described Ravel's attitude in a memoir: 'For Ravel, setting a poem meant transforming it into expressive recitative, exalting the inflexions of speech to the state of song, exalting all the possibilities of the word, but not subjugating it. Ravel made himself the servant of the poet.' How like Debussy's

Below: One of Naum Gabo's designs for *La Chatte* (1927). Diaghilev here matched one of the most recent art styles, Russian Constructivism, and the newest materials – scenery and costumes were made in part from celluloid – with music by the young French composer Henri Sauguet. Choreography was by Balanchine, and the work was a great success.

expressed attitude to opera this sounds. And indeed, while exploiting to the full the colors of his orchestral palette, Ravel's score remains subservient to the poems, content to paint a glowing background against which the soprano line stands out in clear relief.

The piano *Sonatine*, begun in 1903 and completed in 1905, was, for the Italian critic Guido Pannain, Ravel's masterpiece. 'In the actual musical quality of the Sonatine,' he wrote, 'the same Ravel as elsewhere can be seen, but the true miracle of this miniature jewel lies in the perfection of the ensemble, that harmony between the part and the whole which is at once the cross and the reward of all artistic creation.'

Overlapping the composition of the *Sonatine* are the *Miroirs*, pieces for the piano on which Ravel worked in 1904 and 1905. Of them he wrote: 'They mark a change in my harmonic evolution considerable enough to have disconcerted musicians who till then were the most accustomed to my manner.' The five pieces extend the descriptive element of *Jeux d'eau* almost into the field of program-music. Each is dedicated to one of 'Les Apaches,' a group of Parisian friends which included Ravel, as well as Ricardo Viñes, who gave their first public performance, and the critic M. D. Calvocoressi. The first piece, 'Noctuelles,' is inscribed to the poet Léon-Paul Fargue. In its fluttering movement it evokes the nocturnal flight of moths. Ravel himself had an especial fondness for the second piece, 'Oiseaux tristes,' which was in fact the first piece of the collection to be written. In it he sought to evoke 'birds lost in the torpor of a dark forest in the hottest hours of summer.' Its dedication is to Viñes. The seascape of the third piece, 'Une Barque sur l'océan,' deploys the pianistic innovations of the much better-known *Jeux d'eau* on a broader canvas. Ravel orchestrated the piece in 1906. 'The Jester's Aubade' is the nearest English equivalent to Ravel's Spanish title of 'Alborada del gracioso' for the fourth piece. Here, the brilliant piano writing, the volatile changes of mood, clear-cut rhythms and bright harmonic coloring, all paint one of Ravel's most vivid musical pictures. The dedication is to Calvocoressi. Ravel orchestrated the 'Alborada' in 1918. The fifth and final piece, 'La Vallée des cloches,' dedicated to the composer Maurice Delage, one of Ravel's few pupils, is the most restrained. With its subtle suggestion of distant bells, it evokes an almost monastic calm.

Below: Mikhail Larionov's design for Ravel's *The Peacock*, a projected ballet based on Renard's *Histoires naturelles* which never saw the light of day.

By the time Ravel reached his thirtieth birthday on 7 March 1905, his stature as a composer must have been obvious to many of his musical compatriots, but not, so it seems, to the hierarchy of the Paris Conservatoire. The episode of Ravel's fifth attempt at the Prix de Rome is now part of French musical history. He had failed in four previous attempts and did not compete in 1904. By eliminating him in the preliminary round of the 1905 competition, the jury hoisted themselves with their own petard. Worse still, all six finalists were pupils of the undistinguished Charles Lenepveu, who happened also to be a member of the jury. The musicians of Paris took sides. The two most eminent – Fauré and Debussy – supported Ravel. The scandal that ensued had practical results: Théodore Dubois resigned as director of the Conservatoire and Fauré was appointed in his place.

•The pre-war decade•

To this period belongs another Ravel work that is unique in its genre – the lovely *Introduction et Allegro* for harp, 'with accompaniment of string quartet, flute and clarinet.' It originated in the rivalry between two harp manufacturers: Pleyel, whose chromatic harp was perfected in 1903, and Erard, who continued to make the more traditional kind. Ravel's piece was commissioned by Erards and inscribed to their director, Albert Blondel. It was first heard in Paris on 22 February 1907, when the soloist was Micheline Kahn.

More radical were the *Histoires naturelles* which Ravel composed in 1906, five settings of

Right: The symbolist poet Stéphane Mallarmé by James McNeill Whistler, used as the frontispiece for a book of his poems, 1893.

Far right: Frontispiece by Félicien Rops for Louis Bertrand's prose-poems *Gaspard de la nuit; fantaisies à la manière de Rembrandt et de Callot*, published in 1868 and the inspiration for Ravel's piano work of the same name, written forty years later.

prose-poems from a sophisticated bestiary by Jules Renard. Of them, Ravel wrote: 'For a long time I had been attracted by the clear, direct language and deep hidden poetry of these sketches by Jules Renard. The text itself demanded a particular kind of declamation, closely bound to the inflexions of the French language. The first performance of the *Histoires naturelles* at the Société Nationale [12 January 1907, by Jane Bathori and Ravel] provoked a real scandal, which gave rise to lively polemics in the musical press at the time.'

In fact, part of the audience jeered and hissed at that première. Today the cycle is generally recognized as the typical work of a fastidious master at his most exacting. Like Debussy in *Pelléas*, Ravel, with similar economy, paints the scene as well as projecting the text.

The experience Ravel gained in the word-setting of such works as *Shéhérazade* and *Histoires naturelles* served him well in his two operatic scores. Already in 1906, he had worked on *La Cloche engloutie*, a French adaptation of Gerhart Hauptmann's play *Die versunkene Glocke*, yet despite intermittent returns to it until the outbreak of the First World War, it remained unwritten. But in 1907, a year in which the French capital fairly sizzled with musical activity, the year in which Diaghilev made his first assault upon Paris, not yet with his Ballets Russes, but with a festival of Russian music in which Rimsky-Korsakov and Glazunov appeared as conductors of their own music, Ravel was inspired to plan and complete the first of his two operas.

Franc-Nohain's one-act comedy *L'Heure espagnole* had had an immediate success when it was first staged at the Odéon in 1904. As soon as Ravel obtained the author's permission to set it as an opera, the German's bell-foundry was abandoned for an hour in the shop of Franc-Nohain's Spanish watchmaker. The score was completed in five months, between May and September 1907, but its first performance did not take place until 19 May 1911, when it was given at the Paris Opéra Comique. With its precision of language and witty *double ententdres*, Ravel found in *L'Heure espagnole* a libretto ideally suited to his temperament and art. Evoking in its setting the Spain that, through his mother, was ever close to his heart, it provides twentieth-century opera with a one-act masterpiece.

In 1907, however, before the completion of this work, Ravel had already composed another musical tribute to Spain, his orchestral *Rapsodie espagnole*. Since most of Ravel's orchestral work began as piano music which he later scored, it is of interest to note that even the *Rapsodie espagnole*, his first original orchestral score, with the exception of the early *Ouverture de Shéhérazade* (1898), is not free of a transcribed element. One section, the 'Habanera,' is none other than the first of the two long unpublished *Sites auriculaires* for two pianos (1895-7) magically scored. The *Rapsodie espagnole* is Ravel at his most colorful and impressionistic, though there is nothing vague or indefinite about the material he employs.

Ravel's own piano-duet version of the *Rapsodie espagnole* preceded publication of the orchestral score, but the piano duet which more firmly established Ravel's place in the repertoire of four-hand works is *Ma Mère l'Oye* (Mother

Goose), begun in 1908. A close friend and frequent visitor to the home of Cyprien and Ida Godebski, Ravel became the very willing nursery playmate and reader of fairy tales to their children, Mimie and Jean, to whom *Ma Mère l'Oye* is inscribed. In the original piano-duet form, the work consists of *Cinq pièces enfantines*. Ravel wrote of them: 'The plan to evoke in these pieces the poetry of childhood led me naturally to simplify my style and to make my writing leaner.' In 1911 Ravel scored the duet as a *Suite* for double woodwind, two horns, percussion, harp and strings. Later that year, he added a 'Prélude,' a 'Danse de la Toupie' and linking interludes to make up the ballet, for which he himself wrote the scenario. It is, however, still the original scored five-movement *Suite* that is most often heard in the concert room. The brilliant sound of the apotheosis of 'Le jardin féerique' is out of all proportion to the modesty of the orchestral forces required.

In *Gaspard de la nuit*, 'trois poèmes pour piano d'après Aloysius Bertrand,' completed between May and September 1908, Ravel created his greatest piano work. The literary inspiration of the three pieces is drawn from a text which in its miniature perfection resembles the art of Fabergé. The book which gives the piano suite its title is by Louis Bertrand (1807-41), better known by the more Romantic sounding variant of his Christian name, Aloysius Bertrand, a remarkable precursor of the Romantic movement, who, failing as a journalist, devoted what remained of a regrettably short and ailing life to composing a few poems and the Romantic pen-pictures collected under the title of *Gaspard de la nuit*, the sobriquet of the supposed author of these *fantaisies à la manière de Callot* – otherwise the devil. Forgotten by or unknown to the other literary lions of the nineteenth century, the provincial Bertrand was virtually rediscovered by Baudelaire, who admitted that *Gaspard de la nuit* inspired him to write *Le Spleen de Paris*, his own collection of *petits poèmes en prose*. Mallarmé is also known to have commented on *Gaspard's* vitality, telling his daughter: 'Prends Bertrand, on y trouve de tout.'

Ravel's suite, first performed by Viñes in January 1909, reflects in terms of the keyboard three of Bertrand's perfectly chiseled *fantaisies*. And yet, they are more than mere musical impressions. Their piano writing is of high virtuosity, but as precise as the wording of the texts they illustrate. Nowhere in the entire range of music has splashing water been more beautifully suggested than in 'Ondine,' the first of the three pieces, except perhaps in his own earlier *Jeux d'eau*. The fluttering patterns heard at the outset maintain their exact shape in different parts of the keyboard as a unifying feature throughout the piece. (Ravel himself miscalculated the shape in measures 5, 6, 7, 8, 24, 25, 26 and 28, until his pupil Emile Passani pointed this out to him. Ravel immediately authorized the correction, though this has yet to reach the printed edition.) This motif and wider-ranging figuration are the background to an almost unbroken

LA CARPE.
Dans vos viviers, dans vos étangs,
Carpes, que vous vivez longtemps !
Est-ce que la mort vous oublie,
Poissons de la mélancolie.

Above: La Carpe, a woodcut by Raoul Dufy to illustrate Guillaume Apollinaire's *Le Bestiaire*. Poulenc, who later set four of these poems as songs, was one of several composers to base works on Apollinaire's poetry.

Left: Lithograph illustration by Henri de Toulouse-Lautrec from Jules Renard's *Histoires naturelles*, published in 1899. Ravel set the poems as solo songs with piano accompaniment in 1906 and their first performance resulted in violent controversy as to the merits of his music as compared with Debussy's.

melodic line, which Ravel's iridescent harmonies invest with a prismatic quality. Similar unity is imposed on 'Le Gibet' by the syncopated repetition of an octave B flat. Here, too, a continuous line of expressive melody unfolds, but against a desolate, expressionless background. In contrast to the fluidity of 'Ondine,' 'Le Gibet' is static, a fantasia on one sound which tolls its way through the piece with never varying rhythm, like a death-knell. 'Scarbo' is different again; episodic, kaleidoscopic and hallucinatory, its nervous, fitful progress catches to perfection the macabre mood of the text. To a friend, Ravel wrote that in 'Scarbo' he had tried to write a piece more difficult than Balakirev's *Islamey*. In 'Scarbo,' Ravel achieved far more than that.

• *Daphnis et Chloé* •

It was in 1907 that Calvocoressi introduced Ravel to Diaghilev. Two years later Diaghilev invited Ravel to compose a ballet on a scenario by Fokine, and three years later he completed *Daphnis et Chloé*, which he himself described as a 'choreographic symphony.' 'In writing it,' recorded Ravel, 'I sought to compose a broad musical fresco, less concerned with archaic fidelity than with loyalty to the Greece of my dreams,' which in many ways resembled that imagined and depicted by French artists of the latter part of the eighteenth century. The work is built symphonically on a very strict tonal plan by means of a few themes, the develop-

Left: Advertisement for the first performance of Ravel's ballet *Daphnis et Chloé*, commissioned by Diaghilev and premièred on 5 June 1912 with choreography by Fokine and sets designed by Léon Bakst. The overall program mixes avant-garde with Romantic composers.

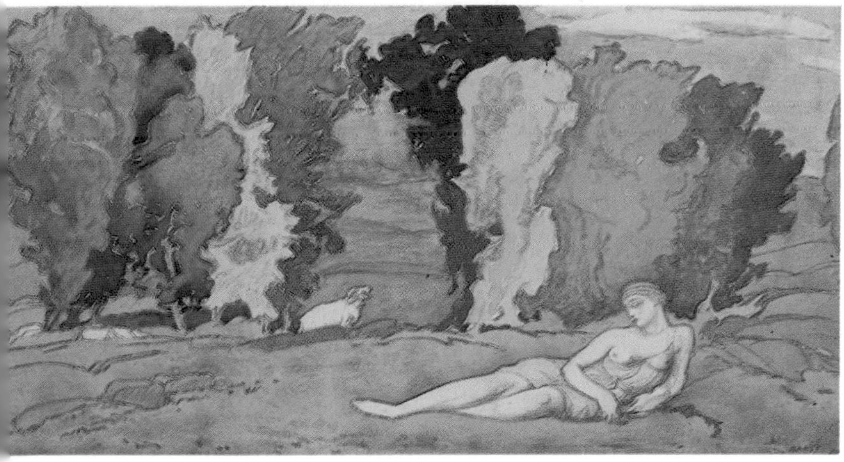

Above: Watercolor designs by Léon Bakst for *Daphnis et Chloé*. Bakst, a well-established artist in his own right, became one of Diaghilev's in-house designers, producing designs for many of the impresario's productions.

ment of which ensures the work's homogeneity.' The three parts of the work follow the three scenes of Fokine's scenario, based on the tale by Longus, which Ravel would certainly have known in Amyot's delightful old French.

The first performance of the complete ballet was conducted by Pierre Monteux for Diaghilev's Ballets Russes at the Paris Théâtre du Châtelet, on 8 June 1912. The choreography, like the scenario, was by Fokine, the décor and costumes by Bakst. The staging of *Daphnis et Chloé* did not go smoothly. Not only was Ravel late in completing the score, but he found certain disparities between his conception of the work and its visual realization. Unfavorable criticisms of the score may be charitably ascribed to inadequate rehearsals, for the two suites Ravel extracted from the ballet never failed to please. The initial impact for the ballet was undoubtedly eclipsed by Nijinsky's interpretation of Debussy's *Faune* in the same season. *Daphnis et Chloé* was a very much costlier score to realize, as was made clear in the summer of 1914, when Diaghilev proposed to skimp the chorus for the performance of the ballet in London. This led to a politely acrimonious exchange of letters between composer and impresario, which appeared as correspondence in *The Times*.

Between the inception of *Daphnis* and its completion, Ravel wrote another work, now as precious to pianists in its original form as to conductors in Ravel's orchestration: the *Valses nobles et sentimentales*, composed in 1911 and scored in 1912. The composer himself remarked that the title of the *Valses* was sufficient indication of his intention to compose a chain of waltzes in the manner of Schubert. The work evokes his model superficially – in rhythmic character, mood and even chromatic idiom –

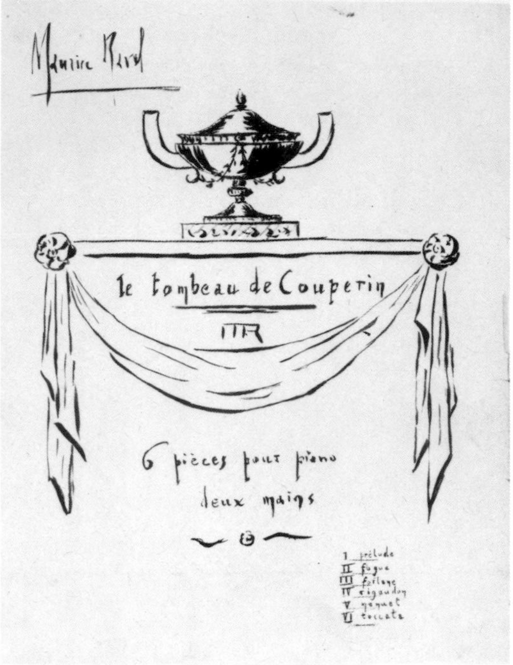

Above: Ravel and Stravinsky, who met in Paris in 1909. Stravinsky, who had come to Paris with Diaghilev, joined 'Les Apaches' the same year. The two young composers collaborated on a ballet version of Musorgsky's *Khovanschina* in 1913, and they greatly respected each other's work.

Above right: The original frontispiece, drawn by Ravel himself, for *Le Tombeau de Couperin*, written between 1914 and 1917. The six movements, harking back to the eighteenth-century with their baroque forms, reflect a neoclassical approach common among the avant garde at the time.

but it remains typically Ravelian in melody and harmony. Coming after *Gaspard de la nuit*, the high point of Ravel's pianistic virtuosity, the *Valses*, as befits their scope, are composed in a much leaner style. In Ravel's words, 'the virtuosity which was at the heart of *Gaspard de la nuit* is succeeded by definitely clearer writing, which strengthens the harmonies and sharpens the outlines.'

Ravel orchestrated the *Valses* in two weeks, and, at the instigation of the dancer Trouhanova, who wished to include the work in a series of four dance recitals, he also supplied the scenario for *Adélaïde, ou le langage des fleurs*, as the balletic version of the *Valses* is called. Apart from the tutti of the rather boisterous initial *Valse* and the ebullient seventh, the orchestral score is one of fastidious refinement. Both piano and orchestral version of the *Valses* bear a motto from Henri de Régnier: '. . . le plaisir délicieux et toujours nouveau d'une occupation inutile' (the delicious and ever new pleasure of a purposeless occupation).

If Ravel's *Shéhérazade* is the score in which he most nearly approaches the musical thought and manner of Debussy, his *Trois poèmes de Stéphane Mallarmé* are indebted for their scoring and a certain spacing of the sound, but not for their essential musical thought, to another of Ravel's contemporaries – Arnold Schoenberg. It was in 1913, when Ravel was staying at Clarens, that Stravinsky showed him his own *Trois poèmes de la lyrique japonaise*. Stravinsky had derived the idea of these settings, for voice accompanied by piano quintet, flutes and clarinets, from Schoenberg's *Pierrot lunaire*. Fascinated by the extraordinary refinement of Stravinsky's score and its variety of instrumental color, Ravel entered the lists with his *Trois poèmes de Stéphane Mallarmé*. All three were composed in 1913, the year in which, curiously enough, Debussy set the first two poems, 'Soupir' and 'Placet futile,' for voice and piano. Ravel's three settings are the quintessence of his art. In their suggestion of harmonic richness, they look back to his previous works; in their flowing lines and crystal concision, they look forward to the leaner manner of his later music. Ravel's scoring is for piano quintet, two flutes (one doubling piccolo) and two clarinets (one doubling bass clarinet).

•The First World War•

During the period leading up to the First World War, Ravel lived in a flat with his widowed mother and his younger brother, Edouard, in the Avenue Carnot, close by the Place de l'Etoile in Paris. He remained devoted to the Basque coast where he was born, and Saint-Jean-de-Luz became his regular summer resort. It was there he composed his *Trio*, for piano, violin and cello, between 3 April and 7 August 1914, and it was there that he heard the news of the declaration of war. The *Trio* captivated all who heard it. Jacques Durand, Ravel's publisher, refers in his memoirs to its revelation at a rehearsal at the home of the cellist Joseph Salmon, with Enesco as violinist and Casella at the piano, as an unforgettable event. The official first performance was at an SMI Concert given in aid of the Red Cross at the Salle Gaveau on 28 January 1915, when the players were Casella, Enescu and Feuillard.

Ravel was approaching forty when war was declared, and he was eligible for service. In September 1914 he had written to a friend from Saint-Jean-de-Luz that he had put five months' work into five weeks because he had wanted to finish his *Trio* before being called up. Although he had been exempted from military service at the age of twenty, Ravel was now anxious to enlist along with most of his friends and his brother Edouard. But he was turned down, and this depressed him. In September 1914 Ravel was already caring for wounded soldiers in Saint-Jean-de-Luz. That winter he composed his *Trois chansons* for mixed choir without accompaniment, on his own texts: 'Nicolette,' 'Trois beaux oiseaux du paradis' and 'Ronde,' of which the undoubted gem is the wistful central *chanson*, with its moving allusion to a lover who has gone to the wars and will never return. This was the first to be completed, in December 1914. The two outer songs were added in February 1915. The following month, Ravel succeeded in enlisting – as a truck-driver – and he served at Verdun during 1916. His war service did not last long, but it took its toll, both morally and physically. The period of depression following his demobilization was much aggravated by the loss of his mother, who died on 5 January 1917.

That year Ravel received a temporary discharge from his military duties. Despite his low morale, he returned to composing and in November completed a work he had begun in 1914, the piano suite, *Le Tombeau de Couperin*. In October 1914 he had announced to Roland-Manuel, among other projects, 'two series of piano pieces.' The first of these was to be a *Suite française* – 'no, not what you think: there will be no "Marseillaise," but there will be a Forlane, a Gigue; no Tango, however.' From this it can be seen that Ravel conceived a French suite containing early dance forms like those of his eighteenth-century precursors. Although he disclaimed the 'Marseillaise' at the inception of his suite, its final form shows Ravel's patriotic feelings, for each movement bears a dedication honoring the memory of a musician friend who died for France. In the title of *Le Tombeau de Couperin*, Ravel revived the eighteenth-century custom of writing a memorial piece for a famous musical predecessor, evoking in its dance forms the *Ordres* of François Couperin.

Le Tombeau de Couperin was one of the first fruits of this period of unpheaval in Ravel's life, caused by the war, the death of his mother, and the move from the Avenue Carnot flat to a villa in Saint-Cloud, which he shared with his brother Edouard. While there is nothing sad about the music, a new-found simplicity of line and purity of expression reflect the profound change that had been wrought in Ravel.

Another work, perhaps more deeply related in its fevered endings to the First World War, is *La Valse*. Ravel described it as 'a kind of apotheosis of the Viennese waltz with which there mingled in my mind the impression of a fantastic and fatal whirling.' As early as 1906 he had toyed with the idea of a work for two pianos which he intended to call *Wien* and in which he wished to present various aspects of the waltz in one clear and unified form. At the time he felt unequal to the task. In 1917 Diaghilev had proposed another collaboration, despite the slight disagreement at the time of the London performance of *Daphnis et Chloé*, but it was not until 1919 that Ravel decided to return

Below left: Princesse Armande de Polignac, one of the many patrons who, at the turn of the century, commissioned music for private entertainment and provided a valued source of income for up-and-coming composers.

Below: First page of the first edition of *Chansons madécasses* (Madagascan Songs), dated 1926, and, even at this late date, first performed at a private *soirée*.

again to the waltz idea which had haunted him ten years earlier. That winter he retired to a friend's villa in the Ardèche region, where he worked on *La Valse*, completing it in March 1920. Ravel's scenario reads: 'Through rifts in the eddying clouds are glimpsed waltzing couples. Gradually the clouds disperse and an immense hall is seen, thronged with a whirling crowd. The stage is gradually illuminated. The light of the chandeliers bursts forth at the *fortissimo*. An Imperial Court, about 1855.'

Diaghilev rejected *La Valse*. To him, it was a waltz and little else, with no spectacular development or choreographic variety. His refusal to stage the work caused the final break between the two men. Ravel was mortally offended and, even as late as 1925, on meeting Diaghilev at Monte Carlo, challenged him to a duel. Diaghilev's loss was the concert room's gain, for *La Valse* has become a repertory piece of many of the world's greatest orchestras. Scored for triple wind, two harps and a large array of percussion, *La Valse* consists in the main of two *crescendi*: the first, a long chain of contrasted waltzes; the second, a short and vehement recapitulation of the previous section, finishing in a furious and rather savage intoxication of sound and rhythm.

An event which took place early in 1920, when Ravel was at work on *La Valse*, sheds light on one aspect of his personality. On 15 January the official list of nominations for the Légion d'honneur published Ravel's name as a Chevalier. He was horrified and went to un-

Above: Design for the front cover of *Habanera*, one of Ravel's early but distinctive examples of piano work. The Spanish title reflects his lifelong attachment to Spain.

Below: Two costume designs by Léon Leyritz for *Boléro*. The first performance of this production took place in Paris on 31 December 1941 with new choreography by Serge Lifar to replace Nijinska's original version. Ravel wrote *Boléro* in response to Ida Rubinstein's request for a ballet of Spanish character.

usual lengths to be removed from the list and refuse the intended honor. When his old friend Erik Satie, probably thinking of the solid success of Ravel's *Trio*, uttered his famous jibe 'Ravel refuses the Légion d'honneur, but all of his music accepts it,' he was forgetting the deep resentment of officialdom that Ravel had felt ever since he had been prevented from competing for the Prix de Rome, ostensibly for his modernist tendencies, as late as 1905, when he was already a much admired composer.

•The late style•

In 1920 Ravel acquired his final home at Monfort-l'Amaury. There, on the side of a damp hill, commanding a view of the little church tower and of the surrounding woods, stands Le Belvédère, the house Ravel moved into in 1921, and where he lived until his death in 1937. At the time he took possession of Le Belvédère, Ravel had two commissions to fulfill. For *Le Tombeau de Claude Debussy*, a musical supplement to a Debussy memorial number of *La Revue musicale*, he wrote at its editor's behest, a Duo for violin and cello. This became the first movement of the *Sonate pour violin et violoncelle, en quatre parties*, of which Ravel wrote: 'I think that this Sonata marks a turning-point in the evolution of my career. The stripping off of inessentials is carried to an extreme limit. Harmonic charm is renounced, with an increasingly marked reaction in favor of melody.' These words should prepare the listener for the essentially lean style of the Sonata, begun in April 1920 and completed in February 1922.

The other commission was one mooted much earlier, when, sometime during the First World War, Colette submitted a libretto to Jacques Rouché, the director of the Paris Opéra. He suggested several composers who might be able to set it, but only Ravel's name aroused any enthusiasm in her: she remembered him from the salon of Mme de Saint-Marceaux. A copy of the text sent to Ravel in 1916, when he was on war service, failed to reach him. A second copy sent in 1917 fared better, and Ravel agreed to set Colette's *L'Enfant et les sortilèges* (The Child and the Spells), a subject utterly appropriate to him. A letter from Ravel to Colette written in 1919 showed that the score was taking shape in his mind, and by 1921 some of it was actually set down. Only Ravel's contractual obligation compelled him to concentrate on the opera during 1924, so that the score would be ready for the scheduled first performance at Monte Carlo on 21 March the next year.

Ravel's previous one-act opera, *L'Heure espagnole*, composed in 1907-9, belonged to his earlier, harmonically opulent manner. The almost chamber-music refinement of *L'Enfant et les sortilèges*, which, despite its orchestra of considerable size, omits every inessential note or color, allies it to the esthetic of his later and leaner style. In the seven years it took Ravel to complete *L'Enfant*, musical art had traveled far, and so had Ravel. If his already refined art had been further distilled, it had also acquired new elements. He admitted to having treated Colette's tale in the manner of an American musical comedy, confessing to a mixture of styles which included Massenet, Puccini, Monteverdi and one that he could not have absorbed earlier – jazz. He achieved the synthesis brilliantly in a score which, for all its surface sophistication, is curiously moving in its fundamentally childlike simplicity, from the gently meandering fourths and fifths of the two oboes which introduce the bored and restless child to his own touching final utterance of 'Maman!' which ends the opera.

If, as Ravel approached fifty, his music became more concentrated and direct in expression, its flow, too, became less free. He was, however, much in demand as a famous composer who could play his own piano music. He paid several visits to England between 1922 and 1932, Oxford bestowing on him an honorary Mus.D. in 1928, the year he returned from an American tour.

On the first of his post-war visits to London, he attended a *musicale* at which Jelly d'Arányi, the Hungarian violinist who lived in London, and Hans Kindler played his Duo. After it, Ravel asked the violinist to play some Hungarian gypsy tunes. That was the origin of his *Tzigane*, a *rapsodie de concert*, composed for

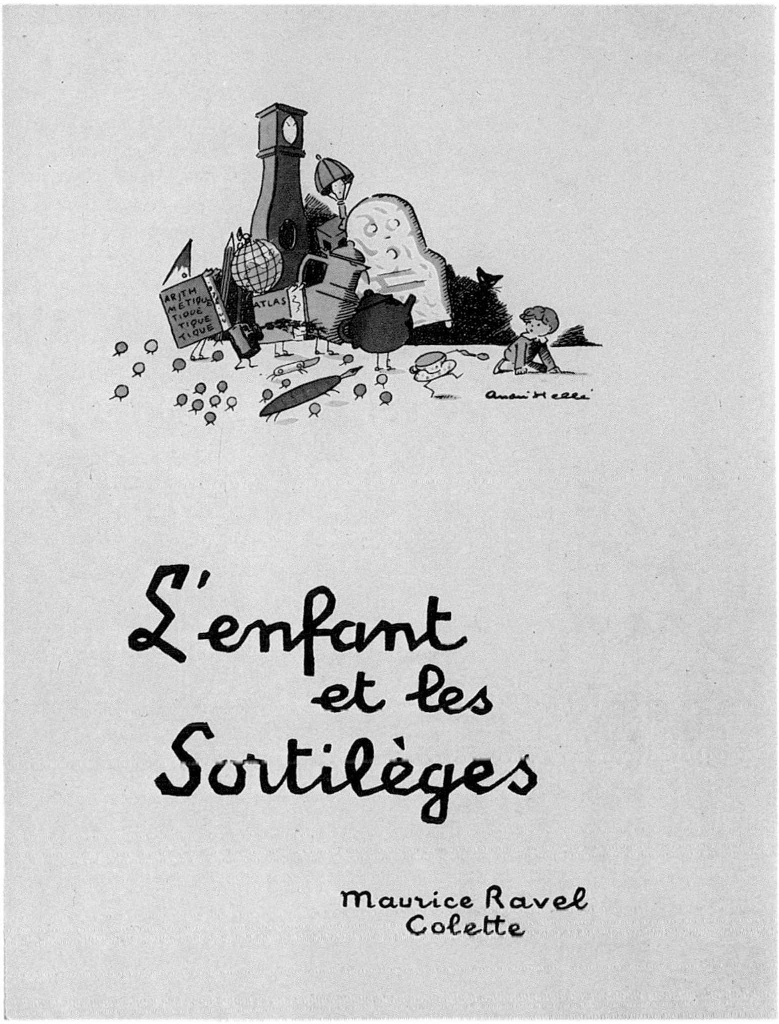

Above: Title-page designed by André Hellé for the first edition of Ravel's opera *L'Enfant et les sortilèges*, with a libretto by Colette.

Left: Colette, holding a dog, at Auteuil around 1925.

Opposite: Ravel at his home at Montfort-l'Amaury outside Paris, where he lived from 1921 until his death.

Jelly d'Arányi and completed two years later in 1924. That year, Hélène Jourdan-Morhange received a postcard from Ravel: 'Come quickly with your violin and the 24 Caprices of Paganini.' Working on the *Tzigane*, and fascinated as ever by the technical resources of the solo instrument, he sought to include every possible violinistic device in this show-piece. Earlier, when Mme Jourdan-Morhange had taxed him with the difficulty of the violin and cello Duo, which made it accessible to only a few virtuosi, Ravel's reply had been: 'So much the better. Then I will not be assassinated by amateurs!' Certainly, few amateurs tackle *Tzigane*, which exceeds in difficulty similar virtuoso works by such violinist composers as Sarasate, Wieniawski and even the redoutable Paganini.

The work is in the traditional form of the Hungarian czárdás, comprising two sections, a *lassú* and a *friss* – the first slow, and the second more animated. *Tzigane* opens with a long cadenza for the solo violin, announcing in its improvisatory course the principal themes. In the accompanied second section, speed and difficulties increase. Jelly d'Arányi gave the first performance with piano (Ravel) in London on 26 April 1924, and with orchestra in Paris on 30 November of that year.

A work more typical of the later Ravel occupied him in 1925 and 1926: the *Chansons madécasses* for voice, flute, cello and piano. Ravel wrote of them: '[They] seem to me to bring a new, dramatic – even erotic – element, introduced by the very subject of Parny's poems. It is a kind of quartet in which the voice has the principal part. Simplicity rules.' The author of the prose-poems, Evariste Désiré de Forges, Vicomte de Parny (1753-1814), was a Creole born on the island of Réunion, and his *Douze chansons* purport to be translations from the native Malagasy. The occasion to set three of them came when Mrs Elizabeth Sprague Coolidge commissioned Ravel, via Hans Kindler, to compose 'a cycle of songs of his own choosing, scored, if possible, for voice with accompaniment of flute, cello and piano.' The lean, astringent style of the Duo is again apparent in Ravel's cycle, as well as the master of orchestration who successfully draws the most astonishing effect of timbre from the accompanying ensemble. Ravel himself commented on the independence of the parts in the *Chansons* as being more marked than in the Duo. He went on: 'I subjected myself to this independence in writing a Sonata for violin and piano, essentially incompatible instruments, which here, far from balancing their contrasts, bring out this very incompatibility.' In fact, the *Sonate pour violon et piano* was begun earlier, in 1923, though not completed until 1927.

Between visits to America and England in 1928, Ravel began a work which more than any other made him world famous. Again, in his own words: 'In 1928, at the request of Mme Ida Rubinstein, I composed a *boléro* for orchestra. It is a rather slow dance, and uniform throughout in its melody, harmony and rhythm, the latter tapped ceaselessly by the side-drum. The only element of variety is supplied by the orchestral *crescendo*.' Ravel's *Boléro* conforms to neither the rhythm nor the tempo of the traditional Spanish dance of that name. When the composer Joaquín Nin pointed out that Ravel's tempo was twice as slow as that of a real *boléro*, Ravel replied: 'That has no importance at all!' And certainly it did not prevent the piece from becoming a wild success in two

Above: Ravel with the Russian soprano Nina Koshetz, on a boat voyage to the USA in 1928. This was one of many concert tours, in the course of which he also visited several European cities.

continents immediately after it caused a sensation at the Paris Opéra, when Mme Rubinstein presented it there on 22 November 1928 in a scenario by Bronislava Nijinska.

No sooner was *Boléro* circling the world than Ravel embarked on another unusual voyage of composition – a pair of piano concertos, worked on simultaneously and completed within a year of each other. These two late works are shining examples of Ravel's twofold skill, models of both piano and orchestral writing, however difficult some of the problems set individual orchestral soloists.

Begun in 1929, the *Concerto pour la main gauche* was a commission from the Austrian pianist, Paul Wittgenstein, who had lost his right arm in the First World War. It was first performed by its dedicatee in Vienna with the Vienna Symphony Orchestra under Robert Heger on 5 January 1932. In 1931, at the time of its composition, Ravel described the two-hand *Concerto pour piano et orchestre*: 'It is a Concerto in the truest sense of the word. I mean that it is written very much in the same spirit as those of Mozart and Saint-Saëns. The music of a concerto, in my opinion, should be light-hearted and brilliant, and not aim at profundity or at dramatic effects.' He went on to admit that the work contained touches of jazz, 'but not many.' The orchestral demands of this essentially gay piece are moderate: double woodwind, two horns, one trumpet, one trombone, three percussion players, harp and strings; but several of the principals' parts – oboe, bassoon, trumpet and harp, for example – call for high virtuosity. The concerto is dedicated to Marguerite Long, who gave its first performance in Paris at a Concert Lamoureux under Ravel's direction on 14 January 1932.

In the four months following the première of the Concerto, Ravel undertook a tour with Marguerite Long in which they performed the work in some twenty cities. After it, Ravel enjoyed an extended holiday on his beloved Basque coast, contemplating two commissions: a ballet on the subject of Ali Baba and the Forty Thieves, for Ida Rubinstein, and music for a film, *Don Quichotte*, with Chaliapin in the title-role. Both subjects would have seemed to be ideal for the now world-famous composer of *Shéhérazade* and numerous works of Spanish inspiration. Unhappily, in October 1932, Ravel was injured in a taxi collision in Paris. His recovery proved to be superficial, and although on 17 January 1933 he was able to conduct the Paris première of the *Concerto pour la main gauche* for Wittgenstein, his condition deteriorated. The three songs of *Don Quichotte à Dulcinée* on texts by Paul Morand are all of the film commission that Ravel was able to complete. They were to be his swansong.

In 1933 Ravel showed signs of brain trouble, a delayed result of the motor accident. The form his tragic ailment took was an inability to co-ordinate his thought with its outward expression in muscular movement and speech, an inability to put pen to paper and partial loss of memory. Months of rest only effected temporary improvement in his condition. Aware of music he still wanted to write, he was unable to set it down. Friends rallied around him, among them Ida Rubinstein, who arranged for him to take a trip to Spain and north Africa in 1935. That and a further trip to Spain in 1936 were Ravel's final pleasures, but his condition continued to worsen. In 1937, he was admitted to a Paris clinic for a delicate brain operation, from which he never recovered. He died in the early hours of 28 December.

Below: Drawing by Albert Moreau of Ravel on his death-bed, dated 28 December 1937.

Above: Costume designs by Multzer, showing the Bumble Bee, the Grasshopper and the Ladybird, for Roussel's ballet *Le Festin de l'araignée.* Roussel wrote a number of ballets, each different in style; *Le Festin* shows him at his most 'impressionistic.'

• Albert Roussel •

Albert Roussel, apart from Debussy, Ravel and Fauré, the one remaining French composer of commanding stature in the first part of the twentieth century, was born into a well-to-do middle-class family in Tourcoing, in northern France, on 5 April 1869. He died in Royan on 23 August 1937, having composed, in all, some eighty works, which establish his right to be considered alongside his two great contemporaries, Debussy, his senior by seven years, and Ravel, six years his junior. The young Roussel quested after distant lands at an early age. In 1884, he went to the Collège Stanislas in Paris to prepare for the Naval College. But music already claimed an earlier loyalty, for his sorrowing widowed mother had taught the child Albert the rudiments of music and *solfège.* Then, piano and music lessons had continued with a local lady organist at Tourcoing. In Paris another organist, the elderly Jules Stolz, who directed music at the Collège Stanislas, on recognizing Roussel's feeling for music introduced him to the music of Bach, Mozart, Beethoven and Chopin. Visits to the opera further extended his musical career. After two years of naval training, during which music had to be neglected, he became a midshipman second class and embarked on the frigate *Iphigénie* for a ten-month cruise which took in the Middle East. Then, his transfer to the battleship *Dévastation* gave him access to a piano. He tried to assimilate Durand's *Treatise on Harmony,* but what he called its excessive complication defeated him. In 1891, Roussel's health obliged him to take convalescent leave, which he spent in Tunis. After this break, he served on the *Melpomène,* the last of the French Navy's sailing-ships.

His next posting was to the cruiser *Victorieuse,* based in Cherbourg, where Roussel took a room with a piano. There he made chamber music with friends, playing Beethoven and later Romantic piano trios. And there, on Christmas Day, 1892, a work of his own had its first public performance at the Sainte-Trinité Church – an Andante for violin, viola, cello and organ. The following year Roussel composed a 'Marche Nuptiale,' which an ensign on board, Adolphe Calvé, brother of the famous singer Emma Calvé, offered to show to the conductor Colonne. Some days later, returning from Paris, Calvé reported that Colonne's advice was that Roussel should abandon the sea and devote himself entirely to music. Thirty years later, Calvé confessed that Colonne had never seen the manuscript, and that the advice was his own. He took a considerable risk, although Roussel was hardly the type to change course without greater encouragement than Colonne's approbation.

In 1894, while he was on leave, Roussel sought out Jules Koszul, director of the Conservatoire at Roubaix, where his family now lived, and showed him some of his work. Koszul agreed to give him harmony lessons. Roussel now threw himself into musical study, and, before long, opted to quit the Navy for music. The French Admiralty accepted his resignation on 23 June 1894, and that October saw him settled in a flat in Paris. He was twenty-five and on the threshold of a musical career, but at an age when most composers are already masters of their technical craft Roussel was still a student. Koszul gave Roussel an introduction to Eugène Gigout, with whom he began working as soon as he arrived in Paris.

Studies were intensified in 1898 when Roussel began working with Vincent d'Indy in composition, orchestration and history of music at the Schola Cantorum, and in 1902 d'Indy appointed Roussel professor of counterpoint there. Among his pupils were Roland-Manuel, the friend of and early authority on Ravel, and, most surprising of all, Erik Satie, an even later starter in serious musical study, for this colorful character decided in his fortieth year to resume basic musical studies and enrolled at the Schola in 1905, where he graduated in 1908 with a Diploma in Counterpoint signed by d'Indy and Roussel.

That year, on 17 April, Roussel married Blanche Preisach, a Parisian of Alsatian origin, and the marriage was one of the happiest imaginable. In September of the following year, the former naval officer was enticed back to the Orient for a four-year honeymoon-holiday, in the course of which the Roussels visited India, Ceylon, Singapore, Saigon and, auspiciously, the ruins at Angkor. On their return to Paris in 1910, Roussel completed the Suite, op.14, for piano, which he had begun before his departure.

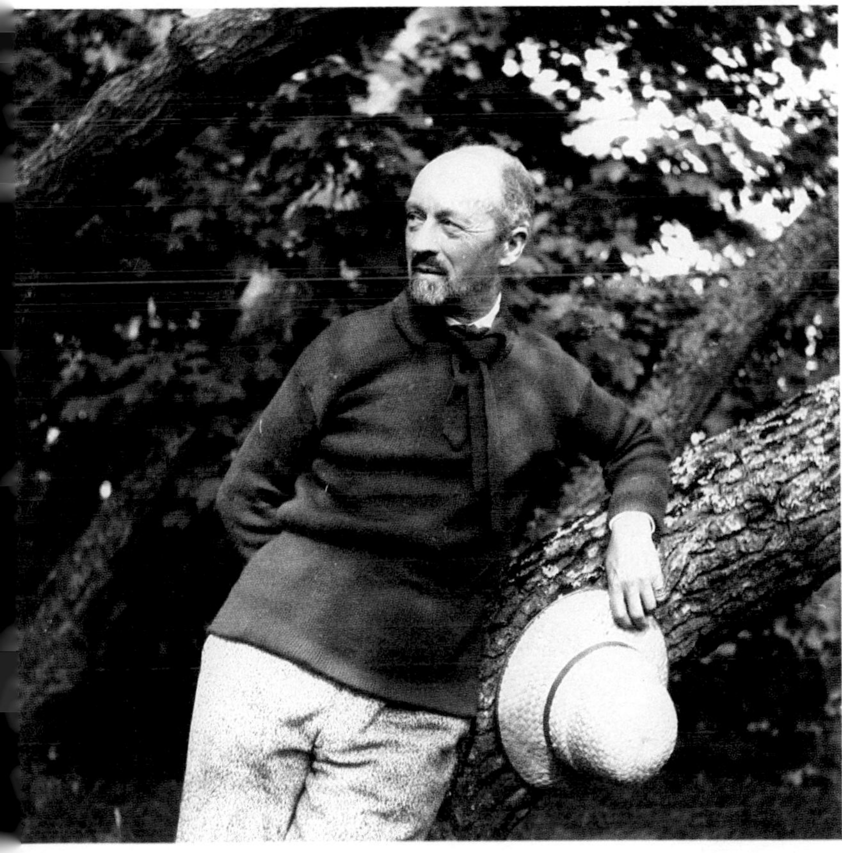

Above: Roussel at Varengeville. Near the end of his life he wrote: 'For several years I have reflected upon my art. . . . I had been captivated by impressionism, and my music was linked, too much perhaps, with extrinsic elements and a technique of picturesqueness, which – I discovered later on – was detrimental to its specific truth. I resolved, therefore, to endow my harmonies with a wider scope, and get nearer to the idea of a music intended and constructed to be self-sufficient.'

Top: A painting by Claude Monet of Varengeville, on the Normandy coast. Roussel lived near here, at Vasterival, from 1922 almost until his death, and it was here that he was eventually buried in the sailors' cemetery.

It was, however, with the succeeding op.15, *Evocations*, begun in 1910 and completed on holiday in Tunis in 1911, that Roussel achieved real distinction. The three *Evocations*, first performed on 18 May 1912 under Rhené-Baton at the Société Nationale, were inspired by Roussel's memories of India.

Roussel was now approached by Jacques Rouché, director of the Paris Théâtre des Arts, with a commission for a ballet. Despite, rather than because of, his personal wealth and affluence, Rouché was an impresario of genius, with an extraordinary flair for artistic marriages and theatrical successes. Witnessing the growing popularity of ballet, thanks to Diaghilev's Ballets Russes, Rouché sought to mount appropriate ballets in his modestly sized theater with its thirty-two-piece orchestra. At first Roussel hesitated but, persuaded by his wife, he accepted Rouché's offer. The chosen scenario, by Gilbert de Voisins, unfolds in the intimacy of a walled garden and is a fantasy of insect life. Nothing could be farther from the distant horizons of *Evocations* than *Le Festin de l'araignée* (The Spider's Banquet), op.17, yet they are divided only by the *Sonatine*, op.16, for piano, composed in September 1912. The ballet occupied Roussel from October to December of that year. Whereas *Evocations* were long pondered, *Le Festin* must have come to Roussel with ease. The little entomological drama around the spider's web inspired him to a delightful masterpiece with its own haunting, atmospheric quality. The first performance was an unqualified success, and Rouché, now director of the Paris Opéra, asked Roussel for a large-scale work suited to the larger house. This time he did not have to ask twice, for the idea of an opera-ballet had haunted Roussel since his visit to India in 1909.

Its composition, begun in Paris in 1914, was interrupted by the First World War, and *Pad-*

mâvatî did not reach the Opéra until Rouché produced it there on 1 June 1923. Its première further enhanced Roussel's prestige, and the opera broke new ground in the facility with which Roussel appropriately deployed Hindu scales, not only in his melodic lines, but also in their supporting harmonic structures. A slighly older French composer, Maurice Emmanuel (1862-1938) used Hindu modes in his Fourth Piano Sonatina (1920) and Olivier Messiaen (b.1908) has used them consistently in more recent years, but Roussel anticipated them both in his *Padmâvatî*.

To mark the fiftieth anniversary of the Boston Symphony Orchestra, which fell in 1930, Serge Koussevitzky crowned his admiration for Roussel and his music, already manifest in several prestigious performances, by commissioning a symphony from him. Roussel worked on his *Troisième Symphonie*, op.42, during 1929, the year in which a veritable Roussel Festival in Paris marked his sixtieth birthday. Like Debussy's *Prélude à l'après-midi d'un faune*, the symphony is a key work in the history of French music – if not in musical history generally, like the earlier work – for it disposes finally of the idea that French music lacks the solid architectural qualities of the Germanic, that it only excels in wit, charm and gracefulness, and that it is essentially a shallow, if not superficial art. In this work Roussel showed that symphonic form and a truly contemporary idiom were not incompatible with his national musical heritage, and that a Frenchman could find as valid expression in a symphony as in 'impressionism' or pastiche. Koussevitzky conducted the first performance in Boston on 17 October 1930, and Roussel was present to witness its triumph.

He was soon to experience another resounding success. Before and after his visit to Boston in 1930, Roussel worked on the first of his two 'classical' ballets. Once again, it was composed at the instigation of his faithful and discriminating admirer Jacques Rouché. Based on the same classical myth as Strauss's *Ariadne auf Naxos*, Roussel's *Bacchus et Ariane*, op.43, is musically more akin to a recent French ancestor, Ravel's *Daphnis et Chloé*, particularly in the matter of the bacchanale with which it ends.

By 1937 Roussel's health was deteriorating, and after completing his String Trio, op.58 in

Above: Portrait photograph of Erik Satie, taken in 1895.

Left: Picasso (center front, wearing a cap, with scene-painters, sitting on the back-drop curtain that he had designed for Satie's ballet *Parade*. The première on 18 May 1917 caused a great stir, and Satie found himself celebrated as a composer of some standing, rapidly attracting several disciples, who formed themselves into the group 'Les Six.'

July, he was obliged, sorrowfully, to quit the home at Vasterival in Normandy in which he had written his best music and spent his happiest hours. Sensing that he would not return there, Roussel destroyed his papers and sketches, and went to stay at Royan, where he began the composition of a Trio for oboe, clarinet and bassoon, which remained incomplete. He took to his bed on 13 August, and died ten days later. He lies buried as he intended, in the little cemetery at Varengeville-sur-Mer, where his tomb overlooks his beloved sea. In the pantheon of French composers, his place is assured.

• Erik Satie •

Erik Satie, who was born to a French father and Scottish mother at Honfleur on 17 May 1866, occupies a strange position in French music. Thirty-four at the turn of the century, Debussy's junior by four years and Ravel's senior by nine, Satie seems more of a twentieth-century figure than either of them. In his lifetime and since, they have overshadowed him, but Satie's brief period of glory has been prolonged by the devotion of those who recognize in him a kind of father-figure, justifying, perhaps, in his elevation to this rank, their own shortness of musical breath and modest scope of achievement. For, considered on its own, Satie's output of music is slender in more ways than one. And yet, no account of French music in the twentieth century would be complete without a consideration of some of his musical activities.

They began with piano lessons in Honfleur from the local organist, a product of the Ecole Niedermeyer, and so an enthusiast for plainsong and the modes. They were continued at the Paris Conservatoire in 1879, after Satie rejoined his father in Paris. Between 1872, when Erik's mother died, and 1878, he and his younger brother had been sent to live with their grandparents in Honfleur. Erik's father remarried in 1879, and although the second Mme Satie was herself a piano-teacher, Erik does not seem to have been drawn to his stepmother. Nor, however, did he distinguish himself at the Conservatoire. With hindsight, it is possible to understand his gradual formation as a solitary, both as a person and in his music. At home, he was subjected to a surfeit of music, because both his stepmother and, encouraged by her, his father, had pretensions as composers. Conventional in their musical taste, the elder Saties sought to influence the growing youth. But Erik's taste was for the unconventional – he himself changed the 'c' in his Christian name to a 'k' – and he reacted against the common thing, whether the music-making in his home and at the concerts to which he was dragged, or the kind of music towards which his studies at the Conservatoire were directed. Whereas Debussy before him and Ravel after him also reacted against the conventional, they stayed the course, giving evidence of original genius before severing links with the institution. Not so Satie.

Satie's eccentricity and introspection began before he had acquired any real compositional technique. A phase of religious mysticism began in 1886, by which time he had composed a few piano pieces. Four *Ogives* resulted from his study of Gothic art and his meditations in Notre-Dame, at a time when he earned the nickname of 'Monsieur le Pauvre.' Then, in 1887, he came under the influence of 'Sâr' Joséphin Péladan, leader of the resuscitated Rosicrucian sect. This was also the year of his *Trois sarabandes* with their unresolved harmonies. Similarly empirical successions may be found in the music of Chabrier, to whom Satie addressed an unacknowledged copy of the *Sarabandes*; but, despite Ravel's own admitted indebtedness to Chabrier, it is Satie who is generally credited as the harmonic pioneer. Debussy may well have known of the Satie *Sarabandes* when he composed the 'Sarabande' of *Pour le piano*, just as Ravel may have remembered Satie's *Gymnopédies* (1888) when writing the waltz in which Beauty and the Beast converse in *Ma Mère l'Oye* (1908).

That Ravel should have performed a *Gymnopédie* and a *Sarabande* by Satie in 1911 and that Debussy should have scored the first and third *Gymnopédies* for orchestra in the same year shows at least the regard they had for their strange colleague. Debussy met him in 1891, when Satie became pianist at the Auberge du Clou. By this time, Satie had also become the official musician of the Paris Rosicrucians, abandoning bars and key signatures in the various ritualistic small-scale works he wrote for them.

From this time until his death in 1925, Satie presents a complex and perplexing character to the musical historian. Quarreling with Péladan, Satie formed his own 'Eglise Metropolitaine

Below left: Picasso's design, of Cubist character, for the Paris Manager in the first production of *Parade*.

Below: Massine as the Chinese Conjurer in the first performance of *Parade*. The ballet was to have been the coming-together of several of Diaghilev's protégés, including Picasso, Satie, Massine and Cocteau, but in the event, Cocteau's text was very much altered, and he had little say in the final character of the production.

d'Art de Jésus Conducteur,' setting himself up as its 'Parcier' and 'Maître de Chapelle,' issuing edicts and excommunicating those who crossed his path. The same *folie de grandeur* must have inspired his three abortive attempts to be elected to the Académie des Beaux-Arts – in 1892, to the seat of Ernest Guiraud, in 1894 to Gounod's, and in 1896 to that of Ambroise Thomas. Meanwhile, earning his living as a café pianist and chansonnier-accompanist, Satie composed a spate of piano music, amusingly if not extravagantly titled, but all of short duration. In 1898, Satie took a room in the suburb of Arcueil-Cachan, whence he walked to Paris and back daily, visiting Debussy once a week to use his piano.

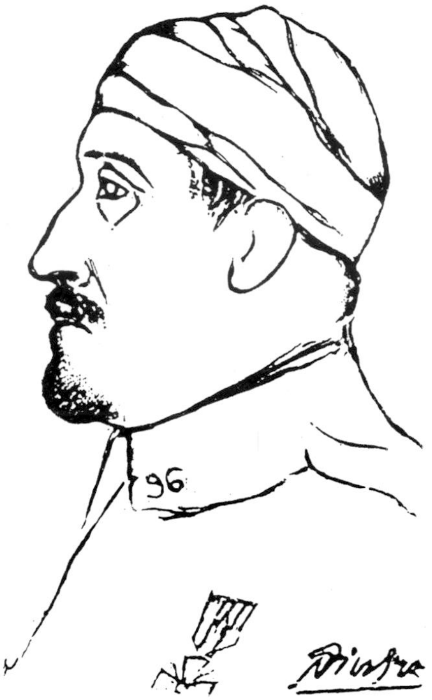

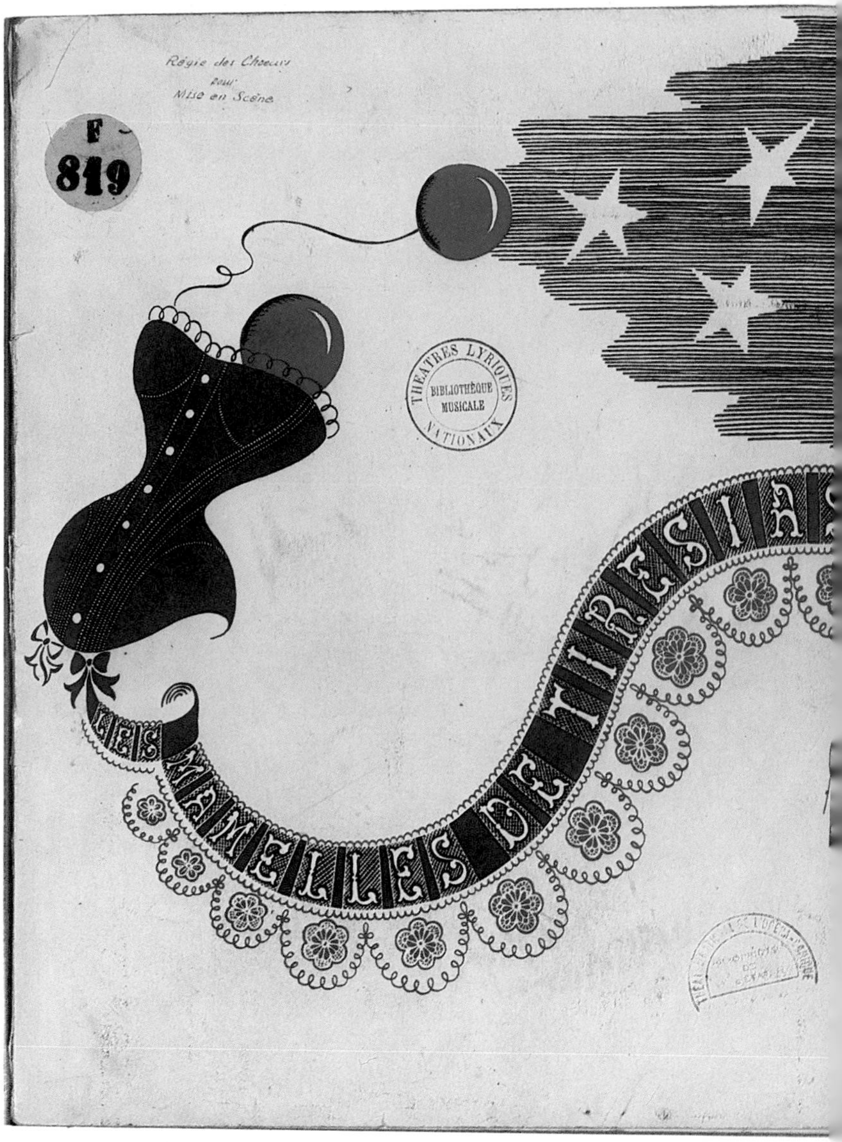

Far left: Drawing by Picasso of Guillaume Apollinaire (d.1917), his head bandaged from a war wound. The father-figure of the avant garde in the early years of the century, Apollinaire remained influential after his death, into the twenties. His 1916 play, *Les Mamelles de Tirésias*, was the basis of Poulenc's opera.

Above: Design by Erté for the title-page of Poulenc's opera *Les Mamelles de Tirésias*, a colorful comedy first produced at the Opéra Comique on 3 June 1947.

To 1905 belongs the completion of *Trois morceaux en forme de poire* (seven, in fact) for piano duet. It is rumored that he so titled them after Debussy, to whom he had shown them, hinted that they lacked form (or shape). But Satie, well aware of his limitations, decided in the same year to make up for his technical shortcomings by enrolling for further musical study at the Schola Cantorum. There, he gained his Diploma in Counterpoint, signed by d'Indy and Roussel with the mention 'Très bien.' But Satie's contrapuntal facility never exceeded that of a competent student.

Already before the outbreak of the First World War, Satie's ostensible debunking of what he saw as the pretentiousness of such influential movements as Wagnerism, Symbolism and Impressionism, made him a kind of rallying point for younger musicians. From 1914 date the twenty delightful pages for piano of *Sports et divertissements*, amusingly enhanced by Satie's texts and each backed by the colored drawings of Charles Martin. It was in 1914, too, that Satie met Jean Cocteau, who was to become spokesman for a widely bruited group of young composers after the war. The Satie–Cocteau collaboration began in 1915 with the composition of *Parade*, described on the title-page as 'Ballet réaliste.' Commissioned by Diaghilev, it brought together Satie's first orchestral score, Picasso's first stage designs, Massine's first choreography and Cocteau's first attempt, as scenario-writer, to express himself on several different levels. In the printed program, Guillaume Apollinaire prophetically described the purposeful integration of these different elements in *Parade* as a kind of *sur-réalisme*, the first known use of that term.

Satie's other 'major' work is *Socrate*, the 'drame symphonique' on which he worked at the beginning of 1917. In the bland serenity with which it unfolds, *Socrate* fulfills the desire Satie expressed to his young friend Valentine Gross that it should be 'white and pure as Antiquity.' In 1920, Satie wrote his *Musique d'ameublement*, to be played between the acts of a Max Jacob play, a kind of background music not intended to be listened to. It heralded the score of *Relâche*, the *ballet instantanéiste* with a film sequence, in which Satie's collaborators for Rolf de Maré's Ballet Suédois were Francis Picabia and René Clair. Like *Parade* in 1917, *Relâche* occasioned a scandal at its première on 30 November 1924.

But Satie was not physically well enough to relish even that. For years, he had sought refuge from frustrations of various kinds in alcohol. Cirrhosis of the liver claimed him in his sixtieth year, and pleurisy, finally, on 1 July 1925. From the unrelated harmonies of his *Sarabandes* to his Surrealist musical experiments and background music, Satie was a pioneer, but always surrounded by other musicians with greater practical ability. Even if the sum total of his own music amounts to surprisingly little, French music in the first quarter of the century would have been far less diverting without the fascinating personality of Erik Satie.

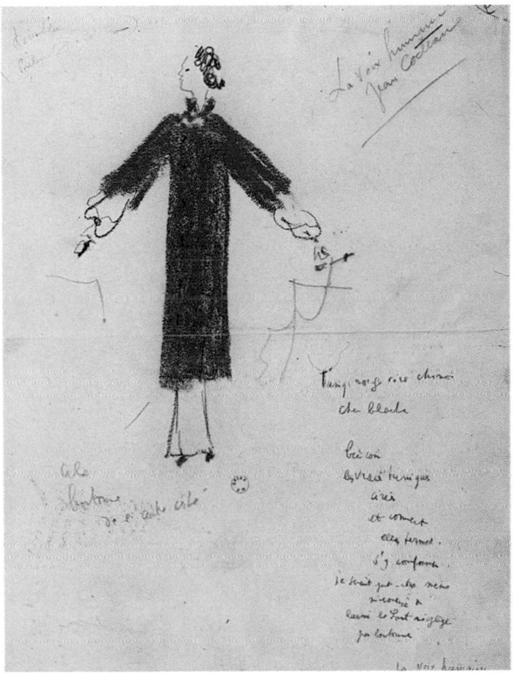

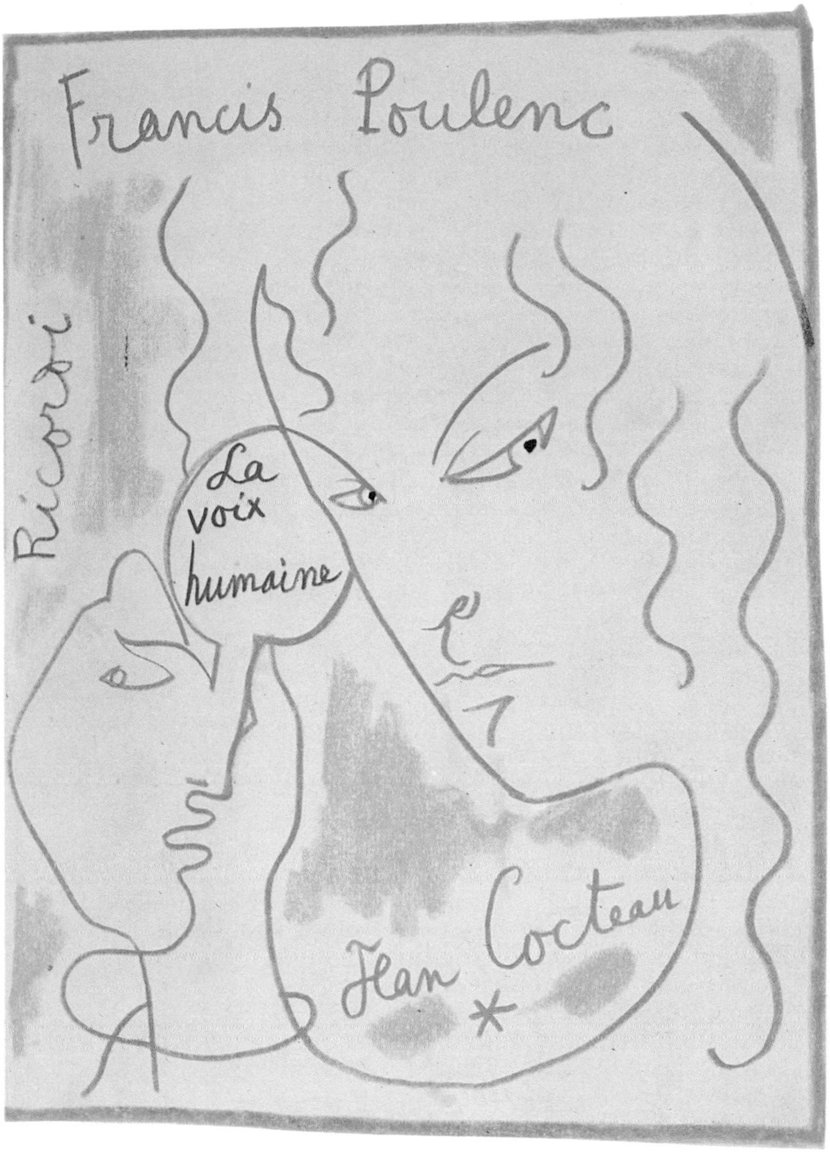

Above and left: Much later in their careers Cocteau and Poulenc collaborated again, this time on an opera, *La Voix humaine*, produced in 1958. Cocteau's designs (of the costume for the only character and of the cover of the score) reflect the serious nature of the work – one side of a telephone conversation between a woman and the lover who is rejecting her.

• Les Six •

By the time of Erik Satie's death in 1925, the members of Les Six had already gone their separate musical ways, but they remained bound by friendship, rather than a common esthetic for the rest of their lives. It was with Satie that three of them – Louis Durey, Georges Auric and Arthur Honegger – had met in 1917 and discussed the possibility of giving joint concerts of their music, the first of which took place on 6 June 1917. They were soon joined by Germaine Tailleferre and Francis Poulenc, and a little later by Darius Milhaud. The group was complete; Satie was their spiritual mentor, and Cocteau their spokesman and impresario of genius.

Louis Durey, the eldest of Les Six, died at the age of ninety-one in 1979, hardly known outside his native France except for his association with the group. His early music leaves no doubt that he could never have subscribed wholeheartedly to the esthetic of the circus and *café-concert.* Elegant settings of Saint-Léger and other texts of literary merit, chamber music and piano pieces, much of it still unpublished, make up about half of his output of 108 listed works. But for the latter part of his life, Durey became better known for the music of more popular intent that he wrote as a confirmed radical, having joined the French Communist Party in 1936 and become general secretary of the Fédération Musicale Populaire in 1937.

Arthur Honegger, next in order of seniority, French by birth but Swiss by parentage, enjoyed dual nationality. A composer of chamber music, sonatas and quartets before he joined Les Six, Honegger's fame was established in 1921 with the première of *Le Roi David*, the symphonic psalm which made his name abroad. It showed that Bach and Handel rather than Satie and Chabrier were his musical idols. *Pacific 231* (1923), the first of three *mouvements symphoniques*, reached even wider audiences, unlike its successors, *Rugby* (1928) and the otherwise untitled *No.3* (1932-3). Then, a succession of five symphonies continued to show a consistently serious view of music. The First (1930) was commissioned by Koussevitzky for Boston, the Second (1941), for string orchestra with optional trumpet, is a war work, born under oppression and colored by it, for Honegger, although a Swiss subject, suffered only a little less than his French colleagues during the years of German occupation. The Third (1945/6), the *Symphonie liturgique*, also had its roots in Honegger's reactions to the Second World War, and is no more light-hearted a work. The Fourth, *Deliciae Basilienses* (1946), is a sunnier tribute to his compatriot Paul Sacher and his Basle Chamber Orchestra. The Fifth, *Di tre rè* (1950/1), commissioned by the Koussevitzky Foundation, concluded a solid series of symphonic achievement, far removed from the supposed collective ideals of Les Six.

Le Roi David, too, had its successors involving choir and soloists as well as orchestra, notably *Jeanne d'Arc au bûcher* (1935), on a text by Paul Claudel, commissioned by Ida Rubinstein. Its successors in this genre were the oratorio *La Danse des mortes* (1938) also on a text by Claudel, *Nicolas de Flue* (1939-40) and *Une Cantate de Noël* (1953), effectively his musical testament.

Germaine Tailleferre, the one woman in the group, was a brilliant student at the Paris Conservatoire. Sponsored by Darius Milhaud, her immediate junior among Les Six, she shared in their exploits, without ever losing the grace and femininity which distinguish her scores, notably her *Concertino pour harpe* (1928), a reminder that Ravel counseled her in orchestration.

Darius Milhaud began musical studies as a child violinist. After matriculating at Aix-en-Provence, he entered the Paris Conservatoire as a violin student, but soon felt drawn towards composition. His earliest compositions date from 1910, when he was eighteen. The outbreak of war in 1914 prevented Milhaud from entering for the Prix de Rome. Rejected on medical grounds from military service – rheumatoid arthritis crippled him most of his adult life – Milhaud was consoled by an invitation from his friend Paul Claudel, newly appointed French Minister in Brazil, to go to Rio as his secretary. Returning to France, by way of New York, in 1918, Milhaud soon became an active member of Les Six. Like his colleagues, he developed in his own way, music pouring from him in a generous stream until his death in his eighty-second year.

Milhaud presents a complex, many-sided musical personality, for he wrote in many styles. The score of his which has, perhaps, the strongest claim to survival is that of his ballet *La Création du monde* (1923). It represents yet another facet of its many-sided composer. When the Ballet Suédois produced it at the Théâtre des Champs-Elysées in October 1924, *La Création du monde* took Paris by surprise, for its score was based on jazz.

Totally different by nature and temperament was Francis Poulenc, a Parisian-born who, in the days of Les Six, most nearly approached in his music the ideals proclaimed by Satie and then Cocteau. He started piano lessons at four; at twelve, he played reasonably well, and at fifteen he was a pupil of Ricardo Viñes. Through the piano he became acquainted with music, old and new, and it became the medium through which he found his own expression as a composer. The miniature *Trois mouvements perpétuels* (1918) and *La Bestiaire* (1919), tiny settings from Guillaume Apollinaire's *Cortège d'Orphée*, remain typical of what he did best – piano pieces for the drawing-room and settings of aphoristic verse, perfectly matched by his repeated two-measure phrases. One side of Poulenc never lost the spontaneous gaiety which

Above: Group portrait of Les Six and their champion, Jean Cocteau. From left to right: Francis Poulenc, Germaine Tailleferre, Louis Durey, Cocteau himself, Darius Milhaud and Arthur Honegger. Georges Auric, in his absence, is represented by Cocteau's caricature of him on the wall behind the group.

Right: Cocteau's own caricature drawing of Les Six, showing himself at the center of the group.

marked his early music, but the passage of years revealed a romantic quality formerly held in check or masked by gentle irony; this is most noticeable in the song-settings of Apollinaire, Aragon, Eluard, Louise de Vilmorin – perhaps the most important part of his *oeuvre*.

In the years leading up to the Second World War, Poulenc gave evidence of his gifts as melodist and miniaturist in a multitude of charming piano pieces and songs. He also worked on wider canvases, but these cost him far greater effort, for the long melodic arabesque was not his forte. In his larger works, melodic and other motifs succeed each other in a kind of panorama, repeated but never developed in the way usually associated with large-scale composition. This is true of the *Aubade* (1929) for piano and eighteen instruments, the first to be heard of his concerted works, as it is of the Piano Concerto (1949), which was his last, and certainly true of the intervening Concerto for two pianos (1932) and Organ Concerto (1938), which has become the most popular of all. Of Poulenc's dozen chamber works, the ten involving wind instruments seem to have come more naturally to him than the two string sonatas (violin and piano, and cello and piano), which caused him greater concern and proved more difficult to complete.

Poulenc composed two ballets: *Les Biches* (1923) and *Les Animaux modèles* (1942), of which the first has become famous. He also composed three operas: *Les Mamelles de Tirésias* (1944), *Dialogues des carmélites* (1957) and *La Voix humaine* (1959). His success with the first, on a Surrealist text by Apollinaire, and the third, on a monologue by Jean Cocteau, might have been anticipated. What surprised was his equal success with the lofty, religious libretto based on a work by Georges Bernanos. Only when this, his largest and longest work, was acclaimed at its La Scala première (26 January 1957) did his declaration, soon after the liberation of Paris in 1944, that he was primarily a composer of religious music, make sense. The path to it began in 1936, when, on 16 August, Poulenc's friend the composer Pierre-Octave Ferroud was killed in a motor accident in Hungary. Poulenc heard the news while on holiday at Uzerche, in the Auvergne country. Deeply affected, he paid a visit to the nearby shrine of the Black Virgin of Rocamadour. There he experienced a kind of recall to the paternal religion which he had neglected since his father's death in 1920. The same evening he began composing his *Litanies à la Vierge noire*, his first religious work. Other works on sacred texts followed, before, during and after the war, but in 1950, Poulenc broke new ground with a *Stabat Mater* for soprano, mixed choir and orchestra. It was followed in 1960 by his *Gloria* for identical forces, and finally, by the *Sept répons des ténèbres* in 1961, two years before his death.

Georges Auric, the youngest of Les Six and Poulenc's close friend, studied both at the Paris Conservatoire and at the Schola Cantorum. Like Poulenc, he became very involved with the activities of Les Six, and this is reflected in the music he wrote in the 1920s, of which the three ballets *Les Fâcheux* (1923-4), *Les Matelots* (1924) and *Pastorale* (1925) are typical. In more abstract instrumental compositions, Auric admitted some of the newer tendencies of the time, but he eventually found his truest musical *métier* in the world of film music. The waltz from *Le Moulin Rouge* has deservedly become world famous.

Below left: Scene from *Les Mariés de la Tour Eiffel*, a tongue-in-cheek fantasy-ballet commissioned by Rolf de Maré for the Ballet Suédois. The overall conception was Cocteau's, and he also collaborated with Börlin on the choreography; the masks and costumes were designed by Jean Hugo, the scenery by Irène Lagut, and the music was an assembly of pieces by Les Six, all of whom provided individual numbers, except for Durey, to whom the idea did not appeal. Soon after *Les Mariés*, which was not an outstanding success, Les Six began to go their separate ways.

Below: Scene from Cocteau's film *Orphée* (1950) which had incidental music by Auric; he remained the only one of Les Six to continue collaborating with Cocteau in his later career as a film-maker.

SERGEI RACHMANINOV

ROBERT THRELFALL

Opposite: Sergei Rachmaninov (1873-1943) at the piano, a portrait by Boris Chaliapin.

The date of Sergei Rachmaninov's birth, adjusted from the Old Style calendar used in pre-1918 Russia, becomes 1 April rather than 20 March 1873. Sergei was the second son (fourth of the six children) born to Vasily Rachmaninov and his wife, Lyubov Butakova. The parents shared a military background, but Arkady Rachmaninov, Sergei's paternal grandfather, was an amateur musician of high standing and a pianist of some accomplishment; he had been a pupil of John Field. Unfortunately, Vasily Rachmaninov squandered not only his own money but also that of his wife, and at the time of Sergei's birth only two of their properties remained: Semyonovo, where Sergei was born, and Oneg.

Semyonovo in its turn was sold, and Sergei's early years were spent not far from the city of Novgorod at Oneg, until that estate too was disposed of in 1882. Meanwhile, Sergei's first music lessons were imparted by his mother, a strict disciplinarian of orderly habits, and it was understood that he, like his father and paternal grandfather, should commence his future career as an officer cadet in the Army. However, even in those early days he evidently displayed a sufficiently unusual facility at the piano for Anna Ornatskaya, a young graduate from the St Petersburg Conservatory, to be engaged to train him properly.

After the estate at Oneg was sold, the family moved to an apartment in St Petersburg. Soon after, as the result of diphtheria, from which Sergei and his elder brother Vladimir quickly recovered, the family lost their second eldest daughter, Sofiya. Tension between the parents now reached breaking-point: Vasily left both home and city and never met his wife again. However, Sergei had been enrolled at the St Petersburg Conservatory, and there seems to have been no further thought of a military career for him. In addition, his eldest sister, Elena, was the possessor of a contralto voice of exceptional beauty, and she introduced him, in the role of accompanist, to the music of Tchaikovsky and others. Unfortunately, her early death in 1885 set short term to this pleasure.

Meanwhile it had become evident that the break-up of the parental home had affected Sergei. At the Conservatory his natural talent easily saw him through his musical examinations. In general subjects, however, his results were so poor that he was threatened with expulsion. On the advice of Alexander Ziloti, son of one of Vasily Rachmaninov's many sisters and a pianist who had been a pupil of Liszt, Sergei was sent at once to Moscow and placed under the control of the man to whom Ziloti owed his own early training – Nikolai Zverev, a famous teacher of the piano (and a no less famous disciplinarian), who was accustomed to board his more promising pupils in his own house. Although he left home with many misgivings, in later life Rachmaninov recognized the immense value of Zverev's training. Apart from intensive work at the keyboard (which included acquaintance with the standard classics of chamber music and symphony through four-hand transcriptions) there were regular visits to concerts and opera, ballet and plays. Above all, there were the Sunday evenings when Zverev entertained at home, all the stars of Moscow musical life coming as his guests, including such world-famous musicians as Anton Rubinstein and Tchaikovsky himself. Before such an audience Zverev's boarders, including the young Sergei, had the privilege of performing.

During the summers Zverev and his pupils spent their time away from Moscow – usually south, in the Crimea. There the new pupils were given basic instruction in harmony, so that on their return they were ready to enter the harmony class of Anton Arensky. This first contact with the raw material of music stimulated Sergei into some early attempts at composition, not only pieces for piano solo but even a *Scherzo* for orchestra. Of the few miscellaneous piano pieces, since published posthumously in Russia, all except one (which was later reworked for cello and piano) were subsequently ignored by their author. No characteristics of the mature writer are found here, save perhaps in the choice of certain keys which he always favored; indeed none of the posthumous works adds anything of significance, despite their occasional interest, to the official canon. At this time Rachmaninov also made a piano-duet arrangement of Tchaikovsky's recently published 'Manfred' Symphony, and this was subsequently played to the composer by Sergei and a fellow-pupil at Zverev's home.

In 1888, when he was fifteen, Sergei passed into his cousin Ziloti's class for advanced piano lessons at the Conservatory and simultaneously commenced the study of counterpoint with Taneyev. However, before any other musical development could take place, a fresh crisis

Top: Lyubov Butakova, Rachmaninov's mother, who gave the composer his first piano lessons, though he was destined for a military career.

Right: Rachmaninov's father, Vasily.

Below: Rachmaninov at the piano.

blew up. Zverev had always considered Sergei as a pianist pure and simple, and in his view composition was a waste of such brilliant pianistic gifts. Hence, Sergei's request for a room with a piano of his own to facilitate his writing, undisturbed by his fellow-pupils' interminable piano practice, precipitated a major row, so serious that he immediately withdrew from Zverev's house. After a short spell in lodgings with a student friend, he turned to his aunt Varvara Satina (another of his father's sisters), who received him warmly and treated him as one of her own family. There he made his home, despite his mother's suggestion that he should return to St Petersburg and study again at that rival Conservatory with Anton Rubinstein and Rimsky-Korsakov.

• Early success •

In the congenial surroundings offered by the Satin family, composition proved very much easier. A number of songs and miscellaneous piano pieces were written, and Sergei received his first commission, an arrangement for piano duet of Tchaikovsky's *Sleeping Beauty* ballet music. A youthful symphony dating from 1891 progressed no further than its first movement, wherein the influence of Mendelssohn, notable in the early *Scherzo*, was replaced by an equally pale imitation of Tchaikovsky. Arensky, under whose eye this symphony was begun, was not pleased with what he saw; much more promising and effective was a symphonic poem based on A. Tolstoy's ballad *Prince Rostislav* and completed a few months later. The warm dedication to Arensky may indicate that the work met his approval; only its lack of any deep expression of the composer's most characteristic style denies it a higher place among his most appreciated works.

The same year, Rachmaninov completed his largest work yet, the First Piano Concerto – his 'official' opus 1. He also passed the examinations in piano playing and fugal composition a year in advance and prepared to complete the Conservatory course in 1892. In the meantime he had appeared as both composer and pianist at a chamber-music concert, and shortly afterwards he played the first movement of his concerto with the Conservatory orchestra. The final stage in his youthful success was his completion in full score, in a mere three weeks, of the one-act opera *Aleko*, a task set for the examination finals (this manuscript score runs to well over a hundred pages). The work was enthusiastically accepted by the examining panel, which included Tchaikovsky. Rachmaninov was awarded the Great Gold Medal of the Conservatory; perhaps he received almost equal pleasure at being reconciled with his old tutor Zverev. The latter also introduced him to a publisher, a firm which not only immediately bought the new opera and other lesser works, but continued to publish his compositions for more than twenty years. Rachmaninov was no longer a student but now a 'Free Artist,' in the words of his Conservatory diploma.

The summer of 1892 passed in a way familiar to many young and newly qualified musicians: private lessons, proof-reading and the arrangement of the new opera for piano and voices. However, some original piano pieces were also composed, including the Prelude in C sharp minor, and during that autumn Rachmaninov appeared at a concert which he subsequently considered to be the commencement of his public career as a pianist. The new piano pieces played were instantly successful; although they were sold outright, thus earning him no royalties, they spread their author's fame far and wide and ensured that wherever he traveled he was welcomed and acclaimed.

A dozen of these new piano works were published, the five *Morceaux de fantaisie* in 1892 and the seven slightly less successful *Morceaux de salon* just over a year later. It was the first of these sets, including not only the famous Prelude but the almost equally well-known 'Elegy,' 'Melody,' 'Polichinelle' and 'Serenade,' which spread the author's fame so effectively. Brilliant, not too difficult and, at their best, sufficiently different (at that time) to attract and hold attention, these pieces quickly achieved a popularity perhaps in part out of proportion to their intrinsic value. The Prelude in C sharp minor is the exception, inasmuch as its complete realization of the composer's mood of characteristic and reflective melancholy in terms of an entirely appropriate piano sonority revealed his unmistakable personal style at a stroke. The 'three-handed' (and four-line) layout may derive from Liszt, but the harmonic richness and progressions are Rachmaninov's own. In his last years the composer presented revised and much altered versions of three of these early pieces ('Melody,' 'Serenade' and 'Humoresque'); he never needed to amplify the 'Prelude' (though he did make an arrangement of it for two pianos) and he continued all his life to play it, however grudgingly at times, to his expectant audiences, most of whom were glad to have heard for once an authentic performance of this popular masterpiece.

The First Concerto, however, fared less well. Despite the capable and idiomatic piano writing, supported by rather less experienced orchestration, Rachmaninov soon decided that the score as a whole was too immature to survive in its early form; it was a quarter of a century, however, before he was able to take up the work for revision. By then, with the Second and Third Concertos completed, the revised version became a re-creation stylistically somewhat at variance with its content; it remains less well known, though on its comparatively rare hearings it cannot be judged unattractive.

In 1892, however, both the First Concerto and the Orchestral Intermezzo from *Aleko* met with success; in the course of the next twelve months the Orchestral Dances from the opera were performed separately, as a prelude to the prestigious staging of the whole work early in 1893 at the Bolshoi Theater in Moscow in the presence of Tchaikovsky. It is not surprising, then, given Rachmaninov's natural gift for handling the orchestra (for nowhere do we learn of his receiving any extensive or specialized tuition in this complicated subject), that in the summer of 1893 he composed the first orchestral work by which he wished to be remembered – another symphonic poem, entitled *The Rock*. Ostensibly a musical treatment of lines from Lermontov (placed as an epigraph on the score), the work is in fact based on Chekhov's story *Along the Road*, which uses the same motto. *The Rock*, which reveals complete orchestral mastery and a keen awareness of beauty of sound, was immediately accepted for publication and performance. It also won the admiration of Tchaikovsky, but his untimely death curtailed plans for performances of it to be included in his next European tour.

Above: Rachmaninov (second from left) and his two fellow pupils Presman and Maximov together with their music teacher Nikolai Zverev, in the latter's flat where Rachmaninov lived while he was a pupil at the Moscow Conservatory.

Tchaikovsky's death moved Rachmaninov to compose the first of his two major chamber works. This is the *Trio élégiaque*, written 'in memory of a great artist' (Tchaikovsky had himself marked the death of his friend Nikolai Rubinstein by the composition of a piano trio of equally extended proportions). 'While working on it,' wrote Rachmaninov, 'all my thoughts, feelings and energy were devoted to it,' and the sincerity of expression in the work is unmistakable. This Trio consists of three movements, of which the second (originally introducing a part for the harmonium) is an extensive set of variations, while the third is on a shorter scale. The ending recalls the opening theme, yet the

Below: Fyodor Chaliapin, standing with his dog by a busy fairground, painted by Natalia Goncharova. Rachmaninov met Chaliapin while engaged as conductor by the Moscow Private Russian Opera Company in 1897-8, and they became close friends. Later the two men studied the operas of Rimsky-Korsakov and Musorgsky together.

Bottom: Pond, 1902, by V. Borisov Musatov, an evocation of calm reflected in several of Rachmaninov's twelve songs published that year, the year of his marriage.

work as a whole remained unbalanced. Rachmaninov returned to this bulky score more than once, making a number of cuts each time. He completely rewrote one of the variations, modifying several details elsewhere and carrying out some welcome thinning of the texture, particularly in the piano part.

Meanwhile he had begun another work, a *Caprice* based on gypsy themes. First cast into the form of a piano duet, the work was completed in orchestral form in 1894, by which time he had also heard *The Rock* performed. The brilliant and effective *Caprice* failed to satisfy the composer, however, and in later years he stated his intention to revise the work, although he never in fact carried this out. By the time it was played in public late in 1895, Rachmaninov had completed the massive manuscript of his largest work so far, his First Symphony, based on Russian ecclesiastical chants.

While awaiting the first performance of this major composition, Rachmaninov published the six *Moments musicaux* in 1896. These show a more advanced piano style than his early sets of piano pieces, and while some look back in character to these, some rise to a higher level, especially the second and most typical, for which Rachmaninov always retained a special liking; already a much more polished execution is needed to do effective justice to the piece. He also completed a short concert tour and another commissioned piano-duet arrangement, this time of Glazunov's Sixth Symphony. It was Glazunov who conducted Rachmaninov's symphony early in 1897, and the reception of the work must have been a blow to its composer. For reasons not easy to identify, the performance (in St Petersburg, where works of the Moscow school were naturally suspect) was a complete failure. The composer withheld the score from publication for the rest of his life and became the prey to depression which effectively stifled new composition for several years.

• Depression and release •

Whatever the reasons for its early failure, it is now clear that the First Symphony stands at the apex of Rachmaninov's first period of creation. He was so disheartened after the première that although he retained the piano-duet version of the work he suppressed the manuscript full score, which has remained unlocated to this day. The orchestral parts used for the first performance in St Petersburg were the basis for a reconstruction carried out not long after the composer's death, however, so that it is now possible to assess the work fairly despite its author's ban. If the second and third movements clearly reveal the influence of Tchaikovsky, much of the first and last movements are fully typical of Rachmaninov himself: the pithy fragments from which the movements are built; the intensely burning lyricism, with its sweeping melodies; the tragic final coda (with its reference

to the 'Dies irae,' perhaps the earliest of several in his output). By the finish, the overwhelming impression is that of reliving a real and vivid experience, although at times the expression lacks the subtlety and smoothness of transition so notable in the two later symphonies.

Fortunately, at this juncture, another musical activity opened up. Rachmaninov undertook the post of opera conductor with a private company operating in Moscow; here he not only revealed interpretative gifts with the baton, but he also formed a long-lasting friendship with the young bass Fyodor Chaliapin, then at the threshold of his own brilliant career. Meanwhile, one result of the increasing fame of the C sharp minor Prelude was an invitation from the London Philharmonic Society to introduce his orchestral and solo piano works in person. This Rachmaninov did in 1899, promising to return the following year with a new concerto, having considered the First inadequate for his London début.

On his return to Russia depression seized him again, but from this he was finally and completely cured by the personal treatment of a hypnotist–physician, Nikolai Dahl, who was also an amateur musician. Completion of the promised Second Concerto (now dedicated in gratitude to Dahl) was delayed a year. It was first played in Moscow in 1900 in incomplete form, but with this major score the corner was finally turned, and its author's fame was set on the firm base which has lasted to this day. When it is presented with the majestic pianism of its author or such close associates as his cousin Alexander Ziloti, the success of the Second Concerto (op.18, in C minor) is understandable, yet the work has also proved an attractive vehicle for even the youngest generation of interpreters. Although a refined performance can still rediscover much more than superficial beauty in the colorful score, its broad lines, glorious melodies and exciting orchestral support can survive even comparatively inexperienced handling. The steady, measured tread of the first movement; the almost immobile, dreaming melodies of the second; the apotheosis of the principal theme at the end of the finale: all these and many other memorable features have combined to grant the work a lasting popularity, matched only, among other non-Classical concertos, by Grieg's or Tchaikovsky's First.

For another whole year the flow of fresh composition continued in full spate, and then Rachmaninov's personal life moved into accord with his artistic success when, in 1902, he married his cousin Natalya Satina. After an extended honeymoon tour of Europe they settled

Left: Title-page of Rachmaninov's Prelude in C sharp minor, written in 1892 – a tremendously successful concert piece which established the composer's reputation virtually overnight. Rachmaninov dedicated the work to Arensky, his harmony teacher.

Above: Front cover of the *Moments musicaux*, six pieces requiring considerable performance technique. It is typical that these comparatively early works should have such a conventional title, keeping well within an established pianistic tradition.

in Moscow, while the composer set in order his recent new works and introduced them at a number of concert appearances. They included his second and last large-scale piece of chamber music, the Sonata for cello and piano, written in 1901 at the same time as the Second Concerto, which it closely resembles in texture and piano style. The morbid moods which permeate the *Trio élégiaque* are here replaced with warmth and vivacity combined with characteristic sweeps of melody.

•Opera and song•

Rachmaninov now turned again to opera. During the next few years he not only completed two one-act operas, *The Miserly Knight* and *Francesca da Rimini*, but he also accepted the post of conductor at the Bolshoi Theater. Here a number of successful performances were given under his baton, many involving collaboration with Chaliapin. *Aleko* was revived with Chaliapin in the title-role, but for the first performances of the two newer works another singer had to be engaged as Chaliapin could not prepare them in the time available. *Aleko*, for all

its still attractive qualities, remains a work of promise rather than fulfillment, and the later pair have similarly failed to maintain a place in the repertory, though every revival, whether in concert or broadcast form, reveals a quantity of Rachmaninov's best music hampered by basically undramatic libretti. A promising project, *Monna Vanna*, unfortunately remained unfinished.

Rachmaninov's songs, however, are another matter. The concise yet inevitable nature of the realization of that three-part unity – the poem, the voice line and the piano part – which is the touchstone of every genuinely inspired solo song, frequently appears in the eighty-three to be found as we turn the pages of Rachmaninov's vocal anthology. In the majority of cases Rachmaninov chose the verses of nineteenth-century authors such as Pushkin and Tolstoy; the Russian poets Fet, Tyutchev and Apukhtin also appear and occasionally the later writers Balmont, Merezhkovsky and Golenishchev-Kutuzov. A few French (de Musset, Victor Hugo) and German (Heine, Goethe) poems occur, but always in Russian translation. The refinement and increasing subtlety of detail that developed in the piano pieces is also seen in the transition from youth to maturity in the songs. Recent piano compositions had included the Variations on Chopin's C minor Prelude, dating from 1902-3, and ten Preludes published in 1903. These are perhaps more immediately attractive than many of the preceding piano works and are very effective without necessarily being as difficult as the second of the *Moments musicaux*. The Prelude in G minor soon took its place as second only to that in C sharp minor in popularity; those in B flat, D minor and major and, in particular, the last of the set – that in G flat – are all of special value and are as rewarding to player as to listener. In both song-writing and solo piano music, when Rachmaninov left Russia in 1917 an abrupt break occurs, and the series of transcriptions later made by the concert pianist is only paralleled by a few settings of Russian folksongs; no original songs were composed during the last quarter-century of the composer's life.

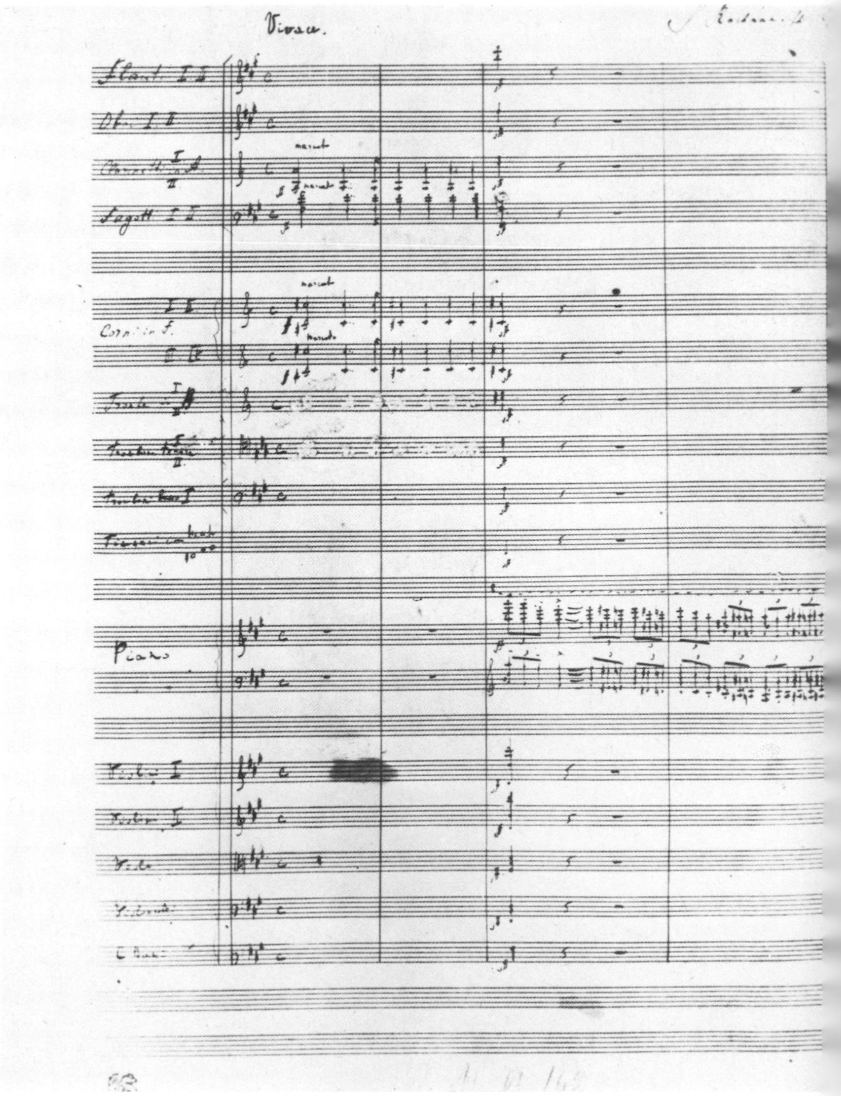

Above all it is Rachmaninov's gift of melody that has determined the songs most popular with both singers and audiences. 'In the silence of the secret night,' 'The harvest of sorrow' and the setting of Pushkin's 'Georgian Song' are as well known as the early piano pieces which appeared at about the same time. Other lesser-known but equally attractive works include some of the Heine settings, in particular 'The dream,' 'The isle,' where simplicity of setting matches Shelley's words, and the virtuoso, though less subtle, 'Spring waters.' The magical setting of 'The answer' and, most famous of all, 'Lilacs,' should not distract us from the melodies of 'How fair this spot' and several other songs in the set of twelve composed in 1902, when Rachmaninov and his wife were on their honeymoon. 'Christ is risen' and 'To the children' are justly famous, but 'The heart's secret,' 'Before my window' and especially 'When yesterday we met' are surely of equal value. In his last collection of songs, published by 1917, Rachmaninov was inspired by the famous singers with whom he had been associated, and thus he has left us a memorial, often as vivid as an actual recording, of the voices in question. 'The raising of Lazarus' and 'The poet,' for example, give a portrayal of the bass Fyodor Chaliapin, while 'The morn of life' and 'What wealth of rapture' were written with the tenor Leonid Sobinov in mind. 'Discord' portrays the dramatic soprano Felia Litvin; the wordless 'Vocalise' immortalizes the coloratura soprano Antonina Nezhdanova; but it is perhaps above all from 'Daisies' and the last-composed song of the book, 'Dreams,' that we obtain some idea of the art of their first interpreters – Nina Koshetz with the composer at the piano.

Opposite left: Rachmaninov's hands at the keyboard.

Opposite right: Opening page of the First Piano Concerto, in F sharp minor, written between 1890 and 1891, as later revised by the composer.

Top: Rachmaninov in his study, 1904-5. During this period most of his summers were spent on the Satins' estate at Ivanovka.

Above: Rachmaninov at the wheel of his car in 1910.

• Last decade in Russia •

The unsettled conditions at the Bolshoi Theater following the 1905 disturbances in Moscow led Rachmaninov to resign from his official post there. He considered other operatic projects and conducted various concerts, but finally, in February 1906, he retired, first to Italy, then to Dresden, to devote himself exclusively to composition. In Dresden he worked for three years on a number of major projects with a diligence only interrupted by a few concert tours, which took him to Paris, London and Berlin, among other places, where he played his Second Piano Concerto.

Probably the least successful of these projects was the First Piano Sonata, said to have been based on an expression of the principal characters in the Faust legend. The composer's fear that the work would be played 'by nobody because of its length and difficulty' has not been fulfilled, but the massive work still awaits a worthy interpreter of its poetry and drama. There are also some who consider the Second Symphony less successful than the First; however, the expertise gained in the dozen intervening years ensured greater finish in a work exceptionally full of detail. The characteristic melodies are longer in span than in the earlier work. The two middle movements now reflect the personality of Rachmaninov himself, while Tchaikovsky's influence has retreated to the background; the ending crowns the leading theme of the last movement with a jubilant conclusion far removed from the menace of the First Symphony's closing bars. Shortly after, in 1909, there appeared the symphonic poem, 'based on Böcklin's famous picture' – *The Isle of the Dead*. Here, despite the predominantly gray coloration and deliberately monotonous effect (set into relief by the passionate central interlude), is to be found one of the undoubted highlights of Rachmaninov's orchestral writing as a means of creating atmosphere.

The outstanding new work of this period, however, was the Third Piano Concerto. This was written for his first American tour, a series of twenty-six engagements during the season 1909-10, which separated him for three months from his wife and family (two daughters had been born to them, Irina in 1903 and Tatyana in 1907). If less immediately attractive to some than the Second Concerto, the melodies of the Third are surely as beautiful; the orchestra's part is even more subtly responsive, and the filigree detail, both of piano part and of the score as a whole, provides evidence of compositional mastery of a higher degree. The opening few pages alone are sufficiently eloquent proof of all this. The work is now in the repertoire of almost as many pianists as the Second, even though it naturally falls into place in serious rather than in popular programs. Despite its difficulty, it has now engaged the attention of many young interpreters, striving to unravel the intricate – but extremely rewarding – solo part.

So successful were Rachmaninov's first appearances in America that he was immediately offered return engagements for the following season and even the conductorship of the Boston Symphony Orchestra. However, he was not yet ready to accept such duties, and on his return to Russia (where he now inherited the Satins' estate at Ivanovka, to his great joy) he resumed the disciplines of composition, alternating with conducting and concert tours featuring his own works for piano. Thirteen more Preludes, making a total of twenty-four, appeared in 1911. They reflect a deepening in both thought and style, and some are of a difficulty which is bound to restrict performance, but those in G major, B major and G sharp minor, to list but three, have maintained a deservedly popular status ever since their first appearance. Nine *Etudes-tableaux* (a title peculiar to Rachmaninov) were written the next year, but three were withdrawn before publication: nos.3 and 5 appeared only posthumously and no.4 was rewritten by the composer and published in a later collection. There is little if any

difference in style, scope or content between the remaining six of these pieces and the preludes finished a year earlier; if nos.2 and 8 are the more immediately attractive, nos.6 and 7 are most likely to engage and retain the pianist's interest. A much more substantial work for solo piano, the Second Sonata, which is similar to the massive First, was completed in 1913. Rachmaninov revised the work in 1931, not only cutting it in length but thinning the texture of some of the more intricate passages.

Probably the peak of all Rachmaninov's work as a composer so far was reached in his setting of Balmont's Russian version of Edgar Allan Poe's poem *The Bells* as a four-movement choral symphony; this was completed late in 1913 and received its first performance the following year. In scope and elaboration of technique *The Bells* has justly been named Rachmaninov's most complex creation; it was the score the composer cherished above all his works. The overall mood of resigned pessimism as the work progresses reflects a salient feature of so much of his best work that the high quality of the result seems inevitable.

During the early months of the First World War Rachmaninov was involved in a number of charity concerts, but at the beginning of 1915 he turned to composition once again and quickly completed his *Vespers*, or *All-night Vigil* for unaccompanied voices, a work of the same high quality as *The Bells*, even though of a perhaps more restricted appeal. Here Rachmaninov reaches one of the unquestioned summits of his art, though in its austerity of medium and style the work is far removed from his usually accepted image of concert brilliance.

There were to be personal losses in this year, with the deaths of Taneyev, his one-time professor, Skriabin, with whom he had been a student at the Conservatory, and his publisher, Gutheil. In 1916 Rachmaninov's father, Vasily, for whom he retained much affection despite his abandonment of the home, also died. During these two years and the early part of 1917, concert tours and charity concerts continued – time being found, however, for the composition of some more songs and piano pieces, including a second set of *Etudes-tableaux*. Besides the rewritten no.4 of the earlier set, now numbered 6, this set includes, in nos.3 and 5, two of the very finest pieces Rachmaninov wrote for piano; all nine display a command of keyboard technique which has not been surpassed, although many have endeavored to follow his example. He was also drafting his Fourth Concerto, but all these activities ceased with the outbreak of the Russian Revolution later in the year; only the long-contemplated rewriting of the First Piano Concerto was carried out while Rachmaninov cast about for some means of leaving the country, having little sympathy with the new régime. An invitation to give piano recitals in Stockholm provided the opportunity he sought, and the whole family emigrated at the end of the year, settling first in Stockholm, then in Copenhagen. By the middle of 1918 it had become evident to Rachmaninov that as an

Above and left: Photographs taken early this century of paintings in the church of John the Baptist, Kostroma, and of the Holy Trinity church in the Zhitny Monastery at Ostashkov. The pervasive influence of the Orthodox church is revealed in Rachmaninov's two major religious works, the *Liturgy of St John Chrysostom*, 1910, and the great *Vespers* of 1915.

exile the only career immediately open to him was that of a concert pianist. To equip himself for this new life he hurriedly studied some suitable programs of miscellaneous piano music (for years his recitals had consisted of his own compositions only). At the same time no less than three attractive offers reached him from America. Now, although not accepting any of the specific proposals put forward, he sailed for America with his family, confident that there his future was to lie.

•A new life•

Once settled in America, where he was welcomed by all who remembered him from his early fame and previous visit, it did not take long for Rachmaninov as a pianist to rise quickly to an eminence which he maintained until his death. His exceptional gifts of musicianship and personality – in addition to his physical resilience – resulted in year after year of travel backward and forward across that great country, and tours of Europe and the United Kingdom were also fitted into the schedule, demanding fifty to a hundred appearances every year. What this new life could not accommodate was original composition, which demanded the kind of peace and relaxation denied to the traveling virtuoso. Instead he commenced a series of attractive recital transcriptions, marking time, as it were, until a sabbatical year which he had planned for 1926.

Then at last, taking up the extensive sketches he had brought with him when he left Russia, Rachmaninov wrote the Fourth Piano Concerto, which he introduced early the following year together with some vivid Russian folksong arrangements. Unfortunately, despite the composer's authoritative pianism (and Stokowski's conducting), this new work failed to gain favorable recognition, and Rachmaninov returned to the concert treadmill for another five years devoid of original composition. The indifferent reception of the Fourth Concerto, due partly, no doubt, to its unexpectedly muted quality as compared to its predecessors, led the composer to rewrite substantial portions and make a number of cuts before first publication. Still unsatisfied, Rachmaninov soon neglected the Fourth himself; but at the end of his life he returned to the score and produced a final version (which he then recorded) over a quarter of a century after the first draft. As a result, the Fourth Concerto has remained in the shadow cast by the more assertive Second and Third, a reflection not only of the history of the work but also of the music itself. To enquiring study, however, the work responds with limitless fascination for its completely different solutions to the perennial problems of balance and texture, not to mention for the mastery of its composition *per se*.

During all this period, developments in recording technique had also provided intensive work; first Ampico player-piano rolls, then Edison and finally Victor records were enriched with some of Rachmaninov's own more famous solos and his equally famous renderings of items drawn from the classical repertory, as well as all his works for piano and orchestra. Meanwhile, the increasing success (and extent) of the European wing of his travels had led Rachmaninov to spend several summers in France while another plan was slowly carried into effect. This was the building of a home in Switzerland, on the shore of Lake Lucerne, where the composer hoped to find peace at last and where indeed, for a space, this was granted to him.

In 1931 he had found time to revise his Second Piano Sonata and to compose a set of variations on the theme 'La Folia,' as used by many earlier writers, including Corelli. If the earlier 'Chopin' Variations are a solo piano counterpart to the Second Concerto (and the First Sonata a similar study for the Third Concerto), the 'Corelli' Variations are a preliminary canter for the *Paganini Rhapsody*. The lightening of texture in the revision of the Second Sonata, and the variety of styles as already found in the 'Chopin' Variations, combine in the 'Corelli

Below: B. Kustodiyev's painting showing the beginning of the Russian Revolution in 1917. Rachmaninov saw no possibility of continuing his career in Russia and sought the first opportunity to leave the country.

Variations' to form an attractive work stamped with the characteristic harmony and pianistic skill of its author. The *Paganini Rhapsody* followed three years later.

• *Rhapsody on a Theme of Paganini* •

It was not until the spring of 1934 that the new home, the Villa Senar (named thus after *SE*rgei and *NA*talya *R*achmaninov), was at last finished and ready for occupation. During the summer of that year, with the rare facility that attended the composition of only his most successful works, Rachmaninov wrote the *Rhapsody on a Theme of Paganini*, his final work for piano and orchestra.

In the standard repertory of works for piano and orchestra, those not in the full three-movement concerto form are comparatively rare. There are a few compositions by Schumann and Mendelssohn, but these resemble single movements which have progressed no further; Liszt's *Totentanz*, a set of free variations on 'Dies irae,' the old plainchant sequence from the Mass for the Dead, is not only his finest composition for piano and orchestra but also one of the few models for Rachmaninov's *Rhapsody*. Originally Rachmaninov was uncertain as to the most suitable title for his own new work; 'Symphonic Variations' and 'Fantasia' were two rejected ideas. Be that as it may, the work consists of a brief introduction with twenty-four variations. In his application of the Lisztian model, however, Rachmaninov groups his work quite clearly into three well-defined sections. The first and last of these retain the key and character of Paganini's theme, the last of his *Caprices*, on which fresh and ever changing light is thrown in dazzling sequence; the middle group (consisting of variations 11-18) is a great contrast in both mood and color, and it thus fulfills some of the functions of the slow middle movement of a concerto while still further developing the argument. The whole work, in its author's words, 'is the size of a piano concerto . . . and is rather difficult.'

The world première took place in Baltimore on 7 November 1934, with Rachmaninov himself at the piano and his 'best orchestra' – that of Philadelphia – under the direction of his friend Leopold Stokowski. This time there was no doubt; audiences received the *Rhapsody* with wild enthusiasm. In the autumn of 1937 there opened another chapter in the history of the work. The composer outlined to the choreographer Mikhail Fokine his idea for a ballet based on the legend of Paganini who, Faust-like, was said to have 'sold himself to the evil spirit in exchange for perfection in art.' By the summer of 1939 work was finished and *Paganini*, 'Fantastic Ballet in Three Scenes by S. Rachmaninoff and M. Fokine,' was first presented in London at the Royal Opera House, Covent Garden, on 30 June.

• Last years •

Following the successful introduction of the *Rhapsody* during the 1934-5 season, the summer vacations at Senar went on to inspire the composition of the Third Symphony (1935-6). In common with other works by Rachmaninov at this period, a lightening of the texture is combined with an increased brilliance of orchestral detail and handling. There are three movements, the middle one combining slow and fast features and separating the other two, one basically lyrical, the other vigorous, on the lines first traced by César Franck. This telescoping of the usual four-movement form reduces the overall length without detracting from the essentially characteristic voice of the whole score. Perhaps its most memorable passages are the long lines of melody that close the first and second movements and the gradual build-up of speed and tension in the last pages of the third.

Only qualified success greeted the Third Symphony in the 1936-7 concert season, but performances continued to follow in Rachmaninov's wake as he returned to his international concert routine for a few more years. In 1939 New York celebrated the thirtieth anniversary of his first visit with a triptych of concerts at which Rachmaninov not only played all his concerted works (except the Fourth Concerto, retained for revision) but also conducted his Third Symphony and, for the first time in over twenty years, *The Bells*.

The following summer, withdrawn not to war-torn Europe but to a quiet retreat on Long Island, Rachmaninov wrote his only score to

Right: Rachmaninov at the piano in 1936. Concert tours, both in America and throughout Europe, gave him little opportunity to compose in the last few years of his life. A virtuoso pianist with a remarkable technique, he concentrated for the most part on performances of his own works, but his interpretations of Chopin were renowned as were his renderings of other nineteenth-century virtuoso piano pieces.

be 'born' in the United States, the *Symphonic Dances*, which were performed early in 1941. With its dark glitter, its references to the 'Dies irae' chant (which also occurred in *The Isle of the Dead*) as well as to earlier compositions of his own (*The Bells* and *Vespers*), this triptych – probably having some programmatic content such as Morning–Noon–Evening – forms a fitting conclusion to Rachmaninov's orchestral *oeuvre*. It had an indifferent reception at first, but is now recognized as one of his major works.

During the summer of 1941 Rachmaninov was at last able to give a third and final setting to his Fourth Concerto, which he forthwith recorded and played in concert the following season. By then America had been attacked and was also at war. Spending the summer of 1942 in California, Rachmaninov decided to settle there and to retire after his 1942-3 season. In January, however, it became plain that he was in failing health. By mid-February 1943 the tour had reached Knoxville, Tennessee, where he gave his last recital; tests showed that he was in the fatal grip of an advanced and inoperable form of cancer, and Rachmaninov died in his home in Beverly Hills on 28 March 1943, a few days before his seventieth birthday. It was over fifty years since that concert in 1892 which he had considered the start of his career; hardly six weeks had passed since the recital which closed his public life. If, as he once wrote to a friend in Russia, he prayed only to be allowed to work up to his last days, surely his prayer had been heard.

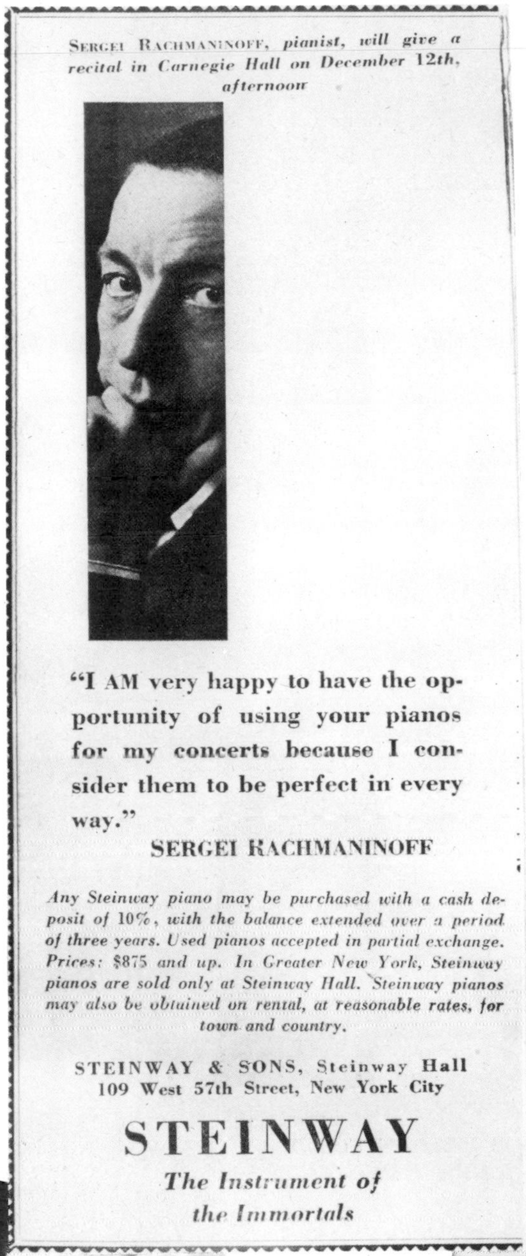

Left: When Rachmaninov settled in America in November 1919 he was given a piano by the Steinway company. This advertisement for Steinway pianos also mentions one of Rachmaninov's many recitals in New York.

Left: Rachmaninov on one of his many concert tours, this one in 1931 when he was on his way to Europe. He kept up his concert commitments, which included rigorous annual tours, from 1918 to 1943, the year of his death.

GALLEN
1894.

JEAN SIBELIUS

ROBERT LAYTON

Opposite: Jean Sibelius (1865-1957), painted in 1894 by Akseli Gallen-Kallela.

Sibelius is more closely identified with his natural environment than almost any other composer. Two themes run through his art: an overpowering and all-consuming love of nature and the northern landscape, and a preoccupation with the mythology enshrined in the Finnish national epic, the *Kalevala*. Yet he is more than a mere nature-poet-cum-nationalist. His musical personality is by far the most powerful to have emerged in any of the Scandinavian countries, but – more to the point – his seven symphonies, and such tone-poems as *Pohjola's Daughter* and *Tapiola*, show an altogether exceptional feeling for form. This is all the more remarkable when one considers that he sprang from virtually virgin soil, without the stimulus of a strong national tradition or even a great deal of musical activity.

From 1582 to 1809 Finland was a Grand Duchy of Sweden, and its outlook and cultural values were predominantly Swedish. When, following the Treaty of Tilsit of 1807, Finland became part of Tsarist Russia, the stage was set for the growth of national self-consciousness. This soon gathered momentum in literature with Elias Lönnrot's collection of folk poetry, *Kantele* (1831), and the epic myths of the *Kalevala* (1835). The so-called 'Father of Finnish music' was Fredrik Pacius (1809-91), a German-born composer who came to Finland by way of the Stockholm Opera and settled there in 1834. He and Martin Wegelius (1846-1906), Sibelius's teacher, did their best to make Helsinki a more lively musical center, though it was not until 1882 that Robert Kajanus (1856-1933) put the Helsinki Orchestra on a permanent footing. It is against this background and the relatively pale, wholly conventional music of his predecessors, the only worthwhile exception being Bernhard Crusell (1775-1838), that Sibelius's achievement can be measured.

Johan Julius Christian Sibelius was born on 8 December 1865 at Hämeenlinna, a small garrison town in south central Finland. His father, a doctor, died during the cholera epidemic that swept Finland in 1867-8; no doubt his propensity for alcohol lowered his resistance, and his extravagance left the family in penurious circumstances. Janne, as he was called, was the middle child of three, all of whom showed musical aptitude. The family spoke Swedish, and it was not until he was about eight that Sibelius began to learn Finnish. When he was eleven, his mother entered him in the Hämeenlinna Normaalilyseo, the first school in the country to use Finnish instead of Swedish as the teaching language. This was to prove of vital importance to him, as knowledge of the Finnish language opened up the whole repertory of national mythology enshrined in the *Kalevala*. However, Sibelius was not wholly at ease in Finnish until his twenties; Swedish was his mother tongue and he spoke it with greater fluency even in his maturity. It was to the great lyric poets writing in Swedish, and in particular Johan Ludvig Runeberg (1804-77) that he most often turned in his songs.

His first love was the violin, and his first composition, *Vattendroppar* (Water Drops), for violin and cello pizzicato, was written before he was ten. However, he did not begin to study in earnest until he was fourteen, when the local bandmaster, Gustav Levander, took him in hand. Hämeenlinna was cut off from the mainstream of music-making, but Janne's younger brother Christian played the cello, and his sister Linda the piano. Together with friends, they acquired a thorough knowledge of the Viennese classics, in particular Haydn and Beethoven, and Sibelius himself wrote prolifically for various chamber combinations. More than two dozen works are recorded, including a piece for the unlikely mixture of violin, cello, piano and harmonium.

Like so many composers, Sibelius gave greater priority to music than to his general studies. However, he gained the necessary qualifications to enroll in the Faculty of Law in Helsinki in 1885. But after a few months he turned his undivided energies to music, studying composition with Wegelius and the violin with Hermann Csillag and Mitrofan Wasilyeff. He had also by this time come to be known as Jean. His seafaring uncle, Johan, had gallicized his name during his travels, and Sibelius, on coming across some of his visiting-cards, took up the idea of 'internationalizing' his name. By the late 1880s, even though the violin consumed both his energies and ambitions, it became obvious that his true path was that of the composer. But he still cherished plans as a violinist, and while in Vienna in 1890-1 he even auditioned for the Philharmonic.

The interest in looking at the early output of an artist lies as much in discovering what he outgrew as in observing those individual

Above: The violin class of the Helsinki School of Music, run by Martin Wegelius. Sibelius (back left), who played second violin in the school's string quartet, attended Helsinki University from 1885 to 1889 and at the time had high hopes of becoming a solo violinist.

Right: Portrait photograph of Sibelius, about 1888.

characteristics we recognize from his maturity. Sibelius's juvenilia show three influences. First, there are the Viennese classics, which dominate a good deal of the thematic material in the earlier works and the formal layout of nearly all of them. The 1885 String Quartet in E flat begins like a Haydn quartet, and Sibelius's sense of form is already discernible. Second, there is the Scandinavian tradition, chiefly as expressed by Grieg and Svendsen. The F major Violin Sonata, probably from 1889, is one early instance of an influence that persisted through to the *King Christian II* music (1898) and the *Arioso*, op.3 (now known to be as late as 1908). Third, and most important, there is the influence of Tchaikovsky. Harmonies that remind one of the Russian master surface as early as the String Trio in G minor of 1885, and the influence can be felt not only in the Second Symphony (1902) and the Violin Concerto (1903, revised 1905), but as late as the *Suite mignonne* (1921), whose Polka could have come straight out of a Tchaikovsky ballet. Of course, these are not the only influences: Sibelius was much affected by a performance of Bruckner's Third Symphony which he heard in Vienna in 1890, and this finds its echo in the first movement of *Kullervo* two years later.

At first Sibelius had entertained the idea of continuing his studies at St Petersburg, with

Left: Front page of the first edition, dated 1892, of seven solo song-settings of poems by Johan Ludvig Runeberg (1804-77). Most of Sibelius's choral works and part-songs were written to Finnish texts, but for solo songs he often chose poems by Swedish 'nature' poets, whose interest in nature he shared; Runeberg was one of the foremost of these; and this was Sibelius's first published work.

Rimsky-Korsakov. Wegelius was set against this, and in the autumn of 1889 Sibelius set out for Berlin to study with Albert Becker. A strict contrapuntist of the old school, Becker subjected his pupil to a rigorous and no doubt chastening discipline. But if Sibelius complained of Becker's pedantry and found Berlin itself uncongenial, he was brought into contact with music-making of a high order. He heard *Tannhäuser*, *Meistersinger*, von Bülow playing Beethoven sonatas. Strauss's *Don Juan* at this time had its première, the Joachim Quartet played late Beethoven, and so on. Creatively it was a fallow period, but he worked on the B flat Quartet, op.4, and a Piano Quintet in G minor, written at the instigation of Ferruccio Busoni. The latter had taught in Helsinki in 1888, and the two had become close friends. When, in the autumn of 1890, Sibelius decided to continue his studies in Vienna rather than Berlin, Busoni provided him with a letter of introduction to Brahms, albeit to no avail. He had lessons from Karl Goldmark and Robert Fuchs and took his first steps as an orchestral composer with an overture which earned him Goldmark's acclaim. It was at this period that the first ideas for the symphony *Kullervo* came to him.

• Early success •

Sibelius was twenty-seven when *Kullervo* was first performed in April 1893. It served to put him firmly on the musical map as the white hope of Finnish music. No Finn had ever measured himself against so big a canvas: *Kullervo* is a five-movement work for two soloists, male chorus and orchestra, on a Mahlerian scale of some seventy minutes' duration, though it was written before Mahler's 'Resurrection' Symphony saw the light of day. Considering that this was his first attempt at an extended orchestral piece, *Kullervo* is a remarkable achievement. Although there are flickerings of originality in the chamber music, this symphony speaks with distinctive accents and an individual voice.

Indeed, what is so striking about the work is not so much its immaturity or faltering proportions, but the astonishing assurance of its language and its immediate sense of identity. The long centerpiece, 'Kullervo and his Sister,' suggests that Sibelius might well have developed into a more than respectable opera composer had he so chosen. However, his pilgrimage to Bayreuth in 1894 made him realize the futility of his own operatic ambitions. His dramatic sense was better fitted to the contrast and concentration of the sonata form than to the lyric stage. *Veenen luominen* – to which *The Swan of Tuonela* began life as the prelude – was his first attempt at an opera, and *Jungfrun i tornet* (The Maiden in the Tower, 1897) did reach the stage; but Sibelius was dissatisfied with it and never returned to the medium. Even so, for all his self-doubts, Sibelius's early letters reveal a basic confidence in his exceptional creative powers: but if he was to contribute to a genre, his work must be of unique quality.

Like Kajanus's 'Aino' Symphony, which Sibelius had heard in Berlin, *Kullervo* was the first of many of his own works to draw on the *Kalevala* for its inspiration. Its success led to other commissions – the symphonic poem *En Saga* (A Legend) and the *Karelia* overture and orchestral suite – and gave Sibelius the necessary confidence to marry and make a home of his own. His friendship with the Järnefelt family, and above all their daughter, Aino, had developed during his student days in Helsinki; the marriage to Aino in 1892 was to last until the composer's death, sixty-five years later.

Now that he had family responsibilities, Sibelius had to earn a living, and for some years gave classes at the Conservatory. In 1897 he was elected as director of music at the University, but the decision was subsequently overturned in favor of Robert Kajanus. This is worth mentioning because the state pension which the Finnish Senate voted Sibelius some months later was partly an acknowledgement of his creative achievements, but also a gesture to meet the body of opinion which felt that he had been badly treated. Some years later this award was turned into a life pension, but Sibelius lived extravagantly, and his finances remained precarious right up until the 1920s. Throughout the intervening period, private patronage had to be mobilized on his behalf.

For all the success of *Kullervo*, Sibelius was slow to turn to a purely instrumental symphony. His next major orchestral work, *The Four Legends*, op.22 (1895), was programmatic, and Karl Flodin, who had been lavish in his praises of *Kullervo*, now pressed him to turn to absolute music rather than 'pictorial and mystical visions.' It was no doubt high time that Sibelius measured himself against the challenge of the pure symphony, and further stimulus to do so may have been provided by the appearance in

1896 of a symphony by the then nineteen-year-old Finnish composer Ernest Mielck (1877-99), fresh from studies with Bruch. But Sibelius bided his time: he had been dissatisfied with *En Saga* and withdrew it after its successful première, and he was likewise set against any further performance of *Kullervo*.

The First Symphony was not completed until 1899, but it was immediately clear that Sibelius had made enormous strides since *Kullervo*, not only in his mastery of the orchestra but in terms of the concentration of his material. The organic cohesion which informs the first movement is of a much higher order than anything

Below: Drawing of Sibelius at the piano by Eero Järnefelt, dated 1892. The artist was the brother of Sibelius's wife, Aino, whom he married that same year. The influential Järnefelt family shared Sibelius's nationalist interest and were keen promoters of the Finnish language.

Left: Frost, by Hugo Simberg, 1895. The combined Nordic national interests of nature and myth were reflected in Finnish art just as much as in music or literature.

Below: Manuscript page from *Kullervo*, Sibelius's first major symphonic success, written in the winter of 1892 and first performed in April 1893. It was the first of many works to have been inspired by the *Kalevala*, the great collection of Finnish folklore and legend.

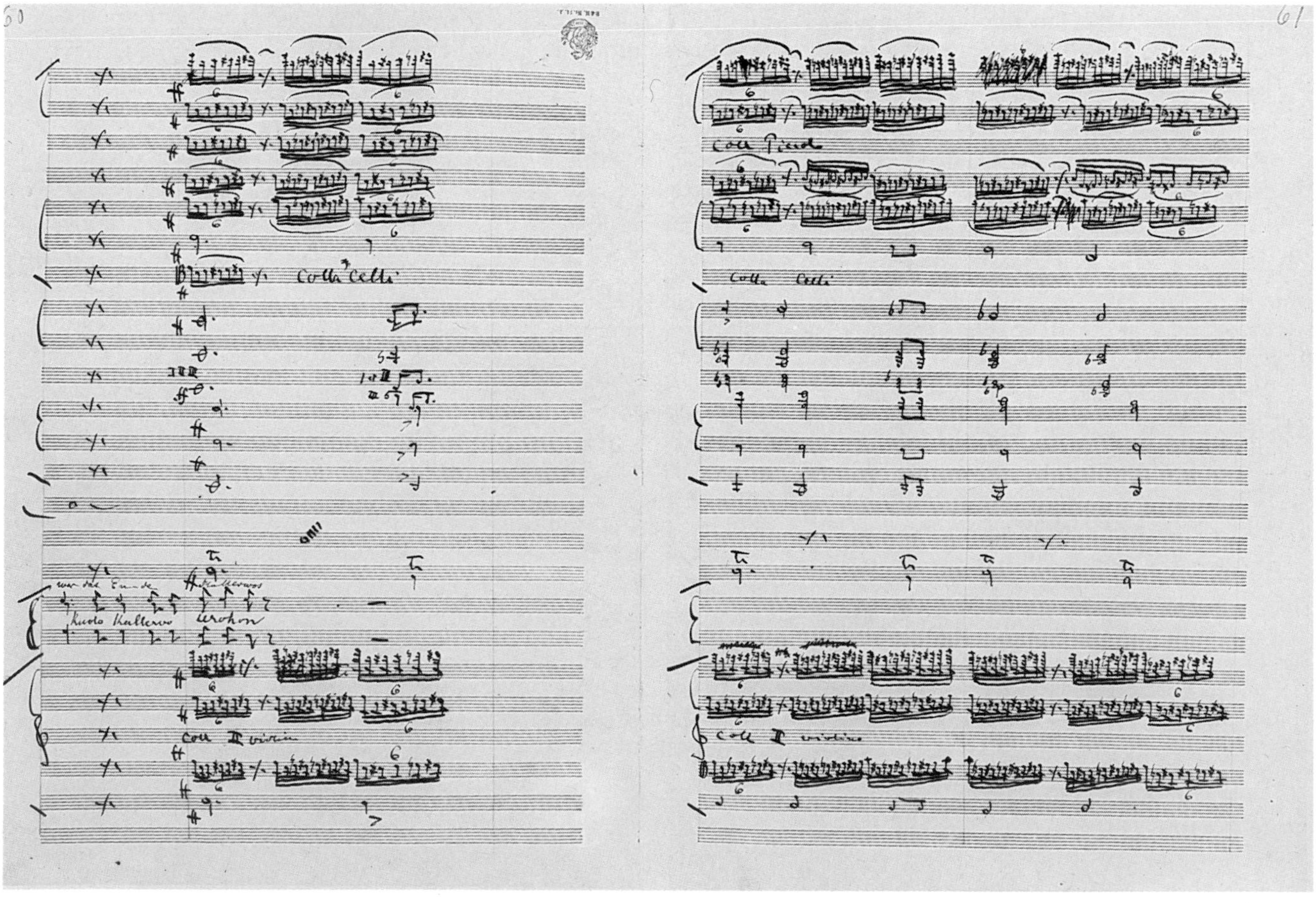

he had done before, with the possible exception of 'Lemminkäinen's Return,' the last of the *Four Legends*. It is a measure of his achievement that one is hardly ever aware of the artifice behind the art; no seams or joins obtrude. The second theme, for example, begins with an idea on the flutes and an icily sparkling accompaniment on *tremolando* strings and harp. The idea actually comes from the clarinet solo heard at the very beginning, but so subtle is the transformation that one is barely conscious of it aurally. It is in the second movement that Tchaikovsky has the strongest resonances, though the coloring and personality of Sibelius are always in evidence. There are also echoes of other Russians here and there: as Balakirev is suggested in the first of the *Legends*, so Borodin appears in the scherzo of the First Symphony.

• International fame •

In 1898 Sibelius acquired a continental publisher, Breitkopf & Härtel, whose efforts on his behalf were to do much to advance his cause in Europe during the first decade of the present century (although he was to sell them *Valse triste*, written in 1903 for his brother-in-law's play, *Kuolema*, on derisory terms, and in so doing lose a small fortune). But his appearance with Kajanus and the Helsinki Orchestra on their first European tour in 1900 was his first major step to international fame. *The Swan of Tuonela* and the newly composed First Symphony were well received. Moreover, at a time when the Russians were tightening their grip on Finland, eroding what little autonomy it retained, *Finlandia* – composed in 1899 for a Press Pension Fund pageant – had become a rallying-point for patriotic sentiment; its importance in terms of Finnish national self-awareness was immeasurable, and its success did much to alert foreign opinion to the cause of Finnish independence.

Sibelius's reputation continued to grow with his new mastery. In England Henry Wood included the *King Christian II* music at a Promenade Concert in 1901, Granville Bantock conducted the First Symphony in 1905 and in the same year Hans Richter gave the Second, completed in 1902, with the Hallé Orchestra. Sibelius went to Heidelberg to conduct *The Swan of Tuonela* and 'Lemminkäinen's Return.' Busoni invited him to direct performances of *En Saga*, in its revised and definitive form, and of the Second Symphony in his New Music Concerts in Berlin, where the Violin Concerto received its first performance with no less a conductor than Richard Strauss.

With the Second Symphony Sibelius set aside the models he had used previously and took up the challenge of the symphonic principle as such. Although in terms of musical language it speaks with much the same accents as the First, there are some important differences which point the way to the future. The orchestra is leaner and more classical, without harp, bass drum or cymbals, and the thematic substance has an even stronger organic coherence, although there was still a programmatic inspi-

Below: Symposium, 1894, by Akseli Gallen-Kallela. The painting shows Sibelius (far right) together with the artist himself (standing) and Robert Kajanus, a Finnish musician and conductor. Kajanus formed a lasting and fruitful friendship with Sibelius, in spite of the fact that the former was preferred for the post of director of music at Helsinki University. The fact that the three men are here shown drinking is not accidental. Heavy drinking was a problem throughout Sibelius's career.

ration: in the summer of 1901 Sibelius had told his friend Axel Carpelan that he planned a work based on *The Divine Comedy*. This was hardly surprising, since he had not long returned from Italy, where his sketchbooks had rapidly filled with various projects, including an orchestral piece on the Don Juan legend (the opening theme of the second movement was intended for this). The Dante tone-poem never came to fruition, but there is a lushness of idiom in the Second Symphony which gives it a sunnier, more relaxed atmosphere than the First, and the Italian stay may account for the fact that the light is softer and warmer. Yet underneath, the geniality hides a granite-like strength. Such is the subtlety of the first movement that few commentators seem to be able to agree where the second theme actually begins. The slow movement and finale are also sonata structures, and the scherzo, more extended than the one in the First Symphony, is inspired by the example of Beethoven in his Seventh. Sibelius repeats the trio, as did Beethoven, but rather than finish the movement with a restatement of the scherzo section, he fashions a link into the finale. In a sense Sibelius's development as a symphonist really begins with the Second Symphony.

The Violin Concerto marks the end of his first period, though even here he treats sonata form with freedom and flexibility: none of its processes is handled mechanically. Nor did Sibelius's love affair with the violin end with the Concerto. Even as late as 1910 a diary entry records: 'Dreamed I was a virtuoso.' His mastery is clearly evident from the quality of his writing in the Concerto itself, as well as in the evocative *Serenades* and the wartime *Humoreskes*. At the time of the First World War he was contemplating a second violin concerto, but this came to nothing.

These were productive but turbulent years; mounting debts and bouts of heavy drinking imposed a considerable measure of domestic strain. In 1904 Sibelius bought land at Järvenpää, some 35 kilometers outside Helsinki, where he built a villa, which he named Ainola, after his wife, and where he spent the remainder of his days. His success was bringing in its train a variety of commissions – the Royal Philharmonic Society commissioned a new symphony, there were commissions for incidental music for Maeterlinck's *Pelléas et Mélisande* (1905), Hjalmar Procopé's *Belshazzar's Feast* (1906) and Strindberg's *Swanwhite* (1908). He also produced two of his greatest tone-poems, *Pohjola's Daughter* (1906) and *Nightride and Sunrise* (1908). It was with his Third Symphony (1904-7), however, that Sibelius began to move away from the main currents of his day.

In the first movement of the Second, Sibelius had shown a flair for form that was unusual, and from now on each of the symphonies is totally fresh in its approach to structure: one cannot distill from the earlier symphonies any set of rules to be applied to the later ones. It is equally difficult to foresee, from the vantage-point of one, the character of the next. Moreover, the Third, like the later symphonies, is

Lördagen d. 4 November:

Festrepresentation

i Svenska Teatern kl. 7,30 e. m.

Program:

1) **Tannhäusermarschen** (utföres af Filharmoniska Sällskapets orkester).
2) **Prolog** (af prof. O. M. Reuter och Kyösti Larson).
3) **Tablåer från forntiden.** Orden af EINO LEINO och JALMARI FINNE. Musiken komponerad af J. SIBELIUS. Tablåerna arrangerade af KAARLO BERGBOM.
   1) Ouverture.
   2) Musik.
   3) Tablå (Wäinämöinen fröjdar naturen med sin sång, Kaleva och Pohjola folket.)
   4) Musik.
   5) Tablå (Finska folket döpes).
   6) Musik.
   7) Tablå (Från hertig Johans hof).
   8) Musik.
   9) Tablå (Finnarne i 30-åriga kriget).
   10) Musik.
   11) Tablå (Under stora ofreden).
   12) Musik.
   13) Tablå (Finland uppvaknar).
4) **Konsertafdelning.**
5) **„Dröm och värklighet"** eller **„Den stora Ankan".** Revy.

Under mellanakterna lottförsäljning.

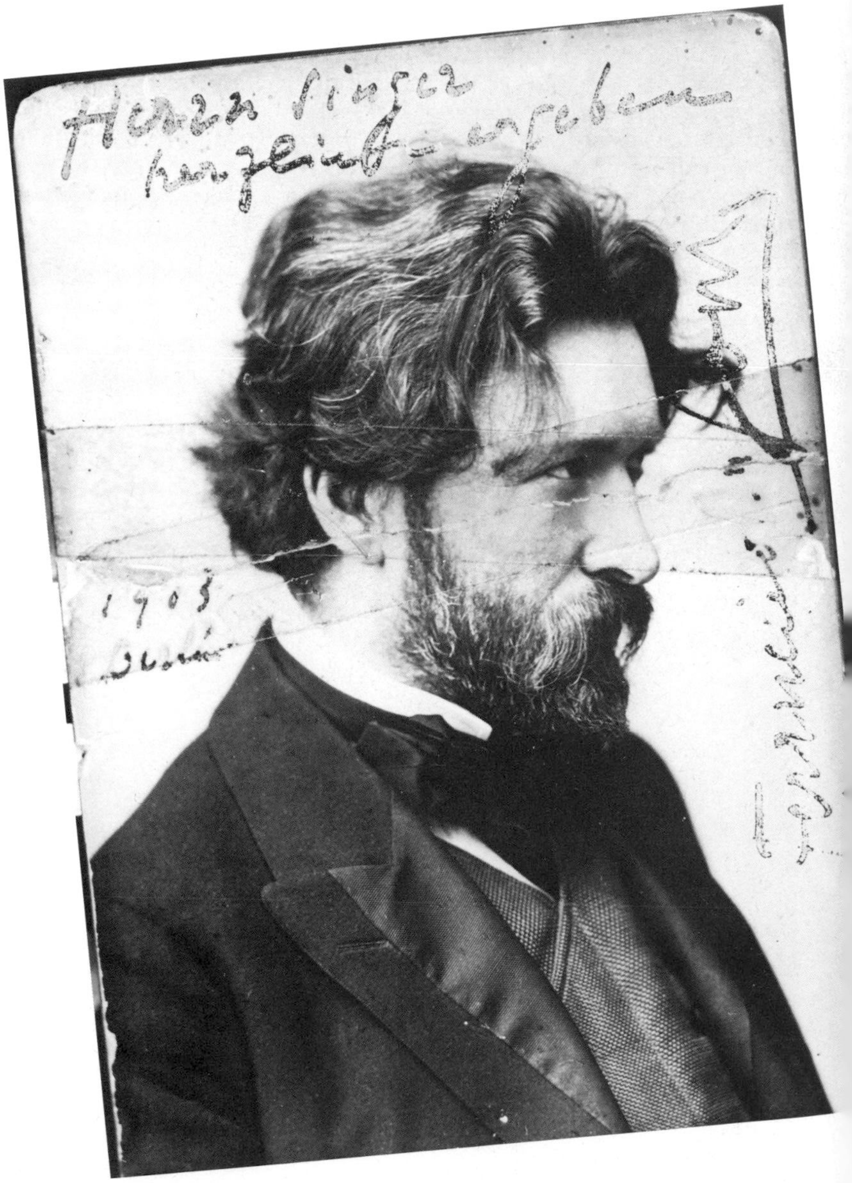

Opposite: Advertisement for the first performance of *Finlandia* in 1899. In spite of the composer's nationalist interests, the advertisement is in Swedish, then the most commonly spoken language. *Finlandia* rapidly became a symbol of patriotism.

Above: Sibelius with his daughter Ruth in 1901.

Opposite: Photograph (1903) of Ferruccio Busoni, Sibelius's great friend and advisor, who taught at Wegelius's Music School in Helsinki for a time and who gave Sibelius every encouragement both at this stage of his career and later on. The photograph is inscribed to the Hungarian pianist Richard Singer.

totally at variance with the artistic climate of its day. Unlike such great contemporaries as Mahler, Skriabin, Strauss or Schoenberg, Sibelius chose not to develop denser chromatic textures but rather to turn away from the richer colors of the post-Romantic palette.

In a diary entry some years later Sibelius compares a symphony to a river and speaks of the innumerable tributaries that form the river before it broadens majestically and flows into the sea. It is this image that expresses his view of symphonic thought: the movement of the river water is the flow of the musical ideas, and the river-bed that they form is the symphonic structure. The first movement of the Third Symphony has a natural flow, uninterrupted by the flamboyant rhetorical gestures of the First; its idiom is pure and its contours firm; the opulence of early Sibelius gives way to a more restrained palette, the glowing hues yield to more subtle pastel colorings. The symphony is more concentrated than its predecessors; the number of movements is reduced from four to three by telescoping the scherzo and finale. The first movement retains a sonata-form outline, but each of the component sections is denser. In fact, the dimensions of the whole work reflect this greater concentration: the symphony lasts thirty minutes as opposed to the forty of its predecessor. The big Romantic gestures, the passionate violin cantilenas and the massive brass are all replaced by much lighter textures. Perhaps his contact with the ideas of Busoni, with his new classicism (*Junge Klassizität*), played a part; Sibelius much later in life declared his belief that classicism was the way of the future.

Like the Sixth, the Third has never found great popular favor, and it is entirely at variance with the Mahlerian view of the symphony. It was shortly after its first performance that Mahler visited Helsinki, and it must have been with the Third in mind that Sibelius made his oft-quoted remark to Mahler: 'When our conversation touched upon the symphony, I said that I admired its style and severity of form and the profound logic that created an inner connection between all the motifs.' Mahler's response was quite the opposite: 'No!' he said, 'The symphony must be like the world! It must be all-embracing.'

•The Fourth Symphony •

It was on a visit to London in 1908 that Sibelius noticed pains in his throat, and in the subsequent months he was fearful that the tumor that was diagnosed would prove malignant and recurring: he underwent a number of operations. The Fourth Symphony (1909-11) and the austere works which followed in its train, such as *The Bard* and *Luonnotar*, are obviously the product of a bitter spiritual experience, and their severity can be related in no small measure to his illness. It seems that in the Fourth Symphony Sibelius had looked into the abyss and was driven by an intensified sense of creative urgency to concentrate only on the barest essentials. The bleakness and astringency of the Fourth Symphony earned it the title of the 'Barkbröd' Symphony, a reference to the hard times when peasants were forced to use the bark of trees to eke out their flour. It certainly posed problems for its first audiences. In Sweden it was hissed, and it scandalized America when it reached there, although Toscanini's response when the work was greeted with derision was to mount an immediate repeat.

If the Third had 'severity of form,' how much more austere and uncompromising is the language of the Fourth! Indeed, the distance Sibelius covered in the four years that separate their completion is incomparably greater than the ground he had covered from *Kullervo* to no.3. For these earlier symphonies, along with such tone-poems as *Pohjola's Daughter* and *Nightride and Sunrise*, reflect a confident, ordered world held in rein by strong classical instincts. As with Mahler, also confronted with the prospect of death, which in his case, alas, claimed him, Sibelius's thoughts turned inwards. In his Ninth Symphony Mahler, too, refined his musical language: both composers reached a point where they were prepared to

Opposite: Oil cartoon of *Elias Lönnrot and the Singer of Tales* by Akseli Gallen-Kallela, 1913. Lönnrot was the man who compiled the *Kalevala*, the collection of Finnish epic myths that formed the backbone of Finland's folklore.

Opposite below: Akseli Gallen-Kallela's painting *Väinämöisenlähtö*, 1896-1906, depicting one of the *Kalevala* legends.

dispense with the trappings of flamboyant rhetoric in favor of monosyllabic truths, and both (to quote Hans Redlich) 'reach the threshold of atonality by fitfully employing the whole-tone scale, that destructive ferment and arch-enemy of tonal cohesion.'

In the Fourth Symphony the middle section of the first movement certainly contains some of the most searching and mysterious music Sibelius ever penned and comes close to indeterminate tonality. And everywhere compression is the order of the day. The note (A) on which the first movement ends is immediately echoed at the beginning of the scherzo, though it is seen in the light of F major, but the result is rather like sunrays breaking through the heavy clouds of the Scandinavian winter. Much has been written about Sibelius's feeling for nature, and the opening of the slow movement conveys both the intimacy and the grandeur of the northern landscape. It is the emotional centerpiece of the work and conveys a sense of communion with nature and a rapt awareness of its sounds and smells. The closing measures of the whole work, among the most desolate in all of Sibelius's work with the possible exception of *Tapiola*, carry this a stage further, for they seem to present us not with the hostility of nature, but rather with its total indifference.

Tautness is the keynote of much of the music written in the wake of the Fourth Symphony. *The Bard* (1913), a tone-poem of the utmost concentration of mood, has a similar terse simplicity of musical substance. It is one of Sibelius's most elusive scores, rich in atmosphere and interesting in its formal layout; in its change of mood halfway through, it almost suggests the sonnet. Another case of extreme compression is the set of three piano sonatinas, op.67, in the first of which the outline of a sonata-style movement is cast in a few simple brush-strokes like a Japanese painting, the whole movement lasting about one and a half minutes. Generally speaking, however, Sibelius was ill-at-ease with the piano, and with rare exceptions his most characteristic thoughts did not find their way into his piano music. In this respect he may be said to resemble Berlioz, whose *Symphonie fantastique* he so much admired, and whose lack of interest in the piano went further still, in that he hardly wrote for the keyboard at all.

•Travel and war•

Travel continued to be both a stimulus and a burden. Much though Sibelius loved both Ainola and Finland, the musical climate was insular. Conducting had in fact become something of a surrogate for his violin playing, and he directed many great orchestras. His visits to Germany and the other Scandinavian countries were frequent, and his love of Italy remained unabated. When he was in England, he heard Debussy's *Nocturnes* for the first time and the First Symphony of Elgar. It was at this period that he returned for the first – and only – occasion in his maturity to the quartet medium, with his *Voces intimae* (1909), one of his purest utterances. At one time there were rumors of another quartet, and part of the Fourth Symphony was originally sketched in this form.

Foreign honors also came his way. The Imperial Academy of Music in Vienna offered him its Chair of Composition in 1912, which he declined, while in 1914 Yale University offered him an honorary doctorate, and in that year he visited the United States to conduct a new work that his American host, Carl Stoeckel, had commissioned. This was *The Oceanides*, the only one of Sibelius's tone-poems not to have been directly inspired by Finnish mythology. He was overwhelmed by the lavishness of American hospitality and the luxury with which he was surrounded. Moreover, he was quite astonished at being so well known. ('I have never, before or after, lived such a wonderful life,' he told his biographer, Karl Ekman.)

Right: The Finnish pavilion, designed by Gesellius, Lindgren and Saarinen, at the Paris World's Fair of 1900. Sibelius visited the Fair himself, and three of his works were performed there and were very well received – the culmination of a European concert tour that Kajanus had arranged for the Helsinki Philharmonic Orchestra.

By the time Sibelius had returned home, Europe was poised for the 1914-18 war, which had two practical effects on Sibelius's life. First, when Russia entered the war, Sibelius became an enemy alien as far as Germany was concerned, for Finland was still a Russian province. Cut off from the income owed him by his German publisher, Breitkopf & Härtel, Sibelius was forced to expend his creative energies on a large quantity of trivial pieces for piano, and violin and piano, aimed at the domestic market. Second, the war limited his ability to travel; above all, it cut him off from conducting (and hearing) great international orchestras.

The war years did, however, find him working on one masterpiece – the Fifth Symphony. Although in its definitive form the Fifth is one of his most popular works, it appears in its initial stages to have given him more trouble than any other of his works. It was first heard

in its four-movement form on his fiftieth birthday (8 December 1915), which was celebrated almost as a national holiday. He thoroughly overhauled it, linking the first two movements, for a performance the following year, but even then he was dissatisfied and continued to work on it until it reached its final form in 1919. And if the Fourth was unpredictable, the same must be said of the Fifth. Each of the symphonies shows a continuing search for new formal means, and in none was this more thorough or prolonged than in the Fifth. The first ideas began to surface in Sibelius's mind before the outbreak of the First World War, and in its definitive form the first movement of the Fifth is perhaps the most original in all Sibelius's work, combining as it does features of a sonata-style movement and a scherzo. It has a sweep and grandeur – and an expansiveness – that is quite unexpected after the austerity of the Fourth.

•The 1920s•

Even after the war and the newly won independence of Finland, Sibelius was still in economic difficulties. Hyperinflation in post-war Germany naturally wrought havoc with the royalties that Breitkopf & Härtel owed him, and small pieces of a lighter nature, such as the *Suite champêtre* and the *Suite mignonne*, continued to pour from his pen: he still hoped to compose another *Valse triste*. His position was only eased with the advent of mechanical performing rights and the payment of royalties on performance, innovations which came into force internationally during the early 1920s.

timpani and strings), plus the relative luxury of a harp. As in the Third Symphony, the strings bear the main brunt of the argument, and they open the movement with polyphony of a remarkable serenity. The main weight of the work is borne by the outer movements; the allegretto has a gentle, pastoral nature, and though neither the scherzo nor the finale offers the physical excitement of the Fifth or the Seventh, one has the feeling of mysterious and powerful

The post-war scene was also very different from the musical world of Sibelius's youth and middle years, and there is no doubt that he felt its spirit to be alien, that he was (to use his own words in respect of the Sixth Symphony) offering 'pure spring water' at a time when others were mixing cocktails of various hues. Nonetheless, these years saw the composition of his four last major works: the Sixth and Seventh Symphonies, the incidental music to Shakespeare's *The Tempest* and the symphonic poem *Tapiola*.

The Sixth Symphony seems remote in character from the Fifth, yet it now appears that their origins were interrelated; the researches of Erik Tawaststjerna have revealed that material intended for the Sixth Symphony found its way into the Fifth and vice versa. The Sixth has never enjoyed the popularity of its immediate neighbors, for it lacks the heroic countenance of the earlier and the stern epic majesty of the later. Its language is as purified of rhetoric as it is possible to imagine. The scoring is more restrained than that of the Fifth, in spite of the fact that it calls for the normal Sibelian orchestra (double woodwind plus bass clarinet, four horns, three trumpets and trombones,

Opposite far left: Sibelius in 1907 having breakfast at 'Ainola,' the villa that he built in 1904 at Järvenpää near Helsinki, and which he named after his wife.

Opposite: In the garden at 'Ainola.' Sibelius lived there from 1905 until his death in 1957.

Opposite: Sibelius with his wife at 'Ainola.'

undercurrents just beneath the surface. In its purity of utterance and its euphony, the Sixth Symphony stands just as much outside time as its neighbors and transcends the period in a way that few works of the 1920s succeed in doing.

The Seventh Symphony followed the Sixth in 1924, after a gap of only a year. Unlike any of its predecessors, the Seventh is in one continuous movement; and unlike any previous attempt at writing a one-movement symphony, the work emphatically does not sound like four separate movements played without a break. Admittedly there are passages that have the character of a scherzo or a slow section, but it is quite impossible to say where one section ends and another begins, so complete is Sibelius's mastery of transition and his control of simultaneous tempi. It is, in fact, the climax of a lifetime's work in this particular field; one thinks of it as a constantly growing entity in which the thematic metamorphosis works at such a level of sophistication that one is scarcely conscious of it.

When it was first performed, at a concert in Stockholm in March 1924, which included the First Symphony and the Violin Concerto, it was simply billed 'Fantasia Sinfonica,' but by the time it had reached publication, Sibelius's doubts about its symphonic pedigree seem to have been resolved. Discussing the symphonic nature of the Seventh as opposed to *Tapiola* (1926), which at one stage it was fashionable to regard as the Eighth Symphony, Robert Simpson quite rightly points to the absence of movement in the latter – movement invariably generated by the contrast of key centers: 'The symphony is like a great planet in orbit, its movements vast, inexorable, seemingly imperceptible to its inhabitants. But, you may object, the Finnish forests of Tapiola are on the surface of such a planet, revolving. Yes, but we never leave them, we are filled with expectation and nothing but a great wind arises. There is no real sense of movement. The symphony has both the cosmic motion of the Earth and the teeming activity that is upon it; we are made to observe one or the other at the composer's will. Indeed, observe is not the right word – we experience these extremes, and when one is operative, the other does not exist for us.' The formal layout of the Seventh Symphony has been described in various ways – exposition, development, scherzo and so on – but there is general agreement that these formal labels are primitive, and that the symphony is a single individual organism, unique in the history not only of Scandinavian music but of the symphony itself. The way in which the thematic substance of the symphony is constantly renewed is an unfailing source of wonder; everything seems organically related to everything else, and yet can be traced back to ideas thrown up in the opening movement. If *Tapiola*, the last major work to come from Sibelius's pen, inhabits an unpeopled, sunless world, the Seventh Symphony, with its glowing C major ending, is a heroic affirmation of the human spirit and a crowning summation of his symphonic achievement.

• Years of silence •

After the mid-1920s Sibelius ceased to travel and, to all intents and purposes, compose. There were many invitations – offers from America and England – but all were declined. Rumors of an Eighth Symphony persisted for many years, and its publication was promised after his death. It would seem that it was as good as complete by 1930, for a note survives to a copyist to whom he had sent the first thirty-two pages, which he describes as being about an eighth of the work, so that in its finished form it would have been roughly the length of the Second Symphony. Only a few measures survive.

What, one wonders, lies behind this failure of creative nerve? Sibelius was an artist who had always subjected his work to the most searching self-criticism, and he was plagued with self-doubt even though he was fully conscious of his own genius. His was a complex and many-faceted personality. He was a compound of arrogance, vanity and pride, and yet vulnerable to self-questioning and depression. In these darker moments – and his diaries become increasingly black – he entertained fears for his own equilibrium, and with his increasing isolation from the music of his contemporaries, his depression only gathered force. The cult of Sibelius in the Anglo-Saxon world put additional pressures on him; in England and America he was hailed as a symphonist of the order of Brahms and second only to Beethoven, while in Germany and France he was neglected. Moreover, during the stress of the war years he had resumed drinking, which he had given up at the time of his throat operation just as he had renounced cigars, and this addiction had undoubtedly taken its toll. A nervous tremor made the act of writing a laborious process.

It is obvious from the achievement of *Tapiola* and the last two symphonies that Sibelius's standards and artistic sights were higher than ever, and to reach or surpass them more difficult than before. Just as he had striven not to write one note too many, and not to continue when there was no more to be said, he may well have felt that the precept by which he had been guided in his symphonies must apply to his life's work: that what he had composed in the Eighth Symphony did not materially extend the vision of the Seventh and *Tapiola*.

Sibelius lived in virtual seclusion throughout his last three decades, although he remained by far the best-known Finn, and many people who would never otherwise have been aware of Finland's existence or her nationalist aspirations became so on his account. Death came on 20 September 1957, three months short of his ninety-second birthday. Only a day or so before, he had taken a walk, and cranes had circled over his head as if making their farewell. He died in the evening, while in Helsinki Sir Malcolm Sargent was conducting his Fifth Symphony, and he was buried in his villa's grounds at Järvenpää, where he had lived for more than half a century.

The History of Recorded Sound

The discovery of ways of recording music has been of crucial significance to audiences and performers, and recording has even affected methods of composition. Edison's phonograph, invented in 1877, was originally sold as a dictating machine for offices, but its value for preserving history was soon realized, and by 1890 it had been used to record the voices of great men and also the speech, songs, war-cries and folklore of disappearing American tribes. Early in the next century Béla Bartók also adopted the Edison machine for the recordings of folksong which so greatly influenced his own music.

Emile Berliner in 1887 invented a 'grammophone' that recorded on to a flat disk, and from this matrix record unlimited duplicate recordings could be pressed. Gramophones came on the market in the 1890s – the HMV 'Trademark model' (*below right*) was launched in 1898 – and the first records of music were issued before the turn of the century. The real breakthrough came with the first recordings by Caruso, starting in 1902, which won the new invention great popularity, although it was still some years before instrumental music, let alone orchestral music, could be recorded satisfactorily.

Since that time, the story of musical recording is one of continuous technical improvements up to the laserscanned Compact Disks of today, while records have brought a vast repertory of music to much wider audiences all round the world and have set far higher standards of performance. As a result, composers are able to take for granted a level of musical knowledge in their audiences and a degree of virtuosity in their performers that would have been unthinkable in the past. At the same time, since the introduction in the 1950s of magnetic tape for recording, composers of the avant garde – as well as pop musicians – have brought recording techniques into the process of composition itself.

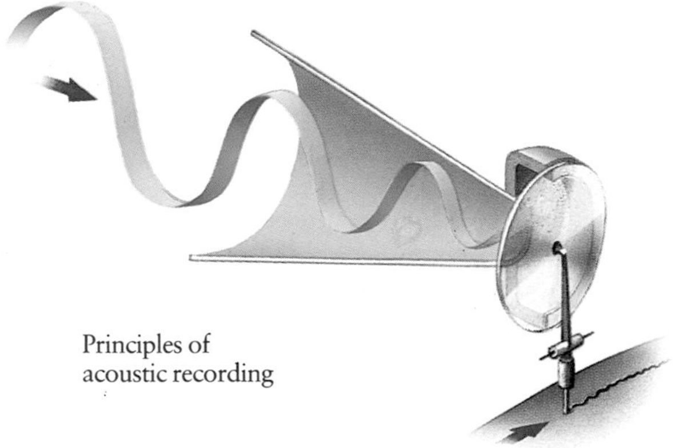

Principles of acoustic recording

Sound is transmitted by pressure waves in the air, and the essence of sound recording is to convert these air waves into mechanical waves and store them in such a way that they can be reissued again as sound. Edison's phonograph used the variation in the depth of wax cut to reproduce the sound wave (the 'hill and dale' method), but on early disks sound was reproduced by lateral deviations in the special groove. In acoustic recording the air pressure wave is collected by a special horn and delivered to a diaphragm, where it sets up a mechanical vibration, in roughly the same pattern as the air wave. The diaphragm transmits this pattern to a cutting 'needle,' which re-forms it in the soft matrix disk. In playing the record made from the matrix the process is reversed, using a horn to amplify the sound picked up from the groove by the needle.

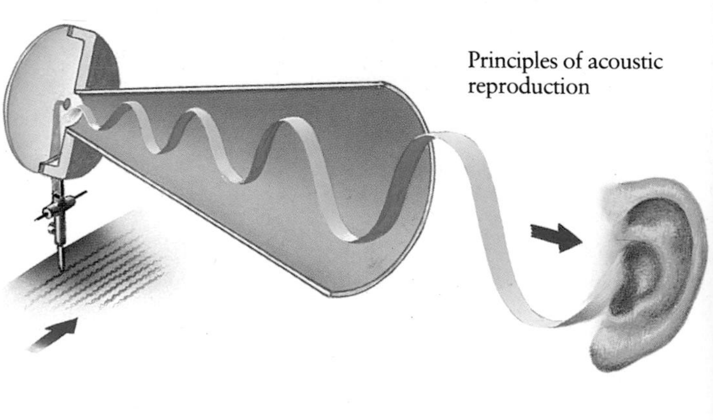

Principles of acoustic reproduction

The development of electrical recording was a major step forward. The first electrically recorded disks were issued in the early 1920s and showed a marked improvement in balance and spatial sense, but the tone tended to be metallic, although the use of fiber needles (instead of steel) produced a better sound. At first these records were generally reproduced by the acoustic method, but by the late twenties all-electric record-players were widely available; HMV had made one as early as 1920, and the Brunswick 'Panatrope' was launched in the USA in 1925. From 1930 numerous models were made (like the cabinet gramophone, *right*), which gave excellent sound reproduction.

Development continued, and the ideal of high-fidelity sound came a step nearer with the launch in 1944 by Decca of Full Frequency Range Recording (FFRR), a sound system improved in every way so as to capture a wider range of frequencies and give more faithful tonal quality.
The gramophone was now setting new standards for musical performance, in particular with such conductors as Toscanini, Stokowski and Beecham, and a vast repertory of classical music had become available on 78 r.p.m. discs, including instrumental, vocal and chamber music as well as the orchestral repertoire and many complete operas and oratorios.

In the early years of acoustic recording only a limited range of sound frequencies could be reproduced, and the quality of recorded sound was therefore quite variable. Certainly one of the reasons Caruso was so successful was that the range and quality of his tenor voice were ideal for this means of reproduction. Orchestral or chamber music sounded very unsatisfactory, and amateurs still got to know such works through versions for keyboard – generally arrangements for piano duet. Various mechanical pianos, most operated by paper rolls, came on the market at the end of the nineteeth century, and these enabled less accomplished players to get to know more difficult works. The critic Ernest Newman gave his blessing to the 'pianola,' but ignored the gramophone. Technical improvements had, however, made great strides by 1920, when Beatrice Harrison recorded Elgar's Cello Concerto with the composer (*above*); the different shaped horns for capturing the solo cello and the more diffused sound of the orchestra should be noted. By now, many of the most distinguished musicians had accepted the gramophone and took part in recording sessions, though by 1922 there were still no symphonies available on the Columbia label, and only one on HMV – the pioneer recording of Beethoven's Fifth by the Berlin Philharmonic under Nikisch, issued in 1913 on eight single-sided discs. Gramophones and records had become much less expensive, and the record companies were opening up a large market for popular vocal and dance-band music. At the same time they gradually increased the repertory of classical recorded music.

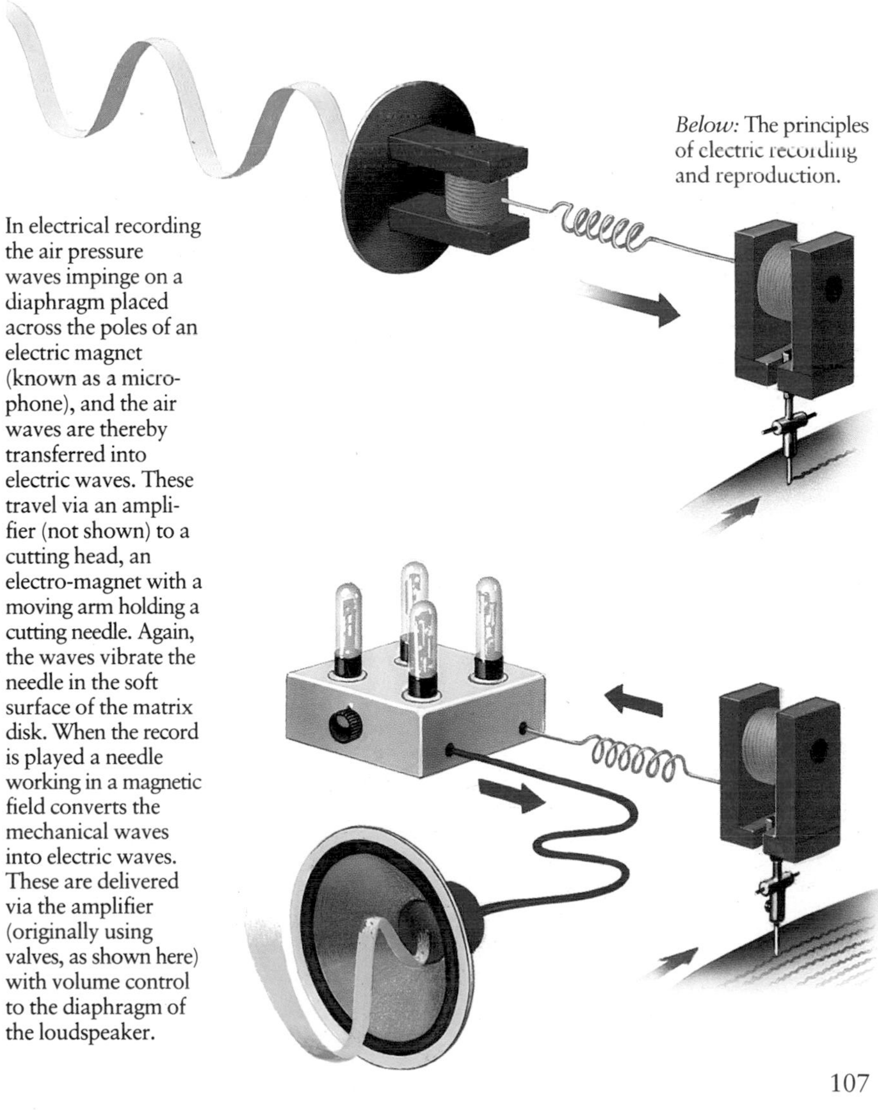

Below: The principles of electric recording and reproduction.

In electrical recording the air pressure waves impinge on a diaphragm placed across the poles of an electric magnet (known as a microphone), and the air waves are thereby transferred into electric waves. These travel via an amplifier (not shown) to a cutting head, an electro-magnet with a moving arm holding a cutting needle. Again, the waves vibrate the needle in the soft surface of the matrix disk. When the record is played a needle working in a magnetic field converts the mechanical waves into electric waves. These are delivered via the amplifier (originally using valves, as shown here) with volume control to the diaphragm of the loudspeaker.

Two men conceived the idea in 1877 of a 'talking machine,' but the Frenchman C. Cros, who had worked out all the theory, did not construct a practical cylinder model, while Thomas Alva Edison produced his working 'phonograph.' The name was taken from an existing method of office shorthand – phonography – and by 1890 improved phonographs were in use in hundreds of thousands of offices in the United States and elsewhere. The original Edison tinfoil phonograph was hand-cranked; it was improved first by the addition of a flywheel and, later, a weight-driven gravity motor. It was not until 1893 that a British inventor applied a spring motor to it. By this time the recording medium was wax, and the addition of a shaver made it possible to erase a previous impression to allow further use.

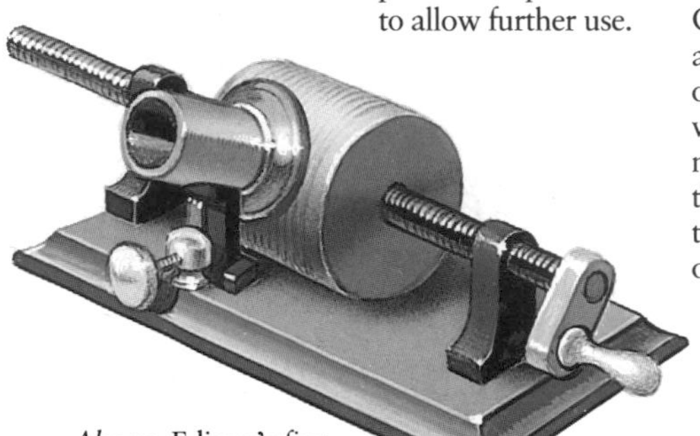

Above: Edison's first tinfoil cylinder phonograph (1877). This had a brass drum, about 4 inches in diameter, threaded on a rod. To record, the person spoke into the mouthpiece while rotating the handle.

Above: Hand-driven Berliner gramophone (1893). The first gramophone using disk records had been manufactured in Germany in 1889 as a toy. As the volume of sound produced was low, Berliner models provided for the use of hearing tubes by the addition of an outlet globe.

Below: The Gramophone Company's HMV 'Trademark' model, fitted with a spring motor. It was used in the famous trademark painted in 1899 by Francis Barraud, showing a dog listening to 'His Master's Voice.'

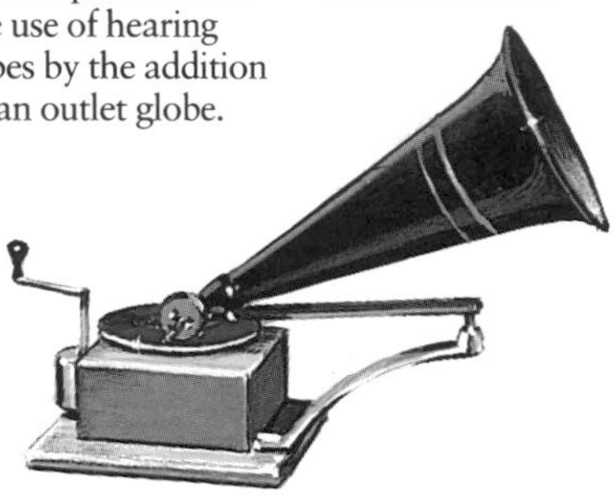

Below: Gramophone from the late 1920s. Large horn systems for playing disk records improved their efficiency, producing more volume of sound, but there was no facility for improving tone other than the use of fiber or thorn needles. By now most recordings were electrically produced, and all-electric reproducers were beginning to be available. However, acoustic machines were still made, particularly portable machines.

Below: Electric gramophone, *c.*1930, housed in a cabinet. This played disks using an electric pickup and valve amplifier feeding a loudspeaker. Electric reproduction of electrical recordings was a great improvement over the acoustic method, and the tone control was an effective way to correct response and produce a more natural sound. A development from the electric gramophone was the 'radiogram,' which also incorporated a radio tuner feeding into the same amplifier and loudspeaker.

The long-play 'microgroove' disk and stereophonic sound

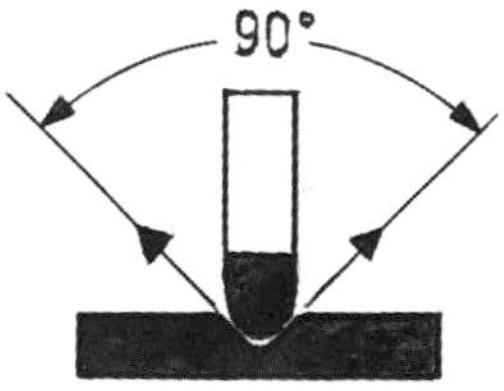

Right: In essence the principle of stereo reproduction combines the 'hill and dale' form of grooves in the Edison phonograph with the lateral waves of the Berliner disk, each channel picking up the movement of the tracking needle in one direction. However, to do precisely that presented technical problems – overcome by tilting the axes at 45° from vertical and horizontal (*left*); movement in one axis is picked up by the channel on the left, that on the other by the one on the right.

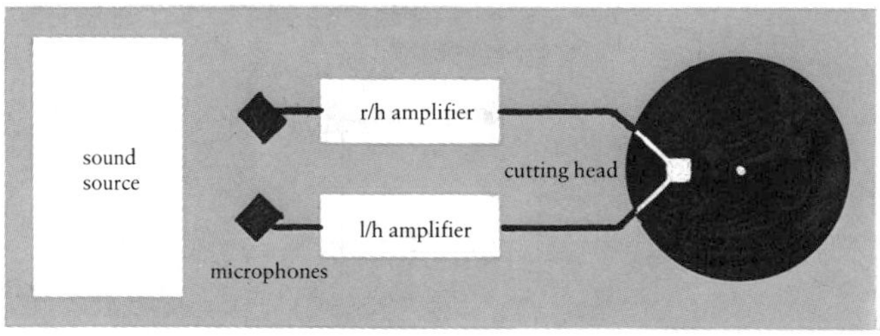

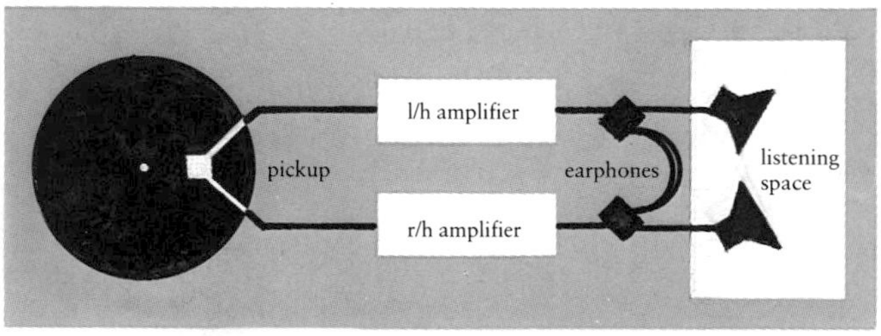

Despite all the improvements in sound quality achieved, the 12-inch 78 r.p.m. disk with about 100 grooves per inch was limited to at most six minutes of music per side. This barrier was broken by the introduction in 1946 of the LP (long-play) record by Columbia Records in the USA, soon followed by companies in Europe.

The new records offered some 23 minutes per side on a 12-inch disk, using a 'fine groove' technique (about 240 per inch) and rotating at 33⅓ r.p.m. The disks were pressed in vinyl plastic and played with a polished and shaped stylus carried in a light pickup, thus reducing surface noise and prolonging the life of the LP disk.

The next ten years saw the revolutionary introduction of magnetic tape as the recording medium and, in 1956, the launching of stereophonic records. Just as binocular vision allows the perception of depth and distance, so listening with two ears gives the hearer a sense not only of direction, but also of depth and space of sound. By collecting the sounds at points to left and right of the center, holding it in separate channels and reproducing it through two loudspeakers (or even through earphones), the illusion of depth and direction can be given. The practical problem was to find a way of playing back both channels through one stylus.

Although the theory and means of stereophonic recording and reproduction had been established by the British engineer A. D. Blumlein by 1931, it was another quarter of a century before the 45/45 system (described above) was developed by Arthur Haddy of Decca and the Westrex Corporation for use in the home.

The most striking demonstration of the new system came with recordings of operas, where the depth and direction that stereo gave allowed for fully developed productions. But the real gain was in the sense of space that was given to all recorded music, instrumental, vocal and orchestral.

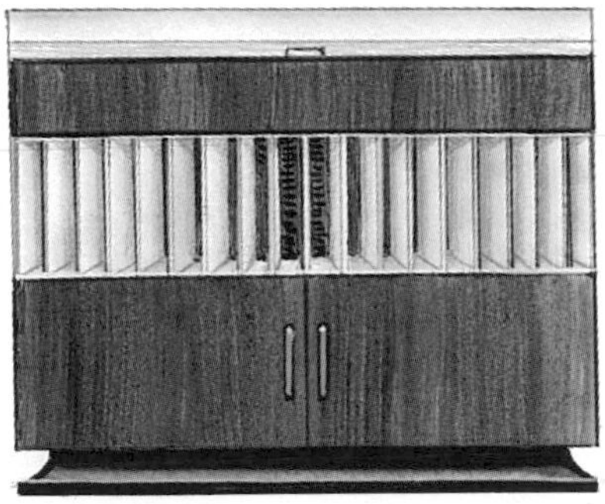

Above: The Decola reproducer (1946), designed by Decca engineers to take full advantage of their FFRR system. Three 12-inch loudspeakers were fitted, connected in parallel in an acoustic chamber with flared grill.

The introduction in the 1950s of magnetic tape brought the first fundamentally new technique to the record industry since Edison. The electric waves generated by the sound are not stored in the form of mechanical waves, but are converted by the transducer in the recording head into corresponding magnetic flux variations that magnetize the particles on the tape. Again a reverse process is used to play back the sound through an amplifier and loudspeaker.

Above: Revox open-reel tape recorder, developed from the machines that became available in the 1950s.

Magnetized steel wire was used for recording as early as 1900, and by 1935 the German AEG company had developed BASF coated magnetic tape.

Below: Long-play records and stereo high-fidelity systems revolutionized the record player. Shown here is a playing-deck made in the 1980s by Linn Products fitted with tangential pickup arm; compare the vertical tracking disk player (*right*).

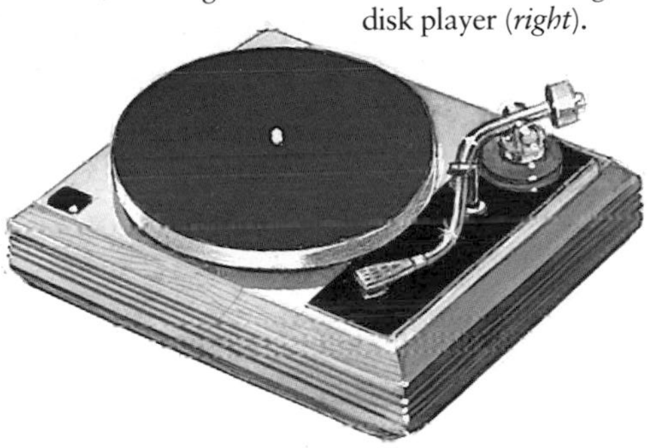

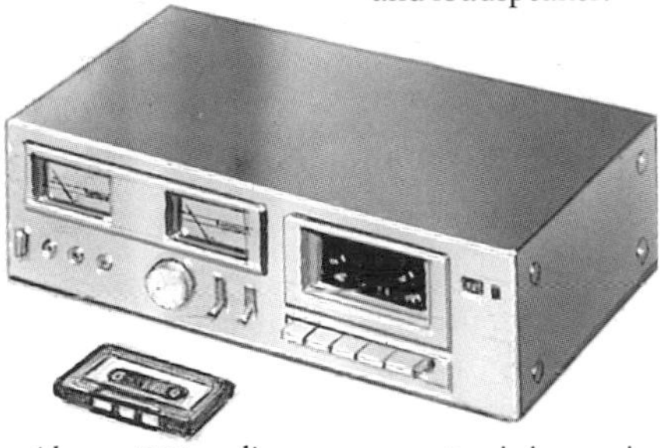

Above: JVC audio tape cassette deck (front loading). Soon after the introduction of tape for recording, containers, known as 'cartridges,' became available, but these have been largely superseded by the Compact Cassette system introduced by Philips in 1963. Today the sale of recordings as tape cassettes is increasing at the expense of disks, particularly since the introduction in the late 1970s of the Sony 'Walkman,' a player fitted with earphones, which has been widely imitated. However, the ease with which tapes can be duplicated has made piracy a very serious problem for the record industry.

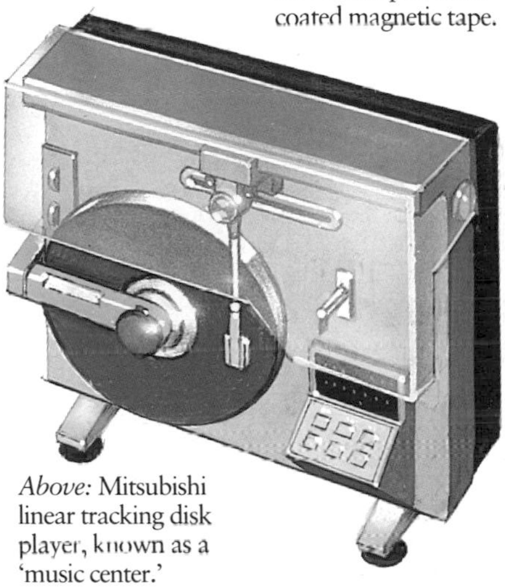

Above: Mitsubishi linear tracking disk player, known as a 'music center.'

Below: One format for the Philips-Sony Compact Disk (CD). On a disk measuring only 12cm, made of clear PVC 1.2mm thick, the digital sound signals are pressed into the surface, on one side only, in the form of tiny pits measuring only 0.6 microns across. The tracks spiral outwards from the center and are scanned by an infra-red laser built into the unit. Up to 60 minutes of stereo music per disk are available. Dirt and minor scratches do not impair the quality of replay, and as there is no physical contact between disk and laser, there is no wear on the record.

The conversion from the conventional, 'analog,' recording method into digital signals is called pulse coded modulation (PCM). It is not possible for the home user to record onto Compact Disks, but a considerable prerecorded repertoire became available in 1983. This laser-scanned CD system is a major step forward in audio history, as it offers very high sound quality. Some historic performances are now also being transferred to CD, although no music-lover will discard an existing library of outstanding recordings, as many will never be transferred.

Above: The control room in EMI's no.1 recording studio in London during the recording in 1978 of William Mathias's *This Worlde's Joie.* In the foreground the balance engineer is making adjustments, while the producer (*right*) studies the score. The introduction of magnetic tape allowed recording engineers to develop editing techniques that were impossible when the matrix was being cut as the music was played. Much imaginative use is made of these in pop music, though in classical music editing is largely confined to eliminating any mistakes.

EDWARD ELGAR AND RALPH VAUGHAN WILLIAMS

JERROLD NORTHROP MOORE & MICHAEL KENNEDY

Opposite: Portrait of Edward Elgar (1857-1934) in 1913 by Sir Philip Burne-Jones.

Edward Elgar was born in a country cottage at Broadheath, near Worcester, on 2 June 1857. The rich agricultural and pastoral countryside of the English West Midlands was to exercise a permanent influence upon him, so it is quite right that Elgar should be regarded as one of the outstanding 'nationalist' composers, for reasons which go far deeper than politics.

Elgar's father, an itinerant piano-tuner and later the proprietor of a music shop, was a talented and versatile musician, but unambitious. His mother, a yeoman farmer's daughter from the neighboring county of Herefordshire, was a stronger character. Founding her own philosophy on the cycles of nature and seasons in the countryside, she encouraged her children in every way to realize themselves as individuals. The eldest son was to have been a botanist or doctor, but he fell victim to scarlet fever at the age of fifteen, when Edward was almost seven. Two daughters came next, both of whom were to marry and lead normal lives, the second as mother of a large family, and then followed Edward, the only one of the children to be born in the country at Broadheath. Before and after Broadheath the family lived across the river in the small cathedral city of Worcester, and all the other children were born there.

After Edward came another son, who was recognized as a musical genius almost from his cradle. He was a special ally of Edward, but died at the age of seven, two years after the eldest son. Finally came the youngest son, who would take over the father's music business, and the youngest daughter, who would become a Dominican nun and rise to be Mother General of her Order in England, for the Elgar children were brought up as Roman Catholics, entirely through their mother's influence. The father, by inclination a free-thinker, supplemented his income by playing the organ in the local Catholic church: his wife became interested, was converted after the birth of her first child, and raised all the children in her new faith, despite her husband's ineffectual but oft-expressed opposition.

The deaths of Elgar's brothers may have marked the start of his ambition to realize himself in some distinctive way: 'I told my mother once when I was young that I wouldn't be content until I received a letter addressed to "Edward Elgar, England."' At the age of twelve he conceived a dramatic allegory with music, to involve his brother and sisters as actors and musicians with the parents as spectators: 'The scene was a "Woodland Glade," intersected by a brook; the higher side of this was our fairyland; beyond, small and distant, was the ordinary life which we forgot as often as possible. The characters on crossing the stream entered fairyland and were transfigured.' The action showed the two 'Old People' charmed to sleep by the music of 'Fairy Pipers' and then awakened with glittering lights to youth recovered with the insights of childhood. This allegory contains much that foreshadows the mature composer; in particular, the plot closely resembles Cardinal Newman's poem of Catholic dying and after-life, *The Dream of Gerontius*, which was to provide the text for Elgar's choral masterpiece thirty years later.

Elgar's schooling ended when he was fifteen, and a year spent in a lawyer's office merely confirmed his overwhelming desire to become a musician. He taught the violin and the piano, succeeded his father as organist of the Catholic church, and gained a wide experience of practical performance in the many musical groups that flourished in and around Worcester. Occasionally he made the 120-mile journey to London, where he was able to hear the music of more advanced composers who were to influence his own style, including Berlioz, Schumann, Wagner and Brahms.

As a composer, young Elgar was essentially self-taught. He became a ready hand at writing short works in all forms, and in these early works the bases of his own style began slowly to emerge: repeating rhythms in short compass, melody in sequences (a larger form of repeating), and a propensity for moving his harmonies toward sub-dominant (fourth interval) rather than dominant (fifth interval) relations. But whenever he aimed toward a large structure, he could not achieve it. His work as a local musician continued for more than fifteen years, from the end of his schooling until he married in 1889. His wife, his senior by nearly nine years, was Caroline Alice Roberts, the daughter of a major-general and a knight, and she was an Anglican. Against the daunting prospect of, in those days, such glaring social and religious differences, she proved the ideal companion and encourager. Elgar's important creative life coincided precisely with the thirty years of his marriage.

Above: Elgar established a wind quintet with friends: seated are Frank Exton and Frank Elgar (Edward's youngest brother); standing are William Leicester, Edward Elgar and Hubert Leicester. Elgar wrote: 'We met on Sunday afternoons, and it was an understood thing that we should have a new piece every week. The sermons in our church used to take at least half an hour and I spent the time composing the thing for the afternoon.'

•The 1890s•

The overture *Froissart* of 1890 heralded one of the fundamental characteristics of Elgar's music – aspiration which could ennoble. The score does not yet contain his favorite musical direction, *nobilmente*, but its beginnings can be heard in the ardent, clean harmonies, the nimble melodies and rhythms typical of all the best early Elgar. In form, the work is a sonata structure, with strong exposition and recapitulation, separated by a weak central development.

The development of musical ideas held the key to achieving the large forms which Elgar constantly pursued. Partly for this reason, he turned to choral music; a libretto and a plot automatically solve many of the largest formal problems. The England of his day was also widely endowed with choral societies and festivals, which provided the clearest path for a local composer to gain national fame.

In the sequence of Elgar's choral subjects one can trace the developing outlook of the man himself. In 1893 came a short cantata on *The Black Knight*, Longfellow's translation of a German ballad about a mysterious outsider who rides to defeat the king's son and topple the old kingdom. It was a powerful allegory of Elgar's own desire to invade the established musical world of his day. *The Black Knight's* fund of warm melody made it a quick success with choral societies in the English Midlands, and by 1896 Elgar was writing two large choral works side by side. In one, a short oratorio on the story in St John's Gospel of Christ healing the blind man, Christ is depicted as another outsider, and when the blind man's eyes are opened, he too finds himself rejected by the people who were better pleased to have him blind. (Elgar called the work *Lux Christi*, but his publisher, Novello, fearing the Latin and therefore Catholic overtones in a basically Protestant community, persuaded him to change it to *The Light of Life*.) For the other, a large-scale dramatic cantata, Elgar chose the Norse hero King Olaf, the only Christian among the Saga heroes. Again, Elgar's treatment emphasizes the cost of vision in a purblind and often violent world. *King Olaf* drew from him incomparably the most powerful music he had written up to this time.

His next dramatic cantata was written for one of the two greatest English choral festivals, at Leeds, in 1898. The subject was Caractacus, the ancient Briton who in legend defended his homeland in the Malvern Hills – close to where Elgar himself lived – against the invading Romans. The choice showed Elgar's propensity to prefer a landscape setting to an adequate dramatic action, and it misfired for several reasons, one the historical defeat of the hero. From the outset of Elgar's libretto (concocted with the aid of a friend) Caractacus is losing, and his fortunes decline steadily until he is captured, enchained and transported to Rome. Only by the unbelievable good nature of Elgar's Roman emperor is he set free. So the hero is not only defeated but humiliated. *Caractacus* was as true a reflection of Elgar's private fears as *The Black Knight* had been of his hopes.

All this time Elgar really wanted to write a major orchestral work in which he could project himself directly. That raised squarely the problem of abstract construction on a large scale, for which his self-tuition had not entirely prepared him. One of his schemes was a symphony based on the career of General Charles Gordon, whose death at Khartoum a few years earlier had taken personal heroism to the verge of insanity, but the orchestral project which he ultimately completed was founded on an almost diametrically opposed notion. One evening in October 1898 his wife drew his attention to a passage which he himself would not otherwise have noticed in his piano extemporization. When she asked what it was, he answered, 'Nothing – but something might be made of it.' He called this mysterious theme 'Enigma,' to signify a quality of black inchoateness. Attempts by later listeners to regard the 'Enigma' as a riddle which may be solved by finding some well-known tune to fit as counter-melody have never succeeded, because they are misguided: the circumstance of the 'Enigma' invention shows that Elgar himself had at first no consciousness of any entity, so there could be no question of any deliberate concealment by polyphony, cipher, or any other device.

What Elgar proceeded to make of his enigma was one of the most celebrated developments in nineteenth-century music. The development came, however, not directly in his own voice, but by a series of variations to show what each of fourteen 'friends' would make of it – 'if they were asses enough to compose.' The fourteenth 'friend' he allowed to be himself: his own solution was reached only through the imagined solutions of others. The 'Enigma' Variations is thus one of the subtlest self-portraits in music, with a remarkable quality of gradual self-discovery as the 'friends' are one by one consulted and conclusions drawn. The work carried Elgar's name throughout the English-speaking musical world. For the man himself, at the age of forty-one, it inaugurated at long last his creative maturity.

Left: Elgar married Caroline Alice Roberts on 8 May 1889 at the Brompton Oratory in London. They settled briefly in Kensington before impecunious circumstances forced them to return to Worcestershire. It was really only after his marriage, with the great support of his wife, that his composition took on a significant character.

•1899-1902•

Elgar did not instantly turn to the long-desired symphony. Instead he fulfilled a commission for the Norwich Festival in October 1899 with a series of solo songs with orchestra entitled *Sea Pictures*. The dark ocean moods are here made the vehicle of a self-exploration in which the strongest elements are sleep and dreams, a theme carried further in the following year with a setting of Cardinal Newman's *The Dream of Gerontius* for the Birmingham Festival. The 'old man' here is the ultimate outsider – on the verge of death in Part I, in Part II entering the after-life, seeing demons and angels on his way to Judgment. Elgar's acquaintance with the poem went back at least to 1887, when he possessed a copy annotated with copies of the markings made by General Gordon in his own copy just before his death at Khartoum.

The Dream of Gerontius is Elgar's choral masterpiece. Throughout the months of its composition he himself was aware of the extraordinary power of the subject for his music. In the solo writing he developed the arioso style begun in *King Olaf* and continued in *Caractacus* to a new sustained power; this and the subtly chromatic choral writing are set within a matchless design. In the original conception Elgar kept the listener outside at the moment when the Soul goes before God for Judgment. Then his friend August Jaeger (depicted as 'Nimrod' in the 'Enigma' Variations) made him see that this was the climax. The unforgettable depiction was accomplished entirely through Elgar's mastery of the orchestra. It was *Gerontius* more than any other work that took Elgar's fame abroad, and in Germany, after the first festival performance there, Richard Strauss hailed him as 'Meister Elgar, the first English progressivist.'

Elgar's next work, written in the winter of 1900-1, formed as complete a contrast as possible. It was the overture *Cockaigne*, op.40, a portrayal of Cockney London which shows Elgar in his happiest, most extrovert mood. *Cockaigne* makes use of a genetic theme hidden inside the work, 'an echo of some noble melody,' Elgar wrote, 'first suggested to me one dark day in the [London] Guildhall, looking at the memorials of the city's great past . . .'

One reshaping of this theme provides the primary motif at the overture's very beginning; a big upward leap at the end of the phrase sounded for the critic Donald Tovey 'a magnificent cockney accent in that pause on the high C.' Soon the 'Guildhall' melody itself appears between primary and secondary themes – a secret source of both, but at present only a part of the unfolding texture. The 'Guildhall' octave opens the second subject, more lyrical than anything heard thus far, and Elgar suggested that it might represent a pair of young lovers out to see the city sights.

The central development section, as with other Elgar works in sonata form, keeps on extending the variations; the primary subject is converted first to a rumbustious military band, and then to a witty parody of an out-of-tune Salvation Army band, but the *Cockaigne* development has solemnity too, when the second ('lovers') subject is simplified to suggest the spaces of a large church. Recapitulation mixes the original primary and secondary themes with the musical experiences of the development, and at the end it is the 'Guildhall' melody which is revealed at last as the progenitor of the whole work – with the orchestra now supported with full organ. Even so, it is a vigorous, lighthearted 'enigma,' posed and solved by a master inventor and master orchestrator, well on the

Above: Elgar playing golf.

road to the composer's dream of turning private experience to the highest forms of his art.

While writing *Cockaigne*, Elgar evolved another melody which was to achieve fame to a degree unparalleled by anything else he wrote. He himself described it as 'a tune that comes once in a lifetime.' At first he thought the great melody might lead him to his symphony. Instead he used it as the Trio-tune in 'Pomp and Circumstance,' a quick march for full orchestra. He explained to an interviewer: '. . . I like to look on the composer's vocation as the old troubadours or bards did. In those days it was no disgrace to a man to be turned on to step in front of an army and inspire the people with a song. For my own part, I know that there are a lot of people who like to celebrate events with music. To these people I have given tunes. Is that wrong? Why should I write a fugue or something which won't appeal to anyone, when the people yearn for things which stir them?'

That was Elgar in his 'popular' mood. There were to be five 'Pomp and Circumstance' Marches in all – two in 1901, a third in 1904, a fourth in 1907 and the fifth as late as 1930. The remainder of 1901 was devoted to smaller works. In the autumn, in response to a request from the Irish writer George Moore, came a big funeral march for a play by Moore and W. B. Yeats on the Irish legend *Grania and Diarmid*. The size of Elgar's work, dwarfing the sixteen-member theater pit band which was to play it, measured the darkness of the composer's inner mood in these first years of real success and real exposure.

At the end of 1901 came his only solo piano work of any size, the *Concert Allegro*, written at the insistence of the pianist Fanny Davies. It was not a great success, and it was not published during his lifetime. The early months of 1902 were devoted to the *Coronation Ode* for Edward VII. The première of the *Ode* was delayed by the King's illness, but when it was heard it achieved huge popular success – especially the 'Land of hope and glory' finale based on 'Pomp and Circumstance' no.1.

•*The Apostles*: 1903-6•

Elgar accepted an invitation to write for the Birmingham Festival of 1903. This time his choice of subject went back to a remark made in his boyhood by a Catholic schoolmaster: 'The Apostles were poor men, young men, at the time of their calling; perhaps before the descent of the Holy Ghost not cleverer than some of you here.' It was *the* story of human inspiration, with a central appeal to a self-taught creative artist. What the end would be, how far to take the story, he felt the music ought to show him. Thus the entire *Apostles* project became, without his fully realizing it, a gigantic

Below: A Music Lesson, by Frank Huddleston Potter (1845-87).

Above: The Concert by Tissot (1836-1902). Not a public concert this, but a private salon gathering, as common in late Victorian England as in Paris where the concept originated, and popular with the aristocracy and wealthier upper classes to which Elgar, the typical 'English gentleman,' aspired.

Left: Title-page of the first edition of *Salut d'Amour*, a piano piece (op.12) written in 1888 and then dedicated to his daughter Carice, born in September 1890. The work was a typical salon piece and proved to be most popular.

wager – that the strength of his inspiration at the beginning would guide his art to a new and grander result than anything yet achieved. He planned a trilogy of oratorios to match Wagner's *Der Ring des Nibelungen*.

He began shaping the music and libretto side by side, each evolving in terms of the other. He was his own librettist, selecting quotations from the most diverse biblical sources, putting them together line by line to evolve the psychological portraits of the Apostles who appealed to him most strongly. First among these was Judas, and that fact gives some clue to the deep uncertainty in the composer himself. Elgar saw Judas not as evil incarnate, but as the misguided intellectual; impatient to see his Lord's triumph, he would force the divine hand by betraying Christ into a situation in which he must show divinity to escape. Elgar had thought of writing something about Judas at the time of *Gerontius*, and the music for Gerontius's Angel of the Agony was originally designed for Judas – a telling insight into the composer's own identification.

To balance Judas, Elgar chose as his strong Apostle Peter, the rock of Christ's Church. Between them he wanted a conversion story, since the theme of conversion is at the center of the apostles' story; the figure he found for this was Mary Magdalene, the sinner who was supposed to have washed Christ's feet with her tears. But Elgar's Mary Magdalene turned out to be his

Above: The Three Choirs Festival at Gloucester, September 1913; Charles Sanford Terry conducts the Festival Orchestra brass players on the roof of the Cathedral porch, playing Elgar's arrangement of Chorales from the *St Matthew Passion*.

Right: Members of the Sheffield Choir pose with Sir Edward Elgar (left) at a railroad station in the United States during their concert tour in April 1911.

greatest failure, seemingly because he himself could not face the implications of real conversion; at each of the points where Mary Magdalene's character should develop, Elgar inserted an interrupting episode about Peter. But if *The Apostles* contains the worst of Elgar's oratorio-writing, it also contains the best. The grandly simple choral Prologue, the evocation of Eastern night and sunrise, the compulsion and despair of Judas, and the greatest choral ensemble of his career in the concluding 'Ascension' are all worthy to stand beside any biblical setting, from Bach's *St Matthew Passion* onward.

The plan of the original *Apostles* was too big to be carried out in time for the Birmingham Festival in October 1903, and the full portrayal of Peter had to be held over to a second oratorio planned for Birmingham in three years time. Meanwhile Elgar went back to his hope for a symphony, but again he was faced with a deadline, for it had been decided to pay him the extraordinary tribute of a three-day festival at Covent Garden, devoted entirely to his works, in March 1904. He hoped to finish the symphony for it, but this proved impossible. So he shaped the musical impressions of his first trip to Italy in the winter of 1903-4 into his last and largest concert overture, *In the South*. It was another sonata structure, but so embellished with extra episodes and so richly orchestrated as to approach the music of Richard Strauss. The principle which shapes *In the South,* however, is not Straussian at all, for once again Elgar shaped his own impressions – a shepherd and his pipe, an old Roman road, a 'canto popolare' – toward the abstract design he was seeking.

The Elgar Festival in March 1904 was a great success, and later in the year Elgar was knighted. After much persuasion he accepted a professorship at the new University of Birmingham. But he had no experience of university life, and his lectures, though full of creative insight and autobiographical interest, were widely criticized, especially by those who resented his home truths about the lack of brilliance in the musical history of England. After three years he thankfully resigned.

Using a figure recalled from a chance hearing during a holiday in Wales, Elgar wrote the brilliant *Introduction and Allegro* for strings at the beginning of 1905. The *Introduction* places the 'Welsh' figure casually, as if it is only one among many impressions. The *Allegro* then vigorously develops it in a series of variants which never refer directly to the 'Welsh' theme at all until a triumphant coda reveals it as the progenitor of all that has intervened. The *Introduction and Allegro* is thus a telling essay on the whole subject of recollection and nostalgia, matters which give Elgar's style its greatest mature individuality.

The quick achievement of the 'Welsh' work showed that Elgar was at last fully equipped to translate his impressions into the symphony he had sought over so many years, but the need to write the second *Apostles* oratorio for Birmingham intervened. Eventually entitled *The Kingdom*, it began with the portrayal of Peter left over from the first *Apostles*. Again there was unforgettable music – an orchestral Prelude delineating Peter's history and character by linking descriptive motives in a masterful pattern,

the descent of inspiration in tongues of fire on the day of Pentecost, Peter's fine address to all the people. But all the best parts of *The Kingdom* had been sketched in 1902 for the original *Apostles*. Where and how to end the new work became an ever more pressing question as Elgar's ability to draw inspiration from the whole subject waned. In the end he narrowly avoided nervous breakdown and produced barely half of his announced design of *The Kingdom*. Plans to finish the *Apostles* trilogy with an oratorio on the Last Judgment came to nothing. The wish for the symphony would be denied no longer.

Far right: Portrait photograph of Elgar by Lambert of Bath.

Right: Elgar sitting with his friend Gustav Holst; both shared an interest in British folksong. Elgar said, of himself, 'I *am* folksong'; Holst preferred to conduct detailed research into the subject.

• Symphonic works •

The month of Elgar's fiftieth birthday, June 1907, found him arranging the earliest music of his life, written originally for the family play in childhood, as two suites entitled *The Wand of Youth*. That wand seemed a talisman indeed when in the same month he produced the 'great beautiful tune' which became the motto-theme of his First Symphony.

Beginning with the motto-theme, stated *nobilmente e semplice* in A flat major, he brought against it an *allegro* theme of opposing character – aggressive, chromatic, and in the farthest possible tonality from A flat, D minor. The psychological distance separating the motto from the rest of the allegro measured out the field on which the symphony's subsequent action would take place. The two middle movements are based on the same arrangement of notes transfigured by tempo and rhythm: what Elgar himself described as 'a sort of scherzo' in 1/2 time, and a profound adagio, which the Hungarian conductor Hans Richter (to whom the work was dedicated) compared with the slow movements of Beethoven. The journey of discovery comes full circle with a finale which returns to the sonata form of the first movement, and in the end to the motto-theme itself. 'There is no programme,' Elgar wrote of the Symphony, 'beyond a wide experience of human life with a great charity (love) and a *massive* hope in the future.'

Elgar's next big orchestral achievement was the Violin Concerto of 1910, which stands at the very center of his creative achievement. In the first movement there is reason to think that the composer felt the primary theme as a heroic, masculine subject. The second theme is actually designated 'Windflower,' and he named after it one of his closest friends, Alice Stuart-Wortley. The orchestra presents a world of 'fact' through an opening exposition; in a second exposition the violin enters to embroider this fact with its solo fantasy. In development an extended crescendo of primary invitation is answered with secondary denial (*fortissimo*, in the minor, harshly scored), and in recapitulation the primary theme stands as far from its secondary opposite as ever.

The slow movement presents a calmer character. The single hint of passion at the movement's climax is instantly hushed, as a mother might tuck up a child disturbed by its dreams. The finale, full of the winds of autumn, again presents two expositions; the second widens the separation between the movement's primary and secondary themes. In place of development, this music returns to the slow movement's climax, now passionately repeated three times. But there is no answer, and in place of recapitulation the music goes further back, to first movement themes. These 'the violin sadly thinks over' (in Elgar's words) in an extended cadenza accompanied by a reduced orchestra softly 'thrumming' with three or four fingers rustling over the strings. As in the first movement, the heroic primary theme stands alone at the end.

Something like a final cycle is presented in the Second Symphony, written within a few months of the Violin Concerto. Again the canvas is large. But where the climax in the First Symphony was at the end, and the climax in the Violin Concerto was in the quiet center, in the Second Symphony the climax comes right at the beginning. Everything after slides inevitably away. The cyclic design is more subtly used than in the First Symphony, more covertly than in the Violin Concerto. In the Second Symphony a 'ghost' figure resembling the opening of *Gerontius* rises quietly in the center of the first movement. After a second movement of immense funereal tread, the 'ghost' appears again at the center of a manic 'rondo,' roaring its denial against the highly wrought fabric of the symphony. At the end of a calming finale, a plunging figure from the beginning emerges in a long sunset glow of farewell. The Second Symphony's reception in May 1911 was less than enthusiastic; what Elgar was saying now his contemporaries did not wish to hear. By a sharp irony, at the time of the coronation of King George v soon afterwards, Elgar was given his country's highest decoration for creative achievement, the Order of Merit.

Above: Watercolor of Elgar by Percy Anderson, painted in 1915, around the time of *The Starlight Express.*

Right: Title-page, of the piano duet version of Elgar's overture *Cockaigne*, written in 1901. The images of London are a clue to the Edwardians' view of themselves: apart from the familiar monuments – St Paul's, Big Ben, Piccadilly Circus and Staples Inn – there are jousting knights, Robin Hood, a golfer and an Indian Army parade.

• Last compositions •

At the beginning of 1912 Elgar moved his family away from his native West Midlands to take up residence in a grand, expensive London house. He had accepted chief conductorship of the London Symphony Orchestra, but he was no more equipped with the wide repertory of a professional conductor than he had been with the skills of a university professor, and after two years the orchestra terminated the engagement. Partly to pay his now heavy expenses, Elgar wrote the music to an 'Imperial Masque' celebrating the coronation of King George v as Emperor of India. *The Crown of India* thus became the chief item in a music-hall entertainment. Meanwhile, Elgar sought to realize a long-standing ambition in setting Arthur O'Shaughnessy's ode *The Music Makers* for chorus and orchestra. His plan was to introduce telling quotations from his own works – the 'Enigma' Variations, *Sea Pictures*, *Gerontius*, *The Apostles*, the Violin Concerto and both symphonies – at appropriate points in the text. But the liberal quotations from his finest ideas overbalanced his present powers of invention, as was recognized at the first performance, in the Birmingham Festival of 1912.

Elgar's next experiment also realized an old plan. It was to draw a musical portrait of Shakespeare's Falstaff, the old rogue who expects his own weakness to be tolerated when his boon companion, Prince Hal, becomes king. For this large-scale 'Symphonic Study' Elgar turned his old style inside out. Where the basis of his musical argument had hitherto been traditional diatonic melody and harmony, now the basis was chromatic; diatonic music here was reserved for the innocence that was inevitably traduced. *Falstaff* puzzled listeners at its first performance at the Leeds Festival in October 1913, and it has never gained real popularity. Elgar himself said it was his finest work, and it richly repays the effort needed to make its acquaintance.

The outbreak of the First World War destroyed Elgar's world as thoroughly as his music had foreseen it would. Returning to 'public' music, he devised three recitations with orchestra on the fall of Belgium, a symphonic prelude, *Polonia*, to commemorate Poland, and a setting of poems by Kipling, *The Fringes of the Fleet*, for another music-hall entertainment. Then 'public'

Above: The Old Bedford, one of London's most famous music halls, by Walter Sickert (1860-1942).

music combined more closely with Elgar's private promptings in *The Spirit of England*, three choral settings of war poems by Laurence Binyon. The third, 'For the Fallen,' is the last and most compelling of all Elgar's slow marches, a dirge for civilization written with a fine simplicity to appeal to every kind of understanding. It was his last attempt at public utterance on a large scale, and it is incomparably his finest.

Retrospection haunted the elaborate music Elgar wrote for a children's Christmas fantasy play, *The Starlight Express*, at the end of 1915. The play's thesis was that only children have the 'starlight' sympathy needed by the shattered world. It revived exactly the thesis of his old family play of childhood, and he laced his score with themes from *The Wand of Youth*. The result is stage music of the highest sensitivity. Retrospection was combined with escapism in a small ballet of Pan and Echo written a year later at the request of a friend, based on Charles Conder's painting *The Sanguine Fan*.

The real synthesis of escape and nostalgia came at the end of the war, in an isolated cottage, Brinkwells, in Sussex, where Elgar realized a dream of many years to write chamber music. A sonata for violin and piano, a string quartet and a piano quintet rapidly succeeded one another through the later months of 1918 and the first of 1919. The music contains much of what Elgar's wife described as 'wood magic.' Stylistically it is the testament of a vanished age, and was so recognized by the thin postwar audiences who attended the few performances. The chamber music was extended in a final orchestral work, the Cello Concerto of 1919. Here the orchestra, confined largely to the top and bottom of its extremities, opens a vast central emptiness in which the solo instrument wanders through four brief, deeply felt movements. It is a brilliant solution to the old problem of cello concertos – how to allow the soloist to be heard through the modern symphony orchestra. And it is the music of ultimate farewell, as clearly as Mahler's *Song of the Earth* and Strauss's *Four Last Songs*.

Five months after the Cello Concerto's première, Elgar's wife died. Without her support and almost mothering encouragement, all the ghosts of his old insecurities rose up to haunt him, and he could not find the courage to write another major work. Only his growing friendship with Bernard Shaw led to the appearance of a few small works beginning in 1930, the *Severn Suite* (for brass band, later orchestrated) and the *Nursery Suite*, both based on old sketches. Then he met a much younger woman who showed an affection which promised to renew the inspiration of his life with Lady Elgar. In his mid-seventies he planned his first opera, on Ben Jonson's play *The Devil is an Ass*, and at the same time began his Third Symphony. Neither of these very brave attempts to confront the world of the 1930s with a revival of his old genius was far advanced before final illness overtook him. He died on 23 February 1934.

Elgar's place in musical history is a paradox. He was the first British composer since Purcell to achieve international status, yet he had no pupils and no true stylistic successors. Like Bach, he summed up an age, but he lived into an era which dismissed his Romantic view of the artist as hero and visionary. He can be compared with the older 'nationalist' composers – Liszt, Grieg, Dvořák and (head and shoulders over the others) Brahms. But Elgar's style shares much with his contemporaries – Richard Strauss, Mahler, Sibelius, even Debussy, even Puccini. All these faced the question of abstract versus program music, the gradual breaking up of the traditional tonal language and of the nineteenth-century world at a time when their own styles were already formed.

Of all his important contemporaries, Elgar was the eldest, and he responded to the challenge least well. But this failure to move with the times is a vital part of what gives his music its individuality – the note of nostalgia, of belatedly looking over lost worlds which may have existed fully only in the fondest, most secret imaginings. That is what gives his music its permanent place in the tradition he himself so profoundly honored.

•Vaughan Williams•

Where upbringing and musical education are concerned, the only common factor shared by Elgar and Vaughan Williams is that both were born in villages in the heart of England's Three Choirs country: Elgar at Broadheath, Ralph Vaughan Williams on 12 October 1872 at Down Ampney, near Cirencester, in Gloucestershire, where his father was the vicar. The Vaughan Williams family had a legal tradition; Ralph's mother was descended from two of the most notable of English eighteenth- and nineteenth-century families, the Wedgwoods and the Darwins. When his father died in 1875, it was natural that his mother should take her three small children back to her Wedgwood parents' home at Leith Hill Place, just outside Dorking, in Surrey. There Vaughan Williams spent his childhood and his school holidays, first from a preparatory school in Brighton, later from Charterhouse at Godalming, in Surrey. Painting, ceramics, science and literature may have been part of his family background, but scarcely music. Yet at the age of six he composed a short piano piece, and two years later took a correspondence course in music at Edinburgh University, passing two examinations. More piano lessons followed, and the violin. At Charterhouse he played in the school orchestra and was allowed to use the school hall for a concert of compositions by himself and a friend. At Leith Hill Place an organ was installed, on which he could practice, although he was never very proficient.

Above: Vaughan Williams playing the viola with his friends Nicholas and Ivor Gatty in the garden of their father's vicarage at Hooton Roberts, Yorkshire, about 1900. Vaughan Williams and his wife Adeline spent many holidays here when they were first married.

When Vaughan Williams left Charterhouse in 1890 just before his eighteenth birthday, he was allowed to go direct to the Royal College of Music in London instead of entering a university as convention demanded. At the college he studied composition under Parry, then probably the leading British composer. Whatever Vaughan Williams may have learned in the study, his musical education benefited at this time from a broadening of his acquaintance with music. He had heard Wagner's *Die Walküre* at Munich in August 1890 and had been swept off his feet. Now Parry lent him the scores of works by Wagner and Brahms and made him study Beethoven quartets. Fellow-students introduced him to the seductive delights of *Carmen* and Verdi's Requiem.

In 1892, perhaps as a result of some kind of bargain with his family, he moved to Trinity College, Cambridge, but continued to have weekly lessons with Parry. His teacher at Cambridge was the church-music composer Charles Wood – 'the finest technical instructor I have ever known,' Vaughan Williams said, and he entered fully into university musical life; some of his own compositions were performed at the University Music Club. Then, in the autumn of 1895, having obtained his university degree, he returned to the Royal College of Music for a further year. Parry was now the director, so Stanford became Vaughan Williams's teacher. Master and pupil clashed violently, the former intolerant, discouraging and bigoted, the latter obstinate and, as he himself confessed, unteachable. Yet an affectionate relationship developed, perhaps as a result of Vaughan Williams's determination not to be bullied and to argue with the older man. It is interesting to note that Stanford wanted Vaughan Williams to go to Italy to study opera.

However, it was not a teacher but a fellow-student who was to have the greatest influence on Vaughan Williams from 1895. This was Gustav Holst, two years his junior, from a background as different as Vaughan Williams's was from Elgar's. Vaughan Williams was tall, hand-

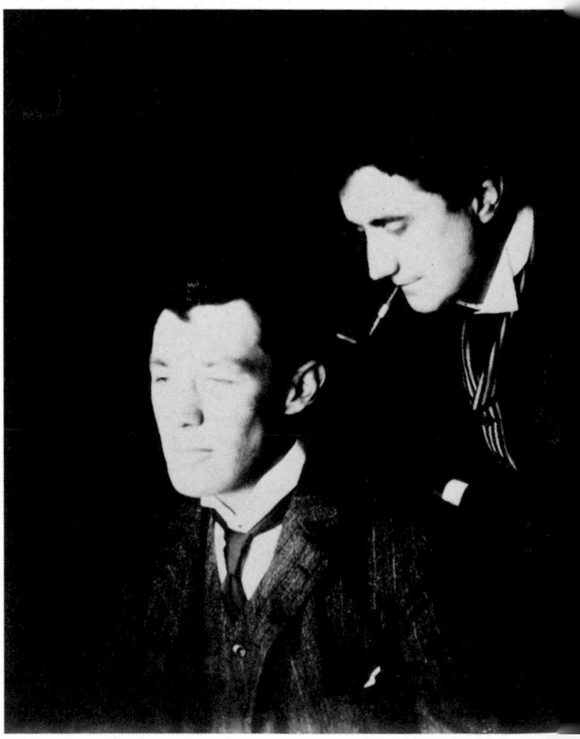

Right: Vaughan Williams with his cousin Ralph Wedgwood; they formed part of the 'Reading Party' along with other friends at Cambridge – George Macaulay Trevelyan, George E. Moore and Maurice Amos.

some and clumsy, widely read and reasonably well-off financially. Holst was small, short-sighted and short of money. Both were fearlessly honest and determined to make themselves into great composers. From almost the start of their friendship they gave each other composition lessons, playing to each other the sketches of their works and criticizing them with the utmost candor.

To gain some kind of practical experience, Vaughan Williams became organist of a London church, St Barnabas at South Lambeth. Holst, meanwhile, became a trombonist in theater orchestras, pier bands and, later, in the Carl Rosa Opera and Scottish orchestras. After Vaughan Williams married Adeline Fisher in October 1897 he gave up the Lambeth post. They spent their honeymoon in Berlin, principally because he had discovered that Wagner's *Ring* was being performed there without cuts, but also in the hope of finding a new teacher. He was recommended to study with Max Bruch, an unlikely master-and-pupil combination if ever there was one. But it worked, at least to the extent that Bruch encouraged him, 'and I had never had much encouragement before.'

On returning to England, Vaughan Williams bought a house in London. From 1897 to 1899 he worked at a setting of the Mass for his degree exercise to become a doctor of music of Cambridge University. A string quartet was composed in 1898 and most of the Serenade for small orchestra. Other projects were a setting of Swinburne's *The Garden of Proserpine* for soprano, chorus and orchestra, a quintet for clarinet, horn, violin, cello and piano, and, in 1900, the *Bucolic Suite* for orchestra. There were also several songs and part-songs, often written for, and first performed by, friends in choral societies. Most of the orchestral works were also performed but, with the exception of some of the vocal music, all these early works were later withdrawn and none of them was published. Among these efforts was one gem, however, a song, 'Linden Lea,' of such freshness and vernal charm that to this day people mistake it for a genuine folksong.

• Folksong •

Vaughan Williams's first expedition to collect authentic folksongs so impressed him that in the autumn of 1902 he gave in Bournemouth a series of lectures containing the essence of his 'nationalist' creed: 'When English musicians learn to . . . write and play for the sake of the music and for the sake of nothing else [as he maintained the singers of folksongs did], then I think that the music which is latent amongst us will come to the fore.' Between 1903 and 1913, Vaughan Williams collected over eight hundred folksongs and variants. He did not think or believe that collecting folksongs would turn him into a great composer, yet he was so excited by the rich crop of tunes he collected near King's Lynn in 1905 that he planned a 'Norfolk symphony.' This emerged as three *Norfolk Rhapsodies*, of which only the first, in a revised version, was allowed to survive beyond 1914; he had also completed another orchestral work in 1904, the symphonic impression *In the Fen Country*, but he was to revise it three times before its first performance in 1909. At this period Vaughan Williams was also setting sonnets by D. G. Rossetti, including the beautiful 'Silent Noon.' Yet, despite having been picked out by several critics as the most promising of the younger generation of English composers, he told Holst that he feared all his invention was gone. Holst refuted this, but suggested ways in which they could 'go into training' to make their music as beautiful as possible. He added: 'I am sure that after a few months' steady grind we should have made the beginning of our own "atmosphere" and so should not feel the need of going abroad so much. For it is all that makes up an atmosphere that we lack in England. . . .'

In December 1904 Vaughan Williams promoted a London concert of songs by Holst and

Below: Vaughan Williams with Gustav Holst on one of their frequent walking tours. In 1905 they had each made a setting of the lines 'Darest thou, now O Soul, walk out with me toward the unknown region?' from Whitman's *Whispers of Heavenly Death*; they decided Vaughan Williams's was the better and it was submitted to the Leeds Festival, where it was performed in 1907.

himself. The first performances of two Vaughan Williams cycles were given: Rossetti's *The House of Life* and the R. L. Stevenson settings, *Songs of Travel*, the latter being immediately singled out for their poetic originality and sturdiness. But there was to be a gap of more than two years before Vaughan Williams wrote any further large-scale works, the reason being an invitation to be the music editor of a new hymn book. He decided that the book should become a thesaurus of the finest hymn-tunes in existence; where an existing tune could not be fitted to words of a particular meter, a new one was commissioned. But when *The English Hymnal* was published in 1906, it caused immense controversy because it was regarded as 'High Church,' veering towards Anglo-Catholicism. Bishops preached sermons against it and banned it from their sees, but it gradually made ground. Agnostic though he was, Vaughan Williams acknowledged that at that period many British people came into contact with music only through their weekly visit to church. He interpreted his task as ensuring that the music should therefore be good.

By the time of his thirty-fourth birthday in 1906, despite all his steady effort, Vaughan Williams's creative reputation rested only on a handful of songs. He was dissatisfied with his work, and it may have been at this time that he wrote to Elgar asking for lessons in orchestration, to be politely refused. Unlike the self-taught Elgar, the highly educated Vaughan Williams continued to search for a teacher. After hearing Delius's Piano Concerto in October

Above: Tipperary, an evocation of the popular wartime song by Walter Sickert.

Right: Gustav Holst in 1914, painted by M. Woodforde. Much of Holst's time was spent teaching; he was musical director of St Paul's Girls' School from 1905 until the year of his death, and was musical director of Morley College for Working Men and Women from 1907.

1907, he wrote to the composer, hoping that 'if you saw my work you might be able to suggest ways in which I could improve myself . . .' Delius agreed to see him, and Vaughan Williams played to him the big Whitman work on which he had been engaged since 1903 and which became *A Sea Symphony*, but nothing came of the encounter. A critic-friend advised him to go and study with d'Indy, but another suggested Ravel, by no means well known at that date. A meeting was arranged, and in January 1908 Vaughan Williams went to Paris for three months, having lessons from the younger man on four or five days each week for several hours at a time. After an initial misunderstanding, they liked each other, and Vaughan Williams wrote home that Ravel was 'exactly what I was looking for . . . He showed me how to orchestrate in points of colour rather than in lines.'

•A personal style•

Whereas one may easily exaggerate the influence of the folksong collecting on Vaughan Williams's music – he was, after all, writing modal tunes while still a Stanford pupil at the Royal College of Music – it is not possible to overstress the significance of the Ravel studies. Somehow, in Paris, he found his true musical language. Vaughan Williams himself put it bluntly: 'I came home with a bad attack of French fever and wrote a string quartet which caused a friend to say that I must have been having tea with Debussy and a song-cycle with several atmospheric effects.' The quartet (no.1 in G minor) does indeed echo Debussy in the slow movement; elsewhere, its flattened sixths and sevenths show the absorption of folksong inflections into a personal style. But whereas this pleasing work is a mixture of not yet fully digested influences, the song-cycle is a masterpiece. It took its title, *On Wenlock Edge*, from the first of the six poems from A. E. Housman's *A Shropshire Lad*, which Vaughan Williams set for tenor, string quartet and piano. The variety of tone-color extracted from this combination, the naturalistic word-setting, the Ravel-inspired picture of Bredon Hill both in summer and in winter, with the chiming of bells so skillfully woven into the texture – these are but some of the best features of a work that had the additional cachet of a first performance by Gervase Elwes, one of the foremost exponents of Gerontius in Elgar's choral work.

The quartet and the song-cycle were performed for the first time in November 1909. Less than a year later, two other works by Vaughan Williams had their first performances. In September 1910, at the Gloucester Festival, he conducted his *Fantasia on a Theme by Thomas Tallis* for strings, a work he was to revise twice within the next decade, and which thereafter took its place alongside Elgar's *Introduction and Allegro* as an outstanding example of writing for strings. Its grave beauty of sound, designed for a cathedral acoustic, hallows this meeting of two English musical minds across the gulf of three hundred and fifty years. Then, on his thirty-eighth birthday, 12 October 1910, Vaughan Williams conducted at the Leeds Festival his *Sea Symphony*, which had been revised many times between 1903 and its completion in 1909. Ungainly and gauche though some of this work may be, its vigor and sincerity, its nobility and mystical vision, its combination of physical exhilaration and spiritual exploration, and above

Above: Landscape at Chirk (Shropshire), *c.*1912, by Augustus John. Vaughan Williams's song-cycle *On Wenlock Edge*, 1909, which sets six poems from A. E. Housman's *A Shropshire Lad* for tenor, string quartet and piano, is one of his first masterpieces.

Left: Photograph of Vaughan Williams at Bolzano, in the Italian Alps, taken by his wife Adeline.

Left: Portrait of Vaughan Williams in 1920, photographed by Lambert of Bath.

Right: Caricature drawing of Vaughan Williams by Kapp, 1914.

all its profuse inventiveness, have not diminished with the passing of time.

Inventiveness was Vaughan Williams's keynote for the next four years, as if the months with Ravel, followed by personal successes, had undammed the source. There were two further works for the Three Choirs Festival: the *Five Mystical Songs* (1911), settings of George Herbert for baritone, chorus and orchestra and, for the same forces, the *Fantasia on Christmas Carols* (1912). He began (but never finished) music for the dancer Isadora Duncan; he wrote a string quintet in 1912; he arranged more folksongs for publication and, between 1910 and 1914, wrote his first opera, *Hugh the Drover*, in which folksongs are used in a story of Gloucestershire village life during the Napoleonic Wars. In 1909 he wrote the incidental music to a Cambridge University production of Aristophanes' *The Wasps* and in 1913 he was the composer for Frank Benson's season of Shakespeare at Stratford-upon-Avon. He also composed a symphony, the 'London.'

In 1912 he crystallized his musical creed in a famous article, 'Who wants the English composer?' – 'Have we not all about us forms of musical expression which we can purify and raise to the level of great art? . . . We must cultivate a sense of musical citizenship . . . The composer must not shut himself up and think about art, he must live with his fellows and make his art an expression of the whole life of the community.' This sounds almost like the doctrine of a Communist composer, yet no one was more jealous of an artist's personal freedom, more resistant to external pressures, more truly liberal. He was advocating not state-controlled composition, but music which reflected national experience.

His 'London' Symphony was a demonstration of his beliefs, raising to the level of great art the lavender-seller's cry, the hunger march of the unemployed, the Cockney pub-crawler's accordion-playing, the Westminster chimes and the jingle of the hansom cab – all this to music betraying the influence not only of folksong and Elgar, but also of Debussy, Stravinsky and Charpentier, for this English composer, like his predecessors and successors from Dunstable to Britten, always had an ear alert to catch what was happening beyond the English Channel. The symphony was first played on 27 March 1914. Four months later, what was happening beyond the Channel was war between England

Left: The first performance of Vaughan Williams's ballet, *Old King Cole*, which took place at Trinity College as part of the Cambridge Festival of 1923. The Festival was largely organized by the local Cambridge branch (of which Vaughan Williams was president) of the English Folk Dance and Song Society.

Above: Vaughan Williams and his wife Adeline with Gustav Holst and friends. Dorothy Longman (left) was a violinist, Vally Lasker and Nora Day were both music teachers at St Paul's Girls' School with Holst, and were always willing to perform new compositions.

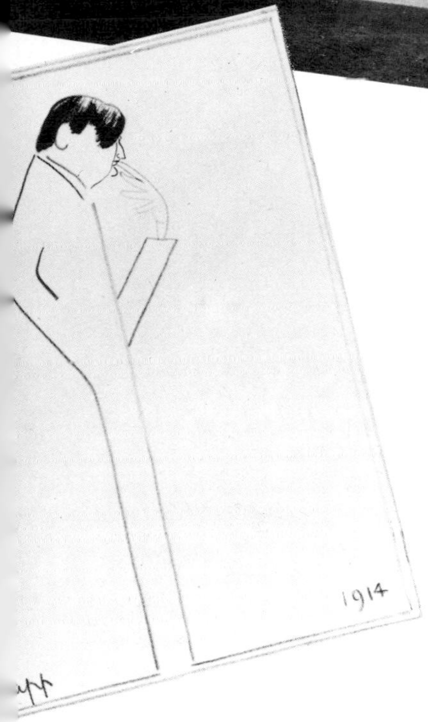

and Germany. Vaughan Williams, within eight months of his forty-second birthday, at once joined the army and wrote no more music for nearly five years while he served in France and elsewhere.

•A post-war world•

Vaughan Williams went to war at a time when he was widely regarded as the leading figure of the post-Elgar generation of British composers. When he returned to musical life in 1919, it was to a new world, a world which so distressed Elgar that he virtually fell silent. Vaughan Williams was invited to teach composition at the Royal College and became conductor of the Bach Choir in London, and he eased himself back into his creative kingdom by revising several pre-war works, including the 'London' Symphony, which was twice conducted in 1918 by a rising young English conductor, Adrian Boult, who at the same time also elevated Elgar's Second Symphony to the place it had failed to achieve in its earliest performances. Among Vaughan Williams's 'carry-over' works from 1914 were the ballad-opera *Hugh the Drover*, the *Four Hymns* for tenor, piano and viola, and the Romance for violin and orchestra *The Lark Ascending*. The last-named, redolent as it is of the essence of English nature poetry, perhaps owes its musical atmosphere to French music, since the writing for solo violin is curiously reminiscent of Debussy and even anticipates the latter's Violin Sonata of 1916-17.

France, in the shape of its northern landscape, was also the inspiration of Vaughan Williams's first major post-war work, *A Pastoral Symphony*, sketched while he was on active service in 1916 and completed in 1921. Because of its title and its modal harmonic style, this masterwork was for long – and still often is – regarded merely as a bucolic daydream. A less superficial hearing will easily uncover its impassioned overtones of war, for there is no doubt that, contained within the music's tranquillity, is a profound and deeply moving threnody for those who died in their hundreds of thousands – a war requiem without words, to be compared with Elgar's Cello Concerto. It was followed by the Mass in G minor, for soloist and unaccompanied double choir, another composition in which the first impression of austerity gives way, after closer acquaintance, to a perception of its burning intensity.

Vaughan Williams's response to another text, the familiar words of Bunyan's *Pilgrim's Progress*, had first manifested itself in 1906, when he wrote incidental music for an amateur dramatic adaptation. He always believed that the work could form the basis of an opera, and his first attempt to put it on the stage was in 1922, when he set the brief episode *The Shepherds of the Delectable Mountains.* Favorite texts were, in fact, the basis of his varied and important output in the 1920s. His style was now less opulent than it had been up to 1914, his scoring for orchestra sparer, his harmony marked with more asperity. The prevailing spirit of neoclassicism touched him in the Violin Concerto (1925), but it is the coloristic influence of Ravel which can again be detected in *Flos Campi*, a suite for viola, small orchestra and small wordless chorus. This work was inspired by the *Song of Solomon*, in its sensuous rather than its spiritual connotation, and its potent mixture of austerity, eroticism and barbarity is an effective answer to those who allege that Vaughan Williams had no technique with which to convey a wide and subtle variety of tone color. The short oratorio *Sancta Civitas* (1923-5) is a crucial work which looks back in places to the expansiveness of *A Sea Symphony* and forward to the violence of the ballet (or masque) *Job.*

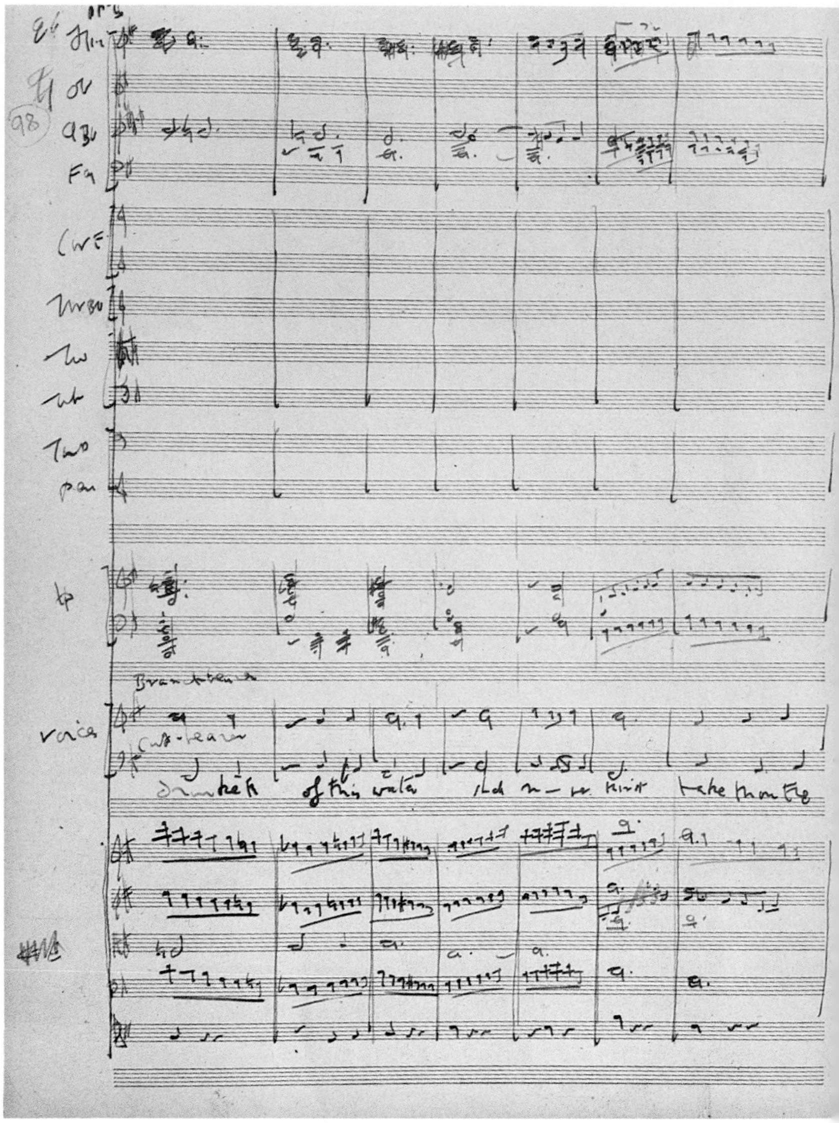

To compose *Job*, Vaughan Williams laid aside three operas, which, amazing as it may seem, he was composing almost simultaneously – four if one counts intermittent labor on *The Pilgrim's Progress.* In 1924 he had begun a Falstaff opera based on *The Merry Wives of Windsor*, which was eventually to become *Sir John in Love*; in 1925 he started to set, practically line for line, J. M. Synge's *Riders to the Sea*; and in 1927 he began a comic opera to be called *The Poisoned Kiss*, in which the influence of jazz mingles with echoes of folksong. But when in 1927 Geoffrey Keynes, the Blake scholar, suggested commemorating the centenary of the artist-poet's death by a ballet based on his illustrations of the Book of Job, Vaughan Williams was immediately enthusiastic. While a stage presentation hung fire, Vaughan Williams's enthusiasm burned on, and he completed the score to his own scenario. It was first performed as a concert suite for large orchestra at the 1930 Norwich Festival and was recognized by some critics for what it is now unreservedly thought to be – one of Vaughan Williams's finest, most spacious and inspired works, summing up in its violence, grandeur, pastoral tranquillity and visionary eloquence all that he meant to the history of English music. *Job* was first staged as a ballet in July 1931, with choreography by Ninette de Valois.

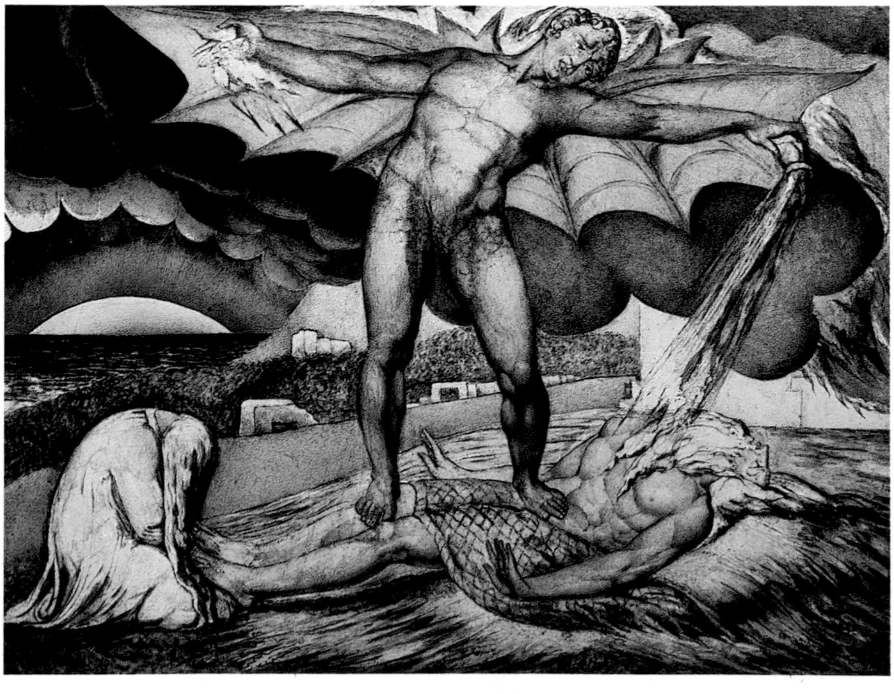

To his regret, Vaughan Williams had to leave London in 1929. His wife's crippling illness demanded a quieter life, and they settled in a bungalow in Dorking. However, there was no diminution of his activities. In 1931 he completed his Piano Concerto, and three of his operas were staged during the 1930s, all by amateurs and none with outstanding success. His major work of the decade, however, was the F minor Symphony, no.4. This was begun in 1931, finished in 1934 and conducted by Boult in 1935. Its impact on the critics was sensational. Unmindful, it would seem, of the brassy dissonances which erupt from parts of *Sancta Civitas*, *Job* and the Piano Concerto, they were surprised by this symphony's almost unremitting harshness of utterance. It was widely interpreted as a sermon in sound on the European situation, where Fascist dictators were practicing for world war, but although the music is susceptible to this interpretation, the composer denied it. It has been seen as a self-portrait – those who played or sang under him at the Leith Hill Festival would have recognized his sudden terrifying outbursts of rage – but he himself regarded it as an attempt to write a classical symphony in a modern idiom. The model was Beethoven's Fifth Symphony, as is clearly shown by the use of short motifs on which the whole structure is founded and by the connecting passage between scherzo and finale. The effect is brilliantly exhilarating, and an outstanding feature of this concise and precisely calculated score is that there is not a wasted note. Compared with some other excursions to the wilder shores of dissonance, it is no doubt basically conservative; but in a good performance it can still make an audience feel as if it has been communally kicked in the stomach. Appointment to the Order of Merit in 1935 epitomized the place Vaughan Williams now occupied in British music after Elgar's death the previous year – which had also seen the relatively early death of Gustav Holst.

•Shadows of war•

For his real sermon on the dangers of war, Vaughan Williams took as his text in 1936 the Bible, Whitman and John Bright and brought them together in the choral work *Dona Nobis Pacem*. This, however, ends optimistically with a vision of a united world, the soprano's still, small voice uttering a prayer for peace. It was the prelude to a new lyrical phase in Vaughan Williams's music. In 1938 he composed the *Serenade to Music*, with words taken from *The Merchant of Venice*, and the music is so beautiful, the work so cunningly constructed, that it may be counted among the few supreme metamorphoses of Shakespeare into music. Its calm, moonspangled mood was carried over into the masque *The Bridal Day* (1938-9) and the *Five Variants of Dives and Lazarus* (1939).

At the outbreak of the Second World War, Vaughan Williams engaged in a new challenge, composing film music, first for *49th Parallel* (a story about a Nazi submarine crew on the loose in Canada) and later for several other films on war themes. His 'private' creative work from 1938 had been concentrated on a new symphony, to be no.5 in D. The symphony was first played in June 1943, and its predominantly peaceful and serene mood seemed at that time to be a vision of a heavenly city beyond any earthly chance of attainment.

If anyone was tempted to regard the Fifth Symphony as its composer's last will and testament, coming after his nationally celebrated seventieth birthday, events were to prove them wide of the mark. It was followed by a Second String Quartet (after a gap of over thirty years), an Oboe Concerto and the *Thanksgiving for Victory*. From 1944 to 1947 he worked on another symphony, no.6 in E minor, which was to confound the critics as effectively as had no.4. For after the benedictions of no.5, here came a Vaughan Williams full of vitality and venom, writing a scherzo which sounded like a hell's kitchen of wartime parodies and progressing from the concentrated energy of the opening movement, by way of a slow movement in which an ominous drum rhythm finally spreads overwhelmingly to the full orchestra, to a spectral finale played *pianissimo* throughout. This finale seemed to many to be a vision of desol-

Opposite: Page from the manuscript score of *The Pilgrim's Progress*, an opera eventually performed at Covent Garden as part of the Festival of Britain celebrations in 1951. However, Vaughan Williams had written incidental music for Bunyan's text as early as 1906, and the idea of an opera had occupied him intermittently ever since.

Opposite bottom: Satan Smiting Job with Sore Boils by William Blake (1757-1827). Vaughan Williams's ballet *Job*, first performed as a concert suite, was written to commemorate the centenary of Blake's death in 1927.

Left: John Piper's stage design for Scene 1, 'The Earth,' from *Job*. The first ballet production took place at Sadler's Wells on 20 May 1948, choreographed by Ninette de Valois, and with David Davenport as Job and Robert Helpmann as Satan.

ation, of a world laid waste, as Hiroshima and Nagasaki had been in 1945, by man's deadliest weapon. Again the composer denied any such inspiration; in his mind, this finale was an agnostic's vision of eternity.

Having depicted a spiritual wasteland in music, Vaughan Williams next turned his attention to a human tragedy in a waste landscape when he wrote the score for the film *Scott of the Antarctic*. But his preoccupation was the completion of his long-planned opera *The Pilgrim's Progress*. This was produced at Covent Garden in 1951 as part of the Festival of Britain, a post-war affirmation of Britain's resurgence in manufacturing and the arts. The production was poor, although Vaughan Williams gallantly defended it. He knew that the work had not been a success, but he was adamant that this was the kind of opera that he wanted to write; and to those in sympathy with his music this work has a special and powerful appeal in spite of its flaws.

The Covent Garden débâcle coincided with the death of Vaughan Williams's wife. Characteristically he declared, 'I'm not going to be a hermit,' and refused to cancel any engagements. He was busy with the symphony he had decided to evolve from the Scott music, and he finished the *Sinfonia Antartica* in 1952, the year of his eightieth birthday. Sculpted by Epstein and painted by Sir Gerald Kelly, he was now the undisputed head of England's music,

Opposite: Vaughan Williams with a group of friends at the Three Choirs Festival in Gloucester, 1937. He is standing between the composers Herbert Howells and Rutland Boughton, the latter famous for his fairy-opera *The Immortal Hour* (1922).

Bottom: Vaughan Williams conducting *England's Pleasant Land*, a pageant-play written by E. M. Forster with music by several composers. Vaughan Williams was to use material from the two pieces he wrote for the pageant in his Fifth Symphony, 1943.

Below: Scene from the first production of *Sir John in Love*, based, like Verdi's *Falstaff* on Shakespeare's *The Merry Wives of Windsor*. It was composed during 1924-8, and the première took place at the Royal College of Music on 21 March 1929.

being not merely a composer but active in many other ways, whether as chairman of the English Folk Dance and Song Society or president of the Society for the Promotion of New Music or still conductor each spring of the Leith Hill Musical Festival, at which his performances of the Bach Passions, though contradictory to everything now known as 'authentic,' were an unforgettable experience. In the last five years of his life he married again, returned to live in London so that he could more easily attend concerts, operas, films and art galleries, wrote two more symphonies, several songs, a violin sonata, music for the Queen's coronation, a Christmas Cantata and a Tuba Concerto. On his desk in 1958, when he died suddenly and peacefully in his eighty-sixth year, was the completed first draft of a new opera.

•The legacy•

Vaughan Williams was a conservative, yet he achieved a kind of revolution. His nationalism was never insular – to read his artistic credo is to understand that his wish was that English music should stand on its own feet, not lean for support on foreign models. Only through being oneself, he believed, and appealing to one's fellow-countrymen, could a composer achieve an international voice. It may be said that in the latter respect he himself partially failed; but the music of Vaughan Williams is known outside his own country far more widely than many Britons realize. He took his inspiration, as has been shown, from many sources, and always claimed, paradoxically, that music need not be original provided that a composer had something original to say. He continued in his later years to be keenly responsive to what others were composing. Where Debussy and Stravinsky had once been influences, Hindemith, Bartók and Shostakovich took their place, yet all were transformed into pure Vaughan Williams. Though he affected to despise Mahler, his own symphonies 'embrace everything' as copiously and daringly as the Austrian's. Like Mahler, he was an 'intuitive' composer, a visionary and a poet in sound. His symphonies cover a time-span of half a century, and each, on its first appearance, made a profound and durable impression, although the last two have been consistently underrated. In its very different way, Vaughan Williams's last symphony is as enigmatic and cryptical as Shostakovich's.

But before all else Vaughan Williams was a composer who, like Britten, wanted his music to be 'of use' to his contemporaries. He provided works for all manner of occasions, from the elaborate professionalism of the symphony orchestra and the opera house to Women's Institute choirs and the players of bamboo pipes and mouth-organs. He wrote choral music for the superb festival choirs of Leeds and Huddersfield, for the small but expert amateur choir which Holst formed at Thaxted, and for the enthusiastic, dedicated amateurs who rehearsed throughout the winter in order to take part in the Leith Hill Festival in the spring. The hieratic splendor and lyrical poetry of Vaughan Williams's choral music are in line of descent from the age of Tallis and Byrd. He preferred a narrative modal means of expression to elaborate contrapuntal textures, but by sheer force of personality he delivered a powerful and uplifting message. Of his operas, only *Riders to the Sea*, is tentatively established in the repertoire. He wanted success on the stage almost more than anything else, but only achieved it incontrovertibly with *Job*, a ballet like no other. Yet there is no more lyrical love music in English opera than is to be found in *Hugh the Drover*, the beauties of *Sir John in Love* are many, and *The Pilgrim's Progress* has an appeal which is as potent as it is difficult to analyze.

In such a long list of works there are bound to be peaks and troughs, the inspired and the humdrum. Yet the least of Vaughan Williams's works contains, in Parry's phrase, 'something characteristic,' and the greatest of them are among the glories of English art. He and his dearest friend Holst both succeeded in their aim 'to become an English composer,' and they provided for others that 'atmosphere' which they had found lacking in the Britain of their youth. Whenever the immense resurgence of composition in Britain in the twentieth century is surveyed and assessed, two names will always lead the rest – Elgar and Vaughan Williams.

LEOŠ JANÁČEK AND ZOLTÁN KODÁLY

MALCOLM RAYMENT

Opposite: Leoš Janáček (1854-1928) by Gustav Böhm, 1926.

Although deeply patriotic, passionately involved with their native folk music, and to some extent sharing similar backgrounds, Janáček and Kodály differed greatly in character and in approach to composition. Whereas the Czech was impetuous, speaking quickly and abruptly, the Hungarian gave much thought to his pronouncements, expressing them slowly, with carefully chosen words, and this difference is reflected in their scores. Those of Janáček, especially the later ones, not only border on illegibility but give the impression of a composer ruled more by instinct then by a comprehensive grasp of his craft. He did not regard his mature works as being unalterably finished, and he frequently made changes before or after a performance. Kodály's well-written scores, on the other hand, were polished to his entire satisfaction; he would not have released them otherwise.

Despite the difference of methods, it is Janáček who is the more important composer. Having at last found his true path after a period of many years, he continued to pursue it with untiring energy to the end of his life, whereas Kodály composed little of major importance after the outbreak of the Second World War. By then, as he once said, there were more important matters to occupy his mind. Kodály was referring to his work in connection with folk music and, still more, to the musical education of the youth of Hungary – a field he revolutionized, with spectacular results. Thus the great promise held out by his earlier compositions, some of them unquestionably among the masterpieces of our century, was to remain unfulfilled. The world in general may be the poorer for this, but, as was his intention, Hungary gained.

Leoš Eugen Janáček was born on 3 July 1854 at Hukvaldy, a village in the north-eastern part of Moravia, not far from the Polish-Silesian border. He was the tenth of fourteen children, only nine of whom survived infancy. His impetuous nature seems to have been inherited from his grandfather, Jiří Janáček (1778-1848), a schoolmaster and organist, for there is little evidence of it in the character of Jiří Janáček junior (1815-66), the father of the future composer. Janáček's father also became a schoolteacher, having studied the organ and piano in addition to singing under the local choirmaster at Velky Petravald. When only sixteen, he secured a post at a school in Neplachovice, near Opava. There he was persuaded to give free music lessons to a gifted boy, who, as a result of the tuition, gained a scholarship enabling him to further his education. This kindly act was to prove very beneficial to Leoš Janáček, for the boy, Pavel Křížkovský, who was later to be regarded as the founder of modern Czech choral music, also became the most influential and beneficial of Leoš Janáček's teachers.

In addition to his father, Janáček's mother was also an accomplished musician, and we may be sure that there were many opportunities of hearing folk music in the village. Janáček's childhood at Hukvaldy was at least an adequate preparation for his future career, although at the local school he did not distinguish himself as an outstanding pupil. However, his fine alto voice, coupled no doubt with a little help from Křížkovský, enabled him to get a scholarship to the St Augustine Abbey in Brno, a venerable institution with Křížkovský as its director of music. So it was that Janáček became the choir's principal alto and lived as a 'Blue Boy,' as the choristers were known. Within a year Janáček's father died, but an uncle and, it is said, Křížkovský himself, gave financial support, thus enabling the boy to complete his education at the junior secondary school, and afterwards to study and eventually take a degree at the Czech Teachers' Institute.

It had always been intended that Janáček should continue the family tradition by becoming a teacher. Initially he remained at the Institute for two years, thereby completing the prescribed probationary period. The Institute's director, Emilian Schulz, later to become Janáček's father-in-law, was second only to Křížkovský in fostering the young man's talents, and both recommended he should move on to the Organ School at Prague in the autumn of 1874. The director, František Skuherský, a professor of composition, was a broadminded musician who both welcomed and taught new techniques. The course at the Organ School was for three years, but Janáček was allowed to skip the first. In the event he managed to cram the syllabus of the next two years into no more than nine months. He nearly did not last that long, however. To earn some money he became a critic, and among the concerts he attended was a choral one conducted by Skuherský. Janáček was unimpressed and said as much in print, whereupon he was dismissed from the school.

Fortunately, he was soon taken back, for he was regarded by Skuherský as the best of his composition pupils. This was by no means the only occasion on which Janáček endangered his career or damaged his prospects by his fiercely outspoken opinions. In an unsigned criticism he even described his own performances as pianist at a concert as 'unforgivable,' while the hostile view he took of an opera by Karel Kovařovič, soon to become conductor of the Prague National Opera, undoubtedly delayed the presentation there of his own opera *Jenůfa*. At Prague, in addition to composition and organ-playing, Janáček studied harmony, counterpoint, fugue and improvisation. The fact that he could master all these to examination level in so short a time – and he passed with distinction – says much for his technical ability.

Above: Janáček with his future wife Zdenka Schulzová, then aged fifteen, just before their marriage in 1881. The marriage underwent a certain amount of strain, and the couple separated for two years after the birth of their daughter Olga in 1882.

• Early career •

Returning to Brno in the summer of 1875, Janáček re-entered the Teachers' Institute in order to take his degree, and then stayed on as a teacher. It was only now that he began to realize that teaching might become a secondary activity and that composition might be his true vocation. Those around him, Emilian Schulz especially, may well have persuaded him in this direction, but if he was to become a composer he needed further training and experience of as wide a range of music as possible. For this reason he was given leave from the Teachers' Institute to study at the Leipzig Conservatory in the autumn of 1879. He stayed only six months, but during that time he took further studies in harmony and counterpoint as well as piano and organ; he attended concerts and became acquainted with the late works of Beethoven, Bach cantatas and the symphonies of Schubert and Schumann. Perhaps most important of all, he composed a large number of pieces, some of which were more than mere exercises.

After only a few months he felt he had learned all that Leipzig could teach him. A more pressing reason for his hasty return to Brno was probably Emilian Schulz's daughter, Zdenka. Separation from her had made him very unhappy in the German city. Despite this, however, Janáček, who still had leave to come, enrolled at the Vienna Conservatory at the beginning of April 1880. His stay in the Austrian capital was even shorter than that in Leipzig, and little that might be called beneficial resulted from it. Admittedly, he could have come home with a testimonial, but he did not wait to receive it after the disappointment of having his new violin sonata – his second, since he had already composed one in Leipzig – rejected for entry in a prizewinning competition on the grounds of being too academic. After returning to Brno in June, he announced his engagement to Zdenka Schulzová on 13 July. Exactly a year later they were married when he was twenty-seven and she not quite sixteen.

Of the works composed prior to Janáček's marriage, many are lost. Probably the majority of these were destroyed by him, for he was well aware that they were of little value. Perhaps the best-known compositions of this period are the *Suite* (1877) and *Idyll* (1878), another suite, both for string orchestra and much influenced by Dvořák, for whom Janáček had the highest admiration. More important are the choruses, particularly those for male voices. While a few of these are folksong settings, it was more usual for Janáček to take a folk text and clothe it in original music. The main reason for Janáček's early comparative success in this medium was that he had ideal models in Křížkovský's decidedly nationalistic male-voice choruses, which achieved far wider recognition than this com-

Right: Janáček as a student, around 1879.

poser's sacred works. For all their merits, Janáček's youthful choruses are a long way from equaling Křížkovský's.

After returning from Vienna to Brno, Janáček threw himself wholeheartedly into the city's musical life, which at the time was German-dominated. In addition to his teaching, he was the conductor of two male-voice choirs – the Svatopluk and Brno Beseda. He enlarged the second of these by adding women's voices and then formed an amateur orchestra to go with it. The next step was a music school to help raise the orchestra's standards. Soon an ensemble that had been a kind of social glee club, suddenly found itself performing Beethoven's *Missa Solemnis* and works by Dvořák. Another of Janáček's ambitious ventures was the formation of an Organ School on similar lines to the one in Prague. Here again the organ was only one of many subjects, and Janáček himself took third-year students in composition. In 1919 the Brno Beseda and the Organ School were to merge, becoming the Brno Conservatory. One of Janáček's dearest wishes was then fulfilled.

Left: Janáček's daughter Olga; the composer dedicated his opera *Jenůfa* to her and played a piano version to her, but she died before seeing the opera performed.

Below: A concert program including works by Janáček, for performance on 12 December 1880 by the Beseda choir in Brno. Always an innovator, Janáček had changed the choir from an all-male to a mixed-voice choir when he became its conductor in 1877. This particular concert also includes works by Křížkovský, Pivoda and Dvořák, whose music Janáček was keen to promote, as well as Smetana's *Vltava*.

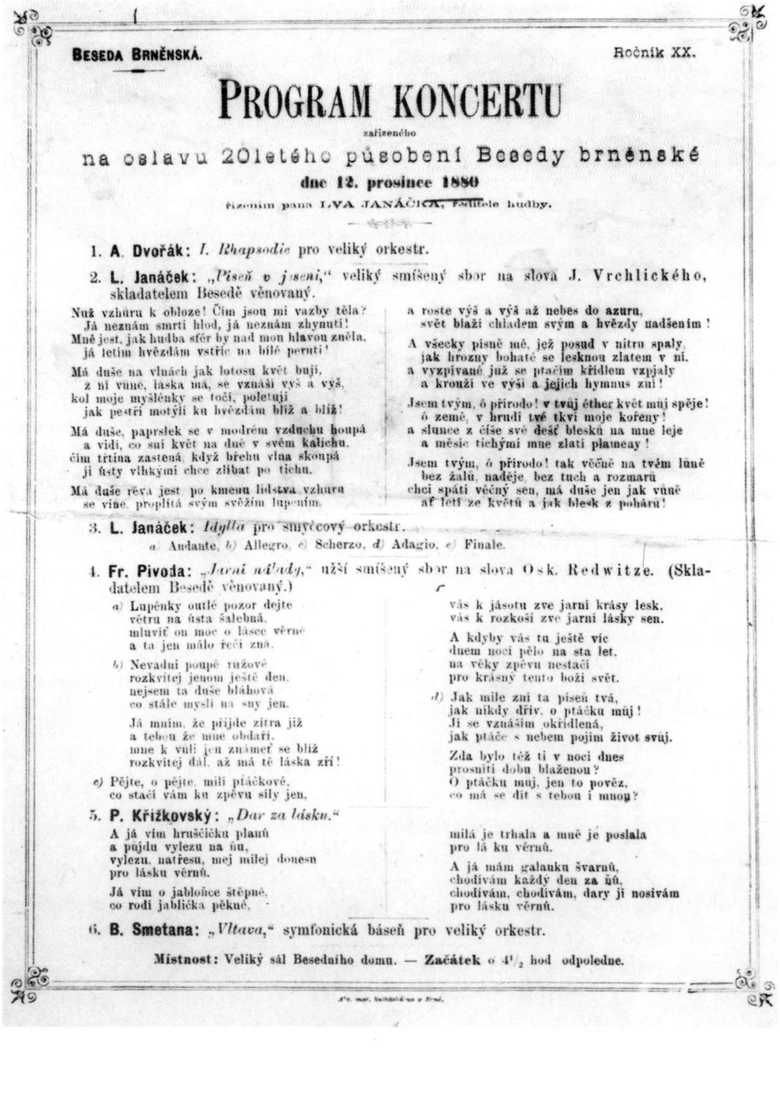

BESEDA BRNĚNSKÁ. Ročník XX.

PROGRAM KONCERTU

zařízeného

na oslavu 20letého působení Besedy brněnské

dne 12. prosince 1880

řízením pana LVA JANÁČKA, řiditele hudby.

1. **A. Dvořák:** *I. Rhapsodie* pro veliký orkestr.

2. **L. Janáček:** „*Píseň v jeseni*," veliký smíšený sbor na slova J. Vrchlického, skladatelem Besedě věnovaný.

Nuž vzhůru k obloze! Čím jsou mi vazby těla?
Já neznám smrti hlod, já neznám zhynutí!
Mně jest, jak hudba sfér by nad mou hlavou zněla,
já letím hvězdám vstříc na bílé peruti!

Má duše na vlnách jak lotosu květ buji,
z ní vůně, láska má, se vznáší výš a výš,
kol moje myšlénky se točí, poletují
jak pestří motýli ku hvězdám blíž a blíž!

Má duše, paprslek se v modrém vzduchu houpá
a vidí, co sní květ na dně v svém kalichu,
čím třtina zastená, když břehu vlna skoupá
ji ústy vlhkými chce zlíbat po tichu.

Má duše réva jest po kmenu lidstva vzhůru
se vine, proplítá svým svěžím lupením

a roste výš a výš až nebes do azuru,
svět blaží chladem svým a hvězdy nadšením!

A všecky písně mé, jež posud v nitru spaly,
jak hrozny bohaté se lesknou zlatem v ní,
a vyzpívané již se ptačím křídlem vzpjaly
a krouží ve výši a jejich hymnus zní!

Jsem tvým, ó přírodo! v tvůj éther květ můj spěje!
ó země, v hrudi tvé tkví moje kořeny!
a slunce z číše své dešť blesků na mne leje
a měsíc tichými mne zlatí plameny!

Jsem tvým, ó přírodo! tak věčně na tvém lůně
bez žalů, naděje, bez tuch a rozmarů
chci spáti věčný sen, má duše jen jak vůně
ať letí ze květů a jak blesk z pohárů!

3. **L. Janáček:** *Idylla* pro smyčcový orkestr.
a) Andante, b) Allegro, c) Scherzo, d) Adagio, e) Finale.

4. **Fr. Pivoda:** „*Jarní nálady*," užší smíšený sbor na slova Osk. Redwitze. (Skladatelem Besedě věnovaný.)

a) Lupénky outlé pozor dejte
větru na ústa šalebná,
mluviť on moc o lásce věrné
a ta jen málo řeči zná.

b) Nevadni poupě růžové
rozkvítej jenom ještě den,
nejsem ta duše bláhová
co stále myslí na sny jen.

Já mním, že přijde zítra již
a tebou že mne obdaří,
mne k vůli jen známeť se blíž
rozkvítej dál, až má tě láska zří!

c) Pějte, o pějte, milí ptáčkové,
co stačí vám ku zpěvu síly jen,

vás k jásotu zve jarní krásy lesk,
vás k rozkoši zve jarní lásky sen.

A kdyby vás tu ještě víc
dnem nocí pělo na sta let,
na věky zpěvu nestačí
pro krásný tento boží svět.

d) Jak mile zní ta píseň tvá,
jak nikdy dřív, o ptáčku můj!
Ji se vznáším okřídlená,
jak ptáče s nebem pojím život svůj.

Zda bylo též ti v noci dnes
prosníti dobu blaženou?
O ptáčku můj, jen to pověz,
co má se dít s tebou i mnou?

5. **P. Křížkovský:** „*Dar za lásku.*"

A já vím hruščičku planú
a půjdu vylezu na ňu,
vylezu, natřesu, mej milej donesu
pro lásku věrnú.

Já vím o jabloňce štěpné,
co rodí jablíčka pěkné,

milá je trhala a mně je poslala
pro lá ku věrnú.

A já mám galanku švarnú,
chodívám každý den za ňú,
chodívám, chodívám, dary jí nosívám
pro lásku věrnú.

6. **B. Smetana:** „*Vltava*," symfonická báseň pro veliký orkestr.

Místnost: Veliký sál Besedního domu. — **Začátek** o $4^1/_2$ hod odpoledne.

• Folk music and the first operas •

Although during his youth in Hukvaldy he must have heard a great deal of folk music and had introduced it into his early choruses, it was only in 1885 that Janáček began a serious study of the subject. With characteristic enthusiasm, he dedicated himself to his researches, which, some four years later, led him also to study folk speech. He filled many notebooks with exclamations, questions, answers and short sentences overheard in the countryside and market-place. All were written down in musical notation, often with an indication of the mood of the speaker. Thus the same words would appear in a variety of notations.

What interested Janáček was not the words themselves, but the meaning conveyed by the inflection with which they were uttered. He claimed these told him far more about the speaker's emotions than the actual words used. Soon this study became extended to incorporate the sounds of animals and, more especially, birds. Here again he indicated the circumstances. There is, needless to say, a very great difference between the bark of a dog greeting his master and one challenging an intruder. These speech studies may have been begun as a supplement to those of folksong, but they turned out to be of equal, if not greater, importance to the composer's future development.

In the realm of folk music Janáček naturally concentrated on his native Moravia, especially the eastern part from which he hailed. The folk music of this region, utterly different from that of Bohemia and even western Moravia, has much in common with that of Slovakia, often being freer in meter and consequently much less four-square. Also it is not restricted to the usual major or minor scales which form the basis of so much Western music. The study of the music and speech of his own people did much to increase Janáček's nationalist feelings, but, far more important, it enabled him to find his true path as a composer. Inevitably the process was a slow one. It is one thing to collect folk music, but quite another to become so permeated with it that its contours become second nature in creative work. As a composer Janáček had been a diehard and a conservative. Thanks to his researches, he was to become a revolutionary, not by linking himself to any avant-garde movement, but by creating and then developing an idiom that was, and has remained, unique. By the time this process began he had already passed his thirtieth birthday.

One unfortunate result of the composer's upsurge of nationalist feelings was a deterioration in his relationship with his wife, Zdenka. Of German ancestry, she had been brought up very much in the German tradition. Admittedly she and Janáček spoke together in Czech, but some elder members of her family regarded this language as 'fit only for servants.' Their daughter Olga was born on 15 August 1882, and their son Vladimir on 16 May 1888, after separation and reconciliation. Both children were adored by their father, but the boy died of scarlet fever in November 1890, and Olga did not live to see her twenty-first birthday; she died after a long illness on 27 February 1903. At least she had the satisfaction of hearing *Jenůfa*, for Janáček played it to her on the piano, although she did not live to see it performed. The opera was dedicated to her.

With his involvement in activities in Brno it is not surprising that Janáček composed relatively little during the earlier part of the 1880s. Again, the most significant compositions of the period are unaccompanied choruses, the majority for male voices. Towards the end of the decade his compositional activities increased. In particular, he set to work on the first of his nine operas. The subject was the legendary Šárka, an amazon-like warrior capable of tender feelings. Faced with the choice between love and duty, however, she decides on the latter. The libretto by Julius Zeyer was written for Dvořák, who had been contemplating an opera on this subject. When he decided not to proceed, Janáček seized on Zeyer's text, made numerous changes to it, and composed his opera between January and August 1887. He submitted the work in short score to Dvořák for criticism and, acting on his advice, rewrote it the following year. Only then did he ask Zeyer's permission to set the text. Understandably, and particularly in view of the changes that had been made, this was refused.

The refusal was a severe blow to the composer, for he had much faith in this work. It became further doomed when Fibich's opera on the same subject (although not to the same libretto) appeared in 1895 and was soon acclaimed. Despite these setbacks, Janáček made a third version of the opera sometime before 1918, revising it yet again in 1925, the year of its first performance. *Šárka* is the earliest major work to reveal Janáček's characteristic personality, although it is difficult to know how much of the completed work, if any at all, was in the original version or the rewritten one of 1888. Typical of Janáček, however, is his disregard of practical considerations. The opera contains barely an hour of music, and the last of its three acts takes only fifteen minutes or so.

The years that followed *Šárka* saw the first published fruits of Janáček's explorations into folk music with the appearance of the *Hanákian Dances* for piano or orchestra, and more especially, *A Bouquet of Moravian, Slovakian and Czech Folksongs*. This contains 195 songs collected jointly by the composer and František Bartoš. Other collections, including *Folksongs of Moravia* (a volume containing no less than 2,057 songs) and *Hukvaldy Folk Poetry in Songs*, were in preparation, but the folk-based work to become most widely known was *Dances from Lašsko* for orchestra. This set, which also derives from the area of Hukvaldy, was incorporated into a folkloristic ballet, *Rákosz Rákoczy*, which was performed with much success in Prague during 1891.

Above: Design by the Czech artist Alfons Mucha, an almost exact contemporary of Janáček, for a poster for the Spring Festival of Song held in Prague in 1910.

Opposite top: Design by A. V. Hrska for *Jenůfa*, whose first performance took place in Brno on 21 January 1904, though the work, based on the play *Her Foster-daughter* by Gabriela Preissová, was begun as early as 1894.

Opposite: Cover of Janáček's collection of *Folksongs of Moravia*.

Opposite right: Maria Jeritza, a singer of great renown, in the title-role of *Jenůfa* in the production at the Vienna Hofoper in 1918.

In the same year Janáček composed his second opera *Počátek románu* (The Beginning of a Romance). This lightweight one-act comedy incorporating folksongs dissatisfied the composer – given his way he would have destroyed it – yet strangely enough it was the only one of his operas he ever conducted. While he fully approved of folk-music arrangements, even if they involved a full symphony orchestra as in the *Dances from Lašsko*, he totally disapproved of their being used to bolster up the material of the work, unless – in a choral work or more particularly an opera – the dramatic situation demanded them. Even then, Janáček preferred to compose his own 'folk music'; contrary to widespread belief, the wedding chorus in *Jenůfa* is not a folksong, although it may be said to have almost become one since it was composed. Even casting aside Janáček's objection, *The Beginning of a Romance* is a slight and thoroughly untypical work. Perhaps its most significant aspect, for the future at least, was that the libretto was based on a story by Gabriela Preissová, whose play *Její pastorkyňa*, (Her Foster-daughter) was to become the basis of Janáček's next opera.

LEOŠ JANÁČEK
Moravská lidová poesie v písních
G.1087.f.
RAHA 1947 - HUDEBNÍ MATICE UMĚLECKÉ BESEDY V PRAZE (362)

It is not known when Janáček first met Gabriela Preissová or came to know her play, which had its première in Prague towards the end of 1890. He may well have seen it when it was staged in Brno early in 1892. At any rate, he must have been at work on this third opera by the beginning of 1894, since its intended, although afterwards rejected, overture was complete by 31 January of that year. *Her Foster-daughter*, or *Jenůfa*, as it became known outside Czechoslovakia, occupied the composer for the next ten years (there was further time spent on revisions in 1906, 1911 and 1916). On at least two occasions it seems to have been completed, although not to Janáček's satisfaction. This is understandable, for his personal idiom was developing rapidly during this period, as the cantata *Amarus* shows. Probably finished in 1898 and certainly performed in 1900, *Amarus* was the most mature and individual large-scale work that Janáček had yet produced. Even so, it hardly prepares one for the enormous advance that *Jenůfa* represents.

With this drama, set in a Moravian village, Janáček reached full maturity. The plot itself, full of ill-directed love and turning on the murder of Jenůfa's illegitimate baby, is unquestionably among the most intense and moving to have found its way into an opera house. In musical terms Janáček's studies of folk music and speech resulted in penetrating characterization, while his dramatic feeling allowed the action to move hardly less quickly than in the original play. Although not the greatest of his operatic scores, *Jenůfa* is a masterpiece, a view that many in the audience seem to have taken when the opera was performed for the first time on 21 January 1904 in Brno. It was the year of the composer's fiftieth birthday.

•1905-15•

Unfortunately there were to be no further performances of *Jenůfa* for another twelve years. However, even before witnessing its successful opening in Brno, Janáček had begun his fourth opera, *Osud* (Fate, or Destiny). Unlike its predecessor, *Osud* was written very quickly, the score being completed in the spring of 1905. Janáček was never to hear this work, for the first performance (and that only a broadcast) took place in 1934, after his death. Not until 1958 was the opera staged. The reason for its rejection was the libretto, a psychological drama put together by Janáček himself and Fedora Bartošová. The central character is an opera composer and teacher of composition. Despite this, and although much of the plot is based on real-life incidents, there is no autobiographical content. The libretto may be confused and lacking in conviction, but operas with greater disadvantages in this respect have succeeded in holding the stage. That *Osud* should have been so neglected is the more regrettable because the score is worthy to stand beside that of *Jenůfa*. The repeated refusals of Prague to present the latter opera added much to the composer's frustration at this time, but the difficulties that stood in its way were largely of his own making. Kovařovič had been antagonized and was unwilling to forgive. Moreover, he found fault with the score.

Janáček soon returned to instrumental and choral composition, the first major work completed after *Osud* being '1.x.1905,' a sonata for piano in three movements, bearing the subtitle 'Zulice' (From the Street). Unfortunately this work, which is among the composer's finest for the keyboard, has come down to us incomplete. It was inspired by the tragic death of a Czech worker during a clash between German and Czech demonstrators in Brno, the issue being the proposed establishment there of a Czech university. The army was called in to intervene and František Pavlík was mortally wounded on the steps of the Beseda building. The first performance of the work was scheduled for the following January, but while the pianist, Ludmíla Tučková, was having her final run through, Janáček grabbed the last movement and burned it. Consequently she was able to play only the first two movements. These she performed privately a little later in Prague, again in the composer's presence. This time he at least waited to the end before throwing all that was left of the manuscript into the Vltava river. In the light of her previous experience the pianist had fortunately taken the precaution of making copies of the movements that had survived the first performance, and later Janáček himself authorized their publication.

The sonata was followed by three of Janáček's finest male choruses, *Kantor Halfar*, *Maryčka Magdónová* and *Sedmdesát Tisíc* (Seventy Thousand), all settings of texts by the Moravian postman–poet, Petr Bezruč (1867-1958), an ardent patriot who attacked injustice and oppression in his poems. This was perfect material for Janáček, and such is the scale of these works that they may be said to amount to symphonic poems for voices. The first two were introduced to the world by the Moravian Teachers' Chorus, an ensemble on the threshold of an international reputation and still in existence today. Even for this fine chorus the difficulties

Opposite: Manuscript sketch for *Jenůfa*, here written in piano version. The wild scoring is typical of Janáček's writing.

Above: A striking woodcut portrait of Janáček by Jean Lebedeff.

Below: Janáček (center) in 1914, surrounded by the graduates and professors of the Organ School in Brno, which he had founded in 1881.

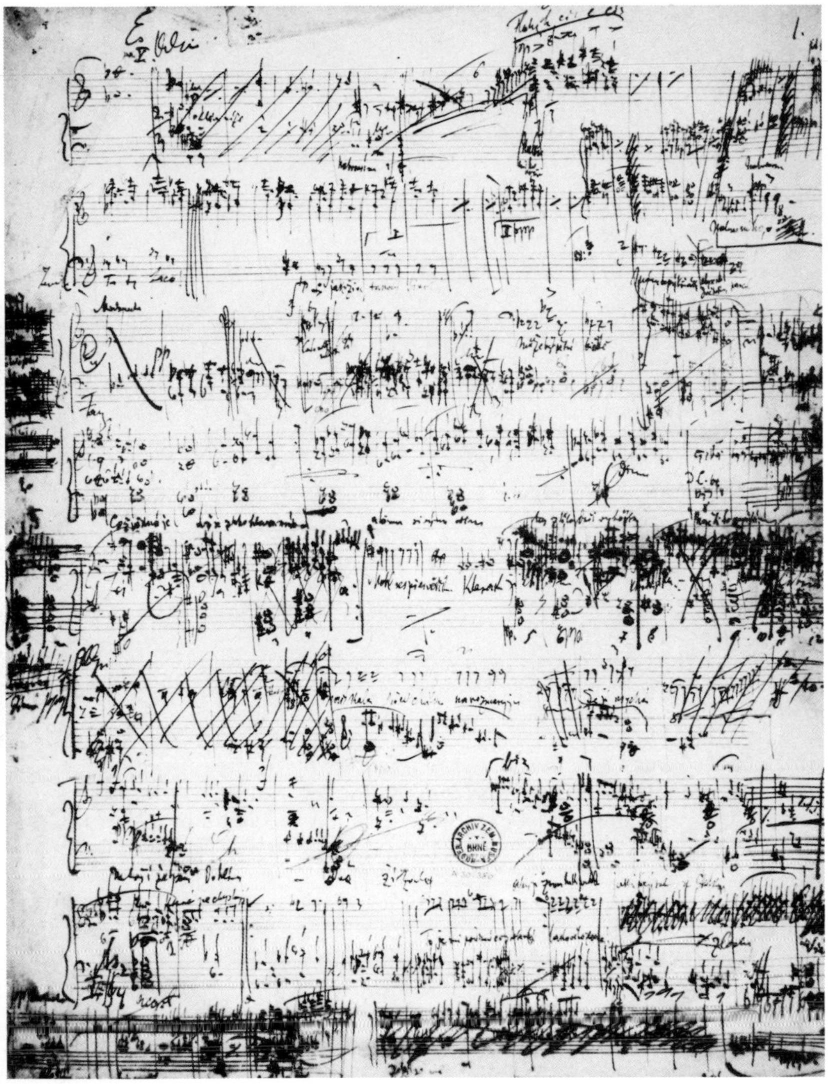

of *Seventy Thousand* initially seemed insurmountable and, as a result, the first performance was given by the Prague Teachers' Chorus. Another important work of this period is *Po Zarostlém Chodníčku* (On the Overgrown Path) for piano, a set of fifteen pieces in two volumes. The ten in the first volume have titles, and these reveal that the inspiration for most, if not all, of the pieces lay in the experiences of Janáček's youth at Hukvaldy. Composition was spread over the years 1901-11, and initially the first seven pieces were intended for the harmonium.

Notwithstanding Janáček's frustrations in the operatic field, he began a fifth opera in 1908. This was *Výlet pána Broučka do Měsíce* (Mr Brouček's Excursion to the Moon), based on the character created by Svatopluk Čech. At first, no doubt because of the reaction to his text of *Osud*, Janáček took no part in the preparation of the libretto. Six others did so, and the efforts of five of them were deemed unsatisfactory by the composer. This largely explains why *Mr Brouček's Excursion to the Moon* – a short piece intended to fill only half an evening – lay uncompleted until 1917.

During these years Janáček composed several of the works for which he is well-known today. In the instrumental field they include *Pohádka* (Fairy Tale) for cello and piano, and the Violin Sonata, both of which were later to be revised, as well as the orchestral ballad *Šumařovo dítě* (The Fiddler's Child). *Taras Bulba*, described as a rhapsody for orchestra despite being in three movements, was begun in 1915 but not completed until three years later. Vocal compositions of this period include the cantata *Na Soláni Čarták* (Čarták on the Soláň) and the much longer *Věčne Evangelium* (The Eternal Gospel). During the First World War the Moravian Teachers' Chorus was temporarily disbanded, and the composer turned his attention to female voices, producing three outstanding works for them: *Hradčanské písničky* (Songs of Hradčany), *Vlčí Stopa* (The Wolf's Trail) and *Kašpar Rucký*.

• Romance and fame •

It was during this time that two events occurred that were to change Janáček's life. In 1915, while on a visit to Hukvaldy, he met Kamila Stösslová, the wife of an antique-dealer. Two years later they met again at the Moravian spa of Luchačovice during a holiday with their respective spouses. Despite the difference in their ages – he was her senior by thirty-eight years – Janáček fell passionately in love with her. On his own repeated admission she became the inspiration for many of his future compositions. The other all-important event was that in Prague Kovařovič finally relented. He agreed, subject to certain changes being made – they were mostly advantageous – not only to present *Jenůfa* at the Prague National Opera, but to conduct it himself. So it was that the curtain at last went up on this opera in the Czech capital on 26 May 1916.

It is no exaggeration to say that overnight Janáček became a national rather than just a provincial composer. He was soon to become an international one, for, even in time of war, Prague was the gateway to the outside world. Within two years, and with the war still raging, *Jenůfa* was in the repertory of the Vienna Hofoper with no less a singer than Marie Jeritza in the title-role. In Cologne, Otto Klemperer conducted the work five days after the cessation of hostilities. In 1924, *Jenůfa* was performed in Berlin, with Erich Kleiber at the helm, and at the Metropolitan in New York under Arthur Bodanzky. By 1926 the opera was in the repertory of no less than seventy opera houses. There can be little doubt that 26 May 1916 was the most important day in Janáček's whole career; he was by then almost sixty-two and had just over twelve years left to him.

They were to prove hectic ones, for, far from taking life easier after his long delayed breakthrough, the composer redoubled his efforts, producing a whole series of masterpieces at tremendous speed. Indeed, some of these works, the operas in particular, suggest that his pen could not keep pace with his thoughts and in-

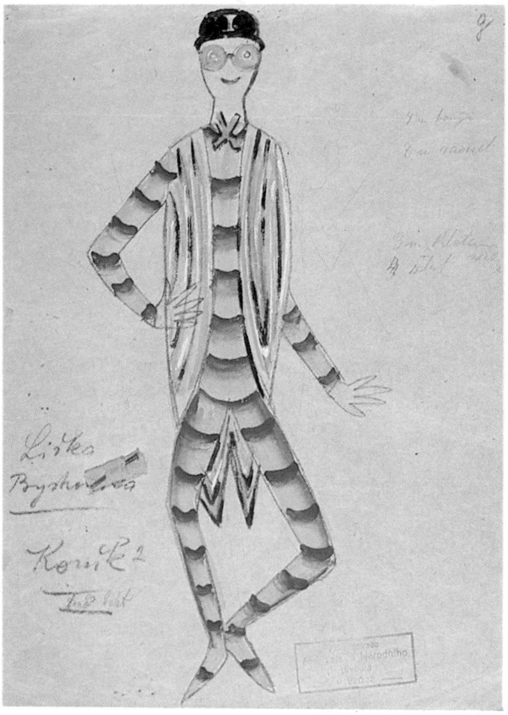

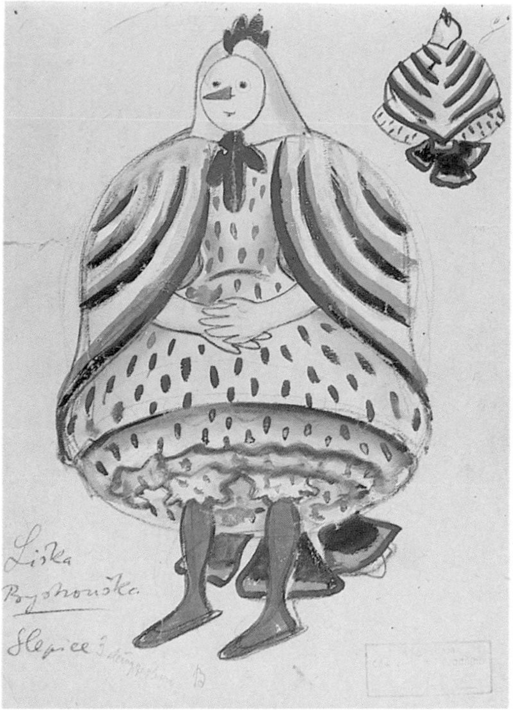

Right: Costume designs by Josef Čapek for the caterpillar, the hen, the bat and the woodcutter for the opera *The Cunning Little Vixen*, first performed on 6 November 1924. Janáček specified that he wanted children to sing some of the animal parts.

ventive powers. His hastily scrawled manuscripts, most of them on plain paper (as opposed to music paper with staves) provide further and conclusive evidence of this. In addition Janáček continued his efforts to make Brno a leading musical center. When Czechoslovakia gained independence in 1918, he immediately applied for, and was granted, permission to transform the Organ School into a State Conservatory. The next year saw the birth of a regular series of Philharmonic Concerts in the city, as well as the engagement of a top-ranking conductor in František Neumann, who also served the Opera, while in 1922 the Society of Moravian Composers was founded with Janáček as its president. It must not be supposed that Janáček's intense involvement in the musical life of the Moravian capital resulted in his being cut off from events in the outside world. During the 1920s he traveled more extensively than he had since his student days. On three occasions he went abroad to attend Festivals of the International Society for Contemporary Music, at which his music was now performed. He was, therefore, well aware of what composers of other nationalities were writing in idioms very different from his own; needless to say, he held very strong opinions concerning the value of these compositions. For instance, he fully recognized the genius of Alban Berg. When that composer's opera *Wozzeck* was adversely criticized in Prague, Janáček sprang to its defence. In this respect it is an interesting fact that Schoenberg held Janáček's *Kát'a Kabanová* in similar esteem.

At the time of the success of *Jenůfa* in Prague there were two major works requiring completion, *Mr Brouček's Excursion to the Moon* and *Taras Bulba*. Not only was the first of these finished in 1917, but in the same year Janáček added *Výlet pána Broučka do xv Století* (Mr Brouček's Excursion to the Fifteenth Century), thereby making one opera, *Výlety páně Broučkovy* (Mr Brouček's Excursions) that fills an evening. Janáček's intention was to produce a satirical work exposing a type of petit-bourgeois character well known in Prague but to be found almost anywhere.

Mr Brouček (literally, Mr Beetle), a landlord, is a boastful character, full of his own importance and imagined superiority. An *habitué* of the Vikárka Inn in the precincts of St Vitus Cathedral in Prague, he frequently imbibes too liberally. Then, in a drunken sleep, he has fantastic dreams that lead on from the preposterous theories he has propounded earlier in the evening; hence his appearances on the moon and in Prague during the Hussite period. Janáček said he intended to convey the message that we should cast out the Broučeks of this world wherever we find them, and especially when we find them in ourselves. All the same, and for all his boastfulness, gluttony and cowardice, audiences cannot help finding Mr Brouček an amusing and to some extent lovable character. Many people regard *Mr Brouček's Excursions* as the weakest of Janáček's mature operas, but given a good production it can be very effective and entertaining.

•*Taras Bulba*•

The other work needing completion in 1916 was the orchestral rhapsody, *Taras Bulba*. The idea of composing a work on this subject had been in Janáček's mind for at least ten years before he began the project in 1915, and it took another three years to complete. The composition is based on the Ukrainian legend of the Cossack leader, Taras Bulba, and his sons Andrij

and Ostopov, all of whom died in the war against the Poles in 1682. The composer, who was very much a Russophile, stated: 'Not because he killed his first son for having betrayed his country, nor for the martyr's death of his second son, but because he said that in the whole world there are neither fires nor tortures strong enough to destroy the Russian nation; for those words, spoken by the famous Cossack leader, Taras Bulba, as he was being burned at the stake, did I compose this Rhapsody after the legend retold by Gogol.'

Only the briefest indication of the story is given in the score's preface, and no attempt is made to relate incidents to specific musical sections. From this it can be presumed that Janáček considered his music self-sufficient. The few programmatic explanations of his instrumental works that he did give were usually unreliable and sometimes contradictory. In the case of *Taras Bulba*, however, he described the programmatic significance of certain motifs and passages to the conductor Jaroslav Vogel, following a performance in Prague. Consequently, in this particular instance, there can be no doubting the validity of the composer's comments.

The first movement, 'The Death of Andrij,' concerns the Battle of Dubno, during which Andrij, who has previously fallen in love with the Polish commander's daughter, deserts and fights against his own people. He is captured and killed by his father. The opening theme, begun by the cor anglais and continued by an oboe and a solo violin, is intended to describe Andrij's feelings as he enters the besieged town at night by means of a secret underground passage. At the end of this section, and just before the quiet entry of the organ, a motif that is to become of the utmost importance is heard on the woodwind. It consists of five notes – the fourth note being sustained – and initially it represents Andrij's fear of discovery. In shortened form, but still with five notes, it is heard against the organ passage, which itself is intended to suggest the starving inhabitants of the town at prayer. The motif of Andrij's fear continues to dominate the next section, which is in much faster tempo, and finally dies away on the violins. At this point Andrij finds the girl, and a love scene follows. During this the sound of the clashing swords (wooden sticks on a suspended cymbal) is briefly heard from the other side of the battlements, but the lovers

Above: Design by Čapek for the Lawyer's office in *The Makropoulos Case*, one of Janáček's last operas, whose first performance took place on 18 December 1926. The opera was based on the play of the same name by Karel Čapek, brother of the artist.

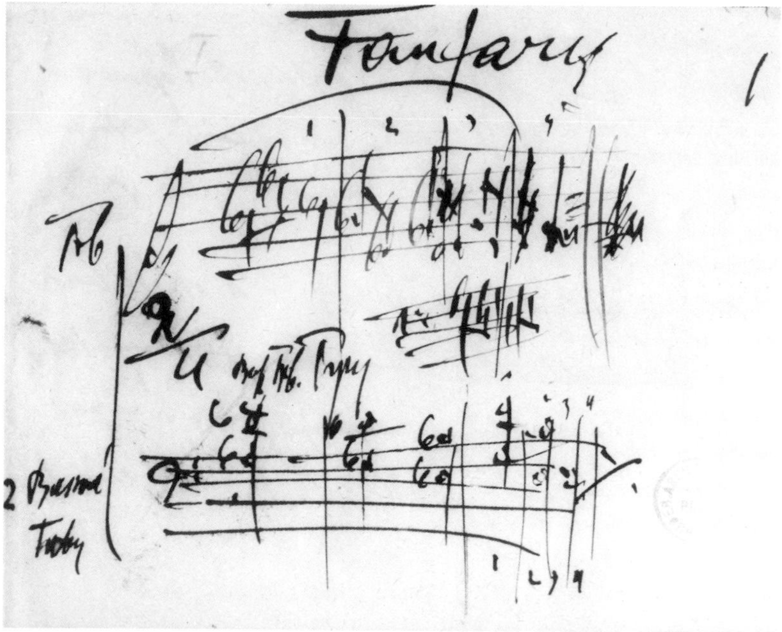

Top: Janáček's sketch for the 'Fanfare' movement of the *Sinfonietta*, written in 1926. By this stage of his career he had stopped using ruled staves, writing in his own. His scoring, though it looks erratic, was actually extremely accurate.

Above: Janáček and his wife in Venice with J. Mikota. They visited the city in 1925 when Janáček's First Quartet was performed (and well received) as part of the chamber-music section of the ISCM Festival there.

remain oblivious to the fighting. There is an abrupt change of atmosphere as Taras's theme is thundered out for the first time by the trombones and tuba, but according to Janáček the lovers, stricken by pangs of conscience, only imagine his presence at this point. From this theme a battle sequence is developed. It ends with a sudden silence as Andrij, who has taken no part in the fighting, comes face to face with his father. Meekly he dismounts from his horse and accepts death, while still thinking of his beloved. Finally Taras gallops away to continue the fight.

The second movement, 'The Death of Ostopov,' provides an excellent example of Janáček's reliance on short motifs of the kind he might well have entered into his speech notebooks. Almost the whole movement derives from three basic ideas, and of these only the third is sufficiently extended to merit being described as a theme. In the introductory section the first motif of six notes is played by the violins and violas against a harp accompaniment and quiet woodwind chords. When the tempo increases, the second motif is introduced by the strings. It, too, consists of six notes, but much of the time only the last four are used. This section, according to the composer, describes a battle on horseback. Next, the initial tempo is resumed and the first motif returns, but now it is supplemented by the four-note idea from the second. During a brief reference to the battle music, Ostopov is captured. To the accompaniment of the initial motif, a sad theme (the movement's third important piece of material) is intended to suggest a procession as Ostopov is led away to Warsaw to be executed. The battle music returns once more, but now it is transformed into a wild dance of victory by the Poles. A chordal theme, deriving from the preceding sad one and given to the trombones, symbolizes Taras's appearance among the crowd in Warsaw. Finally the shrill tones of the little high-pitched E flat clarinet depict the tortured Ostopov calling for his father, who witnesses the execution.

'The Prophecy and Death of Taras Bulba' is the title of the third movement. After taking a terrible revenge for the murder of his second son, Taras himself has been captured and is about to be burned at the stake. The opening theme, Janáček said, depicts his suffering, but a more important piece of material is the phrase of four notes (the last two at the same pitch) played almost immediately by the horns and soon taken over by other instruments. In its original form, varied or with extensions, it is rarely absent from the score. Soon it becomes augmented (played in longer note values), and this tender version is intended to show Taras's thoughts of his comrades, still in battle. A very fast section, still using the same motif, signifies another dance of victory by the Poles, but suddenly Taras's own theme from the first movement, again on the trombones and tuba, cuts through. This theme remains in the forefront throughout the next section, during which Taras has the satisfaction of witnessing his warriors escaping from the enemy. After a brief silence their fanfares are heard in the distance and the theme of Taras's suffering returns. Then, following a brief and fiery passage, comes the coda, and with it the hero's prophecy. Its beginning coincides with the re-entry of the organ, which has not been heard since the first movement. Taras's vision of a glorious victory for his people begins with further variants of the principal motif, all of them fairly easy to recognize despite their extensions, but new material is added in the closing stages. The accompaniments are worthy of special note, since they are very typical of the composer. The figuration used is often of the type produced by cimbalom players improvising (they play a kind of stringed instrument with sticks) in folk ensembles, and there can be little doubt that the composer was much influenced by this style of playing. The opening of the final movement provides a good example of it, the cellos beginning the figuration, which they afterwards share with the violins and violas.

• 1918-23 •

At last accepted, both nationally and internationally, as a major composer, Janáček went his own way during the last ten years of his life, caring nothing for convention and little for the practical considerations of music-making. Among the chamber works of this period are some in which hitherto untried instrumental combinations are explored; but even the long-established medium of the string quartet was to be treated in a new and individual way, often involving immense technical difficulties for the players. Another very fine male chorus *Česká Legie* (The Czech Legion) appeared a week after the Armistice of 1918, and early the following year the composer finished his only song-cycle *Zápisník Zmizelého* (The Diary of

One who Disappeared). The text sets verses printed in a local newspaper and said to have been written by a village lad who disappeared without trace. The verses, written in Moravian dialect, were contained in a diary left in the boy's room. They revealed that he had been seduced by a gypsy girl, who had borne him a son. After much heart-searching he decided that his only course was to leave home and throw in his lot with the gypsy community.

Much later the authenticity of these poems, and hence the events they describe, came under question; a professional writer attached to the newspaper was believed to be the true author. Janáček, of course, did not know this, and it would probably have made no difference if he had, for the verses fired his imagination. The result is among his greatest works; it is also one that ideally requires a semi-dramatic presentation. *The Diary of One who Disappeared* is principally a song-cycle for tenor and piano, but the words of the gypsy girl are sung by an alto, who is instructed to arrive and depart as inconspicuously as possible during the course of the performance. In addition, the atmosphere is heightened during the seduction sequence by an off-stage trio of female voices.

The only sizable new work to appear in 1920 was the symphonic poem *Balada Blanická* (The Ballad of Blanik). It is not one of the composer's more significant compositions of this period, when he was mainly occupied with his sixth opera, *Kát'a Kabanová*, which he completed early in 1921. Based on Ostrovsky's play *The Storm*, this is the most conventional of Janáček's later operas in so far as the plot is concerned, but the treatment it receives is anything but conventional. The main love scene takes place in the wings, while on the stage the audience sees the secondary pair of lovers. As usual with Janáček, the action is fast-moving; indeed, at the point where Kát'a commits suicide by throwing herself into the Volga, it is too quick, for she is brought out of the river in far less time than it would take to drown. Producers usually get over this difficulty by making it appear that she has struck her head in her fall. Because of the intensity of the score, built out of severely limited amounts of basic material, and the brilliance of the characterization, many people regard *Kát'a Kabanová* as Janáček's finest opera.

The year 1922 was a relatively lean one, for although Janáček began another opera, he completed only some folksong settings for piano and his last major composition for male-voice chorus, this time with the addition of a soprano soloist. The chorus is a setting of Rabindranath Tagore's *The Wandering Madman (Potulný Šílenec)*. The Bengali poet had visited Prague the previous year and given a public recitation of some of his work. Janáček, who had been present, was greatly impressed by Tagore's poems and personality.

The new opera was *Příhody Lišky Bystroušky* (The Cunning Little Vixen). Once again the local newspaper supplied the composer with

Right: Janáček in 1927 in the garden of the Organ School at Brno.

Below: Design by František Hlavica for a stage-set for Janáček's last opera, *From the House of the Dead*, after Dostoyevsky's novel of the same name, first performed in Brno on 12 April 1930.

his subject, which this time was in the form of a strip cartoon with verse captions. The first performance took place in Brno during November 1924. With a cast representing animals, birds and insects in addition to humans, the opera makes exceptional demands upon the producer and, since ballet plays an important role, on the choreographer too. Parallels are drawn between various members of the animal kingdom and their human counterparts – indeed Janáček intended certain roles, such as the badger and the parson, to be taken by the same singer. As is usual with the composer's late works, the score derives largely from short, pithy motifs, but the influence of Moravian folk music remains strong; it is heightened by the text, which is in Moravian dialect. No folk tunes are incorporated, but the chorus of the cubs, for instance, could well be mistaken for one.

Contemporary with *The Cunning Little Vixen* is the First String Quartet, which the composer described as being 'after Tolstoy's *Kreutzer Sonata*,' but he gave no explanation of the music's relation to this tragedy. He did, however, volunteer the information that the quartet had its origin in a piano trio composed in 1908 and revised the following year. The extent of the relationship between the two works cannot be assessed, since the trio is among the composer's lost manuscripts – it may well have been destroyed by him – but certainly the quartet is very much in the style of Janáček's last period and one of the masterpieces from it. Less successful was the 'Danube' Symphony, which Janáček began sometime in 1923. It caused him much trouble and he never succeeded in putting the final touches to it. Eventually completed by his pupil Osvald Chlubna and first performed in 1948, it remains a curiosity rather than an achievement.

• Last works •

In 1924 Janáček celebrated his seventieth birthday by composing one of his best-known works – the wind sextet he called *Mládí* (Youth). The title is appropriate, not only because it reflects the composer's youthful vigor, but also because in this work he looks back to his early days as a 'Blue Boy' at the St Augustine Abbey in Brno. His principal concern, however, was his eighth opera, the Czech title of which is *Věc Makropulos.* Since *věc* literally means 'thing,' the opera is usually known as *The Makropoulos Case* or *The Makropoulos Affair*, although the 'thing' is in fact an alchemical 'formula.'

The opera occupied Janáček for more than two years before it was finally completed in December 1925. Once again, he had chosen a highly unconventional subject. *Věc Makropulos* is a play by Karel Čapek, who in another play, *R. U. R.*, was the first to use the word 'robot' (the initials stand for Rossum's Universal Robots). The central character is a woman who has lived for more than three hundred years, thanks to her father's having discovered the formula of the elixir of life. Still retaining her youthful beauty, she is an operatic prima donna, yet life has lost its meaning for her; the action takes place in a lawyer's office, a theater and a hotel, and much of it is bound up with legal wrangling.

Čapek himself tried to dissuade Janáček from turning his play into an opera, believing it to be poor material, but the composer was fascinated by the character of Elina Makropoulos. Unlike Bernard Shaw, who expressed the opposite view in *Back to Methuselah*, the composer did not believe such longevity would be beneficial – a matter the two men probably discussed when they met in London in 1926. Shortly before the end of the opera, the heroine gives up the document containing the formula – the *věc* of the title – which is then burned. The score has great power, while the idiom is more cosmopolitan than in Janáček's other works for the stage.

Two other important compositions also date from 1925. One of them, the Concertino for piano and six instruments (three strings and three wind), is similar in spirit to *Mládí*. The other, *Říkadla*, began in the form of a trio for singer, piano and clarinet (or viola) and ended up employing nine singers and an instrumental ensemble of ten players; an ocarina and a toy drum are among the instruments used. Here again the title does not lend itself to translation; perhaps the nearest we can get is *Ditties and Nonsense Rhymes*, although *Sayings and Nursery Rhymes* has also been used.

To 1926 belong three major works – the *Capriccio*, the *Sinfonietta* and the *Glagolitic Mass*. Like the Concertino, the *Capriccio* is a small-scale piano concerto, but written for a pianist who has lost his right arm. The accompanying 'orchestra' employs the extraordinary combination of flute (doubling piccolo), two trumpets, a tenor tuba (euphonium) and three trombones. This is perhaps the most eccentric of all Janáček's works. More important is the *Sinfonietta*, a work that has become widely popular despite the cost of mounting performances. The title notwithstanding, Janáček's work, his finest for orchestra, requires a very large ensemble in which the brass section is expanded to include twelve ordinary

Right: Votive altarpiece (*c.* 1400) of Archbishop Očko of Vlašim, showing the Virgin and Saints including Saint Wenceslas. Early in his career Janáček had written several sacred choral pieces, then turned to opera as his major vocal output. However, he returned to the idiom with the tremendous *Glagolitic Mass*, written in 1927 in response to the millennium of St Wenceslas (the patron saint of Czechoslovakia). It was based on a text in Old Slavonic, the language which flourished during Prague's medieval 'Golden Age.'

trumpets, two bass trumpets, two tenor tubas, four trombones and a bass tuba. The main reason for these forces is that the work grew out of some fanfares which the composer wrote for the Sokol Gymnastic Festival in Prague.

Equally important is the *Glagolitic Mass*, which the composer sketched out in barely two weeks during a holiday at Luhačovice. As he put it, there was nothing else to do but compose since the rain was incessant. The millennium of St Vaclav (Wenceslas) was approaching, and Janáček chose to set the Old Slavonic text that was in use in the time of the king who was to become patron saint of Bohemia and Moravia. To translate this text into the tongue of the most western Slavs, the monks Cyril and Methodius had found it necessary to invent a new alphabet; they called it the Glagolitic alphabet, hence the Mass's title. Needless to say, it is unlike any other Mass ever written – its vitality is tremendous.

During 1927 Janáček worked on his last opera, again choosing an unlikely subject. This time it was Dostoyevsky's autobiographical novel *Z Mrtvého Domu* (From the House of the Dead). As was his usual custom, Janáček treated the text with great freedom, fusing two or more characters into one and allotting incidents to whichever suited his purpose. He did not even prepare a libretto in advance, but worked directly from the novel in the original Russian while composing the music – on occasion he even forgot to translate. Deeply moved by the predicament of the unfortunate inhabitants of the Siberian prison camp, the composer poured out some of the most intense music that even he had yet written. In 1928 he was still working on the opera, and the starkness of the musical language led people to believe that it was still unfinished at the time of his death. A certain amount of filling in and adjusting was deemed necessary, and this task was undertaken by Osvald Chlubna and another former pupil, Břetislava Bakala, who, as a conductor, was to become a great champion of Janáček's music. These two also supplied an optimistic ending to the work in the form of a 'freedom' chorus. Nowadays it is realized that virtually no touching up was needed and that the 'freedom' chorus was contradictory to Janáček's intentions. It is no longer heard.

By the beginning of 1928 Janáček considered *From the House of the Dead* to be finished, although he was to return to it later. In the meantime he composed his Second String Quartet, his last major instrumental work. It bears the title *Listy Důvěrné* (Intimate Letters), and in it he expresses his feelings for Kamila Stösslová, at the same time giving the work an autobiographical content. No verbal program, however, can begin to match the expression of the music itself, written at white heat in little more than three weeks. Technically it is extremely difficult to play, and for a long time it did not gain a place in the general repertory. Initially, performances were restricted almost entirely to leading Czech ensembles, and even these players made cuts to parts of the last movement, considering it to be unplayable.

In the summer of 1928 Janáček returned to his native Hukvaldy for a holiday with Kamila and her son. One day the boy got lost, and the composer embarked on a strenuous search for him; in helping to find the child he caught a chill which developed into pneumonia. Six days later, on 12 August, he died. It can be truly said that he never grew old.

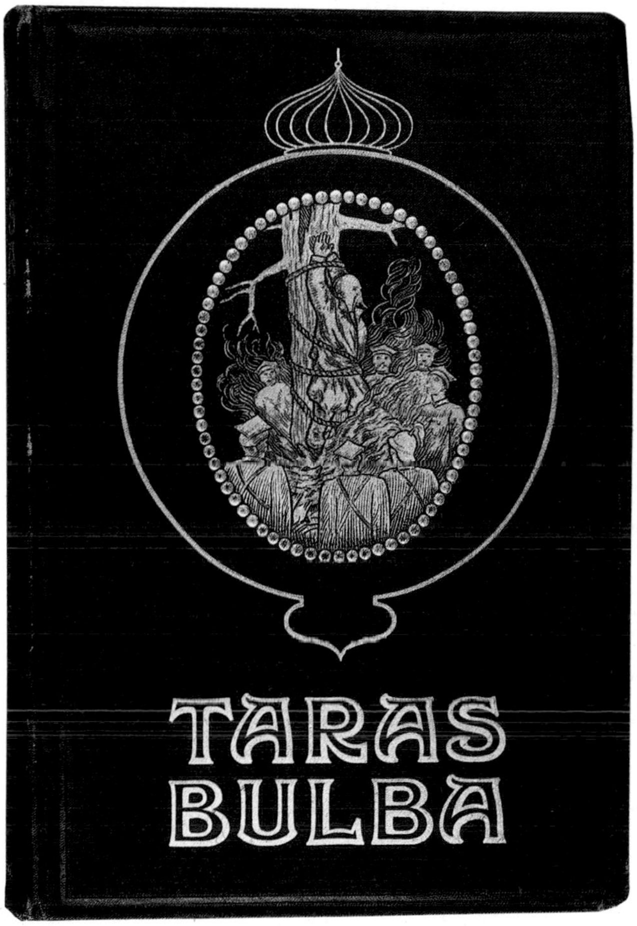

Far right: Front cover of an English edition (dated 1900) of Gogol's *Taras Bulba*, showing the hero burning at the stake, punishment for the retribution he took on his enemies to avenge the murder of his son.

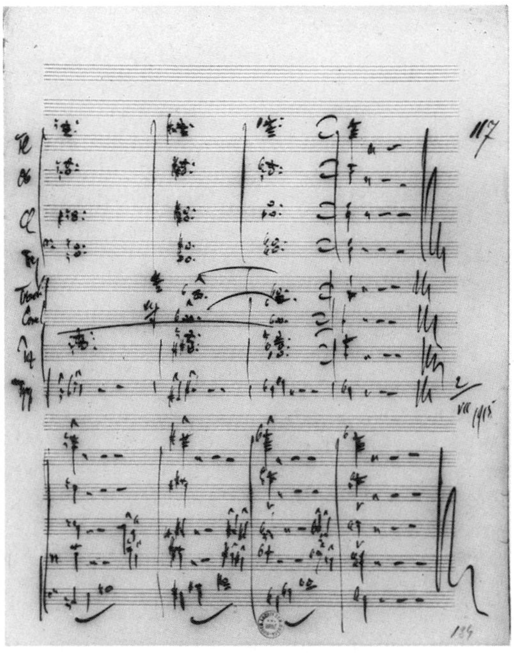

Right: Last page of the autograph score of *Taras Bulba*, a programmatic piece in three movements that Janáček described as a 'Rhapsody,' based on Gogol's retelling of the legend of Taras Bulba and his two sons who died for the Russian cause in 1682.

• Zoltán Kodály •

Right: Zoltán Kodály (left) with Arturo Toscanini in 1928. Toscanini greatly admired the work Kodály was doing, both in terms of his composing and his research, and he was one of the first to include *Háry János* in his concert repertoire. Kodály dedicated *Summer Evening* to the great conductor, who later encouraged him to rework the piece, which he did most successfully.

Zoltán Kodály, unlike Janáček, did not experience any struggle against poverty in his youth. His father Frigyes, as an employee of the railway, was a respected citizen who earned a reasonable salary. He was also a good violinist, while his wife Paulina was a singer as well as an accomplished pianist. With friends participating, chamber music was often performed in the house. There were three children, Zoltán being the second. He was born on 16 December 1882 at Kecskemét, which is to the east of Budapest on the great Hungarian Plain. After being promoted to the rank of station-master, Frigyes was posted to Galánta, a town on the railway between Pozsony (Bratislava) and Budapest, and now in Czechoslovakia. It was here that Zoltán attended primary school and, as he said later, spent the best seven years of his life. To what extent he came into contact with folk music at this time is difficult to assess, since gypsy music was regarded as folk music, especially in towns. All the same, it is probable that the boy heard something of the local folk music as well, particularly from his colleagues at school, and certainly it is significant that he returned to Galánta for his first folksong collecting expedition.

In 1892 Frigyes Kodály was transferred to Nagyszombat in north-western Hungary (now Trnava in Czechoslovakia). Here Zoltán attended grammar school, showing an exceptional capacity for languages, and at the same time he started studying music outside school hours. He began with the piano, but then changed to the violin and viola in order to play in the school orchestra. Next he took up the cello, mastering its technique with the aid of an instruction book. He also began to study scores, including Bach's *Well-tempered Clavier*, and his earliest compositions, none of which has come down to us, date from this time. When he was fourteen he wrote an overture for the school orchestra, performed in February 1898. The event was noted in a Pozsony newspaper, with the comment that the piece revealed a dynamic talent. At the time Kodály had not even heard a professional orchestra.

While Kodály's parents did everything possible to encourage his love of music, they had no intention of allowing him to take it up on a professional basis. He was given a choice between law and schoolmastering, and decided on the latter. When, at the turn of the century, Kodály went to Budapest, he chose as his university subjects Hungarian and German language and literature. At the same time he entered the Academy of Music, where he studied composition under János Koessler, a distinguished teacher whose pupils included Dohnányi, Bartók, and Weiner. Like Janáček at the Organ School in Prague, Kodály was also given the opportunity of beginning his course from the second year, but he chose instead to start at the beginning. After four years, in each of which he came first in the examinations, Kodály was awarded his Diploma in Composition and a traveling scholarship which took him to Berlin; but he was still not satisfied and returned to the Academy for a refresher course while he completed his degree at the University. He then continued this side of his education at the Eötvös College for outstanding students, where he perfected his knowledge of English, French and German, and also took up the music of language as a specialist subject.

• Kodály and Bartók •

His formal education completed, Kodály took a room across the Danube in Buda, and there made his momentous decision to explore the folk music of Hungary. Before doing so he composed the *Adagio* for violin and piano, the earliest of his well-known works. In that it is devoid of Hungarian characteristics, this work is thoroughly untypical, but it achieved enormous popularity, for a long time remaining the most frequently performed of Kodály's compositions. Kodály once commented that, had he continued in this vein, life would have been very much easier for him.

It was in 1905, the year that the Adagio was composed, that Kodály and Bartók met and became friends. Theirs was to become one of the most productive partnerships between composers. It was not limited to folksong collecting and editing; each was stimulated by the other in his effort to produce a genuinely Hungarian music to replace the late Romantic type of composition that had hitherto flourished in the country. They met at the house of Mrs Emma Sándor, an intelligent woman of exceptional sensitivity in artistic matters. She had a talent for composition, and many of her pieces were performed. In fact, she composed one of the variations in the finale of Kodály's First String Quartet. But in the summer of 1905 Kodály revisited Galánta, collecting about a hundred and fifty folksongs, after which he was joined by Bartók in his researches. Later the pair were assisted by Emma Sándor herself. Little did they realize the vastness of the task they had set themselves, for genuine Hungarian folk music was virtually unknown outside small villages or places where the Hungarian population formed a majority. It soon became evident that a lifetime's work faced them.

Early in 1906 Kodály's *Nyári Este* (Summer Evening) for orchestra was performed. It was dedicated to Arturo Toscanini, without whose encouragement, the composer said, it would not have been completed. There is little evidence of the influence of Hungarian folk music on this work, which we know today in its revised version of 1930. Later in 1906 came the second folk music expedition, after which Kodály visited Paris and came into contact for the first time with the music of Debussy. This was a revelation to him, and he immediately recommended that Bartók study it. Debussy's influence on both composers was strong and lasting, and one of Kodály's next compositions bore the title 'Méditation sur un motif de Claude Debussy.' In the meantime Kodály had returned to the Academy, this time as a professor.

Not until 1909 did Kodály complete his first truly major work, the First String Quartet. The craftsmanship is masterly, but the content could never have existed without the explorations into folk music. In 1910 came the Sonata for cello and piano, an equally outstanding work, while other compositions of this period include the sets of *Piano Pieces* and several songs. However, none of these works was offered performance; Bartók's compositions, too, had been denied a hearing. Accordingly, the two composers decided to organize a pair of concerts devoted to their own works. The pianist was to be Bartók himself, but Kodály did not regard himself as sufficiently proficient on the cello to participate, and, anyway, a string quartet was needed. To the rescue came four students, only one of whom – the cellist Jenö Kerpely – was out of his teens. They threw themselves into their task with enthusiasm and without thought of reward, holding nearly a hundred rehearsals. Thus the First String Quartets of both Kodály and Bartók received their first performances, and the young players began their route to international fame as the Hungarian Quartet.

In Budapest the two concerts were noted but created little interest. There were some who were impressed, but most of the professional critics were shocked, particularly by Kodály's pieces. The most notable of the favorable reviews came from the composer and critic Béla Reinitz, who later was to play an important role in the careers of both composers. He prophesied that the time would come when Kodály would be numbered among the most illustrious Hungarians – today the dates of the concerts – 17 and 19 March – are set aside to celebrate the twin birthdays of modern Hungarian music. The year 1910 was also memorable for Kodály for a very different reason. That year he married Emma Sándor, his senior by many years.

• War and politics •

Although the compositions of Kodály and Bartók made almost no headway in their own country, they attracted attention abroad. In particular, Kodály's First String Quartet was widely performed during the years immediately preceding the First World War, while shortly afterwards there were performances in America. The collecting of folksongs also went ahead on an expanding scale, and a vast treasure was discovered in the Székely villages of Transylvania; by 1912 some three thousand songs had been noted down. Clearly it was time to publish the results of these labors, but in Budapest this project was turned down.

Kodály had composed little since 1910, but with his other activities, particularly the collecting of folksongs, restricted by the outbreak of war, he took up his pen once more. After further vocal compositions came the finest of

Below: Kodály in Switzerland, 1914.

Bottom: Kodály with Béla Bartók in 1908.

his instrumental works to date. They include the Duo for violin and cello, the Sonata for unaccompanied cello, and the Second String Quartet, a far more concentrated work than its predecessor. Of these, the Sonata is the most striking – nothing of comparable importance had been composed for the solo cello since the sonatas of Bach, and Kodály's is permeated with the spirit of Hungarian folk music. Indeed there are times when the impression of a full folk ensemble is given. To realize his intention Kodály adopted the old device of *scordatura*, or abnormal tuning. While the upper strings of the cello remain at their usual pitch, the two bottom ones are both lowered by a semitone. This opens up an entirely different range of harmonic possibilities. It also makes the piece very difficult for anyone trying to get to know it at the piano, since some notes have to be transposed while others remain at the written pitch.

In the field of chamber music Kodály achieved great distinction with a limited number of works. He was to write only one more important composition in this category – the *Serenade* for two violins and viola. This work, another masterpiece, was completed early in 1920, but before then there was to be an important, though short-lived, turn of events in Hungary, for the end of the war was followed by a period of Communist rule, during which musical administration was placed in the hands of Béla Reinitz. He called on Dohnányi, Kodály and Bartók as his advisers, appointing the first as the Academy's director, and the second as its deputy director. Kodály naturally saw this as an opportunity to bring in his own ideas on musical education, but in summer 1919 the régime was overthrown and capitalism was restored. Not only were Kodály's efforts at the Academy in vain, but he found himself at the center of a witch-hunt.

Reinitz went into voluntary exile, and Dohnányi, who had been abroad when the new arrangements were made, was exonerated, but Kodály was suspended, pending an inquiry into his conduct. Characteristically, Bartók, who was not called upon to explain his actions, made an official protest, pointing out that he was as much responsible as Kodály for the steps that had been taken. The accusations made against Kodály were ludicrous, one of them being that he had used a rubber stamp on documents instead of appending his own signature. It became all too obvious that the matter was being used as a means of paying off old scores. Eventually, and after repeated suspensions from duty at the Academy, Kodály was cleared, but all the same he was reduced in rank.

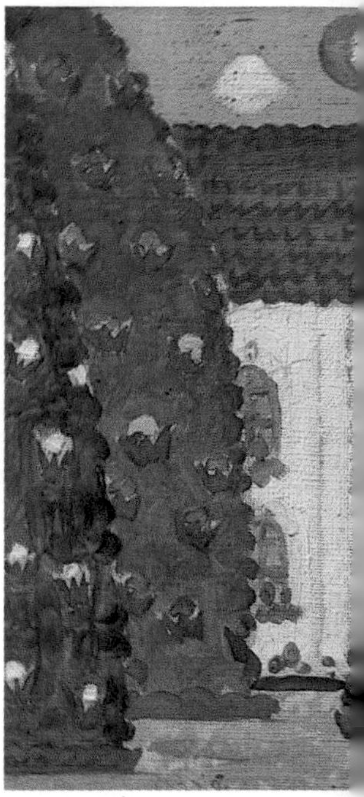

Above: Set design by Gustav Olah for the first performance of *Háry János*. This scene (which forms the second movement of the orchestral suite) is set in the courtyard of the imperial palace in Vienna. As Janós cannot distinguish between a courtyard and a farmyard, the Empress is seen feeding the livestock, which includes a double-headed eagle.

Left: János Kmetty's painting of the town of Kecskemét, where Kodály was born.

• *Psalmus Hungaricus* •

In 1923 the fiftieth anniversary of Budapest was to be celebrated – until 1873 there had been the three towns of Buda, Pest and Óbuda – and Dohnányi, Bartók and Kodály were all commissioned to write celebratory works. Dohnányi produced an overture incorporating the national anthem, while Bartók wrote his *Dance Suite*. Kodály had planned to use dances himself, but changed his mind on learning of Bartók's work. He chose instead to set a text by the sixteenth-century Hungarian poet Mihály Kecskeméti (Michael of Kecskemét). That the poet hailed from his own birthplace probably had little to do with Kodály's choice, but he was certainly much drawn to the poem, which is a paraphrase of Psalm 55 with additional commentary. Much of it mirrored Kodály's personal feelings at the time. For instance: 'I could have borne so sore an affliction, were it an enemy that had reproached me . . . but it was thou, my friend, whom I trusted. Thou art the man who would have struck me down.' In his *Psalmus Hungaricus* for tenor soloist, chorus and orchestra, Kodály makes his final reply to the charges made against him, particularly that of unpatriotic conduct. Moreover, the performance on 19 November 1923 was an unqualified success; at long last the voices of disapproval were silenced, if only temporarily.

In the course of preparing the *Psalmus*, Kodály had discovered the Budapest chorus to be sadly depleted in numbers, and he decided to incorporate a short chorus of children's voices from a Budapest boys' school. He was so stimulated by the results that he began to be specially concerned with children, who, to quote his own words, 'had been growing up in conditions of an utter musical corruption that is worse than illiteracy.' This situation he set out to remedy. He began by writing two choruses for the boys' school, *Villö* (The Straw Guy) and *Túrót*

Eszik a Cigány (See the Gypsies), and the highly successful performance of these works proved his point that it was not enthusiasm but suitable material that was lacking. So began the very large series of compositions of folksong settings for children's voices, soon to be extended to choral groups of male, female and mixed voices.

•Dramas and dances•

Psalmus Hungaricus was quick to win acclaim abroad. In the late 1920s Kodály conducted it in Amsterdam, London and at the Three Choirs Festival at Gloucester. Meanwhile *Háry Janós* had been completed and performed. Although often called an opera, this is more a play with music – a *Singspiel*, in fact. The hero, Janós (John) Háry, as we would call him (in Hungary the given name comes after the family name), is an elderly peasant who delights in telling stories about his youth, when as a Hussar he fought against and defeated Napoleon's invading armies. As a storyteller he is an artist, for his imagination knows no bounds, at least so far as his own deeds are concerned. But when it comes to the settings of his tales this same imagination is very limited. Thus the Emperor's court in Vienna differs little from the best room in the village. The preposterous humor of the stage action is brilliantly matched by a score consisting partly of original music and partly of folksong settings. Theatrical performances outside Hungary are rare, but the orchestral suite has long since become firmly established in the concert-hall repertory. Another work, the *Theater Overture* published in 1927, was originally intended to serve as the prelude to *Háry Janós*.

Even before completing *Háry Janós*, Kodály was working on another piece for the stage,

Above: Poster advertising the first performance of *Háry János* in Budapest in 1926. Kodaly also produced a six-movement orchestral suite from the music, and this had its first performance in Barcelona on 24 March 1927, another boost to Kodály's already well-established international reputation.

although it was not finished until 1932. Its English title, *The Spinning-Room*, is an inadequate translation of the Hungarian *Székely Fonó*, since it omits the all-important point that the setting is a Székely village. Kodály's purpose was to give some of the folksongs discovered there as natural a setting as possible; he himself said that such music loses much of its meaning when performed out of context in a concert hall. Twenty-seven songs, the majority choral, are contained within a single act divided into seven scenes. No use is made of recitative, which the composer said would have been a violation of the work's style. Consequently, the musical items, all with their original texts, are linked by passages of speech. The plot, such as it is, serves merely to give continuity to the sequence of folksong settings.

The work Kodály put aside in 1923 in favor of Bartók's *Dance Suite* came to fruition in 1927 as *Dances of Marosszék*, initially for solo piano. The orchestral version appeared three years later, although the two were conceived simultaneously. *Dances of Galánta*, one of the composer's most widely performed works, was written to celebrate the eightieth anniversary of the Budapest Philharmonic Society in 1933. It forms a companion piece to *Dances of Marosszék*, but the earlier composition is based on genuine Transylvanian folk material, while the later one derives from a volume of gypsy tunes published at the beginning of the nineteenth century. At that period and earlier it was customary for the military to hold festive evenings of feasting, drinking and dancing in villages, the idea being to give young lads a starry-eyed impression of army life, and so persuade them to enlist. The music played by the gypsy ensembles on these occasions was known as *Verbunkos* (Recruiting dances), and for a very long time it passed as the true folk music of Hungary. Kodály and Bartók were to prove otherwise, yet neither, unlike some of their more fanatical followers, scorned this *Verbunkos* music. On the contrary, both made occasional use of it, or of its idiom, in their own works, as in the 'Intermezzo' from Kodály's *Háry János*.

• Later works •

The *Budavári Te Deum*, the next major work after *Dances of Galánta*, was written to celebrate the two hundred and fiftieth anniversary of the recovery of Buda Castle from the Turks. This large-scale setting of the traditional Latin text for soloists, chorus and orchestra continues to some extent in the vein of *Psalmus Hungaricus*. The debt to Hungarian folk music remains unmistakable, but at the same time the work with its fugal sections testifies to Kodály's great interest in the music of earlier periods, the Baroque in particular. Appropriately, the first performance, which took place in September 1936, was given in Budapest Cathedral. Two months later Adrian Boult conducted it in London, and the following year it was included in the Three Choirs Festival. The year 1937 also saw the publication of Kodály's very important book *Hungarian Folk Music*.

Among the many small pieces written during the late 1930s was 'The Peacock,' a setting for male voices of an old Hungarian folksong, but using a new and politically powerful text by the poet Enre Ady. When the Concertgebouw Orchestra of Amsterdam commissioned Kodály to write a work celebrating its fiftieth anniversary in 1939, he returned to 'The Peacock,' using the tune as the basis of his *Variations on a Hungarian Folksong*. With good reason, this is widely considered the greatest of Kodály's orchestral compositions. On a large scale, it consists of a substantial introduction followed by sixteen variations and a finale that incorporates a new theme, albeit one related to the original melody. In the opening bars the tune of 'The Peacock' is heard in simplified form. Not until the closing stage of the introduction does it appear in full on the oboe, by which time it is clothed in a fairly elaborate contrapuntal texture. In addition to the very high level of invention, there is a masterly use of orchestral color.

Above: Poster advertising the first performance of Kodály's *Seven easy children's choruses* published in 1936. The musical education of children was one of Kodály's prime concerns, and in later life he organized a series of schools where music was given special emphasis. Children were taught to sing music at sight, to write out in musical notation tunes played or sung to them, and from memory alone to transpose into different keys.

At almost the same time as the commission from Holland came another from the Chicago Symphony Orchestra for a work with which to celebrate its Golden Jubilee Season. The result was the *Concerto for Orchestra*, smaller and very different from the *Variations on a Hungarian Folksong*. The *Concerto*, which is in a single movement, may be said to develop the baroque tendencies that characterize the *Budavári Te Deum*, while in both mood and construction it has much in common with the old *concerto grosso*, in which small groups of instruments are contrasted against a full ensemble. Folk idioms play a smaller role here than in most of the composer's work, although their influence is still detectable. The *Concerto for Orchestra* is less typical than the composer's other mature orchestral works, and perhaps for this reason it has not maintained a similar place in repertory.

Unlike Bartók, who saw no reason to remain in Hungary and so emigrated to America, Kodály spent the years of the Second World War in Budapest. During the siege of that city not even the air-raids could at first keep him from going about his business, but eventually he and his wife were forced to take refuge in a convent, afterwards moving to the air-raid shelter under the opera house. It was in a cloakroom in this building that his *Missa Brevis* had its first performance. Conceived in 1942 for solo organ, it was rewritten two years later for a solo sextet, chorus and orchestra or organ. The solo group includes three sopranos, two of whom have fairly small roles and may be drawn from the chorus. The trio sections for these three high voices are among the most effective in the work, which is not as short as its title might imply. In addition to the usual sections of the Mass (including the Credo, which is often omitted in a Missa Brevis), there is an introductory Introit leading into the Kyrie as well as an 'Ite missa est.' The construction of the work is on symphonic lines, with material from the first half reappearing in reverse order during the second.

The *Missa Brevis*, so far as is known, is the last of Kodály's masterpieces on a grand scale. With the arrival of peace, the composer set about rebuilding the musical life of his country. He became president of the Musicians' Union, chairman of the board of directors of the Academy of Music, a member of the Academy of Sciences, and he was even chosen by the National Assembly to sit in Parliament. Education of the youth of Hungary remained his major concern, and soon he had organized a number of special schools throughout the country at which music was given equal priority with general subjects.

Kodály also made many trips abroad in order to conduct and give lectures. No wonder major works virtually ceased, although the flow of small choral pieces and educational compositions continued. He did, however, write a third stage work, *Czinka Panna*, to a libretto by Béla Balázs, who long before had supplied the text of Bartók's opera, *Bluebeard's Castle*. Mystery surrounds *Czinka Panna*, which has remained unpublished even though it entered the repertory of the Budapest Opera in March 1948. It was withdrawn after only two performances – and even these were incomplete – the reason given being that there were historic distortions in the libretto. Another unpublished work about which very little is known is *At the Martyrs' Grave*, for chorus and orchestra, Kodály's tribute to the victims of the war.

In November 1958 Kodály lost his wife, Emma. It was her wish that he should quickly remarry, and it has even been said that she chose her successor. Whether or not this was so, Kodály married Sarolta Peczely, a student at the Academy, late in 1959. Emma's junior by approximately eighty years, she was to be of great assistance to the elderly composer, enabling him to continue with his activities both at home and abroad. Two years later, in 1961, the musical world was surprised by the announcement that Kodály had completed the symphony he was known to have planned many years before.

Dedicated to the memory of Toscanini, the Symphony was first performed under Ferenc Fricsay at Lucerne in August 1961, but although it was praised at the time, it has not held its place in the repertory to anything like the same extent as the composer's other major works. It is a typical product, with its roots firmly based in folk music, but somewhat lacking in vitality; perhaps its protracted birth may have been the cause. After its completion Kodály continued as before, composing more choral and educational pieces. He had just planned a further trip abroad when he died suddenly in Budapest on 6 March 1967. He had been active until the end.

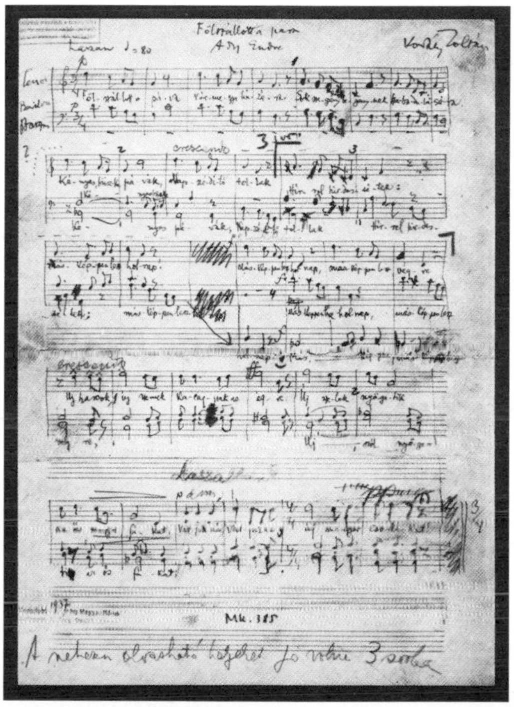

Far left: Kodály conducting, photographed by Auerbach. The composer visited England in 1960 to receive an honorary degree in music from Oxford, where he conducted his *Te Deum*, performed by the Merton College Kodály Choir.

Left: Autograph score of the first page of 'The Peacock,' dated 1937, a setting for male-voice choir of an old Hungarian folksong with new words by the poet Enre Ady.

Below: Scene from *The Spinning-Room*, Kodály's second operatic work, which makes extensive use of folksongs, linked by speech rather than recitative. It was first performed in Budapest on 24 April 1932.

sainte Cécile
max ernst / 23

MEANING AND FUNCTION IN TWENTIETH-CENTURY MUSIC

WILFRID MELLERS

Opposite: Saint Cecilia, the traditional patron saint of music, by Max Ernst, 1923.

There is today a widespread belief that music – and the civilization of which music is a part – has reached some kind of crisis. We live, we say, in an age of transition; and while every age is a transition from one era to another, at some times we are more aware than at others not only of the pace of, but also of the necessity for, change. The awareness of crisis is not, in music as in anything else, peculiar to our own times; we may point as parallels to the end of the fourteenth or the beginning of the seventeenth century, and we can learn something from considering in what ways our crisis resembles, and in what ways it differs from, these earlier crises. There are, however, reasons for believing that the crisis in our own time is more acute than similar ones in Europe's past, if only because our inability to deal psychologically with so much physical change in so short a time may lead to our extinction. As heirs to the European Renaissance we find that man's conscious awareness of his power and glory is inevitably complemented by an awareness of his frailty and pathos. Post-Renaissance man is, in Sir John Davies's words, 'a proud and yet a wretched thing.'

Our problems are of comparatively recent date and are mostly of our own making. In so-called primitive societies there are no doubts about the 'meaning' and function of art for the simple reason that art, in our sense of the word, was and is an irrelevant concept; creative activity is identified with living. When Eskimo children blow into empty tubs used by their parents for the storage of whale-oil, thereby creating a fascinating interplay of sonorities, they are not merely indulging in a giggly game, but are carrying out a procedure of deep ritual significance. Recognizing their part in the ultimate mystery of Being itself, they effect, through their rhythmically patterned inhalation and exhalation, a tribute that pays back to God the breath of life. All the time God is inspiring animate nature with its vital force – such is the literal meaning of the word *inspiration*. The Eskimos' ritual game ensures that God will not be left disastrously breath*less*. The African Bushmen who live in the Kalahari Desert create a (to us) weird music by emulating the twitters and chitters of birds, the grunts and grizzles of beasts; in becoming, in sound and movement, their totemic creatures they employ disguise and illusion in a propitiatory act, conquering fear of the unknown by making a gesture of reverence to the beings on whom they rely for subsistence. The music they make is an aural complement to the visual masks they may wear; in being metamorphosed, aurally, visually and corporeally, into Nature they acquire some of the attributes of divinity. Similarly, the Australian Aborigine, in the emptiness of the Outback, uses magical, pre-articulate syllables to invoke natural phenomena – the sun, moon, cloud or water – on which minimal existence depends. The magic vocables, chanted against the 'everlasting' drone of the dijiridu and accompanied by the metrical clicking of sticks, dramatize the basic fact of life: the beating of the pulse, the thudding of the heart. As for many more sophisticated peoples, music is not a gracious adornment of the surface of life which those who are lucky may have as a bonus. On the contrary, life depends on it, for without music the sun might cease to promote fecundity, the moon to control the tides. Without bread, some people might starve; without music, the world itself might come to a stop. So, as the Zuni Indians put it, 'We sing and dance for the good of the City'; and the magical properties of art cannot be separated from its more mundane functions as succor in labor and solace in play. Some African tribes use their drums to converse and to convey messages over immense distances; praise and dispraise songs serve some of the functions of gossip and the popular press. Everyone makes music for worship and for work or play; and although some may acquire greater skills than others and be honored for them, they are 'makers' who act for the good of the community rather than for personal reward.

If we turn to our European heritage, it would seem that even in the relatively sophisticated societies of medieval Europe the situation was not radically different. The professional composer scarcely existed; musicians were supported by the Church to fulfill what was considered a basic human need, and most composers were also clerics. Secular composers were usually amateur and often, like the troubadours, aristocratic. Common people also made music for love or work or play or magic. They lived by music in a spiritual, not material, sense, though expert performers, especially of dance music, were sometimes rewarded for special services to the community.

It is in the wake of the Renaissance, with the establishment of a humanistic rather than – or

Right: Two musical instruments used by the Australian Aborigines: the dijiridu, a drone pipe made from the hollowed-out branch of a tree, and two sticks that are rhythmically clicked together to provide accompaniment for traditional Aborigine dances.

Opposite: African drummers in Chad, North Africa, while taking part in a funeral dance, demonstrate their native drums, crucial to the ritualistic tribal dances typical of most African countries even today. The sophisticated complexity of rhythm that is achieved with the most simple of means is quite unknown in traditional Western music.

as well as – a religious ethic, that the notion of art in our modern sense takes root. As social groups grew larger and more amorphous, it was evident that humanist values must inevitably imply what we now call democracy. The question as to what 'works' of art are 'for,' and who is responsible for them, grows complicated. It might be the State, the public world which needs artifacts first to define and then to bolster its values; it might be a highly trained minority of individuals capable both of creating and of 'appreciating' these artifacts. The common nineteenth-century belief was in a division between the artist as Solitary Heart in a world increasingly inimical, and the purveyor of aural commodities for the delectation of *hoi polloi*. 'Artists' are concerned with the relationship between time and value; 'entertainers' while away time that is valueless. In simpler terms the split had been manifest as early as the mid-eighteenth century. For instance we have record of a performance in 1742 of Handel's exquisite *Acis and Galatea* – a beautiful and subtle work which nonetheless does not demand extreme concentration from its audience – wherein Mrs Arne obliged with intermittent songs, 'accompanied on the Violin by Mr Arne, who will introduce Comic Interludes, intended to give Relief to that Grave Attention necessary to be kept up in Serious Performances.' We can hardly be surprised that Hawkins, in his preface to the second edition of Boyce's *Cathedral Music*, points out that 'composers who are to live by the favour of the Public have two styles of composition, the one for their own private delight, the other for the Gratification of the many.'

In 1787 Dr Burney, grand panjandrum of eighteenth-century music and arbiter of taste, defined music as 'an Innocent Luxury, unnecessary indeed to our existence, but a great Improvement and Gratification of the Sense of Hearing.' How appalling that definition would have seemed to Beethoven, who believed that his music could affect human destiny; or to Bach, for whom music was 'an harmonious euphony for the glory of God and the instruction of my neighbor.' For that matter how incomprehensible it would have seemed to the 'savages' discussed at the beginning of this essay.

It may seem naïve, in the light of our current sophistications, to speak thus crudely of a divorce between art and entertainment; nonetheless our ambivalences and ambiguities are related to that fundamental split in that they spring from our doubts about belief. There have been many hazardous moments in the history of music: the twilight of the Middle Ages, when the Gothic motet resorted to desperate strategies of mathematical ingenuity in an attempt to hold together foundering values; the shift from the traditional vocal polyphony of the Renaissance to the incipiently operatic style of the Monteverdian madrigal when, at the beginning of the seventeenth century, the modern world was being born; the change of gear from the man-imposed unities of the High Baroque to the revolutionary dualities (speaking both politically and musically) of the sonata principle of the Classical age. Yet, being derived from the stable values of the past, change was feasible because it could be seen to be necessary, if not overtly logical; whereas the technological revolutions of the past half-century have so undermined values that we no longer know what we believe in, nor even what we would like to believe in.

• Diversity •

Our confusion is reflected in the fact that today so many diverse activities are covered by a single word. Confining our attention for the moment merely to 'art' music, we can see that 'music' in our society may mean plainchant, Machaut, Byrd, Handel, Wagner, Debussy, Stravinsky, Webern, Cage, Berio or Stockhausen, since the work of all these and many more composers is intermittently performed. Some of them incarnate the values of pasts which are still present since they were, in Ezra Pound's phrase, 'news that *stays* news.' Others presumably reflect values from our volatile present. Yet what conclusions could we come to about that present on the evidence of the music? Some of the music created in the second and third decades of the twentieth century seems as desperately fragmented and as precariously controlled by mathematical law as the Gothic motet at the end of the Middle Ages; one thinks of the music of Webern. Yet at precisely the same date music was also being created which seems stably rooted in traditional modal techniques found in rural and agrarian communities, bolstered by religious, usually Christian, faith; one thinks of much of the music of Vaughan Williams.

Left: For Eskimos, the drum had a more specific function than the mere production of rhythmic effect; the traditional method for Eskimos to settle arguments was to try and outsing each other – accompanied by drumming – in front of the whole village. Each Eskimo would have his own personal song, believing it endowed with spiritual powers personal to himself. The Eskimos of North-west Greenland, where this photograph was taken in 1980, are aware of their unusual tradition and recently went on a tour of Denmark and Europe.

Above: Performance of *Jeita* by François Bayle, in the Jeita cave in Lebanon, probably in the autumn of 1969, when Stockhausen was also giving a series of concerts there. Music in the open air has become a recognized feature today, ranging from pop festivals through jazz to conscious attempts to make use of the advantages of natural surroundings in musical terms. Bayle is here concerned with causing the listener to relate pure synthetic sound to natural sound when the two are juxtaposed – to respond to the motion and vibration of energy in the Universe.

Twenty years later there were composers such as Shostakovich and Rubbra for whom the notion of the symphony as a thematic and tonal evolution towards a consummated end was still stimulating, though at the same time to composers such as Boulez and Berio symphonic form was moribund and irrelevant. We cannot say that to open-eared (and open-minded) listeners the one kind of music – Webern's or Vaughan Williams's, Shostakovich's or Boulez's – convinces more or less than the other. Degrees of conviction depend on talent and ability rather than on the acceptance of one program or another. In some sense all these kinds of music must be 'right' because they are validated by the experience of some twentieth-century listeners.

• Fusion •

Such catholicity acquires deeper significance in the context of the ultimate fusion which jells from the confusion of the genres. Much of the art music of our time derives from our self-conscious obsession with 'head' and intellect. In the various types of serial music practiced by

Schoenberg, Berg, Webern, Boulez, Babbitt and Stockhausen optimism may have soured, but a fanatical confidence in solutions survives: *this* is the way to make music, we are told, given the world we live in and the assumptions we live by; or at least it ought to be if only more people wanted to listen to it.

Contemporary with all these types of 'head' music have been kinds of music which assert the primacy of the body rather than the intellect; which *go on*, overriding nervous twitch and cerebral stasis. Black and white jazz and white and black rock and pop are of course not unaffected by the more conscious contrivances of art music; indeed in its brief history jazz has encapsulated evolutionary processes which in art music have covered several centuries, as is evident if one reflects on the sequence of, say, Willie Johnson as primitive bluesman, Jimmy Yancey as barrelhouse boogie pianist, Louis Armstrong as improvising New Orleans trumpeter, Duke Ellington as sophisticated New York bandsman, and the heroes of modern jazz, such as Charlie Parker, Thelonious Monk, Miles Davis, Cecil Taylor, Ornette Coleman and Keith Jarret as re-creators and transmuters of all those past traditions. Pop musicians have in an even briefer span of time veered from variously rewarding forms of escape (Bing Crosby, Frank Sinatra, Sarah Vaughan) to disparate types of youth ritual (the Beatles, the Rolling Stones, Pink Floyd), to individualized sexual aggression (Elvis Presley), to protest, personal confession and reaffirmation (Bob Dylan, Joni Mitchell, Randy Newman, David Bowie). Nor are the publics for these widely assorted types of music, or even the techniques employed within them, mutually exclusive. As the obvious barriers between age-groups and classes are whittled down, so consanguinities between avant-garde art music, 'progressive' pop and 'free' jazz cannot be gainsaid, whether we consider them irrefutable or irremediable. The racks in record shops reflect this confusion; the works of a David Bedford, a Terry Riley, a Philip Glass, or even Stockhausen himself, may be found on both sides of the art/pop fence.

Certainly, the career of Stockhausen, who has claims to be considered the most central if not necessarily the 'greatest' living composer, bears significantly on this creative synthesis. He started as one of the 'headiest' of modern composers: an heir to Webern who employed electrophonic techniques to ensure a totality of serialization too complex to be embraced by the human mind unaided. The communication of the 'work' of art seemed to be exhausted, along with the modern ego that had created it. Some kind of a return to *Homo ludens* and to the life of instinct was unavoidable; and this is what we find in much of Stockhausen's later work, some of which relies, without resource to notated sounds, purely on the response of performers to verbal directives. In particular *Stimmung* – in this case a piece which is notated, if unconventionally – calls for more detailed comment as a testament of our time.

Above: Stockhausen directing an outdoor performance of his work *Inori*. The open air has advantages in the performance of some electronic music. Certain modern pieces are so complex logistically that there are problems of space and, on occasion, acoustics, when these are confined to the concert hall.

Left: Stockhausen conducting the first performance of *Sirius* at the outdoor festival at Aix-en-Provence, 1977.

Below: Interest and research into the nature of sound, harmony, pitch and timbre, has led composers to create their own musical instruments. Here Lou Harrison and William Colvig demonstrate a droning drum, one of the instruments they have built. Harrison's extremely varied career has not deflected his interest or research into relative pitch. His early studies with Schoenberg and the implied acceptance of 'equal temperament' have given way to a belief in just intonation, following his intense studies of music of Oriental cultures in Tokyo, Taiwan and Korea.

• *Stimmung* •

The title may be translated as 'tuning,' and in technical terms that is precisely what happens. Six human voices tune themselves to the pure harmonic series or musical spectrum, the voice of Nature herself, and are assisted to do so by an almost inaudible but perfect overtone series on tape. The return to acoustical basics is interesting, for Schoenbergian chromatic serialism had been feasible only on the basis of equal temperament. If each semitone is equal to the other, none can be precisely in tune with Nature, whose truth Stockhausen would reveal. That he uses electrophonic tape to help him and us defines the difference between him and the authentic shaman of some primitive tribe. Stockhausen as shaman is a musician–scientist–priest who offers a helping hand or ear to fallible mortals, thereby admitting to their imperfection.

The technical and physical process of tuning is thus also a metaphysical process whereby the individual becomes part of the cosmos – like those Eskimos and Kalahari Bushmen referred

Right: John Cage's 'Prepared Piano.' Much of Cage's music is percussive in effect and his 'prepared piano' reflects this. Various objects inserted between the strings alter the nature of the sound produced from one of pitch to one that is primarily of impact. The pitch of a prepared piano is often unexpected and unpredictable, and in Cage's terms becomes secondary to the importance of the rhythmic possibilities of the instrument.

to earlier, and despite or because of the terrifying complexity of electronic industrialism. Moreover, this simultaneously scientific and magical act turns out to be social as well as religious, for tuning to the universe is complemented by a process whereby the separate voices tune to one another in rhythm, dynamic and timbre as well as pitch, this communion between human creatures being effected by the invocation of eleven magic names and by way of the vowels of the phonetic alphabet, which overrides articulate, localized speech. Once a magic name has been called by a singer at will, it is repeated until 'renewed identity is achieved.' The process is strictly comparable with the naming ceremonies among primitive peoples and today's children; with the invoking of the 'sensual speech' through a 'music of the vowels,' as practiced by some Amerindians; with the tuning ceremonies of Tibetan monks; and even with the transformations of medieval alchemy, which sought renewal from the Sacred Stone. This is not so much a composition in the Western sense as a ritual experience. The recorded performance lasts seventy-five minutes and could theoretically go on for ever, as could Japanese Buddhist or Tibetan chant. The last five minutes take us full circle, emulating the Eskimos in handing back to God the expiration of breath.

The significance of *Stimmung* and of Stockhausen's work in general may be that it reveals that modern science and ancient magic are far from being the opposite poles that rational Enlightenment had supposed them to be. *Stimmung* releases us from chronometric time, from Locke's 'common measure of duration,' not merely by reinstating the mythological time within which primitive peoples live, but also by giving musical meaning to modern theories of space-time and relativity, to cosmological and astronomical time, and above all to those biological clocks that we now know to function, independently of chronometers, within the human subconscious, and apparently within the senses of beasts, birds, insects and even plants.

So, if *Stimmung* is magic, it is magic that stems from the heart of our scientific technocracy and suggests relationships with the non-Western musics of our increasingly global village that may prove valid rather than evasory. Should this be so we might consider *Stimmung* – and other comparable works such as *Trans*, *Sirius* and the vast mythological, science-fictional opera-sequence to which Stockhausen expects to devote the rest of his life – as authentic heirs to the progressively dedogmatized passions of Western man, as represented in particular by Bach, Beethoven and Wagner; and we might even come to believe that Stockhausen has transcended the 'failure' of Wagner's disciple Schoenberg who, in *Moses und Aron*, created an opera about the artist as prophet and priest, but left it unfinished because he came to the conviction that music, given its sensual nature, must inevitably betray the Word within the word. The last line of the text that Schoenberg

Far left: Harry Partch with the 'Bamboo Marimba' which he invented and built himself. He was a largely self-taught musician, whose research into natural pitch led him to invent his own tuning system, rejecting European values, and to compose for his own instruments, of which he invented and constructed a considerable number, mainly idiophones and chordophones. He only allowed his compositions to be played by his own group of musicians, the 'Gate 5 Ensemble,' and wrote much of his music for theatrical performance.

Above left: This instrument, comprising a cycle wheel used in conjunction with a drum, was created by Peter Maxwell Davies to take part in his music for Ken Russell's film *The Devils*, 1971. Subsequently the music was performed as a *Concert Suite* for instrumental ensemble and soprano *obbligato*.

set is 'O Word, O Word that I lack.' If Stockhausen has found that Word, that will not make his intrinsic musical achievement greater than that of Schoenberg, let alone Wagner, Beethoven and Bach. It might, however, mean that his estimate of himself as the most crucially significant composer of our time will be justified.

•Americans•

Stockhausen offers, from the heart of Europe, perhaps the most radical reassessment of our 'human predicament.' Yet the universal inclusiveness implicit in his work had been manifest considerably earlier in the music of some composers of the New World who, precisely because America *was* new, could see the shape of things to come more clearly than could Europeans, blinkered by their multifarious past. Even a profoundly Beethovenian, Faustian humanist like Charles Ives, living in the polyglot society of the United States, could find a partial resolution of sonata conflict in what he called 'an oriental contemplation and forsaking of works.' His 'Concord' Sonata generates, in his marvelous phrase, 'a kind of furious calm.' At once pragmatically empirical and mystical, it is preoccupied with personal struggle and growth while at the same time democratically 'accepting the universe,' the tawdry and the trivial along with the tragic and the sublime, the babel of the streets and the inchoate noises of the natural world along with Beethoven's Fifth Symphony. The sonata principle is remade in Ives's many-stranded, polymodal, polymetrical heterophony, whereby melodic lines (*phoni* or voices) are thrown together heterogeneously. The democratic inclusiveness of Ives's musical technique bears directly on his status as artist: he refused to sell his works as commodities, and made his (substantial) living in the insurance business, which he genuinely regarded as an amelioration of the human condition. Such an achievement, in a world 'distracted from distraction by distraction,' may justifiably be called noble.

Hardly less impressive is the achievement of Edgard Varèse, in this case an exiled European who made his home in New York and created sound structures complementary to the aural environment of an American industrial city. Interestingly enough, Varèse compared his compositional processes both to the arcane procedures of alchemy and to the mechanics of rock and crystal formation. Ives's career was in part frustrated by misunderstanding and neglect, Varèse's by the fact that his approach to composition, even in the first two decades of the century, anticipated techniques which were to be fully realizable only with the development of electrophonics. Though Varèse had a fanatical if small coterie of disciples, he completed few works. The time was not yet ripe, though the authority and power of those works remains unanswerable.

Varèse represents a radically different approach to composition, which is at once new and very old. One could say the same of that senior West-Coast radical Harry Partch, in whose work we find a comparable rejection of 'Europe' and of industrial technocracy in favor of the clown-saints of Japanese Kabuki, the metrical complexities of Polynesian, Asiatic and African percussion and the purity of monophonic just intonation. According to Partch, equally tempered Western music, having been based on an acoustical lie, must inevitably tend to corruption. His major work, *Delusion of the Fury*, concerns the disintegration of the West and the possibility of revival through a synthesis of disparate worlds, American, African, Polynesian, Asiatic – and European too, of course, since Europe is where most Americans came from. Cage's early prepared piano music attempts something similar, technically, psychologically

and philosophically; and if his later 'happenings' carry the non-principles of American Zen to a point at which the baby is thrown out with the bath-water, we can appreciate their logic in a global context.

At a more superficial level a minor composer like Henry Cowell became consciously involved in an attempt to create a world music, employing ethnic, non-Western techniques along with his Western heritage. Brought up in the Midwestern farming country, he played folk fiddle as a boy and was early familiar with primitively indigenous American hymnody. At the same time he acquired expertise on many exotic instruments during his peregrinations around the world, rightly believing that only by way of practical experience could aural and oral cultures be relevant to our literacy. We must mention, too, that fine Californian composer Lou Harrison, who graduated from Stravinskian neoclassicism and Schoenbergian serialism to the sundry serialisms of pitch and meter typical of oriental monody, and from tempered to just intonation. He, too, has deepened and modified his compositional skills by practical experience of building and playing what we might think of as exotic instruments.

Both composition and performance are thus not esoteric, but a philosophical as well as a musical statement. When, in the *Suite for symphonic strings*, Harrison fuses traditional Renaissance polyphony with the melodic principles of liturgical monody both Western and Eastern; or when, in his *Concerto for violin and percussion*, he mates sophisticated chromaticism with folk-like modal monody and quasi-oriental polymeters, he is making an imaginative statement about the nature of harmonious life. In more recent works, such as the *Rondo Pacifico*, Harrison makes testaments explicitly social and philosophical, and even overtly political: for here the dedication to monophony and just intonation is an approach to universal peace and understanding – a common language at a deeper level than Esperanto, though Harrison embraces that cause also.

It is significant that these veerings from the West are not, in the States, a recent phenomenon. Ives, Varèse, Partch and Cowell were regarded as Grand Old American Eccentrics, wild men who were in fact younger in heart than most men twenty or thirty years their junior. Conlon Nancarrow is another pioneering backwoodsman who throughout a longish life has produced music conceived exclusively for the player piano. Like Varèse, though without actually calling on electrophonic aid, he created an electrifying pre-electric music, which in this case combines the corporeal immediacy of barrelhouse boogie with the abstractions of higher mathematics, as readily calculable on his pianola rolls as on graph paper. We could not hope for a more startling synthesis of the body's immediacy with the head's intellectual contrivance; he might be called the first cybernetic composer in that his music involves 'systems of control and communication in animals and machines.'

Not surprisingly, Nancarrow, after years of neglect, has become something of a cult figure, at the same time as other very old, orientally and astrologically biased expatriates such as Dane Rudhyar and Leo Ornstein have been enthusiastically rediscovered.

• Process music •

All these composers are concerned with process rather than progress. During the 1960s and 1970s Process Music became a genre in a more specialized sense, associated in its most distinguished form with Steve Reich. His work stands at the opposite pole to Webern's post-European fragmentation, precariously and exiguously held together by mathematical law. Whatever one thinks of Reich's music, it is neither fragmented nor discontinuous, though the fact that it *goes on* does not mean it achieves, or even seeks, a return to Bach's physiologically integrated wholeness. Reich says that 'a performance for us' – and each piece is conceived for and executed by his group – 'is a situation where all the musicians including myself attempt to set aside our individual thoughts and feelings of the moment, and try to focus our minds and bodies on the realization of one continuous musical process . . . The momentary state of mind of the performers while playing is largely determined by the ongoing composed slowly changing music.' Reich is inviting us to exist in the musical activity while it happens, to have no identity apart from it; both rhythm and tonal centers are revived 'in the process of people singing and playing instruments.' Such a conception of living in the musical moment is profoundly African. This is not conditioned by the fact that for a time Reich lived and studied on the African continent; he rather chose to live there because his musical-philosophical interests are what they are.

There is, strictly speaking, a 'world' of difference between the members of an African tribe engaging in such activity because it is part of social and religious commitments on which they have been nurtured, and a group of Western musicians doing it because they are disillusioned with their own traditions, religious, social and musical. Still, the proof of the pudding is in the hearing; if the music works, it is because the performers' dedication is beyond the range of what Reich calls 'the old exoticism trip.' The new-old music becomes the seed of a new-old way of life – as Varèse's music had been, with less physiological immediacy. In Reich's *Drumming and Music for Eighteen Instruments*, the infinitely slow exfoliation of metrical patterns and basic, usually pentatonic, melodic formulae, in their tingling orchestration of xylophones, marimbas, pianos and electric organs, powerfully enhances, rather than engulfs, consciousness. As with Chopi xylophone ensembles or Balinese gamelan, nerves and senses are activated as one becomes part of

Opposite top: Bob Dylan at the open-air Blackbushe Concert, 1977. Dylan's unique style derives ultimately from a synthesis of folk-song, blues and rock.

Opposite bottom: The Beatles at the EMI Abbey Road studio in 1967. Almost legendary in their fame and popularity, this Liverpool group first made a name for themselves in the early sixties with pop music deriving largely from American rhythm and blues and rock 'n roll. Their music developed to reflect an interest in jazz, electronics, Far Eastern and Indian music.

Left: Steve Reich at the Salle Favart, Paris, 25 September 1980. His particular interest concerns the possibilities inherent in multiplying instrumental sound using live and recorded versions of the same piece of music or the same instrument. He has also been considerably influenced by ethnic African music.

Above: The eminent Indian musician Ravi Shankar, playing the sitar. In the background on the left is Yehudi Menuhin playing the violin. The two met to give a joint performance for the United Nations Human Rights Day concert. Ravi Shankar has now won acclaim, not just for his superb sitar-playing but also for his efforts at integrating Eastern culture with Western through his concert tours. Yehudi Menuhin has done much for the same cause, as well as mixing musical idioms by performing with the jazz violinist Stephane Grappelli. Both musicians see improvisation as a key element of musical performance.

Above: David Bedford conducting. Bedford is an English composer with an interest in working with amateur performers, children and pop musicians. In order to do this he uses a simplified method of notation, and his music is easily comprehensible and simple in form and style, though his instrumentation is often unconventional.

a process beyond the ego, yet triggered off by human intelligence. When we are in the presence of these highly disciplined performers we share in the stimulation which the intricacy of the unfolding pattern gives them. There is no improvisation; yet subservience to process proves liberating, even jolly, and this is worth being grateful for, when so much of today's art querulously laments.

It would seem that commitment and skill are of the esssence; and this is relevant too to the tribal pop music of young people, to which Steve Reich's process music forms an intellectual's complement. The ubiquity of the phenomenon, at many different levels, should make us pause before we dismiss even the brashest manifestation of pop anti-culture. If we look at the world around us – or more probably obtain a kaleidoscopic glimpse of it by pressing a button on the television – we are made inescapably aware that modern technology, for all the blessings it has showered on us, has much to answer for. We see beautiful black Africans surrendering their natural grace of bodily movement as, lined up like crazy automata, they goose-step Nazi-wise in a parade of armored dinosaurs, enjoying – heaven help them and still more us – the 'benefits' of Western siphylization, to use Joyce's all-too-apposite pun. We hear politicians on all sides mouthing their platitudes while millions die of starvation which the cost of one useless neutron bomb could alleviate; we cringe at the contemplation of human crassness to which even the genius of Dean Swift would have been satirically inadequate.

Is it to be wondered that the rebellious young have banded themselves into singing and dancing 'groups' or tribes, at first designated merely as pre-human Birds, Animals, Beatles or Monkees, but now more cataclysmically as Boom Town Rats, the Clash, the Enemy, the Stranglers, and even (ultimate irony) the Police. Turning the tables, the young in their various kinds of tribal pop have used industrial technology against the very world that made it, seeking to obliterate 'consciousness,' that starry crown of Western achievement. Their music could not exist but for the mechanical apparatus made possible only by the world they affect to despise. Yet their contempt is not baseless, and their mistrust, if not contempt, was – as we have seen – anticipated not merely by old artists of the New World but also, as much as seventy years back, by Europeans such as Stravinsky and Bartók, Picasso and Modigliani, who discovered in 'primitive' arts values relevant to our humanity, but forgotten, to our cost.

Looking back, we cannot but remark on the durability of jazz. Why did the music of a black, alienated, persecuted, dispossessed race, transmuted in a white technocracy, speak so potently over more than a hundred years to people over the whole of the so-called civilized world? It must have been because we recognized in this music buried aspects of ourselves: aspects which reasserted the primacy of the body in a world grown heady on its intellect; aspects which were prepared to accept the violence of dispossession in a society wherein material possessions had become the be-all and end-all of aspiration.

•The future•

Up to the nineteenth century, or even later, almost all the music performed in a given community was contemporary. Yet for the past fifty or sixty years, perhaps for most of this century, contemporary music has formed only a tiny proportion of the music performed in the concert repertory, while at the same time our musical diet has engulfed a gradually widening spectrum of the music of Europe's past. Today,

Right: Terry Riley at a concert in Paris, 21 July 1982. Riley is another musician whose work spans different cultures: he pursues his own identity outside the mainstream of American contemporary music, landing almost on the pop side of the musical fence, but absorbing exotic influences, particularly from Japan and Indonesia, along the way.

with the advance of radio and recording, passively educated musical people are expected to have some acquaintance with the music of six hundred years of European history. But this, though a tall order, is by no means the end, for we now travel through space almost as easily as through time, and in our global villages achieve contact with, if no more than defective understanding of, the music of an astonishing diversity of cultures. Our sound-museum is world-wide, whizzing us from the frozen wastes of Alaska to the fecundities of the Amazonian jungle, as well as tantalizing us with echoes of the great Oriental cultures of India, China, Asia and Japan, not to mention the still vigorous folk music of Europe.

Although such promiscuity is disturbing, it has also its creatively positive aspects. As ethnic musics of heterogeneous natures and cultures meld and jell in our global village, so improvisation re-enters 'art' music, and 'serious' composers once more look for active participation as well as passive response. It is no longer merely a matter of I (the Artist) here and Them (the public) over there. The barriers are broken down not only between art and entertainment, but also between private artists and public communities; between the various genres of artistic creation, professional and amateur, élitist and popular.

To this there are economic and, indirectly, political consequences, for in our complex mechanistic society everything is commodity-based and everything costs a great deal of money. But since the computer will one day, perhaps quite soon, make working for our living an anachronism, we shall ultimately have to face the problem of how to fill the deserts of our leisure. There can be no answer except creative activity of one kind or another. So all we can know of the future of music is that amateur, professional and commercial interests will have to be more vigorously integrated than they have been over the past hundred years. To all three fields commitment and skill are relevant concepts, and we must deprecate any too glib distinctions between Art and Commerce. Schoenberg and Gershwin were both composers of genius who had nothing in common except talent in and commitment to the different, even opposed, worlds in which they operated – apart from the fact that they were both Jewish and, in Hollywood, improbably, played table-tennis together. It is comforting to reflect that the Beatles and Bob Dylan, still the pop artists most unequivocally endowed with genius, were also among the most materially successful; and although few 'serious' composers as good as Strauss and Britten emulate them in becoming millionaires, none is in danger of starvation.

Our problem, confronted as we are by so many and such contradictory possibilities, is not musical but philosophical. Although our world, exacerbated by temporary upheavals, may baffle and frighten us, this is not all loss, since fear also excites, and we teeter between hazard and hope. Paradoxically, technology not only offers opportunities for complete metamorphoses in human potential; it also presents us with unwontedly efficient means of preserving the past on disk, computer and audio-visual tape. This gives us a chance to keep our options open, and so safeguards us from despair on the one hand, and from an inanely euphoric reliance on our technical expertise on the other. As long as we keep our ears, hearts and minds open, in that order, we have a fair chance of recognizing that the Beatles are 'better than' the Monkees, just as Duke Ellington's band was 'better than' Paul Whiteman's, Beethoven better than Hummel, Bach than Telemann. We come back to the fact that in the long run it is a question of belief, not of moral choice. We must value what is truly alive, the more so because our plastic-electric age has produced in 'muzak' a phenomenon which inverts music's human essence in that it is meant to be *not listened to*. The mind boggles at the mind-bending of which we are capable in thus deliberately fostering amnesia. We are left reflecting that although all music is in a sense propaganda, propaganda for life is better than propaganda for death. Let us keep our ears open as we wait to hear whether the future will bring unimaginable marvels, submission to computerized routine, or total annihilation. It is true that while there is life there is hope. That is why it is important that we should recognize life when musically we hear it, and should foster the committed and the skillful in whatever genre they may operate.

It has been attempted here to define the 'landscape' of the contemporary musical scene, and to uncover the impulses that shape it. This seems the more important because these volumes are concerned not with the total landscape but only with the heritage of art music. This is in itself a daunting enough assignment; nonetheless, our perspectives will be distorted if we ignore the context within which that heritage has been manifest. If there is substance in what is said here, it would seem that such segregation will not be possible much longer. The interaction of the genres should strengthen rather than weaken our great Western tradition.

Above: A rehearsal of music theater by the Argentinian composer Mauricio Kagel in the Cloître St Louis at the Aix-en-Provence Festival, July 1981. The surreal quality of this picture is echoed in some of Kagel's works; his interest in exploring a considerable and unexpected range of sound possibilities leads to music of a diverse and sometimes bizarre nature, which has on occasion annoyed the critics. Kagel is a founder-member of the Cologne Ensemble for New Music, established to perform contemporary works, his own among them. He also conducts his own music.

The Growth of Jazz

The years following the First World War are known as the Jazz Age, and during that time jazz took both America and Europe by storm. It had grown out of ragtime and the soulful – but also violent and erotic – blues of the American Blacks combined with the White American tradition of brass-band playing, and it flourished and developed in a number of centers, notably New Orleans and Chicago. Thanks, at first, to recordings, then to live performances and tours, the impact of jazz on the main development of Western 'classical' music was strong, not only on American composers such as Copland, but also in Berlin (Weill, Hindemith) and, particularly, in Paris (on Satie, Stravinsky, Ravel and many others), while it remained nevertheless a quite separate tradition with its own dynamic of development.

Above: The Original Dixieland Jazz Band was formed in Chicago in 1916 of White jazz musicians from New Orleans. A year later they moved to New York, where they scored a huge success with their version of the New Orleans style. It was through the O.D.J.B. that the word 'jazz' became known all over the world.

Right: Jack Laine's Reliance Band in 1910. This was one of many White brass bands playing in the early years of the century.

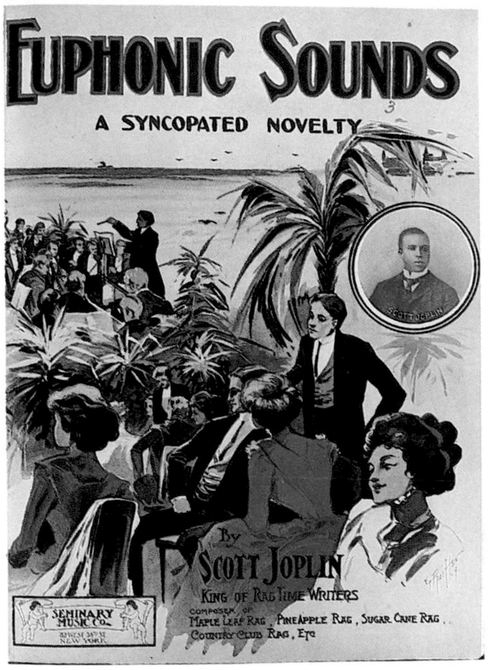

Above and right: Music-covers of two of Scott Joplin's rags. Ragtime influenced jazz, but there is a clear difference: rags were composed, while jazz is improvised. The essence of ragtime, which flourished at the turn of the century, was the clash between the straightforward rhythm of the bass and the internally syncopated melodic line above it.

Below: 'King' Oliver's Creole Jazz Band in Chicago. Oliver (1885-1938), a cornet player, came to Chicago from New Orleans in 1918 and started this band in 1922.

Left: One of the classic recordings of 1923-4 by 'King' Oliver's Creole Jazz Band. Oliver founded his first band in 1920 and was joined in 1922 by Louis Armstrong, who stayed with him until 1924. Oliver, who gave Armstrong his first cornet, remained his lifelong idol, though they adopted widely differing styles of cornet playing, Oliver matching a clipped melodic line to a four-square rhythmic beat, while Armstrong produced a flowing melodic line with increasing rhythmic irregularity against the underlying pulse.

Right: Jazz Hot No.1 by the Cubist artist Kupka (1935). The Cubist and Futurist painters adopted the idea of jazz, both for its strong rhythm and for its flouting of all the conventions.

Above: Rag-Time Parade, a suite of pieces from Erik Satie's 'realist ballet' *Parade*, premièred in 1917. Although jazz was not performed in Paris until the following year, Satie clearly understood its underlying mood – 'it shouts its sorrows' – and rhythms from jazz and ragtime, as well as themes from the popular music-halls, are built into the score of *Parade*, an example followed by many composers.

Right: Scene from *Prodigal Son (In Ragtime)*, a recent work performed by the London Festival Ballet to Scott Joplin's music. The rediscovery of Joplin (1868-1917) in recent years has revealed a musician whose dearest aim was to break into the conventional musical world. The 'King of Ragtime's' most famous piece, 'Maple Leaf Rag,' appeared in 1899, but by the time of his death he had completed two ragtime operas, both lost, and was working on a symphony in ragtime.

Right: Jelly Roll Morton (1885-1941). Morton was for many years an itinerant musician, based on New Orleans, before settling in Los Angeles and, finally, Chicago, where he made his first recordings in 1923. In his work with bands such as the Red Hot Peppers (with whom he recorded in 1926-7) he emerged as the first real composer of jazz: he himself shaped the improvisations of the players in their solo 'breaks,' creating a more complex polyphony that alternated and contrasted with the homophonic 'choruses.'

Above: Django Reinhardt (1910-53, second from right), the outstanding European jazz musician in the 1920s, with the Hot Club de France.

Below: Bix Beiderbecke (1903-31). Beiderbecke was a cornet player based in Chicago, one of the first White jazz musicians to win the wholehearted admiration of Black performers – for the warmth of his unique timbre and his introspective manner in such classics as 'Singin' the Blues,' 1927. He was also a self-taught pianist and composer.

Above: The Marable Band on a riverboat, including Fate Marable (piano), Johnny St Cyr (banjo) and Louis Armstrong (cornet).

Above: Fletcher Henderson (1898-1952). One of the best known band-leaders and arrangers of the 1920s, Henderson was influential through recordings, his appearances at the Roseland Ballroom in New York, and his work with soloists such as Armstrong.

Below: One of the Mississippi riverboats, which were cradles of jazz during its formative years.

Above: Louis 'Satchmo' Armstrong (1900-71). The lyrical sound of Armstrong's trumpet playing and his gravelly-voiced singing emerged from a classic jazz background. Born in New Orleans, he played with Marable on the riverboats, with Oliver in Chicago and with Henderson in New York. It was with the big bands in the twenties that he developed his own virtuoso solo style – in which first short bursts, then whole phrases seem to contradict and disrupt the underlying jazz beat, only to return and merge with it again.

Right: Playbill for Armstrong's London appearance on his first European tour in 1932. Armstrong, who four years earlier had turned from the cornet to the trumpet, had already made numerous recordings, and now his magnetic personality drew him into show business. He appeared in almost fifty films, but continued to tour with his All Stars throughout the post-war years.

Left: The O.D.J.B. (led by the cornetist Nick La Rocca, center) in London on their first English tour in 1919. Even more than their recordings, it was the presence of American bands in Europe after World War I that ushered in the Jazz Age.

Right: Scene from the film version of George Gershwin's opera *Porgy and Bess.* Gershwin (1898-1937), who was a brilliant pianist and songwriter, blended elements of jazz, popular songs and classical orchestral textures in a number of more ambitious works, including *Rhapsody in Blue*, 1924, commissioned by the bandleader Paul Whiteman who was then pursuing the ideal of symphonic jazz, *An American in Paris* and his Piano Concerto, both in 1925, and the Negro opera *Porgy and Bess*, 1935 (the film dates from 1959). Gershwin was one of those rare musicians to cross over from popular to 'classical' music, and his admirers included Schoenberg and Ravel, although the integration of jazz and popular music is one of the typical features of American music.

Above: Duke Ellington (1899-1974). Born in Washington, D.C., where his father was a waiter at the White House, Ellington had none of the archetypal formative experiences of a jazz musician like Armstrong. His big success came in his years (1927-32) at the Cotton Club in Harlem, when he recorded an astonishing number of original compositions.

Right: Ellington at the piano. Ellington's significance lies in his composition far more than his playing; he developed Morton's integration of solos and ensembles, while learning from Henderson the art of preserving the sense of improvisation within written scores. He always had his individual players in mind and was able to create a great variety of textures and timbres, notably in his 'jungle style' of the 1920s and 30s.

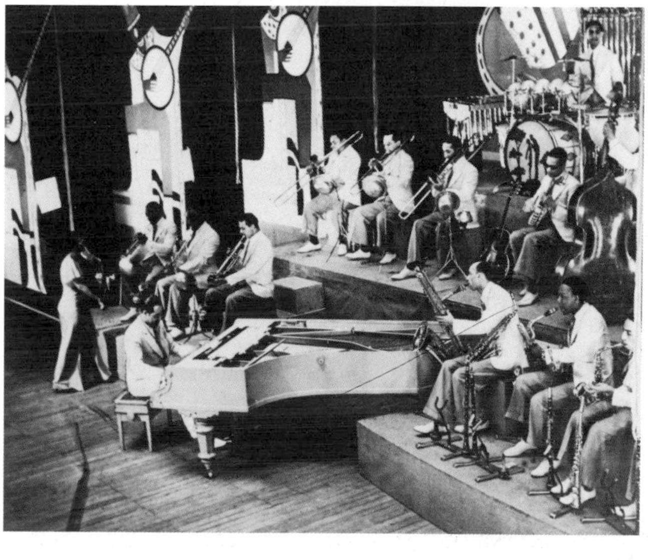

Igor Stravinsky. 1914
Albert Gleizes

IGOR STRAVINSKY

RICHARD ORTON

Opposite: Portrait of Stravinsky by Albert Gleizes, the Cubist painter, 1914. Cubism, beginning around 1908, with its denial of conventional perspective and its determination to present three-dimensionality in a totally new context, was throwing tradition to the wind, and Stravinsky was to follow suit with *The Rite of Spring* in 1913. He was friendly with the Cubist group as a whole and was generally in favor of their aims, but was not enamored of this particular painting, which he described as 'portrait of a nose.'

Igor Stravinsky was born at Oranienbaum in Russia on 17 June 1882. His father, Fyodor Ignatyevich (1843-1902) was a famous singer at the Maryinsky Theater in St Petersburg and was held in high regard both for the quality of his bass voice and for his powerful dramatic presence. Success in the world of music, however, did not persuade Stravinsky's father that this would make the best career for his son, and he insisted that the boy study law. This Igor did, though without a great deal of enthusiasm, and he gained a diploma in law in 1905.

In fact he had already made up his mind what he wanted to do, and he now sought the professional advice of Rimsky-Korsakov, director of the Conservatory, and studied with him for the next three years. He had already composed a Piano Sonata (1903-4) before becoming a regular pupil of Rimsky-Korsakov, and then in 1905-6 he set a text by Pushkin, 'The Faun and the Shepherdess,' for voice and piano, which became his op.2. Two further songs were written the following year, but it is true to say that Stravinsky only began to develop his own musical personality with his *Scherzo fantastique* of 1908, and even more so with *Feu d'artifice* (Fireworks) of the same year.

When the impresario Serge Diaghilev came to organize his second Parisian ballet season for his Ballets Russes, he remembered the brilliant orchestration of *Fireworks*, which he had heard at the Ziloti Concerts. He commissioned a score from the young Stravinsky, *L'Oiseau de feu* (The Firebird), and with its première in 1910 Stravinsky became famous overnight. *Petrushka* received its première in Paris the following year; musically and artistically it explored a very different world from that of *The Firebird.* At the same time, Stravinsky continued to explore vocal music. He had begun the opera *Le Rossignol* (The Nightingale) in 1909, setting it aside when he received the commission for *The Firebird*, but in 1910 he set two poems by Verlaine for voice and piano, which he subsequently orchestrated.

However, the world was jolted into taking note of Stravinsky by a musical event that foreshadowed the confusion, raw energies and cataclysmic devastation of the First World War: the première of his *Le Sacre du printemps* (The Rite of Spring) by the Ballets Russes at the Théâtre des Champs-Elysées in Paris on 29 May 1913. Diaghilev, who had again commissioned the work, had evidently sensed some months before that the powerful rhythms, the constrained melodies, multiple chord formations and yet brilliant instrumentation might overstrain the tolerance even of a curious but passionate Parisian public, and in the event the audience broke out into derisive laughter from the very first measures of the prelude, with its high, straining bassoon melody. Uproar developed as demonstrations and counter-demonstrations ensued. The dancers could not hear their cues, and Nijinsky, the choreographer, shouted out numbers above the pandemonium, trying to keep them in order, while Diaghilev ordered the electricians to flash the house-lights on and off, hoping to quell the disturbance. Stravinsky's ritual of the awakening energies of spring, culminating in a sacrificial dance, had become a harbinger of the tumult of war.

It would be absurd to imagine that *The Rite of Spring* came into being without careful preparation on Stravinsky's part. Yet several circumstances point to the extraordinary spontaneity, energy and uniqueness of this work. First, the origin of the ballet was a sudden, fleeting vision that came to Stravinsky while he was preoccupied with the composition of *The Firebird.* The image of a ring of elders, sages of a pagan tribe, watching a young girl dance herself to death as a propitiatory sacrifice to the God of Spring deeply impressed itself on Stravinsky and maintained its intensity until the work was finished three years later. Second, the act of writing the score demanded more of him than he was at first able to achieve. For some time, while he was able to play the final section on the piano, he did not know how to write it down. Third, analysis of the score indicates many features which simply could not have been predicted even from a thorough knowledge of the composer's earlier work. Much later, Stravinsky referred to himself as 'the vessel through which *Le Sacre* passed.' He evidently felt there had been a psychic urgency for this work to be composed. Rarely, if ever again, do we find Stravinsky responding so directly to inner impulse.

It was Stravinsky's practice to compose at the piano, and the manual source of some of his inspirations may be traced. He wrote that 'it is a thousand times better to compose in direct contact with the physical medium of sound than to work in the abstract medium produced by one's imagination.' The first section of *The Rite* on which he worked was 'Les Augures printaniers – danses des adolescentes' (Signs of Spring – Dances of the Young Girls). This is the infamous section, following the introduction, which so provoked that first audience. The heavy, sharply etched string chords, although regular, are punctuated with highly irregular accents reinforced by the addition of eight French horns. The harmony consists of juxtaposing a dominant seventh chord on E flat and a major triad chord on E (spelled F flat in the score), and it comes as no surprise that the spacing of these chords lies naturally under the fingers at the piano keyboard. Alert ears will notice the melodic unfolding of these chords in this and the succeeding dance, the 'Jeu du rapt' (Game of Abduction).

From 'Les Augures printaniers' Stravinsky composed to the end of the first part, called 'Adoration of the Earth,' before turning his attention to the Introduction. This prelude he later regarded as the best music in the whole piece. It represents the gradual reawakening of nature at the beginning of a new year's cycle, the 'scratching, gnawing, wriggling of birds and beasts,' and it is demonstrably the richest section in its musical material. It contains the greatest number of melody types, from the repeated single-note figure, through sub-pentatonic, pentatonic and diatonic melodies, to various types of fully chromatic melody. It contains a very wide range of multiples and subdivisions of the beat. Its tempo ranges from a flexible *lento, tempo rubato* to a rigidly metrical *più mosso*. Its texture ranges from the single instrument (as in the opening bassoon solo), through

Right: Fyodor Ignatyevich Stravinsky, Igor's father, playing the part of Maka Gomenko in Rimsky-Korsakov's opera *May Night*. Stravinsky's father was an opera singer with a noted bass voice, who worked first in Kiev and later in St Petersburg, at the Maryinsky Theater. Although keen for the young Stravinsky to study law, he also encouraged him to pursue his musical studies, arranging for him to start piano lessons when he was nine years old, and taking him to the opera and ballet from his earliest youth.

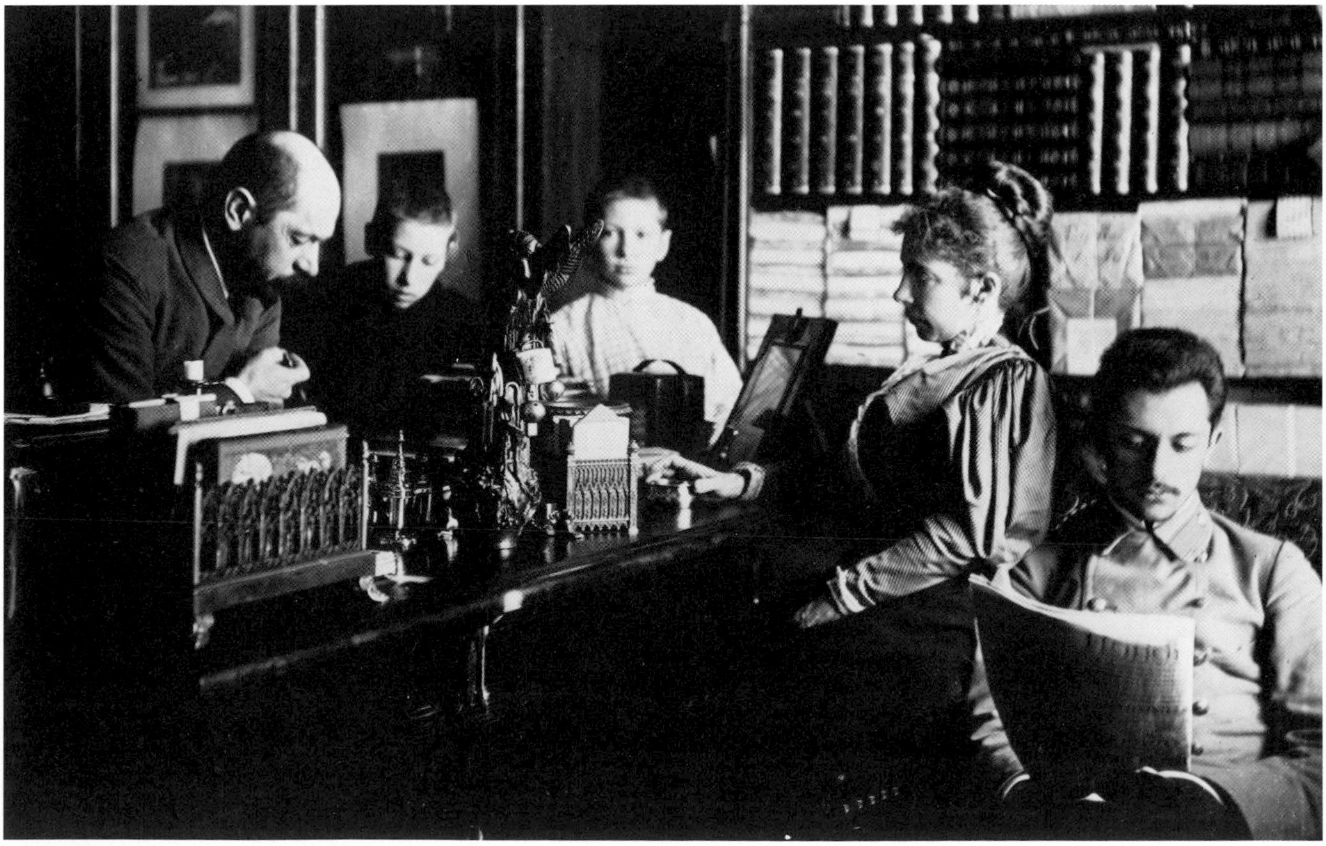

Below: Stravinsky in his father's library, next to his father, with his brothers Guri and Roman and his mother. Guri, the youngest, was also musical and was Igor's favorite brother, but was killed in action on the Rumanian front in 1917.

Left: Stravinsky as a student, probably around the turn of the century. On the wall behind him are pictures of various composers, among them his early hero Beethoven.

combinations of several instruments, to multiple layers of the full orchestra. Its instrumentation is brilliant, achieving a perfect backdrop to the more restricted colors but incisive rhythms of 'Les Augures printaniers,' which follows.

The sketchbook for *The Rite* offers some extraordinary examples of Stravinsky's mode of composition. Ideas leap out from the page; many tiny blocks of notation are gradually combined into more extended musical continuities. In one place he labels the blocks A, B, C, D, and on repetition in the score just writes the appropriate label. In another place he even pokes fun at the repetitions – 'to be continued in the next issue,' he jots down after drafting part of the 'Glorification of the Chosen One.' But these repetitions are never predictable. They do not settle into a pattern one can expect. Phrases are foreshortened or extended asymmetrically, and the meter varies accordingly. Stravinsky's difficulty with the notation of the 'Danse sacrale' was fundamentally one of finding the appropriate combination of changing meters to accommodate this rhythmic maelstrom. 'Music exists when there is rhythm, as life exists when there is a pulse,' he writes in the sketches.

Many remarkable artists were working in Paris at around the time this score was composed. Interestingly, the technical explorations of, for example, Pablo Picasso in painting, or Gertrude Stein in literature, can be understood as parallel to certain innovations in Stravinsky's work. For the viewer the central identity of pictorial space from the Renaissance to the beginning of this century was provided by perspective, still a powerful means of organizing the two-dimensional plane to represent three-dimensional space. Picasso and some of his contemporaries were denying this convention and startling their public into new perceptions. Different perspectives, different 'points of view,' were being adopted on a single canvas, a trait visible in Picasso's *Les Demoiselles d'Avignon* of 1907. In literature the comparable central identity had been provided by narrative, and in Gertrude Stein's work this sense of narrative was breaking down. In music, tonality and the sense of a 'home key' offered a point of reference comparable to perspective and narrative in the other arts; in *The Rite of Spring* we are often confronted with simultaneously different tonal implications. We are frequently pulled to reference points a semitone apart, creating a sense of conflict which, unresolved, induces a continuing tension in the listener.

In the final section of *The Rite* in particular, where the sacrificial virgin dies, there are many such divergent chord-combinations. Here, too, we notice a low irregular thudding on bass instruments and timpani, becoming more regular and insistent as the moment of death draws closer. It appears that Stravinsky associated regularity with constriction and negativity, and irregularity with nature, abundance and the forces of life. The interval of this low, insistent and inevitable pulsing is that of a minor third, and we may find further examples of Stravinsky's use of this interval as a symbol of death in later works.

•Transitional works•

However we regard *The Rite of Spring* now – as a concert piece (the role in which it has been most successful) or as a ballet notoriously difficult to choreograph; as a summing-up of the tensions of the immediate pre-war period or as a final throwing-off of Stravinsky's childhood

Above: Rimsky-Korsakov, who became Stravinsky's tutor and mentor at a critical stage of his career, when he was just beginning to find his own voice. Stravinsky became closely associated with the Korsakov family and their musical gatherings, and he spent some time each year from 1903 to about 1910 (even after his teacher's death in 1908) at their summer home at Lzy.

repressions; as the end of a musical era or as the beginning of a new one – there is no denying its power, its ability to shock and to thrill several generations. While it is true that Stravinsky came to judge few of its pages with more than indifference, it is probably correct to regard it as the most personally expressionistic of his works, and certainly it marked a turning-point in his development. The works of the following years may be regarded as transitional, moving eventually towards an esthetic position usually called 'neoclassicist.'

While returning from a visit to Russia in 1914, Stravinsky found himself stranded in Switzerland by the outbreak of the First World War, and so he remained there until the armistice. The works of this transitional period include the experimental *Three Pieces for String Quartet* of 1914, economical in material and epigrammatic in conception; *Le Renard* (The Fox), a folk-tale from Russia for four singers and chamber orchestra, including a prominent part for cimbalom, composed in 1915-16; the ballet *Les Noces* (The Wedding) and *L'Histoire du soldat* (The Soldier's Tale) for speaker and seven instruments, both of 1918. Among Stravinsky's preoccupations of this period are peasants and animals – there are songs about both as well as the folk-tale and the peasant marriage of *Les Noces* – simplicity, economy and

Opposite: Pages six and seven of the manuscript score of *The Rite of Spring*. These carefully written notes hardly seem in accord with the scandal and protest caused by the first production.

Left: Costume by Nicholas Roerich for *The Rite of Spring*, first performed at the Théâtre des Champs-Elysées, Paris, 29 May 1913.

Opposite: Costume designs by Léon Bakst for the Princess and the Firebird in Stravinsky's ballet *The Firebird*, first performed at the Paris Opéra on 25 June 1910 by the Ballets Russes with choreography by Fokine. Bakst's costume designs highlight the Russian folk element behind the fairy story of *The Firebird*.

variation, and a search for new instrumental combinations. The work that gave him the most trouble from the point of view of instrumentation was undoubtedly *Les Noces*; he wrote out at least some of the score in no fewer than four versions. From the start he had thought of this work as a cantata, and so during the writing of the sketch score had concentrated on the voices. His first attempt at a full instrumental score was for a vast orchestra of nearly a hundred and fifty players; each succeeding version whittled down the numbers and sharpened the clarity of sound until he arrived at the combination we know today, an ensemble of four pianos with pitched and unpitched percussion instruments. *Les Noces* was the most significant product of this period, and had been completely sketched during the course of 1918. It was not until 1923, however, that it was choreographed and given its première in Paris. In the interval several works had appeared, and Stravinsky had been subjected to other influences.

• Neoclassicism •

In 1919 Diaghilev met Stravinsky in Paris and persuaded him to look at a collection of manuscripts which he had brought back from Italy. These were eighteenth-century compositions by a relatively unknown Italian composer, Giovanni Battista Pergolesi. Stravinsky, rather to his surprise, fell in love with the music. Diaghilev proposed that Stravinsky should use it for a new ballet to be based on the traditional hero of the Neapolitan popular theater, Pulcinella, with the scenery and costumes to be provided by Picasso. Stravinsky agreed. He worked at first directly on the copies, adding notes foreign to the eighteenth-century harmony and sketches for instrumentation – a small orchestra omitting clarinets. In general his method was to keep the original melodies and bass lines intact, but to add notes, often by way of *ostinati*, contradicting the original phrase-structure. In addition, he would shorten phrases by elision, or lengthen them by repetition, thus creating a new asymmetrical and idiosyncratic phrase-structure. The result is more than a mere 'arrangement,' but it remains close enough to the chosen models for it to be heard and understood as a twentieth-century 'reinterpretation' of the music of the past.

The term 'neoclassicism' as applied to music was not invented by Stravinsky, but he has become the composer we most associate with the word, used to describe compositions of the present century which revive forms, harmonies, genres and textures from instrumental music of the past, particularly from the period of the seventeenth and eighteenth centuries, though Stravinsky extended his horizons far beyond these limits. There are elements of neoclassicism in works prior to *Pulcinella*; for example, the instrumental chorales of *The Soldier's Tale* are based on Lutheran, even Bachian, chorales. In this work Stravinsky also parodies less obviously 'classical' models – marches and dances, the tango, waltz and ragtime. The last owes its inclusion to an interest in jazz and ragtime initiated by his friend the conductor Ernest Ansermet, who in 1917 brought Stravinsky a collection of sheet music of various bands playing in New York. The ragtime movement in *The Soldier's Tale* was followed by *Ragtime* for cimbalom, percussion and nine instruments in 1918, and the improvisational freedom of jazz also influenced the *Piano Rag Music* and the *Three Pieces for Clarinet*, both composed in 1919. Stravinsky was to return to jazz again with the *Ebony Concerto* composed for the band of Woody Herman in 1945.

We see that *Pulcinella* confirmed Stravinsky in stylistic explorations of the musical past, whether distant in time or very recent. While it may be correct to regard the strictly 'neoclassical' phase as closing with *The Rake's Progress* in 1951, it is worth inquiring at this point why he apparently subjugated his own proven powers of original creation to musical ideas, designs and forms of the past.

This is a thorny problem, and one that has been much discussed. However, it seems not unreasonable to suggest that Stravinsky withdrew himself from conflict, from the dangerous Dionysian energies of *The Rite of Spring*, which had involved a tremendous unleashing of psychic energy. The works of the next few years were either tiny, or settings of words, thus avoiding large-scale formal problems, or were pieces concerning children, animals, or Russian peasant life – things contained within Stravinsky's past experience. It is this phase of Stravinsky's work that the critic Adorno described as a reversion to 'infantilism.' It is not until we come to the *Symphonies of Wind Instruments* of 1920 that we again encounter a relatively abstract work posing real formal problems; and by this time the adventure of neoclassicism had already begun. (Not that this work is itself particularly neoclassical: it is an ingenious patchwork of instrumental sonority-fragments with related tempi, built around a chorale composed to the memory of Claude Debussy.)

There is also no doubt that in part the economic argument for Stravinsky's change of style is a valid one. The Russian Revolution of 1917 cut off all income from his motherland, and Diaghilev stopped paying performance royalties because they could no longer be enforced in law. Stravinsky had a wife and family to support, and there were occasions when he felt desperate for a secure income. The reduced forces for *The Soldier's Tale*, just seven players for a popular theater work, is an indication of his desire to expand the market for his music. Ironically, it received only one performance at the time and was not heard again for five years. Later he began performing his own music in order to obtain higher fees. He began conducting for the first time, nervously and tentatively, with the première of the Octet for wind instruments of 1923, a lively work whose syncopated ending briefly recalls the jazz influence of *Ragtime*.

Another source of Stravinsky's neoclassicism may be his move away from Russia. He was self-exiled from 1914 on, and, as he himself said, he had nothing to go back for. His mother joined him in France in 1922, and he did not return to Russia until he was eighty years old, in 1962. We continue to find Russian themes in his music up until the opera *Mavra*, completed in 1922, but thereafter virtually nothing, apart from perhaps *The Fairy's Kiss*, the *Scherzo à la russe* and some arrangements. Might it not be that the moment of his decision to remain an exile was also the moment he decided to adopt a culture, a history of music, a tradition? Certainly from this period on, for over thirty years, he mined Western music: the medieval period in the Mass, the Cantata; the Baroque in the Octet, the 'Dumbarton Oaks' Concerto; early Classical in *Pulcinella*, parts of *The Rake's Progress*; and high Classical in the Sonata for piano and Symphony in C. Nor are there Russian echoes in the works with mixtures of diverse pastiche elements (*Oedipus Rex*, *Capriccio*) and jazz (the *Ebony Concerto*).

According to the extent to which the composer has relied on his models, neoclassicism removes the struggle to shape the material; an audience's familiarity with the models will assist an appreciation of the new work. In the music of the nineteenth century it had become the rule, in works of serious intent, that the struggle to master the materials was an audible process, heard in the weaving and transformation of themes and motives in a contrapuntal web of an evolving tonal structure. In neoclassicism this development of materials is replaced by an instantaneous distancing of the new from the old. The conflict, the struggle, has been transferred to the audience. For the composer it is a precarious position: if a new work is too close to its model there is evidently no point in recomposing it. If it is too dissimilar, then the use of a model as point of reference will have been lost. This tightrope Stravinsky trod skillfully for three decades.

It would be wrong to imagine that neoclassicism in Stravinsky is one thing. In fact it has many facets. After *Pulcinella*, he returned only once to adapting existing music for a work of

Opposite top: Program for the first performance of *The Rite of Spring*.

Opposite bottom: Stravinsky (seated) with Léonide Massine, Natalia Goncharova, Alexandre Benois and Léon Bakst.

Opposite far right: Matisse (seated) with Massine and model of a nightingale for Stravinsky's ballet *Le Chant du rossignol*, first staged at the Paris Opéra in 1920, with stage designs by Matisse and choreography by Massine. The ballet represented another collaboration with Diaghilev – though it was first written as an orchestral suite a few years earlier, and was first performed as such in Geneva on 6 December 1919.

Above: Scene from the 1920 production of *The Rite of Spring* with new choreography by Massine.

length; in *The Fairy's Kiss*, a ballet score of 1928, he used a series of lesser-known piano pieces and songs by Tchaikovsky. Here his processes of recomposition were broadly similar to those of the earlier adaptation, but the material being so different, a quite dissimilar work is created. He does bring about a unity out of diverse materials, though the music has not enjoyed the popular acclaim of *Pulcinella*. Apart from these two works, Stravinsky's neoclassicism is of a less direct kind, relying more on the reworking of elements of earlier styles – triadic and scalic melody fragments, chordal accompaniments, rhythmic patterns. These he molds into a characteristic style of his own. Above all, it is the rhythmic element in Stravinsky that remains his most recognizable feature.

Neoclassicism, too, changed with the times. We must remember that in the years immediately following the First World War a sense of relief, release and even hysteria provoked a collective tendency toward the frivolous. Neoclassicism in some of its manifestations at this time appears as a surface without depth, the glitter perhaps obscuring an inner hollowness. Some of Stravinsky's works of the 1920s share such characteristics; the Concerto for piano and wind instruments and *Capriccio* are examples. Today it is above all their wit and richness of allusion that sustain them beyond the ephemeral spirit of the times. These were both works that he wrote to perform himself, as solo pianist. The Concerto was written in 1923-4, and when Stravinsky had played it over forty times he felt he needed an alternative concert work. The *Capriccio* for piano and small orchestra was completed in 1929.

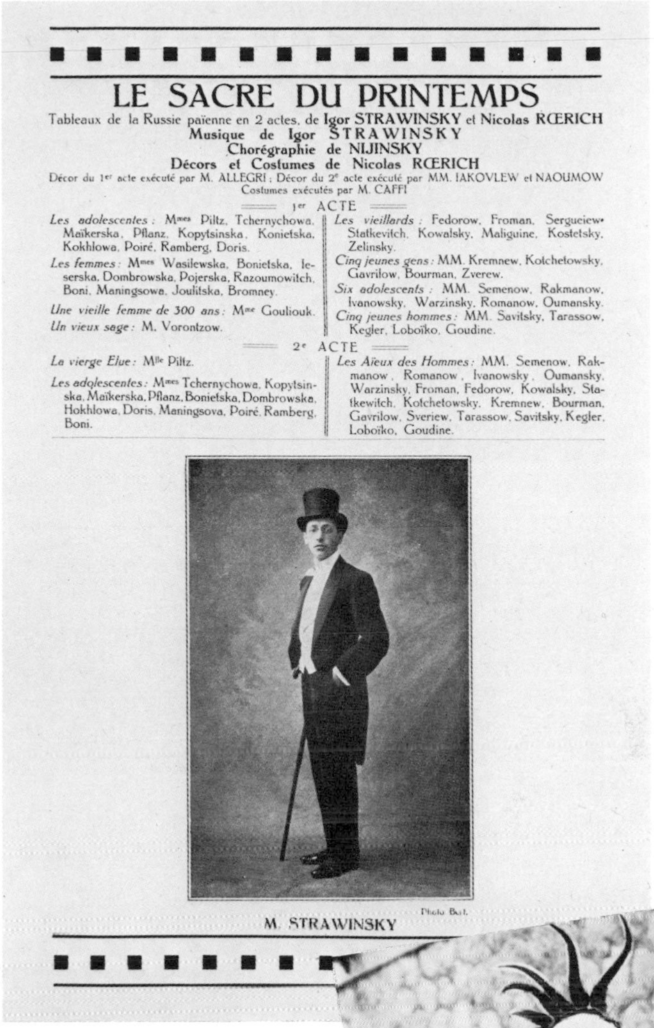
LE SACRE DU PRINTEMPS

Tableaux de la Russie païenne en 2 actes, de **Igor STRAWINSKY** et **Nicolas RŒRICH**

Musique de Igor STRAWINSKY

Chorégraphie de NIJINSKY

Décors et Costumes de Nicolas RŒRICH

Décor du 1er acte exécuté par M. ALLEGRI ; Décor du 2e acte exécuté par MM. IAKOVLEW et NAOUMOW

Costumes exécutés par M. CAFFI

1er ACTE

Les adolescentes : Mmes Piltz, Tchernychowa, Maïkerska, Pflanz, Kopytsinska, Konietska, Kokhlowa, Poiré, Ramberg, Doris.

Les femmes : Mmes Wasilewska, Bonietska, Ieserska, Dombrowska, Pojerska, Razoumowitch, Boni, Maningsowa, Joulitska, Bromney.

Une vieille femme de 300 ans : Mme Gouliouk.

Un vieux sage : M. Vorontzow.

Les vieillards : Fedorow, Froman, Sergueiew, Statkevitch, Kowalsky, Maliguine, Kostetsky, Zelinsky.

Cinq jeunes gens : MM. Kremnew, Kotchetowsky, Gavrilow, Bourman, Zverew.

Six adolescents : MM. Semenow, Rakmanow, Ivanowsky, Warzinsky, Romanow, Oumansky.

Cinq jeunes hommes : MM. Savitsky, Tarassow, Kegler, Loboïko, Goudine.

2e ACTE

La vierge Elue : Mlle Piltz.

Les adolescentes : Mmes Tchernychowa, Kopytsinska, Maïkerska, Pflanz, Bonietska, Dombrowska, Hokhlowa, Doris, Maningsova, Poiré, Ramberg, Boni.

Les Aïeux des Hommes : MM. Semenow, Rakmanow, Romanow, Ivanowsky, Oumansky, Warzinsky, Froman, Fedorow, Kowalsky, Statkewitch, Kotchetowsky, Kremnew, Bourman, Gavrilow, Sveriew, Tarassow, Savitsky, Kegler, Loboïko, Goudine.

Photo Bert.

M. STRAWINSKY

•The late 1920s•

In 1927 Stravinsky embarked on a Greek classical tragic subject, *Oedipus Rex*, a sign of a new seriousness emerging in his work at this time. This static opera, or 'opera-oratorio' as Stravinsky termed it, employed a text by Jean Cocteau, but translated from his French into Latin. In his book *Chronicles of My Life*, first published in Paris in 1935, Stravinsky justifies the use of Latin: 'The choice had the great advantage of giving me a medium not dead, but turned to stone and so monumentalized as to have become immune from all risk of vulgarization.' The main characters, Oedipus, Creon and Jocasta, should be masked, giving the impression of living statues. The male chorus should be seated, their faces concealed. These devices ensure the audience's separation from the stage action. A narrator mediates, intermittently explaining what the audience is to witness: Oedipus's tragic fate – he is married to his mother, having unknowingly killed his father; when he discovers this, he blinds himself by stabbing his eyes with his mother's golden pin.

Musically the work is a great leap forward. It is Stravinsky's longest work up until this time, nearly an hour in duration. The meters are regular, the rhythms reflecting obsession or compulsion rather than variety; great tonal areas are hewn out for symbolic treatment, flat minor keys for tragedy, sharp major keys for jubilation and annunciation. The use of register to illustrate meaning is evident in the many low, somber instrumental and vocal sonorities. The insistent minor third interval appears again as a portent of doom. And, since this is an opera, stylistically Stravinsky has turned to the operatic master he most respected – Verdi's influence can be sensed in the heroic vocal lines of Oedipus and Creon, and especially in Jocasta's aria at the beginning of Act II.

Stravinsky took great pains at this time to stress the necessity for appreciating the ob-

Above: Stage design for *Le Renard*, by Mikhail Larionov. Described as a 'burlesque in song and dance,' it was first performed at the Opéra in May 1922, though it was completed in 1915. The Russian folk element, captured in the scenery and costume design, is also evident in the music.

Opposite: Design by Alexandre Benois for the backcloth in Acts I and IV, 'the Fair,' of *Petrushka*. The première took place on 13 June 1911 in Paris and it has remained one of Stravinsky's most popular ballet scores.

Right: Design by André Bauchant for the backdrop, showing Apollo's chariot, for Stravinsky's neoclassical ballet *Apollon Musagète*. This was first produced in Washington on 27 April 1928, though Diaghilev also produced the ballet the same year in Paris, with choreography by Balanchine – with whom Stravinsky was to work frequently later in his career.

Above: Natalia Goncharova's stage set for *Les Noces*, first produced on 13 July 1923 in Paris with choreography by Bronislava Nijinska. The design reflects the fact that the work is scored for four pianos.

jectivity of musical experience, claiming that '"expression" has never been an inherent property of music,' and it is clear that his preference for the sonorities of wind instruments and piano during most of the 1920s was due to their more 'objective' quality. In a passage about the Octet of 1923 he wrote: 'Wind instruments seem to me to be more apt to render a certain rigidity of the form I had in mind than other instruments – the string instruments, for example, which are less cold and more vague. The suppleness of the string instruments can lend itself to more subtle nuances and can serve better the individual sensibility of the executant in works built on an "emotive" basis.'

This distrust of the flexibility of string instruments was evidently overcome by 1927, when he began composing *Apollon Musagète*, a ballet score using the forces of string orchestra. The Apollonian ideal of order, control and discipline led to a desire to write a *ballet blanc*, a score of the utmost restraint, to be interpreted by four classically trained dancers. Apollo is the leader of the Muses, here represented by Calliope, personifying poetry and rhythm, Polyhymnia representing mime, and Terpsichore, gesture and dance. In the first episode combining all four dancers, a *pas d'action*, Stravinsky symbolizes the intertwining of the Muses with an intricate polyphonic texture, the main theme of which appears canonically at three different speeds. As a whole, the music tends to a unified sonority rather than the succession of contrasts which usually characterizes Stravinsky's work. A passage in a lecture delivered to the University of Harvard in 1940 (later included in *The Poetics of Music*, 1947) might have been written about this ballet: 'What is important for the lucid ordering of the work – for its crystallization – is that all the Dionysian elements which set the imagination of the artists in motion and make the life-sap rise must be properly subjugated before they intoxicate us, and must finally be made to submit to the law: Apollo demands it.'

•After 1930•

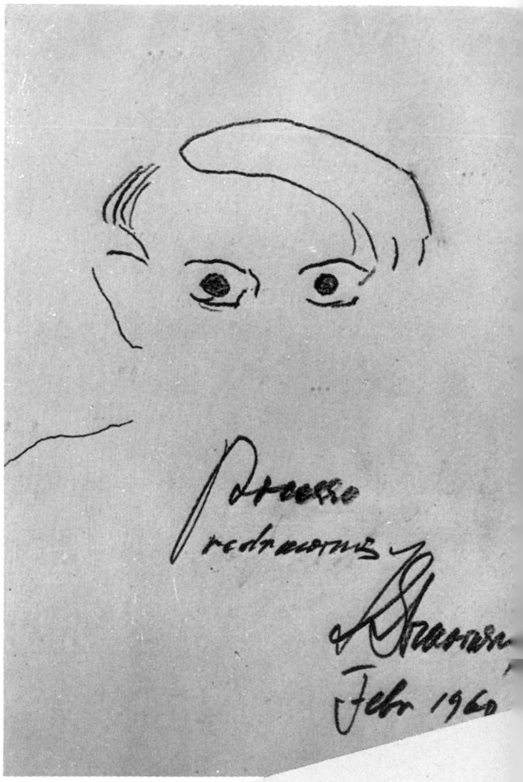

Right: Caricature drawing of Picasso by Stravinsky, remade in 1960. The original dated from 1920.

Opposite: Samuel Dushkin and Stravinsky. The composer was tremendously impressed with Dushkin as a violinist, and composed his Violin Concerto for him in 1931 and his *Duo Concertant* in 1932. They toured Europe together on several occasions, and Dushkin often performed transcriptions he had made of some of Stravinsky's orchestral and stage works.

When Koussevitzky invited Stravinsky to compose a symphonic work to celebrate the fiftieth anniversary of the Boston Symphony Orchestra in 1930, the composer wanted to write a work incorporating extensive polyphonic development without resorting to the Classical symphonic model. His solution was the *Symphony of Psalms*, for mixed chorus and orchestra adding piano and harp but omitting violins and violas. For the first two movements he chose fragments from Psalms 39 and 40, and for the third and final movement the whole of Psalm 150. As in *Oedipus Rex*, he set the text in Latin: the score states that the words should always be sung in this language. The first movement, by way of prelude, implores God's attention: 'Exaudi orationem, Domine' ('Hear my prayer, O Lord'); the second movement declares the Lord's answer ('He hath put a new song in my mouth, even praise unto our God'), and the third movement is itself the 'new song,' a song of unending praise, 'Laudate Dominum.'

The *Symphony of Psalms* continues and develops the tendency to adopt rich, somber, slow-moving sonorities, the softening effect of the chorus making up for the lack of strings. The first movement as a whole demonstrates Stravinsky's skill in molding block textures into a unity. Its tonality hovers around E minor and C major, the alto and soprano lines expressing the plea of the words in an oscillation between E and F a semitone higher. Only at the end of the movement does this melodic aspiration achieve its goal, a high exultant G over an emphatic G major chord. The second movement is a double fugue. This most severe of contrapuntal disciplines is undoubtedly Bachian in spirit, the opening C minor subject differing from Bach's mainly in the type of chromatic movement it employs. The first fugue is an instrumental one in four parts, and it is followed by a choral fugue to the words 'Espectans espectavi Dominum.' This is heard over an orchestral accompaniment which itself contains the first subject. Further interweavings of the material ensue, first the chorus alone, then the orchestra alone, before the forces are combined again for a restatement of the choral subject over a rhythmic variant of the orchestral fugue. The movement ends quietly, expectantly.

The tonality of the third movement revolves around C major, C minor and E flat major. To the words of the Psalm are added some oddly touching 'Allelujahs,' which Stravinsky acknowledged as having their source in the Russian Church services he attended as a child. These 'Allelujahs' and the opening 'Laudate Dominum' are set to slow, quiet music – short, memorable phrases of affecting simplicity. These passages frame the central allegro, which is barbaric and insistent in its rhythms. It reaches a climax at 'Laudate eum in sono tubae,' which breaks off to allow another slow, quiet 'Allelujah' before a return to the mood of the allegro. After a second climax, higher in pitch than before, the speed slackens, and a canonic passage between trebles and basses leads to the 'Laudate eum in cymbalis.' Here, a meter of three half-notes is set against an *ostinato* figure of four half-notes in the lower orchestral lines. The resulting harmonies, avoiding the expected resolution, extend through forty-three measures of celestial timelessness, and at one point there are no fewer than ten separate musical lines. The movement ends as it began, with another quiet 'Allelujah' and the transcendent 'Laudate Dominum' chord of C major, with its high, bright major third in the woodwind.

Whereas up until 1930 the major works of Stravinsky had been composed for the stage, from this period onwards his output was predominantly for the concert hall. For the fifteen years following the composition of the *Symphony of Psalms* Stravinsky kept returning to the paramount forms of the European Classical tradition – the sonata, the symphony and the concerto. To this period belong the Symphony in C and the Symphony in Three Movements, the Violin Concerto and the 'Dumbarton Oaks' Concerto, the *Duo Concertant* and the Sonata for two pianos. It is as if Stravinsky were engrossed with the rediscovery of the works of Bach, Haydn and Beethoven. We know that the first movement of the 'Dumbarton Oaks' Concerto was modeled on the third 'Brandenburg' Concerto of Bach, and that the scores of Haydn and Beethoven symphonies were on Stravinsky's desk at the time he wrote the Symphony in C. At this time Stravinsky came as close as he

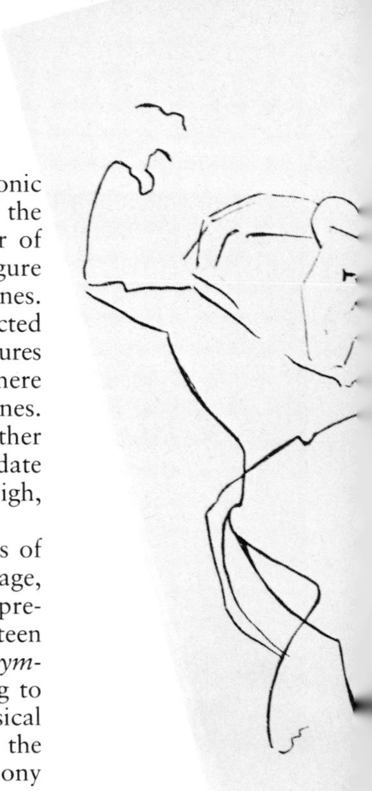

Above: Caricature of Stravinsky conducting by Olga Koussevitzky, second wife of the great conductor, publisher and patron.

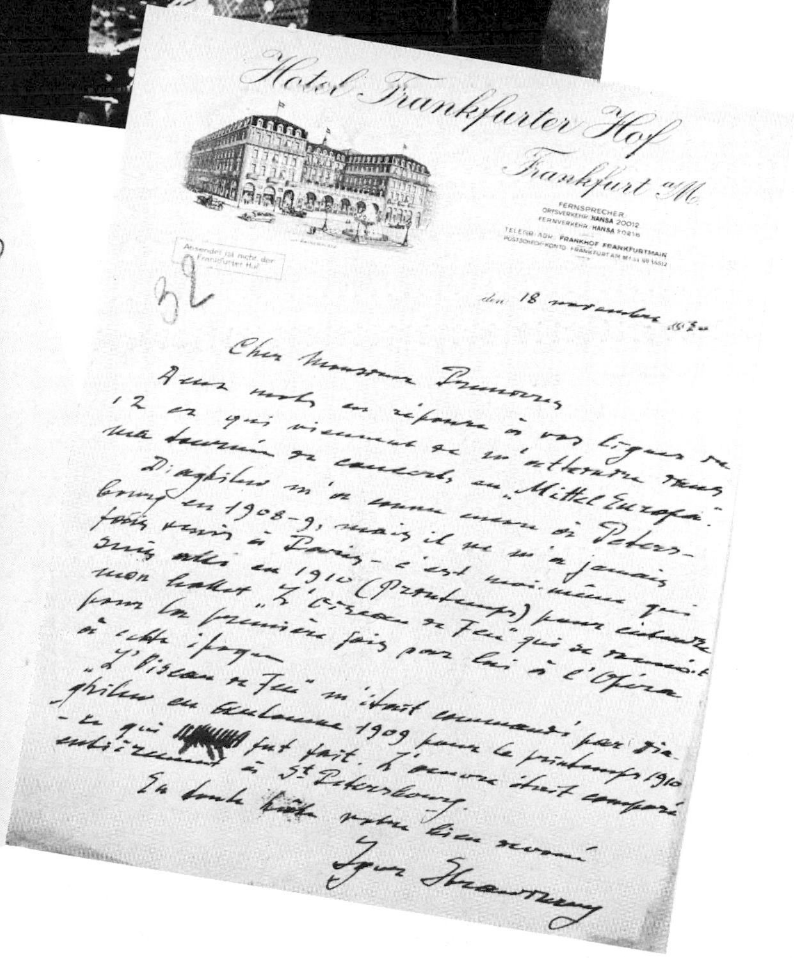

den 18 novembre 1930

Cher Monsieur Brunoire,

Deux mots en réponse à vos lignes du 12 ce qui viennent de m'atteindre pendant ma tournée de concerts en Mittel Europa.

Diaghilew m'a connu déjà à Petersbourg en 1908-9, mais il ne m'a jamais fait venir à Paris – c'est moi-même qui suis allé en 1910 (Printemps) pour entendre mon ballet "L'Oiseau de Feu" qui se donnait pour la première fois par lui à l'Opéra à cette époque.

"L'Oiseau de Feu" m'était commandé par Diaghilew en automne 1909 pour le printemps 1910 – ce qui fut fait. L'oeuvre était composée entièrement à St Petersbourg.

En toute hâte votre bien dévoué

Igor Strawinsky

Above: Autograph letter from Stravinsky concerning his reasons for settling in Paris. The translation runs as follows: 'Diaghilev already knew me in Petersburg in 1908-9, but he never persuaded me to come to Paris. I came of my own accord in 1910 (spring) to hear my ballet *Firebird* which was being premièred at the Opéra at that time. *Firebird* was commissioned from me by Diaghilev in autumn 1909, for the spring of 1910 and was ready then. The work was entirely composed in St Petersburg.' Stravinsky was characteristically disingenuous in denying credit to Diaghilev for bringing him to Paris.

ever did to claiming the symphonic tradition of sonata structure, theme and development, and motto. That there are fewer ballet scores, more for the concert hall, is explained in part by the fact that he was receiving more commissions from the United States than from Europe. Stravinsky moved to America permanently in 1940, halfway through the composition of the Symphony in C. Having taken French nationality in 1934, he took American citizenship in 1945.

There are two notable exceptions to the prevalence of symphonic forms during this period. The first is *Perséphone*, dating from 1934, which Stravinsky called a 'melodrama.' It sets a poem by André Gide for two solo voices, mixed chorus and large orchestra. Although the composer and poet worked together amicably at first, their relationship grew more and more strained, and Gide absented himself from the public performance, apparently disliking the unrealistic stresses given to the poetic lines. This led Stravinsky to write a manifesto explaining his syllabic treatment; he concluded: 'I am on a perfectly sure road. There is nothing to discuss or criticize. One does not criticize someone or something that is functioning. A nose is not manufactured – a nose just *is*. So too is my art.'

The rôle of Persephone is a speaking part, while Eumolpus is sung by a tenor – the tessitura is high, and it is a demanding, dramatic part. Much of the action of the story is conveyed in the words of Persephone, which are given no indication of pitch, or even of rhythm, but are left for the performer to declaim above the music. The transparent scoring of these passages makes it clear that Stravinsky did take pains to allow the words to come across to the audience. The three scenes are headed 'Persephone's Abduction,' 'Persephone in the Underworld,' and 'Persephone Reborn.' Like *The Rite of Spring* it is, of course, a work about the return of spring through sacrifice – yet, how different. Here all is precise, controlled, hieratic. The underlying passion has been transmuted by its filtering through the Greek myth, through the tempered language of Gide, through the device of Persephone's speaking rather than singing; through indeed the clarity of orchestration and harmonic language, which are never themselves threatening as they are in *The Rite*.

The other exception is the ballet *Jeu de cartes* (The Card Game), composed in 1936. With this orchestral score Stravinsky was able to indulge his enjoyment of the game of poker; the court cards of the four suits are characterized, and Stravinsky's own plot devolves upon the dastardly Joker, who does his best to defeat the rules of the game but in the end succumbs. The work sparkles with wit and *joie de vivre*, and there are several examples of musical quotation, from his own and others' works; the main theme of Rossini's *Barber of Seville* overture in the third 'deal' is the most obvious. The score is brightly, even brashly orchestrated, and is highly episodic and non-developmental. Nevertheless, some of its sections prefigure the use of the orchestra in passages of the Symphony in C, composed four years later. Musical unity

Left: Bronze head of Stravinsky by the Italian sculptor Marino Marini, 1950.

is achieved mainly through the simple device of repeating the opening grand processional music at the beginning of subsequent 'deals.'

The 'Dumbarton Oaks' Concerto was a private commission from Mr and Mrs Bliss of Dumbarton Oaks, Washington D.C., to celebrate their thirtieth wedding anniversary in 1938. The first performance was conducted by Stravinsky's lifelong devotee, Nadia Boulanger. It is a work in three movements for fifteen instruments, each of which is treated as a soloist in continually varied instrumental combinations and thematic elaborations. The first movement especially affords an instructive opportunity to observe Stravinsky's rhythmic subtlety. The pulse of this *tempo giusto* may be felt sometimes as quarter-note, sometimes as eighth-note; the listener is tempted to think of even larger units than these by groupings of patterns of half-note or longer durations. The feeling for pulse is disturbed or thrown off-balance by the insertion of groups of notes whose common denominator is a sixteenth-note, at a tempo far too fast to feel as a new pulse. This rhythmic displacement is a major difference from the model of the baroque *concerto grosso*, where a regular meter is ever present. Stravinsky's changing pulse forms a rhythmic counterpart to the harmonic and melodic deviations from the baroque pattern, and ensures the freshness and spontaneity evinced throughout the work.

The two symphonies of 1940 and 1945 lay real claim to be considered as symphonies proper. The Symphony in C has four movements in the traditional mold, and the first invites comparison with Beethoven's Fifth Symphony in its use of the rhythmic motif of that work. This is combined anacrustically with a three-note figure that becomes the unifying feature of the first and last movements. Considered vertically, this B–C–G motto arises from the juxtaposition of C and E chords, and it generates the semitonal harmonic clash which governs so much of the gentle astringency of sound.

The Symphony in Three Movements intensifies the tonal conflict. Here the opening flurry – a C major scale, centered on C – is forced up a semitone to outline the triad of D flat. Whereas the argument of the Symphony in C had been conducted mainly in diatonic terms, here the bitonal clashes of chordal juxtapositions are more prevalent, particularly in the first movement. This features a concertante element for the solo piano. The second movement has a similar role for the harp. In the final movement these two instruments join the orchestra in a summing-up and resolution of the opening tonal conflict in favor of D flat – a consequence, Stravinsky tells us, of the exultation he felt with the Allied victory at the end of the Second World War. Whatever the extra-musical associations here, the greater sense of resolution arises from the nature of the musical materials. Whereas in the earlier symphony the C tonality is modified by that of E, and the two are closely related, in the later work C and D flat are distant, and consequently there is a greater dissonance.

•From neoclassical to serial•

There is some sense of relief in returning to the eighteenth-century operatic conventions of *The Rake's Progress*, composed between 1948 and 1951. The set-piece arias, recitatives, choruses and ensembles do not have to struggle with the dialectics of sonata form, but follow each other in refreshingly varied but related key movements.

It is clear that Stravinsky was delighted with the libretto he received from W. H. Auden and Chester Kallman based on William Hogarth's paintings. The first act sticks closely to the operatic conventions of Hogarth's time, but the composer becomes more adventurous in the second and third acts, as if he is gaining confidence in his ability to combine the various threads of the plot in musical terms. We know that the works of Mozart, especially *Così fan tutte*, were much in Stravinsky's mind and heart during the composition of the *Rake*, but there is also the directness and simplicity of Purcell in some of the choral writing. This willingness to simplify the style to its bare bones creates a truthfulness of expression that can

Left: Stravinsky composing *Threni* in the basement night club of the Hotel Bauer Grunwald in Venice on 16 September 1957. Though he was now an old man, Stravinsky was still lively as ever, eager to assimilate the influences around him. The location is an interesting one, considering that *Threni* is a religious work based on the biblical *Lamentations of Jeremiah*.

Left: Portrait drawing of Stravinsky in Paris by Alberto Giacometti, 12 October 1957.

Opposite: Hogarth's painting *The Madhouse* from his series *The Rake's Progress*, which so impressed Stravinsky that he was inspired to write an opera based on the paintings. The opera, first performed in Venice at La Fenice on 11 September 1951, to a libretto by W. H. Auden and Chester Kallman, represents a watershed in Stravinsky's career. From this point onwards his work took on a new character, revolving around the possibilities inherent in serial music.

only add to the poignancy of, for example, the lullaby of the Bedlam scene in Act III.

The Rake's Progress provided Stravinsky with a kind of stylistic retreat from which he was to emerge into new territory. In the works that follow we perceive a new experimentation with pitches that begins to explore the principles of serial composition laid down by Schoenberg and his two great disciples, Berg and Webern. Serial composition, in its mature formulation, eschews any tonal relationships mainly by insuring that the twelve chromatic notes are constantly rotated in close proximity to each other, never allowing the dominance of any one over the others. In practice, of course, this rarely works exactly, because locally one or more notes are usually given some kind of emphasis, by register, duration, instrumental weight or dynamic. However, serial composition does bring about a constant fluctuation of tonal weight, and it is into this gravity-free environment that Stravinsky cautiously propelled himself.

The relationship between Schoenberg and Stravinsky is intriguing. The two had met as early as 1912, at the time of the appearance of Schoenberg's *Pierrot lunaire* and before the first performance of *The Rite of Spring*. At this time there is no doubt that Stravinsky was highly impressed by Schoenberg's qualities, and at first Schoenberg seemed to reciprocate this respect. However, when Stravinsky's early neoclassical pieces appeared in the 1920s, Schoenberg scorned what he regarded as a cheap dressing-up of the music of the past. While the two composers were never close, there is no real evidence that Stravinsky ever came to regard Schoenberg with the same sort of disdain. Nevertheless, it seems to have come as a shock to many musicians that virtually from the moment of Schoenberg's death in July 1951 Stravinsky began to compose serial music. It was almost as if there were a psychological space which Stravinsky could claim as his own. Stravinsky's new friendship with the young conductor Robert Craft undoubtedly spurred on his serial investigations, which ultimately seem more related to the practice of Webern than to that of Schoenberg himself.

In the beginning, Stravinsky's flirtations with serial technique were rather tentative. In the Cantata (1952) he uses melody forms in mirror and retrograde, which are integral aspects of serial composition, and we see a similar but more developed contrapuntal concern in the Septet which followed. In the *In Memoriam Dylan Thomas* work of 1954 he went further, using a fully serial technique but restricting the basic set of notes to five rather than the full set of twelve. The distinction, however, is theoretical to some extent, since the five notes do fill the chromatic space of a major third and transpositions to other degrees are used.

The ballet *Agon* is especially fascinating in that Stravinsky was able to integrate entirely convincingly both non-serial (even tonal) writing and serial technique. *Agon* was written over a relatively long period, even for Stravinsky – from 1953 to 1957 – which suggests he did not find this integration easy to achieve. In general the work progresses from a diatonic opening to more chromatic material, and then to serial composition, with the opening diatonic fanfare material returning at the end. This unifying device is complemented by an interlude movement which appears between each group of three dances – there are twelve dances in all.

There are many other works in which Stravinsky adopted a form of free serial composition. *Threni*, *Canticum sacrum* and *A Sermon, a Narrative and a Prayer* are examples, but the *Movements for Piano and Orchestra* is undoubtedly the most Webernian of Stravinsky's works. It is a short, concentrated piece in which the brittle sonorities remind us somewhat of the textures of the works of the 1920s. Stravinsky regarded the rhythmic language of this composition as the most complex he had ever employed. Yet the work is curiously anonymous; the series itself and its rhythmic and instrumental manipulations do not have the stamp of their author's personality.

•Achievement•

For most of his creative life Stravinsky adopted a musical language centered on tonal considerations, in the sense that notes, phrases and chords were carefully balanced in relation to

Below: Photograph by Erich Auerbach of Stravinsky rehearsing with the BBC Symphony Orchestra on 8 December 1958 at the Maida Vale Studios. He was renowned for the skill with which he conducted his own music, and in particular for his driving sense of rhythm.

Left: Stravinsky and the cellist Mstislav Rostropovich; another Auerbach photograph, taken at the Royal Academy of Music.

Below: A final portrait photograph of Stravinsky taken in August 1970, a year before he died, at Evian, near Lake Geneva.

definite 'tonic' pitches. These tonics, centers of gravity, might change during the course of a movement – in examples where they do not, as in the *Three Easy Pieces for Piano Duet* of 1921, we see at its most exposed the static patterning which was the foundation of his achievement. The movement from one tonal center to another was not usually modulation in the nineteenth-century sense; it simply changed, instantaneously, like a dancer's leap into a new space. In the mature extended works such as *Oedipus Rex*, the *Symphony of Psalms* and the later symphonies, the succession of tonalities themselves form a network of complex symbolic relationships.

Stravinsky wrote astonishingly successful music for the ballet at all stages of his career, and the balletic metaphor is not purely fortuitous. The dancer has essentially two kinds of space in which to express himself. One is the gestural space immediately surrounding his body – the local space of posture and movement of torso and limbs. The other is the global space of arena or theater. The tension of relationship between a dancer's gestural space and the global space is dynamic, continually evolving and changing. If more than one dancer is present, the gestural and global spaces of each dancer in relation to every other dancer also change in time. Stravinsky's use of local tonal centers around which melody and harmony are patterned is analogous to the gestural space of the dancer, and, like the dancer, Stravinsky can suddenly leap out of this space into a different tonal area. More rarely does he lead us out slowly, step by step, in a procedure akin to Classical modulation.

Stravinsky's achievement thus lies in his mapping of tonal space, activating it by novel rhythmic and structural means, in which the principle of varied repetition is applied to the smallest as well as to the largest elements. His invention, of a high order, was always motivated by the same thought, to overcome the terror of the conflict of the world by borrowing fragments of history and compressing them into a space which he could explore and command. In this light we see that the serial works are informed by the same desire; the new classicism of dodecaphony had to be appropriated too. Stravinsky's wit and sarcasm, his ritual elements and his playfulness, were all bound to one end: to objectify history, to destroy time and so to conquer death.

The Revival of Early Music

Until the late nineteenth century the music of composers such as Monteverdi, Lully and Vivaldi (and, indeed, most of the music of J. S. Bach and Handel) was hardly known, while the music of the Middle Ages had remained buried for centuries. The revival of interest in early music in the years before 1900 can be seen as part of the rejection of late Romanticism in all the arts.

A decisive role in this revival was played by Arnold Dolmetsch (1858-1940), a French-born violin teacher. As a student his interest in early music and early instruments was aroused by the historical concerts on early instruments given at the Conservatoire in Brussels. He began to look for music for viols and other ancient instruments, and he began also to acquire and restore early instruments. After Brussels, Dolmetsch studied at the Royal College of Music and settled in England, where, during the 1890s, he gave concerts on period instruments in his own house, often performing pieces he had discovered in old manuscripts or printed editions. In 1893 he made his first lute, and in 1894 his first keyboard instrument, a clavichord (*above*). He was then encouraged by William Morris, the founder of the English Arts and Crafts movement, to make a harpsichord, and his first such instrument was exhibited at the Arts and Crafts Exhibition of 1896. In the early years of the new century he visited the USA, and he worked in Boston from 1905 to 1911, a period when he made some of his best instruments, including a harpsichord for Busoni. Dolmetsch was equally concerned with earlier playing techniques and with the interpretation of old music, and the modern practice of authentic performance can be traced directly to his influence.

Meanwhile, many composers began to look again at pre-Romantic music as a source for their own compositions, and they made editions and arrangements of early music, although these often bore the character of their own work without any attempt at more objective authenticity. Thus two strands of development complemented one another, the one not being allowed to decline into dry-as-dust antiquarianism, the other being constantly challenged by the rhythms and colors of rediscovered styles of performance and the sonorities of old instruments.

Above: Ferruccio Busoni (1866-1924) by the Futurist painter Boccioni. A phenomenal pianist, influential teacher and theorist, and original composer, Busoni had a profound effect on attitudes to music of the past. In composers such as Mozart and Beethoven he looked for 'classical' values – the architecture of rhythm and sound – rather than for Romantic elegance or emotion. He also awakened a far deeper interest in the polyphony of J. S. Bach, whose works he played, edited and transcribed throughout his career.

Above: Ottorino Respighi (1879-1936), one of a group of Italian composers born around 1880 who followed Verdi's advice to 'turn to the antique in order to make progress.' Despite the eclecticism of his own music, through his editions and arrangements Respighi revived interest in music ranging from Gregorian chant through the Renaissance and Monteverdi to Vivaldi, Tartini, Rameau and Paisiello.

Below: Alfredo Casella (1883-1947) in a portrait by the Metaphysical painter De Chirico. Casella was active as a pianist, editor and composer – certainly the most important of his generation in Italy – and aligned himself with the avant garde both in music (Stravinsky, Bartók, Schoenberg) and art (the Cubist, Futurist and Metaphysical movements); but he had a wide-ranging interest in music of the past, being especally active in the revival of Vivaldi, and also preparing editions of Clementi's symphonies as well as works by Beethoven and Bach.

Juan Gris's design ('Offering to the shepherdess') for a detail of the set of *Les Tentations de la bergère* (*above*), and a *pas de deux* from the ballet (*below right*). This was first performed by Diaghilev's Ballets Russes in 1924 in Monte Carlo with choreography by Bronislava Nijinska. The music was supposedly arranged by Henri Casadesus from music by Michel de Montéclair (1667-1737), although it is far more likely that it was a pastiche by Casadesus himself. As with so much new music, Diaghilev was also the agency through whom music by pre-Romantic composers found an enthusiastic public: *The Good-Humored Ladies* (first performed in 1917) used music by Domenico Scarlatti arranged by Tommasini, while Stravinsky's *Pulcinella* (like the Cimarosa–Respighi ballet *Le Astuzie femminili*, first performed in 1920) was based on pieces by Pergolesi. Though Stravinsky's was the most radical transformation, none of these versions was at all 'authentic,' but they were a major factor in developing a taste for music that had been swamped in the tide of Romanticism.

Above: Costumes by José-Maria Sert for the ballet *Le Astuzie femminili* (Feminine Wiles), choreographed by Massine to an arrangement by Respighi of music by Cimarosa, and first performed by the Ballets Russes in May 1920. Respighi had worked with Diaghilev the previous year, providing a score, arranged from Rossini, for *La Boutique fantasque* (the Fantastic Toyshop), for which the designs had been executed by André Derain and, again, choreography was by Massine. Respighi's interests were extremely broad, and his arrangements of early Romantic music, like those of Casella, shed light on another forgotten period.

Henri Casadesus (1879-1947), shown here tuning a viol, was, with his family, central to the revival of early music in France. In 1901, in collaboration with Saint-Saëns, he founded the Société des Instruments Anciens, and until 1939 the group (*below*) organized many concerts. It is ironical that all of his 'new discoveries' were, almost certainly, written by himself and his brothers, Francis (who also reorganized music in the US army) and Marius (a composer and instrument-maker as well as a player), including pieces they attributed to C. P. E. Bach, to J. C. Bach and to Handel, and even the 'Adelaïde' violin concerto by 'Mozart.' The great violinist Fritz Kreisler followed the same practice in the 1920s with works by 'Padre Martini' and others. Nevertheless, these imaginative works can only have helped the efforts of such real pioneers as Dolmetsch and Nadia Boulanger.

Above: Arnold Dolmetsch with his son Carl (*left*) and assistants in his workshop at Haslemere. On his return from America, Dolmetsch finally settled in England, making his home at Haslemere in Sussex. A trust was set up to support his work, and in 1925 the first Haslemere Festival took place, an event that was continued by his son and still takes place annually today. As well as working on stringed and keyboard instruments, Dolmetsch experimented with making recorders. He perfected his first modern instrument as early as 1905, but did not complete his first full family of recorders until 1926. This was, perhaps, the most influential of all his achievements, in that the recorder, especially since the Dolmetschs and others have succeeded in making an excellent version in plastic, has become one of the keystones of musical education throughout the world, played by millions of children. Dolmetsch also wrote on *The Interpretation of the Music of the XVII and XVIII Centuries*, thus complementing his work as an instrument-maker, and his influence can be heard in many of the more recent performances of old music: groups who specialize in early music will now often use only ancient instruments or replicas of them, so that the timbres of baroque oboes and bassoons, trumpets and trombones, as well as the stringed and keyboard instruments, have become familiar; and performance techniques of the pre-Classical period have also been revived, with less vibrato used by string players, and both singers and instrumentalists ornamenting melodic lines in accordance with correct practice.

Right: Wanda Landowska (1879-1959), the great Polish harpsichordist, who must take the main credit for the instrument's return to popularity in the twentieth century. She was originally a pianist, giving her first public concert in 1903, but from the outset she had championed the music of the seventeenth and eighteenth centuries, especially J. S. Bach, and she soon turned to the harpsichord. However, the sound of the available instruments was very weak (particularly in contrast to the late Romantic pianoforte), and she had Pleyel in Paris make a two-manual harpsichord with a metal frame, constructed like a grand piano, to produce a strong tone. She followed the lead of Dolmetsch in using the harpsichord as a continuo instrument, but also inspired new works from contemporary composers, notably Falla's Chamber Concerto for harpsichord (1926) and Poulenc's *Concert champêtre* (1928). In 1925 she founded the Ecole de Musique Ancienne in Paris, where she worked to redevelop the techniques of harpsichord playing.

Left: Dame Janet Baker and Thomas Hemsley in a performance of Purcell's *Dido and Aeneas*. Purcell's music, like that of so many of his contemporaries, had been almost completely forgotten, and its revival early this century, along with that of the great composers of the English Tudor Renaissance, stimulated composers in England from Vaughan Williams to Britten and Tippett to look again at their native traditions.

Below: Orchestra pit in the Court Theater at Drottningholm, Sweden, during a performance of Haydn's opera *L'Infedeltà delusa*. In this eighteenth-century theater every attempt is made to recreate the atmosphere and sound of authentic period performances, so that even the orchestra appears in the costumes of Mozart's and Haydn's day. Haydn's operas were also works that had fallen into neglect, and they have been revived in more recent years.

Above: Nadia Boulanger (1887-1979), the French composer, conductor and teacher whose pioneering activity was devoted in equal measure to the revival of old music and to the production and performance of new music. She gave up composition after the death of her sister Lili and thereafter directed many performances of French music of the Baroque and Renaissance, and with her superb performances and recordings of Monteverdi's madrigals in the 1930s brought that composer back into public favor. She was also a most influential teacher of composition in Paris and was chosen by Stravinsky to direct the première of his most neoclassical work, the 'Dumbarton Oaks' Concerto, in 1938.

SCHOENBERG, BERG AND WEBERN

PAUL GRIFFITHS

Opposite: The Green Self-Portrait, by Arnold Schoenberg (1874-1951), October 1910. Schoenberg painted all his life, but was particularly active during this stage of his career, exhibiting with the Expressionist group *Der Blaue Reiter*.

Schoenberg occupies an unusual place in our musical culture. Though he is generally regarded as one of the great composers, very few of his works are performed with any frequency. And though the value of his music is widely conceded, the strength of his influence has come to outweigh consideration of his works. Nor is this very surprising. He was, after all, the first composer to make a complete break with the system of major and minor keys that had governed Western music since the Renaissance, and the first to propose a new method of ordering music: twelve-note serialism. He was also one of the very few great teachers of composition, so that his innovations, despite his thoroughly traditional methods of instruction, came to be carried on in the music of a wide circle of pupils, chief among them Berg and Webern.

Arnold Schoenberg was born in Vienna on 13 September 1874, the child of Jewish parents who had come to the imperial capital from Pressburg (Bratislava, in present-day Czechoslovakia). He had violin lessons as a boy, but no formal musical education at a higher level. Instead, he seems to have found his way into music through playing in chamber ensembles with friends, and through some discussions with Alexander von Zemlinsky, his near contemporary and later his brother-in-law. Thus from the first his standards were set by the chamber music of Haydn, Mozart, Beethoven and Brahms, and by the importance of discovering things for himself: here were the roots of his paradoxical nature as a conservative revolutionary, one for whom the great works of the past inspired emulation but not imitation.

Almost from the first this brought him into difficulties. His String Quartet in D major (1897) was well received, but significantly Schoenberg did not allow it to be published, presumably feeling that his own voice was not yet at full strength in what is an amiable and melodious work, recalling the composer's Czech origins in its links with the tradition of Smetana and Dvořák. The first compositions that he did feel to be representative were various songs and the string sextet *Verklärte Nacht* (Transfigured Night), op.4 (1899), and these did meet with resistance. There were protests when the songs were introduced, and the sextet was turned down for performance under the auspices of the Vienna Tonkunstler-Sozietät on the grounds that it contained an unorthodox chord.

So it does, and more than one. Schoenberg's aim here was to extend the harmonic venturings of Wagner's *Tristan und Isolde* in a musical translation of a poem by Richard Dehmel, a writer of sentimental symbolist verse to whom he was much attracted at this period. In form and mood the music follows the poem quite closely. Dehmel writes of a man and woman walking through a wintry wood in the moonlight. The woman suddenly confesses that she is pregnant by another man; she speaks of her earlier dissolute life, her present grief and shame. They walk on, and the man replies in strong, comfortable tones: the child, he says, will be transfigured by their love and become their own. Finally the couple is left striding on in confidence through the bright night.

As a program for a piece of music, Dehmel's poem is more intimate in tone than any that might have appealed at the same time to Richard Strauss, but this is exactly what commended it to Schoenberg, for *Verklärte Nacht* is not only a symphonic poem but also a work of chamber music. The instrumentation – for violins, violas and cellos in pairs – is an inheritance from Brahms, who had written two works for this medium, and Brahms is also the model for the intensive thematic working. This was to become one of the most characteristic features of Schoenberg's art; the piling up of strong melodic lines all bearing the weight of the music's basic themes. In *Verklärte Nacht* such energetic counterpoint is in almost constant struggle with music that wants to linger in lush harmony or exquisite texture. The work is thus not so much a synthesis of Wagner and Brahms, the rival popes of music earlier in the century, but rather a fighting mixture of the two, and in that respect it bears witness to the tension within Schoenberg's mind between the calls of innovation and those of tradition. It was a tension he was never to resolve.

After *Verklärte Nacht* his next major work was the immense cantata *Gurrelieder*, of which the main work of composition was done in 1900-1, though the piece was not finished until 1911. Here Wagner's influence is even more apparent than in the sextet. Like *Tristan*, *Gurrelieder* tells the story of a great and calamitous love between two people made large by a legendary setting: in the castle of Gurre (hence the title) live Waldemar, a medieval king of Denmark, and Tove, his mistress. The work uses the poems of the Danish writer Jens Peter Jacobsen. The first part of the cantata is an exchange of rapturous songs between these two, but it ends with the melancholy tale told by the Wood Dove of Tove's murder at the behest of Waldemar's Queen. In the short central part, the work's pivot, Waldemar curses God for causing him such misery. The third part shows the King and his men condemned to ride the night sky until they are blown aside by the summer wind and lost in the glorious dawn: at this point great choral tableaux are introduced and one extraordinary passage of 'melodrama,' or recitation with music, which is much closer in style to Schoenberg's work of 1911 than that of 1900-1. But for all its stylistic incongruities, *Gurrelieder* moves forward with all the grand confidence of its period, being massively scored for soloists, choirs and an orchestra of unparalleled size.

In 1901, while *Gurrelieder* was in progress, Schoenberg left Vienna for Berlin, where he wrote cabaret songs, scored operettas and did some teaching. He also composed a second symphonic poem, *Pelleas und Melisande*, op.5 (1902-3), apparently unaware that Debussy had recently completed an opera on the same subject. With its full orchestral scoring and its themes representing the characters, *Pelleas* is a more normal symphonic poem than *Verklärte Nacht*, but again it shows Schoenberg's dissatisfaction with program music. The music is thoroughly developed, not least in passages of densely entwined and active counterpoint, and the effect, as in much of Schoenberg's music for the next few years, is often of ideas coming too fast for the forms that fix them.

• New beginnings •

Schoenberg returned to Vienna in 1903 and began private teaching. Alban Berg and Anton Webern became his pupils the following year. Schoenberg was now thirty; his two students were about a decade younger, Berg having been born on 9 February 1885 and Webern on 3 December 1883, both, like Schoenberg, in Vienna. Given their youth, it is not surprising that neither of them had composed anything of much consequence. Berg, who always had a particular feeling for the literary currents of his time, had composed dozens of songs; Webern had produced a variety of songs and instrumental pieces that range from the competent to the inept. What is astonishing, though, is that within a very short time of becoming pupils of Schoenberg both young composers should have been creating much more assuredly and imaginatively, and that they should have gained distinctive voices while contributing to the musical revolution that Schoenberg was in the process of launching. No doubt, too, their sympathy and support was an encouragement to him, though he seems always to have been sure of his artistic mission, and he had already given expression to his combative self-confidence in a work written before he met them, the *Six Orchestral Songs*, op.8 (1904).

Left: Alban Berg, as a young boy in Vienna. The photograph captures completely the character of the Vienna of the early 1900s – a cultural center of long-standing bourgeois tradition.

Opposite: Manuscript score of the opening of 'Mondestrunken' one of the twenty-one poems that comprise *Pierrot lunaire*. The poems are set for speaker/singer and chamber ensemble; the vocal part is given specific 'melody' and rhythm but with instructions to fade off the given pitch; the result is a highly stylized and often disturbing form of sung speech.

The first work he completed after their meeting was his First String Quartet, op.7 (1904-5), in which he achieved two related ambitions: a continuous development of the work's basic themes, and an extension of the conventional sonata-form opening movement so that it embraced within a single span sections corresponding to slow movement, scherzo and finale. Thus cast in one movement, and lasting for three-quarters of an hour, the quartet is one of Schoenberg's most complex works, a great test of concentration and comprehension, although it is still nominally in a key, Schoenberg's favorite one of D minor (this was also the key of *Verklärte Nacht* and *Pelleas und Melisande*). This achievement naturally impressed the composer's young pupils. Webern was influenced by it in his quartet of 1905, the most substantial of the compositions that preceded his op.1, and Berg chose it as principal exhibit in his important article 'Why is Schoenberg's music so hard to understand?,' written two decades later.

Meanwhile, the creative energies of the quartet carried Schoenberg into his First Chamber Symphony in E major, op.9 (1906), which is similarly in one all-encompassing movement, though on a more compact scale. Here, as in *Verklärte Nacht*, Schoenberg takes an orchestral genre into the domain of chamber music, for at a time when Mahler was writing for enormous resources (his Seventh Symphony was also finished in 1906) here was a symphony for fifteen soloists – eight woodwind, two horns and five strings – an ensemble aptly chosen to delineate the music's dense but dynamic textures.

Left: Poster for the first performance of Schoenberg's expressionist *Pierrot lunaire* in Berlin, 16 October 1912. This was to prove a seminal work, opening the eyes of the public to the new possibilities of atonality, which Schoenberg had been experimenting with for the past few years.

Below: Gebet an Pierrot (Prayer to Pierrot), a woodcut by Felix Müller, Leipzig 1913. The use of stark, almost crude, line and the resulting directness and force of the picture are typical of the expressionist tendencies of the period.

•The voyage into atonality •

Once he had completed this work Schoenberg immediately started a Second Chamber Symphony, but this was overtaken by the rapid change in his style and not completed until 1939. Instead, the work that followed was his Second String Quartet, op.10 (1907-8), in which he accomplished another marriage of genres, this time chamber music and song, the third and fourth movements incorporating a soprano voice singing poems by the mystic idealist Stefan George. This turn to song serves to expose very clearly the program of the quartet, which begins with a challenging movement in F sharp minor, continues with a scherzo that includes a popular song giving the message 'all is past,' then reaches towards spiritual calm in the first vocal movement and achieves an emancipation from earthly ties in the song finale. It achieves also an emancipation from tonality, developed still further in the fifteen songs set to poems by George that Schoenberg was beginning at the same time, *Das Buch der hängenden Gärten* (The Book of the Hanging Gardens), op.15 (1908-9), where again the release from key centers is expressive of a release from the world, a voyage into the interior of the personality.

Berg and Webern also found themselves in much the same creative situation. Berg's Piano Sonata, op.1 (1907-8), is a short single movement where melodies of Mahlerian expressive force grapple with chords that threaten and undermine any harmonic stability. And Webern's op.1, his *Passacaglia for Orchestra* (1908), is characteristically more coolly planned in its structure but no less vehement in its emotional climax. For both composers, as for their teacher, the only way forward lay in atonality, in music whose melodies could move without restraint, whose dissonances could be set in progressions that never look for resolution. Like Schoenberg, Webern took the step into the new musical universe with the help of poems by George, which he set in his op.3 and op.4 (1908-9). And Berg's first atonal compositions were also songs, the four of his op.2 (1909-10).

The next problem for all three composers was the creation of instrumental movements without the usual support of tonal harmony. This caused them great difficulty, for in abandoning keys they had also abandoned themes, and it was hard to see how music could make structural sense without clear harmonic movement or thematic development. Inevitably what hap-

Right: Schoenberg's own design for his music drama *Die glückliche Hand*, for the first scene, 'Der Chor.' The work was highly introspective and a typical product of the Second Viennese School. It was first performed at the Vienna Volksoper on 14 October 1924.

Right: Christus Vision, an undated painting by Schoenberg. Religion played an important part in Schoenberg's life and in his work, although two of his major religious compositions, the oratorio *Die Jakobsleiter*, started in 1915, and the opera *Moses und Aron* remained unfinished.

pened was that movements became very short, that they were built from very rapid gestures and from passages of stasis, with very little of a gradual nature, and that the secondary features of music – instrumentation, timbre, loudness – took on a new importance. But it would be absurd to attribute the extreme emotional charge of this music to some sort of technical necessity. There can be no doubt that the works composed by Schoenberg, Berg and Webern in 1908-15, or thereabouts, are as they are because all three composers were venturing into quite new and deep realms of experience. It does not seem inappropriate to compare their endeavors with those of another Viennese, Sigmund Freud, and indeed Schoenberg's largest work from this period, the monodrama *Erwartung* (Expectation), op.17 (1909), is an explicitly Freudian investigation of the intense feelings of terror, hatred, rejection and need within a woman's subconscious.

But the expressive frenzy is certainly no less in the short instrumental movements which make up Schoenberg's *Three Piano Pieces*, op.11, and *Five Orchestral Pieces*, op.16 (both also 1909), Berg's String Quartet, op.3 (1910), and Webern's *Five Movements* for string quartet, op.5 (1909), and *Six Orchestral Pieces*, op.6 (1909-10). In Webern's op.5, for example, the whole range of available string effects – pizzicato, playing with the wood of the bow to achieve a coarse sound, bowing close to the bridge to make the sound thin and strained, playing with a mute – is used to gain decisive changes of character, and the music is either caught in headlong rush or else ethereally calm. In either case the constant change is paradoxically but necessarily marked by obsessive repetition: a rising minor ninth of alarm in the first movement, a single bass note at the start of the third, circling *ostinati* (especially in the third and fourth movements) and harmonies that revolve and reappear. Webern's quartet movements are in all these respects typical of the music being written by all three composers at this time, but in their extreme brevity they belong only to him; the second and fourth movements are miniature adagios of only a dozen or so measures, the centerpiece is a tiny scherzo, and the two outer movements, though more fully developed, are of miniature proportions, in scale quite unlike the two substantial movements that make up Berg's Quartet.

Before long, however, Schoenberg, Berg and Webern were all finding themselves unable to extend a movement beyond the confines of a fragment. Again Webern was the most extreme. His *Six Bagatelles* for string quartet, op.9 (1911-13),

Above: Impression III by Kandinsky, painted in January 1911. The previous year Kandinsky, one of the prime exponents of Expressionism, had begun experimenting with the concept of 'abstract' or non-figurative art, where form and color are used for their own sake, for expressive quality, as in music. *Impression III* was probably done after Kandinsky had heard a concert of Schoenberg's work, which had tremendously impressed him. He began an immediate and intense correspondence with Schoenberg and invited him to teach at the Bauhaus in Weimar – an offer that Schoenberg declined.

and *Five Orchestral Pieces*, op.10 (1911-13), are still more concise extrapolations from op.5 and op.6, and his *Three Little Pieces* for cello and piano, op.11 (1914), conclude with a movement of just twenty notes. The public rhetoric of the works of 1909-10 has been left behind. Webern is now concerned with the still moment and the sigh, having distanced himself also from the feeling of drive that still persisted in the contemporary miniatures of his two colleagues: Schoenberg's *Six Little Piano Pieces*, op.19 (1911), and Berg's *Four Pieces* for clarinet and piano, op.5 (1913).

Not surprisingly, audiences of the time found it very difficult to accommodate themselves to the utterly new music that Schoenberg, Berg and Webern were bringing back from their voyages into atonality and into themselves. Schoenberg's *Five Orchestral Pieces* were given their first performance by Sir Henry Wood in London in 1912 and were received with embarrassment and mockery. The following year Schoenberg himself conducted a concert of music by himself and his pupils in Vienna, and this was the occasion for a riot, sparked off specifically by Berg's *Five Orchestral Songs*, op.4 (1912), settings of short poems by the Viennese eccentric Peter Altenberg, which gave Berg the opportunity to express a characteristic mixture of eroticism and irony, rich romanticism and cool, magical calculation.

Above: Drawing by Fred Dolbin of the Kolisch Quartet, together with Berg (seated in the middle) and Schoenberg (standing on the right). Rudolf Kolisch's daughter became Schoenberg's second wife, and the Kolisch Quartet performed much of Schoenberg's and Berg's work, including several first performances, remaining closely associated with them for many years. Berg gave them sole performance rights in the *Lyric Suite*; after the war they gave regular performances in America and did much to promote the works of the Second Viennese School.

In the face of this incomprehension, Schoenberg wrote a work that gained him, if not success, then at least notoriety and widespread performances: *Pierrot lunaire*, op.21 (1912). Again the work crosses the boundaries between different media. It is chamber music, but written for a small-scale orchestra of two woodwinds, two strings and piano. It is a song-cycle, but it can also be given as a dramatic entertainment with the vocal soloist in costume. Above all, it asks the soloist to tread the line between song and speech, hitting the notated pitches but then drifting away from them. The effect is to create a weird, nocturnal atmosphere where the abnormal is normal, dream is reality, and the reciter can indulge in telling the audience of

Opposite: Newspaper cutting showing the painter Oskar Kokoschka, Schoenberg, Schoenberg's wife and the architect Adolf Loos, celebrating a chance meeting in a Berlin bar around 1922.

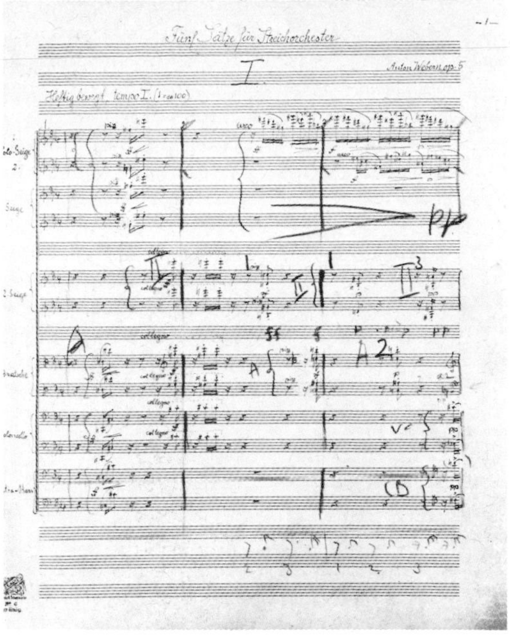

Right: Manuscript score of the first page of the orchestral version of Webern's *Five Movements*, op.5. This was one of his major works, assuming considerable significance because his output was relatively small.

Opposite: Alban Berg and Anton Webern, around 1923.

unspoken fantasies, of murder, blasphemy and profound dislocation. Within the twenty-one numbers of the work the highly pressured emotions of Schoenberg's earlier atonal pieces are encapsulated and to a degree neutralized, though at the same time the more formal nature of the music can be the more abruptly rent when the knife turns.

Another composer might have tried to continue in this fertile vein, but Schoenberg would not allow himself repetition. Between 1913 and 1916 he gradually assembled the set of *Four Orchestral Songs*, op.22, remarkable for their distinctive scorings: the first, for example, uses six clarinets, a small brass group, percussion and full strings without violas. Then he began an oratorio, *Die Jakobsleiter* (Jacob's Ladder), which is explicitly concerned with the need to go ever onward and upward. The work is a drama of the soul, with various individuals coming forward under the regimen of the archangel Gabriel to sing of their spiritual follies and aspirations. Schoenberg's own text, written in 1915, is complete, but he found it impossible to continue the work into its second part, where Gabriel speaks of unity with God as the ultimate aim for every soul, exactly as later the composer would find it impossible to imagine music for the third act of his opera *Moses und Aron. Die Jakobsleiter* was abandoned unfinished in 1922, and though Schoenberg returned to it in 1944 no more music was composed for it.

Berg and Webern, meanwhile, were suffering no such block. Indeed, in his *Three Orchestral Pieces*, op.6 (1914-15), Berg at last achieved what neither of his colleagues had accomplished: large-scale instrumental movements without any tonal underpinning. The first, 'Präludium,' begins in percussion noises, coalesces around a focal pitch, rises to melody, and then slides back to noise. The second, 'Reigen,' is a symphonic waltz, perhaps inspired by the sexual round-dance of Arthur Schnitzler's play of the same name. And the third, 'Marsch' is an immense piece haunted by military fanfares and proceeding steadily towards catastrophe; the date it bears, 'August 1914,' seems quite as significant as the undoubted influence of Mahler, particularly his Sixth Symphony.

•Voices of war•

When the war foreshadowed in the 'Marsch' broke out, all three composers were caught up in it and were obliged to undergo periods of military service, which in Berg's case prepared him for his first opera, *Wozzeck*, op.7 (1917-22). For this the composer turned to a fragmentary play by the early nineteenth-century German dramatist Georg Büchner, whose work was being rediscovered almost a century after his death, and whose theatrical technique was astonishingly forward-looking. The scenes are short, the speech simple and naturalistic, the character-drawing swift and merciless, the imagery stark but richly endowed with symbolism. This was exactly what Berg needed, and he could sympathize completely with Büchner's curious blend of cynicism and compassion, his ruthless exposure of the weakness of his characters and, as a concomitant, his anguished feeling for them and with them.

Wozzeck is a simple soldier, an inadequate man who is the victim of all around him: his flirtatious mistress Marie, who shows her real affection for their child but not for him; the cruelly mocking Captain who delights in showing up Wozzeck's stupidity and trust; the crazed Doctor who saps his strength by using him as a dietary guinea-pig; the brutish Drum Major who boasts scornfully of his conquest of Marie. But all of these are victims too, victims of their own limitations, and if in Büchner's play the Captain and the Doctor are hardly more than puppets, in Berg's opera the strings are revealed and one begins to understand and to be appalled by their mental barrenness.

Such a cast of vividly differentiated characters demands very different kinds of music, as do the locales and situations of the opera, which include everything from a low tavern to a barracks dormitory, from sexual triumph to suicide. Accordingly, the opera makes use of a great variety of means. The voice parts range from song to musical declamation, as well as 'speech-song' in the manner of *Pierrot lunaire* and even ordinary speech. The large orchestra is placed against a military band in one scene, a café ensemble in another, and against the orchestra of Schoenberg's chamber symphonies in yet another. The musical style moves flexibly between pure tonality and the most tearing dissonances. Moreover, as the tragedy hastens towards its end, so the opera becomes more erratic. One interlude in the last act is simply an immense orchestral crescendo on the note B, heard twice, and this terrifying noise is followed without any break by an out-of-tune piano in a quick polka. Later, the scene of Wozzeck's suicide by drowning, ending in unearthly chro-

The first performance of *Wozzeck* took place – after 137 rehearsals – in Berlin on 14 December 1925 at the Unter den Linden opera house (*right*). Berg himself was closely involved with the production, and he kept tight control over the direction of the opera, including lighting, curtain falls etc. The sets (*below and bottom*) were designed by P. Aravantinos, and the first Wozzeck was the baritone Leo Schützendorf (*far right*). The opera scored a tremendous success in Leningrad in 1927, though Vienna, conservative as ever, did not stage a production until 1930.

Staats-Theater

Opernhaus Unter den Linden.

Anfang 7 — Montag, den 14. Dezember 1925. — Anfang 7

14. Karten-Reservesatz. (Außer Abonnement.)

Uraufführung: Georg Büchners

Wozzeck

Oper in drei Akten (15 Szenen) von Alban Berg.
Musikal. Leitung: General-Musikdirektor Erich Kleiber
In Szene gesetzt von Frant Ludwig Hörth

Wozzeck	Leo Schukendorf
Tambourmajor	Friß Soot
Andres	Gerhard Witting
Hauptmann	Waldemar Henke
Doktor	Martin Abendroth
1. Handwerksbursch	Ernst Osterkamp
2. Handwerksbursch	Alfred Borchardt
Der Narr	Marcel Noë
Marie	Sigrid Johanson
Margret	Jessyka Koettrik
Mariens Knabe	Ruth Iris Witting
Soldat	Leonhard Kern

Soldaten und Burschen, Mägde und Dirnen, Kinder.

Gesamtausstattung: P. Aravantinos.

Technische Einrichtung: Georg Linnebach.

Nach dem zweiten Akt findet eine längere Pause statt.

Kein Vorspiel

Anfang 7 Uhr. — Ende nach 9 Uhr.

[illegible]

Oper Am Königsplatz.

Anfang 7½ — Montag, den 14. Dezember 1925. — Anfang 7½

280. Abonnements-Vorstellung.

Tosca

Musikdrama in drei Akten von V. Sardou – L. Illica – G. Giacosa. Deutsch von Max Kalbeck
Musik von Giacomo Puccini.
Musikalische Leitung: Selmar Meyrowitz
Spielleitung: Josef Höpfl

Floria Tosca, berühmte Sängerin	Mafalda Salvatini
Mario Cavaradossi, Maler	Alexander Kirchner
Baron Scarpia, Chef der Polizei	Theodor Scheidl
Cesare Angelotti	Eduard Habich
Der Mesner	Heinrich Schultz
Spoletta, Agent der Polizei	Emil Lücke
Sciarrone, Gendarm	Rudolf Krasa
Ein Hirt	Trude Conrad
Ein Schließer	Rudolf Watzke
Zwei Häscher	Bernhard Sperber
	Albert Wehrle
Roberti, Gerichtsbüttel	Alfred Kunze

Ein Kardinal. Ein Offizier. Ein Sergeant. Soldaten. Damen. Herren. Bürger. Volk usw.

Dekorationen nach Entwürfen von P. Aravantinos in den Werkstätten der Staats-Theater angefertigt. Technische Einrichtung: Georg Linnebach.

Nach dem 1. und 2. Akt je 15 Minuten Pause.

Anfang 7½ Uhr. — Ende gegen 10 Uhr.

[illegible]

Wochenspielplan für:		Opernhaus Unter den Linden	Oper am Königsplatz
Dienstag,	15. Dez.:	279. Ab.-Vorst. 7½ Uhr La Traviata.	291. Ab.-Vorst. 7½ Uhr Mignon.
Mittwoch,	16. „	280. Ab.-Vorst. 8 „ Fidelio.	292. Ab.-Vorst. 7½ „ Die Fledermaus.
Donnerstag,	17. „	281. Ab.-Vorst. 6½ „ Die Meistersinger.	293. Ab.-Vorst. 8 „ Das Christelflein.
Freitag,	18. „	12 Uhr: Sinfonie-Mittags-Konzert. Abends 7½ Uhr 5. Sinfonie-Konzert	294. Ab.-Vorst. 7½ „ Hänsel und Gretel. Klein Idas Blumen
Sonnabend,	19. „	282. Ab.-Vorst. 8 Uhr Wozzeck	295. Ab.-Vorst. 7½ „ Rigoletto.
Sonntag,	20. „	283. Ab.-Vorst. 7 „ Hänsel und Gretel. Klein Idas Blumen	296. Ab.-Vorst. 7 „ Bohème.
Montag,	21. „	284. Ab.-Vorst. 7½ „ Tanzabend. [illegible]	297. Ab.-Vorst. 7 „ Der Evangelimann

line the abandoned melancholy in the poetry of Georg Trakl, who gave this period its most crystalline and most horrifically possessed verse. But thereafter Webern concentrated on religious poetry, while continuing the style he had discovered in the Trakl set: a soprano line frozen in high tension and accompanied by packed instrumental polyphony (in op.14 for a quartet of clarinets and strings). The *Five Sacred Songs* for voice and mixed quintet, op.15 (1917-22), set folk poems; the *Five Canons* for soprano, clarinet and bass clarinet, op.16 (1923-4), have Latin texts appealing to Christ and the Cross; the *Three Traditional Rhymes* for voice and four instruments, op.17 (1924-5), are again naïve expressions of piety; and the *Three Songs* for voice, E flat clarinet and guitar, op.18 (1925), make up a triptych in honor of the Virgin.

•Serialism: Schoenberg•

It is by no means immediately obvious that the two last of these sets are serial compositions whereas the others are not. Webern, for the

matic ripples, is succeeded by an orchestral adagio in D minor, which may be interpreted as the composer's direct entry into his opera in order to express his sympathy with his inadequate hero, that sympathy which alone gives *Wozzeck* not just coherence but tremendous force.

While Berg was engaged on his opera, and Schoenberg struggling with *Die Jakobsleiter*, Webern was devoting his attention exclusively to songs, most of which use small groups of instruments to effect the capture of a lyrical moment, as in the earlier pair of Rilke songs, op.8 (1910). The *Four Songs*, op.13 (1914-18), draw on varied instruments selected from a small orchestra, but are unified by the image in all four poems of the wanderer, exiled far from home, feeling himself apart and eventually finding rest in a vision of the sacrament. This was to be a pattern reflected in Webern's career. The *Six Songs*, op.14 (1917-21), under-

Above: A Russian prisoner of war painted by Egon Schiele in 1916, the year *Wozzeck* was conceived by Berg. Both painter and composer expressed the anguish of the individual at the mercy of military authorities.

moment, easily incorporated the new technique into his present style, but for Schoenberg, who had laboriously worked out the method of serialism, this new way of composing had immediate, far-reaching consequences. For although some tentative approaches towards twelve-note serialism have been pointed out by some analysts in *Die Jakobsleiter* – and indeed in Berg's 'Altenberg' songs, written several years earlier – Schoenberg himself was only aware of his new method as he developed it in his works of 1920-3, in which he came to re-introduce thematic working and formal molds inherited from baroque and classical music. Rather like Stravinsky at this period, he adopted a kind of neoclassicism. The nature of serialism made this almost inevitable, not because the series of twelve notes has to be used as a theme (Schoenberg sometimes does this, sometimes not), but because serialism establishes a framework of order within which thematic working is readily re-established.

How this happens may be simply stated. The twelve notes of the chromatic scale are arranged in a fixed order, the series, which can be used to generate melodies and harmonies. The series may be referred to in a composition in a great variety of ways: as a melodic line that follows the serial ordering of the twelve notes, or as a melody with accompaniment, or as a chord progression, to give some straightforward examples. The possibilities are vast, and certainly the use of the serial method does not impose any particular style, as becomes obvious when one considers the very different serial compositions created by Schoenberg, Berg and Webern, not to mention such later practitioners of the technique as Frank Martin, Luigi Dallapiccola, Pierre Boulez or Milton Babbitt.

As far as Schoenberg was concerned, the serial method provided the means to build large-scale instrumental movements once more – something which he had not found possible since the *Five Orchestral Pieces* of 1909. Significantly, the development of the serial technique came about in three almost purely instrumental works: the *Five Piano Pieces*, op.23, the *Serenade* for septet, op.24 (with a bass voice in one movement), and the *Piano Suite*, op.25, all composed between 1920 and 1923. Of these, the *Suite* was the first fully twelve-note serial composition, the others including non-serial movements as well as movements based on series of more or fewer than twelve notes. And increasingly Schoenberg was returning to the established forms of Viennese classical and light music, not so much in op.23, but quite definitely in the *Serenade*, which includes march and dance movements developing the acid irony of *Pierrot lunaire*, and in the *Suite*, which adapts the baroque model in having a prelude followed by a sequence of dances, while including also a Brahmsian intermezzo.

These works established the character of Schoenberg's early serial music: clear in thematic working and formal movement, close to conventional models of texture and structure, but often spiked with irony. In his next composition, the Wind Quintet, op.26 (1923-4), he took up the four-movement form of chamber-music tradition, with a sonata-form first movement, a scherzo and trio, a slow movement and a rondo finale. The *Suite* for septet, op.29 (1925-6), follows the line of the *Serenade*, both works probably having been designed in part to demonstrate that serial music could be blithe, happy and comic, as indeed it may, though only under the uneasy subterfuge of parody. When the style is more relaxed and assured, as it is in the *Variations for Orchestra*, op.31 (1926-8), and the Third String Quartet, op.30 (1927), then the expressive nature of the music becomes more openly bleak, edgy or angry, and if Schoenberg's music were the only evidence available, then one might well conclude that atonality, whether serial or not, necessarily went along with the expression of predominantly negative emotions.

•Serialism: Webern and Berg•

The works composed at the same time by Berg and Webern show how serialism could be turned to quite different ends – technical, esthetic and expressive – by composers who had already established their own creative worlds. Webern's initial easy adoption of the new method was continued in the String Trio, op.20 (1926-7), the first instrumental work he had finished since the *Three Little Pieces* for cello of 1914. But in his next work, the Symphony, op.21 (1928), he found a quite new style opened up by the serial technique. With its emphasis on intervallic pattern, and with the importance Schoenberg gave to inverting the pattern and turning it backwards, serialism lent itself very naturally to the kind of highly structured music created by the polyphonists of the fifteenth and sixteenth centuries, or at least to a modern use of the same kind of artifice.

Webern's Symphony, totally unlike any other work bearing that much-used title, shows the possibilities with exemplary clarity. Of its two movements, the first is an extremely symmetrical four-part canon, in which the voices are confused by being passed among the ensemble of clarinets, horns, harp and strings. The second movement is again a very formal conceit, being a set of variations which turns back on itself halfway through. Indeed, throughout the work the emphasis is so much on structural matters – on one voice answering another, one variation alluding to another – that the music may easily impress first and foremost as a pure construct in sound devoid of expressive connotations. And Webern himself very clearly delighted in this aspect of his work, in the purity, transparency and simplicity that gives his compositions the perfect rightness of works of nature rather than art.

With Berg the case was different again. Like Webern he was fascinated by the possibilities within music for structural complexity, as is abundantly demonstrated in his *Chamber Concerto* for piano, violin and thirteen wind instruments (1923-5). This work was designed as a present for Schoenberg on his fiftieth birthday and as a celebration of the Viennese 'trinity' of Schoenberg, Berg and Webern. Accordingly, Berg not only filled it with musical mottoes spelling out the three names in pitch letters (e.g. A–[l]–B–A–[n] B–E–[rg] for himself) but also made the number three a central element. There are three movements, three groups of instruments (two soloists and the ensemble), units of thirty measures, and so on. However, where Webern would have brought all this out into

Below: Webern conducting a Mahler symphony. In common with Schoenberg and Berg, Webern found it hard to make a living by composing, since his work was not generally accepted; he therefore resorted to conducting concerts of conventional music – not necessarily highbrow, Johann Strauss was popular – in order to make ends meet.

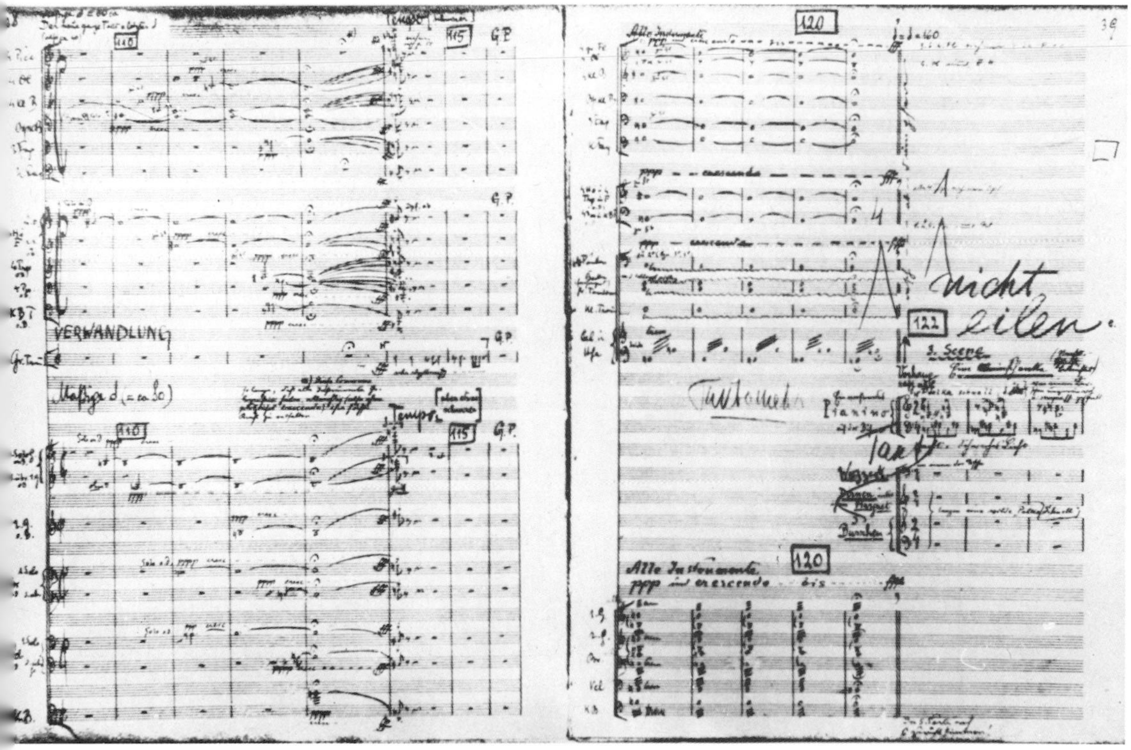

Left: Pages from the autograph score of *Wozzeck*.

Left: The tone-row chart from Schoenberg's Fourth String Quartet, illustrating clearly the concept of serialism that was the fundamental basis of the work of the Second Viennese School.

the open, Berg places it firmly in the background, so that one's first impression of the concerto is almost bound to be that it is a deeply romantic work, powerful and resilient in the first movement with solo piano, moving in the central adagio with solo violin, and relentless in the finale with both soloists.

Though composed after Schoenberg's first serial works, and at a time when the three composers were once more in close contact with each other in Vienna after the separation of the war, Berg's *Chamber Concerto* is not yet serial. Unlike Webern, who began to use the new method almost at once, in 1924, Berg took a while to become convinced that serial composition would be possible for him. He first tested the waters in composing a song, 'Schliesse mir die Augen beide' (Close both my eyes, 1926), and thereby gained the confidence to pursue the technique in his *Lyric Suite* for string quartet (1925-6), which immediately shows how far Berg was from both Schoenberg and Webern in his serial thinking. He allows himself to use several different but related series, to include non-serial movements, and to combine serial working with the rich tonal harmony that had never been wholly absent from his music. This rich harmony here contributes powerfully to the sense that the quartet hides a secret program of affection, love and disaster – as was recognized instinctively long before it was revealed, in the 1970s, that the work was a musical confession to the great love of the latter part of Berg's life, Hanna Fuchs-Robettin.

• Growing reputations •

By this time Schoenberg, Berg and Webern were all beginning to gain a measure of public acceptance, contrasting with the hostility of a decade before, and even with the situation in the immediate post-war years, when Schoenberg had been obliged to found a Society for Private Musical Performances in order to gain a hearing in Vienna for contemporary music.

On 14 December 1925 *Wozzeck* was given its world première in Berlin, conducted by Erich Kleiber; the event made Berg's reputation, and before long his opera was heard all over the world. Neither Schoenberg nor Webern achieved anything like the same fame or material success, but Schoenberg's appointment in 1925 to the Prussian Academy of Arts in Berlin, where he was to take a master-class in composition, was at least a demonstration of official approval, and in 1927 Webern gained security from a regular conducting engagement with Austrian radio. Moreover, the music of all three composers figured prominently on the programs of the annual festivals of the International Society for Contemporary Music, of which the first was held in 1923, and though almost none of their music was recorded for the gramophone, radio stations in Austria, Germany and England gave them an occasional airing.

The new mood is reflected in the public voice Schoenberg was able to adopt in his *Variations for Orchestra*, which were composed for Wilhelm Furtwängler and the Berlin Philharmonic, as well as in his comic opera *Von Heute auf Morgen* (From Today to Tomorrow), op.32 (1928-9). Like other composers of the period, notably Weill and Hindemith, Schoenberg here

Above: Middle section of the triptych *Grossstadt* (Big City) by Otto Dix, 1927-8. Dix, whose ruthless satire laid waste the post-war social and political corruption in Germany, here depicts the bawdy glamour of Berlin nightlife.

Left: Scene from the first production of *Lulu* in Zürich in 1937, starring Nuri Hadzig as Lulu and Albert Emmerich as the Lion-tamer. Berg wanted the première to take place in Berlin, but the rise of Nazism and his evident disfavor made this impossible. However, his friend Erich Kleiber conducted a concert version on 30 November 1934, resigning from his post as director of the Berlin Opera four days later, unable to tolerate the Nazi régime.

applies himself to contemporary society, but the message of his comedy of manners is that modernity by itself is a shallow alternative to thinking for oneself, that modishness is unacceptable, whether in music or in life. The same idea, directed with satirical zest at Stravinsky as the 'little Modernsky,' had already been put forward in the *Three Satires* for chorus, op.28 (1925).

Schoenberg's other operatic project of this period, *Moses und Aron*, is very different, though it too shares fundamental ideas with a choral work, the *Four Pieces*, op.27. For Schoenberg, writing his own libretto, Moses is the man who is gifted with a vision – that of the unfathomable Jewish God – but who lacks the verbal skills to communicate his vision to his people. By contrast, Aaron can make the vision known and acceptable, but only at the cost of compromise with the wonder and spectacle that people expect. The metaphor is, however, more deeply religious and philosophical in meaning. Beyond the problem of communication, the opera is about finding a way to God through obedience, prayer and steadfast commitment to truth. In the third act of the libretto Moses finally comes to express the ultimate goal as 'unity with God,' but as in *Die Jakobsleiter* Schoenberg could find no way of giving this idea a musical realization, and the opera ends, by no means inappropriately, at the conclusion of the second act with Moses lamenting his failure to master language, or rather the failure of language to define the ineffable. It is also appropriate that the opera is a serial composition – Schoenberg's largest, lasting for nearly two hours – since the series is an idea which can be represented in music only partially, its possible forms and powers being, like those of Jehovah, infinite and incomprehensible.

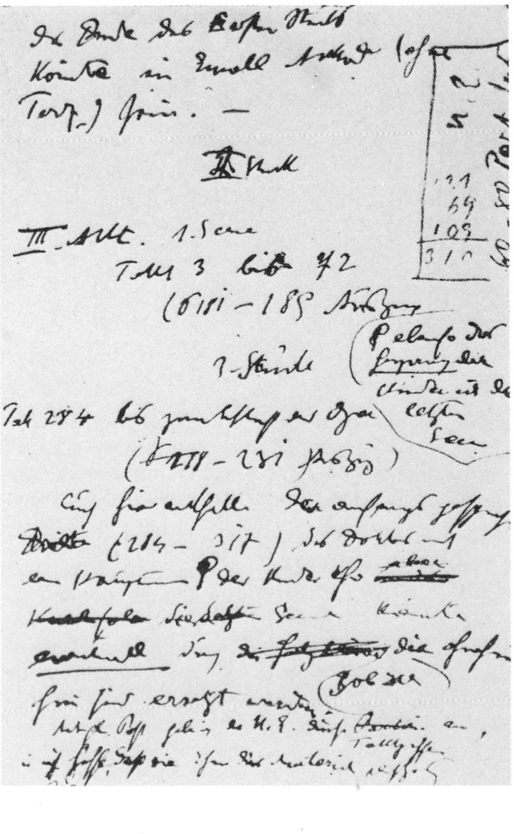

Left: Berg's sketch for *Lulu* Act III, Scene 1.

• *Lulu* and death •

The two completed acts of *Moses und Aron* date from 1930-2 and have much in common, musically and philosophically, with other works of this time, notably the two *Piano Pieces*, op.33 (1928 and 1931), and the *Six Pieces*, op.35, for male chorus (1929-30). Meanwhile Berg was also finding his way towards his second opera, for which he decided to make his own conflation of two plays by Frank Wedekind, pioneer of sexual frankness on the stage. The two plays concern the career of Lulu, a woman who fascinates all the men (and one of the women) with whom she comes into contact, and by compressing the plays into one Berg was able to depict that career in a single arch of rise and fall, marked by a great many musical and dramatic correspondences. For many years, however, an embargo was placed on the unfinished third act by Berg's widow, and only after her death was it possible for the opera to be performed complete; its world première was thus delayed until 24 February 1979, when Pierre Boulez conducted it at the Paris Opéra.

Above: The first performance of *Lulu* given in its entirety, in Paris on 24 February 1979, in a production conducted by Pierre Boulez. Berg died before finishing the opera's third act, but left sketches detailed enough for Erwin Stein to complete it in 1936. Even then, however, Berg's widow withheld publication, and it is only since her death that performance has been possible.

Berg began work on *Lulu* in 1928, but at first progress was slow, partly because it had been two years since he had written anything new. In the intervening time he had orchestrated a group of *Seven Early Songs*, chosen from his output of 1905-8, and arranged three movements of his *Lyric Suite* for string orchestra, answering a request made by his publisher, Emil Hertzka of Universal Edition (on this same occasion Schoenberg orchestrated his Second String Quartet and Webern his *Five Movements*, op.5). The composition of *Lulu* was then interrupted at an early stage when the singer Růžena Herlinger commissioned a concert aria, and Berg wrote *Der Wein* (1929), setting translations by Stefan George of three poems by Baudelaire in praise of wine as a release from restraint and convention. Later on, when the opera was almost complete, Berg set it aside in order to write his Violin Concerto (1935) – another commission, this time from the American violinist Louis Krasner – and when he died in Vienna on Christmas Eve 1935, *Lulu* was still not finished.

Berg's failure to complete his second opera is perhaps partly to be explained by the complexity of the task he had set himself. As with *Wozzeck*, the music is very supple in responding to different dramatic situations, but the scenes are now longer and the musical forms correspondingly more extended. At the same time, the palindromic nature of the action, with Lulu rising to a prestigious marriage and then falling to meet her death as a London prostitute at the hands of Jack the Ripper, called for a long-range control of every aspect of the composition. But equally, Berg seems to have been reluctant to let go of *Lulu*. He put himself into the opera as the composer Alwa, and it is clear that he thought of the work as belonging to Hanna Fuchs-Robettin: it was a world he was unwilling to leave for the reality of his unsatisfactory marriage.

In the summer of 1934, by which time the opera had been finished but not yet orchestrated in full, Berg drew from it a set of five *Symphonic Pieces*. The outer movements, much the weightiest, are concerned with Lulu in relation to two of the other principal characters. In the 'Rondo' and 'Hymn' she belongs to Alwa, who in the opera uses this music to sing a passionate aria of devotion. But though the movement is filled with ripe romantic ardor, Alwa's love is for a poeticized image of Lulu, not for the woman herself. Acceptance of Lulu as she really is comes only from her murderer, Jack the Ripper, at the end of the opera. The 'Adagio' essentially reproduces this passage, complete with the dying words of Lulu's lesbian admirer Countess Geschwitz, and it tells, in the most moving, most tonal music of the entire work, of the unspeakable sadness of human needs and aspirations which are answered only in a despicable criminal death.

Within these great set-pieces are the 'Ostinato,' written to accompany the rapid events of a silent film in the middle of the opera (Schoenberg had earlier written an orchestral accompaniment to an imaginary film scenario, his *Begleitmusik zu einer Lichtspielszene*, op.34, of 1929-30, showing how well music could intensify feelings of dread and terror), and the 'Variations,' which set the location of the final scene in London, using as theme a song by Wedekind. The centerpiece of the suite is Lulu's song from Act II scene 1, which is her single opportunity to express what she believes. In excited coloratura she declares that she is what she is, and has never pretended otherwise; if others were attracted to her, then they knew what they were doing and what they would get out of her. It is perhaps a cynical and pessimistic view of human motivations that the opera and the suite put forward, but for the duration of Berg's music it is the only one possible.

Berg's final work, the Violin Concerto, which he completed only a few months before his death, is again concerned with a heroine and with easeful death, being inscribed 'to the memory of an angel' and inspired by the death at the age of eighteen of Manon Gropius, the daughter of Mahler's widow by her second husband. Like the *Chamber Concerto*, it is not a display-piece but a closely integrated work, divided this time into four movements linked to form two halves. The first seems to invoke memories of the living girl, her charm and vivacity, while the second part presents first catastrophe and then peace, as a Bach chorale is carefully woven into the texture. Berg's ability to accommodate tonal music within his far-ranging serial technique had been displayed before, in a *Tristan* quotation worked into the *Lyric Suite*, and in the Wedekind song included in *Lulu*. In the Violin Concerto, however, the Bach fragment is not only given a place but made to seem the work's natural culmination and home.

The first performance of the Concerto, in Barcelona in April 1936, was due to have been

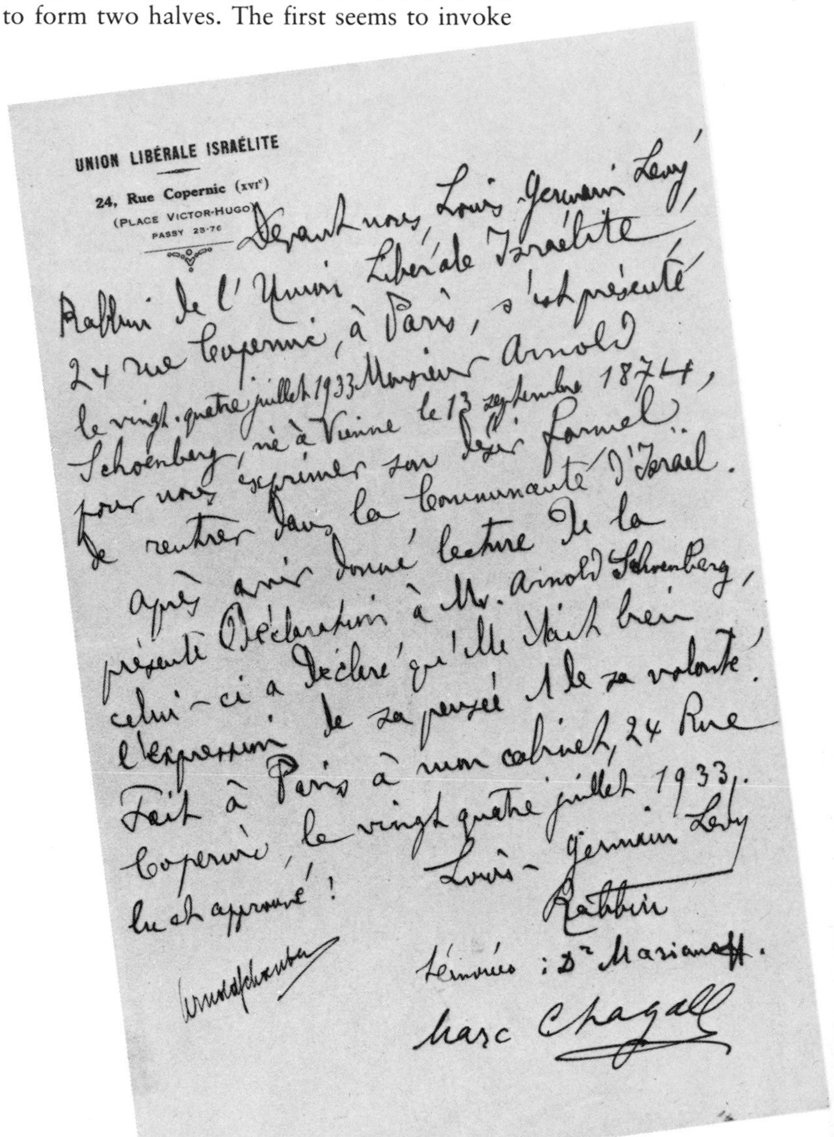

UNION LIBÉRALE ISRAÉLITE
24, Rue Copernic (XVIe)
(PLACE VICTOR-HUGO)
PASSY 29-76

Devant nous, Louis Germain Lévy, Rabbin de l'Union Libérale Israélite 24 rue Copernic, à Paris, s'est présenté le vingt-quatre juillet 1933 Monsieur Arnold Schoenberg, né à Vienne le 13 septembre 1874, pour nous exprimer son désir formel de rentrer dans la Communauté d'Israël.

Après avoir donné lecture de la présente Déclaration à Mr. Arnold Schoenberg, celui-ci a déclaré qu'elle était bien l'expression de sa pensée et de sa volonté.

Fait à Paris à mon cabinet, 24 Rue Copernic, le vingt quatre juillet 1933.

Lu et approuvé!

Arnold Schoenberg

Louis-Germain Lévy
Rabbin

Témoins: Dr Marianoff.

Marc Chagall

Above: Document witnessed by Marc Chagall, verifying Schoenberg's conversion to Judaism in 1933. The document was drawn up in Paris, where Schoenberg spent the summer of that year prior to emigrating to America; this followed his resignation from the Prussian Academy of Arts in the wake of the anti-semitism that was now rife in Berlin.

Right: Portrait drawing of Webern by Hildegard Jone. Webern was so impressed by Jone's poetry, which is of an extremely introspective nature, that from the day he first met her in 1926 he restricted himself in the field of song-writing entirely to settings of her words.

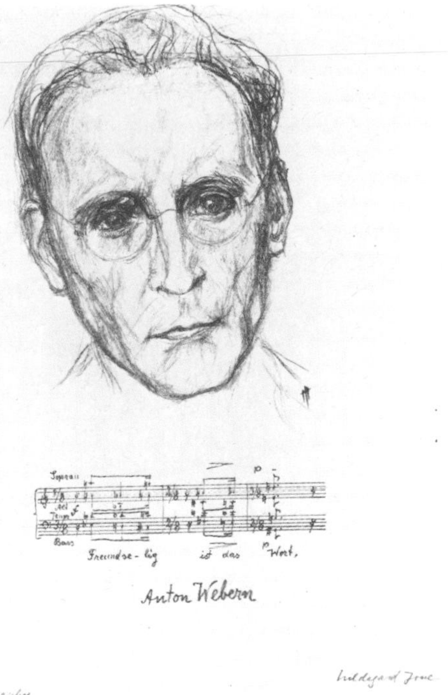

Below: Autograph of Berg's score for his Violin Concerto, written after the death on 22 April 1934 of Alma Mahler's daughter Manon Gropius, to whom Berg dedicated the work. The entry of the Bach chorale is shown on this page.

conducted by Webern, but he found it impossible to face the task of introducing his friend's last work so soon after his death. Schoenberg, too, was deeply saddened by Berg's death, coming so rapidly after he had begun to enjoy some comfort as a result of the success of *Wozzeck*. But before Christmas 1935 the three composers had already been separated by events among the living.

•Schoenberg in America•

In May 1933 Schoenberg had left Berlin, following an announcement from the new Nazi government that Jewish elements were to be removed from the Prussian Academy. He was not at this time a practicing Jew – he had converted to Lutheranism in 1898 – but one of his first acts on fleeing to France was to return to the Jewish faith. Then in October 1933 Schoenberg left with his family for the United States, where he was to remain for the rest of his life.

At the same time he began again to compose tonally, which he had not done for a quarter of a century. His first tonal works were revisions of baroque concertos, one for cello after a harpsichord concerto by Georg Matthias Monn (1932-3) and one for string quartet after a *concerto grosso* by Handel (1933). In both cases Schoenberg's adaptation goes far into the substance of the music, so that the effect is of an outrageous and unstable mixture of the eighteenth century and the twentieth, rather as in Stravinsky's *Pulcinella*. Then came a wholly original *Suite* in G major for string orchestra (1934), followed by a symphonic reinterpretation of the Brahms Piano Quartet in G minor, op.25 (1937), and *Kol nidre* for rabbi (speaker), choir and orchestra, op.39 (1938), which Schoenberg intended for performance in synagogues. For this a tonal style was obviously required, but there was no such clear reason for the return to tonality in the other works: only the composer's discovery that he still had tonal ideas which he wanted to pursue, and his feeling that nothing would be served if he refused himself the pleasure of doing so.

Of course, he continued at the same time to compose serial works, and indeed at this time created two of his greatest achievements with the new method, the Violin Concerto, op.36 (1935-6), and the Fourth String Quartet op.37 (1936). Unlike Berg's almost exactly contemporary work, Schoenberg's Violin Concerto has no program and no leaning towards tonality, which probably accounts for the fact that it is much less well known. It is, however, an extraordinarily brilliant and bizarrely colorful score, clearly displaying in its three movements the composer's penchant for continuous development. The quartet is similarly complex in form, though again the four-movement plan is conventional, and both works show Schoenberg trying to find within serialism some equivalents for the harmonic features that uphold tonal structures, notably those of modulation.

Two portrait drawings by Egon Schiele (1890-1918): Arnold Schoenberg (*above*) and Anton von Webern (*right*).

Opposite: Portrait of Alban Berg by Schoenberg, 1910.

In the year he completed these works, 1936, Schoenberg was appointed a professor at the University of California at Los Angeles, and his teaching duties there, coupled with his determination in learning English, may account for the relative sparseness of his output during the next few years. In 1939 he returned to his Second Chamber Symphony, which he had begun in 1906, and brought it to completion as his op.38, the task no doubt eased by his recent new experience of tonal composition. But his only new work was *Kol nidre* until in 1941 he composed the tonal *Variations on a Recitative* for organ, op.40. Cast in his favorite key of D minor, this is the most substantial of his late tonal works, looking back to the richly expanded tonality of his compositions of the period of the First Quartet and First Chamber Symphony. It is also one of the most weighty and demanding works in the modern organ repertory.

When Schoenberg came to return to serialism again, after a gap of six years, he did so without quite giving up a sense of tonality. His *Ode to Napoleon Bonaparte* for reciter, piano quintet and string orchestra, op.41 (1942), ends in E flat, the key of Beethoven's 'Napoleon' Symphony no.3, and generally seems to reside only a short distance from definite keys; it is also unusually relaxed in its serial method. The Piano Concerto, op.42, written in the same year, is once more fully serial, but even here the feeling of hazy tonality lingers, and the work also looks back to the composer's earlier achievements in conflating the four movements of a symphony into a single span. His next work was again tonal, a *Theme and Variations* in G minor for wind band, op.43 (1943), though here there was an external reason; the piece was written in response to a request from Schoenberg's American publishers, Schirmer, who wanted something that might appeal to the many such bands in American schools and colleges.

•Webern: last years•

Schoenberg's move to Schirmer from the Viennese house of Universal had become inevitable after the Anschluss of 1938. Universal had been publishing Schoenberg's music since the time of *Pierrot lunaire* and in the 1920s had also taken on Berg and Webern, but once Austria

was under Nazi control no Austrian publisher could touch music which had been condemned by the authorities. Just as performances of Schoenberg, Berg and Webern effectively ceased throughout Nazi-influenced Europe, so did publication of their music, and naturally this caused particularly severe difficulties for Webern, who had remained in Vienna and now found himself cut off from friends, from most aspects of musical life, and from any way of making money except by undertaking mundane tasks that Universal put his way.

None of this, however, was reflected in Webern's music. Ever since the Symphony of 1928, his output had been divided between perfectly fashioned instrumental works and settings of verses by Hildegard Jone, whose blend of nature observation and mystical Christian piety he took very much to heart. He met Jone in 1926 and after that meeting completed no work with words by anyone but her, though it was not until 1933-5 that he made his first settings, in two sets each of three songs, his op.23 and op.25. Jone was, however, informed about the progress of his instrumental compositions, particularly the *Concerto for Nine Instruments*, op.24 (1934), of whose interlocking symmetries Webern was particularly proud. Here the twelve-note series is itself generated from a still smaller unit, consisting of only three notes, and the whole work is thus built on a frame that allows only very few choices of harmonic or melodic interval. And this high degree of consistency goes along with a similarly stark restriction of rhythmic units, as well as a didactic presentation of the music through the medium of dissimilar soloists: three woodwind, three brass, two strings and piano.

Though the Concerto is an unusually strictly composed piece, Webern's liking for closely ordered serial construction is also very clear in his subsequent instrumental works: the *Piano Variations*, op.27 (1936), the String Quartet, op.28 (1936-8), and the *Orchestral Variations*, op.30 (1940). The purity of Webern's technique in these works also makes it possible for him to refer to two or more different structural methods at the same time. For instance, the first movement of the quartet is a theme and six variations which also functions as a sonata form without development, and which is composed almost throughout in two-part canon.

Much the same style is to be found in the three choral works in which Webern set poems by Jone: *Das Augenlicht* (The Light of the Eyes), op.26 (1935), the First Cantata, op.29 (1938-9), and the Second Cantata, op.31 (1941-3). The luminous textures and the extreme clarity of Webern's late music are now at the service of poetry which, though hardly of any great merit, is perfectly in accord with Webern's own thinking, delighting in delicacy and religious sentiment, in expressing a fragile moment of spiritual insight. For example, in the central soprano aria of the First Cantata, contained between two choral movements, the soloist sings of maple seeds falling to the ground only to gain new life, and the vocal line is surrounded by a

pattering of falling instrumental phrases in canon with it.

The Second Cantata is on a larger scale, with six movements and a duration of a little more than ten minutes: it is, indeed, the largest composition of an artist who had made the miniature his genre. Webern himself likened it to a Renaissance Mass, though a nearer model might well have been the church cantatas of Bach. The work begins with a recitative and aria for bass soloist, followed by a chorus with solo soprano; then comes a recitative and aria for the soprano, the aria featuring also chorus and *obbligato* violin, and the cantata ends with a canonic chorus. As in the First Cantata, the vocal parts continue the pure tranquillity of the Jone songs, and the orchestral writing, though sometimes weightier than in the earlier work, produces a fine entwining of color beneath and around the voices.

In 1943, the year in which he completed the Second Cantata, Webern was able to attend the première of his *Orchestral Variations* in Winterthur, in Switzerland, but otherwise he lived an isolated existence in Vienna. In the last weeks of the war he and his wife left the city in order to be with their daughters at Mittersill, in the mountains near Salzburg, and there on 15 September 1945, the composer was shot in error by an American soldier. A third cantata, again with words by Jone, was left at a very early, fragmentary stage.

•The survivor•

Schoenberg, eldest of the three, was now the last survivor, and he was in poor health. In 1944 he had written nothing; but in the autumn of 1945 he was well enough to accept a commission from the composer and musical entrepreneur Nathaniel Shilkret, who was involving various composers in a suite based on texts from Genesis. Schoenberg contributed a short *Prelude* for chorus and orchestra, his op.44, in which chaos gives way to divine order in the shape of an eight-part canon. Other items in this curious collaboration were produced by Shilkret himself, Tansman, Milhaud, Toch, Castelnuovo-Tedesco and Stravinsky.

In August 1946 Schoenberg suffered a heart attack which left him an invalid for the remaining five years of his life. The experience of closeness to death left its mark on the String Trio, op.45 (1946), written soon after his recovery and reaching back to the excited intensity of the first atonal works, though by way of the serial method. As in the Piano Concerto, Schoenberg returns here to single-movement form, but the Trio is by no means so clearly divided into sections corresponding to standard movement types; instead it rushes forward in continuous development at high pressure, urgent and visionary in what it has to tell. It was Schoenberg's last chamber work, and his masterpiece in this genre which had always been closest to him.

Top: Schoenberg in 1951.

Above: Schoenberg's autograph sketch for the String Trio, op.45 (1946), written shortly after his heart attack in 1945.

A year later he was compelled to take up his pen again by public rather than private events, specifically by a report from a concentration camp. The whole drama is recreated in his short composition, *A Survivor from Warsaw* for narrator, male chorus and orchestra, op.46: Jews on their way to the gas chambers break spontaneously and unanimously into singing the 'Shema Yisroel,' the command to love the one God. In using heightened speech with music

Left: Four-sided chess set, designed by Schoenberg and clearly a commentary on the Second World War.

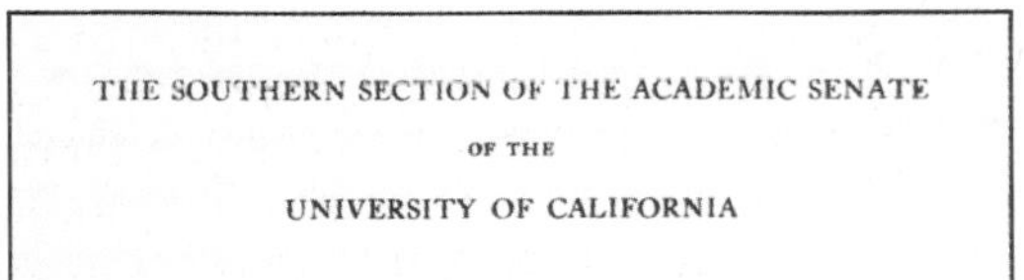
THE SOUTHERN SECTION OF THE ACADEMIC SENATE
OF THE
UNIVERSITY OF CALIFORNIA

Is Pleased to Present

ARNOLD SCHOENBERG
Professor of Music

AS THE

SEVENTEENTH ANNUAL
FACULTY RESEARCH LECTURER

"The Composition with Twelve Tones"

There will be a reception for Professor Schoenberg in the Community Lounge, Kerckhoff Hall, following the lecture.

WEDNESDAY EVENING, AT EIGHT-THIRTY O'CLOCK
March 26, 1941
JOSIAH ROYCE HALL

Left: Poster advertising one of Schoenberg's lectures, given in 1941. On settling in the United States, he was offered the post of professor of music at the University of California in Los Angeles, and this position enabled him to carry on composing while enjoying more financial security than he had been used to in Vienna. He retired from teaching in 1944 at the age of seventy.

here, Schoenberg aligned this work with his most powerful utterances: the final solo from *Gurrelieder*, *Pierrot lunaire*, the stage piece *Die glückliche Hand* (The Lucky Hand), op.18 (1910-13), which had concerned itself with his passionately held convictions of artistic responsibility to the truth, *Die Jakobsleiter*, *Moses und Aron* and most recently the *Ode to Napoleon Bonaparte*, in which Byron's castigation of dictatorship had been newly directed at a contemporary example. When the verbal message was decisively important, it had to break out of its musical containment: the truth was more important than the perfection of the image.

After a final instrumental work, the *Phantasy* for violin and piano, op.47 (1949), Schoenberg returned again to his religious preoccupations. In *Dreimal tausend Jahre* (Three Thousand Years) for unaccompanied choir, op.50a (1949), he looked forward to the re-creation of a people under God in the new state of Israel, and in *De profundis*, op.50b (1950), also for unaccompanied choir, he set the penitential prayer of Psalm 130. His last work, unfinished, was the first of a projected sequence of 'modern psalms' to his own texts; the *Modern Psalm*, op.50c (1950), is scored for speaker, chorus and orchestra, and, like *Moses* and *Die Jakobsleiter*, it breaks off at a point where it would need to speak of unity with God. Instead it ends, most appropriately, with the words 'And still I pray.'

Schoenberg died in Los Angeles on 13 July 1951. He had had the satisfaction of seeing his music received with new interest and acclaim in Europe, particularly in those parts of Europe which had been under Nazi dominion, and he also knew of the excitement with which young composers were discovering the vast new possibilities that lay within the serial method. For some, like Pierre Boulez, who wrote an obituary entitled 'Schoenberg is dead,' he was now a reactionary who clung to the old forms and genres which his own serial method had rendered obsolete. But that was Schoenberg's strength, not his failure; his adherence to the past was not nostalgia but a reverence for enduring virtues while he pressed forever onward.

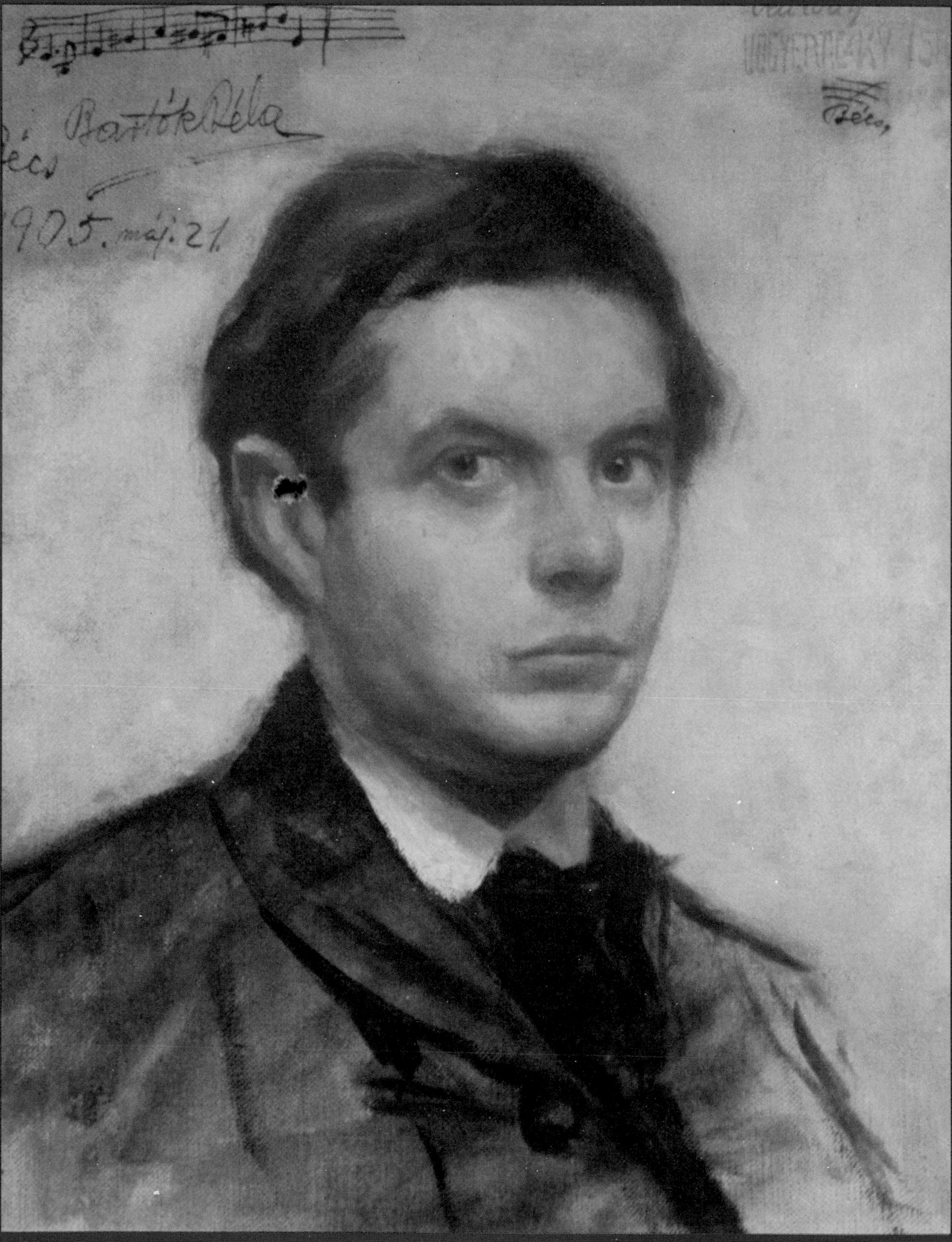
Bartók Béla
1905. máj. 21

BÉLA BARTÓK AND PAUL HINDEMITH

HAMISH MILNE

Opposite: Portrait of Béla Bartók (1881-1945) by István Vedrödy-Vogyeraczky, 1904, with a later dedication date of 21 May 1905. The musical quote is the opening theme in his First Suite for Orchestra, op.3.

The retreat from Romanticism took many paths. If the technique of serialism was to prove the most far-reaching in terms of its influence on subsequent generations of the avant garde, the two great examples of Bartók and Hindemith are enough to remind us that it was not the only solution, nor necessarily the most fruitful. In fact, neither of these masters advocated the abandonment of tonality or key relationships, and both vigorously refuted any classification of their music as 'atonal.' What they both sought, although quite independently, was to free themselves from the traditional constraints and obligations of resolved dissonance without negating the gravitational pull of tonal centers.

The Hungarian Béla Bartók was born in 1881 into circumstances of modest middle-class security in Nagyszentmiklós, a small town in a part of eastern Hungary that was ceded to Rumania after the First World War. His father was head of the agricultural college there, and his mother, Paula Voit, was a schoolteacher and an accomplished amateur pianist. It was she who started young Béla's musical education at the age of five. However, the family situation was reduced to one of precarious insecurity by the early death of Bartók's father in 1888. Paula Bartók assumed sole financial responsibility for the upbringing of Béla and his younger sister, and at first she tried to make ends meet by giving piano lessons in addition to her work at school, but soon she was forced to look further afield for a more remunerative position, and it was not until 1894 that the family had a settled home once again, this time in Pozsony (now Bratislava, in Czechoslovakia).

Inevitably Bartók's education had proceeded rather erratically, but he had by this time already composed a number of small dances and piano pieces. In Pozsony, the leading provincial cultural center, he had sound and systematic teaching from László Erkel (son of Ferenc Erkel, the most celebrated Hungarian composer after Liszt) and later from Anton Hyrtl, and he was able to broaden his general musical experience through the rich concert life of the city. The youthful works composed during this period reflect the Brahmsian tenor of local musical taste at the time and reveal little of Bartók's personality, but they show a confident grasp of conventional styles and forms.

In 1898 he was offered a place at the Vienna Conservatory, but, on the advice of Dohnányi (just four years his senior but something of an idol to Bartók), he rejected the offer and took the far-reaching decision to go instead to the Budapest Academy of Music. There he studied the piano with István Thomán, a former pupil of Liszt. This was a wholly beneficial experience which he remembered with gratitude for the rest of his life, but his relationship with his composition teacher, Jámas Koessler, was less productive. Koessler was a staunch upholder of the Brahmsian tradition, and his strict academic disciplines reduced Bartók to a state of creative impotence. He was roused from this torpor 'as by a lightning stroke' (Bartók's words) by the Budapest première of Richard Strauss's tone-poem *Also sprach Zarathustra*, and he composed a number of grandiloquent works in the Straussian mold, such as the *Scherzo* for piano and orchestra (virtually a fully-fledged concerto) and, most notably, *Kossuth*, a symphonic poem in seven movements based on the life of the Hungarian revolutionary hero. Although *Kossuth* does not withstand comparison with the best of its Straussian models, the great conductor Hans Richter presented it with the Hallé Orchestra in Manchester in 1904, giving the young composer his first public recognition.

As early as 1903, Bartók had declared in a letter to his mother that he had set himself but one objective in life – 'the good of Hungary and of the Hungarian nation.' There were other influences to be assimilated (notably Debussy and, much later, the fastidious clarity of pre-Classical music), but for the time being Bartók struggled towards his goal by welding Hungarian elements on to his current Straussian or, more properly, Lisztian techniques. The Rhapsody no.1 and the Piano Quintet are representative of this stage of his artistic development. There were also setbacks. At the Academy he had been considered first and foremost a pianist, and it was in this capacity that he had to earn his living when his studentship came to an end. A visit to the prestigious Rubinstein Competition in Paris in 1905 ended in humiliation and fiasco. The piano prize was won outright by Wilhelm Backhaus, and the composition prize was withheld altogether, possibly for financial and political reasons. Bartók, who had entered in both categories, was deeply hurt, but beneath his disappointment and wounded pride he dimly felt that the truly Hungarian style he sought, at once personal and national, had not yet crystallized.

•Folk music•

The turning-point came in 1905-6, when, in collaboration with his friend Zoltán Kodály, Bartók began systematic researches into the roots of Hungarian folk music. Both suspected that the superficial melodic and rhythmic mannerisms of the so-called 'Hungarian' style, as evinced by the pieces 'à l'hongroise' by Haydn, Schubert and Brahms, and even by Liszt himself in his *Hungarian Rhapsodies*, derived more from urban gypsy music than from the true indigenous music of the peasants. They initiated a series of expeditions into remote rural regions, where they discovered with amazement an undreamed-of wealth of primitive folk music, barely touched by Western art music.

At first they jotted down the songs roughly by hand, but they soon began to use Edison cylinders to record the peasant songs and dances *in situ* and to transcribe and classify the material at home. Owing to the historical, geographical and ethnic complexities of Eastern Europe, Bartók soon found it necessary to extend his researches to neighboring regions. By the end of his life this passion (for that is what it became) had yielded a collection of over fourteen thousand melodies of Hungarian, Slovak, Rumanian, Croatian, Ruthenian, Turkish, Bulgarian and even African origin. The demands of his promising career as a concert pianist were already becoming irksome to him and when, in 1907, he was offered a position as professor of piano at the Budapest Academy, he was already clear in his mind as to the direction his life was taking. He wrote in his autobiography, 'I particularly welcomed this appointment as it enabled me to settle down at home and pursue my researches into folk music.'

The first fruits of this endeavor appeared in 1907 with some arrangements of Hungarian and Slovak folksongs. Bartók was at pains to point out that the extreme simplicity of the melodies (invariably based upon more primitive scales than the familiar major and minor modes), far from placing constraints on the composer, was a liberating factor; free of conventional harmonic implications, the melodies had nothing to gain by the addition of an accompaniment in the manner of, say, a German folksong setting by Brahms or Schumann. Bartók later likened the simplest approach to that of a jeweler mounting a precious stone in its setting, and there is no better example than his own technique in the eighty-five short piano pieces, *For Children* (1908-9), based on Hungarian

Top: Bartók on a research trip to the village of Darazs, in the county of Nyitra, Czechoslovakia, in 1908. Local peasants were asked to sing into Bartók's two-way Edison wax cylinder sound-recorder.

Above: Professor István Thomán's piano class at the Budapest Academy of Music, 1901. Bartók is standing in the back row, third from the left.

and Slovak tunes. Here the unadorned melody is often repeated three or four times, but in quite different harmonic settings which illuminate fresh aspects of its character. These enchanting miniatures have taken their place alongside Bach's *Anna Magdalena Notebook* and Schumann's *Album for the Young* as a foundation stone of the beginner's repertoire.

Right: Bartók's study notes concerning particular folksongs, taken on a field trip. His early interest in folksong developed after meeting Kodály in 1905 – the two formed a lasting friendship based in part on their enthusiasm for genuine folksong. Although Hungarian folk music had not been ignored by earlier composers, no one had undertaken such specific research into the field.

• Pre-war years •

The years leading up to the First World War were formatively crucial ones for Bartók. A series of piano pieces (*2 Elegies*, *3 Burlesques*, *2 Rumanian Dances*, *4 Dirges* and *7 Sketches*) show radical advances towards his mature style and a personal harmonic language, although the occasional lapses into Lisztian piano style sometimes fit uneasily with the growing terseness of his thematic material. The blatantly experimental *14 Bagatelles* avoid any such pitfalls by reason of their extreme brevity. If there are still parallels with Liszt to be drawn, they are with the laconic and prophetic utterances of his old age. It was this collection that caused Busoni to exclaim, 'At last, something *really* new!' Bartók's fascination with the music of Liszt (part artistic, part patriotic) was an enduring one, and the *Two Portraits* for orchestra are indebted to Liszt's principles of thematic metamorphosis. In another orchestral work of the same period, *Two Pictures* (1910), we find the new influence of Debussy, whose music had been introduced to Bartók through the enthusiasm of his friend Kodály.

Above: Bartók in peasant costume in his home in Budapest around 1910-12, playing his peasant's hurdy-gurdy (a *nyenyere* in Hungarian). His fascination for the folklore of his native land is reflected also in his hand-made peasant furniture, of which he was extremely proud.

In 1907 Bartók went through a severe emotional crisis as a result of his thwarted passion for a young violinist, Stefi Geyer. It seems that their differences were ideological; she was devout, he an atheist. There are a number of autobiographical threads to be traced in his music as a result of this episode, but the most important is the composition of the First String Quartet, which Kodály described as 'a man's return to life after traveling to the very borders of non-existence,' apparently a reference to the fact that Bartók had contemplated suicide over the affair. In later years Bartók expressed some disquiet over 'Wagnerian' elements in this Quartet, but to most listeners it is Beethoven who seems a more tangible source of inspiration in this serious and moving work. The grave fugal opening arouses distant but distinct echoes of Beethoven's Quartet in C sharp minor, op.131, and the masterly freedom with which Beethoven, in his later works, adapted sonata and rondo forms to accommodate specific threads of argument is increasingly to be observed in Bartók's extended instrumental works. Bartók may have felt later that the peasant elements were less naturally absorbed than in the flawless Second Quartet (1915-17), but the work is an entirely worthy start to the magnificent series of six quartets, which have become universally acknowledged classics of twentieth-century music.

In 1909 Bartók married Marta Ziegler, a sixteen-year-old student in his piano class at the Academy, and their son, Béla, was born the following year. By now Bartók was attracting attention among the new guard of intellectuals at home, and a 'Hungarian Evening' in Paris in 1911, where he and Kodály were branded as 'young barbarians,' added a touch of notoriety to his growing international reputation. Bartók's immediate response was his *Allegro Barbaro* for piano, a piece of unbridled ferocity which is typical of a certain strain in his music, although it is unfortunate that this single aspect should have been seized upon by certain critics who could see nothing beyond a nihilistic iconoclasm. Despite this defiant gesture, Bartók was becoming increasingly depressed at the resistance of the musical establishment to his work.

The poet Béla Balázs encouraged him in their collaboration in the same year over Bartók's only opera, *Bluebeard's Castle*, which was submitted for a competition. It was rejected out of hand and this, together with the failure of a New Music Society in Budapest, deepened Bartók's dejection to the extent that he withdrew from public life.

• Dissonance •

Bartók was moving away from a narrow nationalism towards a universal humanism, and the outbreak of war affected him deeply, in the first instance because of its inhuman brutality, and in the second because of the consequent isolation of his research territories. The Suite for piano (1916) may reflect some of his despair, for the third movement (incorporating Arabic scales encountered on a visit to North Africa) has a remorseless violence, while the slow finale evokes something of the desolation of a deserted battlefield. The accelerating tempo of the first three movements is a further instance of his growing concern with overall structure, manifested earlier in the First Quartet and, especially, in *Bluebeard's Castle*.

In 1918 a ballet, *The Wooden Prince*, earned Bartók his first taste of public acclaim at its première at the Budapest Opera, and this, no doubt, encouraged him to embark on his '*pantomime grotesque*,' *The Miraculous Mandarin*. The score has great subtlety of characterization, but the harmonic idiom is now of uncompromising harshness. Nevertheless, it was the lurid violence and sexuality of the scenario (by Melchior Lengyel) rather than any musical 'difficulty' which repeatedly prevented it from reaching the Budapest stage; it was presented successfully in Prague but caused a scandal in Cologne, where the Mayor closed the production after a single performance.

The extreme dissonance of *The Miraculous Mandarin* and the contemporary *Three Studies* for piano reaches its apex in the works of the early 1920s, sometimes referred to as Bartók's 'Expressionist' period. The two Sonatas for violin and piano, despite their vigorous folk-dance rhythms, bring Bartók's music into greater proximity than at any other time with the dodecaphonic music of Schoenberg through their tendency to utilize equally all the notes of the chromatic scale and to avoid repeated exposure of the same notes. Moreover, the lyrical melodies make liberal use of 'octave displacement,' which gives rise to angular leaps of a kind particularly associated with the Second Viennese School.

These were difficult years for Bartók at home. In 1923 he divorced his first wife and married Ditta Pásztory. Also, he was constantly subjected to politically motivated attacks over his ethnographical researches. He had taken little active part in the political upheavals that followed the end of the war, but he had sat on the music committee set up by the short-lived Communist Republic, and this made him automatically suspect in the eyes of Horthy's right-wing administration. As a result, he found himself the subject of ludicrous but damaging accusations in connection with his publications on the racial derivation of folk music and for his association with known Communists such as Béla Balázs, who was now in exile. He seriously considered emigrating, and there is no doubt that, by this time, he could have settled successfully in a number of European capitals. However, his bonds with Hungary were too strong, and he remained in Budapest, although most of his works were premièred abroad, where he made frequent tours as a pianist.

In 1926 he set about replenishing his repertoire for these appearances, and in a summer of furious creative activity completed his First Piano Concerto, the Piano Sonata, *Nine Little Pieces* and the suite *Out of Doors*. In the orchestral *Dance Suite* of 1923 he had triumphantly achieved his goal of 'assimilating the idiom of peasant music so completely that one is able to forget all about it and use it as one's mother tongue.' Although the work celebrates peasant music and dance, all the themes are of Bartók's own devising, and this seamless synthesis of ethnic and personal elements is a notable feature of the piano works of 1926. There are important innovations as well, such as the

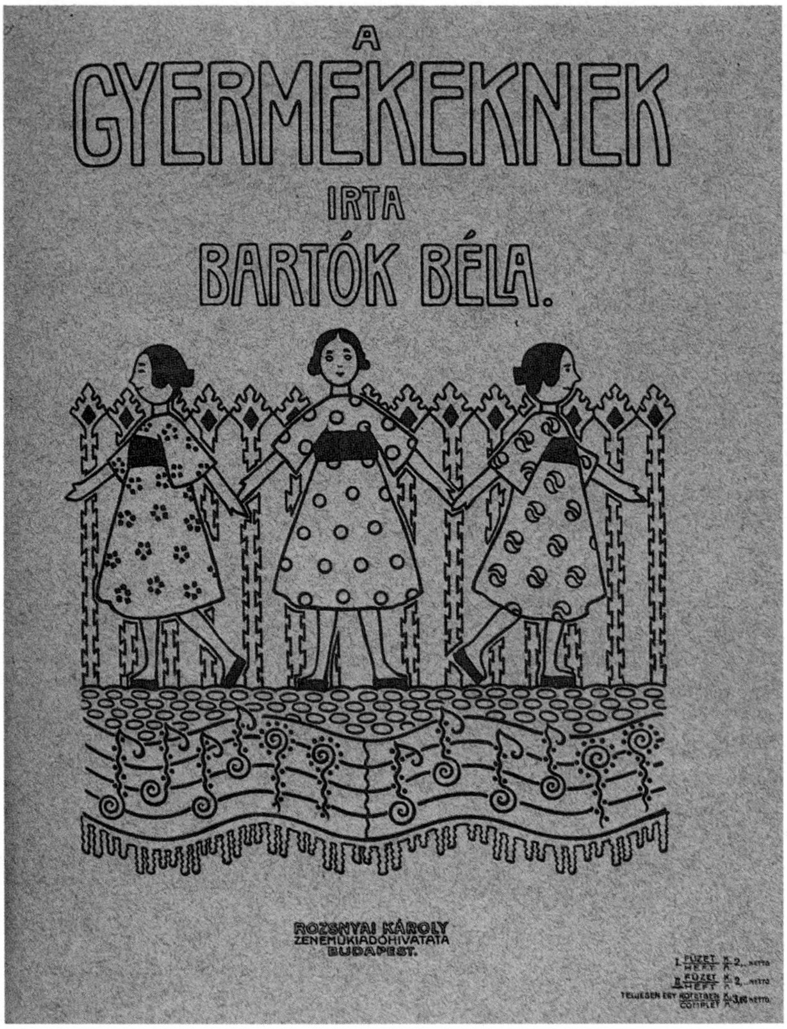

Above: Front cover of the first edition of Bartók's album *For Children*, 1908. Teaching was always an important element for Bartók in his conception of the composer's calling.

emergence (in the 'Night Music' movement from *Out of Doors*) of a totally novel strain of impressionism – an eerie evocation of stillness disturbed by the twittering of insects, the rustle of twigs or the sudden shriek of a bird.

• Classicism •

The rigorous contrapuntal clarity of the *Nine Little Pieces* suggests a leaning towards the objectivity of the 'neoclassical' style then much in vogue, but it more probably stems from Bartók's recent immersion in pre-Classical keyboard music in connection with his teaching duties. In any event, this newly won contrapuntal mastery adds a further rich dimension to the masterpieces of the 1930s, sometimes referred to as his 'classical' period, reflecting a shift in emphasis from emotional expression towards a fastidious balance of style, expression and architecture, although these changes were evolutionary rather than radical.

The Third and Fourth String Quartets, composed in 1927 and 1928 respectively, exemplify this evolutionary process. The Third is the shortest of the six, violent in its percussive rhythm and attack and explosively compressed, not only in its unique single-movement form, but also in its motivic components, which are often cramped within the interval of a fourth. While the Fourth Quartet retains much of the ferocious concentration of its predecessor, its form is extended to five movements: the first and fifth are closely related, likewise the second and fourth, while the central slow movement acts as the keystone of the arch or the middle of the palindrome. The Fifth Quartet, written in 1934, further explores an integrated five-movement structure, and the symmetry of the palindrome governs the architectural geometry of two other important productions of the early 1930s, the Second Piano Concerto and the *Cantata Profana* for soloists, double chorus and orchestra.

During the 1930s Bartók's professional commitments continued to take him abroad a great deal, although most of his composing was done at home in Budapest, where the authorities had thawed slightly. Performances of his new works were now given quite regularly, though generally some years after the European premières. It gave Bartók great satisfaction when, in 1936, he was finally relieved of his teaching duties and offered a research post by the Hungarian Academy of Sciences. This belated recognition of his stature at home was little more than an acknowledgment of his undisputed standing abroad, both as ethnomusicologist and composer. In the later 1930s this reputation was further enhanced by several important commissions. Paul Sacher, the conductor of the Basle Chamber Orchestra, was the instigator of three of Bartók's greatest works of this decade, the *Music for Strings, Percussion and Celesta*, the Sonata for two pianos and percussion; and the *Divertimento* for string orchestra.

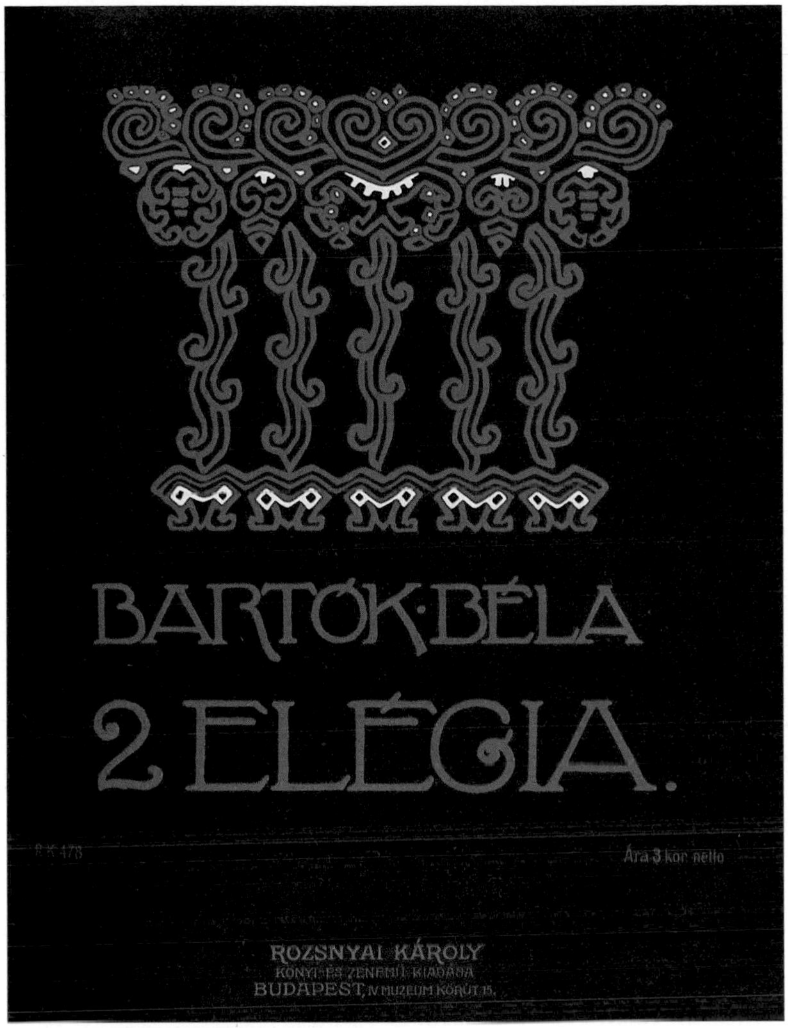

Above: Front cover of Bartók's *Two Elegies*, again a first edition. Both these volumes of piano music were very largely derived from folksong material collected on Bartók's previous research expeditions. The design of the covers deliberately emphasizes these ethnic origins.

Left: Peasant girl who sang for Bartók and was photographed by the composer himself on one of his field trips.

Left: Part of the last page of the original manuscript of Bartók's Viola Concerto, which he never completed, together with his twenty-five-year-old Waterman fountain pen. He began the concerto in 1945, the last year of his life, and it was later completed by Tibor Serly.

The *Music for Strings, Percussion and Celesta* may be Bartók's greatest work. Although Bartók was himself a pianist, his handling of stringed instruments is unrivaled, and the numerous novel techniques (in part derived from his observation of peasant fiddlers) which he had devised in the quartets are exploited still further here. The percussion had risen to previously undreamed-of prominence in the earlier years of the century but, strangely, no one had combined the two families in this way before. Bartók also required the two string orchestras to be separated on the stage by the percussion, so the spatial element adds a further dimension to this unique sound-world. Furthermore, the architectural organism is at once so complex and so unified that many of its subtleties escaped a whole generation of musicologists.

All this would be of no more than academic interest were not the level of artistic and emotional inspiration so unflaggingly sustained and so directly communicated. Analysis can prove unequivocally that the four-movement edifice grows from the halting, plaintive phrases of the opening fugue, but the exalted 'night music' of the adagio or the joyous affirmation of the final dance explains itself unaided. The Sonata for two pianos and percussion is scarcely less original in conception or less compelling in presentation, conjuring an extraordinary wealth and variety of sonorities from its superficially uningratiating resources, while the *Divertimento*, despite its dark-hued slow movement, is one of Bartók's sunniest inspirations.

The awesome mastery and assurance of these works might seem to presuppose a resolution of conflicts in Bartók's personal life but, sadly, this was far from the reality. He had a stubborn moral integrity which forbade him to keep silent in the face of wrong-doing, and he had been one of the first to speak out against the anti-Semitic tendencies of Horthy's administration. The rise of Hitler filled him with grave disquiet – he refused to play in Germany as early as 1933 – and when in 1938 Austria capitulated to the Anschluss, he severed his connections with his Austrian publishers. The idea of leaving Hungary for an uncertain future in a foreign land was intensely painful to him, but after the death of his mother in 1940 he set sail with his wife for America.

Bartók's American years were few. Although he derived some satisfaction from insecure and poorly paid research work at Columbia University, his health was failing and his financial resources dwindling, and it seemed that his creative spirit was broken. In February 1943 he collapsed with a kind of leukemia, but later in the year there was some improvement in his condition and a miraculous resurgence of his creative powers. During the next two years he composed the opulent *Concerto for Orchestra* for Koussevitzky, the gritty Sonata for solo violin for Yehudi Menuhin and the radiant Third Piano Concerto, a parting gift to his wife. The last thirteen measures of the piano concerto still needed orchestrating when he died on 26 September 1945 at West Side Hospital, New York, after a sudden and irreversible relapse.

Bartók's music enjoyed a surge in popularity after his death. Initially this may have been due to the appeal of the *Concerto for Orchestra*, and,

indeed, some of his former advocates deplored what they saw as softness or appeasement in this work and in the Third Piano Concerto. In fact, this euphonious warmth continues a trend already noticeable in works composed before Bartók left Hungary, notably in the Second Violin Concerto and the *Divertimento*. To decry it as cheap populism is sheer intellectual snobbery. If we stand back and look at Bartók's output as a whole, we can see it as a great arch rounding from the naïve Romantic excess of *Kossuth* to the unforced and humane intelligibility of the Third Piano Concerto, having reached its apex in the harshness of the period roughly spanned by *The Miraculous Mandarin* and the Fourth String Quartet. Viewed in this way, the increasing clarity and lucidity of his 'classical' period lead naturally and inevitably to this last American phase.

Bartók followed a lonely road. A proud and unbending man, he was never able to adjust pragmatically to the external pressures of his troubled times and personal circumstances. And yet the power and universality of his music has earned him a place beyond controversy among the great masters of his art.

Right: Bartók recording his composition *Contrasts* with the distinguished Hungarian violinist Joseph Szigeti, and the jazz clarinetist, Benny Goodman, for Columbia Records in New York, 1943. *Contrasts* was specially commissioned for Szigeti and Goodman.

Below left: Bartók in Basle as a guest of his friends Mr and Mrs Sacher. A conductor of distinction, Paul Sacher was always extremely generous as regards financing Bartók and other composers in their times of need and in giving them new musical assignments. He commissioned from Bartók the *Divertimento* (1939).

Below right: Bartók in New York, 1943. His health was deteriorating at the time and he was financially insecure, though receiving support from ASCAP (the American Society of Composers, Authors and Publishers).

Above: Fool in Trance by Paul Klee, 1929. As well as being a painter, Klee was also an accomplished violinist, and he was concerned with musical equivalents in terms of line and color. Many of his works, including this painting, have a musical derivation.

• Paul Hindemith •

The German Paul Hindemith (born in Hanau on 16 November 1895) was a man of a quite different mettle, a pragmatist undaunted by the vicissitudes of life around him. His childhood was not particularly happy, yet neither was it (like Bartók's) traumatically marked by tragedy or bereavement, so his down-to-earth attitudes to the practical and business aspects of professional life can be attributed to a self-reliance engendered by the hurly-burly of a penurious working-class background.

In 1902 his father, Robert Rudolf Emil Hindemith, a house-painter by trade, settled with his wife, Marie Sophie, and their three children in Frankfurt, where he set up his own business in a working-class district. The children seem to have led a somewhat joyless existence. Discipline was strict, and duty took precedence over pleasure. Music was a part of this régime, and Paul started violin lessons at the age of nine. He was fortunate to have as his teacher a very able violinist, Alice Hegner, who passed him on to Adolph Rebner when she left Frankfurt two years later. Rebner was the leading violin teacher at the Hoch Conservatory, and a year later (in 1909) he secured a free place there for his protégé; Hindemith remained there until the end of his studentship in 1917.

Initially Hindemith's official studies were confined to the violin, but in 1912 he started composition lessons, first with Arnold Mendelssohn (a distant relation of the composer), then with Bernard Sekles. Hindemith had hitherto been rather bashful and secretive about his composing (which he had begun by 1910 at the latest), presumably through fear of ridicule, but by the time of his first composition lessons at the Conservatory he had already amassed a formidable portfolio of extended chamber works. None of these has survived intact, but such fragments as have been published suggest a precocious talent at once natural and methodical. Nonetheless, it was a wise decision to

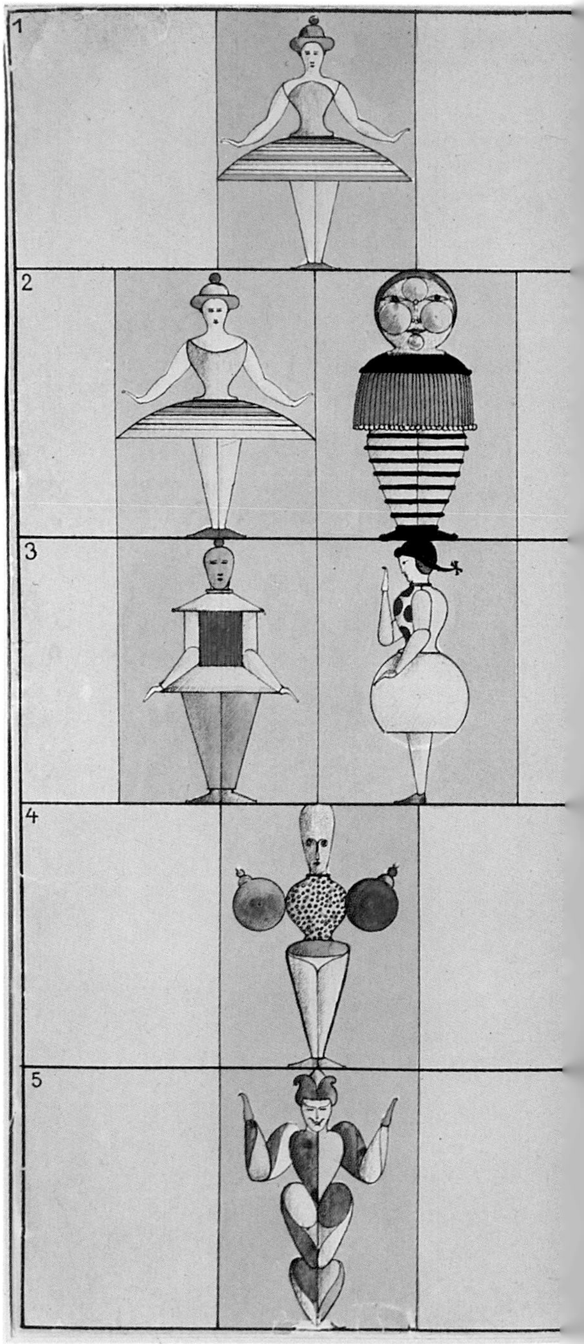

devote himself primarily to his instrumental studies in his first years at the Conservatory, for his commitment to the reality of music-making was to provide a lifelong stimulus to his creative imagination. The viola later superseded the violin as his principal instrument, but he also acquired formidable skills on several others.

His progress was rapid, and in the summer vacation of 1913 he fulfilled his first professional engagement in a light orchestra at a Swiss resort. Just two years later he was given the second violin chair in Rebner's string quartet, and in the same year he was appointed principal violin of the Frankfurt Opera Orchestra, where, within months, he took over as concert-master. An insatiable appetite for work and for involvement with every level of music making was a dominant characteristic in Hindemith from the earliest days, but these jobs were as much a response to financial exigencies as artistic ones. His father had volunteered for military service in 1915 and was killed in Flanders shortly afterwards. The sense of obligation instilled in childhood now asserted itself, and Hindemith instantly assumed financial responsibility for his mother, his sister Toni and his younger brother Rudolf, a promising cello student at the Conservatory. Hindemith was himself called up in 1917, but although he was stationed near the front line he escaped the worst horrors of the war, largely, it seems, through his great good fortune in finding himself under the command of an officer whose passion for chamber music was at least equal to his military ambition.

Most of Hindemith's music composed before the end of the war has either been destroyed or remained unpublished. The *Three Pieces* for

Below: Oscar Schlemmer's designs for Hindemith's *Triadic Ballet*. Originally this was staged by the Bauhaus in 1916; Hindemith collaborated with Kokoschka, and the result was by all accounts a most stylish production. Schlemmer's designs were done for the 1925 production at Donaueschingen – by this time the ballet had been rewritten for mechanical organ, with the organ roll punched by Hindemith himself.

9
10
12
"Triadisch",abgeleitet von Trias = Dreizahl,Dreiklang. Es sind 3 Tänzer (eine Tänzerin und zwei Tänzer,die einzeln,zu zweien oder zu dreien tanzen); drei Hauptfarben der Bühne: citrongelb, weiss und schwarz; es sind zusammen 12 Tänze in zusammen 18 Kostümen.
Das Ballett entstand z.T. schon vor 1914. Teile davon wurden 1916 aufgeführt. Erstaufführung des ganzen Balletts 1922 im Landestheater in Stuttgart. Darauf in Weimar und Dresden. Später (mit Musik zu einer mechanischen Orgel von Paul Hindemith) in Donaueschingen und in einer Revue in Berlin.

cello and piano, op.8, are an exception and suggest (as do certain references in contemporary letters) that he began his career much as one would expect, firmly in the mainstream of German post-Romanticism. Of the immediately preceding generation of composers, Max Reger (1873-1916) has been most often cited as Hindemith's spiritual forerunner. Both composers rejected the prolix expressive continuum of the post-Wagnerians in favor of a rejuvenation of Classical forms (albeit, in Reger's case, on an often massive scale) and looked to J. S. Bach as an esthetic ideal, seeking in their different ways to emulate his sublime balance of linear and harmonic tension. Such ideas were in the air in Germany at the time, not least through the pervasive and prophetic personality of the Italian-born Ferruccio Busoni who, despite his enthusiasm for Liszt, looked back wistfully beyond the sensuous and egocentric emotionalism of the Romantics to the mystical equilibrium and universality of Bach, and forward to the problem of recapturing this inspired objectivity in a truly progressive idiom. Hindemith later expounded views that had much in common with Busoni's.

• Experimentation •

Although the creed and dogmas of Hindemith's maturity were some way off, his apprenticeship was over by the end of the war. In the course of the next few years he experimented with a bewildering variety of styles and techniques, assimilating and rejecting diverse elements from jazz to the Baroque with almost insolent ease. He expressed impatience with the accepted traditions of teaching and performance, rebelling, on the one hand, against Rebner's constant *espressivo* and, on the other, against Sekles's insistence on the established norms of formal procedure.

Few composers have had first-hand acquaintance with a broader spectrum of music. He was playing constantly either at the Opera or in chamber music with friends at the newly established Verein für Theater- und Musikkultur, an early experiment in community arts. His First String Quartet was performed at one of these gatherings, and his kinship with Reger is evident in its quicksand of constantly shifting harmonic implications arising from the convoluted chromaticism of the individual lines. Rather more surprising cross-winds can be detected in the five Sonatas, op.11. The florid melismata of the 'Fantasie' of the Sonata for viola and piano, op.11 no.4, (the largest of the group), recalls Debussy's exotic vein, while the beguiling theme of the ensuing variations has an affectionately Franckian accent. Notwithstanding these and other more or less definable influences, the imposing arrival of the finale in the middle of the uninterrupted chain of variations shows an already formidable and individual command of structure.

From here Hindemith plunged headlong into the 'Expressionism' then much in vogue in Germany. Expressionism covered a variety of artistic trends and tendencies, but all involved some degree of distortion of esthetic norms in laying bare the ego or psyche of the artist, a doctrine almost diametrically opposed to Hindemith's later beliefs but one which fitted well with his prevailing mood of exasperation at the entrenched attitudes of his elders. The earnest

Below left: Drawing by Rudolf Heinrich of the Amar–Hindemith Quartet, dated 31 July 1923. Hindemith played the viola as a member of this quartet from 1922 until 1929. The other players in the drawing are Licco Amar (1st violin), Walter Caspar (2nd violin) and Maurits Frank (cello).

Below: Fugal score on which Hindemith has drawn lions (for his wife, whose birthsign was Leo) to illustrate the fugal entries. Their didactic character is echoed in a great many other scores, all similarly decorated for educational purposes.

Left: Hindemith rehearsing with a celebrity piano quartet, around 1932. The other performers are Bronislaw Huberman, violinist, Pau Casals, cellist, and Artur Schnabel, pianist.

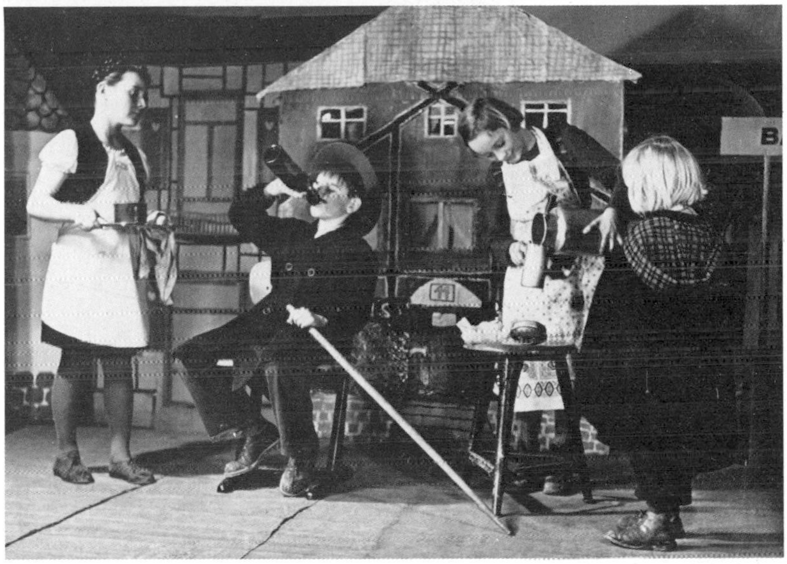

Above: Scene from *Wir bauen eine Stadt*, one of Hindemith's operas written for children. Hindemith sincerely believed in practical teaching from an early age, stressing the importance of involvement for children so that they should have a genuine comprehension of music.

anxiety of the Second String Quartet has much in common with Schoenberg's expressionist vein of ten years earlier, but in the wake of the war a new taste for horror and atrocity, even sadism, entered German Expressionism, and it was from this new wave of writers that Hindemith drew texts for three one-act operas which bolstered his own reputation as a radical. The first of these, *Mörder, Hoffnung der Frauen* (Murderer, Hope of Women, 1919), was by Oscar Kokoschka (a writer as well as a painter in his younger days), and replete with all manner of obscure sexual symbolism, while *Sancta Susanna* (1921), to a story by August Stramm in which a sex-crazed nun strips and ravishes the figure of Christ, makes the censorious repression of Bartók's *The Miraculous Mandarin* seem petty indeed. The ironic parodies of the third, *Das Nusch-Nuschi* (1920), a mildly decadent piece of exotic whimsy, suggest that the violent Puccinian and Straussian outbursts in *Mörder, Hoffnung der Frauen* were prompted less by any real sympathy with the agonizings of the text than by the eagerness of the young composer to try his hand at the latest theatrical fashion. In any event, Hindemith later spoke disparagingly of these first operatic ventures.

• Radicalism •

Hindemith proclaimed his growing musical radicalism with far greater aplomb in the *Kammermusik No.1*, op.24 no.1. The title itself – Chamber Music No.1 – is a provocative expression of his irritation with the soulful reverence that prevailed in Rebner's Quartet (he broke with it in 1921 and became a founder member of the Amar–Hindemith Quartet, which specialized in modern music). A riot of musical nose-thumbing, *Kammermusik No.1* is scored for a motley theater-band of twelve players, who are instructed to sit with their backs to the audience, and its *outré* instrumentation together with its jarring mixture of unrelated keys (polytonality), its shrill noise-effects and its use of jazz and cabaret music were deliberately calculated to offend the rearguard, who wasted no time in branding its composer a decadent upstart. He made further, not entirely convincing, use of jazz in the *Suite 1922* for piano, but in the same year composed the serious and tortured Third String Quartet, which again picks up the expressionist thread of 1920.

Willy Strecker of Schott's publishing house, who had signed up Hindemith principally on the strength of his op.11 sonatas, had mixed feelings about his protégé's progress. 'We are completely mystified by your sudden change of direction,' he wrote in 1920. Hindemith retorted that it was 'all true and natural music, not in the least bit forced,' but it is easy to understand Strecker's increasing unease when confronted with such things as 'quarter-note=600–640, tearing tempo, wild, tone quality is irrelevant,' the heading to the fourth movement of the Solo

Left: Hindemith in old age, probably around 1960.

Viola Sonata, op.25 no.1, of 1922. In that year alone Hindemith composed no less than eleven works, none of which could be described as insubstantial, while his performing activities continued unabated. He had been invited to participate in the new contemporary music festival at Donaueschingen, which had the dual advantage of providing a platform for his own works and enabling him to keep his ear close to the ground of the contemporary scene. His magpie eclecticism continued unabashed and to the borrowings already mentioned should be added the names of Bartók (in the Third String Quartet and the Sonata for viola and piano, op.25 no.4) and the French *enfants terribles*, notably Darius Milhaud (*Kammermusik No.1* and the *Suite 1922*).

The work that marks the end of this period of rebellion and exploration is *Das Marienleben*, a cycle of fifteen songs to poems by Rainer Maria Rilke on events in the life of the Virgin Mary, in which Hindemith renounced all other sources in an attempt to recapture the Classical or, more usually, baroque virtues which were to become the basis of his definitive personal language. Although traces of his expressionist manner linger here and there, and the harmony recognizes possibilities undreamed of in earlier epochs, the shocking gestures and virtuosic egotism have subsided in cool lines of contrapuntal discourse, in which even the solo voice assumes an egalitarian role. The texture begets the form of the individual songs, which in many instances are re-creations of eighteenth-century models. 'The best things I have yet written,' declared Hindemith, and his publishers concurred with relief and enthusiasm.

• Neoclassicism •

This resolution of the hectic experiments of the preceding years in a decisive commitment to neoclassicism suggests that their motivation had not been anarchic or Dadaistic but simply anti-Romantic. Hindemith's greatest gift had been, and was to remain, for the lucid and orderly exposition of arresting ideas rather than the breast-beating passion of the Romantics or the tortured self-revelation of the Expressionists. In the ensuing years of consolidation Hindemith composed six further works entitled *Kammermusik*. All are concertos for a solo instrument with chamber orchestra, but their starting-point is the *concerto grosso* of the eighteenth century (in particular the 'Brandenburg' Concertos of J. S. Bach), and the soloist has an essentially concertante role within the ensemble quite unlike the heroic protagonist of the nineteenth-century concerto. In fact, this resuscitation of Reger's 'back to Bach' call laid Hindemith readily open to jibes of 'Bach with wrong notes.' Their antique flavor is sustained by the remorselessly busy counterpoint and the avoidance of specific emotional suggestion or contrasted themes within movements, and their modernity by the piquancy of harmony and

Opposite: Temptation of St Anthony, a panel from the Isenheim altarpiece by the great German artist Mathias Grünewald (*c.*1455-1528). It was Grünewald who was the inspiration for two of Hindemith's major works: the opera *Mathis der Maler*, based on the life of the painter, which was first performed at the Stadttheater, Zürich, on 28 May 1938; and the *Mathis der Maler* Symphony, completed before the opera and actually based on this particular altarpiece. It is a true example of symphonic program music, each of the three movements describing musically one of the panels of the altar.

Right: The first page from the fifth book of sketches for Hindemith's *Mathis der Maler* Symphony, 1934.

instrumentation. The series is crowned by the *Concerto for Orchestra* of 1925, which deploys its larger forces in small opposing groups.

Classical forms also dominate Hindemith's first full-length opera, *Cardillac* (1926), based on a tale by E. T. A. Hoffmann of a goldsmith who murders his customers in order to regain possession of his precious creations. The librettist, Ferdinand Lion, contained the action in a series of set-pieces which enabled the composer to revive the formulae of Handelian opera and to combine them with eighteenth-century instrumental forms, which he does with such dramatic, even poignant, effect that *Cardillac* has a strong claim to be the most unjustly neglected opera of this century. More than a decade was to pass before Hindemith returned to the operatic stage with such deeply serious purpose, but, in the meantime, he composed two comedies of contemporary manners, *Hin und Zurück* (There and Back Again, 1927) and *Neues vom Tage* (News of the Day, 1928-9), whose witty cynicism and satire provoked a temporary resurgence of the irreverent pranks of the early 1920s.

In 1927 Hindemith accepted a position on the staff of the Hochschule für Musik in Berlin. It was a surprising decision for a man who prided himself on being first and foremost a practical musician, but in 1924 he had married Gertrude Rottenberg (daughter of Ludwig Rottenberg, principal conductor of the Frankfurt Opera, which Hindemith had left the previous year), and he may have felt the need for a regular income from some source. Unlike Bartók, he was not a reluctant teacher, and he took up his new job with crusading vigor. Whereas at nineteen he had made it clear that he 'didn't care a damn' what people thought of his music 'so long as it's genuine and true,' he had by now become uneasy at the growing gulf between modern composers and the general public.

The traditional basis of teaching harmony and composition had become inadequate and irrelevant; Hindemith saw a need to establish new criteria and tried to do this in his teaching. His experiences and conclusions emerged later in two important books, *Unterweisung im Tonsatz* (The Craft of Musical Composition, 1937) and *A Composer's World* (1950). He felt that a *rapprochement* between composer and public could be achieved if composers wrote music with some specific purpose, thereby enlisting the support of enthusiastic amateurs, who were understandably daunted by the esoteric complexities of modern music. *Gebrauchsmusik* (literally 'use-music') was the inelegant term by which Hindemith's work in this field came to be known. It was not a politically motivated venture (in fact, a collaboration with the Communist writer Bertold Brecht ended in acrimony) but a genuinely benevolent social and artistic aspiration. 'The days of composing for the sake of composing are perhaps gone forever. On the other hand, the demand for music is so great that it is urgently necessary for composers and users to come to an understanding with each other,' he said in 1928.

Hindemith was not slow to put his words into practice, composing music for films, mechanical instruments and for amateur choirs and orchestras. The *Five Pieces* for strings, op.44 no.4, are typical of this new *Sing- und Spielmusik* (Sing and Play Music), as he liked to call it. Well within the competence of a well-trained school orchestra, the music eschews condescension in its serious tone, involves all sections of the orchestra in a responsible role and renders its harmonic idiom palatable by its use of rhythmical patterns and phrase-structure familiar from an assumed knowledge of eighteenth-

century counterparts. In the children's opera *Wir bauen eine Stadt* (We're Building a City, 1930) and the *Plöner Musiktag* (Music Day in Plön, 1932), comprising material for a whole day of school music-making, the classical severity of his style is further softened by the use of old German folksong, which introduces a new lyrical and homophonic strain into his music from this time on.

• Nazi opposition •

Although Hindemith's troubles with the Nazis put an end to his pioneering work in the educational field, much of his subsequent work confirms that the *Gebrauchsmusik* episode was not a fleeting idealistic whim but a noble attempt to re-create the nineteenth-century relationship between all the participants in music. His motets and madrigals of the 1950s, for instance, or the series of sonatas which enrich the repertoire of neglected instruments like the tuba and saxophone as well as the more familiar

Left: Hindemith teaching; the photograph probably dates from the 1940s, by which time Hindemith had emigrated to the USA and had a teaching post at Yale University.

winds and strings, testify to his enduring concern for the amateur and student.

The Nazi episode attracted some odium to the composer in the recriminatory post-war years, but if Hindemith did not emerge spotless from this testing time for all German artists his sins were of omission rather than commission. His Aryan credentials were not in question, although there was Jewish blood in his wife's family, but he was denounced as a decadent on the evidence of his early one-act operas and for a parody of a military march in the *Kammermusik No.5*. At first Hindemith saw the posturings of the Nazi cultural authorities as a temporary nuisance and kept a low profile, 'trusting to achieve all the more in the background.' He could be criticized for failing to speak out on behalf of the persecuted, but, on the other hand, he openly maintained friendly associations with Jews in his professional life. The conductor Wilhelm Fürtwangler wrote a courageous and vehement newspaper article in his defence and was promptly dismissed from his posts with the Berlin Opera and Symphony Orchestra. Goebbels himself then launched a vicious personal attack on Hindemith, which virtually sealed his fate in Germany. His music was not specifically banned, but it took more courage or foolhardiness than most promoters could muster to present it.

These events took place in a period of ripe achievement. In 1930 Hindemith had followed his *Kammermusik* series with three further works entitled *Konzertmusik*, which retain the instrumental exuberance of the earlier pieces but with a new mellowness, melodic warmth and grandeur. With the opera *Mathis der Maler* (Mathias the Painter), based on events in the life of the sixteenth-century painter Mathias Grünewald, Hindemith achieved a homogeneity and naturalness of style that allows for vivid characterization of the personae and preserves the artificial divisions of aria, recitative and ensemble without impeding or denying the cumulative momentum of the dramatic action (as sometimes occurs with the more consciously stylized formulae of *Cardillac*). The *Mathis der Maler* Symphony (completed and performed before the opera) is an equally important landmark, but for rather different reasons. Each of the three movements depicts one of the panels of Grünewald's famous Isenheim altarpiece, and in proclaiming this program Hindemith made his peace with Romantic musical ideology (Liszt's *Totentanz*, for example, depicts Orcagna's frescoes of *The Last Judgment*) and assumed his natural place in the Austro-German symphonic tradition. It had been widely assumed that the upheavals of twentieth-century harmony had rendered the form obsolete, but Hindemith, in moving forward from baroque forms, was able to build a coherent and intelligible structure on a chromatic extension of Classical sonata principles.

As Hindemith's position in Germany became untenable, he increasingly took up engagements abroad. He made several visits to Turkey at the invitation of the Turkish government to oversee the organization of the country's musical education, and he shrewdly engaged Bartók to undertake research into the nation's folk music. His legendary facility as a composer remained undiminished and when, during his visit to England in January 1936, King George v died, Hindemith composed his tribute, the *Trauermusik* (Funeral Music) for viola and strings, the next day and performed it the following day.

A final insult was delivered by the Nazis when Hindemith's work was prominently displayed at an exhibition of 'decadent art' under the motto, 'Who eats with Jews, dies of it.' In 1938 he went to Switzerland, but enticing offers from across the Atlantic drew him to America in 1940, and he eventually took up a position at Yale University, where he remained until 1953,

Below: Scene from Hindemith's opera *Die Harmonie der Welt*, first performed at the Munich State Opera in 1957. *Die Harmonie der Welt* concerns Kepler, the Renaissance astronomer who attempted to discover the secret of the 'harmony of the spheres.'

when he retired to Switzerland. He continued to compose prolifically until the year of his death, and when his powers as an instrumentalist waned he took to conducting with the same enthusiastic practicality. He died in a Frankfurt hospital on 28 December 1963.

•Theory and practice•

After his bitter experience under the Nazis Hindemith's objectives in life were greatly simplified – 'good music and a clean conscience,' as he put it. However, in his later years he became more dogmatic in his views and attacked Schoenberg and Stravinsky by testing them against the criteria of his own music. Thus the *enfant terrible* of the early 1920s yielded to the irascible conservative of the post-war years, the grand old man. But his music never ossified. His five-act opera *Die Harmonie der Welt* (The Harmony of the World, 1956-7) does far more than relive the glories of *Mathis der Maler*, and comparisons between the two operas reveal a decelerating but still active exploration of forms and also color (never, in the Debussyan sense, a conspicuous feature of his earlier music).

There is no doubt that Hindemith believed he had established the ground-rules for the only workable and intelligible system of harmony for his time, but his findings have gained little acceptance from subsequent generations of composers, who have been more exercised to disprove their validity than to build on them. Hindemith's starting-point, as expounded in *Unterweisung im Tonsatz*, was the scientific reality of the overtones of the harmonic series, which, according to acoustical laws, he arranged in diminishing relationship to the fundamental note until all twelve notes of the chromatic scale had been allotted their precise degree of importance in relation to the fundamental. From here he used the same acoustic principles to define the relative tension and strength of intervals and chords.

To deny the overwhelming gravitational force of the major triad was, he felt, 'sheer perversity.' Since exactly this has been the avowed intention of several important composers before and since, it is not surprising that his views have been dismissed as sheer dogma. Some opponents have suggested that his theories were a rationalization of his own instinctive procedures and that subsequent works were governed by a compulsion to vindicate those theories. *Ludus Tonalis: Studies in Counterpoint, Tonal Organization and Piano Playing* (1942), together with various revisions of earlier works to conform with his theories, might lend support to this view, but to claim that their didactic purpose necessarily precludes any artistic merit is to deny such merit in Bach's *Well-tempered Clavier* or *The Art of Fugue*.

The threads which run consistently through Hindemith's music and thought – the *Gebrauchsmusik*, the increasing melodic simplicity, the formal clarity, the deliberations on the artist and society, even the harmonic theorizing and insistence on sound technique – all these point to a central desire to communicate with listeners at the most fundamental level. 'The composer is no isolated human being,' he wrote in *The Composer's World*, 'but a member of the human community, and it is his moral duty to use his skill to communicate with his fellow beings.'

By this submission Hindemith's work must be accounted, for the present, a heroic failure. The *Mathis der Maler* Symphony and the *Symphonic Metamorphosis on Themes of Weber* hold a secure place in the orchestral repertoire, and memorable performances – such as David Oistrakh's of the Violin Concerto or Dennis Brain's of the Horn Concerto – continue to make a deep impact through recording, but generally speaking Hindemith's reputation, unlike Bartók's, has declined since his death. It seems safe to say confidently of a composer so generously endowed with technical skill and humane wisdom that his time will come. In the meantime his practical legacy, the sonatas and chamber works, will continue to be played and enjoyed by countless amateurs and students, and this would not have displeased the composer who wrote, 'Once you join an amateur group, you are a member of a great fraternity, whose purpose is the most dignified one you can imagine: to inspire one another and unite in building up a creation that is greater than one's individual needs.'

He said that Schoenberg ignored the fundamental laws of tonality, but many would retort that Hindemith rewrote them to suit his own ends. Bartók, unlike either, was not a theorist and so has avoided the acrimony of partisan scholarship. By empirical means Bartók evolved a personal language every bit as logical and consistent as Hindemith's. Both were idealists and each recognized in himself a need to reach out and communicate with his fellow men. In doing so without compromising their integrity or their individuality they built an unanswerable case for the continuing validity of tonality in the twentieth century.

Above: Scene from *Cardillac*, first performed in Dresden in 1926. This particular photograph was taken at the German première of the revised version of the opera, which took place at the Städtische Bühnen, Frankfurt, in 1953. The story of *Cardillac*, based on a story by E. T. A. Hoffmann, concerns a goldsmith who murders his customers in order to retrieve from them the treasures he has created in the past.

SERGEI PROKOFIEV AND DMITRI SHOSTAKOVICH

GEOFFREY NORRIS

Opposite: Sergei Prokofiev (1891-1953) by Piotr Konchalovsky, 1934.

Sergei Prokofiev and Dmitri Shostakovich were born about half a generation apart, Prokofiev in 1891, Shostakovich in 1906. In the history of twentieth-century Russian music their paths diverge and converge at various times, though they reveal such contrasting temperaments, both musically and personally, that this chapter will deal with each composer individually. Prokofiev's early life was spent in an atmosphere of Russian late Romanticism, to which he reacted sharply as soon as his own style had acquired the strength and character to do so. Shostakovich, on the other hand, was in every sense a child of revolution, born just as the dust was settling after the abortive Russian uprising of 1905 and then pursuing a career that went hand in hand, though frequently differing, with the social and political history of the new Communist state, formed after the October Revolution of 1917.

Prokofiev was a true *enfant terrible*. He was a pianist of exceptional abilities; by nature he had a propensity for iconoclasm; and in his student days in St Petersburg he allied himself with the contemporary artistic movement centered on the Evenings of Contemporary Music, concerts given for and by the Russian avant garde. These factors combined to color such early piano pieces as the *Suggestion diabolique* (1908), the Toccata, op.11 (1912), the *Sarcasms* (1912-14) and the *Visions fugitives* (1915-17) with qualities hailed as progressive by the modernists, but rejected as incomprehensible by the conservatives – spiky, often harshly percussive piano writing, wild virtuosity and a harmonic language of sharp acidity.

We can well imagine the stir such music made in the early years of this century, for Russia was still in the autumn of its Romantic age: Rimsky-Korsakov's opera *The Golden Cockerel* (1909) had only just been produced, Rachmaninov had already settled in the lush idiom which was to dominate the music of his mature years in such works as the Second Symphony (1906-7) and Third Piano Concerto (1909), and Skriabin was composing the heady music of *Prometheus* (1908-10) and his late sonatas.

Prokofiev, then in his early twenties, was, together with Stravinsky, seen as a composer of remarkable innovative flair, and he was to continue to have something fresh and startling to say for many years to come. While his solo piano pieces were attracting attention at private (or at least select) *soirées*, Prokofiev took the wider St Petersburg public by storm with his First Piano Concerto (1911-12), a work which powerfully asserts a strong compositional character in vivid strokes of instrumental and orchestral color, in its firm grasp of structure, its sure feel for melody, and in that touch of devilment which seems to underlie so much of Prokofiev's music.

In fact Prokofiev himself analyzed his style as having several distinct components. First there was a 'classical' element, as he called it, owing much to the Beethoven sonatas he was accustomed to hearing his mother play on the piano, and finding an outlet in such works as the 'Classical' Symphony (no.1, 1916-17), in the shaping of some of his sonatas and concertos, and in his writing of certain 'classical' dance movements such as the gavotte, rigaudon and allemande (included in his *Ten Piano Pieces*, op.12, 1906-13). He also isolated a liking for 'toccata-like' music, a trait which is apparent in his light-footed, scurrying writing throughout his career, but which he pinpointed particularly in the scherzos of his Second (1912-13) and Fifth (1931-2) Piano Concertos, parts of the Third Concerto (1917-21) and in some of his early piano pieces. There is as well a lyrical side to Prokofiev's style, undeniably a prominent feature if we look at the sumptuous, languid melodies of his later works of the 1930s and 1940s – the Fifth Symphony, for example, or parts of the opera *War and Peace*, the cantata *Alexander Nevsky* and the ballet *Romeo and Juliet*. Perhaps in his earlier works pure melody was less important to him, though the lyrical First Violin Concerto (1916-17) is a notable exception, and we can point to music of subdued, contemplative beauty in such early orchestral works as the symphonic tableau *Dreams* (1910) and the *Autumnal Sketch* (1910).

However, in the main, Prokofiev's quest for a new and powerful language led him in the direction of complexity – complexity of harmony, rhythm and orchestration (as for example in the *Scythian Suite* of 1915 or the Second Symphony of 1924-5). And if the First Piano Concerto took St Petersburg by storm, the Second, at its first performance in 1913, caused a positive outrage. 'Half the audience hissed,' recalled Prokofiev, 'the other half applauded.' And one reviewer commented that in his playing of the concerto Prokofiev seemed either to be dusting the keys or striking high and low notes at random. 'This music is enough to drive you mad,' said one couple as they hurried for the exit, doubtless scandalized by the dissonant harmony, the feverish activity of the finale and the huge, ten-minute cadenza in the first movement. The concerto embraced many of those qualities which have come to be termed grotesque: galumphing rhythms, growling basses, distorted melodic lines and instrumental astringency. Prokofiev himself resented the use of the word 'grotesque,' and preferred to describe this facet of his style as 'scherzo-like,' with its implications of burlesque, laughter and mockery.

•Dramatic music•

Burlesque or grotesque, Prokofiev's musical style of the 1910s and 1920s was ideally suited to the satirical mood which, as in Shostakovich's music, was prominent in Russia at the time. Blessed with a wry wit and an infectious sense of fun, Prokofiev was drawn irresistibly into this snook-cocking, leg-pulling atmosphere, a trend most vividly apparent in his sparkling opera *The Love for Three Oranges*, based on a play by the eighteenth-century Italian dramatist Carlo Gozzi. Prokofiev was introduced to the subject by the theater director Vsevolod Meyerhold, who himself had been experimenting with theatrical procedures and was particularly interested in the possibilities of improvisation on stage. He felt a special affinity with Gozzi's work, because in the Venice of the late eighteenth century Gozzi had revived the multifaceted, largely improvisatory *commedia dell' arte*, flying in the face of the more traditional Italian theater represented by Carlo Goldoni; Gozzi's *Love for Three Oranges* was in fact a satire on theatrical conventions of the time. Meyerhold gave Prokofiev an adaptation of Gozzi's play, and Prokofiev read it as he sailed from Russia to the United States, via Japan, in 1918 taking up his voluntary – and in the end temporary – exile in the West after the 1917 October Revolution.

Prokofiev was intrigued by Gozzi's bizarre drama: a melancholy prince is cursed by the sorceress Fata Morgana for laughing at her and is forced to find and fall in love with three oranges. Each orange contains a princess; two die of thirst (for the prince has taken all the oranges into the desert), but the remaining one survives, despite being turned into a rat at nearly the last moment; she is re-transformed by a friendlier magician and marries the prince, so overcoming Fata Morgana's evil powers. The magical elements, the knife-sharp comedy and the sheer absurdity of the story combined to inspire one of Prokofiev's most scintillating scores.

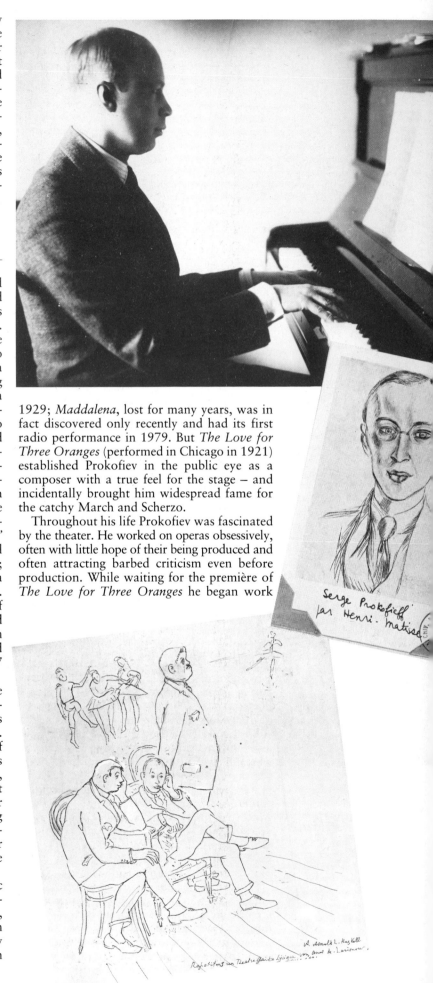

He had already put his considerable dramatic talents to the test in two major operas, *Maddalena* (1911-13) and *The Gambler* (1915-17, revised 1927-8), though neither had yet been produced. *The Gambler*, based on the novel by Dostoyevsky, was first performed in Brussels in 1929; *Maddalena*, lost for many years, was in fact discovered only recently and had its first radio performance in 1979. But *The Love for Three Oranges* (performed in Chicago in 1921) established Prokofiev in the public eye as a composer with a true feel for the stage – and incidentally brought him widespread fame for the catchy March and Scherzo.

Throughout his life Prokofiev was fascinated by the theater. He worked on operas obsessively, often with little hope of their being produced and often attracting barbed criticism even before production. While waiting for the première of *The Love for Three Oranges* he began work

Opposite: Prokofiev playing the piano, probably while he was still in Russia before 1918.

Opposite below: Drawing of Prokofiev by Henri Matisse, probably done around 1920, when Prokofiev had left Russia and was living in Paris. The drawing was used on the front cover of one of the Ballets Russes' programs in 1921.

Below: Scene from *Chout*, with décor by Larionov. The ballet was commissioned by Diaghilev and first performed in Monte Carlo. Prokofiev conducted the first Paris production at the Théâtre Gaité Lyrique on 17 May 1921.

on another opera, *The Fiery Angel* (1919-23, revised 1926-7), based on a lurid story of religious hysteria, torture and demonic possession in sixteenth-century Germany, but it did not reach the stage until 1954, a year after Prokofiev's death. Besides opera, he was attracted to ballet. While in London in 1914, shortly after completing his Second Piano Concerto, Prokofiev met Diaghilev, who conceived the idea of creating a ballet from the concerto's music. Thinking better of it in the cool light of day, Diaghilev instead commissioned an original ballet, *Ala and Lolli* (1914-15), and was later instrumental in having the ballet *Chout* (or *The Tale of the Buffoon*, 1915, revised 1920) performed in Paris and London (1921).

• Return to Russia •

Prokofiev's years away from Russia were not particularly fruitful as regards non-dramatic composition, although he did compose three symphonies: the Second (1924-5), the Third (1928, based on material from the opera *The Fiery Angel*) and the Fourth (1929-30), derived from the ballet *The Prodigal Son*, composed in 1929-30. He also wrote his masterly Third

Opposite: Drawing by Mikhail Larionov of Massine, Prokofiev and Diaghilev. The picture is dedicated to Arnold Haskell, the ballet critic, and was done during rehearsals of Prokoviev's ballet *Chout* in 1921.

Piano Concerto (1917-21), characteristically drawing on themes he had jotted down over a number of years, and completed his set of five concertos with the Fourth, for the left hand (1931, commissioned, but not performed, by the pianist Paul Wittgenstein), and the somewhat diffuse and weaker Fifth (1931-2). In all three concertos there is a certain mellowing of Prokofiev's style; the essential vivacity of the earlier music is there, but it is now tempered by more relaxed lyricism, more euphonious harmonies, smoother textures. These were to be significant aspects of his later music.

In the late 1920s Prokofiev, who had married and settled in Paris in 1923, revisited the Soviet Union, and in the early 1930s he decided to return there. He remained for the rest of his life, and in 1933 received a commission from the Soviet film company Belgoskino to write the music for the film *Lieutenant Kijé*. This gave him the opportunity to put a toe in the waters of the recently reorganized Soviet musical establishment, drawing on his gift for fresh, memorable melody and muscular rhythms, and developing his less abrasive harmonic idiom, which was at once spicy enough to provoke and sustain interest but not too outrageous to offend the new principles of socialist realism.

Lieutenant Kijé is sheer fantasy. It is based on a short story by the critic and writer Yury Tynyanov, and is a satire on the Russian bureaucratic machine. Told with a sharp Gogolian wit, the story is set in the time of Tsar Paul I, famed for his alleged insanity and for a fascination with military spectacle. The important thing to remember about Lieutenant Kijé is that he never existed. He is given life only through an unclear entry in a military register; the Tsar misreads what was in fact a general reference to collective lieutenants, 'poruchiki zhe,' as a reference to one lieutenant in particular, 'Poruchik Kizhe' – Lieutenant Kijé. No subordinate would dare contradict the Tsar, so his entourage indulges his belief in Kijé's existence and invents an eventful life-story for him. Quite early in his fictitious life Kijé commits some trifling offence for which he is flogged and exiled to Siberia, but the Tsar eventually recalls him. He marries, has children, is promoted to the rank of general and is richly rewarded and lavishly decorated. But when the Tsar finally asks to see him, he is made to fall ill and die. As the empty coffin is carried in procession the Tsar remarks, 'Ah, all my best men are dying off.'

Here, then, was a piece of pure whimsy, full of opportunities for musical tongue-in-cheek, to which Prokofiev responded with one of his happiest scores. The film itself was never completed, but Prokofiev, ever resourceful, swiftly compiled the suite of five numbers, which has justifiably become one of his most popular works. Such music – delightfully easy on the ear but with impressive substance and meatiness – stood Prokofiev in good stead for his remaining years in the Soviet Union, and he scored notable successes with many works, among them the ballets *Romeo and Juliet* (1935-6) and *Cinderella* (1940-4), the tale for children *Peter and the Wolf* (1936), the cantata he based on the film score *Alexander Nevsky* (1939), and his comic opera *The Duenna* (1940-1).

Like other Soviet composers Prokofiev was encouraged to write music of an overtly patriotic nature, and he produced such works as the Cantata for the twentieth anniversary of the October Revolution (1936-7), *Hail to Stalin* (1939) and the orchestral *Ode to the End of the War* (1945). During the war itself, he began work on the epic opera *War and Peace*, completed his war-tinged Seventh (1939-42) and Eighth (1939-44) Piano Sonatas and composed his Fifth Symphony (1944), which, like Shostakovich's Seventh, expresses sentiments of hope and resilience: it was a 'symphony of the grandeur of the human spirit.' His Sixth Symphony (1945-7) was a dark, brooding comment on the losses which the war had exacted; and it was perhaps the absence of jubilation in this work, coupled with highly subjective official dissatisfaction with other works (including *War and Peace*), which placed Prokofiev in the forefront of those composers who were condemned in the Zhdanov purges of 1948.

By this time Prokofiev was ill and broken. He had slipped and fallen after conducting the première of the Fifth Symphony in 1945 and never completely recovered. He had no stamina to counter Zhdanov's and Stalin's criticisms with music of fresh artistic invention, and his last works – including the opera *The Story of a Real Man* (1947-8), the ballet *The Tale of the Stone Flower* (1948-53), the choral suite *Winter Bonfire* (1949-50) and the 'festive poem' *The Music of the Volga and the Don* (1951) – show him falling back on his old skills, his natural talents for endearing melody and sparkling, shimmering instrumentation, without any feeling of true conviction or creative spirit. It was a sad irony that he had no opportunity to pick up the threads, as Shostakovich was able to do, in the post-Stalin years, for Prokofiev died on 5 March 1953, the very same day as Stalin himself.

• Dmitri Shostakovich •

When the conductor Nikolai Malko laid down his baton after the première of Shostakovich's First Symphony on 12 May 1926, he said he felt he had 'turned over a new page in the history of symphonic music.' Although we might take this to be no more than a word of encouragement to a young composer, then in his twentieth year, it was in fact a remarkably perceptive comment, accurately forecasting the monumental contribution which Shostakovich was to make to the twentieth-century symphonic repertory. His fifteen symphonies span almost the whole of his creative life, the last being composed in 1971, just four years before his death. Moreover, his close involvement with the symphony pinpoints one key aspect of his musical character. At a time when many major composers were tending to explore new genres and fresh idioms, Shostakovich continued to pour some of his finest music into the traditional molds of the symphony, the sonata, the string quartet and the concerto, making them vehicles for some of his most powerful personal and public statements.

Shostakovich's First Symphony was composed at a crucial stage in Russian musical history. The years immediately after the 1917 October Revolution were exciting, challenging ones, in

Bottom: Stage design for *Chout*, Act v, by Mikhail Larionov.

Below: Two Russian figurines for Prokofiev's *The Love for Three Oranges*, first performed in Chicago at the Auditorium, 30 December 1921, with Prokofiev conducting. These two designs were most probably for the Russian première, which took place in Leningrad in 1926.

the arts no less than in politics and economics. The First Symphony exudes at every turn a youthful zest and a desire to create something new which would break decisively with the past. To be sure, the symphony has points of contact with earlier Russian music: there are echoes of Tchaikovsky in the slow movement, a hint of Rimsky-Korsakov and Glazunov in the transparent, crisp orchestration, a kinship with Prokofiev in its occasional whimsicality and wryness. But, far more strongly than these reminiscences, we hear a voice of striking originality, breathing new life into a genre which, in the early years of this century, had become staid and tired in Russia.

The First Symphony reveals, too, many of the characteristics which were to become prominent in Shostakovich's later music: the use of terse, pithy, thematic cells; an instantly recognizable deployment of parts of the orchestra, notably the bustling strings and a predilection for certain solo instruments; a harmonic pungency; and a confidence and individuality of structure – the First Symphony is in a sense 'monothematic,' each movement drawing on the thematic germ announced by the trumpet

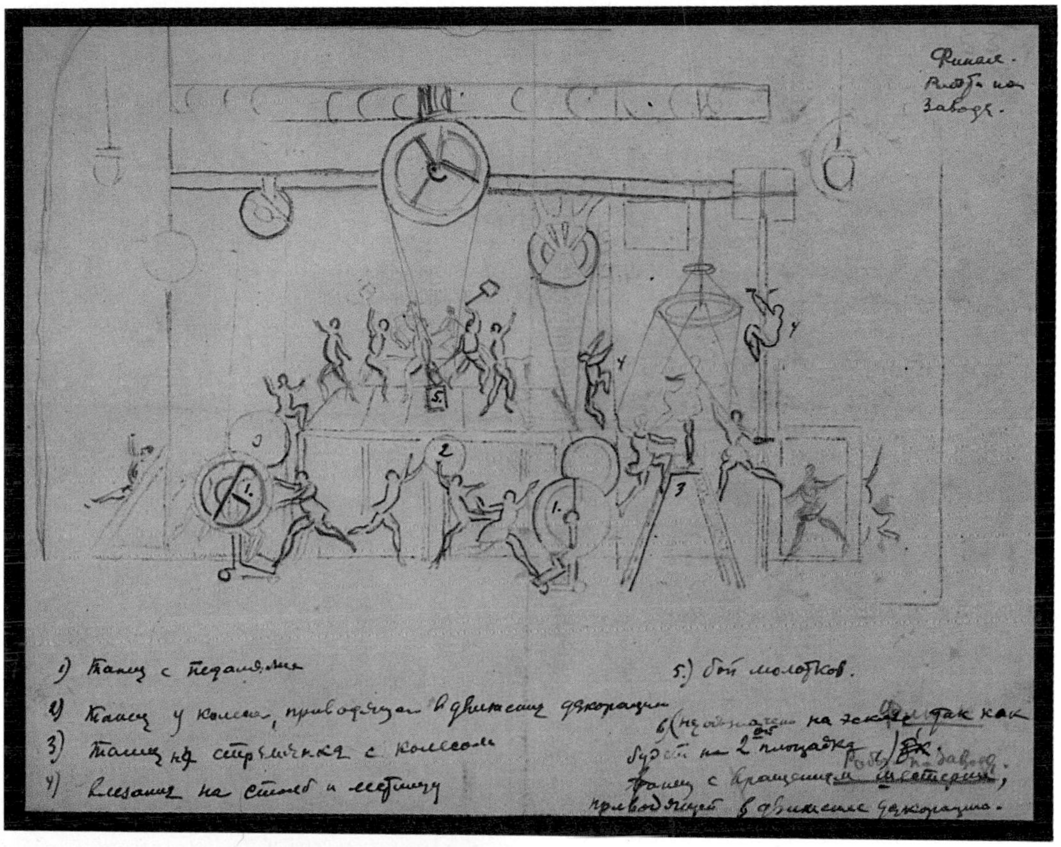

Right: Design by Georgy Yakulov for Prokofiev's ballet *Le Pas d'acier*, composed in 1925-6.

Below: Stage design by V. V. Dmitriev for Prokofiev's *War and Peace*. The première, in which only eight scenes were staged, took place in Leningrad in June 1946.

and the bassoon in the very opening measures. Then there are certain prominent rhythmic traits: for example the dotted pattern of the bassoon's motif at the beginning and the insistent dactylic rhythm – a quarter-note followed by two eighth-notes – which in the First Symphony is most apparent in the predominant theme of the second movement, first hinted at by the cellos in the first measures, then heard in full on the clarinet.

And, lastly, we can detect Shostakovich's penchant for melody. True, Prokofiev once remarked that Shostakovich was 'bereft of melodic invention,' but in such works as the First Symphony (slow movement) and the Second Piano Concerto (second movement) we can hear that Shostakovich could produce melody of unaffected charm when he wanted to – although, as we shall see, his melodic writing, and particularly his vocal writing, was guided by more profound notions than mere pleasantness on the ear. All in all, we can appreciate the First Symphony as very much a work of the

Left: Photograph of (from left to right) Shostakovich, Mayakovsky, Meyerhold and Rodchenko, taken at the time of the production of *The Bedbug* in Moscow. Shostakovich wrote incidental music to Mayakovsky's play, which was performed at the Theater Meyerhold in 1929.

twentieth century. What startling new ground it breaks when compared, say, to the symphonies of Shostakovich's own teacher Glazunov! And in the works which Shostakovich composed immediately after it his style developed more unconventionally still.

•'Contemporary' music•

In the Russia of the 1920s, when composers were avidly seeking a mode of expression to suit the prevailing revolutionary mood, music tended to fall into two principal categories: first there was the 'proletarian,' stylistically traditional, kind favored by the Russian Association of Proletarian Musicians (RAPM); then, in the other camp, there were the more forward-looking, experimental works sponsored by the Association for Contemporary Music (ASM). In the late 1920s Shostakovich allied himself unhesitatingly with the more progressive, 'contemporary' school, influenced by such Western composers as Hindemith, Schoenberg and Berg, whose music was frequently to be heard in Soviet concert halls and opera houses.

The fruits of this period of Shostakovich's creativity were the First Piano Sonata (1926), the succinct *Aphorisms* for solo piano (1927), incidental music to Vladimir Mayakovsky's play *The Bedbug* (1929), the ballets *Bolt* (1930-1) and *The Golden Age* (1927-30) and, above all, the Second (1927) and Third (1929) Symphonies and his opera *The Nose* (1927-8). The symphonies are interesting signs of their time. The Second bears the subtitle 'To October,' the Third is dedicated to '1 May.' In both of them, then, Shostakovich was fired by revolutionary sentiment, the feeling that the Revolution was something to celebrate and be thankful for. But they are not couched in the dull, tub-thumping idiom that dogged so much of the 'proletarian' mass-appeal music produced by composers supporting the RAPM. Rather do they attempt to chart a new course in symphonic music.

Left: Eisenstein's sketch for the final scene of his film *Ivan the Terrible*, for which Prokofiev was commissioned to write the incidental music. The first part of the film was made between 1942-4, the second part in 1945.

Both symphonies are cast in a single movement, a lengthy stretch of abstract orchestral music leading to a concluding chorus. In both cases the choral music is a forthright setting of verse by a contemporary poet. In the Second Symphony Alexander Bezymensky's text tells of the struggle towards the October Revolution, heralding 'the dawn of a new era.' The Third Symphony's text, by Semyon Kirsanov, is a happier expression of the joys of the future Communist state. In the Second Symphony Shostakovich explores the possibilities of polyrhythm and polytonality in an almost unrelievedly dense, complex texture, displaying a new harshness and acerbity and an uncompromisingly modernist use of the orchestra (listen to the frenetic activity – the multifarious independent instrumental lines, the string *glissandi* – about five minutes from the beginning of the symphony). In the Third Symphony the sound is less clogged, the tone of the music more carefree, making use of the exuberant

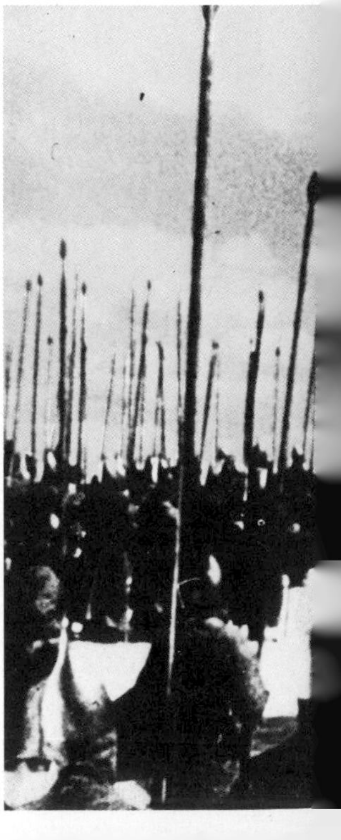

rhythmic and instrumental effects familiar from the First Symphony, and also having features in common with the opera, *The Nose*.

•*The Nose*•

The Nose was written at a time when Soviet operatic music was at a low ebb. Despite the brilliant talents of Russian theater directors of the 1920s, the actual repertory tended to concentrate on the nineteenth-century classics; worthwhile new works were few and far between. Yet here again Shostakovich broke new ground; in the words of one critic, 'he . . . put forward the most interesting musical experiments, based on rhythm and timbre alone . . . he is perhaps the first among Russian opera composers to make his heroes speak not in conventional arias and cantilenas but in living language, setting everyday speech to music. . . .' This 'speaking in living language' had been a facet of Russian vocal writing since the 1860s, when Dargomyzhsky advocated 'musical realism' in his opera *The Stone Guest* and Musorgsky developed – in *Boris Godunov* and some of his mature songs – a kind of 'melodic recitative,' vocal lines closely molded to the inflection of spoken Russian. In *The Nose* Shostakovich adapted this principle to his own modernist style of the moment, producing vocal lines that were animated, nervy and 'brilliantly eccentric,' as the composer Sergei Slonimsky dubbed them.

Shostakovich chose to base his opera on Gogol's short story *The Nose* (1835), largely because of its satirical content, judging that in the 1920s 'an opera on a classical subject would be most topical if that subject had a satirical character,' and his musical style proved to be an ideal counterpart – witty, sharp-edged and bubbling with irrepressible energy. In the music Shostakovich tried to steer away from deliberate parody or irony, preferring to allow the pace and character of the story to dictate the pace and character of the music, and thus creating an opera which is compact in its design, clearly focused in its characterization and telling in its satirical thrusts. Although the story is set in the time of Tsar Nicholas I, the opera is in turn a no less pungent comment on the Russia of the 1920s: the press, the medical profession, the police, the church, the civil service, the pomposity of self-important petty bureaucrats – none of them comes out of the work unscathed.

Yet this satirical trend was soon to run into difficulties. When Lenin had formulated his ideas for the New Economic Policy in 1921, he had correctly realized that he could not effect cultural change as quickly as political, military or economic change; the arts needed time to find their feet. But by the early 1930s, with Stalin in power, the Soviet authorities were seeking to bring the arts under control and to curtail the experimentalism that had been allowed to thrive in the 1920s. In a decree of 1932 the opposing factions of the RAPM and the ASM were brought to heel; a central Union of Soviet Composers was founded, with the power to assert immutable influence over the nature of musical works.

Below: Scene from Prokofiev's ballet *Romeo and Juliet*, first performed at Brno in Czechoslovakia on 30 December 1938. Alongside his interest in film music and contemporary comedy, Prokofiev maintained his devotion to classical ballet and indeed to 'classical' subject-matter generally, as is shown by his opera *War and Peace*.

Left: Still from *Alexander Nevsky*, 1938, another Eisenstein film with music by Prokofiev. The two men worked very closely together, and Prokofiev was present during most of the filming and editing. Occasionally filming was done to fit a pre-recorded sound track, rather than the other way around. Later on Prokofiev re-used the film music in his cantata *Alexander Nevsky*.

•Socialist realism•

The goal of 'socialist realism' was set up, and all composers were expected to aim for it in music 'directed towards the conquering, progressive principles of reality, towards those heroic, bright and beautiful traits which distinguish the spiritual world of Soviet mankind and which must be embodied in musical images full of beauty and life-affirming strength' (quoted from the statutes of the Composers' Union). *The Nose*, and much of Shostakovich's music of the late 1920s, quickly disappeared from the repertory. Like everyone else, he had to reconsider his musical style and try to shape it to these new demands.

As it happens, Shostakovich was nearing completion of his second opera, *Lady Macbeth of the Mtsensk District*, when the decree was proclaimed. He had intended this to be the first part of a trilogy of operas 'dealing with the position of women at different times in Russia,' and he took as his theme a highly colored novella (1865) by Nikolai Leskov telling of the tragic demise of a woman – Katerina Ismailova – desperate to find true love and happiness in the stifling, corrupt atmosphere of the nineteenth-century Russian provinces.

In the music of *Lady Macbeth* some of the caustic bite of *The Nose* survives in such caricature roles as Boris (Katerina's father-in-law, a 'power-loving despot,' as Shostakovich called him) and in the comic scene in the police station (scene 7), which is redolent, as Olin Downes remarked in his review of the opera's New York première (1935), of the Keystone Kops. But above all we sense in this music a new lyrical intensity and passion, particularly in the music of Katerina herself. Of all the characters she is the only one to display genuine human emotions – exasperation, affection, anguish and, at the end, abject despair. And Shostakovich underlines these qualities in music of emotional sincerity and nobility, whether in her cry of boredom in the opening pages of the opera, her passionate entreaties to her lover Sergei, her dream of happiness in the third scene, or the pathetic, falling lines of her final lament, heightened by the gentle simplicity of the accompaniment on the cor anglais.

After its Leningrad première (1934) the opera was hailed as a prime example of the new socialist realism, a model of Soviet opera. Yet only two years later, just after Stalin had seen it on stage for himself, it was condemned in a now notorious *Pravda* editorial entitled 'Chaos instead of music': 'The music quacks, grunts and growls, and suffocates itself in order to express the amatory scenes as naturalistically as possible.' No doubt the sexual explicitness of the stage action of the opera gave Stalin, with all his Victorian prudery, much cause for disgust and repulsion, but the music, too, was condemned, for although Shostakovich had now abandoned the breathless, hyperactive style of *The Nose* and the Second Symphony, he still had recourse on occasion to harsh dissonance and, in the *entr'actes* for example, to music of enormous rhetorical weight.

Lady Macbeth was dropped from the repertory, and was not seen again until it was revived, as *Katerina Ismailova*, in 1963. Realizing that his Fourth Symphony (1935-6) was a closely related companion piece to *Lady Macbeth* in its bold gestures and grim power, its harnessing of lavish orchestral resources and its massive and unorthodox symphonic structure, Shostakovich withdrew it from rehearsal (it was not in fact performed until 1961).

Instead he set to work on a Fifth Symphony (1937), which has been dubbed 'a Soviet artist's reply to just criticism' and which has justly earned a key position in the twentieth-century repertory. We can continue to interpret this symphony in political terms, suspecting 'forced optimism' here, 'resistance to authority' there, but it is much more interesting to look at it in purely musical terms. This 'reply' is couched in a clearer, more direct manner than, say, the Fourth Symphony or *The Nose*; it is essentially euphonious, with a structural and thematic grandeur and nobility. Such a manner by no means compromised Shostakovich's artistic integrity, but rather revealed a maturing per-

Right: Design by Dmitriev for the opera *Lady Macbeth of the Mtsensk District*, composed between 1930 and 1932 and first performed in Leningrad on 22 January 1934.

Left: Portrait of Shostakovich by T. Salakhov.

sonality, a stabilizing of the spirit which had already been evident in such works as the First Piano Concerto (1933) and the Cello Sonata (1934). There was, arguably, no future in the ultra-modernism of Shostakovich's music of the late 1920s; the music of the 1930s, on the other hand, formed a firm foundation on which his later style was built.

In the years immediately after the Fifth Symphony, though they were not especially fruitful, Shostakovich consolidated this style in the cool freshness of the First String Quartet (1935), in the curiously unbalanced Sixth Symphony (1939) and in the magnificent Piano Quintet (1940); he also composed a number of film scores (a constant fascination throughout his life) and completed his edition of Musorgsky's *Boris Godunov* (1939-40).

Then in 1941 the Soviet Union entered the Second World War, with all the dislocation and evacuation that it entailed. As one would expect, the horrors of the war drew from many composers expressions of patriotism, resistance and heroism. Prokofiev, for instance, produced his Fifth and Sixth Symphonies, Myaskovsky his own series of war symphonies (nos.21-23), and Shostakovich wrote his Seventh Symphony (1941), a powerful, defiant work dedicated to the city of Leningrad, which suffered so much during the lengthy siege by German forces.

Perhaps the most frequently discussed aspect of the Seventh Symphony is the protracted first movement, with its long, reiterated march theme (which so irritated Bartók that he lampooned it in his *Concerto for Orchestra*). This passage may be seen as representing the march of hostile invaders, though it has been claimed in the book *Testimony: the Memoirs of Shostakovich* that the symphony portrays not so much the Nazi aggressor as the continuing Stalinist repression within the Soviet Union itself. Be that as it may, the symphony is a demonstrative work about human life and human tragedy, about the resilience of Soviet mankind and about its strength and ability to survive.

The Seventh takes a somewhat different attitude, then, from the Eighth Symphony (1943), written at the height of the war and couched in bleak, bitter, oppressively pessimistic terms, in which the gloom-laden opening measures (resembling the opening of the Fifth Symphony, but now even more deeply searching) set the tone of a work of unremitting darkness, which not even the concluding, seemingly skittish *allegretto* pages can lighten. This grim mood also pervades the Second Piano Trio (1944), written in memory of Shostakovich's friend Ivan Sollertinsky, and only in his opera *The Gamblers* – a planned word-for-word setting of Gogol's play (1836-42) – could he find a lighter touch, though the opera was never completed and the surviving torso was not performed until 1978.

After the war Shostakovich composed his Ninth Symphony (1945), a work whose jaunty turns of phrase (first, third and fifth movements) and untroubled serenity (second movement) seem to express a sense of relief rather than victorious jubilation; as the composer himself said, 'if the Seventh and Eighth Symphonies were tragic and heroic in character, then the Ninth is dominated by a transparent, clear mood.' Only the short *largo* fourth movement hints at anything more ominous. Certainly the Ninth's chirpy humor caused perplexity among those who had expected from Shostakovich something more weighty; and it was to attract even more savage criticism three years later during the cultural purges of 1948. At this time Shostakovich, Prokofiev, Khachaturian and every other Soviet composer of worth were arraigned for so-called 'formalistic' leanings; their music, so the allegations went, had strayed from the path of socialist realism

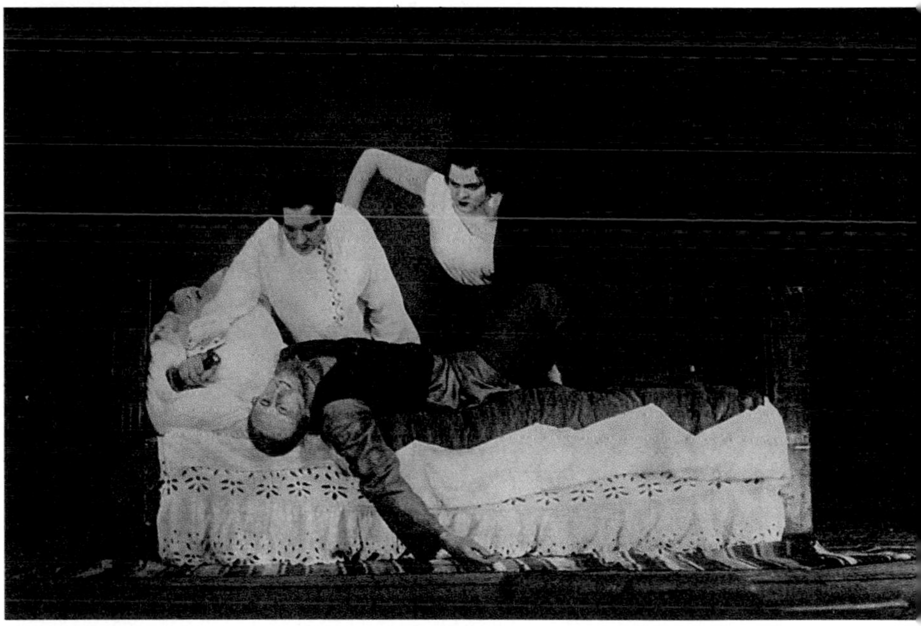

Above: Scene from Eisenstein's own production of *Lady Macbeth of the Mtsensk District*, staged in Moscow in 1934.

Above: Shostakovich composing the Seventh Symphony during the Siege of Leningrad, 1941. Shostakovich threw in his lot with Russia and, unlike many other composers, determined to work within the framework established by the new régime. The Seventh Symphony came to be thought of as an expression of the 'martyrdom' of Leningrad while it was under siege by the Germans.

Right: Poster advertising a concert performance of the Seventh Symphony, 1942, in Moscow. The soldier buying his concert ticket adds poignancy to the picture, and again one is reminded that Shostakovich was thought of as a hero fighting for the Russian cause.

Top right: The first few measures of the final movement of Shostakovich's Seventh Symphony, composed at Kuileyshev; this particular page is signed and dated 24 March 1942 and presents the two main themes of the movement.

and had tended to put itself out of the intellectual reach of the general public. Their music was 'radically wrong,' said Andrei Zhdanov, who was Stalin's commissar for the arts: 'it is anti-people and prefers to cater for the individualistic experience of a clique of esthetes.' Excessive dissonance and complexity drew Zhdanov's contempt; easy melody, euphony and profound human feeling were praised.

In such circumstances it was natural for Shostakovich once again to take stock. A few of the works he was either engaged on or contemplating were plainly not what Zhdanov and Stalin were seeking: the First Violin Concerto (1947-8), with its broad introspective first movement and its huge passacaglia third movement; the song-cycle *From Jewish Folk Poetry* (1948); the Fourth String Quartet (1949). Shostakovich withheld these and presented himself before the public with a handful of film scores and such choral works as the oratorio *Song of the Forests* (1949) and *The Sun Shines on our Motherland* (1952).

•After Stalin•

The opportunity for Shostakovich's more private works to be heard came with the death of Stalin in 1953 and the subsequent thawing of the cultural climate. Even more important, he began work on his Tenth Symphony (1953), thus breaking a symphonic silence of eight years. The Tenth is, many would argue, his greatest symphony, one in which the undercurrents of deep melancholy which flow beneath so much of his earlier music come forcefully to the surface. The symphony is also deeply personal in another sense, for Shostakovich uses as a thematic motif his musical monogram DSCH, derived from the spelling Dmitry SCHostakowitsch and giving in musical notation the sequence D–E flat–C–B. He had used it before and was to use it again; it permeates the Eighth String Quartet (1960), the so-called 'Autobiographical' Quartet which recalls themes from a number of his works; it can be detected towards the end of the second movement of the Sixth Symphony; it occurs in the First Violin Concerto; it underpins the First Cello Concerto (1959); it is prominent in the wry *Preface to the Complete Collection of my Works* (1966); and it is quoted in his enigmatic Fifteenth Symphony (1971), with its additional references to Rossini and Wagner. In the Tenth Symphony the harmonic implications of the motif color the language of the whole work, and it is hammered home to powerfully dramatic effect at the climax of the finale.

As the first symphony of the post-Stalin era, the Tenth was the subject of intense debate. Some critics were troubled by the pessimism of the long first movement; others stressed that composers ought – now – to be guided by their own artistic instincts, as Shostakovich himself was to do in his own later music. From the Tenth Symphony onwards his style became more inward-looking, more anxious to express in musical terms the concerns he had so far kept largely suppressed. It is not surprising, therefore, that we find him concentrating on chamber music; he composed nine string quartets – with ever increasing introspection – in his last decade, and the Viola Sonata (1975) was written in his very last year. He turned, too, to solo song, composing in his last years those spare, despairing song-cycles which stand at the peak of Soviet vocal writing: *Satires* (1960), to words by Sasha Chorny; *Seven Songs on Poems by Alexander Blok* (1967); *Six Poems of Marina Tsvetayeva* (1973); and the *Suite on Verses of Michelangelo Buonarroti* (1974). Significantly, he had prepared an edition of Musorgsky's opera *Khovanshchina* in 1959 and had orchestrated the same composer's *Songs and Dances of Death* in 1962, and his own late songs owe much to the stark realism of Musorgsky's vocal writing.

This concentration on the voice spilled over into two symphonies of Shostakovich's final years, the Thirteenth (1962) and the Fourteenth (1969). Each of the five movements of the Thirteenth Symphony is a setting (for baritone and orchestra) of verse by the poet Yevgeny Yevtushenko dealing with aspects of life in Stalinist Russia. At its première in 1962 the symphony created a furor, not so much because of the music but because of the words, in particular those of the first movement, 'Babiy Yar.' Yevtushenko's poem tells of the massacre of Jews by the Germans at Babiy Yar during the Second World War, though in parts the text also implies anti-Semitism in the Soviet Union.

After the first performance the authorities insisted that two sensitive passages be replaced by new words stressing the Soviet Union's fight against Fascism and emphasizing that the horrors of Babiy Yar took their toll of Russians and Ukrainians, as well as Jews. (Western performances and recordings have reverted to the original text, but the very few subsequent Soviet performances have retained the revisions.) Although the 'Babiy Yar' movement tends to be the center of attention, we shudder none the less at the ironic bitterness of the second movement, 'Humor,' and at the dull thuds of the fourth movement, 'Fears,' as frightening a musical picture of Stalinist terror as we can expect to hear.

Irony, terror, death – these concepts seemed to dominate Shostakovich's later years, and they were expressed no more poignantly than in his Fourteenth Symphony. In this achingly depressing work – in effect a song-cycle scored for soprano and bass soloists with a small orchestra of strings and percussion – Shostakovich set eleven poems by Rilke, García Lorca, Apollinaire and Küchelbeker. Death is the overriding theme, conveyed in terms of sinister drama (as in no.2, García Lorca's *Malagueña*), heart-rendering lyricism (towards the end of no.3, Apollinaire's *Loreley*), chill gloom (no.4, Apollinaire's *The Suicide*; no.10, Rilke's *Death of a Poet*) and martial brutality (no.5, Apollinaire's *On Watch*, with its tense twelve-note xylophone theme at the beginning). Although we can still hear in the Fourteenth Symphony the distinctive rhythmic characteristics, the traits of orchestration and the pithiness and economy of Shostakovich's melodic writing, which were noted as far back as the First Symphony, they are now transmuted into music of almost impenetrable introspection and harrowing intensity.

The music of Shostakovich and Prokofiev stands at the very heart of twentieth-century Russian musical culture. In their early years both composers shared a desire to break with tradition and to forge a style which was original, individual and strikingly assertive. Their careers were of roughly the same length: Prokofiev was sixty-two when he died, Shostakovich sixty-nine. Yet in that time their musical development took quite different courses. Prokofiev, the more outgoing of the two, set out deliberately to shock in his early, flamboyant music, acquired a more restrained grace during his thirties, and in his mature years became established in a style of openness, mellifluence and powerful dramatic flair. Shostakovich is more problematical. After the innovatory First Symphony and the experimental works of the 1920s, he sowed the seeds of a style which has often seemed to conceal more than it revealed about his personality. Yet it was in his music – and particularly in the troubled works of his final years – that he expressed his most profound thoughts, for, as he himself said, 'by studying my music you will find the whole truth about me as a man and as an artist.'

Left: Shostakovich seated in a theater at rehearsal.

CHARLES IVES AND AARON COPLAND

PETER DICKINSON

Opposite: Charles Ives (1874-1954), *c.*1917, photographed in Battery Park, New York, at the height of his business career, near his insurance offices (Ives and Myrick).

Charles Edward Ives has been claimed both as the first distinctively American composer and as the first great composer to emerge from the United States. The music of Ives is certainly distinctively American, reflecting the elements of the definition provided by Henry and Sidney Cowell in their biography, *Charles Ives and His Music* (1955): 'To experiment and to explore has never been revolutionary for an American; he is unaffectedly at home in the unregulated and the untried. In a vast new country experience is direct, intense and various, and so grass-roots creative activity in the United States has been marked by an exuberance and a diversity that are shocking to sensibilities developed in older cultures whose essence is refinement and selectivity. In all the arts Americans quite naturally bring together elements that elsewhere appear as irreconcilable canons of radically opposed thought.'

But Ives was not by any means the first composer to show such American traits. Attitudes associated with Ives can be found as early as colonial times. William Billings (1746-1800), who lived in Boston and worked as a tanner and singing-teacher, was just as opposed to academicism: 'I don't think myself confined to any rules for composition laid down by any that went before me. Nature is the best dictator.' In his part-song 'Jagon,' published in *The Singing Master's Assistant*, 1778, Billings celebrates 'hateful discord' in fourteen measures containing only one consonant chord – an eighteenth-century equivalent of Ives's take-offs to stretch the ears and the mind.

In the nineteenth century Anthony Philip Heinrich (1781-1861), an immigrant from Bohemia known as 'the Beethoven of America,' was a romantic eccentric who drew liberally on local sources for his music. He quoted patriotic songs, including several of Ives's favorites, as did the pianist–composer Louis Moreau Gottschalk (1829-69). Gottschalk was born in New Orleans and was one of the first composers to incorporate Afro-American rhythms in his works. The Black influence in American music began as early as 1619, when the first slaves landed. Ives was profoundly affected – not necessarily at first hand – by Afro-American techniques of a kind which had not been represented accurately in musical notation.

The American sound of Ives arises in part from his uninhibited use of hymns and popular tunes in fashioning sonatas, symphonies and other concert music. William Brooks has compared this technique, more extreme in Ives's work than in that of the European composers who drew on folksong, to Claude Levi-Strauss's structuralist concept of *bricolage* – a form of creativity which builds from disparate elements, or 'bric-à-brac.' Ives's dissonant innovations, anticipating Schoenberg, Bartók and Stravinsky, at once gave him a place in musical history as soon as they became known. But his American sound and experimental ideas are not enough on their own to establish him as a major twentieth-century composer. This is achieved by the extraordinary visionary intensity of his finest scores, products of a deeply spiritual nature. In them Ives succeeded – against all odds – in giving musical expression of almost photographic realism to his and his father's memories of life in the small New England town of Danbury, Connecticut.

It is difficult to separate the originality of Ives's music from the crusade which has been needed to bring it, painfully and gradually, to a public. Ives achieved recognition only after the age of seventy, following years of neglect and misunderstanding, more than twenty years after he had stopped composing. By the time of the Ives centennial in 1974 and the American bicentennial in 1976, his reputation was at its height, and his concerns were relevant to composers all over the world. Ives's music and its sources offer endless scope for musicological investigation, as the flow of books and theses now shows. Ultimate success, almost canonization, has come to a man who must have been one of the most isolated composers in the history of music.

In 1897 Ives wrote an organ prelude on the Christmas hymn, 'Adeste Fideles,' normally sung in English as, 'Oh come, all ye faithful.' Intentionally or not, the title of the piece illustrates his situation in a prophetic way. In Ives's lists of works and on the manuscript the title is 'Adeste Fidelis.' 'Fidelis' is grammatically incorrect, even though Ives took Latin in his first two years at Yale University. It could be a punning reference to the popular march, 'Semper Fidelis,' written in 1888 by John Philip Sousa (1854-1932), but it could also be an attempted singular rather than plural – 'Oh come, faithful one' – referring to Ives on his own, and faithful to his visions. On the manuscript there is a note that Ives played 'Adeste Fidelis' at a Christmas service in 1898: 'Rev. J. B. Lee, others, and Mrs Uhler said it was awful.' In fact the Prelude is ingenious in opening with the melody inverted and then in combining the tune with its inversion. In terms of classical harmony the combination does not agree any more than the two title words agree in Latin. The music is atmospheric, not unlike the transcendental calm of *The Unanswered Question* of 1906, and the same tune appears in 'Decoration Day,' which was considered a masterpiece by Stravinsky in 1966.

• Parallels •

Ives's predicament has only a partial parallel in the ordeals suffered during this century by the major European composers – who were unknown to him. There were protests at first performances of Schoenberg, Bartók and Stravinsky, but however radical their music was at its most advanced phases, they were extending their European traditions and could be accommodated. There was also a professional audience for new music. Ives, in late-nineteenth-century New England, lacked a continuous musical culture and had no audience at all. Instead he had a rich diversity of sources, which he forced into a musical synthesis of a completely original kind.

Folk music revitalized aspects of the central Austro-German tradition through Stravinsky and Bartók: Ives too was a nationalist. Primitive subjects drove Stravinsky to greater dissonance and rhythmic complexity: Ives's realism did the same. Popular melodies were a means towards a democratic art for Bartók, and Ives felt this too. Schoenberg, an exact contemporary of Ives, stated his respect for the American composer who used twelve-tone rows before he did himself – in *Tone Roads No.3* (1915). The innovations of Ives and Schoenberg stem from their acceptance of a pioneering destiny. Schoenberg reluctantly faced the necessity of twelve-tone techniques; Ives felt he could never write obvious music – 'I hear something else.'

What all three major Europeans, who all emigrated to the United States and died there, have in common with Ives is their origin in musical Romanticism: Wagner and Brahms for Schoenberg; Liszt and Strauss for Bartók; Tchaikovsky and Rimsky-Korsakov for Stravinsky. The equivalent for Ives – and here he is unique – was his corpus of popular music, absorbed raw, as opposed to the polished assimilation of Mahler. Even if the Romantic traditions Ives used were in the vernacular, this still did not prevent him from writing a First Symphony – a student work – affected by Dvořák, and a conventional but powerful oratorio, *The Celestial Country*, as late as 1898-9, five years after his first polytonal composition, *Song for Harvest Season*. Ives's innovations coexist with diatonic material, sometimes in the same piece, and he did not always use his full range, from vernacular, pop-art juxtapositions to dissonant tone-clusters.

The hymn-tune background of the Second and Third Symphonies, which are referred to in detail later, suggests another organist–composer, Anton Bruckner (1824-96). But as a pioneer Ives has been compared with the eccentric French composer Erik Satie (1866-1925). Satie was probably the first European composer to use syncopated rhythms arising from ragtime at the turn of the century. Like Ives, he had a productive relationship with popular music, working as a pianist in night clubs, and – at the other extreme – he was ahead of his time in exploring dissonant harmony. Satie too was ridiculed and misunderstood and cloaked himself with defensive behavior. But whereas every note counts in a piece of Satie, Ives, with a larger vision, can embrace confusion. This confusion is what European listeners in the 1960s and 1970s found so stimulating, so foreign to their own narrower traditions.

The most revealing parallel to the creative mind of Ives is not a composer at all, but the Irish writer James Joyce. This was first noticed by Lou Harrison, composer and conductor active in the Ives cause, in 1946. I developed the connection further at the time of the Ives centennial, but of course Ives and Joyce had no direct contact.

Ives disliked the work of the American writer Gertrude Stein (1874-1946) – he deplored the influence of women anyway – but they both pushed their respective media into hitherto unimagined territory. Compare the grand repetitive sweep of Stein's *The Making of Americans* (1906-8) with Ives's 'Concord' Sonata, or the abstraction of *Tender Buttons* (1911) with Ives's exploratory chamber pieces. Both Ives and Stein were ridiculed. It was easier for her, relatively wealthy and living in Paris from 1903 until her death. Ives had to buy his artistic freedom by working in business – life insurance –

Below: Charles's father, George Ives, in bandsman's uniform during the Civil War. A strong character, his musical taste was not conventional and he was inclined to experiment, a feature he evidently passed on to his son.

Bottom: Ives (top row, fourth from left) with the Yale Glee Club in 1898. Ives drew in his own music on many American popular music traditions such as glee-singing and brass band playing.

in New York City, until he had a serious stroke in 1918, brought on by overwork in attempting a double career.

• Musical background •

The strongest musical influence upon Ives was that of his father, George Edward Ives (1845-94) (but we should not ignore the impact of his Yale professor, the conventional and prolific composer Horatio Parker, 1863-1919). A thoroughly trained general musician and an expert band-leader commended by President Lincoln, George Ives was also blessed with an experimental attitude. In the 1880s he got his children to sing a popular song in one key and accompany themselves at the piano in another. He tried to imitate bells with tone-clusters on the piano, and these were also used to imitate drum parts. It was his father's microtonal experiments that formed the basis for one of Ives's late works, *Three Quarter-Tone Pieces for Two Pianos* (1923-4).

When his father died in 1894, Ives lost his greatest ally. His memories of him remained, since the communal music-making of Danbury as well as the wilder experiments had been supervised by George Ives. His letter to a pupil in the 1880s echoes exactly the sentiments of William Billings quoted earlier: 'The older I get and the more I play music and think about it, the more certain I am that many teachers (mostly German) are gradually circumscribing a great art by these rules, rules, rules, with which they wrap up the students' ears and mind as a lady does her hair. . . .'

His son agreed and went further. Teachers can restrict the freedom of music, but so does the profession, according to Charles Ives: 'I personally think that most of the celebrities of world fame are the greatest enemies of music – unless it is going to lie down forever as an emasculated art. . . .'

Ives found reality in functional popular music, which the teachers and the professionals largely ignored: in hymns, whether psalm-tunes, revival hymns at camp-meetings, or four-part church hymns; in band music, especially in its social and musical context; in minstrel tunes and rags, probably heard at traveling shows; in country fiddling for dances; in parlor music generally consisting of popular ballads and the songs of Stephen Foster (1826-64); and in music for small theaters and fairgrounds. Home chamber music in Danbury consisted of Bach, Handel and Beethoven rather than Haydn and Mozart, who were considered too effeminate.

Right: Manuscript of the first page from 'Emerson,' first movement of the 'Concord' Sonata, completed in 1915. The American philosopher and poet Ralph Waldo Emerson (1803-82) was one of Ives's heroes. The sonata was very largely based on the *Emerson Overture*, which he had sketched out in 1907 but never completed.

Below: Ives in the uniform of the Hopkins Grammar School baseball team, 1894.

Bottom: Ives and his business partner Julian Myrick, in their insurance office, with other members of staff.

Ives chafed not only against the academic rules and attempts to impose them, but also against the rigid framework of musical notation and all it represented: 'The eye mustn't guide or enslave the ear too much – any more than the hand should, limited too much by custom. . . . As soon as music goes down on paper it loses its birthright.' From the age of thirteen until 1902, Ives worked continuously as a church organist – a situation where improvisation is required for services, but within limits. In this work he came to know the hymns which meant so much to him. In his piano music, which he played himself largely for himself, improvisation is also a factor. He preferred to play the 'Concord' Sonata differently each time, even after it was published: 'I may always have the pleasure of not finishing it.'

For Ives, the ideas of the music are more important than the exact way in which they are written down – what Ives called the substance

Opposite top: Drawing of Charles Ives by Fred Dolbin.

Opposite below: Church Bells Ringing, Rainy Winter Night, 1917, by the American artist Charles E. Burchfield (1893-1967). Burchfield was one of the artists who, like Ives, rejected European tradition, and even European modernism, to establish a powerfully American contemporary style.

Right: Portrait of James Joyce by Jacques-Emile Blanche, 1935. Several critics have noticed a parallel development in Ives and Joyce; they never actually met, but Joyce's subjective, stream-of-consciousness, prose has affinities with Ives's experimental work, which does not hesitate to incorporate – almost at random – large numbers of diverse musical 'thoughts.'

was to dominate, rather than the manner. Thus he could ignore practicalities in orchestral layout, willfully requiring two conductors, or he could superimpose details which might never be heard, all with a transcendentalist's faith in the outcome. Moreover, it is not only Ives's improvisatory approach to his own playing, both as organist and as pianist, which determined his attitude to borrowed tunes. He attached himself to this heritage like a folk-singer incapable of reading music, relying on his memory. When he quotes the tune 'Nettleton' in his *Memos*, for instance, Ives gets the measuring wrong, starting with a downbeat instead of an upbeat.

Such distortions can result in some ambiguity when more than one tune is suggested. In the third movement of the First Piano Sonata (1901-9), 'Erie,' sung to 'What a Friend we have in Jesus,' and the Stephen Foster song 'Massa's in de Cold Cold Ground' are mixed up. This situation occurs in other works, and Dennis Marshall has drawn attention to motivic links between the selected melodies. It is difficult to establish whether Ives chose the tunes for their resemblances, or whether his improvising instinct operated upon a kind of blurred folk memory which was then swept up in more important issues. This type of confusion also affects the listener, whose associations will be different from those of Ives. Joseph P. Webster's spacious tune to 'In the Sweet By-and-By' – a gospel hymn which dominates the third movement of the Second Orchestral Set and the second movement of the Fourth Symphony – is sometimes mistaken for 'My Bonny Lies Over the Ocean,' possibly, as Michael Alexander has suggested, because of their pentatonic origins. They could come from a common source.

•The 'Concord' Sonata•

One of the most interesting examples of this type of ambiguity in quotation is the Second Piano Sonata. Its full title is 'Concord, Mass., 1840-1860,' and it was mostly composed between 1911 and 1915. The four movements are headed with the names of New England writers Ives particularly identified with – Ralph Waldo Emerson, Nathaniel Hawthorne, Bronson and Louisa May Alcott and Henry David Thoreau. Concord was the village in Massachusetts, not far from Boston, where they lived while developing their transcendentalist ideals.

Each of the four movements depicts Ives's response to the writer, or writers, as acutely as his portraits of popular festivals in the sections of the 'Holidays' Symphony, but obviously less literally. Some aspects of the Sonata have often been discussed – the tone-clusters, some of them gently played with a flat board in the 'Hawthorne' movement; the optional use of a flute for the 'Thoreau' movement, because the writer played that instrument; the frequent appearance of the unifying fate motif from Beethoven's Fifth Symphony.

The genesis of the 'Hawthorne' movement is complex, involving earlier and concurrent sources. Ives often has several versions of an idea, no one of which is final. Some commentators have missed the quoted material from *Country Band March* and *Overture 1776* (1903), used again in *Putnam's Camp* (1912) and in the second movement of the Fourth Symphony (1910-16). The 'Hawthorne' movement of the sonata shares material with these works and is itself reflected in *The Celestial Railroad* (1924?) – the title of a short story by Hawthorne – recorded by Alan Mandel but still not published. There are also connections between the 'Concord' Sonata and the many Studies for piano, which form a kind of sketchbook to illuminate the composer's working method.

Ambiguity in the interaction of sources in the 'Concord' Sonata is reflected in the connections between the fate motif from Beethoven and the two or more hymn-tunes which are linked to it. Everyone notices the Beethoven motif, but familiarity with the slow movement, 'The Alcotts,' shows the descending major third leading into H. C. Zeuner's hymn-tune 'Missionary Chant.' Closer investigation reveals more – the hymn-tune 'Martyn,' by S. B. Marsh, which emerges in the third line of music. All of the melody line in the outer sections of the movement can actually be derived from the Beethoven motif and the two hymns. However, this is not so in the 'Hawthorne' movement, where a hymn emerges in rapt stillness between the outbursts of piano virtuosity. The first phrase of this hymn is 'Martyn,' but the rest of the implied four-phrase hymn-tune in 6.6.6.6. meter is not. Still another hymn-tune is linked to these by its falling major third – 'Dornance' by I. B. Woodbury. This is a principal source of the fourth movement of the Fourth Symphony, thus making a connection with the second movement of that work.

Even after much investigation there are still riddles of quotation which may never be solved. Enough can be gleaned to justify linking Ives's practice to an oral, improvising tradition rather than to the formal, worked-out development of composers from Bach to Brahms. A vernacular tradition found in village fiddlers, in ragging – all kinds of tunes can be treated in this way, as Ben Harney's *Ragtime Instructor* (published in 1897) shows – and later in jazz, is employed. All these examples would be notated, if at all, after the event.

Ives's connections with Afro-American music are rarely stressed, although he was aware of them and they go back to his father. George Ives studied the singing of a Black boy during the Civil War when he was with the army. On returning home, he brought the boy with him and sent him to school in Danbury. Charles never knew the boy, but he noticed the differences between Black and White singing and the treatment of familiar gospel hymns by groups like the Jubilee Singers. He could also remember black-faced comedians ragging their songs before 1892.

In the decade before the First World War Ives wrote most of his music, frenziedly composing at night after work and at weekends, unhindered by an audience. After 1918 his stroke prevented him from doing much more at the office, and he started to sort out his music – a process still being carried on by scholars at Yale under the direction of John Kirkpatrick. The first stage of public recognition began when Ives sent out at his own expense in 1921 copies of the 'Concord' Sonata, with a companion book, 'Essays before a Sonata,' and a single-volume set of 114 Songs.

In 1927 the composer Henry Cowell (1897-1965) wrote to Ives, having seen these scores, and their partnership introduced the second stage. Cowell edited the periodical *New Music*, and Ives generously contributed to the costs and supported performances, by no means restricted to his own works. In 1932 Aaron Copland accompanied Hubert Linscott in *Seven Songs*, still published as a set, and drew favorable attention to Ives. John Kirkpatrick played the 'Concord' Sonata in New York in 1939, where it was hailed as 'the greatest music composed by an American.'

•The Third Symphony•

The fame Ives achieved in his lifetime, however, came to him primarily after the Second World War, in his last decade. In 1946 Lou Harrison conducted the Third Symphony, which was awarded the Pulitzer Prize the following year. Even at this stage Ives maintained his stance about officialdom: 'Prizes are for boys. I'm grown-up.' And, 'Prizes are the badges of mediocrity.' Leonard Bernstein conducted the Second Symphony in 1951 and Stokowski the Fourth in 1965 – all these were first public performances, incredibly delayed.

The recognition that came to Ives with the Third Symphony also affected his hearers as they recognized their own American past, nostalgically evoked. This was something Copland also did in *Appalachian Spring* (1944), and Samuel Barber in *Knoxville: Summer of 1915* (1947). But it is worth approaching the Third Symphony (1901-4) from the point of view of its hymn-tune sources. Most of it originated from organ pieces Ives used in church. He felt this kind of playing weakened the music – 'I seem to have worked with more freedom when I knew the music was not going to be inflicted on others.'

The subtitle of the symphony is 'The Camp Meeting,' which refers to Ives's childhood: 'I

remember, when I was a boy – at the outdoor Camp Meeting services in Redding, all the farmers, their families and field hands, for miles around, would come afoot or in their farm wagons. I remember how the great waves of sound used to come through the trees – when hymns were sung by thousands of "let-out" souls. The music notes and words on paper were as much like what they "were" (at those moments) as the monogram on a man's necktie may be like his face.' Thus a potent source for Ives's varied treatment of the tunes in the Third Symphony is what happened to them in mass singing: 'Most of them knew the words and music by heart, and sang it that way. If they threw the poet or composer around a bit, so much the better for the poetry and the music.' Because of their importance in Ives's stream of consciousness, some of the main hymn-tunes are named here, with alternative names in some cases as well as composers. It is worth tracing these in old hymn-books in order to get to know them on their own terms, as Ives did. John Kirkpatrick and C. W. Henderson have provided many clues in their publications on Charles Ives.

Each movement of the Third Symphony has its own heading. The first is called 'Old Folks Gatherin',' and at least four hymn-tunes intermingle, not necessarily represented by their initial phrases. 'Erie' (What a Friend) by C. C. Converse and 'Azmon' (Denfield) by C. G. Glasser are suggested at the start, but 'Azmon' gains ground as the basis of a fugato in the strings and then horn. 'Woodworth,' by W. F. Bradbury, appears on horns in a new section, but 'Azmon' is varied to a climax. A short pause leads to 'Erie' on the oboe and then, more clearly, on the flute. 'Erie' dominates, though parts of 'Azmon' intrude, and both are heard together at the end of the movement, 'Azmon' complete in the strings with 'Erie' above in flute and oboe.

The second movement is called 'Children's Day.' 'Naomi,' by Lowell Mason, the musical educator and reformer, functions as a *cantus firmus* in horns or bassoon, against simultaneous suggestions of another Mason tune in the first violins. This is 'Fountain,' later to become the basis of Ives's most acclaimed song 'General William Booth enters into Heaven.' The dotted figure passed from woodwind to strings and back at the start of the second section is 'There is a Happy Land,' thought to be an old Hindu air, and a smoother tune in woodwind shortly afterwards comes from 'There's Music in the Air,' a popular song. A section based on dotted rhythms leads to a march with a B minor theme, which ought to be identifiable. A varied recapitulation puts the 'Naomi' *cantus firmus* high up in the flute with 'Fountain' below. 'Erie' enters into it, and so does 'Happy Land,' to end the movement.

The finale is headed 'Communion,' so 'Woodworth,' already met in the first movement, is a realistic communion hymn: 'Just as I am, without one plea, but that Thy blood was shed for me.' Now we notice that 'Naomi' and 'Woodworth' have almost identical first phrases, again creating ambiguity: 'Naomi' in 4/4 starting on the beat, but 'Woodworth' starting with an upbeat and in 6/8. The emphasis on 'Woodworth' – it comes almost complete in the cellos at the end – recalls 'Naomi' from the first movement, although this largo is quite different, approaching the intensity of a Mahler adagio. The last few bars could be heard as a mixture of 'Naomi' and 'Woodworth.'

At the very end Ives asks for the sound of bells, preferably church bells, Henry Cowell thought. This passage for bells, notated in alternating triads of B minor and G sharp minor against perfect cadences in B flat major, jogged the memory of an elderly Bavarian percussionist when he heard it with David Wooldridge in 1954. He claimed to have played the Third Symphony under Gustav Mahler in 1910. It was known that Mahler took a score of the work to Vienna shortly before he died in 1911, but there seems to be no other evidence that he actually conducted it. If he did, it would be an example of American innocence crossing paths with European experience. John Cage (b.1912) studying with Arnold Schoenberg in California in 1933 is another. Schoenberg did not regard Cage as a composer at all, but as an inventor – of genius.

•The legacy•

The quitessential Ives experience was elaborately carried to extremes by Cage in 1967 – in a work, or a happening, called *Musicircus*. Some twenty concerts or more are assembled under one roof and allowed to carry on regardless. People walk around as at a circus, each one getting a different impression. Cage has been influenced by Ives, whose source was, as usual, something that happened with his father. Philip Sutherland, who lived in Danbury at the time, recalled this when talking to Vivian Perlis in 1968: 'They'd be going one way with the band, with another band going the other way round the park here, and the two would clash – that interested Charles Ives very much, but people in Danbury didn't think it was very interesting to see the two bands blending and playing two different tunes.'

In a flash Ives must have realized the potential of that incident. He returns to it again and again. All his most advanced works bring opposing textures together either simultaneously or in violent alternating succession. Notating the resulting clash of meters and tempi gave problems to Ives and his eventual performers. But they provided some of his most adventurous moments – *Three Places in New England*; 'Holidays' Symphony ('Washington's Birthday,' 'Decoration Day,' 'The Fourth of July,' and 'Thanksgiving'); two 'Contemplations' (*The Unanswered Question* and *Central Park in the Dark*); the Second Orchestral Set; and the Fourth Symphony. These large-scale confrontations are the unforgettable legacy of Ives.

Top: Charles Ives, 1947.

Center: Virgil Thomson, photographed by Lee Miller. He studied in Paris with Boulanger and collaborated with Gertrude Stein on two operas, while many of the sources of his music are purely American – Baptist hymns, traditional songs, pop tunes and southern spirituals.

Top: Nadia Boulanger.

Center: Copland in the thirties.

Bottom: A Cecil Beaton photograph of the American Ballet Theater group. Copland is here seated on the right, with Oliver Smith standing next to him. Lucia Chase is seated in the foreground.

•Aaron Copland•

Aaron Copland, born in 1900 in Brooklyn, is the most distinguished and successful American composer of the generation following Ives. He could only follow Ives in a chronological sense, however, since Ives's music was unknown, or almost unknown, during his youth. There is a tantalizing story about Copland's glimpsing a copy of the 'Concord' Sonata in the New York studio of his teacher Rubin Goldmark (1872-1936), which must have been just before Copland left for Paris in the spring of 1921. Goldmark discouraged him from studying the work. What would have happened to Copland, Ives and American music if his teacher had given him the copy?

Copland had no musical father like George Ives to inspire him, but his elder brother and sister took lessons. His father was a Lithuanian immigrant who ran a successful department store known as 'The Macy's of Brooklyn,' and who was also president of the local synagogue. His mother, too, was of Russian origin, suggesting a comparison between Copland and Stravinsky, reaching back into their ancestry. The Russian Jewish connection Copland shares with George Gershwin. Gershwin too was born in Brooklyn and also studied with Goldmark – but he only survived three lessons.

Like Ives, but in a more straightforward way, Copland drew on popular culture and could be described as a nationalist. As a young man Copland too rebelled against the German type of academicism. Goldmark was of Austro-German descent and studied in Vienna. At Yale Ives had been misunderstood by Horatio Parker, who had studied in Munich with Rheinberger. Goldmark's bias turned Copland towards French music several years before he went to France and became the first American pupil of Nadia Boulanger (1887-1979). Her role in training leading American composers was well established, as Copland was followed by Virgil Thomson, Walter Piston, Roy Harris, Marc Blitzstein, Elliott Carter and many more.

Before he went to Paris, Copland had written some polished piano pieces and songs showing an awareness of Debussy, Ravel and Skriabin. Some of this juvenilia had to be written down to the level of his teacher, just like Ives, but the published pieces are good enough to suggest that Copland had more need to grow up in a cosmopolitan atmosphere than to change direction. The first of these is a scherzo called *The Cat and the Mouse*, which Copland, a well-trained pianist if not a virtuoso, played himself. This work was a turning-point, more than once. Goldmark had no criteria by which to judge it, but after a performance Copland gave in Paris, Debussy's publisher Durand offered to publish it. This scherzo and the *Passacaglia* (1921-2) were the first of Copland's works to be heard in his own country after his return.

The Cat and the Mouse is full of programmatic touches, witty snippets suggesting the later composer of film-music. The piano textures and especially the whole-tone chords probably stem from Debussy, particularly the funereal passage at the end. The opening of Debussy's ballet *Jeux* (1913) is a possible source, but Copland and Debussy must certainly have known *The Sorcerer's Apprentice* (1897), the highly original as well as popular tone-poem by Paul Dukas.

In 1922, a year after the performance of the scherzo, two songs about love, written before Copland went to Paris, were performed there. 'Old Poem' is a setting of a Chinese poem translated by Arthur Waley. The atmosphere is beautifully sustained, as in some of Duparc's songs, but the harmony of sevenths and ninths comes from Ravel, in particular his popular *Habanera* (1895). The second song is 'Pastorale,' composed a year after 'Old Poem' and now showing marked Copland melodic characteristics – rising intervals of a major seventh, and a major ninth in the voice – as well as harmonic derivation from Skriabin. The opening chord is only one note removed from Skriabin's mystic chord, but the piano texture anticipates that of the first of the Emily Dickinson songs (1949-50).

The two songs and the scherzo are not diminished by reference to their technical sources, which are mostly assimilated. The qualities of the mature Copland are emerging – using the simplest means to achieve a precise sound. The *Passacaglia*, written during Copland's first year with Nadia Boulanger and dedicated to her, is less consistent. But in spite of arpeggios suggesting Fauré, dotted rhythms and whole-tone patterns from Debussy's *Préludes* and even a Franckian peroration, the gritty passacaglia bass focused on tritones is put through its paces in the same cumulative sectional layout used later in the Piano Variations of 1930. And even that work's theme is clearly a response to the one used for variations in Stravinsky's Octet, and the wide chords stem from his *Symphonies of Wind Instruments*. The *Passacaglia* is a rehearsal for the Variations, a major landmark in American piano music, and Copland had to wait to absorb Stravinsky and the intransigent sound of Edgard Varèse before he could produce it.

Copland singled out two qualities about Nadia Boulanger: her 'consuming love for music' and her ability to 'inspire a pupil with confidence in his own powers.' He also paid tribute to her encyclopedic knowledge of music of all periods. She was not satisfied merely to supervise Copland's composition, but took his career in hand – and perhaps risked her own – when she commissioned the Symphony for Organ and Orchestra for her first American tour. She played the organ part in 1925 with the New York Philharmonic under Walter Damrosch. He was the conductor who had insulted Ives in 1910 when he found the second movement of his First Symphony too hard to get through at a rehearsal. Damrosch's insult to Copland turned out to be remarkably valuable publicity. Fearing the wrath of the subscribers, Damrosch had turned to the audience immediately after the performance and said: 'If a young man at the age of twenty-three can write a symphony like that, in five years he will be ready to commit murder.'

Dedicated to Boulanger, the Symphony has three movements: prelude, scherzo and finale. The prelude opens and closes with a flute solo related to the atmosphere of Debussy's Trio for flute, viola and harp, but the warmth of the first violin melody is Copland's own. So are the high spirits of the scherzo, prompted less by *The Rite of Spring* (1913) than by Satie's *Parade* (1917) and some of the works of Milhaud, whom Copland must have found sympathetic, because he was a Jew with a similar lyrical gift and had celebrated jazz in his ballet *La Création du monde* (1923). The finale shows the results of studying counterpoint and fugue, one of Boulanger's specialities. A single line, with a minor triadic motif, builds to a rhetorical climax where the soloist comes in. The minor third is converted into a dry static bass *ostinato* for much of the *allegro* section, a tactic of Stravinsky's at this period and later, and reflected in other composers such as Poulenc. Again these neoclassical hallmarks do not detract from an exhilarating work in the rare medium of organ and orchestra, which ought to be heard more often.

• Developing an American audience •

Jazz was to be Copland's next phase. The conductor of the Boston Symphony Orchestra, Serge Koussevitzky, was impressed by the Symphony and commissioned a new work. This was *Music for the Theater* (1925), full of jazz mannerisms following the lead of John Alden Carpenter, the concerns of George Antheil, whom Copland admired, and the sensational success of Gershwin's *Rhapsody in Blue* the year before. Copland drew on jazz – and had done so earlier in his *Moods* for piano, 1920-1 – because he wanted his music to be as recognizably American as possible. This idea sustained his Piano Concerto (1926), which he played himself with the Boston Orchestra under Koussevitzky. Philip Hale, critic for the *Boston Herald*, wrote: 'If this concerto shows the present condition of Mr Copland's mind, he is on the wrong track . . . we found little to attract, little to admire, much to repel . . . .' In 1931 Ives called Mr Hale 'a nice and dear old lady in Boston.' Because Hale accused Ives of having been influenced by Stravinsky, Prokofiev or Hindemith (all impossible), Ives concluded: '. . . he is either a fool or a crook.' Incidents like this illustrate the ignorant philistinism of established critics at the time.

After the Piano Concerto, Copland's jazz interests became more generalized into popular forms, especially Latin-American. This was encouraged by visiting Mexico for the first time in 1932, and by his friendship with the Mexican composer Carlos Chávez (1899-1978), whose

Above: Copland in London rehearsing for a concert in 1980. He was an extremely proficient conductor, quite exacting but with an experimental attitude to rhythm. Rhythm has always been a key factor in his compositions, the means whereby he transformed many of his borrowed sources of melody.

tough, folksy sound he admired and perhaps imitated. One result was the orchestral piece *El Salón México* (1933-6). This Spanish magnetism had affected French composers from Bizet and Chabrier to Debussy, Ravel and Milhaud.

Copland, like Ives, had a business instinct, but unlike Ives he applied it to the musical profession. They both had a passionate commitment to improving the lot of the ordinary person – Copland wrote a *Fanfare for the Common Man*, conducted in 1943 by Eugene Goossens, the man who mounted the first two movements of Ives's Fourth Symphony in 1927. Ives pioneered life insurance for the common man and in 1912 wrote a widely used pamphlet for insurance agents called 'The Amount to Carry.' Copland crystallized his concern into lectures for the ordinary listener given at The New School for Social Research, New York City. These became *What to Listen for in Music* – a best-selling book in at least six languages. The emphatic preposition 'for' implies that listening is an active and not a passive task.

Copland continued to visit Europe during the later 1920s and early 1930s. He began to feel that 'it was worth the effort to say what I had to say in the simplest possible terms,' although in 1967 he resented the way this remark had been oversimplified and used to discredit his and other people's tougher music. He was interested in Hindemith's *Gebrauchsmusik* in Germany and came across Kurt Weill's *Threepenny Opera*. Both composers had responded to the fashions of the 1920s, including jazz, and wanted to make their music more functional and direct. In 1933 Copland wrote about Ives for the periodical *Modern Music*. He linked the neglect of Ives to the problems facing every single American composer: 'for men of the stature of Ives an audience must be found, or American music will never be born.' By 1967

Copland could say: 'Ives has pre-empted the place once held by Edward MacDowell as the first truly significant composer of serious music in our country.'

Before Ives could break through to that position, and with him American music as a whole, an audience had to be built up. Copland, as composer, performer, writer and propagandist, did more than anyone else to make this happen. He reached the large public with his ballets *Billy the Kid* (1938) and *Rodeo* (1942) and put to good use what he had learned from Hindemith's approach and the example of Virgil Thomson in eight film scores between 1939 and 1961. When he began to conduct as well, the public loved him, and the stage was set for his role as America's cultural ambassador and dean of American composers.

•Theater and poetry•

Quiet City, for cor anglais, trumpet and string orchestra, is typical of Copland's finely spun, relaxed manner of the later 1930s. It started

life in the theater. In 1939 Copland's friend Harold Clurman was directing a production of Irwin Shaw's play called *Quiet City*, about a lonely Jewish youth – a jazz trumpeter – but also concerned with 'the night-thoughts of many different kinds of people in a great city.' (*Night Thoughts* is the title of Copland's 1972 piano piece.) The concert piece skillfully stitches together sections of the incidental music, and Wilfrid Mellers finds the result 'both Negroid in its blue notes and Jewish in its incantatory repetitions.'

The blue notes are built into the Mixolydian mode on C, which is used for the work's outer sections. The main melodies are all related and are still memorable even though they recur slightly differently. The opening in the strings, followed by cor anglais, sounds preludial, but is not. These sustained sounds are in four-part counterpoint based on the motivic interval of a perfect fourth, which provides chords too. The trumpet's tensely repeated single notes are a diminution of the rhythm of the main melody which comes next on the cor anglais, and the tune itself is soon treated this way. Cadenzas in triplets in both solo instruments separately are related to the perfect fourth – still a clean interval after so many centuries of harmony based on thirds – and soloists and strings interact closely in the work's single climax, part of a rhythmic passacaglia lasting through four measures, before soft recapitulations.

Copland's instrumental spacing is unique. It has been heard as an image of the vast spaces of the prairies, or the endlessly long avenues of New York City: it is also the expression of one of Nadia Boulanger's goals in composition – the long line. (Both of these aspects are also present in the work of Roy Harris.) In an interview with Philip Ramey in 1980, Copland described *Appalachian Spring* as 'plain, singing, comparatively uncomplicated and slightly folksy. Direct and approachable.'

By 1950 Copland was at a turning-point. This was marked by the *Twelve Poems of Emily Dickinson* (1830-86), which Stravinsky singled out as 'distinctly American and very lovely pastoral lyricism.' The New England recluse who wrote 1,775 poems and only had six published in her lifetime suggests a parallel to the Ives saga. Her regular use of hymn meters for verse reveals the power of these sources, as for Ives, and she too suffered for her originality and awaited discovery – which only came after her death. Copland, from a quite different, Jewish, background but one with a type of alienation in common, chose twelve of her poems to make one of the finest song-cycles for voice and piano in the English language.

In the same year as these songs, which are clearly based on tonality, Copland started to use serial techniques in his Quartet for piano and strings. Stravinsky was still occupied with *The Rake's Progress* and only after that began to move in a serial direction. Roger Sessions, Copland's colleague from the days of the Copland–

Above: Cradling Wheat, 1938, by Thomas Hart Benton (1889-1975). His paintings emphasize the vernacular traditions of the American countryside and echo many of the nationalistic sentiments embodied in Copland's music.

Left: Oliver Smith's design for Copland's ballet *Rodeo*, first performed at the Metropolitan Opera House, New York, on 16 October 1942. *Rodeo* was typical of Copland's work in its popular images and its colorful rendering of an American way of life.

Left: Scene from *Billy the Kid*, first performed in 1938 with scenery and costumes designed by Jarel French. Copland's ballets reached wide audiences and exerted a far-reaching influence on the public – it was mainly through these popular works that he gained recognition as a composer.

Sessions concerts in 1928-31, only got there in 1953. Ironically, the Piano Quartet is dedicated to Elizabeth Sprague Coolidge, who wrote to Mrs Ives in 1921 to say that she 'did not in the least understand' Ives's music and found nothing in it which she liked.

Some observers have pointed out the discrepancy between the serious Copland of the Piano Variations, the 'Vitebsk' Trio, or the 'Short' Symphony, and the composer of the popular ballets and film scores. In his works since 1950 Copland seems to have been determined to go further in technical advancement and yet keep his popular image. He perhaps hoped to be fashionable with the musical profession without losing his public. But the diversity between works that results from this versatility is negligible compared with what has now been allowed Ives, sometimes in the same work; and Schoenberg, after all, wrote tonal music following his first twelve-tone piece in 1923.

In an interview with me at Keele University in 1976, Copland explained his own position: 'It's nice to vary the attack, so to speak, by sometimes addressing a highly sophisticated audience with a musical style that one knows is not acceptable to the great mass of people, and then to turn around and write something for a school chorus or orchestra for a different kind of public and a different occasion. Not all composers are able to do that. I happen to think that I was able to and I found it relaxing not to be always at the top of my form trying to write the great masterpiece of the age.' That account seems completely convincing, and so does the music. The listener is hardly aware of any serial workings in the Piano Quartet, but the Piano Fantasy (1957) went further. Copland then arranged his Piano Variations for orchestra, perhaps in the hope of bringing the orchestral public into touch with his sterner visions, but the orchestral piece is not as successful as the *Symphonic Ode* from the same period.

In 1962 Copland was commissioned by *Life* magazine to write an easy piano piece. All his lucid diatonic characteristics emerge in *Down a Country Lane*, and in the same year his twelve-tone orchestral work, *Connotations*, was written for the opening season of the New York Philharmonic in the new Lincoln Center. Leonard Bernstein, who conducted it, was concerned that Copland had 'tried to catch up with twelve-tone music just as it was becoming old-fashioned to the young.' Copland was undeterred. For the medium of band, particularly associated with diatonic popular music, he wrote *Emblems* (1964), and followed it with the orchestral *Inscape* (1967). All these pieces suggest the influence of Varèse, whose music reached the concert hall again in the 1960s after a long gap since the 1920s and '30s.

Copland seemed to be closing the circle by reflecting the influences of his youth – New York in the 1920s. The avant-garde, dissonant works of that period – especially those by Varèse and Ruggles – were standing up well to the test of time. So was Ives. Elliott Carter (b.1908) had met Ives in 1924, unlike Copland, and found it a disturbing experience, later changing his views about Ives's music several times. In the 1960s and '70s Carter too was looking back to the heroic 1920s: he had passed through neoclassicism, touched on the American movement, bypassed serialism, and finally achieved a Varèsian hard edge in his later works.

During the 1970s Copland's pace slowed down, except for his conducting, until he ceased to compose – another connection with Ives. Like Stravinsky in later life, he wrote a few tributes to friends: a Duo for flute and piano; two threnodies, one for Stravinsky's death. Like Ives he tidied up some aspects of his work, without of course anything like the same need. The Duo was done in a violin and piano version; eight of the Emily Dickinson songs were scored for voice and chamber orchestra; some early pieces were published for the first time and others completed from existing sketches. *Proclamation*, begun in 1973, was completed in 1982, when Copland described it as a 'rather stern-sounding piece, in what has not inappropriately been termed my "laying-the-law-down " style.'

Below: Copland taking a class in composition at Tanglewood, Mass., venue for the annual Berkshire Music Center summer school of instruction, founded by Koussevitzky in 1940. Copland acted as chairman of the faculty from the early forties until he retired in 1965.

That approach to the keyboard was much in evidence with three solo pieces which formed landmarks in Copland's career: the Variations, the Sonata and the Fantasy. The Sonata (1939-41) was Leonard Bernstein's favorite Copland work. The declamatory first movement, the bouncing varied meters of the vivace and the spare lyricism of the slow finale all have echoes in Bernstein's own music on and off Broadway.

In 1972 Copland wrote another extended piece in serious vein for his own instrument. *Night Thoughts*, which begins and ends quietly, was an unusual response to a commission for the Van Cliburn Quadrennial Competition of 1973. The composer told me in 1975 that he intended to write 'a test of musicality in varied textures' rather than a showpiece. *Night Thoughts* has fourteen changes of tempo or meter, apart from *ritenuto* marks, in its length of some six minutes. Two of these changes are metrical modulations of the type pioneered by Elliott Carter. When I performed this work in Copland's presence at Keele University in 1976, he asked me to preface it with *In Evening Air*, a shorter and simpler piece which had been published at about the same time. I later made the first recording of both pieces together, again at his request. Copland seemed to associate the two pieces with each other, and I got the impression they were contemporary. At the end of *In Evening Air* he quotes a couplet from the American poet Theodore Roethke: 'I see, in evening air, how slowly dark comes down on what we do.' This suggests the winding down of Copland's own creative life, and chimes with the title *Night Thoughts* – a more challenging statement of a similar inner melancholy. However, I later discovered that *In Evening Air* was not written at the same time as *Night Thoughts* at all, but was arranged in 1969 from a film score, *The Cummington Story*, written in 1945. It shows Copland's contentment in parallel channels, simple and complex, that he was able to be vague about the years separating the two pieces. They could have been written together. The subtitle of *Night Thoughts* is 'Homage to Ives,' which Copland added 'because of the work's Ivesian flavor.' This was a recognition, in what was to be Copland's last substantial piece, of the importance of Ives and what he stood for in American music – a piece, with its rock-like sonorities, worthy of Ives's idealism, where the listener is told to 'stand up and use your ears like a man.'

In 1980, in a birthday tribute, Lawrence Starr suggested: 'The accelerating rediscovery of Ives may also be somewhat responsible for the weakening of Copland's previously undisputed position at the forefront of American composers.' This need not be so. Ives and Copland can be regarded as complementary. Everything about each composer adds up to a major achievement of international proportions, although both composers have their American detractors. At the same time, I wrote: 'In an age of neurotic soul-searching and tension, Copland's music of affirmation is a beacon of optimism worthy of the best in the American spirit. Everyone who cares about the state of music today, or is involved in teaching, performing or composing, must be grateful to him for what he has achieved and what he has stood for as man and composer for over half a century.'

Right: Page from the autograph manuscript of Copland's Piano Quartet, written in 1950. The appearance of the score is businesslike and direct – both qualities that could describe Copland himself. In this work he used twelve-tone techniques for the first time, but he never abandoned traditional harmony, continuing to use it as a basis for musical exploration.

In the same year Frank R. Rossiter assessed the position of Ives in relation to his American society: 'Today it is widely believed, especially by those who admire his music, that Ives had the best of both worlds – the normal American world and the world of the avant garde. But this is a sentimental view. It ignores the hard choice with which Ives's society confronted him at the turn of the century – a choice between being an artist and a good American. Ives chose to be a good American.' In a century when creative artists have often been at odds with the establishment for political or personal reasons, Aaron Copland has come nearer than any other American composer to having it both ways.

Below: Copland (right) with three of his distinguished contemporaries: Roy Harris, Roger Sessions and Elliott Carter.

Opera in the Twentieth Century

Opera has become one of the most popular forms of musical experience in the twentieth century. Recordings – from Caruso to modern stereophonic productions – have helped familiarize audiences with opera, while its dramatic and visual content have also obviously contributed to its popularity, so that the development of cinema and, subsequently, television, have been important factors in this success story.

But opera has also responded to the social and political developments of the twentieth century and has not been content simply to preserve the works of the past. These have, of course, continued to feature largely in the repertoires of the great opera houses, but new productions and new interpretations permit audiences to see the old works in a new light. Furthermore, contemporary composers have, in many cases, been stimulated by this interest to write works of social and political relevance. These have not always been greeted with enthusiasm, especially by audiences for whom vocal display is the main purpose of opera. Nevertheless, the fact that composers have been prepared to risk unfavorable criticism for this very reason suggests that twentieth-century opera is healthy and likely to continue to flourish in the years to come.

Right: Francis Poulenc's *Dialogues des carmélites*, premièred at La Scala, Milan in January 1957, brought to the operatic stage a work by a master of conveying the moods of words, as well as a subject that in earlier times would have scarcely been thought suitable for opera: the experiences of a group of Carmelite nuns prior to their execution during the French Revolution; and it created a new kind of realism in a medium often criticized for its apparent escapism.

Wagner's operas have remained a major force in the twentieth century and, despite their vast scale, they are in the repertory of all the world's great opera houses. Since 1950 the operas have been subject to radical reinterpretation even at the annual Bayreuth Festival founded by the composer himself in 1876. In the 1950s the elaborate stage effects envisaged by Wagner were rejected in the productions of his grandson Wieland Wagner in favor of symbolic minimal scenery and lighting. Above is a scene from his production of *Tristan und Isolde*. For the Bayreuth centenary production of *Der Ring des Nibelungen*, the French producer Patrice Chéreau returned to a much more lavish style of production (*top right*), although his use of nineteenth-century costumes for many of the characters gave the work a strong political content, closer perhaps to the composer's original intentions, but which nevertheless scandalized a considerable section of the audience. This production, conducted by Pierre Boulez, reached a world-wide audience in a televised version.

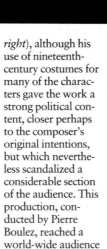

Left: A scene from Visconti's Covent Garden production of Verdi's *Don Carlo*. Today's audiences demand far greater qualities of acting from opera singers than was the case in the past, so that the producer assumes a far larger role. Many notable productions have been the work of film directors, including Visconti, Schlesinger and Zeffirelli.

Right: Benjamin Britten's *Peter Grimes* (1945) was a landmark for English opera, heralding the first native operatic composer of such stature since Purcell. The work itself was a commission from Serge Koussevitzky in memory of his wife Natalie and was indeed begun while the composer was still in America. An essentially English provincial story has now become a great international success, through both the BBC Television production, shown here in rehearsal, and the orchestral *Sea Interludes* which the composer arranged from the opera and which have entered the symphonic repertoire of orchestras throughout the world. In this way the opera has touched thousands who may never have set foot inside an opera house.

Right: A new depth has been given to opera by the collaboration of artists of such stature as David Hockney, whose sets for Stravinsky's *The Rake's Progress* not only give great visual stimulus but also add intellectual dimension to the production. The scenery is now an integral part of the presentation, and vitally important to the overall coherence of the producer's conception.

Left: The nineteenth century was the great period of opera house building in Europe and America, and subsequently, where houses were badly damaged or even destroyed in World War II, the tendency was to recreate the past and rebuild them exactly as before. Only in the younger countries, for the most part, has there been scope for exciting new developments, and Jørn Utzon's opera house (1959-73) in Sydney, Australia, has become a landmark throughout the world for its adventurous, if controversial, style of architecture, showing that opera is very much a part of the cultural life of the twentieth century in that country. At the same time, the building of this particular house demonstrated that a country which had formerly imported most of its music and exported most of its talent, including many great opera singers, to the outside world, could now boast a flourishing and firmly rooted musical culture of its own.

Opera in the twentieth century has frequently conveyed a powerful political message. The work of Kurt Weill (1900-50), particularly in his collaborations with the playwright Bertold Brecht, was marked by a strong sense of satire in the cause of socialism. Weill was greatly assisted by the talent of his wife, the actress and singer Lotte Lenya, shown (*above*) in her role in *The Rise and Fall of the City of Mahagonny*, first performed in 1927.

Below: There is a strong social and political message in *Intolleranza 1960* by Luigi Nono (b. 1924), first performed in 1961 in his native Venice. This set by Josef Svoboda was used in the 1969 Boston production. Nono's music is marked by a profound sense of humanity in opposition to totalitarianism, of freedom and individuality in opposition to violence, enslavement to money and the trappings of an acquisitive, capitalist society.

Above: Die Bassariden by Hans Werner Henze (b. 1926), first performed in 1966, was strongly influenced by Henze's commitment to the ideals of the New Left and the socialist revolution. The Bassarids or maenads – followers of Dionysus – of classical antiquity are used as an allegory in this modern indictment of the capitalist system. Henze wrote it in an increasing mood of 'ecstatic pessimism,' and it marks a turning-point in his musical development.

Below: Scene from *Die Soldaten* (1965) by Bernd Alois Zimmermann (1918-70). Like Berg's *Wozzeck* (based on Büchner's play), Zimmermann's opera, with its military background, is based on a revolutionary play – by J. M. R. Lenz (1751-92). It concerns the ruin of an innocent young girl by a vicious aristocrat and involves jealousy, violence and class rivalry. Although this comes close to a conventional opera plot, Zimmermann sets his opera in French Flanders 'yesterday, today or tomorrow,' and the relevance of the message is underlined by Svoboda's powerful sets (for the 1969 Munich production). Musically, the opera is a synthesis of many of the new techniques available to modern composers. Zimmermann, who taught at the Musikhochschule in Cologne, introduced a seminar on stage and film music into the curriculum – one of the first to acknowledge this vast new area of musical development.

Above: The Mines of Sulphur (1965) by Richard Rodney Bennett (b. 1936) to a libretto by Beverley Cross, though it has no overt political message, concerns greed, murder and retribution. In its treatment of the violence of human passions it is in the tradition of the operas of Britten – to whom it is dedicated. It is, in the composer's words, 'a genuinely English opera, but English in the tough, dark way of the seventeenth century.'

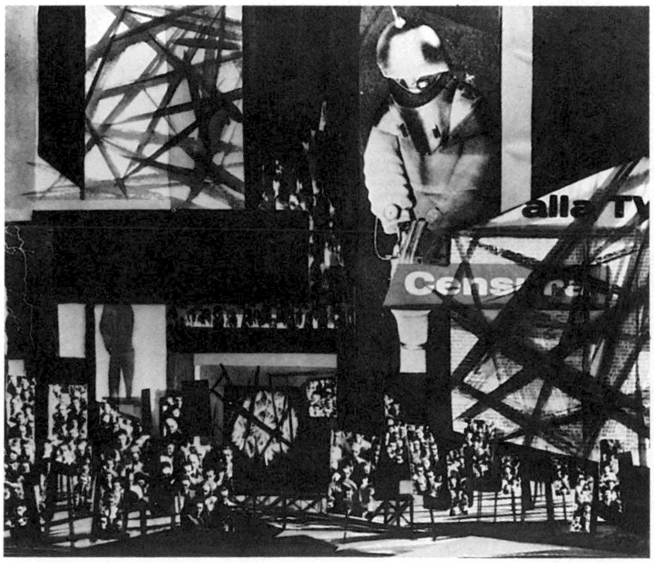

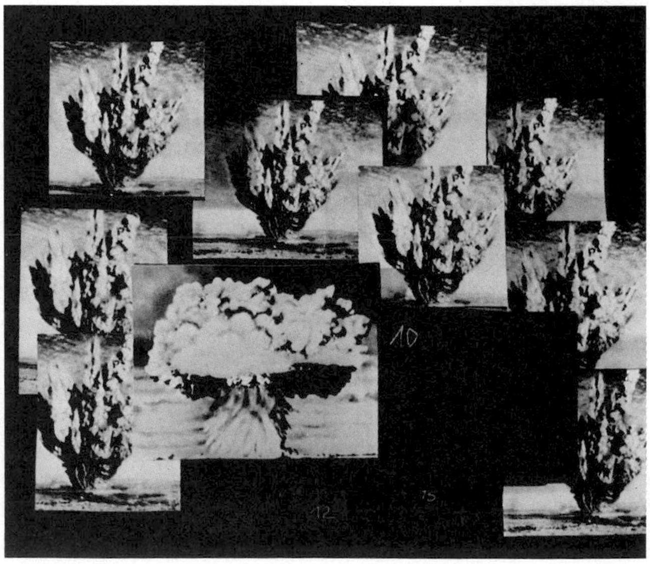

One of the greatest areas of development in opera in the twentieth century has been the revival of interest in pre-Classical works, especially those of Monteverdi and Cavalli, whose *La Calisto* is shown here (*left*) in a production at Glyndebourne. Before such works can be performed, however, orchestral parts have to be reconstructed and copied out, and vocal lines written out in modern notation. In many cases there is no definitive manuscript from which to work, so that scholars disagree on the question of which instruments are to be used, while there is considerable scope for variation in the decoration or embellishment of the vocal line on the part of the singers. As far as staging is concerned, since spectacle was an essential element in these early operas, considerable use of stage machinery and special effects is called for.

Revivals of early opera are enhanced by performances in original theaters that have survived, such as the Court Theater at Drottningholm in Sweden (*right*). Here the entire atmosphere of the early performances can be recreated, and it makes it possible to appreciate accurately the balance between the various forces involved – especially that of orchestra to vocalists – in early opera, as well as providing ideal conditions for the conventions of that opera, which are often foreign to today's audience.

Recordings have greatly extended the audience for opera, and the vivid production effects made possible by stereophonic sound add to the sense of drama; the Decca recording of Wagner's *Ring* under Georg Solti was an outstanding example of this technique. At left is a recording session in Vienna, and at right the thunder-machine used to such powerful effect in *Das Rheingold*.

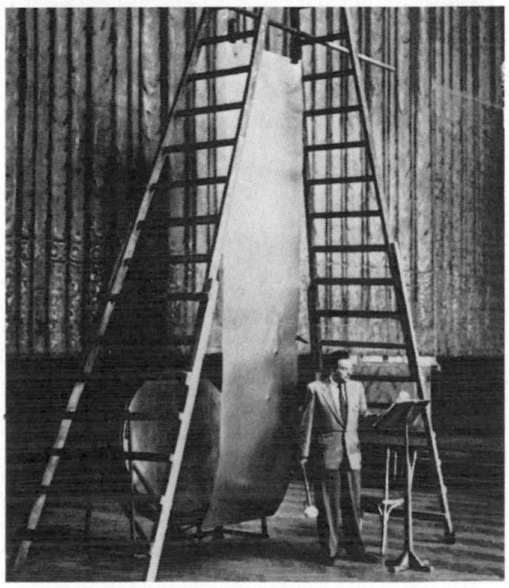

WILLIAM WALTON, MICHAEL TIPPETT AND BENJAMIN BRITTEN

MICHAEL KENNEDY

Opposite: Benjamin Britten (1913-76) rehearsing at Aldeburgh in 1973.

These three English composers were born within eleven years of each other – William Walton in 1902, Michael Tippett in 1905 and Benjamin Britten in 1913 – and each has been regarded at some time as the leader of his generation of English composers. To Walton this distinction came early, from roughly 1929 to 1940. With Britten the peak of fame came almost overnight in 1945, and he remained on the summit until his death in 1976. Tippett, the latest developer of the three, had to wait until he was almost in his seventies for universal recognition. The fluctuations in their reputations over the past twenty-five years reflect the fickleness of critical and public acclaim in the world of music.

William Walton was born, in poorer circumstances than either Tippett or Britten, on 29 March 1902 in the Lancashire mill town of Oldham, where his father, Charles Walton, was a teacher of singing and a church organist and choirmaster. Charles Walton had been one of the first intake of students at the Royal Manchester College of Music, established in 1893. A bass-baritone pupil of Andrew Black, he married Louisa Turner, an amateur singer, in 1898. William, their second son and second of their four children, showed early musical promise and was taught the violin and piano. There is a family legend that he could sing before he could talk and he eventually sang solos in his father's church choir.

Anxious that the boy should have a better education than that provided by the local school, Charles Walton sent for application forms when he read a newspaper advertisement of voice trials for probationer choristers at Christ Church, Oxford. Because of a mishap, Mrs Walton and her nine-year-old son missed the first train to Oxford and arrived after the examinations had been held. However, the organist consented to hear William, who was at once accepted for the choir school, where he remained for six years, from 1912 to 1918. In 1914, when he was twelve, Walton began to compose. In 1916 he wrote two part-songs, settings of Shakespeare, one of which ('Tell me where is fancy bred?') was for soprano and tenor voices with an accompaniment of three violins and piano.

The Dean of Christ Church, Dr Thomas Strong, was the first in a line of Walton benefactors. When war began in August 1914, Charles Walton's income decreased as there were fewer singing pupils, but Dr Strong, who was a doctor of music as well as of divinity and also a good pianist, personally paid the school fees not met by William's scholarship award. After Sunday morning service Strong would allow the choristers to explore his extensive music library and to play his piano. Sometimes he would play to them; Walton, in a tribute to him in 1949, recalled his playing them Schoenberg's *Six Little Pieces*: 'They caused a great deal of mirth amongst us and he fairly bubbled with amusement . . . He was much more open-minded and knowledgeable about [modern music] than many professional musicians, and if he joked and made fun of it, it was from knowledge and not prejudice.'

In 1918 Walton entered Christ Church as an undergraduate with financial assistance from a fund which Strong controlled. He spent much of his time studying scores by Stravinsky, Bartók, Debussy, Prokofiev and Ravel – 'to the detriment,' he admitted, 'of my scholarly studies in Latin, Greek and algebra.' The inevitable result was that he failed to pass the important Responsions examination on three occasions and was 'sent down' for two of the three terms in 1920. He did, however, obtain the degree of Bachelor of Music that year.

His musical experiences at this formative period were not confined to Oxford. His father took him to the Hallé Concerts in Manchester, where the first orchestral work he heard was the suite from Tchaikovsky's *Nutcracker* ballet. In Manchester, too, in 1916 and 1917 Sir Thomas Beecham staged two famous seasons of opera, and Walton was 'bowled over' by the colorful productions of *Boris Godunov* and *The Golden Cockerel*. Even more significant, though, was the month's holiday he spent in Italy in 1920, when, subsidized by Dr Strong, he accompanied the Sitwells.

Walton had first met Sacheverell Sitwell, youngest of the three talented children of Sir George Sitwell of Renishaw Hall, Derbyshire, at Oxford in 1918. 'Sachie' was five years older than Walton and even at twenty-one was a fervent discoverer of genius. He insisted that his elder brother Osbert should go up to Christ Church early in 1919 to hear part of the Piano Quartet that Walton had composed in 1918-19 and had dedicated to Dr Strong. The Sitwells took Walton into a new world. He became involved with them in trying to promote a concert of music by their protégé Bernard van Dieren;

they arranged for Walton's songs to be performed in London at a *soirée* in the home of Lady Glenconner; his parents in Oldham were astonished to receive letters informing them that their William had been invited to Lady Ottoline Morell's home at Garsington and that he had found the new Satie ballet, *Parade*, 'very marvellous.' Very soon he numbered among his friends the poets and writers Siegfried Sassoon, Roy Campbell and T. S. Eliot, the painter Wyndham Lewis, and the musicians and critics Cecil Gray, Lord Berners and Philip Heseltine.

•The twenties and thirties•

Leaving Oxford at the age of eighteen, Walton became 'adopted, or elected, brother' to the Sitwell brothers and their poet sister Edith and lived with them in Chelsea. The Sitwells championed all that was new in the arts and waged continuous war against philistinism and the academic 'Establishment.' They resolutely opposed all attempts to persuade Walton to enter one of the London colleges of music; this caused some consternation in Oldham, but eventually Charles Walton was persuaded that 'Willie knew best.' The Sitwells and other friends provided Walton with a reasonable annual income, which enabled him to concentrate on composing; and this he did, either in Chelsea or at Amalfi in Italy, a country he loved from the moment he first saw it.

If they kept him untainted by any academy, the Sitwells were anxious that Walton should meet influential teachers. An attempt to interest Busoni in his work failed, but in 1921 he was having lessons from the conductor Ernest Ansermet (1883-1964) and from the critic and teacher Edward J. Dent (1876-1951). Dent was first president in 1922 of the International Society for Contemporary Music and was probably helpful in the selection of Walton's String Quartet for the Society's first festival at Salzburg in August 1923. (Among other works performed at the festival were Berg's String Quartet, Janáček's Violin Sonata and Bartók's Violin Sonata no.2.) The work made little impression, but two months earlier, in London, Walton had had his first taste of public controversy when *Façade* received its first public performance.

Façade was, and is, a remarkable and original work. It was devised in November 1921 as a private experimental entertainment. Poems by Edith Sitwell were declaimed through a megaphone to an accompaniment (or commentary) of Walton's music, scored for a small chamber ensemble. The poems were not 'set to music' as songs, but the words inevitably attracted some rhythm from the music. The Aeolian Hall performance on 12 June 1923 attracted a good deal of hostile and rather silly press comment and was used for publicity by both friends and foes. It seemed then to be just another manifestation of the 'bright young things' element of the 1920s. But three years later it was received with acclamation and has never looked back.

It would be no surprise if posterity were to decide that *Façade* was Walton's finest achievement. It is one of those rare works of art which capture the spirit of an age, yet transcend mere topicality. The jazzy flavor of the music, the parodies of folksong, of Rossini, of music-hall

Below left: Paul Hindemith playing the viola. A most gifted violist, he gave the first performance of Walton's Viola Concerto at a Promenade Concert after it had been turned down by Lionel Tertis, for whom Walton had in fact written the work. Later Walton was to honor Hindemith by writing variations (1962-3) on a theme taken from the opening of the slow movement of his Cello Concerto.

Below: Walton's music being recorded for Olivier's film *Hamlet*, released in 1948. The advent of film-sound provided a whole new range of possibilities for Walton, although recording the music itself was a complicated venture – the sound track had to tally exactly with the action on the screen, and timing was therefore crucial.

songs, the fanfares and hornpipes and yodeling were all highly appropriate in the context of 1922, yet they are such good musical jokes and satires that they survive. And beneath the surface wit and charm lies a serious lyrical strand, the forerunner of the bitter-sweet lyricism which runs throughout Walton's work. The music, rescored for larger orchestra, has had much success as a ballet, but the original version, with its sparer scoring, is to be preferred. Its progenitors were *Parade* and Stravinsky's *The Soldier's Tale* (Walton had not heard Schoenberg's *Pierrot lunaire*). The work as a whole has undergone much revision, only six of the original eighteen items surviving into the published score of 1951, and as late as 1979 Walton reworked some numbers, including one which had not been heard since 1923. It is apparent, therefore, that *Façade* was a continual obsession, which is scarcely surprising since it is quintessential Walton.

After *Façade* Walton flirted with various styles, writing several works which ended in the fire. But his overture *Portsmouth Point* (1925), a brash portrait of an eighteenth-century nautical scene etched with Stravinskian rhythms, spicy harmonies and brassy instrumentation, was a success when performed at the ISCM Festival in Zürich in 1926. He then achieved maturity with a full exploitation of his personal vein of lyricism in the Viola Concerto, written at Amalfi in 1928-9. This work was suggested to him by Sir Thomas Beecham as a vehicle for the great viola virtuoso Lionel Tertis. But Tertis declined it – to his shame, as he admitted later – because he thought it did not suit the instrument. (Walton himself put it more bluntly: 'He thought it was too modern, God knows why.') Instead the soloist at the first performance, in London, was Paul Hindemith. The groundplan is very similar to that of Elgar's Cello Concerto; a contemplative first movement and a quicksilver scherzo are followed by a finale in which the predominant mood is nostalgic, but Elgar's ripe romanticism is replaced by Walton's bitter-sweet lyricism.

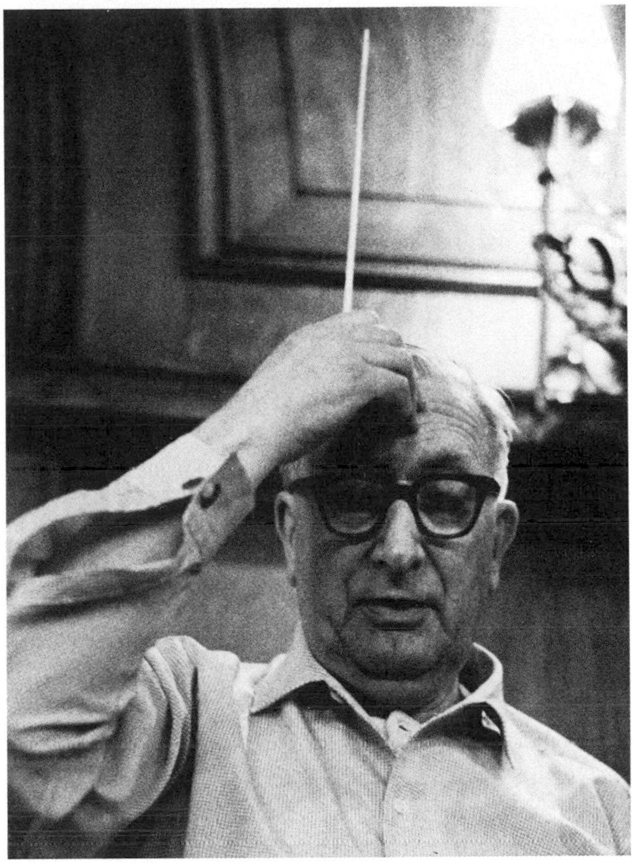

Right: Walton conducting at the first rehearsal of his 'Hindemith' Variations with the Royal Philharmonic Orchestra, 6 March 1963.

Above: Scene from Walton's one-act opera *The Bear*, which had its première at Aldeburgh in 1967. The particular version illustrated here was the 1972 English Opera Group production. *The Bear* is a witty, effervescent comedy, based on a Chekhov play.

Portsmouth Point and the Viola Concerto showed that there were two principal strands in Walton's musical make-up – a scherzando vein, with irregular and spiky rhythms, and a broader melodic vein tinged with cynical melancholy. The concerto also established Walton as a major force in English music before he had reached the age of thirty and dispelled any impression, caused by the aura of frivolity surrounding *Façade*, that he was a lightweight. His next work, the oratorio *Belshazzar's Feast*, caused a far greater sensation than the concerto. Where the purely instrumental work was a private musing, the choral piece was a public oration, delivered with shattering force at one of Britain's temples of choralism, the Leeds Festival, in 1931.

Originally commissioned for radio, *Belshazzar's Feast* grew in scale as it developed. A compact libretto, compiled from biblical sources by Osbert Sitwell, enabled Walton to narrate the drama with exemplary concision. Powerful and brilliant writing for chorus and for the orchestral brass – there is only one soloist, a baritone – and the sheer dynamic force of the music led to a general verdict that here was the greatest and most revolutionary English choral work since Elgar's *The Dream of Gerontius*. Walton, as in the Viola Concerto, had again demonstrated his ability to write music in traditional forms and yet to give the impression of novelty: *Belshazzar's Feast* has a Handelian splendor; it borrows ideas from Mendelssohn's *Elijah*; and its big central orchestral march is in

Above: Portrait of William Walton by Michael Ayrton, 1948. The composer had spent much of his time in Italy since the 1920s and moved permanently to the island of Ischia in 1948 when he married.

Right: Design detail by John Armstrong for one of the backdrops for *Façade*. Armstrong's designs were for the production first staged by the Camargo Society at the Cambridge Theatre on 26 April 1931, with choreography by Frederick Ashton. The scenery was reused in the 1948 Sadler's Wells production.

the ceremonial manner of Elgar. It was almost as if Walton was making a declaration of independence from the Sitwells. They regarded Elgar as an outdated, overblown relic of an imperial past, yet Walton admired and emulated him. The oratorio form was regarded in the 1920s as thoroughly *démodé*, a reminder of Victorian piety and hypocrisy, yet here was Walton at the age of thirty injecting new life into it. What would he do next? The answer, of course, had to be a symphony, another form frequently declared by progressives to be dead, but which resolutely refused to lie down.

Rivalry always played a part in Walton's approach to composition. He claimed to have written his Piano Quartet to see if he could have as much success with it as Herbert Howells had had with his. The Viola Concerto was his reply to Hindemith's *Kammermusik No.5*. When the conductor Sir Hamilton Harty asked Walton to write a symphony for the Hallé Orchestra, he began work on it early in 1932, and when progress was slow, he admitted that new impetus came from a desire 'not to be done in by old Elgar's no.3' (a symphony commissioned in 1932 by the BBC, but which never progressed beyond fragmentary sketches). By 1934 three movements were written and the finale partially finished. For some reason Walton was persuaded to allow the symphony to be performed – three times – without the finale. It was first played in full on 6 November 1935.

The First Symphony is Walton's biggest orchestral work in length and density of scoring. Its turbulent, passionate mood was linked by

Right: Walton conducting the band of the Coldstream Guards at Windsor on 17 September 1969. Walton's music, which can be both witty and lyrical, has also drawn on the popular English tradition of music for military band, particularly in the pieces he has written for national occasions – such as the *Crown Imperial* Coronation March, 1937, and the *Orb and Sceptre* Coronation March, 1953.

Above: Still photograph from Laurence Olivier's film *Richard III*, made in 1955 with music by Walton. Walton had previously collaborated with Olivier on films of two other Shakespeare plays, *Henry V*, 1943-4, and *Hamlet*, 1947.

commentators to the international political climate, but Walton denied the connection, and all the evidence now suggests that its emotional roots lie in an intimate personal relationship. In four movements, heroic in scale, the work was at first compared with Beethoven and Sibelius. Today it seems more accurate to relate it to the symphonic ethos of Prokofiev and Shostakovich. But whatever its stylistic affinities, it is unmistakably Walton's voice that addresses – and sometimes harangues – us, and, like *Belshazzar's Feast*, it has in half a century lost little of its power to rivet an audience's attention with the cogency and splendor of its musical argument.

As far as Britain was concerned, Walton at the age of thirty-three was the outstanding figure of the epoch, and he had achieved this position by means of a very small number of works, each skillfully wrought. Although he frequently described himself as being lazy, Walton's prime virtues were his fastidious craftsmanship and his highly developed capacity for self-criticism. There are no glib solutions in his music. Even as a boy at Oxford, his fanatical concentration on the task in hand had impressed his friend the South African poet Roy Campbell. 'What he did give me, even then,' Campbell wrote in his *Light on a Dark Horse* (1951), 'was a sense of vocation and how a man can live for his art.' In 1937 Walton was commissioned by Heifetz to write a violin concerto, by the BBC to compose a Coronation March (*Crown Imperial*) and by the Leeds Festival to write *In Honour of the City of London*, and he was given his first honorary degree.

The Violin Concerto, though closely related to the Viola Concerto in its structure and effulgent lyricism, marked an advance in Walton's powers as an orchestrator, and it is possible that this was a beneficial result of the discipline of writing film music since 1934. The Violin Concerto has a certainty, a glitter and a resonance which are new to Walton's music. It was the climax of an eventful decade in his career; he seemed thereafter deliberately to subject himself to certain disciplines. He contemplated composing a string quartet, he wrote a suite of piano duets which he later orchestrated (*Music for Children*), and he transcribed Bach for a ballet, *The Wise Virgins*. But the outbreak of the Second World War prevented further creative experiments: he was directed into the film division of the Ministry of Information and wrote the music for several documentary and patriotic films. Of these the best were Olivier's *Henry v* (1944) and *The First of the Few* (1942), a biography of the designer of the Spitfire fighter aircraft. The *Spitfire Prelude and Fugue* is a splendid example of Walton's ability to conscript *Portsmouth Point* into military uniform.

•After the war•

The String Quartet and another chamber work, the Violin Sonata, eventually appeared in 1947 and 1949. There was music for Olivier's film *Hamlet* and a *Te Deum* and another March for the 1953 Coronation service. No second symphony followed, however, and no more concertos. There was a feeling that Walton was written out, a spent force. English criticism, having hailed Walton as the 'white hope' up to 1939, now discarded him. It had found a new savior of English music in the younger composer Benjamin Britten, whose opera *Peter Grimes*, first produced in 1945, heralded a new dawn. Ironically, however, the chief reason for Walton's silence was that – stimulated by the success of *Peter Grimes* – he too was working on a large-scale opera, commissioned by the BBC early in 1947. This was *Troilus and Cressida*, to a libretto by Christopher Hassall. Also, Walton married in 1948 and settled on the island of Ischia. This meant that the long and laborious task of putting the libretto into shape had to be undertaken by correspondence. The music was not begun until 1950 and the opera not completed until September 1954.

The first performance at Covent Garden in December 1954 was an unhappy occasion. There had been disagreements between Walton and the conductor, Sir Malcolm Sargent, and the production was in many respects unsatisfactory. The opera was damned with faint praise by the critics, several of whom said that a composer in 1954 had no business to be writing Romantic operas in the Wagnerian mold. The analogy was wrong, for in its Italianate passion the work comes nearer to Verdi and Puccini. The failure of *Troilus and Cressida*, then and when it was revived in 1976 after four years of revision, wounded Walton deeply. It is difficult not to conclude, however, that the opera is flawed, not because it is in an outdated style – it is in Walton's own style, through and through – but because he did not always respond to the florid libretto with genuine imaginative zest. Although much of *Troilus* has a dark, smoldering beauty unlike anything else he wrote, the best Walton opera is his one-act comedy *The Bear* (1965-7) based on Chekhov, in which the sparkle and wit of *Façade* recur; the best of *Troilus* is to be found in its influence on the amorous and glamorously scored Cello Concerto of 1956.

After the Cello Concerto came a series of commissioned orchestral works: the Second Symphony (1959-60); the *Partita* (1957); the *Variations on a Theme by Hindemith* (1962-3); and the *Improvisations on an Impromptu of Benjamin Britten* (1969). These are all brilliant in style, with 'objectivity' replacing the turbulent emotionalism of the pre-1939 works, and all are scored with increased mastery. There were also the song-cycles *Anon. in Love* (1959) and *A Song for the Lord Mayor's Table* (1962; with orchestra 1970), the choral works *The Twelve* (1965, to a poem by Auden) and *Missa Brevis* (1966), and several slighter works. The assumption sometimes made that Walton 'dried up' after the 1950s is false; never a fast worker, he kept up a steady flow of works. In 1965 he had an operation for lung cancer, fortunately diagnosed at an early stage. But there was no creative flowering as there was in the case of Richard Strauss. He was appointed to the Order of Merit (O. M.) in 1967, two years after Benjamin Britten, and continued to live quietly, still revising his works, until his death in 1983.

•Michael Tippett•

For a profuse late flowering we must turn to the music of Michael Tippett, born in London on 2 January 1905, the son of middle-class parents who could afford to send him to a preparatory school, from which he won a scholarship to Fettes College, Edinburgh. After two unhappy years there he moved to Stamford Grammar School in Lincolnshire. Although he had no musical training, he surprised his parents on leaving school by announcing that he intended to be a composer. From 1923 to 1928 he attended the Royal College of Music, studying composition under Charles Wood and C. H. Kitson. He then settled near Oxted, Surrey, undertaking part-time schoolteaching and putting on operas and choral works with the local dramatic society. In April 1930 a concert of his own works was given, including a string quartet, which so dissatisfied him on hearing it performed that he persuaded R. O. Morris, a professor at the Royal College of Music and brother-in-law of Vaughan Williams, to give him further lessons in composition.

Another significant event was a request for Tippett to take charge of the music at workcamps for unemployed ironstone miners at the village of Boosbeck, East Yorkshire. In 1933 he conducted these men in a performance of *The Beggar's Opera* and in the following year in his own ballad-opera *Robin Hood*. This encounter with the effects of the Depression shocked him into radical left-wing views; he became conductor of the South London (Morley College) Orchestra, which gave concerts in aid of musicians put out of work by the arrival of talking-

Opposite left: Scene from *The Midsummer Marriage*, which Tippett completed in 1952, having worked on libretto and music since 1946. It was first performed on 27 January 1955 with stage designs by Barbara Hepworth. Tippett wrote the libretto himself, as he did for many of his works, feeling himself best able to express his basic concern that social, political and even domestic problems all stem from a misunderstanding of self, a general misapprehension or ignorance of the intellect and emotion.

Opposite right: Portrait photograph of Michael Tippett by Cecil Beaton.

Opposite below: Scene from *King Priam*, first performed at Coventry's Belgrade Theatre on 29 May 1962. In his later work opera has become one of Tippett's main concerns, and he evidently sees it as the best way to express his views and ideas. *King Priam* is based on Homer, though the libretto itself was written by Tippett, as was by now his custom.

films, and of two choirs run by the Royal Arsenal Cooperative Society, affiliated to the Labour Party. For a few months in 1935 he became a member of the Communist Party, but left because he could not persuade his branch to accept his Trotskyist views. However, as the barbarous nature of both Communism and Fascism began to manifest itself in international affairs, he realized that his Trotskyism provided no answer. In addition, in 1938-9 he renewed an earlier interest in the writings of Jung and later conducted his own analysis. After the outbreak of war in 1939 he joined the Peace Pledge Union, a pacifist organization founded five years earlier; in 1940 he applied for registration as a conscientious objector. At the same time he was appointed director of music at Morley College.

Whereas Walton in the 1930s was a composer in the nineteenth-century mold, working out his hectic emotional life in his music, Tippett was growing into the socially conscious artist characteristic of the later twentieth century. To a greater extent than Britten, Tippett throughout his career has considered his role in relation to the world around him, asking, in his own words, 'has the reality of my imagination any lasting relation to the reality of those events which immediately affect the lives of men?' Britten's answer to this question was a decision, 'To be useful, and to the living,' but Britten made his political statements within the context

of his music, at any rate after his early twenties. Tippett reached the same conclusion, but in a more complex way. He was so horrified by what he saw in the North in 1932 that he wondered if he had 'the right' to turn away from such reality by writing abstract music. His dilemma was solved 'by the fact that the actual drive of one's needs as an artist was so great that it forced me back to the studio for the purpose of writing music, although I was quite certain that, at some point, music could have a direct relation also to the compassion that was so deep in my own heart.'

An anonymous music critic who went to the Tippett concert at Oxted in 1930 was unusually percipient. Mentioning the composer's 'remarkable gift,' he concluded: 'Probably Michael Tippett will prefer to put all behind him and go on to fresh ideas. They will surely be worth it.' This is what Tippett did, realizing that he had to acquire and develop a technique. His reverence for contrapuntal textures, for fugue, for long melodies and for Classical Beethovenian structures shows how hard he disciplined himself. In 1934-5 he wrote the first work he still acknowledges, the String Quartet no.1 (known now in the 1943 revision, in which a new first

movement replaced the original first and second movements). Here it is the rhythmical fugal finale which most clearly points the way ahead.

The First Piano Sonata (1936-7) was played in London by Phyllis Sellick in November 1937. Although a recording of the sonata was issued in 1941, the work, later revised, made less impact than the Concerto for double string orchestra of 1938-9. This was Tippett's first masterpiece, in which he achieved a memorable synthesis of his principal musical influences at that time: the syncopation and asymmetrical rhythms of the madrigalian composers and of Stravinsky; the jazz and folksongs; and the long, sinuous melodies which, because of their buoyant underlying rhythm, seem to float on air. These compositions, together with the Second String Quartet of 1941-2, represent the 'abstract' works of this first period.

The first of Tippett's overtly 'political' – or, better, humanitarian – statements was begun in 1938-9 when, encouraged by T. S. Eliot, he wrote his own text for an oratorio. He had been deeply moved by the fate of a seventeen-year-old Polish Jew, Herschel Grynsban, who, while taking refuge in Paris in November 1938, killed a Nazi diplomat in protest against the persecution of his parents. He was imprisoned and never heard of again. The Nazi response was a pogrom. Tippett started to compose the music the day after war was declared in 1939. 'I felt I had to express collective feelings,' he said, 'and that could only be done by collective tunes such as the negro spirituals, for these tunes contain a deposit of generations of common experience.' The use of five spirituals, comparable with Bach's use of Lutheran chorales in the Passions, is one of the most remarkable features of *A Child of Our Time*. The work also symbolizes Tippett's Jungian belief in the 'shadow' and the 'light' in every personality, only through knowledge of which can one become whole. The oratorio was completed in 1941 but not performed until three years later, by which time he had written his cantata *Boyhood's End*, a setting of W. H. Hudson for tenor and piano, first performed at Morley College in June 1943 by Peter Pears and Benjamin Britten.

This was also the month in which Tippett was sentenced to three months' imprisonment for failing to comply with the conditions of his registration as a conscientious objector, although he maintained that he served his country better as a musician than as a worker on the land or in the fire service. After two months in Wormwood Scrubs he was released. 'Prison is not a creative experience at any point,' he wrote at the time, 'except perhaps in human contacts. I daresay it will seem less wasteful when one looks back. . . .' On release he returned to his work at Morley College, where the choral concerts he conducted became famous, and it was through him, in 1946, that Monteverdi's Vespers had its first British performance.

•Post-war works•

The first performance of *A Child of Our Time* in 1944 had established Tippett as a major composer, and it was followed by the Symphony no.1 (1944-5), the Third String Quartet (1945-6), and the *Little Music for Strings* (1946). In 1948 the composer was commissioned by the BBC to write an orchestral work, the Suite in D, to celebrate the birth of Prince Charles. In 1951 one of his most impassioned creations, the song cycle *The Heart's Assurance*, was first performed at a Festival of Britain concert by Pears and Britten. Characteristic of all these works is a radiant, wide-ranging lyricism, gushing forth as from a spring. This radiant quality is present, too, in the magnificent *Fantasia Concertante on a Theme of Corelli* for strings (1953), where the eighteenth-century *concerto grosso* is trans-

Opposite: Scenes from Tippett's *The Ice Break*, 1977 (*top*), and *The Knot Garden*, 1970 (*below*), both first performed at the Royal Opera House, Covent Garden. While the one opera has a space-age setting and the other is based on an Elizabethan idea, both incorporate elements of blues, boogie-woogie and jazz to produce a truly cross-cultural mix of musical references.

Below left. Model for Britten's opera *The Rape of Lucretia*; the design was by John Piper, and the first performance took place at Glyndebourne on 2 July 1946, conducted by Ansermet.

Below: Kenneth Green's costume design for the name part in *Peter Grimes*, premièred on 7 June 1945 at Sadler's Wells, with Peter Pears gaining instant recognition for his striking performance as Grimes. The opera used English village life as a vehicle for the moral subject of the story, 'innocence a prey to violence, the outsider a prey to society.'

Right: Benjamin Britten and Peter Pears at the Windmill, Snape. Pears and Britten had worked in close association since 1939 when they both emigrated to America. They returned to England again in 1942, settling first in Snape on the Suffolk coast, and moving to Aldeburgh in 1946.

Below: Britten with W. H. Auden. The two originally met when working together in the Post Office Film Unit in the thirties. They collaborated on a few song cycles, in which Britten set Auden's words to music, and the operetta *Paul Bunyan* (1941) was set to an Auden libretto – though the work was quickly withdrawn.

formed into twentieth-century music and where the radiance becomes ecstasy.

The primal source of this increasingly 'beautiful' strain in Tippett's music was revealed in 1955 in his opera *The Midsummer Marriage.* On its first appearance it was widely considered to be incomprehensible, but the issue of a recording in 1971, followed five years later by a sensitive Welsh National Opera production, led one critic to write, 'The difficulties have simply vanished.' In *The Midsummer Marriage* Tippett again explored his Jungian thesis of shadow and light, in this case suggesting that people's marital difficulties arise usually from lack of self-knowledge. To this he added the conflict between the young generation and its elders, with overtones of magic and mythology. Dance plays a major part in his scheme and the *Ritual Dances*, which are heard regularly in the concert hall, are typical of the opera's abundant vitality and melodic fertility – indeed, the work is in itself a fertility rite.

Having completed the opera, Tippett, with that ruthless sense of creative exploration he seems to have inherited from Vaughan Williams and Holst, radically varied his style. After the Piano Concerto of 1953-5, which is related to *The Midsummer Marriage*, there came in 1956-7 the Second Symphony, in which the harmony is no longer principally diatonic, the argument is tauter, the orchestration sparer and more sectionalized. This process is carried a stage further in the opera *King Priam* (1958-61), written, like Britten's *War Requiem*, for the consecration of the new Coventry Cathedral and dealing with the effects of war on human relationships. Where the first opera was profuse, *King Priam* is economical. The singing is declamatory rather than lyrical; the orchestration, instead of being highly ornate and rich, is reduced at times to a single instrument – guitar or piano – and sometimes to a concertante group, brass or woodwind. Similar instrumental procedures are followed in the *Concerto for Orchestra* (1962-3). Yet when one hears Achilles' blood-curling war-cry at the end of Act II of *King Priam*, one realizes that it comes from the same mind, using the same musical procedure, which invented the rapturous Monteverdian ecstasies of Mark's love-song in Act I of *The Midsummer Marriage*.

Left: Scene from *The Turn of the Screw*, with Peter Pears as Quint and Jennifer Vyvyan as the Governess. The first production was staged at La Fenice, Venice, under Britten himself, on 14 September 1954. The libretto was written by Myfanwy Piper, adapting the original Henry James novella. After the large-scale operatic works *Billy Budd* and *Gloriana*, Britten here returned to the concept of chamber opera.

If the *Shires Suite* (1962) marks another stylistic turning-point for Tippett, the climactic work of this period is *The Vision of St Augustine* (1963-5), for baritone, chorus and orchestra, in which the mystical element is expressed by the use of note-clusters, extremely ornamented vocalization and densely woven textures. With this reassertion of the English choral tradition, Tippett felt free to begin his third opera, *The Knot Garden*. Blues and boogie-woogie are part of the musical inspiration. The characters – a woman 'freedom-fighter,' a tycoon with a wife who takes a whip to him, a fake psychoanalyst and a homosexual couple, one of them black – may seem to be relentlessly *de nos jours*, but *The Knot Garden* is already a period-piece, for it belongs to the 1960s, the decade of Beatlemania, of the Vietnam war and its anti-war backlash among the youth of America, of 'make love not war' while the tendency to violent demonstration intensified, the decade of increasing awareness of racial tensions culminating in the murder (and near-canonization by the oppressed) of Martin Luther King.

It is a question for posterity whether the music of *The Knot Garden* and its successor *The Ice Break* is sufficiently strong to overcome the handicap of a rapidly outdating modishness and gaucheness in the libretti – in *A Child of Our Time*, *The Midsummer Marriage* and *King Priam* it has proved strong enough. It is certainly an explanation for Tippett's success in the United States since 1973, which has led to commissions from Chicago (Fourth Symphony) and Boston (a choral work not yet completed).

Tippett's later instrumental works are perhaps more accessible – the Third Symphony (1970-2), with its quotations from Beethoven and its soprano blues, the Fourth Symphony (1976-7), compact and regenerative, the Third Piano Sonata (1972-3) and the Fourth String Quartet (1977-9), versatile in technique and returning to the lyricism of *The Midsummer Marriage*. A theme from the quartet recurs significantly in the 'Triple' Concerto for violin, viola and cello (1979-80), the crown of Tippett's seventh decade and one of the most beautiful and original works of our time. He followed it with the huge choral work *The Mask of Time*, a testament on the most ambitious scale – nothing less than an account (his own libretto again) of the beginnings of the universe and a contemplation of mankind's role and destiny. Completed when he was nearly eighty, it is an extraordinary demonstration of Tippett's unabated mental vigor and vitality, extended to embrace a fifth opera, *New Year*.

• Benjamin Britten •

Benjamin Britten was born in Lowestoft, Suffolk, on 22 November 1913, son of a dentist whose wife was a gifted musician. The youngest of four children, Benjamin's obvious musical gifts were fostered from the start. He composed prolifically from the age of five and studied the piano and the viola. In 1924 and 1927, at the Norwich Triennial Festival, he heard compositions by the violist Frank Bridge which profoundly stirred him. Through his viola teacher he gained an introduction to Bridge and became his private pupil. Bridge subjected Britten's natural musicianship to the rigors of the acquisition of a painstaking technique and at the same time opened the boy's ears to a wide range of contemporary music – Bartók, Stravinsky, and Schoenberg – which no academic establishment of the day would have countenanced.

When at length Britten entered the Royal College of Music in 1930, he felt stifled by the

Below: Still from *Night Mail*, a film produced under the direction of John Grierson by the Post Office Film Unit. Britten collaborated with Auden on this film, and here began their friendship – they had much in common, particularly their political ideas, and were both pacifists. Auden, seeing no future in his own country, invited Britten, together with Peter Pears, to join him in America.

Above: Britten conducting at a Promenade Concert in 1973 at the Royal Albert Hall. It was typical for Britten, a brilliant conductor, to include the Proms in his range of activities. Throughout his career one of his major concerns was the appreciation and enjoyment of music by people from all walks of life, and the Proms were clearly effective in their popularization of music.

Right: Scene from *Owen Wingrave*, written specially for BBC Television and first broadcast on 16 May 1971. Like *The Turn of the Screw*, this is another adaptation of Henry James, but very different in style.

lack of encouragement both of his wish to explore his European contemporaries' work and his desire for performance of his own music. Only one of his works, *Sinfonietta* (1932), was performed at the College while he was a student and then only after it had been played elsewhere. Towards the end of his college days he arranged some of his juvenilia into the *Simple Symphony* (1933-4) for strings, which has since become one of his best-known works. In 1934 his *Phantasy* for oboe quartet was selected for performance at the ISCM festival in Florence. Earlier that year his choral variations *A Boy Was Born* were broadcast and hailed by several critics as evidence of the emergence of a major new talent. In some ways, harmonically and structurally in particular, *Sinfonietta* and *A Boy Was Born* are more 'progressive' than most of Britten's later works. They point to the kind of composer he might have become had he been allowed, as he wished, to study with Berg in Vienna.

In 1935 Britten was invited to write music for documentary films made by the small Post Office Film Unit, of which the leading light was the Scottish-born director John Grierson. At this time Britten also met Paul Rotha, William Coldstream, and the poet W. H. Auden, with whom he collaborated on two celebrated short films, *Coal Face* and *Night Mail*. It was here that Britten developed his liking for working as a member of a dedicated team, something that was to be a feature of his later operatic productions. Through Auden, with whom he shared a homosexual nature, Britten met a group of left-wing artists and writers. His political commitment was never as wholehearted as theirs – pacifism, nurtured by Bridge, was another matter – and unlike Tippett he had no searing personal revelation of the effects of poverty and deprivation.

Britten composed music for events organized by the Peace Pledge Union, but he did not participate, as Auden did, in the Spanish Civil War because he would not indulge in any activities involving war, even the non-combatant activities undertaken by some pacifists. His chief collaboration with Auden was the symphonic song-cycle *Our Hunting Fathers* (1936) for soprano and orchestra. This dual attack on cruelty to animals and birds and, by analogy, on the Nazis' treatment of the Jews shocked the 1936 Norwich Festival audience and has never occupied a prominent position among Britten's works, even though it is one of the most daring, exciting and original pieces he wrote. On the other hand the *Variations on a Theme of Frank Bridge*, composed in 1937 for the Salzburg Festival, was an immediate success.

•America and War•

Although Auden could not persuade Britten to go to Spain, he persuaded him and his friend the tenor Peter Pears to leave Britain in 1939

for North America, the intention being to settle there permanently. Whereas Auden was disillusioned with the intellectual and political climate of Britain, Britten was convinced that he had no future as a composer in his native country. He had been distressed and wounded by the critical reception of his music as displaying mere 'facility' and a gift for pastiche. Even the 'Frank Bridge' Variations had been praised for the parodies of Rossini and Johann Strauss rather than for the deeper, Mahlerian element in a masterly work.

From 1939 to 1942 Britten and Pears were in America, living for some of the time with Auden in a New York artists' commune, until they tired of its dirtiness and the cultivated bohemianism of its inhabitants. (Essentially puritanical, Britten followed a lifelong routine of cold baths, physical exercise, hard work and plain food.) While in America, Britten completed his song-cycle *Les Illuminations* (1938-9), an ornate and brilliant setting of Rimbaud's French text, and his Violin Concerto (1938-9), similar in mood to Walton's exactly contemporary work. He also composed the short and dramatic *Sinfonia da Requiem* (1940), the *Diversions* (1940) for piano (left hand), the *Seven Sonnets of Michelangelo* (1940) – to Italian words – for tenor and piano, the First String Quartet (1941), and the operetta *Paul Bunyan* (1940-1). Auden was the librettist for this delightful work, in which the two exiled Englishmen somehow penetrated to the core of American folklore. It was a failure at the time, but was revised and revived at the end of Britten's life.

In 1942 homesickness and a sense of guilt over the wartime plight of Britain impelled Britten and Pears back to England, where, as conscientious objectors, they were directed – by a more sensible tribunal, evidently, than had dealt with Tippett – to give recitals for factory workers and soldiers. The first performance of the *Michelangelo Sonnets* and of the *Serenade* for tenor, horn and strings (1943) in blitzed London re-established Britten in the forefront of English music. Already it could be seen that he differed from Walton and Tippett in that he was himself a brilliant executant, one of the finest of pianists and no mean conductor. Nearly all his works were written for friends to perform, tailored to their special needs, and he had developed the practicing musician's delight in providing both a challenge and a reward rolled into one. With his fertile (but always hard-won) inventiveness, he was able to appeal to a wide cross-section of the sophisticated musical

Below: One of John Piper's designs for *Death in Venice*, showing the interior of St Mark's Basilica. This was one of Britten's last major works and represents the culmination of a long association with John Piper and his wife Myfanwy. *Death in Venice* was written for the Maltings concert hall at Snape and was first performed there on 16 June 1973.

public, and he also reached a wider audience, for he had a natural affinity with children's musical tastes and abilities and wrote for them in an unpatronizing and absorbing manner.

•Aldeburgh and opera•

Although he kept a flat in London, Britten worked best and felt most at ease in Suffolk. With Pears he settled first at Snape, and later in Aldeburgh. It is the latter, disguised as 'the Borough,' which is the location of his opera *Peter Grimes*, adapted from the poem by George Crabbe. Produced at Sadler's Wells in June 1945 – not without fierce opposition from within the company – this opera is a landmark in British music, for it was the first operatic work on this scale by an Englishman to take not only London but continental capitals by storm. With its fine choruses, its dramatic central role and its evocative orchestral score, *Peter Grimes* became a household name.

The schism caused by the production led many famous singers to leave Sadler's Wells and to join Britten's new foundation, the English Opera Group. At roughly the same time he also decided to found a festival at Aldeburgh. The first was held in 1948, and the event grew into one of the most enterprising and varied of annual festivals. Henceforward a major new Britten work could nearly always be expected for first performance each June. Aldeburgh became the hub of Britten's universe, and he emerged only for some special occasion or for a tour abroad.

Britten's first two chamber operas, *The Rape of Lucretia* and *Albert Herring*, completed before the festival was inaugurated, were produced at Glyndebourne. His next two operas – excepting the children's work *Let's Make an Opera!* – were on a larger scale and were first performed at Covent Garden. *Billy Budd*, an adaptation of Melville's story, was written for the 1951 Festival of Britain and *Gloriana* for the Coronation of Queen Elizabeth II in 1953. Britten's rapid rise to a pre-eminent position and the blinkered adulation of his works by a highly vocal group of critics and musicians provoked a reaction, as it was bound to do, and the anti-Britten faction had its revenge with *Gloriana*, which was deemed to be a tasteless insult to the Sovereign because it showed her predecessor Elizabeth I not only as a great ruler but as a woman capable of vanity, cruelty and pettiness. No surprise to students of history, one might have thought, but it was enough to taint *Gloriana*, even though audiences after the first night liked the opera, especially when it was restaged some years later. Though it contains highly effective music, especially in the contrast of pageantry and ceremonial with private relationships, it remains the only opera by Britten that has not been recorded.

For his next stage work Britten returned in 1954 to chamber opera, an adaptation of Henry James's ghost story *The Turn of the Screw* – a study, like *Billy Budd*, of various facets of evil and emotional claustrophobia. It has become one of his most frequently performed operas, but no Britten work, before or after, achieved the initial success and acclaim of *War Requiem* (1961), first performed in the new Coventry Cathedral in 1962. This public declaration of his pacifism took the form of a large-scale setting of the Latin Mass for the Dead, for soprano, mixed chorus and boys' choir, into which were interpolated chamber-settings of the war poems of Wilfred Owen for tenor and baritone soloists. Britten's gift for vivid, easily memorable musical imagery was here fully and fruitfully deployed, and the work was swiftly in demand for choral societies. Although its popularity waned, its high position in Britten's output is unlikely to be challenged. Like *Belshazzar's Feast* and *A Child of Our Time*, it is a reaffirmation of the English choral tradition. Britten had meanwhile completed his setting of *A Midsummer Night's Dream* (1959-60), which deserves to be ranked among the most successful transferences of Shakespeare into music.

The 1960s were dominated by two strands in Britten's development. His close personal friendship with and artistic admiration for the Russian cellist Rostropovich resulted in a sonata, three suites for unaccompanied cello and a Cello Symphony, which is probably his greatest orchestral work, though its difficulties have frightened off all but the most intrepid cellists. And a visit in 1956 to the Far East, where Britten heard gamelan music in Bali and saw a Noh play in Japan, bore fruit in 1964 when the first of three 'church parables,' *Curlew River*, was performed (it was dedicated to Michael Tippett). The highly stylized production combined elements of medieval mystery plays – such as Britten had already explored attractively in *Noye's Fludde* (1957) – with the ritual of Noh drama. The exotic scoring featured special instrumental timbres, a development continued in the second and third parables, *The Burning Fiery Furnace* (1966) and *The Prodigal Son* (1968). In producing these works in Orford

Above: Peter Pears as the Mad Woman in *Curlew River*, first performed at Orford Church, Suffolk, under Britten's direction on 12 June 1964. Pears worked with Britten in a unique partnership for more than thirty-five years, and took part in the first performance of virtually all his vocal works.

Above: Britten conducting a performance of the *War Requiem* in Ottobeuren Basilica, in southern Germany, with Dietrich Fischer-Dieskau and Peter Pears, on 6 September 1964. Britten had been a conscientious objector during the war, and the *Requiem* expresses his pacifism and the idea of reconciliation.

Right: Scene from *A Midsummer Night's Dream* first performed at Aldeburgh on 9 June 1960.

Far right: Scene from *Noye's Fludde*, with Owen Brannigan as Noah, first produced at Orford Church on 17 June 1958. Much of Britten's work was specifically directed at amateur performers, and several works, including *Noye's Fludde* and *Let's Make an Opera!*, are written for children, with very few adult parts.

Church, Britten was able to work with a small team of like-minded enthusiasts, as he had in the film unit thirty years earlier. Yet he was not deaf to the noise on the campus of youth which had stirred Tippett. In Britten's case the response was again to tell a pacifist parable, another operatic adaptation of Henry James. In *Owen Wingrave* the son of a military family rebels against family tradition and meets a coward's fate. The work, another study in the betrayal of innocence, was first produced on television in 1971 and later at Covent Garden.

From 1971 to 1973 Britten devoted most of his energies to the completion of an opera he had long contemplated, to a libretto based on Thomas Mann's novella *Death in Venice*. His energies were now sapped by failing health, and he took himself to the physical limit to finish the score before having an operation to replace a heart valve. This was only partially successful, a stroke during the surgery leaving him unable to play the piano and able to work only for a short, exhausting spell each day. Yet over a period of two years he revised some early works, including *Paul Bunyan*, composed three vocal works, the *Suite on English Folk Tunes* and his Third String Quartet. In June 1976 he was created a life peer; he died on 4 December 1976.

Britten's melodic gift, his basic conservatism, his ability to give a new twist to an old device or form, his fertile imagination, his brilliant sense of a tightly unified structure, his understanding of the true nature of individual instruments and voices, his compassion for the outsiders in society (stemming from the dark side of his own complex and insecure personality), his flair for giving artistic validity to sado-masochism in operatic plots and characters – these are the principal hallmarks of an immensely gifted all-round musician. In such joyous celebrations as his *Spring Symphony*, in the haunted world of *The Turn of the Screw*, in the Janáček-like study of a community persecuting an individual which is *Peter Grimes*, in the profound glimpses of the mysteries in his own creative make-up afforded by *Billy Budd* and *Death in Venice*, in the courageous fatalism of the Third String Quartet, Britten brought to his art poetry, technique and topicality. Whether he is the greatest, the most lasting, of the three composers discussed here is a question for future generations to debate. That he reached far into the hearts and minds of his contemporaries is beyond argument.

OLIVIER MESSIAEN AND PIERRE BOULEZ

ROBERT SHERLAW JOHNSON

Opposite: Olivier Messiaen (b.1908) taking notes during a field-trip to research birdsong, probably in the Dordogne, photographed by Edouard Boubat. Birdsong came to be an absolutely essential element in Messiaen's music – sometimes used purely as a melodic basis, sometimes with great accuracy and for its own sake.

Olivier Messiaen was born at Avignon in 1908 of literary parents. His mother, Cécile Sauvage, was a poetess and wrote for her unborn child a series of poems, *L'Âme en bourgeon* (The Budding Soul), full of love and premonitions of greatness. His father, Pierre Messiaen, was best known for his critical translations of Shakespeare into French. Although neither of his parents was a musician, Olivier showed an aptitude for music at an early age; his first composition was a piano piece, written when he was nine years old and inspired by Tennyson's poem, *The Lady of Shalott*. The family moved to Grenoble in 1914, and after the First World War to Paris. In 1919, Messiaen entered the Paris Conservatoire, where he studied with such teachers as Marcel Dupré and Paul Dukas until 1930. There he received prizes in most of the subjects which he studied, including the organ and, of course, composition.

Messiaen was appointed organist at the church of La Sainte Trinité in Paris in 1930, and it is hardly surprising that, as a result, much of his major early work up to 1939 was for the organ. The principal organ works of this period were *Le Banquet céleste* (The Celestial Banquet, 1928), adapted from a piece for orchestra; *L'Ascension* (The Ascension, 1934), also arranged from an orchestral version written the previous year; *La Nativité du Seigneur* (The Birth of the Lord, 1935) and *Les Corps glorieux* (The Glorious Body, subtitled 'Seven brief visions of the life of the Resurrected,' 1939). Besides his organ music, his other important work of this period consisted of the early *Préludes* for piano (1929) and two song-cycles, each setting his own words for soprano and piano: *Poèmes pour Mi* (Poems for Mi, 1939), dedicated to his first wife, the violinist Claire Delbos; and *Chants de terre et de ciel* (Songs of Earth and Sky, 1938), written for the birth of his son, Pascal.

Messiaen joined the army at the outbreak of the Second World War, and he was taken prisoner by the Germans in 1940. After his repatriation on health grounds in 1941 he turned his attention principally to orchestral and piano works. However, the *Quatuor pour la fin du temps* (Quartet for the End of Time), for clarinet, violin, cello and piano, was written in the prisoner-of-war camp in 1940 and first performed there by himself and three musical compatriots. It was entirely due to the circumstances in which he found himself that this particular combination of instruments was forced upon him. He never afterwards wrote chamber music, always preferring solo piano or the more sonorous possibilities of the orchestra. Organ music was not entirely neglected after the war, but it no longer formed the most significant portion of his output.

On his return to Paris in 1942 Messiaen was appointed professor of harmony at the Paris Conservatoire. In the following year he started giving private composition classes at the house of a friend, Guy-Bernard Delapierre. These continued until 1947, when he received the more important appointment of professor of analysis, esthetic and rhythm at the Conservatoire, and he continued his composition classes there under this title. Darius Milhaud was appointed professor of composition in that same year, so that it was not until Milhaud's retirement in 1966 that Messiaen was officially appointed professor of composition. Messiaen's early classes included a number of pupils who were later to achieve fame in their own right, notably Pierre Boulez, Karlheinz Stockhausen and Yvonne Loriod, for whom he was to write all his piano works from 1943 onwards and whom he married in 1962 after the death of his first wife in 1959.

In Paris during these years he worked on a number of major works: *Visions de l'Amen* (Visions of Amen, 1943), for two pianos expressing seven different 'Amens'; *Trois Petites Liturgies de la Présence Divine* (Three Little Liturgies of the Divine Presence, 1944), for women's voices, piano and *ondes Martenot*, strings and percussion; and *Vingt Regards sur l'Enfant-Jésus* (Twenty Glances at the Child Jesus, 1944), for piano solo. In spite of the Catholic, Christian significance of the subjects of most of his works up to this time, he wrote practically no liturgical music, always preferring a symbolic approach in music written for the concert hall or, in the case of the organ music, to accompany the liturgy, rather than to form an integral part of it.

Between 1945 and 1949 he produced three works which form a trilogy on the subject of love and death. The first of these, *Harawi*, for soprano and piano, is based on Peruvian mythology and religious symbolism; the others, *Turangalîla-symphonie* for large orchestra including a piano and *Cinq Rechants* (Five Re-

Left: Messiaen (*extreme right*) at the Paris Conservatoire in a class taken by Paul Dukas. Other members of the class shown here were P. Maillard-Verger, Elsa Barraine, Yves Desportes, Tony Aubin, Georges Favre, R. Duclos, G. Hugon, Maurice Duruflé, Claude Arrieu and Pierre Revel. Messiaen's musical background was certainly conventional, with little to indicate the direction he would take.

frains) for twelve solo voices, derive their symbolism from a number of sources: Hindu religion, stories of Edgar Allan Poe, Orpheus and other love-myths. Running through the whole trilogy is the Celtic story of Tristan and Yseult; Messiaen had Wagner's version at the back of his mind, although there are no conscious musical quotations from Wagner's work.

The titles reflect the breadth of Messiaen's sources and his individuality of technique. *Harawi* is the Quechuan word for a love song which leads to the lovers' death, and the work is subtitled 'Songs of Love and Death.' The poems, by the composer himself, are strongly influenced by Surrealism, and in addition to the French text Messiaen adds onomatopoeic words to represent the sound of the dancers' ankle-bells, incantations, and so forth. Some of this added text bears a resemblance to Quechuan. *Turangalîla* is a Sanskrit word combining the rhythm of time (*Turanga*) and the processes of love (*Lîla*) or life itself, to suggest, again, complexities of love and death. *Rechant*, a created word, is paired with 'chant' (song) in the alternating patterns of the text, but is more like 'refrain' than 'antistrophe' – Messiaen uses the Greek term in his later *Chronochromie*.

• Later works •

Until *Et exspecto resurrectionem mortuorum* (And I look for the Resurrection of the Dead, 1964), for an orchestra of wind instruments and metal percussion (1964), little of Messiaen's music after 1944 used Christian symbolism. In 1949 he produced a number of experimental piano pieces: *Cantéjodayâ*, an exploration of Hindu rhythms which was composed during the summer at Tanglewood, in Massachusetts; and the *Quatre Etudes de rythme* (Four Studies of Rhythm). He returned briefly to Christian symbolism again in *Messe de la Pentecôte* (Mass of the Pentecost, 1950) for organ and *Livre d'orgue* (Organ Book, 1952), but subsequent works were mainly concerned with birdsong, a growing preoccupation of the composer since the *Quatuor* of 1940. From this period emerged the major works for piano and orchestra: *Réveil des oiseaux* (Awakening of the Birds, 1953); *Oiseaux exotiques* (Exotic Birds, 1956); *Sept Haï-Kaï* (Seven Haiku, 1962), written after a visit to Japan; and *Couleurs de la cité céleste* (Colors of the Celestial City, 1964), as well as *Catalogue d'oiseaux* (Catalogue of Birds, 1956-8), thirteen pieces for piano solo, and *Chronochromie* (Color of Time, 1958-9) for orchestra without piano.

Since *Et exspecto* Messiaen again produced a number of large works which returned to the use of Christian symbolism: *La Transfiguration de Notre Seigneur Jésus-Christ* (The Transfiguration of Our Lord Jesus Christ, 1969), for choir, instrumental soloists and orchestra; *Méditations sur le mystère de la Sainte Trinité* (Meditations on the Mystery of the Holy Trinity,

Below: Messiaen at the piano with a practice organ pedal-board, in his conventional bourgeois home in Paris. His parents did not hesitate to encourage Messiaen's musical interests; his mother, Cécile Sauvage, was a poet and his father an English teacher.

1969), for organ; and *Des Canyons aux étoiles* (From the Canyons to the Stars, 1970-4), for piano and orchestra, inspired in part by the Utah landscape of the American West. In addition he wrote a further piece for piano solo as a sequel to *Catalogue d'oiseaux* – *La Fauvette des jardins* (The Warbler of the Gardens, 1970).

In 1983 Messiaen completed his single opera, *St François d'Assise*, on an even grander scale than the *Turangalîla-symphonie*, employing an orchestra of a hundred and twenty players, including three *ondes Martenot*, and a chorus of a hundred and fifty in addition to the soloists. The work is in eight scenes, divided into three acts, and is an apotheosis of the themes that have run through the composer's life's work: an ecstatic mysticism; birdsong; instrumentation and rhythmic devices taken from oriental traditions. There is also a recorded organ improvisation based on his mother's work, *L'Âme en bourgeon*.

•Color and mode•

The formative influences on Messiaen's music at various times in his development as a composer have been varied. One of the most important influences present since his youth is a strong sense of the association of color and sound. This association led him to develop a unique conception of mode during the 1930s. In his early music this took the form of artificial scale-systems, which he called 'modes of limited transposition.' By dividing the octave into two, three or four equal parts and dividing each of these parts into the same groups of tones and semitones, a scale is formed which can be transposed only a limited number of times before the original scale is repeated. Messiaen explained these and other systems in his *Technique de mon langage musical* (Technique of my Musical Language, 1944, or see *Messiaen* by Robert Sherlaw Johnson).

Messiaen made much use of these modes in his music, from the early *Le Banquet céleste* for organ, his first published work, until *Cinq Rechants*, and many of his unique harmonic combinations are based on them. They do not form a substitute for tonality, as he does not base a whole piece on a single mode, but he contrasts them with one another in the same piece, in either juxtaposition or superimposition.

From *La Nativité du Seigneur* of 1935 he used, in addition, rhythmic patterns derived from Greek meters and from thirteenth-century Indian talas. These are frequently built up into superimposed repetitive patterns of different lengths, providing a rhythmic modal background to more important and varied material in a similar way to successions of harmonies based on the modes of limited transposition. These Indian rhythms (which were tabulated in connection with an article on Indian music in Lavignac's *Encyclopédie de la musique dictionnaire de la conservatoire*, 1924) consist, in many cases, of irregular patterns, implying no regular accent which can be defined by constant time signatures and bars. Messiaen's aim in using them, in fact, was to avoid rhythms depending on a regular meter (or a division of time), and often to create a sense of timelessness. The title of the *Quatuor pour la fin du temps*, in fact, was intended to have a double meaning, implying not only the end of time in the apocalyptic sense but also in musical terms.

After 1948 Messiaen made hardly any use of his early modes until *Catalogue d'oiseaux* for piano solo. During the intervening years he experimented with an extension of serial processes and with the use of material derived from birdsong. It was in 1944 that Boulez joined his harmony classes at the Conservatoire, during the course of which Messiaen, analyzing Berg's

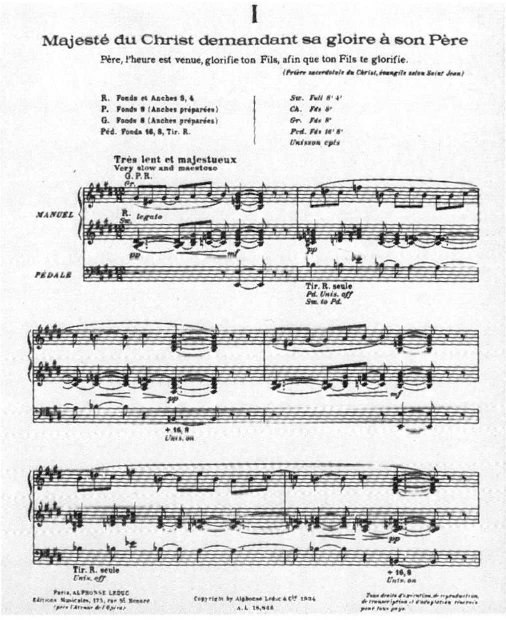

Left: First page of the printed score of *L'Ascension*, originally written as an orchestral work in 1933, and arranged for organ in 1934. Catholicism has always been important to Messiaen, and this work, though an early one, already shows a commitment to religion that was to be echoed throughout his career – as were some of the other notable features here: the richness of harmony and complexity of rhythm.

Lyric Suite, spoke strongly against Schoenberg's and Berg's practice of serializing pitch while still adhering to classical conceptions of rhythm and form. This had an influence not only on the early work of his pupils of that time (including Boulez) but also on his own music in the later part of the decade.

•Serial processes•

In 1949-50, in the second of the four *Etudes de rythme* for piano – 'Mode de valeurs et d'intensités' – Messiaen used series of durations, intensities and timbres combined with three twelve-note pitch series. But in spite of its notional connection with serialism, it is significant that he described the work as being based on a mode rather than a series, the mode consisting of the three pitch series, to each of which is assigned a unique register, duration, intensity and attack. In Schoenbergian serialism, the series actually defines a series of interval relationships between each note and the next, which means that the series can be freely transposed, inverted or turned backwards so long as the order of intervals is preserved. Because, in the case of Messiaen's mode, the notes are defined by their own unique characteristics and not by an interval relationship between them, their ordering in relation to each other can be free. This is a fundamental difference in conception between Messiaen's work and that of Schoenberg or Berg, which justifies the composer's own use of the term 'modal' in connection with the piece, rather than 'serial.' In subsequent works Messiaen made use of permutated or freely ordered groups of the twelve notes of the chromatic scale (especially in his *Livre d'orgue*, 1952). These twelve-note groups, unlike the Schoenbergian series, do not underlie the structure of the music; they create a contrast of color, in the way that the modes of limited transposition did in Messiaen's earlier music. They are more properly thought of collectively as a different kind of mode – a twelve-note or chromatic mode. However, Messiaen did also use a serial process with note durations. Discussing *Chronochromie* (1960), the composer wrote that 'the "temporal" or rhythmic material consists of 32 different durations which are used in symmetrical interversions, while always retaining their original order. The permutations thus obtained are heard either separately, or fragmentarily, or superimposed three by three.'

In spite of Messiaen's continual preoccupation with rhythm, the concept of mode in his music is far more general, embracing also the way in which rhythmic patterns are used. It is necessary with *Catalogue d'oiseaux* to consider rhythms, harmonies, tonalities, birdsong types, as well as modes of limited transposition and twelve-note modes as contributing to an all-embracing mode which characterizes each of the pieces.

• Birdsong •

Messiaen's preoccupation with birdsong began when he was fifteen years old, when he noted down his first example while on holiday in the Aube district. Before *Quatuor pour la fin du temps*, however, there are only hints of birdsong style in his music. From the time of the *Quatuor* onwards birdsong appears in most of his works, and frequently the names of the birds from which the songs are derived appear on the score. From 1953 to 1960 he wrote a group of works in which birdsong forms the principal material. It is the only source of material in the first of these, *Réveil des oiseaux* for piano and orchestra, which is an impression of birdsong from midnight to midday.

The second piece, *Oiseaux exotiques*, for piano, wind and percussion, mixes birdsongs from North and South America and from the East, and combines them in the two long tutti passages with Indian and Greek rhythms played by the percussion section. In this and in most works, Messiaen simply used birdsong as a source of melodic ideas, without regard to their association in nature, but *Réveil des oiseaux* and especially *Catalogue d'oiseaux*, are more concerned with realism.

Messiaen's concern for realism in his representation of birdsong has been a source of misunderstanding. He has claimed to have translated their songs into music as accurately as possible, while allowing for the fact that they must be slowed up and transposed down in pitch in order to make them intelligible on a human timescale and within the normal range of human perception of pitch. His method, at the time of writing *Catalogue d'oiseaux*, was to go into the country with only manuscript paper and pen and note down directly, 'like an exercise in aural training' (as he expressed it), the songs which he heard, while identifying the singer with the aid of pictures of the bird, or sometimes enlisting the help of a local ornithological expert. There is no doubt that his researches were most careful and thorough, so that it is not difficult, in most cases, to relate Messiaen's interpretation to the original birdsongs.

• *Catalogue d'oiseaux* •

There is a distinct development in Messiaen's representation of birdsong, especially over the period from *Réveil des oiseaux* to *Catalogue d'oiseaux*. In works up to and including *Réveil des oiseaux*, he generally confined himself to a purely melodic representation of a bird's song. *Oiseaux exotiques* was the first composition to make extensive use of a harmonic representation of the timbre, and this is refined still further in *Catalogue d'oiseaux*. He went further than merely using dissonant harmonies to suggest the more raucous bird calls and consonant harmony to suggest the sweeter ones: many subtle shades in between these two extremes are also represented.

Below: Messiaen's notes of birdsong. He recorded each sound as accurately as possible, using musical notation, and has only recently resorted to the use of a tape recorder.

Catalogue d'oiseaux was the result of many journeys to different parts of France in search

little literal repetition of material in the thematic sense; shape and form result from relationships between types of material and from a sense of line, continuity and growth which is present in each piece. The birdsongs and calls can be divided into four main groups: calls, usually homophonic, dissonant and atonal in character, some short (tawny owl, quail), others longer and more varied (herring gull, raven); short repetitive song-patterns (chaffinch, golden oriole); varied song-patterns, either melodic (blackbird) or declamatory in style (nightingale, song thrush), sometimes with tonal implications; and long passages of 'chattering' birdsong, continuous or broken up, some centering on a particular note or notes (skylark), others free (reed warbler, blackcap). Other material is either contrasted with birdsong in character, or is related to it by means of harmonic characteristics such as in the first piece, 'Chocard des Alpes,' where the harmonic character of both birdsong and other material is highly dissonant and atonal.

Some pieces in *Catalogue d'oiseaux* employ a large number of birdsongs, while others use only a few. In addition, in some, the principal bird of the title appears to feature very little, while having a notable effect on the piece as a whole. In 'Le Traquet Stapazin' (the black-eared wheatear), for instance, the bird of the title is confined to brusque interjections which break up the otherwise calm flow and continuity of the piece. In 'Le Merle bleu,' on the other hand, there are only four birdsongs or calls used, and the blue rock thrush has the predominant role. Besides the blue rock thrush, the other birds used are the swift (*martinet noir*), the

Above: An informal picture of Messiaen at home, taken by Auerbach in 1967.

Right: Scene from the ballet *Oiseaux exotiques*, first performed at the Württembergisches Staatstheater, Stuttgart, on 5 May 1967, with choreography by John Cranko; the dancer was Marcia Haydée. The music was not originally intended as a ballet, and indeed Messiaen has never written ballet music, generally shunning most forms of dramatic music in favor of choral or orchestral work. *Oiseaux exotiques* is not a precise rendering of birdsong but represents a fusion of different bird song-types.

of the songs of birds which are specific to a particular locality. Each of its thirteen pieces sets out to paint (as he put it) a portrait of a particular bird, together with other birds to be found in the same locality. Some of the songs used are inevitably those of birds found in more than one locality; hence the blackbird, the song-thrush, the nightingale, the robin and others are to be found in more than one piece. In addition to birdsong, he also invoked natural sounds associated with the bird's habitat: the sea in 'Le Merle bleu' (the blue rock thrush) and 'Le Courlis cendré' (the curlew), for instance, or the sounds of frogs and insects from the swamp in 'La Rousserolle effarvatte' (the reed warbler). Or he created impressions of night, as in 'La Chouette hulotte' (the tawny owl) and 'L'Alouette-Lulu' (the woodlark), or of natural phenomena such as rock formations in 'Le Chocard des Alpes' (the alpine chough) and 'Le Merle de roche' (the rock thrush). Some pieces cover the events of a period of time, the most extensive in this respect being 'La Rousserolle effarvatte,' which takes us through a period of twenty-seven hours, from midnight to 3 a.m. on the following day.

With such an enormous variety of material it would appear, at first sight, impossible to impose a sense of order and coherence on the pieces of *Catalogue d'oiseaux*. Indeed, there is

Left: Messaien, seated at the piano, teaching a class. His musical analysis classes at the Paris Conservatoire were world-famous for their precision, detail and lucidity, and his in-depth investigation of *The Rite of Spring* was particularly well known.

Below: Messiaen in Luxembourg, March 1982.

Above: Yvonne Loriod, long associated with Messiaen as a faithful interpreter of his music, having played at most of his premières. She married Messiaen after the death of his first wife.

herring gull (*goéland argenté*) and the theckla lark (*cochevis de theckla*). Thus the four types of birdsong previously described are represented: swift (short call); herring gull (varied call); blue rock thrush (melodic); theckla lark ('chattering'). Although most of the other pieces in the set use more varied material, they achieve a strong coherence by means of a predominant musical quality (sometimes a sense of tonality) to which material is related or contrasted. This quality is what was earlier referred to as the 'general mode' of the piece.

• Influence •

Messiaen is undoubtedly one of the most important composers of the twentieth century, and yet he has remained completely independent of any school or circle of composers. One may point to his founding of the group La Jeune France, in 1936, together with André Jolivet (1905-74), Yves Baudrier (b.1906) and Daniel-Lesur (b.1908), as an exception to this, but that group grew out of the friendship that existed among the four composers and of the general esthetic aims as set out in their manifesto of 1936, rather than from common compositional ideals shared by them.

And yet Messiaen has undoubtedly influenced the development of modern music for a large part of the present century, from before the Second World War to the present day, and indeed he has played a paramount role in that development. On the one hand his works reach an ever growing number of listeners, and young musicians in particular. On the other there is his teaching, which has gone far beyond the boundaries of France. He himself has taught in Hungary, the USA, Germany, Bulgaria and Argentina, and pupils have also come to him from all over the world. In this respect his appointment as professor of composition at the

Paris Conservatoire in 1966 was merely giving official recognition to a function he had been exercising for more than twenty years, since he started giving his lessons in the home of Guy-Bernard Delapierre. Those early lessons inspired the pupils to call themselves 'Les Flèches' (the arrows), and it is significant that among them was Pierre Boulez, and that in his teaching Messiaen first used Stravinsky's *The Rite of Spring* for purposes of analysis. For these two links alone – even if there were no other reason – it is appropriate that we should turn next to Pierre Boulez, whose important analysis of *The Rite of Spring*, though differing from that of Messiaen, nevertheless was clearly inspired by his teacher.

• Pierre Boulez •

Pierre Boulez was born in Montbrison in the Loire in 1925. His father, a steel industrialist, destined him for a scientific career. He studied higher mathematics in Lyons to prepare for admission to the Paris Ecole Polytechnique. At the same time, he continued his musical studies and made such progress that he decided to join the Paris Conservatoire in 1942, against his father's wishes. He came into contact with Messiaen through his harmony class in 1944 and remained with him for a year. Messiaen's original approach to composition and to the music of others was a revelation. It is not surprising that Boulez's *Trois Psalmodies* for piano, written in 1945, should show some influence of Messiaen's modal approach to composition, while also relating to Schoenberg's *Three Piano Pieces*, op.11.

The influence on Boulez of Messiaen's views on serialism which he propounded in these classes has already been mentioned, but it was René Leibowitz's performances of Schoenberg's Wind Quintet in Paris in 1945 which fired Boulez with the enthusiasm to discover more about serial techniques and to adopt them in his own composition. After leaving Messiaen's class he went to Leibowitz to study serial technique, but like Messiaen, he quickly came to believe that Schoenberg's use of classical forms, textures and rhythms was anomalous and misconceived. It was to Webern's music that Boulez turned as the stimulus for his future development. Webern had been tragically killed just after the end of the war in 1945, and because the Nazis had tried to suppress his influence, he had been allowed few pupils in his later life. His music had received very few performances, and his direct personal influence on others was extremely limited. After the war, however, the upsurge of interest in his music amongst younger composers, fostered in part by René Leibowitz, made him one of the most influential figures of the time. Boulez did not confine himself merely to imitating or carrying on from where Webern left off. He saw in his music the possibility of generating serially all the linear (melodic) and vertical (harmonic) elements of a piece and quickly evolved his own methods of using the series. One of the most striking contrasts between Boulez's and Webern's work lies in the elaboration and effusiveness of the former in contrast to the sparseness and economy of the latter.

Besides Messiaen and Webern, two other composers had a formative influence on Boulez's development as a composer: Debussy and Stravinsky. His music often displays a Debussyan delicacy and sense of color, but it was what Boulez has referred to as Debussy's 'collage' forms that were the main influence on him. Debussy, in his later works such as *Jeux*, creates forms which involve constantly changing material from one section to another, but little repetition of ideas in a literal form. The effect is like different colored beads on a chain, some of which may resemble their neighbors, but will rarely relate closely to beads spaced some distant apart. From Stravinsky Boulez took rhythmic procedures which are also to be found in Messiaen: the use of short rhythmic patterns or cells, which can be expanded or contracted.

Below: Messiaen and Boulez together in the church of Notre Dame du Liban, Paris, in 1966. Boulez was a pupil of Messiaen's, studying analysis and composition along with other young composers including Yvette Grimaud, Jean-Louis Martinet and Maurice Le Roux. Messiaen became one of Boulez's greatest champions, giving him encouragement as a composer and staunch support in various projects, including the Domaine Musical, which Boulez founded in 1954 for the promotion of contemporary music.

• Fixed structures •

Although there is a certain amount of motivic working in Boulez's earlier compositions, in his mature works the form is not defined by thematic or motivic repetition. In this respect his music follows principles similar to those of Messiaen's later music, where one recognizes references to earlier material by texture, rhythmic shape, melodic shape or some other characteristic. We have seen how, in *Catalogue d'oiseaux*, musical coherence is provided in part by correspondences between types of birdsong rather than exact repetitions of particular birdsong phrases. Very rarely does the same bird repeat the same song exactly. In connection with his own music, Boulez speaks of four kinds of texture, or structural organization: monody (single lines), homophony (chord structures), polyphony (combinations of monodies and/or homophonies) and heterophony. The first three of these have obvious parallels in classical music in melody, harmony and counterpoint, but the fourth – heterophony – is a concept which is traditionally foreign to Western music.

Heterophony is used in some Eastern music, where the same basic melodic line may be simultaneously decorated by a number of different performers. This type of heterophony is called by Boulez 'decorative heterophony.' For his

own procedures, however, he uses the term 'structural heterophony,' implying that the independent behavior of each strand in the texture is governed by the structure of the basic series and is not the result of free decoration.

The Sonatina for flute and piano (1946 – all earlier works have been withdrawn), the first two piano sonatas (1946 and 1947-8), and the two cantatas *La Visage nuptial* (The Nuptial Face, 1946-7) and *Le Soleil des eaux* (The Sun of the Waters, 1948) represent the extant compositions of the period before Boulez came under the influence of the principles underlying Messiaen's 'Mode de valeurs et d'intensités.' In two works which have since been withdrawn – *Livre pour quatuor* (Book for Quartet, 1948-9) and *Polyphonie X* (1951) – Boulez moves decisively in the direction of total serialism, but the significance of 'Mode de valeurs' is borne out by his use of one of the twelve-note groups of the mode which Messiaen uses in this piece as the serial basis for *Structures Ia* for two pianos (1951-2). Like Messiaen, Boulez assigns different durations, from one to twelve thirty-second notes, to each note of the series, but unlike Messiaen, he regards the series as being capable of manipulation in the manner of the Second Viennese School, that is, subject to transposition, inversion and retrogression. In addition, he applies serial processes to intensities and attacks.

The result of the processes which Boulez uses in *Structures, livre I* is somewhat mechanistic; the composer retains control over the registers of notes and of the vertical density of the music but of very little else. In the following work which he wrote – *Le Marteau sans maître* (The Hammer without a Master) for contralto, alto flute, xylorimba, vibraphone, unpitched percussion, guitar and viola (1953) – he employs more flexible processes which allow for a greater variety of textures and rhythmic structures among the various movements. Boulez sets three poems by René Char: 'L'Artisanat furieux' (The Angry Artisan), 'Bourreaux de solitude' (Executioners of Solitude) and 'Bel édifice et les pressentiments' (Beautiful Building and the Forebodings). Two of these settings give rise to connected instrumental movements, and the third is set twice. Each setting has its own rhythmic and melodic treatment, which is carried over, in the case of the first two poems, into the instrumental movements which follow from them. 'L'Artisanat furieux' is florid in style, using different divisions of irregular durations; 'Bourreaux de solitude' is more pointillistic in style, with a regular unit of rhythmic value from which rhythmic patterns are built up, and 'Bel édifice' is more rhapsodic in style with some obvious use of homophony. The second setting of this poem forms part of the last movement, which brings together elements from all three types of movement.

• Directed chance •

Among the works which followed *Le Marteau*, one which must be mentioned is the Piano Sonata no.3 (1955-7), only two movements of which have been published to date. In his earlier serial procedures Boulez sometimes employed sections of commentary which were interpolated into the mainstream of a movement. In addition, situations could be arrived at where

Left: Boulez conducting rehearsals for the first complete performance of *Lulu* at the Paris Opéra in 1979. He is acknowledged as one of the greatest interpreters of the music of the Second Viennese School, particularly that of Schoenberg and Berg.

Below: Boulez pictured in front of a drawing by Cocteau of Stravinsky playing *The Rite of Spring*. Stravinsky has been a considerable influence on Boulez, alongside Debussy and Schoenberg. The notion of Boulez as Stravinsky's successor is held by many of his admirers.

there was more than one possible continuation. Both of these situations are reflected in the Third Sonata by allowing the performer some choice in the final form of the work.

The series for the Third Sonata is considered to be cyclic, that is to say the end could be joined on to the beginning, so that one may start anywhere in the series. (It is a matter of some interest that Berg often considered his series in this way whereas Schoenberg and Webern did not; for them there was a defined beginning and end to the series.) This cyclic quality is reflected in the overall form of the second *formant* of the sonata, 'Trope.' There are four sections, corresponding to the four divisions of the series, and the pianist may start with any section, playing the others in order. The position of two of the sections may be interchanged, reflecting the structural similarity and interchangeability of two of the cells of the series.

The third *formant*, 'Constellation-Miroir,' is divided into a number of sections which must be played in a fixed order, but within each section there are a number of fragments which can be played in a number of different orders. Here Boulez allows the performer to choose one of the different possibilities which may arise at a given point in the composition.

These controlled chance (or aleatory) elements have become a feature of many of Boulez's works since 1956. In spite of the association of Boulez with other aleatory composers – Stockhausen, Cage, Pousseur and others – there is an essential distinction between the freedom that Boulez allows and the frequently random elements which occur in the music of some other composers (notably Stockhausen and Cage). For Boulez, choices must be made; nothing in the end is left to chance (although decisions by the performer may be left until the actual performance), so that it is arguable whether Boulez's later music is aleatory in the strict sense of the word.

• Le Soleil des eaux •

An important factor in Messiaen's music up to the time of *Turangalîla* was a growing interest in Surrealism. This is apparent in the poems which he wrote for his own song-cycles, *Poèmes pour Mi* and *Chants de terre et de ciel*, as well as in his own prefaces to the scores of the *Quatuor* and *Vingt Regards sur l'Enfant-Jésus*. It became all-pervasive in the music and poetry of *Harawi* and *Cinq Rechants* as well as in the music to and in his writings about *Turangalîla* and other works. Surrealism was principally an artistic and literary movement which flourished in the twenties and thirties. It was essentially an attempt to portray the world of the subconscious through a symbolism which often involved the violent juxtaposition of opposites. This is particularly apparent in the music of *Turangalîla* in its sharp contrasts, particularly of dissonance and sensuality, reflecting the underlying contrast of love and death, of joy and pain. Boulez also became interested in Surrealism at this time, but the consequences of this are more apparent in his choice of poetry for setting rather than in the music itself. *Le Soleil des eaux* is in fact one of three works which set poems by the Surrealist poet René Char, the others being *Le Visage nuptial* and *Le Marteau sans maître*.

Le Soleil des eaux started life as incidental music for a radio play of the same name by René Char. Out of this music Boulez adapted two movements for soprano, tenor, bass and chamber orchestra, 'Complainte du lézard amoureux' (Lay of the Lizard in Love) and 'La Sorgue' (The River Sorgue), which were first performed in a concert version in 1950. It was revised for full orchestra with the addition of choral parts for soprano, tenor and bass in 1958 and performed in this version at Darmstadt in that same year (this is the version which has been recorded). The piece was further fully revised in 1965 for soprano solo, full chorus and orchestra. The writing for voices, which varies from spoken phrases through half-spoken, half-sung intonation to fully sung passages in the 1958 version, becomes fully sung in the 1965 version. The poems were inspired by Char's native region of Provence. 'Complainte

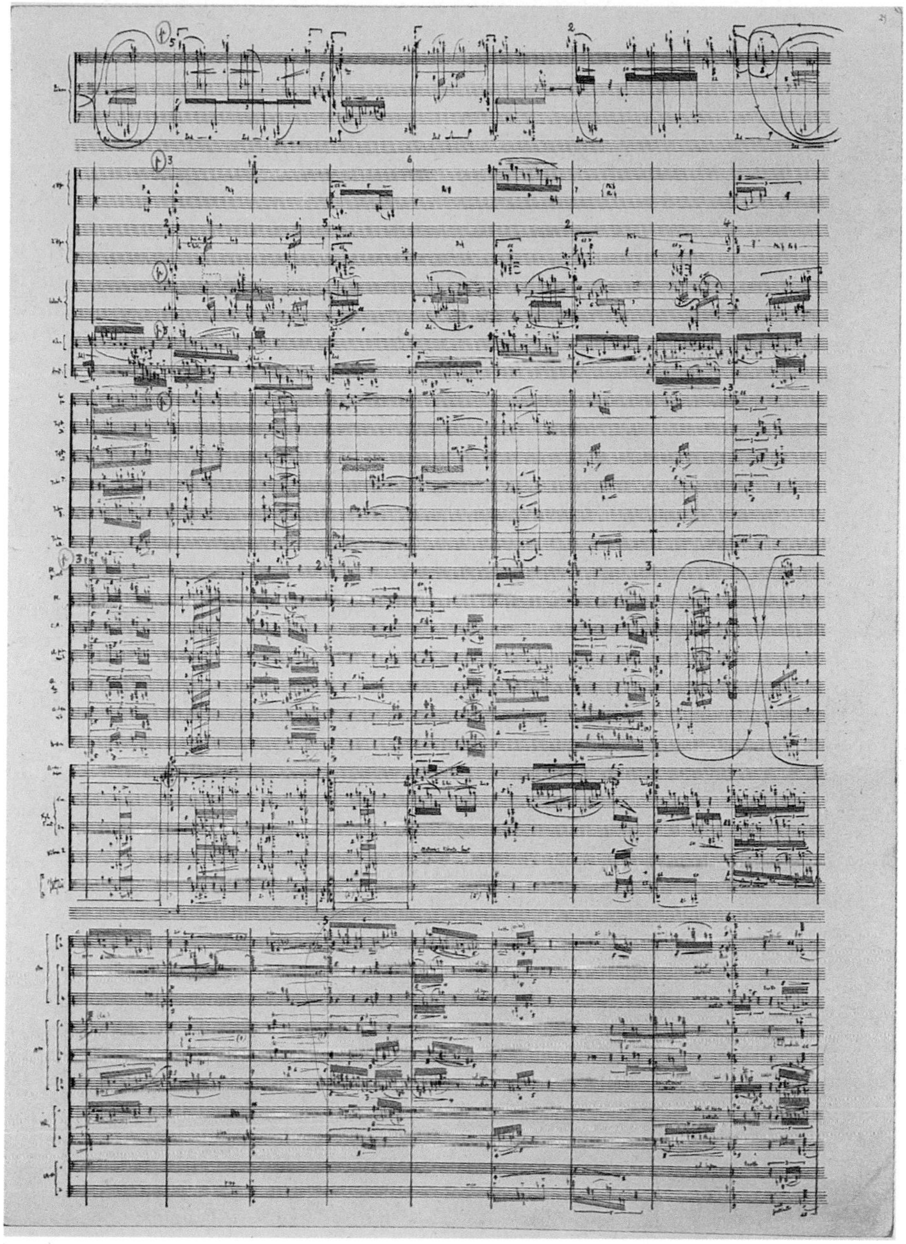

Above: Page from the score of *Tombeau à la mémoire du prince Max Egon zu Fürstenberg* from *Pli selon pli*. Boulez has a great ear for orchestral sonorities and is constantly interested in revising his own work, of which he is constructively critical.

du lézard amoureux' describes the fears of a lizard looking lovingly at a goldfinch picking at a sunflower, in danger from the hunter who is out shooting. In the original play the river Sorgue, a source of livelihood to the fishermen who live on its banks, is threatened by pollution; the poem 'La Sorgue,' therefore, is descriptive of the river itself as well as of its spiritual qualities of strength and purpose.

The setting of the first poem tends to alternate passages for the orchestra with passages for the soprano. Only one stanza – the second – is set fully with orchestral accompaniment, the others being set as solo monodies with some overlapping with the orchestral passages that precede or follow. The orchestral passages are of different lengths, but the vocal passages diminish in length as the movement proceeds. There are seven stanzas in the poem. After an orchestral introduction the first three stanzas are set without a break (the second being accompanied). The next orchestral interlude is followed by a monodic setting of the fourth and fifth stanzas, the next interlude by a setting of the sixth stanza. After the next interlude, the seventh stanza is broken up into three lines and one line, by a three-measure orchestral interpolation. The soprano is allowed to finish the movement on her own.

Contrasts of texture, varying between the partial polyphony of the opening, the monody of the soloist and homophonic blocks, are readily apparent, although they are not used as systematically in this instance to define the shape of the movement as is the case in later music. The eleven short stanzas of the second movement each begin with the word 'Rivière.' The mere repetition of the word is sufficient to act as a demarcating refrain, but the music also underlines the structure of the poem by treating each stanza differently. The treatment may vary during the course of a stanza, but each begins in a distinctive way, as follows: 1 Full choir, spoken, homophonic; 2 Solos, sung, monodic; 3 Tutti, sung, polyphonic; 4 Tutti, spoken, canonic; 5 Groups of three (sopranos and tenors), half-spoken, against tutti basses, spoken; 6 Tutti, sung, homophonic; 7 Solo bass, sung, against tutti tenors, then sopranos, spoken; 8 Solo tenor, then soprano, sung, against tutti sopranos, then basses, then tenors, spoken; 9 Solo bass and soprano, sung, against tutti tenors, spoken; 10 Two tenors and basses, half-spoken, polyphonic; 11 Full choir, spoken, homophonic (as 1), but leading to tutti tenors and basses, sung, against solo soprano, spoken.

In setting the poems, Boulez indulges in some interesting word-painting. The solo monodies of the soprano in the first movement enhance the intimacy and the monologue character of the poem. The violence of 'La Sorgue' is suggested by the shouted invocations of the first stanza and of the last, with its reference to 'this mad prison world.' In the orchestral introduction to the second movement Boulez uses different-sized groups of soprano voices in unison, without words, 'like an instrument in the orchestra' (as he marks on the score). Debussy's use of a wordless women's chorus in 'Sirènes' had already been reflected at the end of Messiaen's 'Le Merle bleu,' where the composer asks for an effect 'like a distant choir of women's voices,' and there is also a precedent in Ravel's original ballet music for *Daphnis and Chloé*, which uses a mixed chorus. Whereas Debussy's and Ravel's intentions are impressionistic, however, it could be argued that Boulez's intention is to depersonalize the voice by reducing it to equality with the orchestra to symbolize the dehumanizing influence of industrialization, implicit in the poem 'La Sorgue.'

Perhaps the most striking piece of word-painting occurs in the first movement after the

Left: Boulez is a very skilled conductor and is noted for the intellectual clarity of his interpretations, particularly of the works of Wagner, Debussy and Stravinsky.

Below: Boulez with the Ensemble Intercontemporain during a rehearsal at IRCAM of *Repons*, one of his more recent enterprises.

third stanza, which ends with the words 'the waving grasses of the fields.' The orchestral interlude which follows is heterophonic in style, with several different instrumental timbres chasing each other around the same group of twelve different notes, suggesting a field of long grass wafted by the wind, causing it to change continually in its internal detail, while retaining the same overall pattern. This heterophonic-like passage resolves on to a sustained chord, which consists of the twelve notes used in the section.

In spite of an athematic method of composition, Boulez, as in many other works, preserves a sense of line which, especially in the voice, is distinctly melodic in its characteristics.

Repetitions of particular shapes are apparent, although the interval and rhythmic structure which define them may be radically altered from one appearance to the next. Except where a decisive division between sections is intended, Boulez carries the ear through from one section of the music to the next by the use of common notes. In the first movement, especially, where the alternating soprano and orchestral passages could be in danger of creating a fragmentary effect, the soprano monodies are dovetailed with the preceding and following orchestral interludes, not only by overlaps, but by groups of notes common to both soprano and orchestra at the overlap points.

Once one becomes accustomed to Boulez's athematicism, the shape of his music becomes very clear. In common with the music of other French composers, in fact, his shows a clarity of texture with a strong sense of color, together with a sensitive treatment of the voice as an essentially melodic instrument.

• Conducting and directing •

In addition to his activities as a composer, Boulez has of course played an important role as a conductor, especially in the works of Debussy, Stravinsky and Schoenberg. His famous – or rather infamous – concerts in Paris, that began in 1953 as the Concerts du Petit-Marigny and then became the Concerts du Domaine Musical the following year, made him feel that the artistic climate in France at that time was not sufficiently responsive – one might even say developed – to assimilate the music he was propagating, so he made a conscious decision to work outside France. Other creative artists had the same problem at the time, and took the same decision.

Boulez went to Germany in 1959, but his career rapidly took on an international dimension, and he did much pioneer work in bringing what is still regarded as avant-garde music to the concert platform. He had a particularly long and fruitful association with the BBC Symphony Orchestra in London, which produced some memorable concerts, especially of works he particularly admired. It must also be admitted, however, that he could be a less than inspiring conductor of the standard repertoire pieces by composers for whom he felt little enthusiasm, and involvement with an institution like the BBC requires that the repertoire be covered.

This ought not to surprise us, in view of Boulez's evident sympathies. But it did mean that many of the subsequent attempts by Boulez to return to his own country and its musical life were doomed to failure. There was a highly successful production of *Wozzeck* at the Paris Opéra in 1962, but this was an isolated incident, because two years later Boulez had a direct confrontation with the Gaullist Minister of Culture, André Malraux, after which he vowed that he would never work in France again. Even the Gaullist régime had to come to an end, however, and under De Gaulle's successor, Georges Pompidou, a vast cultural center was planned in the eastern part of central Paris, on the site of what had been Les Halles, the capital's food market.

The center is now operational, bears the name of Georges Pompidou, and boasts IRCAM, a financially independent center for contemporary music, established in 1975 and presided over by Pierre Boulez. Included in the Institute's wide research program are investigations into the relationship of music with neurophysiology, linguistics and sociology. For many of his admirers Boulez has at last taken his rightful place, and as one eminent music critic has written: '[if IRCAM is successful] it will be a milestone in the history of Western music as crucial as the advent of the airplane has been in the field of transport. IRCAM will probably succeed in pushing out the frontiers of sound as drastically as the great explorers of the Renaissance succeeded in expanding man's knowledge of the Earth.' High hopes indeed.

Left: Boulez and Giuseppe de Giugno in one of the IRCAM studios.

EDGARD VARÈSE AND KARLHEINZ STOCKHAUSEN

PAUL GRIFFITHS

Opposite: The Large Glass, 1915-23, by Marcel Duchamp, also entitled 'The Bride stripped bare by her bachelors, even.' Early in his career, Duchamp had spearheaded the Dada movement, which with its attempt to undermine all conventional and traditional aspects of art, rapidly became an international movement. It sowed the seeds of Surrealism, based on the more constructive notion of giving free rein to the unconscious and irrational – hence Duchamp's interpretations of 'ready-made' objects as art. The career of Edgard Varèse has much in common with that of Duchamp. Both were Frenchmen who emigrated to the USA, and both were so radical that the full force of their influence was felt only by a much younger generation.

Varèse and Stockhausen are the two great explorers of music in the twentieth century. And though in many respects their interests and achievements differ widely, the music of both is very often concerned with a search for new sounds and a search for new structures to contain those new sounds. In particular, the whole history of electronic music owes a great deal to them: to Varèse as prophet and instigator, to Stockhausen as practitioner and developer in a whole range of works.

Indeed, electronic music was something to which Varèse was looking forward from as early as 1916, when he said to a newspaper interviewer: 'We also need new instruments very badly . . . Musicians should take up this question in deep earnest with the help of machinery specialists.' At this time he had recently arrived in New York from his native France. He was thirty-two; he had left Europe in the grip of the First World War, and he was ready to make a new start. Most of his music remained behind and was lost: only a song to a poem by Verlaine, 'Un grand sommeil noir' (A great black sleep), survived because it had been published in 1906. Otherwise, his output began with the work he wrote to celebrate his arrival on the other side of the Atlantic, *Amériques* (Americas) for large orchestra (1918-21), the title chosen 'as symbolic of discoveries – new worlds on earth, in the sky, or in the minds of men.'

Varèse was born in Paris on 22 December 1883 and christened Edgard Victor Achille Charles (later he was sometimes to anglicize his first name as Edgar). He spent his early childhood partly in Paris and partly in Burgundy, where he was strongly impressed by the Romanesque architecture of churches and cathedrals. Then, in 1893, the family moved to Turin, where Varèse's father tried to direct Edgard's studies towards a business career.

But the young composer had already chosen his path, and in 1903, after fierce arguments with his father, he left home for Paris, there to study with the composers Albert Roussel and Charles Widor, and with the early-music specialist Charles Bordes. Four years later he moved to Berlin, where he gained the admiration of Richard Strauss and of Busoni, whose radical ideas about new musical possibilities coincided with his own. He also got to know the recent atonal music of Schoenberg, and when he returned to Paris in 1913 he brought news of this to another close acquaintance, Debussy. Meanwhile he was also composing: the opera *Oedipus und die Sphinx* (1909-13), after a play by Hofmannsthal, was the biggest of the works that disappeared during the war; the symphonic poem *Bourgogne* (1908) was retained by the composer, but destroyed by him towards the end of his life.

Thus, ignoring the early and unrepresentative song, Varèse appears at once fully formed in his *Amériques*. Although this work contains plain echoes of the music Varèse had just heard in Europe – Stravinsky's *The Rite of Spring*, Debussy's *Jeux* and Schoenberg's *Five Orchestral Pieces*, op.16 – it just as clearly announces a new musical personality. The huge orchestra is particularly rich in percussion instruments, requiring nine players apart from the two timpanists, and introducing a siren in addition to the more normal drums, cymbals, triangles, gongs, tuned instruments (xylophone, glockenspiel, celesta) and so on. Moreover, the work is engaged in a continuous onward movement, propelled by colossal masses of sound and regions of immense contrast.

During the next ten years Varèse followed up the 'discoveries' of *Amériques*, occasionally even drawing on its musical ideas and setting them free to develop in new contexts. Its immediate successors were a pair of songs setting Surrealist poetry for soprano and small orchestra under the title *Offrandes* (Offerings. 1921), and *Hyperprism* (1922-3), in which Varèse not only indulged his fancy for the scientific (a 'hyperprism' is a four-dimensional object) but also introduced a kind of mixed chamber ensemble which has been much imitated: the work is scored for two high woodwinds, seven brass and seven percussionists. This orchestra was well suited to the sort of music Varèse wanted to write, with insistent repetitions of a single note, searing high dissonances, brutal climaxes and complex textures of unrelated rhythms. *Intégrales* (1924-5) was composed for a similar formation, between works which effectively split the Varèsian orchestra into its constituent halves: *Octandre* for seven wind and double bass (1923), and *Ionisation* for thirteen percussion players (1929-31).

Ionisation, again with a 'scientific' title, was the first work created by a Western composer for percussion ensemble, and as such it dramatizes Varèse's quest for new means of produc-

ing sounds (he was already in contact with Maurice Martenot and with others who were trying to build electronic musical instruments). The ensemble is an enlargement of that deployed within *Amériques*, including two sirens, various kinds of drum and cymbal, anvils, gongs and other instruments which produce sounds of indefinite pitch; the tuned instruments – piano, glockenspiel and tubular bells – are reserved for the bell-like sounds with which the piece ends. And so before those final pages the music is concerned not at all with melody and harmony but only with the rhythms, sounds and textures to be generated by 'noises,' though Varèse compensates for the strangeness of the material by making the structure unusually clear: a rhythmic theme in the 'tambour militaire' (military drum), first heard near the beginning, marks out the main stages of the musical development.

•The tape recorder•

After *Ionisation* Varèse composed *Ecuatorial* (1932-4), setting a Maya incantation for bass voice with an orchestra including two of Martenot's electronic instruments, and the flute solo *Densité 21.5* (1936), so called because it was written for a platinum flute, platinum having the density 21.5. Then, however, he was silent for more than a decade. For although his music had gained him success and notoriety in America and abroad – Stokowski had conducted *Intégrales* and a second work for large orchestra, *Arcana* (1925-7) – he had still not found the new instruments he needed. He spent a lot of time on a project called *Espace* (Space), which was to involve simultaneous broadcasts by performers all around the globe, but he completed nothing until the development of the tape recorder brought him what he had been seeking for three decades.

As Varèse – and others in the 1930s, including Hindemith and Milhaud – had realized, the future of electronic music would depend not on specially manufactured instruments like Martenot's but on the direct manipulation of recorded sound. Experiments with disks had been conducted by various people, the most sophisticated being by the French composer and technician Pierre Schaeffer, who discovered the novel effects that could be obtained by playing recordings at different speeds, playing them backwards, or excising fragments of sounds. It was Schaeffer who created the first pieces of real electronic music in 1948, using recordings on disk, and who established the first studio for electronic music at French Radio. But disk recording was a cumbersome medium for electronic music. The tape recorder, which became commercially available at the beginning of the fifties, made all the processes of transformation and editing very much easier, and it was when Varèse was given a tape recorder, in 1953, that he pressed ahead with his new work, *Déserts* (?1950-4).

Déserts was the first musical composition to combine the new medium with the old. There are four sections for a typically Varèsian orchestra of wind, piano and percussion, linked by three interpolations of music on tape, which Varèse completed in Schaeffer's studio in 1954. The impression is of windows that look out into the new, though paradoxically the orchestral music is much more subtle and imaginative than the electronic. Perhaps, now that the new means were available, Varèse was disappointed by what could be achieved. Certainly the brave

Left: 'Edgar Varèse, Futurist Composer' was the caption of this early publicity photo. Varèse's musical training was conventional, but he rapidly established himself in Paris as a young 'modern,' associating with Duchamp, Picabia and the other Dadaists. His formation of the International Composers Guild in 1921 for the performance of contemporary music expressed his concern for the development and encouragement of musical experiment, later to be frustrated by the lack of suitable electronic means of sound production and variation.

Below: Pierre Schaeffer in 1951. Schaeffer, a pioneer in the field of musical electronics, invited Varèse to produce *Déserts* at the RTF Studio in Paris in 1954. This was the first 'electronic' work that Varèse produced after he had received a gift of a tape recorder.

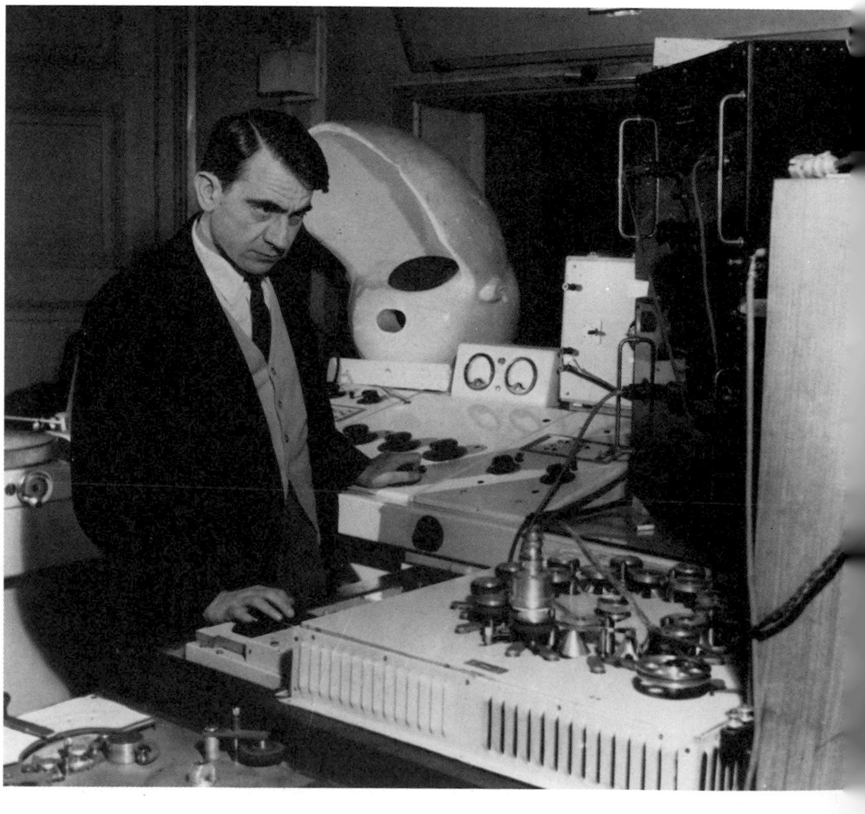

optimism of *Amériques* has been left far behind in a work which concerns 'not only physical deserts of sand, sea, mountains and snow, outer space, deserted city streets . . . but also this distant inner space . . . where man is alone in a world of mystery and essential solitude.'

• Karlheinz Stockhausen •

However, there were in the early 1950s other composers much more confident about the potentials of new musical techniques, among them Karlheinz Stockhausen. Stockhausen was born on 22 August 1928 in Burg Mödrath, near Cologne, and he studied in that city at the Music Academy. Much more significant, however, was his visit to the summer school at Darmstadt in 1951. There he met two contemporaries who were exploring the possibilities of Schoenberg's serialism, Luigi Nono and Karel Goeyvaerts, and there he heard and was fascinated by a new piano piece by Olivier Messiaen, *Mode de valeurs et d'intensités*. He responded to these influences in his *Kreuzspiel* (Crossplay) for oboe, bass clarinet, piano and three percussion players (1951), and in January 1952 he went to Paris to study with Messiaen, also meeting Boulez and spending some time in Schaeffer's studio.

Right: Karlheinz Stockhausen in an electronic studio in 1958. His earlier introduction to Schaeffer in Paris had inspired him to experiment with taped sound, not using Schaeffer's *musique concrète* method but generating new sound by purely electronic means. He continued, however, a parallel practice of composing for conventional instruments.

For Stockhausen the near-simultaneous introduction to serialism and to electronic music was decisive. The new medium appeared to offer unlimited possibilities for the generation of sounds, and Stockhausen imagined he might be able to create with it music which was absolutely determined in all points of pitch, duration, loudness and tone color; he made two approaches to this ideal in his *Elektronische Studien* of 1953-4, composed in the new studio at Cologne. All the sounds in these pieces were made by purely electronic means, whereas Varèse, following the practice of Schaeffer and his colleagues, started out in *Déserts* from existing recordings, of factory noises, metallic vibrations, conventional instruments, etc. (Schaeffer's term for this latter technique was *musique concrète*.) The polarity between the two methods, and between the rival studios of Paris and Cologne, was to persist until Stockhausen himself created a work using both synthetic and recorded material, his *Gesang der Jünglinge* (Song of the Boys, 1955-6), where the sounds of a boy's singing voice are interlaced and fused with those created solely with electronic equipment.

But meanwhile Stockhausen was also composing for traditional instruments. The first work in his official catalogue, *Kontra-Punkte* (1952-3), is based on a simple idea of leveling out; an original group of ten diverse instruments is gradually reduced to a solo piano, and the music also progressively moves towards stable central areas of pitch and volume. This bald scheme, however, is enlivened by a virtuoso interplay of quick melodic invention, and the music's boldness and brilliance, contrasting with the confined, constructive designs of other young composers investigating serialism at the time, brought Stockhausen to the forefront of the musical avant garde, along with Luigi Nono and Pierre Boulez. He further confirmed the keenness of his imagination, and his extraordinary knack of finding a fruitful new system of composition for each new work, in two sets of piano pieces (1952-3 and 1954-5), the first fast, elaborate and precise in the manner of *Kontra-Punkte*, the second exploiting all the physical, human features of musical performance that had been missing from music created on tape.

The commanding, positive feeling conveyed by Stockhausen's next group of works, dating from the mid-1950s, is testimony not only to his own confidence but also to the brave sureness with which the whole avant garde was pushing back the frontiers. *Gesang der Jünglinge* is among the few outstanding works of music on tape, a graphic image of the boys held in Nebuchadnezzar's burning, fiery furnace, with flickerings of a voice in prayer heard among sounds that are totally new and strange. It is also successful in its attempt to integrate the vocal sounds and the electronic, so that sometimes one is not sure which is which; human language and artificial sound thus become extremes in a continuum.

There is the same mastery of creative aim and technique in the instrumental works on which Stockhausen worked at the same time: *Zeitmasse* (1955-6) for five woodwinds, *Gruppen* (Groups, 1955-7) for three orchestras and *Klavierstück XI* (Piano piece XI, 1956). Like the second group of piano pieces, *Zeitmasse* happily adapts itself to human rather than mechanical means of measurement. The title means simply 'tempi,' and the music juggles constantly with a variety of speeds among its five instrumental lines, played by flute, oboe, cor anglais, clarinet and bassoon. Moreover, the tempi are relative: 'as fast as possible,' 'as slow as possible (within one breath),' and so on. Co-ordination among the five instruments, therefore, cannot be exact, and this moderate opening of his music to the fortuitous was to have wide repercussions within and beyond the composer's later music. Indeed, *Klavierstück XI* already shows a much greater component of chance. The piece is notated as nineteen separate fragments on a large sheet of paper, the performer being free to play these in any order.

Gruppen has connections with both these works. Like *Zeitmasse*, it is a play of distinct bands of time in different motions, in this case using three orchestras, each under its own conductor. And like *Klavierstück XI*, it benefits from Stockhausen's studies of acoustics at the time, which gave him new ideas about musical form. The variability of the piano piece was suggested by the uncertainty one must have about the constituents of any complex sound; the weighting of the elements is unpredictable, exactly as the weighting of harmonics within, say, a clarinet sound will also be unpredictable. *Gruppen*, rather similarly but on a much larger scale, is the magnified image of a sequence of complex sounds, colored by a versatile use of orchestras each containing woodwind, brass, strings and percussion, including one tuned instrument. But, quite typically, the theorizing about musical time and timbre composition is vivified by the drama with which Stockhausen wields his resources. The use of three orchestras may have been suggested originally by the need to establish different tempi at the same time, but the result in *Gruppen* is an exhilarating essay in musical stereophony; ideally the audience should be surrounded by the ensembles, which at the exultant climax toss brass chords among themselves.

• *Poème* and *Kontakte* •

No doubt the confidence of Stockhausen and his contemporaries had its effect also on Varèse, now in his seventies but still alert to new musical developments. In 1957 he was invited to compose an electronic work to be played in the Philips Pavilion at the 1958 World Fair in Brussels. The pavilion was to be designed by Le Corbusier, with the help of an assistant who had already applied musical ideas to architecture and who was soon to make his own mark in the musical world, Iannis Xenakis. Varèse eagerly accepted the opportunity, and created for the pavilion his *Poème électronique*, music on tape designed to be heard through an array of four hundred loudspeakers. Unfortunately, Le Corbusier's building was destroyed when the exhibition was over, so one cannot reconstruct the original effect of Varèse's music. Nevertheless, and though the piece is only eight minutes long, it is a highly arresting collage of industrial, synthetic, instrumental and vocal sounds, a complete justification of all the composer's optimistic expectations from the new medium.

But, whether he was too old to take further advantage of electronic music or because the techniques were still primitive, Varèse left it to his juniors to continue the exploration, and Stockhausen was fully prepared to take on the mantle. Once more he engaged himself on a big electronic work, *Kontakte* (1959-60), and once more the electronic composition was surrounded by others for instruments: *Zyklus* for solo percussionist (1959), *Refrain* for three players (1959) and *Carré* for four ensembles of voices and instruments (1959-60). Just as *Gesang der Jünglinge* had been an integration of vocal and electronic sounds, so *Kontakte* mingles the electronic with the instrumental, but in a different way. The tape was composed wholly by artificial means, and yet some of its sounds seem to belong to the known world of percussion instruments. These resemblances Stockhausen

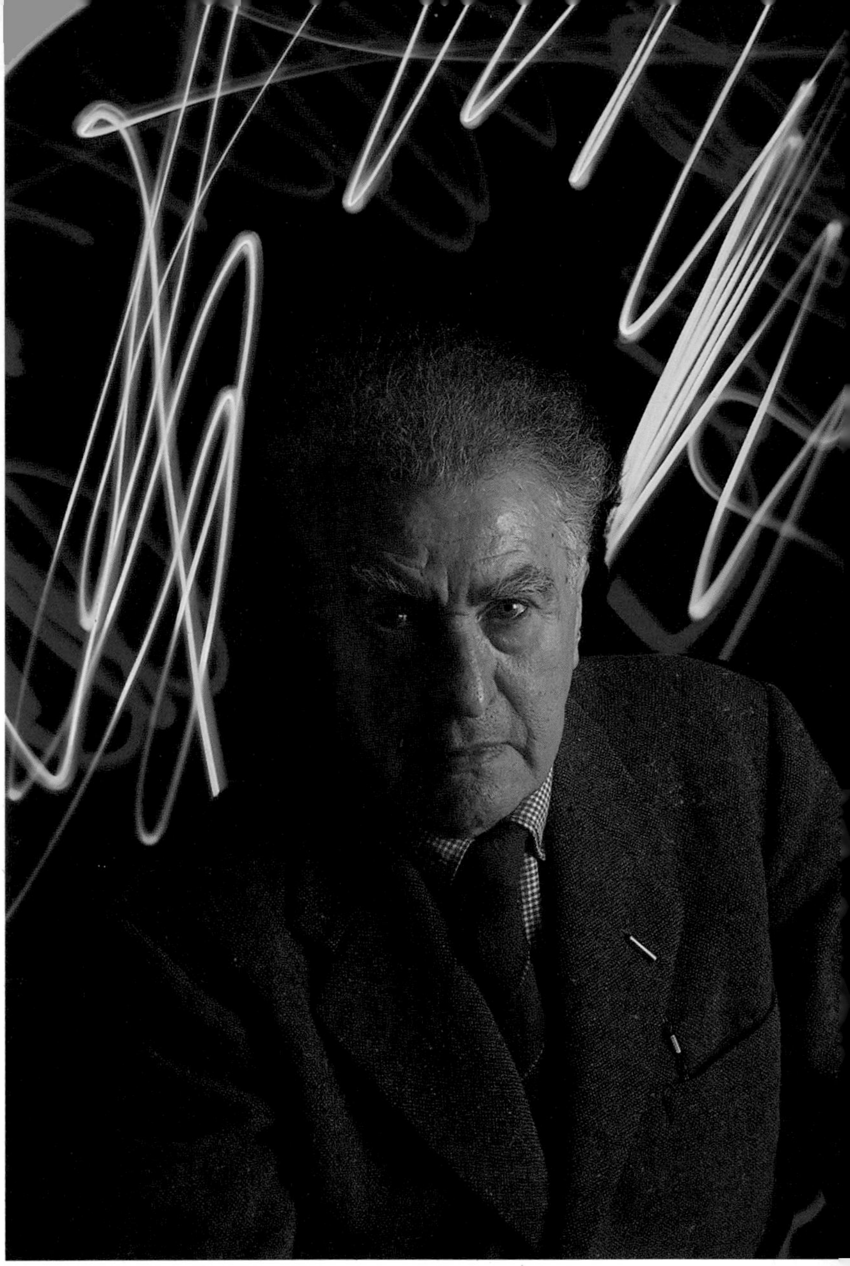

Above: Varèse in front of a light sculpture. Electronic means were employed in art as well as in music – most often for kinetic sculpture.

accentuates by having a pianist and a percussionist play along with the tape (which, however, can also be heard by itself). In his own striking phrases, they 'provide orientation, perspective to hearing; they function as traffic signs in the unlimited space of the newly discovered electronic sound world.' And the vast extent of that world is displayed in the work's perpetual newness, which is maintained throughout a period of more than half an hour.

Kontakte marks the beginning of Stockhausen's move towards works of long duration, for although *Zyklus* and *Refrain* are both quite short – the former a virtuoso test piece for percussionists, the latter a brilliant jewel of trills and chimes from piano, celesta and vibraphone – *Carré* can extend for more than an hour. It is by no means simply a re-run of *Gruppen* with four ensembles instead of three; the time-scale is much slower, and where *Gruppen* was filled with activity, *Carré* centers itself on sustained sounds, on events which linger.

The impression now is not of observing the music but of being immersed in it, of living in the present of the sounds as they arrive, not using memory to relate and predict. This is also true of *Kontakte*, and it gave Stockhausen a new conception of musical form as a sequence of 'moments,' each existing for itself, the listener being free to respond to different moments with different levels of attention, instead of being invited to follow a musical argument through all its stages.

Below: Stockhausen, photographed by Auerbach, in London to prepare for the British première of *Inori*, which took place in January 1973 at the London Coliseum. *Inori* is written in traditional notation – a return to a convention that Stockhausen had rejected several years earlier and taken up again a few works previous to this one. *Inori* also makes the first tentative steps in the direction of music drama, a form that has occupied Stockhausen ever since.

• Moment-form •

The idea of moment-form received its fullest expression in the work entitled *Momente* (1961-4), scored for a solo soprano with four choruses, eight brass, two electronic organs and three percussion players, of which Stockhausen wrote that it is 'no self-contained work with unequivocally fixed beginning, formal structure and ending, but a polyvalent composition containing independent events. Unity and continuity are less the outcome of obvious similarities than of an immanent concentration on the present, as uninterrupted as possible.' Accordingly, as he had done earlier in the *Klavierstück XI* but now on a much larger scale, the composer allows for the 'moments' of the work to be assembled in various possible orders, although the permutations are severely limited, and indeed the composition is quite decisively shaped in three groupings of moments, these focusing in turn on sound quality, on melody and on aspects of duration. Moreover, the definitive version of the work, completed in 1972, adopts a much more theatrical and public tone, so that the effect is of a dramatic ceremonial rather than, as in the original version, of a voyage through the forever surprising territories of sound to be obtained from what might appear rather limited resources.

The emphasis on discovering new sounds – on 'timbre composition' in Stockhausen's terms – is very much a feature of both the original *Momente* and of *Carré*, and it was obviously stimulated by the composer's experience in making *Kontakte*. It is also in complete accord with the principles of 'moment-form,' which encourages the listener to relish each new sound as it arrives instead of trying to relate events to each other.

At the same time, the works of this period saw a change in Stockhausen's approach to the task of composition, and again his work in the electronic studio may well have been influential. A composer creating an electronic work must learn to work in partnership with technicians; thus Stockhausen had had his assistant Cornelius Cardew work up much of the detail in *Carré*, keeping control over the work by establishing first the basic design and then supervising Cardew's elaboration of it. The obvious next step was to publish a work which was only a design, and this Stockhausen did in the case of *Plus-Minus* (1963), which consists simply of diagrams and instructions without any specification of instruments or any conventional musical notation. And as if anxious to keep the piece in this pristine condition, Stockhausen has hardly ever involved himself in performances of it. It remains among the few of his works that he has not recorded.

The notion of releasing creative control would grow in Stockhausen's mind towards the end of the decade, but for the moment *Plus-Minus* was a sport, and he continued with his explorations of new sound sources. *Mikrophonie I* (1964) is a work for six performers using various implements and electronic equipment to draw a vast range of sounds from a single large tam-tam, or rimless gong. *Mikrophonie II* (1965) has the sounds of a small choir made strange by electronic modulation, creating a cramped, dark world into which the composer sets recorded 'windows' onto the more joyous landscapes of *Gesang der Jünglinge*, *Carré* and *Momente*. *Mixtur* (1964) uses a similar technique of electronic transformation but with an orchestra, and with the more positive feeling of a bounding journey from one completely new texture to another. *Solo* (1965-6) is for a single performer playing against self-recordings gradually built up on tape, so that a continuing musical line divides into counterpoint.

•Departures•

Thus in all these works of the mid-1960s Stockhausen was finding out what could be done with electronic equipment in the concert hall, used there to transform instrumental or vocal sounds instead of being kept in the studio to be employed in the preparation of finished tapes. All four compositions speak of a continuing fascination with the electronic medium, which contrasts with the creative attitude of Varèse in his last years. After completing his *Poème électronique*, Varése worked on various projects associated with themes of death and the night, and in none of these does he seem to have planned an electronic component. In 1961 an unfinished fragment, *Nocturnal*, for soprano, bass chorus and small orchestra, was performed in New York, but this still remained incomplete when Varèse died four and a half years later, on 6 November 1965 in New York. The piece was posthumously edited and completed by Varèse's pupil Chou Wen-chung, but its bleakness, disillusionment and intense despair cannot be hidden, testifying, perhaps, not only to the personal feelings of a composer approaching the age of eighty but also to his sense that electronic music was less exciting in actuality than it had been in prospect.

It is also possible that Varèse was disappointed by the rapid dissipation of the energy and enthusiasm his younger colleagues had evinced in the 1950s, or at least that he was affected by their own comparative unease in the new decade. Stockhausen, Boulez and the rest were by now asserting themselves too powerfully as individuals to maintain a common charter for the future of music for any length of time; the partnership they had felt at the time of *Gruppen* and *Gesang der Jünglinge* was no longer so close or so important. And while Boulez turned increasingly towards his secondary career as a conductor, Stockhausen began to develop his activities as a performer, though unlike Boulez he was playing his own music almost exclusively and was working with his own ensemble, which he formed in the first place to give performances of *Mikrophonie I*. This new experience increased Stockhausen's awareness of the

ways in which performers who are familiar with one another can work together intuitively, responding to each other and engaging in musical dialogue. The phenomenon is perhaps most commonly found among string quartets and jazz bands, but Stockhausen found it operating too within his own group of musicians using conventional instruments (piano, viola, percussion) and electronic equipment. It was to exploit their intuitive skills that he wrote *Prozession* (1967).

For this work he invented a quite new kind of musical notation. The principal symbols are plus, minus and equal signs, indicating an increase, a decrease or an equivalence in loudness, pitch level, duration or complexity of detail. Each musical part – there are four, one for each instrumentalist – consists essentially of a sequence of these symbols, together with indications as to which performer is leading at any given time. These symbols are to be understood as prescriptions for reactions, each player responding either to what he himself has just played or else to what he hears from another. And so the printed musical material is no more than a scheme for a process, a conversation which takes as its topics the composer's earlier works. For whereas in *Mikrophonie II* the quotations from previous compositions were deliberately made alien, in *Prozession* the players take all their initial stimulus from the corpus of Stockhausen's output; the pianist, for example, is directed to refer to the eleven *Klavierstücke* and *Kontakte*, the viola player to *Gesang der Jünglinge*, *Momente* and also *Kontakte*. Thus *Prozession* becomes both a meditation on themes from the past, conducted by the composer in intimate collaboration with his performers, and also, because the transformations involved may be very considerable, a thrust towards

Above: Varèse with a colleague in the Philips Pavilion at the Brussels World Fair of 1958. The Philips Company commissioned Varèse to write a piece of music specifically for their display; Varèse responded with *Poème électronique*, a remarkable example of *musique concrète*, designed to be reproduced through four hundred loudspeakers and first performed on 2 May 1958.

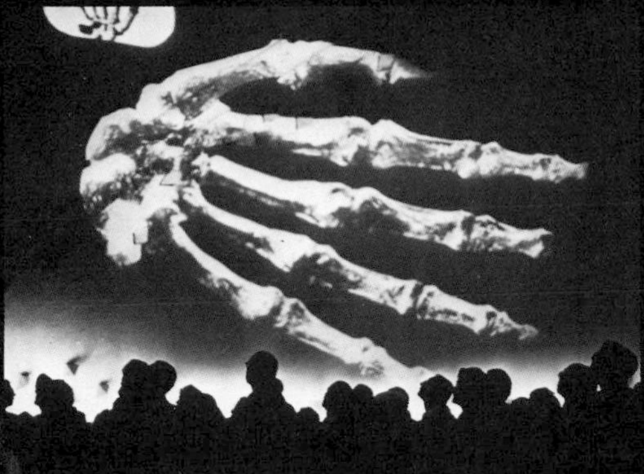

Right: The Philips Pavilion itself, designed by Le Corbusier assisted by the musician and architect Iannis Xenakis, who contributed significantly to the architectural concept, working on the formula of displacement of the straight line so that all planes derive from a curved surface. Above are some of the cinematic images projected inside the pavilion during the performance of *Poème électronique*.

things forever new, unlimited by conventional notation.

No doubt the kind of music-making Stockhausen requires in *Prozession*, dependent on a high degree of attunement among a small group of players, was stimulated in part by his experience of music in Japan, where he made a prolonged stay in 1966. It was there that he composed his third major work of music on tape, *Telemusik*, in which he suddenly found it possible 'to go a step further towards writing not "my" music but a music of the whole world, of all lands and races.' The work has the sounds of Japanese temple instruments – bells and woodblocks – to define the starting-points of its thirty-two sections, but by no means do the references to foreign cultures end there. Much of the piece is created from recordings of the world's music, including Japanese gagaku, Hungarian folk music, Balinese gamelan playing, song from the southern Sahara, and so on. These raw materials are usually combined with each other, and so rendered more or less unrecognizable, by Stockhausen's technique of 'intermodulation,' or projecting one aspect of a recording onto another recording.

Intermodulation – which has its analogue in the live processes of interreaction in *Prozession* – gives rise in *Telemusik* to complex textures and events in which the original recording, when it can be distinguished at all, sounds as if it is being jammed by radio interference. This, coupled with Stockhausen's use of twittering high-frequency tones throughout much of the composition, gives *Telemusik* something of the character of shortwave reception. And though the radio ambience enlarges its claims to being, as Stockhausen describes it, 'a universality of past, present and future, of distant places and spaces,' it is also quite definitely a product of his imagination, and his alone.

Even so, *Telemusik* was, remarkably, the first of Stockhausen's works to claim association with any music outside itself. Hitherto Stockhausen had been at pains to emphasize what most clearly distinguished his music from any other; and indeed part of the excitement of such works as *Kontra-Punkte*, *Gruppen*, *Kontakte*, *Momente* and *Mikrophonie I* comes from the freshness and independence of the composer's approach, renewed on every occasion. *Telemusik* still has this feeling of new ideas caught raw at the moment of conception, but the presence of ethno-musicological recordings from around the world signals the composer's wish to set himself in the context of folk music, if not yet of his Classical heritage.

There followed very soon another attempt at a 'music of the whole world' in his next tape composition, *Hymnen* (1966-7), a work which is in every respect more open than *Telemusik*. It lasts for almost two hours, by comparison with the seventeen and a half minutes of the earlier piece, and its source material, the national anthems of the world, is now freely acknowledged in what is a great festival of quotation. There is also a still stronger feeling of broadcast reception: the well-fashioned scheme of

Telemusik is replaced by an allusive drift of thought, catching on anthems, on sounds imitative of radio interference and on stretches of speech. Furthermore, the four large sections of the work can be interchanged, extended or omitted in performance, and Stockhausen has prepared a version of the work with his own live electronic ensemble participating throughout, imitating what they hear and forging new connections among the disparate materials, as well as another version with orchestra.

Hymnen is the outstanding achievement from an extraordinarily prolific period in Stockhausen's career, the years 1964-7, during which he had opened up various fields of live electronic music, established his own performing ensemble, created two major works in the electronic studio and generalized the notion of the composer's task, giving most attention not to the basic material but to larger processes and relationships. In all this the electronic component was crucial, and it is significant that his two works of this period for conventional instruments, *Stop* for six small orchestra groups (1965) and *Adieu* for wind quintet (1966), are spin-offs from work in the electronic medium; the former is again an image of tuning a radio, scanning different noise textures and revealing single tones and occasional melodic fragments, while *Adieu* is a study in tonal cadences prolonged, distorted and interrupted as if being manipulated on tape.

• Mysticism •

At the same time, *Adieu* introduced into Stockhausen's music a feeling of chamber-musical intimacy contrasting with the outward manner of his earlier works for small complements. This new feeling was continued in *Prozession* and then reached its apogee in *Stimmung* (meaning both 'tuning' and 'mood') for six singers (1968), where the performers face each other in a circle and concern themselves solely with the overtones of a low B flat, dwelling on and in this serene harmony for well over an hour. There is thus an extreme stasis, distant indeed from the racing thought of his music in the fifties and early sixties, a radical consequence of moment-form in the long extension of a single moment. On another level *Stimmung* marks a fundamental change in Stockhausen's musical intentions. Whereas before he had always been reluctant to discuss the purpose of his music, *Stimmung* is quite explicitly designed as a spiritual instrument: the text is studded with the names of divinities worshiped in many cultures (Quetzalcoatl, Venus, Osiris, Jesus, Shiva, Buddha, etc.), and Stockhausen's programme-note for the work speaks of it as a 'winged vehicle voyaging to the cosmic and the divine.'

Stockhausen's willingness to regard his music as facilitating a mystical excursion now rapidly gained ground. His next work, *Kurzwellen* (Shortwaves, 1968), is superficially a development from *Prozession*, with the same plus–minus notation for an ensemble using conventional and electronic instruments, but the source material, instead of coming from his own previous output, is taken from shortwave radio receivers, one for each of the four instrumentalists. As in *Hymnen*, only now in live performance, the music lays itself open to accept and use sounds coming from all over the world, and perhaps indeed beyond it: 'it must be possible for something not of this world to find a way through,' Stockhausen writes, 'something that hitherto could not be found by any radio station on this earth. Let us set out to look for it!' And in *Spiral*, for a soloist with a shortwave receiver (1968), the challenge of the distant unknown is similarly paramount, this time encouraging the virtuoso to excel himself in imitating and responding to the sounds that arrive.

Above left: Stockhausen conducting *Spiral*, 1969, a piece for soloist with shortwave receiver, performed here at the Osaka World Fair, 1970. The work combines aleatory qualities with improvisation, since the soloist relies on the sounds transmitted for the basis of his own performance.

Left: Stockhausen's son Markus playing in his father's work *Sirius* in Cologne in 1978.

Above right: Scene from *Inori*, this time an outdoor performance which took place in Athens in 1978.

Also from 1968, the set of pieces *Aus den sieben Tagen* (From the Seven Days) is even less prescriptive of what will be heard, since here there is no musical notation, no specification of what instruments or voices are to be employed, nothing beyond a few lines of prose poetry for each of the fifteen compositions. The text is intended to influence the group-feeling of the ensemble meditating upon it and to stimulate their capacities for intuitive music-making. It would seem, therefore, that *Aus den sieben Tagen* is the end-point of a progressive abandonment of control that Stockhausen found possible through working with his own group, though in fact authorized performances of the pieces appear to have been quite firmly directed by him, and a second set of text compositions, *Für kommende Zeiten* (For Times to Come, 1968-70), begins to reintroduce more specific directions.

Even so, the appearance in 1970 of a score completely written out in conventional notation – Stockhausen's first since *Momente* – was a perplexing surprise. The work was *Mantra* for two pianists, an hour-long structure of variations on a melody of Stockhausen's composition; and this was again a surprising feature, for not since *Formel* for orchestra (1951) had Stockhausen created music that made play with themes. However, *Mantra* also depended on his more recent experience. The title is a clue to the kind of exaltation which a good performance of the work can induce, always repeating the basic mantra, but always extending into new territory. Also, there is an electronic component which Stockhausen uses to give a quite original kind of harmonic enrichment. Each of the pianists is also required to operate a ring modulator, a device which Stockhausen had employed before (notably in *Mikrophonie II*) and which creates from two inputs an output containing only sum and difference frequencies. If the inputs are harmonically related, then the output will be more or less consonant, but if they are not so related then a strident dissonance will result. In *Mantra*, where the piano sound is usually modulated with a stable sine tone, this has the effect of exposing any harmonic excursion from the central pitch of each section; the further the music departs from its home base, the more clangorous it becomes.

Nevertheless, it was not this discovery that Stockhausen went on to explore so much as the techniques of melodic composition and variation. First he created his most spectacular work of improvisatory music, *Sternklang* (Starsound, 1971), for five electronic groups spread around a public park at night, communicating with each other by means of musical signals. Then came *Trans* (also 1971), the transcription of a dream in which the composer saw a body of orchestral strings bathed in magenta light, sustaining dense chords as a curtain to other sounds. But with his next orchestral work, *Inori* (1973-4), he returned to the variation method of *Mantra* and also confirmed the theatrical turn of his thinking, for the piece has one or two mimes performing attitudes of prayer in company with the orchestral sounds.

Below: One of the first rehearsals for 'Michaels Heimkehr' in Cologne in May 1980. 'Michaels Heimkehr' (Michael's Homecoming) is the third act of *Donnerstag*, (Thursday) one of the works forming the sequence that comprises *Licht*, the project that Stockhausen has been working on for the last few years, and that he anticipates will occupy him for some time to come.

• Music drama •

Nearly all of Stockhausen's works since *Inori* have been music dramas of some kind: even *Atmen gibt das Leben . . .* (Breathing Gives Life, 1974), which began as a simple piece for amateur choirs, was developed in 1977 into a 'choral opera'; and *In Freundschaft* (In Friendship, 1977), otherwise a small, straightforward opus for solo instrumentalist, requires the performer to face in particular directions for particular passages. *Herbstmusik* (1974) is more a mime of autumnal pursuits in the country than a musical composition, though from it the composer extracted an appealing duet for clarinet and viola. Similarly, *Musik im Bauch* (Music in the Belly, 1975), a ceremony for six percussionists, was the source for a set of twelve melodies, *Tierkreis* (Zodiac), which were originally written to be contained in musical boxes used by the performers of the parent work.

These melodies in turn became the fundamental material for Stockhausen's most ambitious work of the mid-1970s, *Sirius* (1975-7), being used there to spin the fabric of a synthesized polyphony which proceeds on tape. The live performers – trumpeter, soprano, bass clarinetist and basso profundo – present themselves in futuristic costume as visitors from the star Sirius, come to Earth to celebrate the seasonal, celestial and biological cycles we experience. The tone, as in much of his work of this period, is high-flown and selfconsciously prophetic, but the musical achievement is extraordinary, not least because it depends on compositional techniques quite different from those of Stockhausen's earlier music. Instead of being concerned primarily with new ways of composing sounds and musical structures, in *Sirius*

Left: 'Jahreslauf' (Course of the Year), a scene from *Dienstag* (Tuesday), another music drama in the *Licht* sequence, this one written in 1977 and performed by the Opéra Comique at the Salle Favart in November 1979, with costumes designed by the fashion designer Kenzo. Stockhausen has clearly been influenced on all sorts of levels by his travels to the Far East.

and other works since 1970 he has examined ways of creating, transforming and combining melodies. And though this might seem a much more conventional pursuit, the nature of Stockhausen's melodies, even as far back as *Formel*, is quite distinctive: there is usually great variety of pitch class (most of his melodies are twelve-note), interval and rhythmic figure, and yet a decided modal feeling persists. Furthermore, in *Sirius* particularly, the allusive merging of the four principal melodies into one another is extremely sophisticated.

Soon after completing *Sirius* Stockhausen began work on a very much larger project, again deriving the music from a small group of basic melodies, and again devoting himself as much to text, drama and production as to musical composition. This new project was *Licht* (Light), intended as a sequence of works occupying the seven evenings of a week, a kind of super-*Ring*. First to be completed was *Donnerstag* (Thursday), which centers on Michael, the archangel, and hence more generally the messenger of God to man. The other principal actors in the drama are Lucifer, Michael's archetypal opponent, and Eva, his mother, protectress and lover. Each of the three is personified by a singer (tenor, bass and soprano), an instrumentalist (trumpeter, trombonist and clarinetist) and a dancer, so that the composer has available a variety of levels on which the action may be played out. For example, the central act of *Donnerstag*, 'Michaels Reise um die Erde' (Michael's Journey Round the Earth, 1978), is essentially a trumpet concerto placed between a play with music ('Michaels Jugend') and an oratorio–ritual ('Michaels Heimkehr'), and the variety of musical means and dramatic styles is carried further in *Samstag* (Saturday, 1985) and *Montag* (Monday, 1988).

Stockhausen has said that *Licht* may occupy him through the 1990s, perhaps to the end of his life. Quite clearly his own personal investment in it is huge, though it may not be too far-fetched also to see this great cycle as the descendant not only of Wagner but also of the musical-dramatic works which Varèse dreamed of but never achieved, of *Espace*, with its global performers, and of *The One-All-Alone*, in which the protagonist was to be an individual granted contact with an extra-terrestrial civilization. Exactly like Varèse, Stockhausen continues to travel where none has been before.

Above: Design for the set for 'Michaels Heimkehr' for La Scala, Milan. The whole cycle of *Licht* is based on a very few musical ideas, which are expanded and developed in different ways. This concept of 'variations on a theme' is a feature of Stockhausen's more recent work.

Rock Music in the Seventies

Rock music, depending largely on the same technology as electronic music, has developed alongside it over the last twenty years or so, but with a very different following. The development of the tape recorder and multi-track recording facilities, the various types of synthesizer, and the electric guitar, symbol of seventies rock music, all enabled musical progress and experiment that simply was not possible earlier on. The wide availability of music through records and the media resulted in enormous audiences and a consequential increase in the amount of music written, the number of rock bands, and the diversity of the sounds they produced. Rock fans developed an expectation from their musicians that encouraged them to improve both their technical expertise and their musical invention – a stimulus to groups and soloists alike to expand their repertoires while still maintaining the essential character of the genre. Recording studios offered rock musicians sophisticated facilities, enlarging the scope of possible sound effects and taking rock way beyond the traditions of live blues and rock 'n roll in which it was rooted.

But live rock was equally important. The seventies saw the rapid development of multi-media rock shows, in which visual and theatrical character often established a band's identity more successfully than its music. Most of the visual displays, and particularly the stunning lighting effects, were dependent on complex electronic processes, often linked to the music being performed. Many of the more experimental musicians in the rock field have experience in mainstream electronics, but have directed their output at the much wider rock audience, thereby encouraging in them an appreciation of serious electronic music.

The visual element is clearly also reflected in record sleeve design. Album covers have become a recognized art-form during the last twenty years, developing from straightforward group photos with superimposed lettering to complex designs associated with psychedelia – and a whole range in between that includes realism, surrealism, comic strip and pop art.

Above: The Beatles with the effigies of themselves that were used in the surreal cartoon film *Yellow Submarine* (1969). To describe them merely as a 'rock group' is to underestimate the *Beatles'* diversity and invention; they had the most dramatic influence on the history of rock. Their early numbers assimilate sources from popular American music – blues, rhythm and blues, rock 'n roll – but their film music of the mid-sixties already showed their interest in experimentation. Under the direction of George Martin, and making the fullest use of new studio recording techniques, they expanded the existing musical vocabulary of rock beyond all expectation.

Above: Pink Floyd. Their reputation was based on spectacular multi-media concerts, and they developed their own electronic systems to match. Their 1980 show *The Wall* is perhaps the culmination of their art, with pre-recorded tapes, light shows and special effects, speakers placed around the audience, and the creation of a massive wall on stage.

Below: Emerson, Lake and Palmer. In the early seventies they dominated the field of 'techno-rock.' Emerson especially, a virtuoso organist, combined technical bravado with aggressive showmanship. Their technical and electronic equipment was extremely sophisticated, and they had a serious interest in mainstream music.

Below: sleeve for *Roxy Music*'s record *Manifesto*, released by Polydor in 1979. One of the more bizarre and eccentric groups, *Roxy*'s popularity was at its height around 1972 with the collaboration of the two key figures, Bryan Ferry and Brian Eno. Eno, a synthesizer wizard, used the instrument more for its treatment and sound possibilities than for its keyboard. While some rock musicians approach their music from a 'classical' background, Eno used his rock experience as a basis for his electronic composition and formed his own record company, Obscure Records, which he uses for the minimalist school of avant-garde music, including that of Terry Riley and Steve Reich. He has also maintained his rock output with solo albums and works as a producer.

Left: Sleeve for the *Beatles'* 1967 record *Sergeant Pepper's Lonely Hearts Club Band* – a landmark in rock recording history. A collage of musical styles, ranging from blues and jazz to electronic and Indian music, and including complex orchestral textures, the LP was conceived as a single entity and composed entirely in the recording studio, using the most recent technology (four-track recording tape) and relying for its effect on cutting up and reassembling the tape itself – an innovatory approach which immediately proved extremely influential. The sleeve, with its Pop Art technique and imagery by Peter Blake, established sleeve design as yet another aspect of the total performance.

Above: Tangerine Dream, a German group whose original line-up in the early seventies performed almost entirely improvised electronic music; vocals were conspicuously absent, and have been in all albums but one. The group approached the rock idiom from a background of avant-garde electronic music, and their serious interest is reflected in the scale and concept of their work. They have given concerts in several cathedrals, whose lofty architecture enhances their performances.

Below: Yes, another technically brilliant British band with classic roots; their compositions range from mainline to rock music – a diversity that for some time hindered their acceptance in the world of rock, but which worked in their favor once the brilliance of their work was recognized. They are now acknowledged (together with *Emerson, Lake and Palmer*) as among the prime exponents of 'flash' or 'techno' rock, with Rick Wakeman rivaling Emerson in his outstanding keyboard techniques.

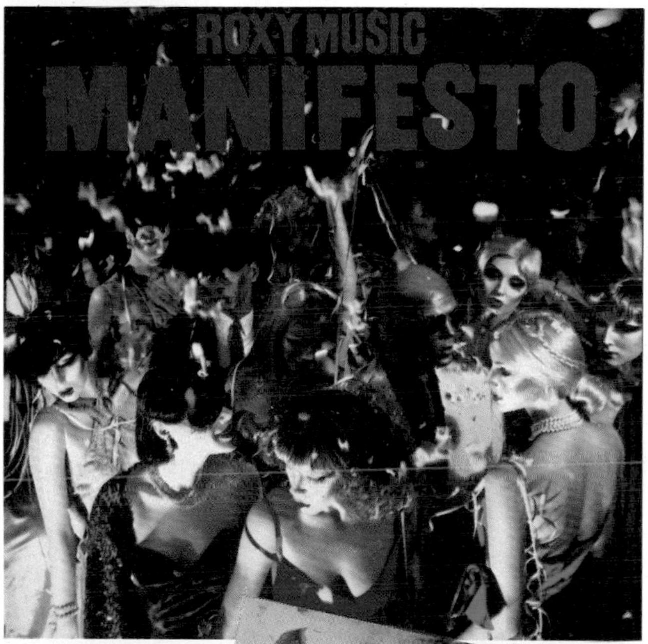

Above: Sleeve of *Yes*'s record *Tormato*. Earlier *Yes* covers featured romantic or surrealist landscapes or made use of their particular logo, developed by Roger Dean, a designer with a fine-art background. Members of many bands have had art-school training and involve themselves with the design of the sleeve as an integral part of the image.

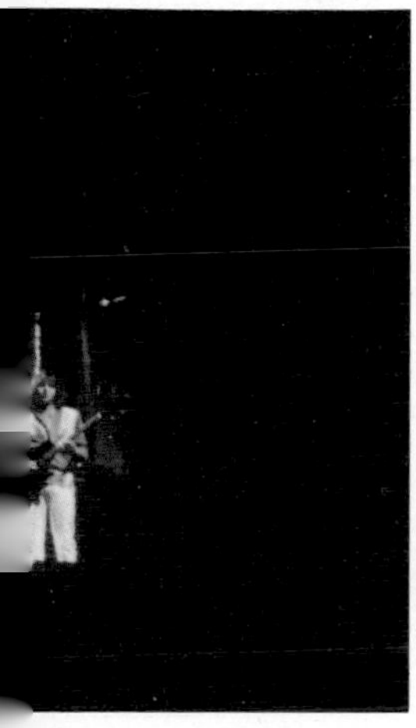

Above: Genesis. The early reputation of the group was based largely on their stage appearance, with flamboyant and outrageous star Peter Gabriel taking the limelight within the group's visual and theatrical performances. Gabriel's departure from the band in 1975 heralded the group's demise in the eyes of the critics, but *Genesis* remained as popular as ever, possibly more so. It is a feature of rock bands that musicians come and go, often leaving one band to join another, so there is a continual cross-fertilization, though generally one or two lead musicians establish a group's identity in musical terms.

Above: Mike Oldfield, whose first album, *Tubular Bells*, released in 1973, brought him instant success. Its popularity increased when it was used as incidental music for the film *The Exorcist*. Oldfield is unusual in that his live performances are extremely rare and he concentrates almost entirely on studio compositions. In *Tubular Bells*, a continuous 50-minute piece, Oldfield used multitrack equipment to overdub virtually all the different instruments played. It was later orchestrated by his colleague the composer David Bedford, and Oldfield has featured on two of Bedford's records.

Above: Crosby, Stills and Nash. These three musicians all brought to the group considerable performing experience from earlier well-established rock bands – the *Byrds*, *Buffalo Springfield* and the *Hollies*. Their first album made them famous almost overnight, and their distinctive sound, particularly Crosby and Nash's harmony singing, made an immediate impact on American rock fans; but this first album was perhaps their most successful, and even the addition to the group in 1969 of guitarist Neil Young (seen with them in this photograph), a fine musician who made brilliant contributions to their performances, did not consolidate their original success, although they still had a following. However, success merely in terms of album sales was not necessarily what they were aiming for – they have always stressed that they should not be thought of as a group or single entity, but rather as individual musicians who work together but are free to go their separate ways. The title of their third album, *Four Way Street*, hinted at this independence, and the group disbanded soon after its release in 1971, though they have had one or two reunions since.

Below: One of the features experimented with by Keith Emerson was feedback, the sound produced when an electronic instrument picks up its own sound from a loudspeaker. The resulting sustained note can be manipulated by using amplifiers, a technique Emerson applied to the electric organ. In the course of his more outrageous performances he has been known to mistreat the instrument grossly, plunging daggers into it and causing it to crash onto the stage. Emerson was also one of the first to use the Moog synthesizer in live performances.

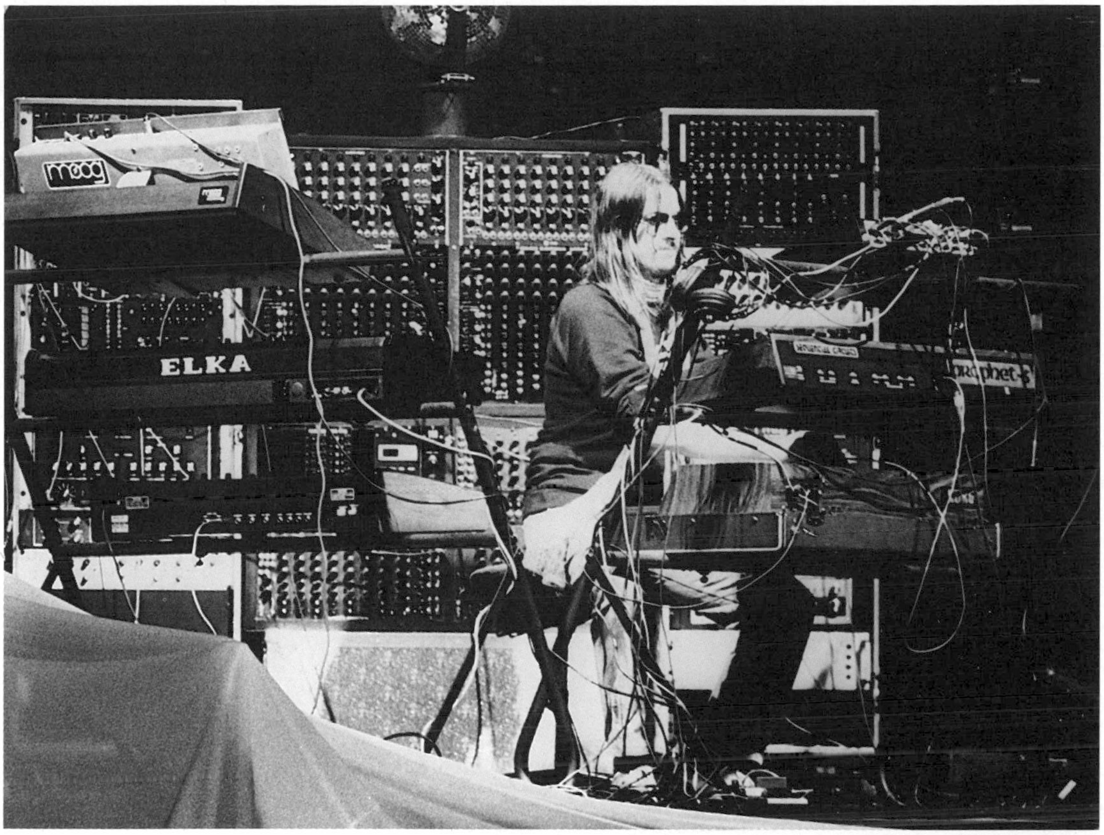

Below: Kraftwerk; the name, meaning 'electrical power plant,' reflects the German group's industrial background and the mechanistic quality of much of their work. Strongly influenced by Stockhausen, Terry Riley and John Cage, as well as *Pink Floyd*, the group's two founder-members, Ralf Hutter and Florian Schneider, left their traditional music studies to build their own studio in Düsseldorf, where they now do all their own recording. The titles of their albums, *Autobahn*, *Radio-Activity*, *Computerworld*, indicate their area of interest, and they are widely respected for their electronic music, while attracting a rock audience as well.

Above: Some of *Tangerine Dream*'s electronic equipment. Edgar Froese and Christoph Franke, who originated the band, both come from West Germany. In 1980 the group gave two performances in East Berlin, apparently the first western rock band to have given a concert in East Germany.

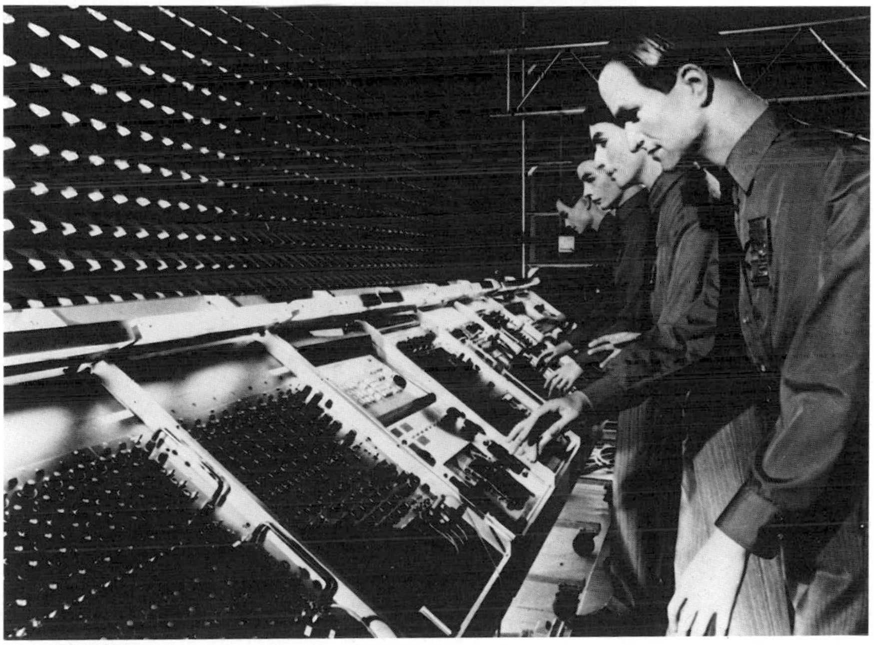

Left: Orchestral Manoeuvres in the Dark, a more recently formed band from Liverpool who issued their first album in 1979. Founder members Andy McClusky and Paul Humphreys had formerly worked together under various different titles including *Id* and *Dalek I Love You*. Both fostered an interest in German groups such as *Can*, *Tangerine Dream* and *Kraftwerk*, with their avant-garde electroacoustic qualities; Humphreys took a course in electrical engineering, and they have equipped their own recording studio, 'The Gramophone Suite,' in Liverpool.

ELECTROACOUSTIC MUSIC

RICHARD ORTON

Opposite: Actions de Lumière et du Son, a 'polytope' by Iannis Xenakis, at the Thermes de Cluny, December 1973. Xenakis's music involves the handling of very large numbers of different elements – hence his term 'stochastic' – he used a computer not to create sounds but to simplify the musical 'arithmetic.' His early training was as an architect, and he worked closely with Le Corbusier on the Philips Pavilion designed for the Brussels World Fair of 1958. His composition, like his architecture, is closely based on theory.

In a remarkably prophetic passage from *The New Atlantis* (1626), Francis Bacon wrote: 'We have also sound-houses, where we practise and demonstrate all sounds, and their generation. We have harmonies which you have not, of quarter-sounds, and lesser slides of sounds. Divers instruments of music likewise to you unknown, some sweeter than you have; together with bells and rings that are dainty and sweet. We represent small sounds as great and deep; likewise great sounds extenuate and sharp; we make divers tremblings and warblings of sounds, which in their original are entire. We represent and imitate all articulate sounds and letters, and the voices and notes of beasts and birds. We have certain helps which set to the ear do further the hearing greatly. We have also divers strange and artificial echoes, reflecting the voice many times, and as it were tossing it: and some that give back the voice louder than it came; some shriller, and some deeper; yea, some rendering the voice differing in the letters or articulate sound from that they receive. We have also means to convey sounds in trunks and pipes, in strange lines and distances.'

Bacon might have been describing the electroacoustic music studio of today. Any sound that can be recorded or expressed mathematically can be created or analyzed; new harmonies can be constructed; new instruments have been created; large sounds can be fragmented, or filtered to become 'extenuate and sharp'; the microphone, loudspeaker and earphones do indeed 'further the hearing greatly,' and there are many ways of conveying sounds through space.

It seems curious to us today that sound recording initially took place without electricity, in the 'talking machines' of the late nineteenth century. Here a needle attached to a membrane traced an acoustic pattern – usually a human voice speaking into a tube – on a hand-rotated waxed cylinder. At about the same time Alexander Graham Bell succeeded in transmitting sounds along a wire by means of electromagnetic induction – the first telephone. Important here was the principle of converting the patterns of air pressure that we perceive as sound into analogous modulations of electrical current which can be transmitted virtually intact over considerable distances. The converse effect, of changing such electrical patterns into acoustic energy, was achieved in the development of the moving-coil loudspeaker, which did not, however, become generally available until about 1926. Another very important step in this chain of technology was the invention, by Lee De Forest in 1906, of the triode valve, which made possible electrical amplification of audio signals.

The most important figure in the prehistory of electroacoustic music must be Thaddeus Cahill, a New York lawyer and inventor, who between 1892 and 1907 developed an amazing musical instrument, the Telharmonium. This was, in effect, the first multiple-keyboard electronic music synthesizer. It had a frequency range of nearly seven octaves, far better than the acoustic recordings of the time. Its electrical apparatus was vast: it weighed about two hundred tons. Its circuits could produce pitches with considerable accuracy, permitting tuning systems other than that of duodecimal equal temperament. It was installed in a building on Broadway, in New York City, called 'Telharmonic Hall,' and a company was set up to administer regular programs for audiences visiting the hall, or subscribers to a telephone circuit who could then hear the performances from their homes. The repertory was in general rather staid, however – Bach, Gounod and Rossini.

In the twenties and thirties a number of electroacoustic instruments for live performance were invented, of which the Hammond organ and the *ondes Martenot* have been the longest surviving. Both have become accepted by successive generations of composers, the variable timbre of the Hammond's drawbar system finding a function as a kind of live-performance synthesizer by the avant garde, and the *ondes Martenot* being included in many works by a wide range of composers, Hindemith, Varèse and Messiaen among them. In Germany the first magnetic tape recorders were developed before the Second World War, but it was not until after the war that these became commercially available and catalyzed the rapid postwar development of electroacoustic music.

It was evidently an idea whose time had come. In October 1948 Pierre Schaeffer, a French radio engineer, broadcast a 'Concert de bruits' (Concert of noises) with five studies in *musique concrète* ('objective' music), including one on the sounds of railway trains and the *Etude aux casseroles*, in which the sound sources were saucepans, canal boats, voices, harmonicas and a piano. Astonishingly, he assembled these compositions, and indeed all his works until 1951, using disk recordings. The most noticeable technical feature is the closed groove, which allows an isolated sound object or one of its fragments to be repeated over and over again as the stylus keeps to the same circular path on the disk. Apart from this hallmark, the compositions are assemblages of what Schaeffer came to call *objets musicaux* (or, later, *objets sonores*).

The young composer Pierre Henry joined Schaeffer in 1949, and they produced together the *Symphonie pour un homme seul* in the following year. That this is a more ambitious work can be seen in its length – twenty-two minutes; its form – it comprises eleven distinct sections or 'movements'; the increased variety of its textures and sound-sources; and also its human, personal associations – for example, the heartbeat – as well as the more mechanical sounds of Schaeffer's previous work. In 1951 Radio-Télévision Française established the first studio designed solely for electroacoustic composition, with Schaeffer at its head. They acquired tape recorders as well as special equipment devised by the engineer Jacques Poullin, for creating the illusion of sounds moving across the space between two loudspeakers, for giving repeated echo-signals to generate artificial reverberation, and for playing tape loops at different speeds.

The compositional output of Pierre Henry began rapidly to outstrip that of the studio's founder. Before he left in 1958 to found the Studio Apsome, Henry composed over sixty electroacoustic works, of which the collection, *Le Microphone bien tempéré* (The Well-tempered Microphone, 1951), and *Le Voile d'Orphée* (The Veil of Orpheus, 1953) are probably best known. The latter work was extracted from a further Schaeffer–Henry collaboration, the opera *Orphée*, for tape and two singers, which appeared in a first version in 1951 but was revised and extended, with the addition of violin and harpsichord, in 1953. Although Schaeffer's compositional output began to fall off, his importance in establishing the theoretical and esthetic basis for the new medium should not be underestimated. His first book, *A la recherche d'une musique concrète* (In Search of a Concrete Music, 1952) recounts the early months of his work in the form of diaries of events as they happened, while in the later sections he seeks to establish a *solfège*, or scale, of musical objects drawn from the 'real,' concrete world.

Below: Pierre Schaeffer. His impact on the musical public has been largely through didactic effort. His background is technical rather than musical – he trained as a telecommunications engineer, working originally for French Radio. He was one of the first to experiment with electronic music in the late forties, coining the phrase *musique concrète* to describe assemblages of recorded sound. He established the 'Club d'essai' in 1951, which became the 'Groupe de recherches musicales' in 1958.

Right: John Cage surrounded by a student audience in the open air. Cage has been at the forefront of American avant-garde music for several decades. He is renowned as a protagonist of aleatory music, where the element of chance supersedes normal musical conventions and the composer has little control over the eventual sound produced.

• Cologne and New York •

While Schaeffer was concentrating on *musique concrète* a very different orientation was developing in Germany. Werner Meyer-Eppler, a physicist who became director of the Institute of Phonetics at Bonn University, had published a book, *Electronic Tone Generation: Electronic Music and Synthetic Speech*, in 1949. The term 'electronic music' here meant any music that could be produced on electronic instruments. He followed this with experiments and practical demonstrations using a 'melochord' invented by Harald Bode and a tape recorder; and in 1951 he joined with Robert Beyer of the Northwest German Radio and Herbert Eimert in presenting a radio program entitled 'The World of Sound of Electronic Music.' As a direct result, an electronic music studio was set up in the Cologne radio station under the direction of Herbert Eimert, becoming fully operational in 1953.

Two years later, Eimert wrote of 'the birth of electronic music.' He saw that through sine-wave synthesis new electronic timbres could be constructed and related to each other in an extension of the principles of Webern's serial composition. He outlined the equipment used in making those constructions and classified electronic sound into six categories: the sine tone; the single note (assembled from several sine tones in harmonic relationship); the note-mixture (assembled from sine tones in non-harmonic relationship); noise; and sound-complexes (by which he meant 'chords'); and the impulse, or click.

Below: Vladimir Ussachevsky with the RCA Mark II electronic music synthesizer – the only one of its kind. Born in Russia, Ussachevsky arrived in the United States in 1930. In 1959 he co-established, with Otto Luening and Milton Babbitt, the Columbia–Princeton Electronic Music Center. He is known primarily for his transformation of existing sound rather than for the production of purely electronic sound.

Eimert claimed that the first compositions of 'real' electronic music, drawn purely from electronic machines, were performed in a concert on Cologne Radio on 19 October 1954. It included his own works together with others by Karlheinz Stockhausen and the Belgian composer Karel Goeyvaerts. Stockhausen's *Studie I*, his first work created in the Cologne studio, was the most developed of these compositions. It is constructed from sine waves alone, the purest of electronic sounds, and the elements of pitch, density, loudness and duration are all serially ordered. It lasts nine and a half minutes and gives a gently transparent effect, the clarity of the middle and upper frequencies dominating the sound-picture. Harmonies close to what we would anachronistically call the augmented triad – of neutral tonality – abound. Stockhausen devised a way of notating these sounds,

which he refined and developed for his next piece, *Studie II* (1954), published by Universal Edition – the first score of electronic music.

Meanwhile, in 1951 in New York, John Cage had set up a project, 'Music for Magnetic Tape,' with fellow composers Earle Brown, Morton Feldman and Christian Wolff, with the help of Louis and Bebe Barron, who had established a private experimental recording studio. The first result of the project was Cage's *Imaginary Landscape no.5*, a four-minute piece completed in January 1952. The score, composed by a method of chance operations derived from the Chinese *Book of Changes* (*I Ching*), contained instructions for splicing together recordings of various durations taken from any forty-two gramophone records. In 1959 Cage wrote: 'The chief technical contribution of my work with tape is in the method of splicing, that is, of cutting the material in a way that affects the attack and decay of sounds recorded. By this method I have attempted to mitigate the purely mechanical effect of electronic vibration in order to heighten the unique element of individual sounds, releasing their delicacy, strength and special characteristics, and also to introduce at times complete transformation of the original materials to create new ones.'

Another four-minute composition, *Williams Mix* (1952), followed. This was an extremely labor-intensive work, requiring nine months of painstaking splicing and editing by the members of the project, for approximately six hundred recordings were used, divided into six categories: city sounds; country sounds; electronic sounds; manually produced sounds, including the playing of musical instruments; wind-produced sounds, including the voice; and small, heavily amplified sounds.

The other composers of the group each completed a work. Earle Brown's *Octet I* (1953) for eight loudspeakers used as its source material the off-cut pieces of tape from Cage's *Williams Mix*, and is an informal, energetic work lasting three and a half minutes. Wolff's *For Magnetic Tape* and Feldman's *Intersection* were also completed in 1953. Although the project concluded with these works, John Cage went on to further involvement with electroacoustic music, and, from 1960 on, continued work with 'live electronic music.'

Elsewhere in New York, and quite independently of Cage's project, a more cautious, even academic approach was beginning. Vladimir Ussachevsky was placed in charge of an Ampex professional tape recorder when, in 1951, it was purchased for the recording of concerts at Columbia University. He realized that it could also be used as an instrument of sound transformation and prepared some experiments which he presented in a concert in May 1952. These first experiments, *Transposition*, *Reverberation*, *Experiment*, *Composition* and *Underwater Waltz*, totaled about nine minutes. *Transposition* is a study made from the lowest note on the pianoforte, recorded and transformed by the octave transpositions achieved by changing the speed of the tape. Repeated transpositions enabled Ussachevsky to obtain a range of sounds from a high hiss to a low resonance below the piano's range. *Reverberation* treats the identical material to 'head reverberation' derived from feeding back the sound from the playback head to the record head of the tape recorder. The other pieces arrange such materials and transformations into little musical structures.

During the summer of 1952 Ussachevsky was joined in further experiments and compositions by his colleague at Columbia, Otto Luening, and together they assembled a group of four works for tape recorder which were included in a concert of contemporary music organized by Leopold Stokowski in the Museum of Modern Art, New York, on 28 October 1952. The works were Ussachevsky's *Sonic Contours* and Luening's *Low Speed*, *Invention* and *Fantasy in Space*. *Sonic Contours* used the piano again as its main sound-source, creating deep gong-like sounds, bells and sustained clusters. *Fantasy in Space* and *Low Speed* used Luening's flute improvisations, with speed change and added reverberation. *Invention* was a con-

Opposite: Luciano Berio at the Studio di Fonologia in Milan in the 1950s. One of the most active of Italian composers, he is also renowned as a conductor. His interest in electrical music led him to persuade Milan Radio to set up, with Bruno Maderna, the first Italian electronic music studio, which he directed until 1961, when he moved to the USA. He was later appointed to the board of IRCAM by Pierre Boulez.

trapuntal work based on a twelve-note row. A review of the concert in the *New York Herald Tribune* ran: 'It has been a long time in coming, but music and the machine are now wed . . . The result is as nothing encountered before. It is the music of fevered dreams, of sensations, called back from the dim past. It is the sound of echo . . . It is vaporous, tantalizing, cushioned. It is in the room and yet not part of it. It is something entirely new. And genesis cannot be described.'

• In the sound studio •

The four groups described – those of Schaeffer, Eimert, Cage and Ussachevsky – are now regarded as having spearheaded activities in electroacoustic music in the early 1950s. Though these turned out to be the most influential, there were, of course, many other artists turning to the possibilities of the new electronic medium. It might even seem that the arrival of the tape recorder only focused attention on developments that were already under way a decade or more earlier. Experiments with film sound-tracks, variable-speed phonographs, and audio-frequency oscillators were certainly undertaken long before the tape recorder appeared on the scene. But it was the ease of sound editing and manipulation of the tape medium that led so many more artists to begin working with these materials.

Moreover, the early ideological division between *musique concrète* and *elektronische Musik* – the one approaching the medium from the recorded sound-object, the other from an abstract compositional principle applied to the control of electronic sound generators – did not maintain its force for long, for in 1955-6 Stockhausen, working in Cologne, produced his *Gesang der Jünglinge*, which utilized a recording of a boy's voice as well as electronic sounds. It became clear that this combination of both recorded and generated sound was a considerable enrichment of resources, and the arguments for the purist approach on either side began to seem rather petty. In practice, the studios that followed amalgamated both the recording technology and also equipment for generating and processing electronic sound, and these, in the light of subsequent developments, became known as 'classical' studios.

It should be emphasized that there are many 'correct' ways to compose a sonic structure in the electronic music studio, but let us take as an example Stockhausen's *Gesang der Jünglinge*. The recorded text, extracted from the Apocrypha to the Book of Daniel, Chapter 3, was sung by a boy. It is the story of the three young men in the fiery furnace, chosen as a parable for the three young composers – Boulez, Nono and Stockhausen himself – under critical fire! In the work certain words of praise are clearly heard and are used as a kind of refrain. However, for much of the rest of the work, the words were cut up, and the individual sound fragments (phones) permutated. Thus, from *jubelt* (rejoice) we also get *telbju*, *lebtuj*, and *blujet*. As Stockhausen remarked, 'The gap between musical sense and word sense is continually variable in the same way as is the relationship between sound and phones; certain permutations allow the sense of the words to come through, even though certain phones are interchanged and so not in their "most meaningful" positions.' The single elements of language Stockhausen then related to the electronic sound elements – a single vowel became a part of the series of harmonic spectra, the simple voiceless consonant an element in the series of 'noises.'

To organize the electronic sounds Stockhausen devised eleven categories: sine tones; sine tones fluctuating in pitch periodically, or 'statistically' (i.e. randomly); sine tones fluctuating in amplitude periodically, or statistically; sine tones fluctuating in both pitch and amplitude periodically, or statistically; filtered white noise of constant density, or of statistically varying density; regular, or irregular filtered noise 'clicks.' To produce some of the more 'statistical' (random, or aleatory) sonic events, unusual tactics were devised. Stockhausen describes how one such event of twenty seconds' duration was made: 'I sat in the studio with two collaborators. Two of us were handling knobs: with one hand, one of us controlled the levels and, with the other hand, the speed of pulses from a pulse generator which were fed

Below: Watcher, 1965, by James Seawright, a kinetic sculpture with a feedback loop – the light display is translated into a bagpipe's skirling sound.

Bottom: Laszlo Moholy-Nagy's *Light Space Modulator*, 1922-30, operated by an electric motor and the precursor of recent electronic sculpture.

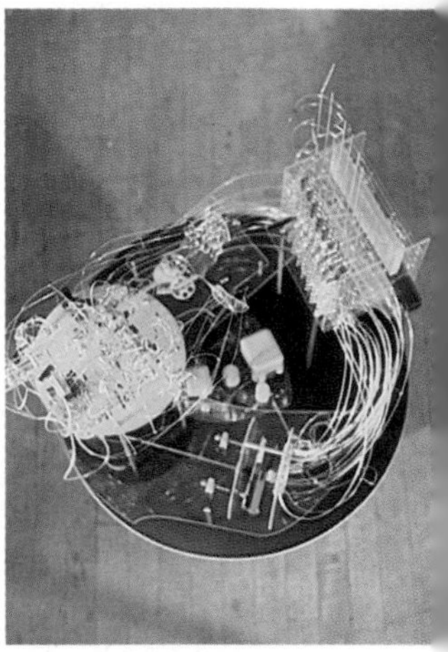

Below: Seawright's *Tetra*, 1966, a set of four electronically connected spoked wheels, which vibrate to produce a singing sound. Seawright worked with Ussachevsky and Moog at the Columbia–Princeton Electronic Music Center, and many of his sculptures have a musical dimension in that they emit, or react to, sound.

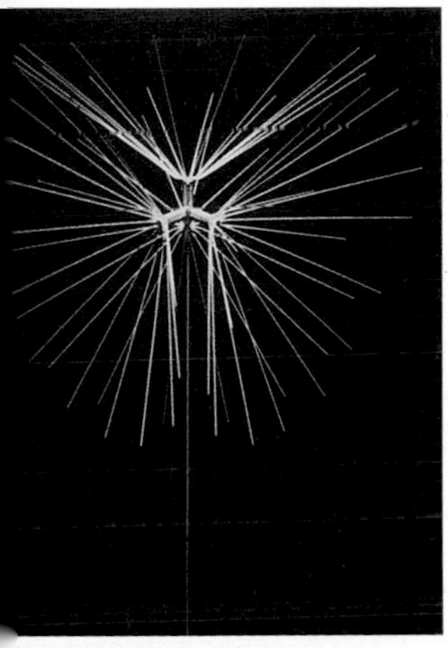

into an electric filter; a second musician had a knob for the levels and another for the frequency of the filter; and the third one would manipulate a potentiometer to draw the envelope – the shape of the whole event – and also record it. I had drawn curves – for example, up down, up-down up-down up-down, up, which had to be followed with the movement of a knob (let's say for loudness) for the twenty-second duration. And during these twenty seconds, another musician had to move the knob for the frequency of the pulses from four to sixteen pulses per second in an irregular curve that I'd drawn on the paper. And the third musician had to move the knob for the frequency of the filter following a third curve.

'So, everyone had a paper on which the different curves were drawn. We said, "Three, two, one, zero," started a stopwatch . . . we'd all do our curves, individually produce one sound layer which was the product of our movements; and this resulted in an aleatoric layer of individual pulses which, in general, speeded up statistically. But you could never at a certain moment say, "*This* pulse will now come with *that* pitch." This was impossible to predetermine. Then we'd make a second, third, fourth, fifth layer – the number of layers was also determined – and I'd synchronize them all together and obtain a new sound. At that time I very often used the image of a *swarm* of bees to describe such a process. You can't say how many bees are in the swarm, but you can see how big or how dense the swarm is, and what envelope it has.'

Above: Mixing panel of the Moog Synthesizer at the Columbia-Princeton Music Center. Robert Moog, who started designing electronic synthesizers in 1954, has worked with Tudor, Cage and Ussachevsky.

Gesang der Jünglinge was originally composed for six loudspeakers or loudspeaker groups placed around and above the listeners. The spatial element is an integral part of the composition, but it has become best known in the stereophonic reduction for gramophone recordings; even here it is a powerful acoustical experience. For broadcasting on the radio back in 1956, Stockhausen had to be content with a mix-down to a single channel.

A piece which similarly fragmented a recording of a voice and restructured the sounds is Luciano Berio's *Thema: Omaggio a Joyce*, made in the Milan studio of Radio Audiozione Italiane (RAI) in 1959. Here the sole sound-material is the voice of Cathy Berberian reading, in English, French and Italian, a passage from James Joyce's *Ulysses*. Berio relates the sonic transformations within the work to three categories of articulation he found in the original material. These articulations are 'discontinuous,' as in 'Goodgod, he never heard inall'; continuous, as in the elongated sibilants of 'Pearls: when she. Liszt's rhapsodies. Hissss'; and periodic, as in 'thnthnthnthn.' All transformations in this work were accomplished by tape editing, superimposition, transpositions and filtering. It was Berio's aim to establish a new relationship between speech and music by effecting a continuous metamorphosis from one to the other.

Henry Pousseur, the Belgian composer, produced *Scambi* (Exchanges), a piece original in form, during two months in Milan in 1957. Its primary sound-source was white noise – the result, Pousseur tells us, of seeking the most asymmetric sound material in order to demonstrate at the level of microstructure those unpredictable properties which he and his colleagues had been composing into their musical structures. He made use of a special device, an amplitude gate, which triggered whenever the amplitude of the continually fluctuating levels of the white noise reached a certain peak. However, instead of making a fixed composition on tape, he produced instead raw compositional materials and instructions which could be further developed, transformed and superimposed in an infinite number of ways. Pousseur himself made two realizations in fixed forms, one six minutes long, the other three minutes; Berio also made two, and other composers have made versions. This solution to an 'open form' concept was the first in the tape medium.

John Cage spent four successful months in Milan in 1958. Not only did he make a new tape composition, *Fontana Mix* (named after his landlady Signora Fontana, as *Williams Mix* had been named after his sponsor Paul Williams), but he also won a large prize of five million lire in a series of television quiz shows, 'Lascia o Raddoppia' (Double or Quits), answering questions on mushrooms. *Fontana Mix*, even more than its predecessors in Cage's tape output, creates an impression of sensory overload. 'Meaningful' sounds flash by at a tremendous rate, like a heightened form of Bergson's 'stream of consciousness.'

Edgard Varèse had predicted the coming importance of electronics for music in the 1930s. For him the tape recorder arrived almost too late; certainly his late electronic works were preceded by a long compositional silence. In two late works, however, he showed himself to be a natural composer for the medium, utilizing both recorded and synthesized sound. *Déserts* (1954) successfully symbolizes not merely deserts of the earth but also the deserts of the mind in a technological world. Sounds of machinery collaged with organ sounds and those reminiscent of human screaming powerfully invoke an industrial desert in which the human being struggles for meaning. And Varèse's last major work, *Poème électronique*, has become a classic of tape music; the spatial design of this work for four hundred loudspeakers and four-channel tape is evident even from the reduction to stereo of the gramophone recording.

Stockhausen's *Kontakte* (1960) represents a peak of classical-studio technique, and is also an early example of the combination of instrumental and tape sound. In the electronic tape Stockhausen was most interested in exploring the perceptual ambiguities that can arise when repeated clicks occur so rapidly that they begin to create a new tone. For *Kontakte* he also devised a new technique, in which already synthesized material is played through a specially constructed revolving loudspeaker and the result is re-recorded on four microphones placed at cardinal points around it. In this way he achieved what he called 'floodsound,' derived from spinning the loudspeaker at high speed. The 'contacts' of the title are those between the known sounds of the piano and percussion on the one hand and those of the 'unknown' tape sounds on the other.

The development of the voltage-control synthesizer in the 1960s meant that electronic devices could be interconnected much more easily and in many more ways than previously, and it led to a tremendous increase in the number of electronic music studios. Most audio devices for the production of electronic sound have dials, knobs or switches to control their operation. For example, an oscillator may have a dial for selecting its frequency (pitch), a knob for controlling its amplitude (loudness), and a series of switches for selecting a waveform, which gives its timbre. By making a number of these manual controls susceptible to voltage control, many more devices can be controlled from a single source. Devices can also be cascaded: one oscillator can be controlling another while in turn being controlled by a third. The six-handed operation necessary to assemble a single sound event of *Gesang der Jünglinge* becomes relatively simple with voltage-controlled equipment.

It was soon realized that a collection of devices, each with one or more control inputs and outputs as well as signal outputs, could be assembled into a comprehensive instrument for the production and treatment of electronic sound. This was achieved in the early 1960s virtually simultaneously by two American designers, Robert Moog and Donald Buchla, and their instruments were called 'modular synthesizers.' These were produced in a range of sizes; the largest were very complex to operate

Right: François Bayle, photographed in January 1980.

Far right: Iannis Xenakis in his study.

Below: Electronic circuit. With the development of microchip technology, the flexibility of electronic media has greatly increased. This printed circuit clearly demonstrates the technological development since 1959, the year of the RCA Mark II synthesizer (*see p.297*).

but permitted a tremendous range of sounds and possibilities for control.

As well as allowing instruments such as oscillators to control themselves, as it were, by cascading, it was necessary to develop a means of applying manual direction to sources of voltage control. The two most popular appeared very early on. One is an ordinary piano-style keyboard which supplies an appropriate voltage according to the location of the key depressed. The other is a 'linear controller,' a special strip above a contact plate; when the finger presses the strip against the plate, the position of contact determines the voltage that is sent to the device being controlled. Another electronic device that followed shortly was the sequencer, which supplies a series or possibly several series of pre set control voltages and runs through them cyclically.

Good examples of the creative use of the voltage-control synthesizer and sequencer are provided by the Californian composer Morton Subotnick (b.1933), using a Buchla system. In *Silver Apples of the Moon*, commissioned by Nonesuch Records, *ostinato* patterns produced by the sequencer create a delicate lattice of sounds in which percussive elements alternate with bell like melodies. Textures gradually emerge, rise to a climax and recede. Throughout his electroacoustic work, Subotnick has paid great attention to timbral nuance. More recently his works have evolved from the use of what he calls 'ghost tapes,' tapes pre-recorded with audio signals which are not heard as such, but which are used instead as control signals for a bank of synthesizer equipment, permitting sophisticated simultaneous control over many instruments.

Towards the end of the 1960s some adventurous pop groups (Pink Floyd, Tangerine Dream) began to use synthesizers. Since then there has been a trend toward developing synthesizers as performance instruments rather than for studio use, and in some ways the use of the devices has become more conservative; they appear more like sophisticated electronic organs than instruments capable of creating radically new sounds or sound processes.

• Live performance •

In the 1950s many commentators had reported how uncomfortable they felt at an auditorium 'performance' of tape music, staring at loudspeakers with complex and perhaps disturbing sound surrounding them. At least if a live performer were involved in making the sounds it was felt there would be some clearly human contact. John Cage was again at the forefront of such developments. In 1960 he composed *Cartridge Music* for amplified 'small sounds.' In this work materials are provided which permit a performer to determine when and how to insert, use or remove certain objects from gramophone cartridges; or alternatively when and how to manipulate amplifiers or other electronic sounds. The piece thus relies entirely on the amplification of 'small,' otherwise inaudible, sounds. Later, contact microphones became available. These are devices which amplify vibrations in solid objects (as opposed to normal microphones, which pick up vibrations in the air). These effectively replaced the use to which Cage put the cartridges in *Cartridge Music*, and they were subsequently used by many composers for live electronic performance in the 1960s and beyond.

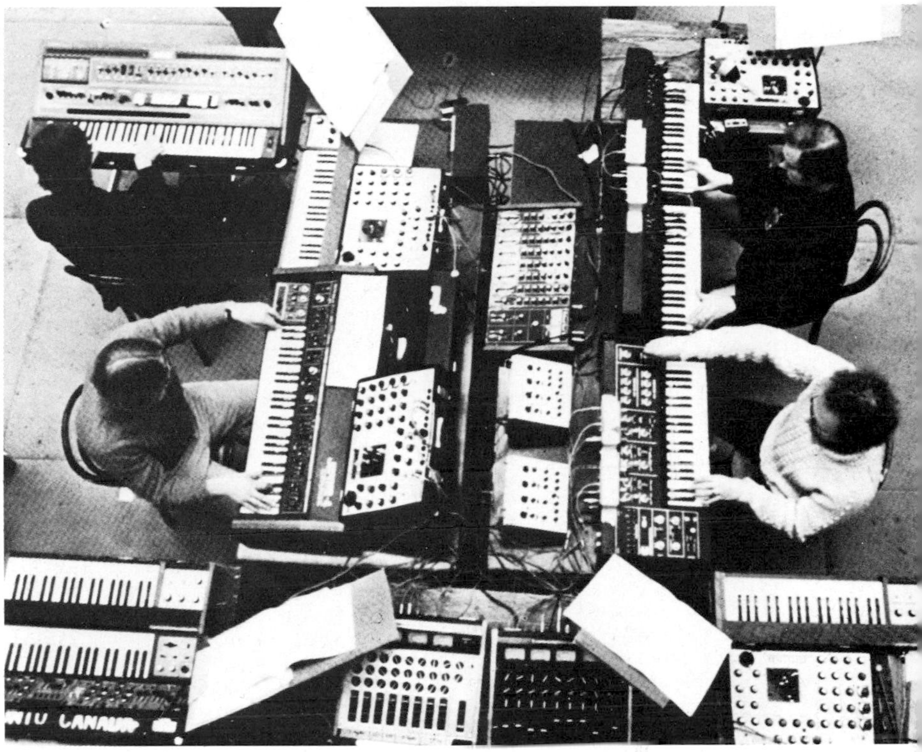

Above: The Canadian Electronic Ensemble, who use a minimum of four keyboards in the performance of their work.

Another seminal live electronic work was Stockhausen's *Mikrophonie I* (1964). In this work a large tam-tam is used as a resonator and source for aural exploration by moving microphones across its surface in prescribed ways, the sounds being further treated by filters and potentiometers before they are heard in the loudspeakers. Six performers are used; two to activate the tam-tam with a variety of auxiliary instruments, two to manipulate the microphone, and two to operate the filters and potentiometers. *Mikrophonie II* (1965) ring-modulates (that is, distorts and transforms) the sounds of a chorus with a Hammond Organ. Stockhausen also uses ring modulators in *Mixtur* (1964) to transform the sounds of an orchestra. Here forty-eight microphones are used to input the sounds to the ring modulators, and sine-wave oscillators are used as auxiliary inputs.

With the intense concentration on live electronic performance in the sixties and seventies, it was perhaps natural that musicians formed groups to pool their resources. In America the most significant was undoubtedly the Sonic Arts Union, comprising Robert Ashley, David Behrman, Alvin Lucier and Gordon Mumma. Robert Ashley's *The Wolfman* (1964) employs a tape to accompany a voice amplified so highly that the feedback generated between loud-

Above: Stockhausen directing a performance of *Sirius* at the open-air festival in Aix-en-Provence in 1977.

speaker and microphone can be modulated by the vocalist's mouth cavities. Gordon Mumma designed his own circuits, and it is important to recognize that in electronic music the equipment configuration or the circuit design had been an integral part of the creative process, as important as a composer's choice of medium (piano, string quartet or orchestra) is in conventional music. In Mumma's *Hornpipe* (1967) a solo French horn plays alone for a definite but unknowable duration while the electronic circuits are building up information on the resonance-response of the auditorium in which the piece is played. At a certain point the circuits become 'saturated,' and from this moment the piece becomes a polyphony of horn with electronic sound, resulting from the synergy of the electroacoustic environment.

Alvin Lucier is perhaps the most original of the four. His *Music for Solo Performer* (1965) employs electroencephalograph (EEG) electrodes which are attached to the performer's scalp. With eyes closed, the performer can learn to produce low-frequency brain waves known as 'alpha' waves, which disappear when there is any form of visual activity in the brain. A low-frequency bandpass filter permits the amplification of these waves and no others. Lucier wrote: 'I realized the value of the EEG situation as a theater element and knew from experience that live sounds are more interesting than taped ones. I was also touched by the image of the immobile if not paralyzed human being who, by merely changing states of visual attention, can activate a large configuration of communication equipment with what appears to be power from a spiritual realm. I found the alpha's quiet thunder extremely beautiful and instead of spoiling it by processing, chose to use it as an active force in the same way one uses the power of a river.' The low frequencies produced by the alpha waves through the loudspeakers were used to resonate percussion instruments placed adjacent to them: cymbals, gongs, bass drums, timpani and packing cases or cardboard boxes. By varying the duration of alpha bursts, and by channeling and mixing the sounds, Lucier was able to achieve a wide variety of sonorities.

Another Lucier work, *Vespers* (1968), employs special echo-location devices known as Sondols, developed originally for use by the blind. These are highly directional gun-like electronic instruments that project beams of intense click-sounds into the auditorium. The frequency of the clicks can be varied very simply by the operator. The four performers enter the darkened auditorium from different sides. By listening carefully to the quality of the echoes from the clicks from their four Sondols, and by pointing them in different directions, the performers build up a quasi-visual mental picture of the space from the auditory image. The task is to meet each other in the center of the auditorium. For an audience it is an uncanny experience, as the performers spray acoustic pellets around the performance space.

In 1958 in Paris, Pierre Schaeffer reorganized his studio to create the 'Groupe de recherches musicales,' which he headed until his retirement in 1966. François Bayle then took over the direction of the group, which has included Luc Ferrari, Bernard Parmegiani, Guy Reibel, Jean Schwarz and Michel Chion. Compositions like Bayle's *L'Experience acoustique* and *Grande polyphonie*, and Parmegiani's *De Natura sonorum* are all, in a sense, didactic works, telling us something of the nature of the electroacoustic experience, and in that sense they lead directly out of Schaeffer's work. The problem of sound diffusion is one that has occupied the group for several years, and a sophisticated loudspeaker system called the 'acousmonium' has been developed. This employs different loudspeaker types and a variety of ways of placing them depending upon the auditorium and the nature of the work to be heard. It also separates frequency-bands in order to obtain a greater clarity. The number of loudspeakers and the variety of the layout creates a kind of 'loudspeaker orchestra.' Another French group, the 'Groupe de musique expérimentale de Bourges' has created an even more diverse loudspeaker system which they call the 'Gmebaphone.' Undoubtedly such frequency-distribution systems will become highly developed.

Above: Work in the IRCAM studios at the Centre Pompidou, Paris.

Right: Pierre Henry's work *Futuristie*, described as an audio-visual homage to the Italian Futurist artist Luigi Russolo.

Below: John Cage and David Tudor. Tudor, a pianist and composer, was one of very few who appreciated Cage's aleatory music right fom the start, and since 1954 they have made several concert tours together.

• Computer music •

There are essentially three ways in which computers can be used for musical composition. The first is to program the computer to generate the data – pitches, durations and so on – to provide a score which is interpreted in the usual way by human performers. The second is to get the computer to output the equivalent of musical wave forms; and the third is to use a computer to control electroacoustic equipment.

The use of a computer to create a musical score was initiated in 1957, when Hiller and Isaacson produced the *Illiac Suite* for String Quartet at the University of Illinois. Here the computer chose what notes and durations should occur according to carefully worked-out, though elementary, 'rules' of composition. A much more sophisticated but essentially similar program was devised by Xenakis in 1961 at the University of Indiana; this was used to create a number of stochastic (meaning 'probability') works for instruments, of which the best known is probably *Atrées* (1962). In both of these cases the computer provided numerical output which was then transcribed manually into musical notation for performance. (In 1974 Donald Byrd wrote a program to transcribe the computer's output automatically.)

The generation of sound waveforms by converting series of numbers into voltages which can then be sent to activate loudspeaker cones has been the subject of continuous research, and a number of high-level languages instructing the computer to compile the desired numerical equivalents of sounds have appeared. Max Mathews, of Bell Telephone Labs, was responsible for several of them – *MUSIC 1*, *2* and *3* were relatively short-lived, *MUSIC 4* and *MUSIC 5* much more influential. *MUSIC 11* (1975) is a highly developed language created by Barry Vercoe at the Massachusetts Institute of Technology. It was written for use by a relatively small computer, the DEC PDP 11, which at once indicates the increasing power and cheaper cost of the newer systems. Compositions created on any of these developing systems are as yet hard to come by, but the works of Jean-Claude Risset, John Chowning, and Barry Vercoe are worth watching out for.

The third category, of a computer controlling electroacoustic instruments, has a much greater diversity, probably because large computers are not required. Today these systems range from small 'personal' computers such as the Apple II controlling specially designed oscillators and other devices, to fully fledged

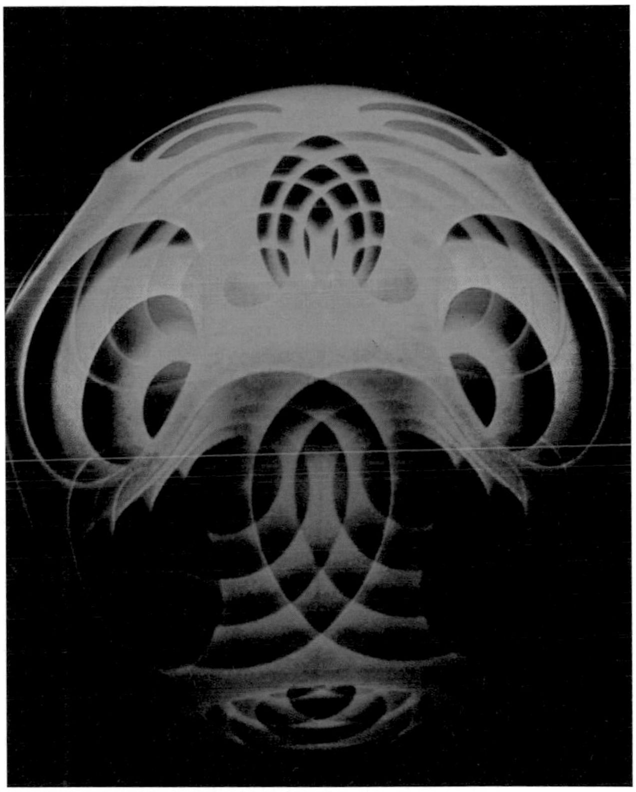

digital synthesizers controlled by computer, like the Australian Fairlight Computer Musical Instrument. The best of these outstrip their analog synthesizer counterparts in terms of both performance and accuracy. The oscillators of analog devices have always tended to drift in pitch as the circuitry warms up with heat dissipation; digital equipment cannot cause such problems. There can be no doubt that highly comprehensive digital instruments point to a musical future that we can only dimly envisage today, although in the best electroacoustic works, whether created in a traditional electronic music studio or on a computer, whether on a synthesizer or on specially designed live electronic circuitry, there has been a marriage of technology with inspired fantasy. We might indeed glimpse in such a phenomenon a hope for the future of our society.

BIOGRAPHICAL DICTIONARY OF COMPOSERS

Albéniz, Isaac (* Camprodon, Lérida, 29 May 1860; † Cambo-les-Bains, 18 May 1909). Spanish composer and pianist. A child prodigy, making his first appearance as a pianist in Madrid at the age of four, Albéniz spent an eventful youth, traveling extensively through Spain, Europe and South and North America studying with various distinguished teachers, including Liszt, and earning a living as a virtuoso, or, if necessary, playing dance music in sailors' bars. He settled in Spain in 1883, where acquaintance with Pedrell moved him to relinquish concert work in favor of composition. In 1890 he lived in London, where he began to write operas to libretti by a banker-patron, then moved to Paris in 1893.

Albéniz's most successful orchestral works are the suite *Catalonia*, the *Rapsodia española*, and a piano concerto, and he wrote some fine songs. He is best known, however, for his piano music, which had a direct influence on the development of the impressionist style in France. There are five piano sonatas, three works entitled *Suite antigua*, two 'Spanish' suites and a *Serenata española*. His greatest achievement, however, was *Iberia*, four books of picturesque pieces evoking different aspects and areas of Spain, but with a depth of musical thought under their decorative polyphony.

Antheil, George (* Trenton, N.J., 8 July 1900; † New York, 12 Feb. 1959). American composer and pianist. In 1920 began private study with Bloch. His first symphony (1920-2) was one of the earliest to incorporate jazz. Antheil left for Europe as a concert pianist, creating scandals with his own works (*Airplane Sonata*, *Sonate Sauvage*), and soon turned wholly to composition. In Paris he became acquainted with Joyce, Picasso, Pound, Satie, Yeats and others, and worked with Léger on the *Ballet mécanique*. From 1936 he worked in Hollywood, composing works that were less avant-garde, more neo-Romantic in style.

Auric, Georges (* Lodève, 15 Feb. 1899; † Paris, 23 July 1983). French composer. Studied at the Paris Conservatoire (1913) and with d'Indy at the Schola Cantorum (1914-16). In 1919 he provided the 'Prélude' for the *Album des six*, marking the foundation of the group. He also worked for Diaghilev and the Ballets Russes, and was one of the pianists at the première of Stravinsky's *Les Noces*. In 1962 he was appointed director of both the Paris Opéra and the Opéra Comique and did much to revitalize opera in the capital. His own works include orchestral pieces, ballets, film scores, incidental music, chamber music, piano pieces and songs.

Babbitt, Milton (* Philadelphia, 10 May 1916). American composer and mathematician. An early attraction to the music of Varèse and Stravinsky gave way to an absorption in that of Schoenberg, Berg and Webern at a time when twelve-tone music was unknown to many and viewed with skepticism by others. In 1946 a paper, *The Function of Set Structure in the Twelve-tone System*, was the first formal and systematic investigation of Schoenberg's compositional method.

Babbitt has developed the synthesizer as a sophisticated composing and performing instrument, but is adamant that the composer should retain control over the fundamentals of composition. In taking the principles of the Second Viennese School to their absolute limits, Babbitt's idiom involves the complete serialization of pitch, rhythm, timbres and dynamics. His best-known piece for synthesizer alone is *Ensembles for Synthesizer*, of 1962-4, but *Philomel* (1964), for soprano and synthesizer, is arguably his most attractive composition; elegance and clarity are features of his works for classical instruments, such as *Ars combinatoria* (1981), in which subtle rhythmic changes develop over a constant pulse.

Bantock, Sir Granville (* London, 7 Aug. 1868; † London, 11 Oct. 1946). English composer. Little of Bantock's vast output of orchestral, vocal, piano and theater music is heard today, although his contemporaries held him in high regard. His best-known work is probably *Fifine at the Fair*, one of many tone-poems. His predilection for oriental subjects led to a number of compositions with exotic themes, including the six song-cycles, *Songs of the East*, and the huge choral *Omar Khayyam*. He composed well over 200 songs, but his greatest contribution was to the repertoire of the unaccompanied chorus, in particular for men's voices. These pieces include a number of arrangements of British folk-songs, in which Bantock took a particular interest.

Barber, Samuel (* West Chester, Pa., 9 Mar. 1910; † New York, 23 Jan. 1981). American composer. He studied piano, composition, conducting and singing at the Curtis Institute in Philadelphia, and went on to win a number of composition prizes. He adhered largely to a lyrical, Romantic style within a loosely Classical framework, becoming one of America's most popular composers. *Dover Beach*, a setting of Matthew Arnold's poem, brought him recognition while still a student, and he continued to write convincingly for the voice in songs, choral works, and operas (*Vanessa*, 1957, and *Antony and Cleopatra*, 1965-6). His most celebrated composition is the *Adagio* (1938), which he arranged for string orchestra from his String Quartet of 1936. His rich harmonic and melodic gifts emerge also in the concertos for violin and for cello and in the early cello sonata. The First Symphony, two *Essays for Orchestra*, a piano sonata and the *Summer Music* for wind quintet are frequently performed, while his theatrical music includes the Overture to *The School for Scandal* and the ballets *Medea* and *Souvenirs*.

Barraqué, Jean (* 17 Jan. 1928; † Paris, 17 Aug. 1973). French composer. Initially a pupil of J. Langlais for harmony and counterpoint, he then followed Messiaen's analysis classes at the Paris Conservatoire (1948-51). For the next three years Barraqué worked for French Radio's research group in *musique concrète*. Although he has used serial technique, Barraqué rejected certain avant-garde ideas such as the aleatoric principle. In fact, there is much in Barraqué's technique that goes back to Debussy and Beethoven, and his music has an essentially lyrical quality. His principal works, apart from a piano sonata (1950-2), are all for voices and instruments.

Bartók, Béla (* Nagyszentmiklós [now Sînnicolaul Mare, Rumania], 25 Mar. 1881; † New York, 26 Sept. 1945. Hungarian composer. *See pp.207-213.*

Bax, Sir Arnold (* Streatham, London, 8 Nov. 1883; † Cork, 3 Oct. 1953). English composer. His music, shot through with Celtic influences, expresses the turbulence, grandeur, and mystery of nature. The frequent complexities of his harmonic style led to a paradoxical relationship with critics: he was regarded in some quarters as too avant-garde for the period, while by the mid-1940s there were others who were dismissing his music as outdated. Much of the struggle to contain his musical emotional temperament may be observed in the seven symphonies, regarded by many as his finest achievement.

Bax wrote in almost every medium except opera, other important orchestral works being the tone-poems *The Garden of Fand*, *Tintagel* and *November Woods*. A wealth of chamber music includes three string quartets, a nonet for harp, woodwind and strings, a clarinet sonata, three violin sonatas and one for viola.

Bayle, François (* Tamatave, Madagascar, 27 Apr. 1932). French composer. Studied with Stockhausen at Darmstadt and Messiaen in Paris. In 1960 he joined the *musique concrète* group at French Radio and directed it from 1966. He has composed some instrumental and vocal pieces, but most of his works are for, or incorporate, tape. He juxtaposes natural and synthetic sounds and wants his listeners to feel the motion and vibration of energy in the universe.

Bedford, David (* London, 4 Aug. 1937). English composer. Studied composition with Berkeley at the Royal Academy of Music and then with Nono in Venice. He became a music teacher in London schools, and there are many works for children among his compositions. He writes simple and direct music, but requires improvisation and unorthodox instruments and playing techniques. Many of his works are based on transposable sets of notes which may be used either melodically or harmonically.

Bennett, Richard Rodney (* Broadstairs, 29 Mar. 1936). English composer and pianist. Studied with Berkeley and Ferguson at the Royal Academy of Music. The feeling for line and texture evident in his early works remains characteristic, hardly affected by two years of study in Paris with Boulez (1957-9). In addition to his classical compositions, which include two symphonies, a piano concerto and three operas, he has written film scores and jazz.

Berg, Alban (* Vienna, 9 Feb. 1885; † Vienna, 24 Dec. 1935. Austrian composer. *See pp.188-201.*

Berio, Luciano (* Oneglia, Imperia, 24 Oct. 1925). Italian composer. Berio first worked as accompanist, conductor and orchestral player; his first compositions were in a tonal, Romantic idiom. In 1950 he married the American singer Cathy Berberian, the chosen interpreter of many of his works. In America in the early 1950s, he reached beyond the concept of classical twelve-note serialism in *Chamber Music*, and made acquaintance in 1952 with the first compositions on tape by Luening and Ussachevsky. His meeting in Basle in 1954 with Maderna, Pousseur and Stockhausen brought him into contact with the post-Webern avant garde. Berio pursued with Maderna an intense though short-lived activity in producing music by electronic means, including *Différences*, a composition juxtaposing musical instruments with electronically 'doctored' tapes of the same instruments. One of his most important pieces is *Circles* (1960), settings of poems by e.e. cummings, in which the soloist

sings approximate pitch intervals. From 1963 to 1970 Berio lived in the USA, working extensively with synthesizers. Compositions of this period include *Sequenze*, in which various solo instruments are alternately directed to exploit their known characteristics and then forbidden to 'sound like themselves.' Other important compositions include the early opera, *Allez-Hop!*, which draws on popular song and blues, and *Laborintus II* (1965), with quotations from Dante, Ezra Pound and T. S. Eliot. His opera *La Vera Storia* had its première in Milan in March 1982.

Berkeley, Sir Lennox (* Boar's Hill, Oxford, 12 May 1903). English composer. Studies with Nadia Boulanger and a predilection for the classics, combined with the influence of contemporary French music (notably Ravel) and of Stravinsky, helped to form Berkeley's style, in which there is no significant trace of 'Englishness' of the Elgar or Vaughan Williams type. His deftness of touch and clarity of texture make it easy to label his idiom as 'Gallic'; there is also a deep, expressive quality in some of the vocal and instrumental works. A subsequent tendency towards a more complex, consciously 'modern' idiom reflects his interest in contemporary developments. His instrumental music includes the Sonatina for violin and piano, op.17, the Sonata for viola and piano, op.22, music for string quartet and pieces for various instruments, while more recent works include *Voices of the Night*, op.86, a guitar concerto, and the Fourth Symphony. He has written four operas, the most successful being *Nelson* and *A Dinner Engagement* (both 1954).

Bernstein, Leonard (* Lawrence, Mass., 25 Aug. 1918). American conductor, composer and pianist. One of the most versatile American musicians of the century, Bernstein has made his name chiefly as a conductor and music educationist, the latter through writing and television. Of a substantial list of compositions, influenced by the music of Milhaud and Stravinsky, by the late nineteenth-century German composers, and also by jazz and popular music, the best known are the comic operetta *Candide*, the musical *West Side Story*, the 'Jeremiah' Symphony (the first of Bernstein's three symphonies) and the *Chichester Psalms*. *Mass*, composed as a dedicatory work for the opening of the John F. Kennedy Center of the Performing Arts in Washington, D.C., created a sensation on its first performance as a result of its bold juxtaposition of liturgical and popular musical elements.

Birtwistle, Harrison (* Accrington, Lancs., 15 July 1934). English composer. A clarinet student at what was then the Royal Manchester College of Music, Birtwistle studied composition with Richard Hall. At first influenced by Stravinsky, Varèse, Webern and medieval music, he composed works of stark ritual form and expression, but he has gradually developed a more organic technique; much of his music relates to myths of birth (physical or esthetic), death and regeneration.

For much of his work Birtwistle has turned to the verse-refrain form found in Greek classical drama – hence titles such as *Refrains and Choruses* (1957) and *Tragoedia* (1965), an aggressively dissonant 'suite' of movements which turned out to be a study for his melodramatic opera *Punch and Judy*. *Verses for Ensembles* (1969) harshly juxtaposes wind, brass and percussion, unusual instrumental sonorities being of prime interest. *The Triumph of Time* (1972) is a large-scale work both in scope and instrumentation. Birtwistle has also experimented with electronic techniques; *Medusa* (1969), for example, uses a mixture of woodwind, strings and electronic tape. More recent works include scores for London's National Theatre, where he became music director in 1975, and the opera *The Mask of Orpheus* (1974-86).

Blacher, Boris (* Nin-chang, China, 6 Jan. 1903; † Berlin, 30 Jan. 1975). German composer of Baltic descent. At first he studied architecture and mathematics in Berlin, but then composition at the Hochschule für Musik (1924-6) and music at Berlin University (1927-31). He subsequently held several posts as a composition teacher. He wrote a great deal of ballet and incidental music, as well as operas and film scores, though it was through his instrumental works that he became known.

Bliss, Sir Arthur (* London, 2 Aug. 1891; † London, 27 Mar. 1975). English composer of American descent. Bliss studied at Cambridge, and had lessons from Stanford, Vaughan Williams and Holst. Influenced by Stravinsky and the French composers, including Ravel and 'Les Six,' his early works, among them *Conversations* and *Rout*, shocked as much as they entertained.

His 'Colour' Symphony of 1921-2 and the choral Pastoral *Lie Strewn the White Flocks* (1928) show Bliss returning to a more personal, sensuous melodic and harmonic style, with *Morning Heroes* (1930), in memory of the fallen, evincing the deeply emotional roots of his musical personality. To the 1930s also belong *Music for Strings*, the Piano Concerto, and his chamber-music masterpieces, the Clarinet Quintet and the Sonata for viola and piano. Of almost equal stature is the Oboe Quintet of 1927. He proved to have a particular flair for film and ballet music; the latter include *Checkmate*, *Miracle in the Gorbals* and *Adam Zero*. His opera *The Olympians* (1949) was followed by an opera for television, *Tobias and the Angel*. Works of the last period include the Violin Concerto, the Cello Concerto, the orchestral *Meditations on a Theme of John Blow* and *Metamorphic Variations*.

Blitzstein, Marc (* Philadelphia, 2 Mar. 1905; † Fort-de-France, Martinique, 22 Jan. 1964). American composer of Russian–Jewish descent. He was the first composer to develop a convincing music-theater idiom representative of American vernacular speech style. Deeply committed to the doctrine of 'art for society's sake,' he devoted much of his talent to social commentary and political satire. Blitzstein studied with Nadia Boulanger in Paris and Schoenberg in Berlin. His greatest public acclaim came from his adaptation of Brecht and Weill's *Die Dreigroschenoper* (1952). His theater scores include the political parody opera *The Cradle Will Rock*, the operas *Triple-Sec*, *Regina*, *The Harpies*, *The Condemned* and *Sacco and Vanzetti* (unfinished), the opera-ballet *Parabola and Circula* and the musical plays *Reuben, Reuben* and *June*. Other works include a choral symphony, *The Airborne*, a ballet, *The Guests*, a cantata for chorus and orchestra, *This is the Garden*, and a symphonic poem for male chorus and orchestra, *Freedom Morning*.

Bloch, Ernest (* Geneva, 24 July 1880; † Portland, Oregon, 15 July 1959). American composer and teacher of Swiss–Jewish birth. Bloch trained as a violinist, studying with Ysaye in Brussels. After some years in Germany and Paris he returned to Switzerland and in 1915 became a professor at the Geneva Conservatory. In 1916 he was invited by the American dancer Maud Allan to conduct the orchestra for her tour of America, and he stayed there, teaching and conducting; he became an American citizen in 1924. Roger Sessions and Elliott Carter are among his best known pupils.

The salient feature of Bloch's music is its ultra-Romantic, expressionist and rhapsodic quality: melody is all-important, its rhythmic freedom and harmonic originality corresponding with the intensity of his musical thought. Indeed, religious fervor is at the heart of his best compositions. The First Piano Quintet makes use of quarter-tones and, with the *Concerto grosso* for strings and piano, is one of his most popular pieces. Other works include the 'Israel' Symphony (with five solo voices), the Violin Concerto and *Concerto symphonique* for piano. Bloch's vocal music includes the opera *Macbeth*, and his chamber music includes two violin sonatas and five string quartets. Late works include the *Suite modale* for flute and piano, three suites for solo cello, and two for violin.

Boulanger, Lili (* Paris, 21 Aug. 1893; † Mézy, nr. Paris, 15 Mar. 1918). French composer. Her death at the age of twenty-four cut short an extremely promising composing career; after lessons with her sister, Nadia, she entered the Paris Conservatoire in 1909, and four years later became the first woman to win the Prix de Rome. Her compositions include the prize-winning cantata, *Faust et Hélène*, a number of psalm settings and other choral works. The pieces show impressionist, as well as occasional oriental influences. Lili Boulanger also wrote an opera based on a Maeterlinck text, *La Princesse Maleine*, and another cantata, *Frédégonde* (1913). There are also some songs, a few orchestral pieces – *Sicilienne*, *Marche gaie* and *Marche funèbre*, *Poème symphonique* – some piano music, a violin sonata and various short instrumental pieces. Among her best works is the psalm setting *Du fond de l'abîme* (1914-17), a vast piece of striking solemnity and grandeur, densely but subtly written, and showing a masterly handling of both large forces and the solo voice.

Boulez, Pierre (* Montbrison, Loire, 26 Mar. 1925). French composer and conductor. *See pp.273-8.*

Bowen, York (* London, 22 Feb. 1884; † London, 23 Nov. 1961). English composer and pianist. Although his principal studies at the Royal Academy of Music were piano and composition, Bowen also played the horn and the viola. An excellent pianist, he composed three piano concertos, as well as a symphonic fantasia, a symphony and a violin concerto. He wrote several works for the viola, including a sonata and a concerto, inspired by the playing of Lionel Tertis, with whom he frequently worked. His chamber music includes a string quartet, a piano trio, a suite for violin and piano and a cello sonata.

Bridge, Frank (* Brighton, 26 Feb. 1879; † Eastbourne, 10 Jan. 1941). English composer, violist and conductor. German Romanticism, absorbed via his teacher, Stanford, together with the music of the French impressionist school, had a profound effect on Bridge's early style; later he was to shed these influences, evolving a more personal idiom not unaffected by the music of the Second Viennese School of composers. In so doing he lost some of the popularity gained initially. Orchestral tone-poems such as *The Sea* and *Summer* show his mastery of orchestration, his fine ear for instrumental, impressionist colors, while the rhapsody *Enter Spring* was a key factor in Benjamin Britten's decision to go to Bridge for composition lessons.

The increasingly chromatic quality of Bridge's writing led to some compositions in a more dissonant style, for example the Piano Sonata, and the *Oration* for cello and orchestra. But the 'advance' to modernism was not a total commitment, the Sonata for cello and piano, for instance, written between 1916 and 1917, being one of his most lyrical and passionately romantic works. The second of his *Three Idylls* for string quartet provides the theme for Britten's celebrated set of variations of 1937.

Britten, Benjamin (Lord) (* Lowestoft, Suffolk, 22 Nov. 1913; † Aldeburgh, 4 Dec. 1976). English composer. *See pp.261-5.*

Busoni, Ferruccio (* Empoli, nr. Florence, 1 Apr. 1866; † Berlin 27 July 1924). German–Italian composer, pianist and teacher. Busoni was born into a musical household, his father being a virtuoso clarinetist and his mother a pianist. He was a child prodigy and at twelve conducted his own *Stabat Mater* in Graz, where his parents had moved. In 1886, he went to Leipzig, where he met Tchaikovsky, Mahler, Grieg, Sinding and Delius; he then taught

for a year in Helsinki, and in 1894 settled in Berlin, which, apart from some years spent in Bologna and Zürich during World War I, remained his home. A bent for philosophical thought and intellectual argument became apparent at an early stage, and his demand for a 'young classicism' was elaborated in his *Entwurf einer neuen Ästhetik der Tonkunst* (Project for a New Musical Esthetic, 1907), in which he rejected the clichés of nineteenth-century musical form and practice. He was much concerned with orchestration and the difficulties of creating something fresh with the old range of instrumentation, while in harmony he broke through the traditional major–minor system, but, unlike Schoenberg, he always kept the audience in mind. Busoni's classical modernism derived from Bach, Beethoven, Berlioz and Liszt rather than Wagner and Debussy, and he was one of the most original musical thinkers and influential teachers at the beginning of the century; Weill and Varèse were among his pupils. His compositions include orchestral works, the operas *Arlecchino*, *Turandot* and the unfinished *Doktor Faust*, as well as many transcriptions for piano, including his celebrated version of Bach's organ works.

Cage, John (* Los Angeles, 5 Sept. 1912). American composer, philosopher and writer on music. He studied with Henry Cowell and then with Schoenberg, but rejected accepted compositional techniques in favor of a radically experimental approach. In the late 1930s he became active in the organization of concert-performances by percussion orchestras and his *First Construction (In Metal)* (1939), includes scoring for bells, gongs, anvils and car brake-drums. He also became interested in the 'prepared' piano, in which pitch and timbre are altered by the attachment of objects made of different materials to the strings. From this it was a logical step to the possibilities of the electronic studio. While some degree of rhythmic control still governed compositions such as the long *Sonatas and Interludes* for prepared piano (1948), subsequent works show Cage basing his compositional methods on the laws of chance. This reached a climax in the Concerto for piano and orchestra (1957-8). From 1951 he also started working with magnetic tape, although his compositions have seldom been purely electronic. Cage's aleatoric principle changes entirely the function of the composer, from being the creator of an inviolate composition to 'assembling' sounds for a performance; a piece such as *HPSCHD* (1967-9) was a gigantic multi-media event, while some of his best work has been in collaboration with Merce Cunningham's dance company.

Caplet, André (* Le Havre, 23 Nov. 1878; † Neuilly-sur-Seine, 22 Apr. 1925). French composer and conductor. After studying at the Paris Conservatoire, Caplet won the Prix de Rome in 1901 and traveled extensively in Europe. Highly esteemed as a conductor, he was asked by Debussy to direct the first performances of *Le Martyre de Saint-Sébastien* and to complete the orchestration. Caplet also made an orchestral version of Debussy's *Children's Corner* suite. Despite a busy conducting career (much of it in the USA) and his early death, he left behind a good deal of music, vocal, choral and orchestral. Its sensitivity and refinement are a response to the music of Debussy, though he was never merely imitative. Caplet was also one of the first composers to use voices in an instrumental manner in chamber music: in his Septet for three female voices and string quartet and a Sonata for voice, cello and piano.

Carpenter, John (* Park Ridge, Ill. 28 Feb. 1876; † Chicago, 26 Apr. 1951). American composer. He studied composition at Harvard with J. K. Paine, graduating in 1897, but worked in his father's firm until 1936. He was asked by Diaghilev to write an American ballet for Monte Carlo – *Skyscrapers* – though it was first given at the Metropolitan Opera House in 1926. There are jazz elements in the ballet, but Carpenter also wrote symphonic works influenced by French impressionism.

Carter, Elliott (* New York, 11 Dec. 1908). American composer. He worked with Walter Piston at Harvard and then studied with Nadia Boulanger in Paris. On his return to America he worked as a music critic. His own composition is modal and polytonal and reveals the influence of Copland, Piston, Hindemith and Stravinsky. Carter used a system of 'metrical modulation' to co-ordinate tempi and their relationship to each other, and it is in the field of rhythm that he became most individual. In 1955 his composition underwent a radical change when he applied serial technique to intervals and intensities. Carter has published a great deal of vocal music, and among his instrumental works are a piano sonata, (1945-6), three string quartets (1951, 1959 and 1971) and his First Symphony (1942, revised 1954).

Casella, Alfredo (* Turin, 15 July 1883; † Rome, 5 Mar. 1947). Italian composer, pianist and conductor. After early essays in composition in the nineteenth-century German tradition, Casella went to Paris at the age of thirteen, remaining there for twenty years before he returned to Italy, advocating a 'return to the pure classicism of our ancestors.' Most of the works of his maturity reflect this concern for craftsmanship and proportion, and display the neoclassical composer's characteristic fondness for contrapuntal writing. Examples are the *Partita* for piano and orchestra (1924-5) and *Scarlattiana* for piano and orchestra (1926), which reflects Casella's contact with the music of 'Les Six.' A few pieces, such as the Piano Sonatina of 1916, show the passing interest Casella had in Schoenberg.

His post-Paris compositions include orchestral, chamber, piano solo and vocal music. As a teacher of piano and of composition, Casella's effect on contemporary and subsequent generations of musicians was considerable; he was, too, a tireless and scrupulous editor of the Classical piano repertoire.

Castelnuovo-Tedesco, Mario (* Florence, 3 Apr. 1895; † Los Angeles, 17 Mar. 1968). Italian composer and pianist. He studied in Florence with Pizzetti and became a prolific composer in all genres; Casella did much to promote his music in Italy and elsewhere. He became an American citizen after moving to the USA in 1939, where he composed scores for several films. Music for the stage figures prominently in his long list of published works, and his orchestral music includes overtures and concertos. He wrote several solo guitar pieces, and other chamber music includes two piano quintets, a concertino for harp and string quartet, two piano trios, and sonatas for violin, clarinet, trumpet and bassoon. His piano music includes a number of 'program' pieces, among them *Sonatina zoologica* and a sonata, while his songs include many settings of Shakespeare.

Chaminade, Cécile (* Paris, 8 Aug. 1857; † Monte Carlo, 18 Apr. 1944). French pianist and composer. After completion of her studies she made frequent concert tours, her own piano compositions featuring prominently in her programs. Her light, elegant style veered to the idiom of salon music. She was a prolific composer, her larger-scale works including a 'symphonie lyrique,' *Les Amazones*, for voices and orchestra, a *Concertstück* for piano and orchestra, a ballet, *Callirhoé*, and two piano trios. Her less ambitious but possibly more successful compositions include a large number of songs and piano pieces.

Chávez, Carlos (* Mexico City, 13 June 1899; † Mexico City, 2 Aug. 1978). Mexican composer, conductor and teacher. He studied with Manuel Ponce, and his compositions from before 1921, mostly for piano, are overtly Romantic, with Schumann as the dominant influence. Chávez then devoted much of his career to the development of a national music idiom. Although only a

handful of his compositions incorporate genuine Mexican folk-themes, the influence of Mexican-Indian dance tunes may be heard in almost all of them. Among his best-known works are the second of his six symphonies, *Sinfonia india*, the First Violin Concerto and the Piano Concerto, and the ballet-music (particularly *El fuego nuevo*, *Xochipili* and *Caballos de vapor, H. P.* – horsepower – which juxtaposes 'machine-age' and 'tropical' music). Other compositions include a concerto for four horns, chamber and piano music, while his political sympathies emerge in such pieces as the 'proletarian symphony' *Llamadas* and the *Cantos de Mexico*. Chávez was a master of orchestration, particularly when writing for wind, and he used strong dynamic contrasts to reinforce unusual instrumental effects. As director of the National Conservatory (1928-34) and the Mexico Symphony Orchestra (1928-48), as well as with his compositions, he played a decisive role in the cultural life of his country.

Coleridge-Taylor, Samuel (* London, 15 Aug. 1875; † Croydon, 1 Sept. 1912). English composer. His father, a native of Sierra Leone, was a doctor; his mother, an Englishwoman, was left to bring Samuel up on her own when her husband returned to Africa.

At the Royal College of Music Coleridge-Taylor trained as a violinist and studied composition under Stanford. Chamber music figures prominently among his student works, most notably the Clarinet Quintet; this won the

approval of Joachim, who performed it with his quartet in 1897 in Berlin. The work which brought him fame and a stream of commissions was *Hiawatha's Wedding Feast* (1898), the first part of a trilogy based on Longfellow's poem. The colorful orchestration and tuneful character of his music shows the strong influence of Dvořák. His most important orchestral composition is the Violin Concerto in G minor, dating from 1912.

Copland, Aaron (* Brooklyn, N.Y., 14 Nov. 1900). American composer. *See pp.241-5.*

Cowell, Henry (* Menlo Park, Cal., 11 Mar. 1897; † Shady, N.Y., 10 Dec. 1965). American composer, pianist, teacher, editor and writer on music. He was largely self-taught and began his career in 1913 as a pianist playing his own compositions. He absorbed widely diverse ethnic influences and was enormously prolific; his works include 19 symphonies, the collection of pieces *Hymn and Fuguing Tune*, as well as an opera, chamber, choral, instrumental and band music. Through his wide-ranging activity he did much to further the cause of American composers.

Dallapiccola, Luigi (* Pisino d'Istria, 3 Feb. 1904; † Florence, 19 Feb. 1975). Italian composer, pianist and writer. Dallapiccola taught the piano for more than thirty years at the Florence Conservatory, and received much active support for the performance of his works from Casella.

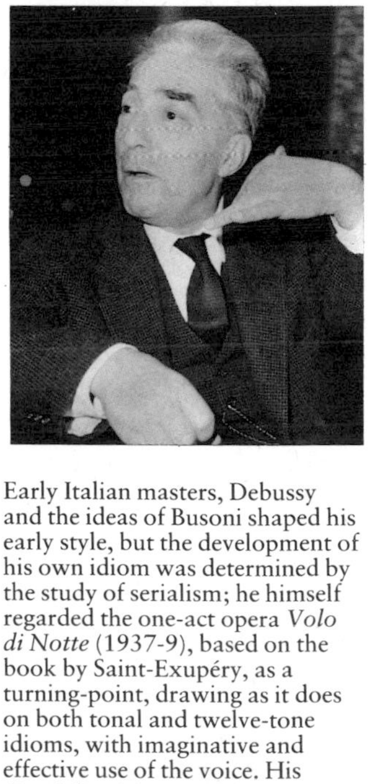

Early Italian masters, Debussy and the ideas of Busoni shaped his early style, but the development of his own idiom was determined by the study of serialism; he himself regarded the one-act opera *Volo di Notte* (1937-9), based on the book by Saint-Exupéry, as a turning-point, drawing as it does on both tonal and twelve-tone idioms, with imaginative and effective use of the voice. His *Canti di prigionia* (1938-41) established his reputation when performed at the ISCM in 1946; a setting of words by Mary Stuart, Boethius and Savonarola, the work epitomizes Dallapiccola's passionate concern for freedom and human welfare, and he established a balance between tonal and atonal elements in the songs, contrasting Bergian expressionism with regular metric pulse.

His most important composition, the opera *Il Prigioniero*, takes up, in more pessimistic terms, the theme of liberty; here twelve-tone technique is used wholeheartedly. Intellectual grasp of formal problems is evident in instrumental works such as the *Due Studi* for violin and piano (1946-7), and the 'ghost-like fugacity' of the *Piccola musica notturna* (1954). *Ulisse* (1960-8) is the most ambitious of his operas, but contains some of his more rebarbative music. Mention must also be made of his *Notebook* of piano pieces composed for his daughter – short, mainly contrapuntal and delicately melodic studies – and of his *Concerto per la notte di Natale*.

Davies, Peter Maxwell (* Manchester, 8 Sept. 1934). English composer. A member, with Birtwistle and Alexander Goehr, of the Manchester New Music Group, he studied with Richard Hall, and later with Petrassi in Rome. Since 1970 Davies has done much of his work in Orkney. This is reflected in a long series of scores based on Orcadian or Scottish subject-matter or music.

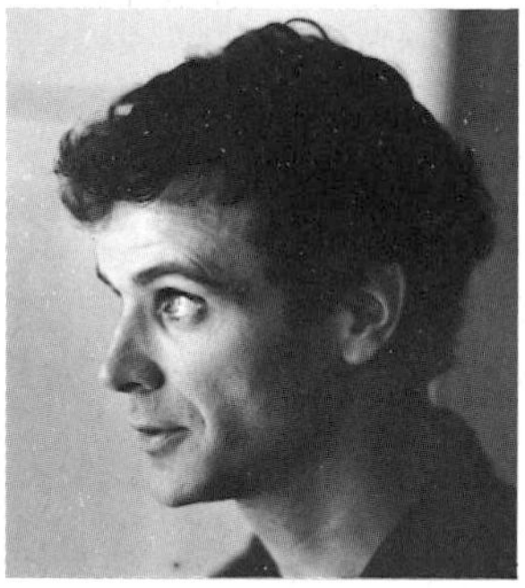

A fascination with pre-Classical music underlies much of Davies's writing, as in *Missa super L'homme armé*; a strong, recurring element of parody may also be encountered, especially in his numerous compositions for music-theater. *Taverner* is a large-scale opera on the life of the sixteenth-century composer, while *The Two Fiddlers* was written for children of the Orkney Islands. The operas *The Lighthouse* and *The Martyrdom of St Magnus*, and *Ave maris stella* are other compositions inspired by this environment. He has also written music for films. Other works are the *Veni sancte spiritus* and *O magnum mysterium*, written in the early 1960s, the Trumpet Sonata, three symphonies, a Sinfonia for chamber orchestra and a string quartet.

Debussy, Claude (* Saint-Germain-en-Laye, 22 Aug. 1862; † Paris, 25 Jan. 1918). French composer. *See pp.35-53.*

Delius, Frederick (* Bradford, 29 Jan. 1862; † Grez-sur-Loing, Seine-et-Marne, 10 June 1934). English composer of German descent. His father did not approve of music as a career, but agreed to lend Delius the money to become an orange grower in Florida in 1884. Later his father financed a course for eighteen months at the Leipzig Conservatory from August 1886. The most important result of this period was not the instruction, but the fact that he composed much music and met Grieg, who persuaded Delius's father to allow his son to continue composing after Leipzig and support him in Paris. In 1897 he settled with Jelka Rosen at Grez-sur-Loing. They married in 1903 and, except during World War I, spent the rest of their lives at Grez.

Delius wrote in a wide variety of media – opera, incidental music, orchestral works, choral and vocal works, chamber and instrumental pieces, and several songs. His musical language developed slowly, over a long period, but took as its point of departure Wagner and Grieg. By the turn of the century, however, his lyric drama *A Village Romeo and Juliet* proclaimed that Delius had reached maturity as a composer, and his distinctive harmonic style, in particular, was now complete. He then wrote three works for his favorite ensemble of soloists, chorus and orchestra: *Appalachia* (1903, original 1896); *Sea Drift* (1903-4), a setting of Walt Whitman, and, perhaps his greatest work, *A Mass of Life* (1904-5), a setting of Nietzsche. However, his best known works remain his orchestral evocations of nature in works such as *Brigg Fair* and *On Hearing the First Cuckoo in Spring*.

Dohnányi, Ernö [Ernst von] (* Pozsony [now Bratislava], 27 July 1877; † New York, 9 Feb. 1960). Hungarian pianist, composer, conductor, teacher and administrator. Dohnányi early established himself as one of Hungary's leading pianists. After being invited by Joachim to teach in Berlin, where he stayed ten years, Dohnányi returned to Hungary and did much to promote the music of other composers, in particular that of Bartók and Kodály.

German Romantic music, and above all Brahms, was the dominating influence on his own music, and only a proportion of his compositions reflect his Hungarian background. Classical forms predominate, imbued with lyrical, expressive Romanticism, and frequently displaying an individual sense of humor, as in the well-known *Variations on a Nursery Song* for piano and orchestra, op.25 (1914).

Dukas, Paul (* Paris, 1 Oct. 1865; † Paris, 17 May, 1935). French composer, music critic and teacher. He composed prolifically in most forms, but was severely self-critical, and later destroyed much of his earlier work. Among the surviving works, the most celebrated is undoubtedly *L'Apprenti sorcier* (The Sorcerer's Apprentice), a witty symphonic scherzo illustrating Goethe's ballad with graphic skill. This was followed by two major works for piano, the vast Sonata and the Variations, Interlude and Finale; both show his mastery of the keyboard. Emotional ardor, coupled with a French poetic sensibility, both expressed within firm formal outlines, characterize his music. His most outstanding contribution to the theater was *Ariane et Barbebleue* (1907): consciously deriving inspiration from Debussy, Dukas drew on much of the language of the impressionist composers, including whole-tone scales and a wordless male chorus; the use of a kind of Wagnerian *leitmotif*, however, ensures that the musical evocation of moods and pictures is integrated within the musical argument of the piece. In 1912 he wrote a *poème dansé*, *La Péri*, its choreographic qualities matched by an opulent, but delicately written orchestral score. Dukas taught at the Conservatoire from 1910 until his death.

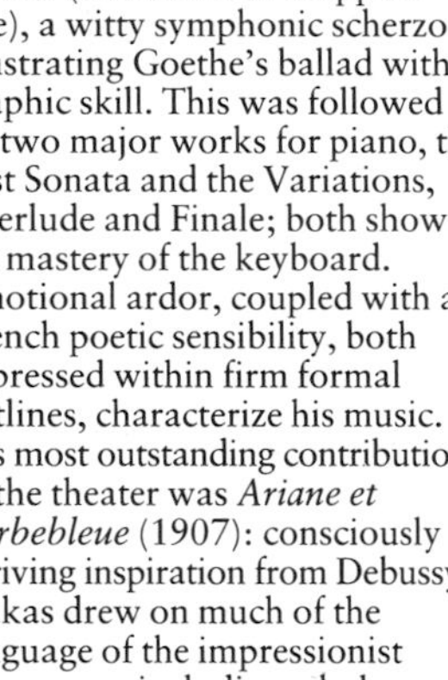

Dutilleux, Henri (* Angers, 22 Jan. 1916). French composer. Dutilleux's earlier works were very derivative (notably from Ravel), and many were destroyed by the composer. The individual qualities of his music, therefore, must be sought in the six major works written since World War II, the Piano Sonata of 1947, the two symphonies (1950 and 1959), the ballet *Le Loup* (1953), *Métaboles* (1964) and *Tout un monde lointain* (1968-70), which has a concertante cello part written for Rostropovich. Dutilleux shows masterly command of orchestral and symphonic techniques and writes in a frequently very dissonant idiom, one contained, however, within a well structured framework. The Piano Sonata remains one of his most impressive compositions, a dramatic work of dynamic contrasts and Ravel-like textures and vital, almost Bartókian rhythms, fused in a highly idiosyncratic manner, its final pages grandiloquently effective. Other works include music for the theater, a few songs, and some instrumental music.

Eimert, Herbert (* Bad Kreuznach, 8 Apr. 1897; † Cologne, 15 Dec. 1972). German composer, theorist and critic. He studied at Cologne Conservatory (1919-24) and University (1924-30), and from 1925 until 1969 (apart from 1933-44) he wrote the program notes for the Gürzenich concerts. Through his work with Westdeutscher Rundfunk he became a pioneer of electronic composition, and in 1951 he founded its studio for electronic music, which he directed until 1962; he brought in Stockhausen as a collaborator from 1953. From 1965 to 1971 he was professor at Cologne Hochmusikschule and directed its electronic music studio.

Eisler, Hanns (* Leipzig, 6 July 1898; † Berlin, 6 Sept. 1962). German composer. He studied under Schoenberg (and on occasion Webern) and from 1927 until 1933 wrote extensively for the Berlin theater and cinema, including working with Brecht. He developed a style of extreme, almost naïve, simplicity, using the political ballad as musical propaganda for Communism. He returned to East Germany after fifteen years of exile, mostly spent in the USA, but his official socialist compositions had lost the bite of his earlier work.

Elgar, Sir Edward (* Broadheath, nr. Worcester, 2 June 1857; † London, 23 Feb. 1934). English composer. *See pp.111-9.*

Enescu, George (* Liveni Vîrnav [now George Enescu], Botoşani district, 19 Aug. 1881; † Paris, 3 or 4 May 1955). Rumanian composer, violinist, conductor and teacher, often known by the French form of his name, Georges Enesco. Enescu graduated from the Vienna Conservatory at the age of twelve, continuing his composition lessons in Paris with Massenet and Fauré. During his international career as a concert violinist, he premièred a number of works – by Bartók, Strauss, Casella, Fauré, Ravel and Saint-Saëns – with the composers themselves at the piano.

While his early compositions show the strong influence of Wagner and Brahms, the most important factor in his musical development was his Rumanian background and his knowledge of Rumanian folk music. A passionate believer in the power of music to communicate, he had no time for developments such as dodecaphony, although he did incorporate the use of quarter-tones – derived from folk music – in some compositions. Enescu developed a distinctive, individual style, with a penchant for polyphonic textures. His works include an opera, three symphonies, chamber music and songs, as well as three violin sonatas and the celebrated orchestral *Rumanian rhapsodies*.

Falla (y Matheu), Manuel de (* Cádiz, 23 Nov. 1876; † Alta Gracia, Argentina, 14 Nov. 1946). Spanish composer. He had lessons in composition from Pedrell, and at the age of twenty-nine won both a piano competition and a competition for a Spanish opera with his *La Vida breve*. There followed seven years in Paris, where he became acquainted with Debussy, Ravel and Dukas; he returned to Madrid in 1914. The war years saw the premières of *Seven Spanish Folk-songs* and of the first versions of the ballets *El Sombrero de tres picos* (The Three-Cornered Hat) and *El Amor brujo* (Love the Magician), as well as *Noches en los jardines de España* (Nights in the Gardens of Spain). These have remained Falla's best-known compositions, and the three movements of the *Noches*, examples of Spanish musical impressionism, show his characteristic use of the piano as an orchestral rather than concerto instrument. In the twenties his style became more austere, though the puppet opera *El Retablo de Maese Pedro* (1923), based on *Don Quixote*, draws on popular folk music. The Concerto for harpsichord (1926), which Falla described as being based on 'ancient Spanish religious and folk tunes,' combines the neoclassicism of Stravinsky and echoes of Domenico Scarlatti with a characteristic intensity of utterance. His only piece for guitar was *Homenaje* (1920), an elegy in honor of Debussy, quoting fleetingly from the French composer's music.

In 1939 Falla left Spain to conduct concerts in Argentina, where he settled for the rest of his life. His most ambitious work *Atlántida*, a scenic cantata, occupied him intermittently for some twenty years, but remained incomplete at his death.

Fauré, Gabriel (* Pamiers, Ariège, 12 May 1845; † Paris, 4 Nov. 1924). French composer. *See pp.19-29.*

Françaix, Jean (* Le Mans, 23 May 1912). French composer and pianist. The child of musical parents, Françaix was a precocious composition student of Nadia Boulanger, writing his first piano work when he was six and his first symphony (later withdrawn) when he was twenty. He has written much vocal, orchestral and instrumental music, as well as operas, ballets and film music, and his facility and seemingly endless melodic inspiration are the hallmarks of his style, seen at its best in works such as the Concertino (1932) and Concerto (1936) for piano and orchestra.

Fricker, Peter Racine (* London, 5 Sept. 1920). English composer. The most prominent British composer to emerge immediately after World War II, Fricker established a reputation as a composer of finely-constructed and concentrated works, quite removed from the pastoral idiom of much English music of the period. He succeeded Tippett as director of Morley College in 1953; since 1964 he has lived and worked in California.

Basically diatonic, with a high degree of dissonance, Fricker's music has moved gradually towards the modified serialism of the Fourth Symphony (1964-6) and a generally sparser, more linear style, governed always by a strong sense of form. *The Vision of Judgment* (1967-8) for chorus and orchestra is one of his most important large-scale compositions, while his other works include concertos for violin, for viola and for piano, chamber, vocal and instrumental music and music for theater, cinema and radio.

Gerhard, Roberto (* Valls, Catalonia, 25 Sept. 1896; † Cambridge, 5 Jan. 1970). Spanish composer, later naturalized British, of Franco-Swiss descent. Gerhard studied piano with Granados and composition with Pedrell; a further five years were spent with Schoenberg. On his return to Barcelona he made his name as a critic, musicologist and composer, works of this period including the Wind Quintet, the Catalan Folk Songs (both 1928) and the ballet *Ariel*

(1936, a collaboration with Miró and the poet Foix). After the Spanish Civil War Gerhard took up residence in Cambridge. Here, recognition came slowly, but with his First Symphony (1952-3) his reputation was firmly established; in it he set out to create a new format for symphonic thought, 'evolving a large-scale work as a continuous train of invention.' Interest now grew in his earlier compositions such as the *Seven Haiku* for voice and instrumental ensemble, the *Don Quixote* ballet music (1941), and, above all, the Violin Concerto (completed 1943). This typifies Gerhard's imaginative blend of Spanish influences, serial and impressionist elements, with a skillful and wide-ranging scoring for percussion instruments that was to become a feature of much of his later work. Gerhard composed five symphonies in all, the Third ('Collages,' 1960), being scored for orchestra and tape. Other tape compositions are the opera *The Duenna* (1945-7), *Audiomobiles I-IV* (1958-9), *Lament for the Death of a Bullfighter* (1959), to words by Lorca, and *Sculptures I-V* (1963). His chamber music includes two string quartets, a nonet for wind instruments and accordion, a cello sonata and the three astrological works written at the end of his life. Other important orchestral works are the Concerto for harpsichord (1955-6), the *Concert for Eight*, *The Plague* (text after Camus) for speaker, chorus and orchestra and the *Concerto for Orchestra* (1965).

Gershwin, George (* Brooklyn, 26 Sept. 1898; † Hollywood, 11 July 1937). American composer, pianist and conductor. From 1912 he studied with Charles Hambitzer, who introduced him to the music of Chopin, Liszt and Debussy. Later he briefly studied theory, harmony, counterpoint and orchestration but acquired only a limited knowledge of these subjects and never became proficient at reading music. Inspired by the examples of Jerome Kern and Irving Berlin, he made his name as a songwriter, setting words by his brother Ira, and his style inaugurated a new era of sophisticated jazz, colored by subtle rhythmic inflections and shot through with a 'delicacy, even dreaminess,' which is uniquely his.

His aspiration as a serious composer advanced when Paul Whiteman commissioned and performed, with Gershwin as soloist, the *Rhapsody in Blue* (1924) for jazz band and piano. Because of his inexperience, the work was orchestrated by Ferde Grofé (though Gershwin claimed to have scored all his later orchestral music).

Musical comedies followed, and then the Concerto for Piano (1925). *An American in Paris* dates from 1928, a second *Rhapsody* from 1931, and the *Cuban Overture* from 1932; in 1935 came what he called his Negro opera, *Porgy and Bess*, which has become a classic.

Ginastera, Alberto (* Buenos Aires, 11 Apr. 1916; † Geneva, 25 June 1983). Argentine composer. Ginastera has achieved international recognition as Argentina's foremost composer, one with firm roots in the South American musical tradition, though modified in later works by his adoption of the techniques of the Second Viennese School. The rhythmic vitality and colorful scoring of Ginastera's music emerges in a work such as the Concertino for harp, while the Piano Sonata of 1952 is at times introspective in character as well as energetic and dance-like. The *Twelve American Preludes* explore widely different facets of piano technique and idioms and pay tribute to composers such as Copland and Villa-Lobos. In 1958 came the Second String Quartet, which increased his reputation abroad and confirmed his adoption of serial methods, the fiery finale still overtly acknowledging its South American ancestry. Full of virtuosic string writing, it opens with cadenzas for each instrument in turn – the quartet is a work of great vigor and intensity, a more avant-garde version of the earlier *Variaciones concertantes* (1953).

Other important works are concertos for piano and for violin, some early ballet scores and the operas *Don Rodrigo* (1963-4), *Bomarzo* (1966-7), and *Beatrix Cenci* (1971), the last a work of some violence, built on atonal and some aleatoric principles.

Glass, Philip (* Baltimore, 31 Jan. 1937). American composer and performer. He studied in the USA and with Nadia Boulanger in Paris (1964-6), where he met Ravi Shankar. The influence of Indian music as well as rock music is evident in the hypnotic rhythmic complexities coupled to extreme harmonic simplicity in his works, generally performed by his own ensemble. His operas *Einstein on the Beach* (1976) and *Akhnaten* (1984) have enjoyed international success.

Glière, Reinhold (* Kiev, 11 Jan. 1875; † Moscow, 23 June 1956). Russian composer. He studied at the Moscow Conservatory until 1900 and was professor of composition there from 1920 until 1941. He tended to prefer the larger forms of opera, ballet, symphony and symphonic poem, always with a pronounced melodic line and often with a heroic Soviet theme. As such he was heir to the Russian Romantic tradition, though at the same time he showed considerable interest in folk culture, particularly of the regions around the Caspian Sea. He was also an accomplished pianist and conductor.

Goehr, Alexander (* Berlin, 10 Aug. 1932). English composer of German birth. His father, the conductor, Walter Goehr, who had studied with Schoenberg, brought the family to England in 1933. Alexander Goehr studied in Manchester, then with Messiaen and Loriod, becoming professor of music at Leeds University (1971) and Cambridge (1976). His cosmopolitan background, reinforced by visits to Darmstadt, has led to the development of a style rooted in the late Romantic and expressionist language of the Second Viennese School and governed by a strong formal sense. Of his early compositions, the Violin Concerto (1962) is in two contrasting movements, the first a set of variations of classical restraint, the second brilliant and dramatic. This was followed by the *Little Symphony* and the *Little Music for Strings* (both 1963). *Arden Must Die*, his first opera, dates from 1966; *Naboth's Vineyard* (a dramatic madrigal) from 1968. In 1970 came the *Symphony in one Movement*; *Shadowplay-2*, for music-theater; the *Sonata about Jerusalem*, and the *Concerto for Eleven Instruments*. Two years later Goehr composed a piano concerto and he has also written notable chamber works.

Grainger, Percy (* Brighton, Melbourne, 8 July 1882; † White Plains, N.Y., 20 Feb. 1961).

Australian–American composer, pianist, folksong collector, writer and teacher. After studying in Australia and in Germany with Busoni, he embarked on a successful career as a soloist, touring extensively. Friendship with Grieg and Delius aroused in him a deep and lasting interest in folk music. His unconventional techniques ranged from the use of free rhythmic devices, as in *Train Music* and *Bush Music*, nonsense words, as in *Irish Tune from County Derry*, speech rhythms, whistling and ensemble extemporization, to unorthodox performance directions. Many of Grainger's pieces exist in a variety of instrumental and vocal arrangements, including a large number for chorus, and they include original works inspired by folk music as well as many freely adapted and imaginatively arranged versions of folk-tunes. He also made settings for Kipling's *Jungle Book*.

Granados, Enrique (* Lérida, 27 July 1867; † at sea, English Channel, 24 Mar. 1916). Spanish composer and pianist. Initially a pupil of Pedrell in Barcelona, in 1887 he went to Paris to study piano with Charles de Bériot. After two years he returned to Barcelona, giving his first recital the following year. In 1898 he had his first great success, in Madrid, with a *zarzuela*, *Maria del Carmen*. He continued to compose and teach at his Academia Granados, founded in 1901, as well as perform, and he knew an even greater success with the piano suite *Goyescas* (1911), which was adapted as an opera, premièred in New York in 1916. His tragic death cut short what he saw as only the beginning of his career as a composer. Piano and vocal works make up the bulk of his *oeuvre*, and he made free use of Spanish folk rhythms and harmonies. Both by his example and his teaching he gave a powerful new impetus to Spanish music.

Hába, Alois (* Vizovice, Moravia, 21 June 1893; † Prague 18 Nov. 1973). Czech composer. He studied in Prague, Vienna and Berlin and by 1920 had evolved his own style of composition based on quarter tones, as well as an ultra-chromatic theory of composition. Hába was also involved in making instruments capable of producing these tones. Among works for the more conventional system of semitones are several string quartets, songs and an opera.

Hahn, Reynaldo (* Caracas, 9 Aug. 1875; † Paris, 28 Jan. 1947). French composer and conductor of Venezuelan birth. Hahn was only eleven when he was accepted by the Paris Conservatoire, where Massenet gave him lessons in composition.

He achieved success in the theater, both as conductor (especially of Mozart operas) and composer, writing incidental music, ballets, operettas and operas. He acquired a reputation in the salons of Paris as a singer to his own accompaniment. The fluent, elegant, but also expressive style which Hahn successfully brought to his many songs appears, too, in the chamber music, a piano quintet and a sonata for violin and piano.

Harrison, Lou (* Portland, Oregon, 14 May 1917). American composer, poet and dancer. He studied with Cowell in San Francisco and Schoenberg in Los Angeles and worked with Cage during World War II, organizing recitals of percussion music while earning his living in a wide variety of ways. He moved to New York in 1943 where he met Virgil Thomson, who promoted his music. He has made a study of Korean and Chinese music, and a refined eclecticism is a hallmark of his style.

Henry, Pierre (* Paris, 9 Dec. 1927). French composer. He studied piano with Nadia Boulanger at the Paris Conservatoire (1938-48), where he also attended Messiaen's classes. He joined Pierre Schaeffer in the electronic studio of French Radio in 1949, and from 1950 to 1958 was head of the *musique concrète* research group. He was the first musician with a formal education to devote himself to electronic techniques. He has written music for a wide variety of uses, including ballet, cinema, radio, television and the church, and many of his more recent works combine music and spectacle. His collaboration with Maurice Béjart's ballet, in particular his *Jerks électroniques* (1967), brought electronic music to a much wider, and enthusiastic, audience.

Henze, Hans Werner (* Gütersloh, 1 July 1926). German composer. Henze has composed in all main media, operas and ballets forming a significant part of his *oeuvre*. Always receptive to musical stimuli, he responded to jazz in early ballet-scores such as *Labyrinth* and *Maratona* (just as in some of the works written after 1966 he absorbed the influence of the Rolling Stones), and to Stravinsky (along with Hindemith and Bartók) in *Rosa Silber* and the First String Quartet. Studies in twelve-tone writing with Leibowitz had a lasting effect, and around the time of the First Symphony and the First Violin Concerto (1947) serial techniques took on greater importance, a trend confirmed in the Piano Variations (1949). Symbolizing Henze's move to Italy in 1953 is the opera *Il Rè cervo* ('King Stag'), a revised version (1962) of *König Hirsch*, on which he had worked between 1952 and 1955. With its fairy-tale setting, free vocal style and successful *mélange* of traditional and contemporary harmonic idioms, it is an important landmark in Henze's career. His alignment with left-wing politics, in some ways a logical extension of the cool, anti-Romantic stance of his operas of the early sixties such as *Elegy for Young Lovers* and *Der junge Lord*, emerged unequivocally in the Sixth Symphony (1969), which quotes from Vietnamese liberation songs and from Theodorakis's 'Hymn to Freedom.'

Henze's avant-garde compositions include *Compases* (a viola concerto with small ensemble, incorporating aleatoric devices) and the Second Violin Concerto, for an ensemble with tape and speaking voices; among his more recent stage works are *We Come to the River* (1974-6), *Orpheus* (1979) and *El Rey de Harlem* (1980).

Hindemith, Paul (* Hanau, 16 Nov. 1895; † Frankfurt-am-Main, 28 Dec. 1963). German composer and violist. *See pp.214-221.*

Holbrooke, Joseph (* Croydon, 5 July 1878; † London, 5 Aug. 1958). English composer. One of the most prolific English composers in the early part of this century, he studied piano and composition at the Royal Academy of Music, thereafter giving frequent performances of contemporary British compositions as well as of his own music. His style draws heavily on the Romantic composers, particularly Wagner, whose influence dominates *The Cauldron of Annwyn*, a trilogy of operas on Welsh legends. The writings of Edgar Allan Poe inspired both the symphonic poem *The Raven* and the ballet *The Red Mask*. A piano concerto displays Holbrooke's dramatic, Romantic idiom and his grasp of orchestral effects and coloring.

Program-music dominates even the chamber music, although Holbrooke succeeds, for the most part, in scaling down the massive effects which characterize his orchestral writing.

Holst, Gustav (* Cheltenham, 21 Sept. 1874; † London, 25 May 1934). English composer and teacher, of Swedish ancestry. Musical talent manifested itself at an early age, and he gained practical experience as an organist and choral conductor before entering the Royal College of Music in 1893, where he studied under Stanford. He was an outstandingly original composer, but it was as a teacher and as a director of music that he achieved the greatest distinction, his pragmatic approach having even greater influence on pupils and other musicians than his own compositions. Holst's involvement with folk music, through his close friend Vaughan Williams, found its most convincing expression in the one-act opera *At the Boar's Head* (1924). While still a young man, he had also felt drawn to oriental subjects, and with characteristic thoroughness undertook studies of Sanskrit and of Indian music, resulting in four sets of choral hymns from the *Rig Veda* and his last opera *Savitri*.

His large-scale works include *The Hymn of Jesus* (1918), the First Choral Symphony (settings of Keats) 1924, *A Choral Fantasia* (R. Bridges) 1930, and, most popular of all his works, *The Planets*, a suite for large orchestra and female chorus.

Honegger, Arthur (* Le Havre, 10 Mar. 1892; † Paris, 27 Nov. 1955. Swiss composer. He studied at the Zürich Conservatory and then at the Conservatoire in Paris, where he met Milhaud, who became one of his fellow-members in the group 'Les Six.' Honegger was more interested in Cocteau's neoclassicism (they collaborated on the opera *Antigone*, 1927) than in the sardonic nihilism of Satie, while Bach's cantatas remained a strong influence in his many biblical works, including *Le Roi David* (1921), *Judith* (1926), *Jeanne d'Arc au bûcher* (1935) and his last work, *Une Cantate de Noël* (1953). He also composed instrumental, chamber and symphonic works.

Huré, Jean (* Gien, Loiret, 17 Sept. 1877; † Paris, 27 Jan. 1930). French composer, organist, pianist and teacher. Huré wrote a number of treatises on keyboard technique, taught at the Paris Conservatoire, and founded an Ecole Normale de Musique. His use of cyclic forms shows the influence of Franck, but his harmonic language shows an awareness of contemporary trends. French folksong, in particular the music of Brittany, emerges as a feature of his style. Chamber music forms an important part of his output, and his other works include three (unpublished) symphonies, sacred and secular songs, and a stage work.

Ibert, Jacques (* Paris, 15 Aug. 1890; † Paris, 5 Feb. 1962). French composer and administrator. Ibert studied with Paul Vidal at the Paris Conservatoire. Works from his early period include *Escales*, written in impressionist vein and less characteristic than his later operas and ballets. Ibert's Gallic wit and grace find expression in orchestral pieces such as *Féerique*, *Overture de fête*, the Concerto for flute, the Concerto for cello and wind and in his incidental music to Labiche's comedy *The Italian Straw Hat*. This material was again used in the orchestral *Divertissement*. The piano music includes a set of ten *Histoires*, of which the most famous is 'Le Petit âne blanc.' Among his most important chamber works are the String Quartet in C (1943), the Trio for viola, cello and harp, and pieces for wind groups. Ibert was director of the French Academy in Rome from 1937 to 1960.

Ireland, John (* Bowdon, Cheshire, 13 Aug. 1879; † Rock Mill, Washington, Sussex, 12 June 1962). English composer, pianist and teacher. He studied at the Royal College of Music (1893-7), principally piano, and then composition with Stanford (1897-1901). He was organist and choirmaster at St Luke's, Chelsea, 1904-26, and from 1923 until 1939 he taught composition at the Royal College of Music. His early music shows a debt to Brahms, but his style altered considerably under the influence of Debussy, Ravel and Stravinsky. Nevertheless, there is an English quality to his mature work, known chiefly through his songs and piano pieces. His orchestral output is small, but the Piano Concerto (1930) is one of the masterpieces of twentieth-century English music.

Ives, Charles (* Danbury, Conn., 20 Oct. 1874; † New York, 19 May 1954). American composer. *See pp.235-240*

Janáček, Leoš (* Hukvaldy, Moravia, 3 July 1854; † Ostrava, 12 Aug. 1928). Czech composer. *See pp.131-143.*

Järnefelt, Armas (* Viipuri, 14 Aug. 1869; † Stockholm, 23 June 1958). Finnish composer and conductor. He studied with Busoni in Helsinki, Becker in Berlin and Massenet in Paris, and in 1907 became conductor of the Royal Opera in Stockholm. He took Swedish nationality, but returned to Finland as director of the National Opera (1932-6) and conductor of the Helsinki Philharmonic Orchestra (1942-3). A champion of Mahler and Schoenberg, his own music is Romantic and often patriotic in character.

Jolivet, André (* Paris, 8 Aug. 1905; † Paris, 20 Dec. 1974). French composer. Influenced chiefly by Varèse, with whom he studied between 1930 and 1933, Jolivet set out in his early compositions to write in a style unrelated to the traditions of Western music. This led to such innovatory works as *Mana* (1935), an unashamedly dissonant suite of six piano pieces that points up one of Jolivet's essential preoccupations, the musical expression of the forces that regulate the world. There followed a short period of music in more conventional idiom, including the *opéra bouffe Dolorès* (1942) and the ballet, *Guignol et Pandore* (1943). The works of his maturity begin with the First Piano Sonata (1945), dedicated to Bartók. Both the Concertino and the Concerto for trumpet reflect the influence of jazz, demonstrating also Jolivet's virtuosic handling of instruments; there are concertos for percussion and for *ondes Martenot* as well as for piano, and the second of his two concertos for cello was written for Rostropovich in 1966. He

wrote three symphonies as well as vocal and choral pieces, an oratorio and theater and ballet music.

Kabalevsky, Dmitri Borisovich (* St Petersburg, 30 Dec. 1904; † Moscow, Feb. 1987). Russian composer. He studied at the Moscow Conservatory from 1925, returning there to teach in 1932. His work is essentially conservative and readily accessible, in accordance with Soviet artistic principles, and his best music is characterized by fluent melodic writing and by vivacious, colorful rhythms. This is evident in the three concertos (for violin, cello and piano) written for young players. The use of folk music is integral to his five operas, which glorify the people's struggle and often incorporate popular Russian peasant and revolutionary songs. His Requiem (1963) is a plea for world peace.

Kagel, Mauricio Raul (* Buenos Aires, 24 Dec. 1931). Argentinian composer. He studied with Ginastera before becoming chorus-master at the Colón Theater and founding a chamber orchestra (1954). Two years later he settled in Cologne, where he joined the Radio electronic music studio and directed the Rheinisches Kammerorchester. He has written conventional music for orchestra, including *Heterophonie* (1959-61), a sextet (1953 and 1957), *Sonant* for three instruments and percussion (1960) and *Anagrama* for voice and orchestra (1955-8), as well as some exclusively electronic pieces such as *Transicións I* and *II* (1959-60), *Antithèse* (1962), and *Ludwig van* (1969) using Beethoven material.

Khachaturian, Aram Ilyich (* Tbilisi, 6 June 1903; † Moscow 1 May 1978). Russian composer. Largely self-taught, Khachaturian entered the Moscow Conservatory at the age of twenty-six and became internationally known for compositions such as the Violin Concerto (1940), the Piano Concerto (1936), and the ballet *Gayane* (1942), which contains the popular 'Saber Dance.' He later wrote a concerto for the cello as well as concert rhapsodies for violin, cello and piano respectively. A Romantic lyricism combined with colorful orchestration and rhythmic drive, stemming from his interest in folk music, render his music attractive and immediately accessible. The Third Symphony (1947) incurred the charge of 'formalism,' and for two years he confined himself to music for the cinema – his *Funeral Ode in Memory of Lenin* is taken from a film score. In 1956 he completed his ballet *Spartacus*, and music from this and from *Gayane* was incorporated in popular suites for the concert hall.

Kilpinen, Yryö (* Helsinki, 4 Feb. 1892; † Helsinki, 2 May 1959). Finnish composer. He studied in Helsinki, Vienna and Berlin. Known in the West by a mere handful of songs, Kilpinen wrote more than 750, as well as some thirty choruses for male voices and some instrumental pieces. Many of the songs are settings in traditional *Lied* form of German poetry, Hugo Wolf being one of the obvious models for a style that changed little over the years; a ballad-like form is sometimes adopted for Finnish texts. Despite the far from radical nature of its language, Kilpinen's music is evocative as well as lyrical, not least in the imaginative piano accompaniments. *Tunturilauluja* – open-air songs – is a large group of songs about the Finnish landscape, and it is settings such as these, of Finnish poetry, which have made Kilpinen's music popular, particularly in his native country.

Kodály, Zoltán (* Kecskemét, 16 Dec. 1882; † Budapest, 6 Mar. 1967). Hungarian composer. *See pp.144-9.*

Koechlin, Charles (* Paris, 27 Nov. 1867; † Le Canadel, Var, 31 Dec. 1950). French composer, teacher and musicologist. A pupil of Massenet and Fauré, he wrote biographies of Fauré and Debussy, and, at their request, orchestrated some of their theater music. He also wrote a number of important treatises on composition. He developed a unique and extremely varied style, adapted to the particular medium for which he was writing, and while Fauré and Debussy are obvious influences, his works are far from being merely derivative. Koechlin aimed at a clear-textured, melodic style, and his chamber music writing alternates between the simple, Fauré-like melodic line of his piano sonatinas and the more harmonically complex *Paysages*.

Alert to contemporary developments he wrote, in his mid-sixties, a *Hymne* for the *ondes Martenot*, and as early as 1915 composed a viola sonata in bitonal idiom for Milhaud, himself an exponent of bitonality. At the age of eighty he experimented, in a set of orchestral interludes, with an 'atonal-serial' style, although he remained strongly in favor of more traditional idioms.

Křenek, Ernst (* Vienna, 23 Aug. 1900). Austrian–American composer. He began his studies in Vienna, but moved to Berlin. His early works were markedly dissonant, and a comic opera of 1923 included elements of jazz. The influence of Bartók is also evident, as well as neoclassical Stravinsky. He wrote the text and music for the opera *Jonny spielt auf* (1925-6), and its première in Leipzig in 1927 was a scandalous success. He emigrated to America when Hitler occupied Vienna and began an academic career while continuing to compose in many musical languages, from serialism to jazz and electronics.

Ligeti, György (* Dicsöszentmárton [now Tîrnăveni], Transylvania, 28 May 1923). Hungarian composer. He studied at the Franz Liszt Academy in Budapest, and in 1949-50 undertook research into Rumanian folk music. He was made a professor at the Academy in 1950, but moved to Vienna in 1956, where he encountered leading avant-garde composers, in particular Stockhausen.

Experiments followed with electronic music, but these did not satisfy his quest for fundamental musical ideas, which he demonstrated in his *Apparitions* of 1958-9, for four-track tape, a work that brought him international recognition. In 1973 he was appointed professor of composition at the Musikhochschule in Hamburg. Aleatoric experiments occur in his *Volumina* (1962) for organ, the density of tone-clusters and duration of passages being left to the performer, and a similar technique is found in *Lux aeterna* (1966), a piece for sixteen solo voices and chorus. With *Lontano* (1967) Ligeti further explored varieties of orchestral textures, producing imaginative sonorities, but he achieved greater unity and cogency of expression in the Second String Quartet. In the Chamber Concerto (1969-70) he demonstrated his predilection for closely-clustered instrumental sounds and created an iridescent, shifting texture, alternately volatile and static. Ligeti replaces traditional ideas of musical argument with superimposed textures, frenzied micro-tonal buzzings, and atmospheric instrumental layering, but despite the apparent density of his harmony, his scores are often remarkable for their lucidity.

Lucier, Alvin (* Nashua, N. H., 14 May 1931). American composer. A graduate of Yale and Brandeis University, he spent two years in Rome on a Fulbright Scholarship (1960-2), and returned to America to an academic career. Co-founder of the Sonic Arts Union in 1966, he is one of the most innovative of the younger electronic composers and gives concerts and lecture demonstraions in addition to his composition and academic work.

Lutoslawski, Witold (* Warsaw, 25 Jan. 1913). Polish composer. He studied at the Warsaw Conservatory, and his style was influenced by Szymanowski, Stravinsky and Bartók. Although he started composing in the 1930s, wider recognition came only when his personal idiom changed radically in 1961, with *Venetian Games*, in which he first used controlled aleatoric techniques. These involve no random happenings on the part of the performer, for Lutoslawski considers the organization and architectural design of a composition to be of paramount importance. Since 1961 his main compositions have been the String Quartet (1964), *Paroles tissées* (1965, written for Peter Pears), the Second Symphony (1967), and the Cello Concerto (1970). In 1972 came the *Preludes and Fugue* for string orchestra, incorporating fugal and canonic procedures, an impressive vindication of controlled aleatoricism, and in 1980 his Concerto for oboe, harp, strings and percussion. Lutoslawski's idiom impresses through its intellectual strength, its imaginative use of orchestral sonorities, and its emotional range and commitment.

McCabe, John (* Huyton, Lancs., 21 Apr. 1939). English composer and pianist. He had composed thirteen symphonies by the time he went to the Liverpool Institute at the age of eleven, then went on to study composition in Manchester and at the Munich Hochschule. He was resident pianist at Cardiff University (1965-8) and has published a book on Bartók's orchestral music. McCabe is a rather eclectic composer, who stands apart from the mainstream of English tradition. Among his mature work is music for voices, theater, chamber works and full-scale orchestral pieces, including three symphonies.

Maderna, Bruno (* Venice, 21 Apr. 1920; † Darmstadt, 13 Nov. 1973). Italian composer and conductor. He played an unequaled part in the early post-war development of Italian music, presiding, as teacher and conductor, over the early careers of Nono, Berio, Donatoni, Aldo Clementi and others. An accomplished violinist and conductor from an early age, Maderna studied composition with, among others, Malipiero and Scherchen, learning from the latter the techniques of dodecaphonism.

He rapidly became an influential force in Italian music, but although he experimented with aleatoricism, he disavowed the more extreme tendencies of the avant garde. He lectured at various important musical centers, and made performing editions of music by Vivaldi, Monteverdi (*Orfeo*), Josquin, Gabrieli and of pieces from the *Fitzwilliam Virginal Book*. His own compositions include a string quartet, concertos for piano and for violin, three concertos for oboe, electronic music, and music combining live and taped sounds. Operas include *Don Perlimplin*, a tape montage for radio, in which the principal characters are played by instruments instead of voices, *Satyricon* and *Hyperion*, which also provided material for concert excerpts, divided into 'Dimensioni' and arias.

Mahler, Gustav (* Kalište, Bohemia, 7 July 1860; † Vienna, 18 May 1911. Austrian composer and conductor. *See Volume III.*

Malipiero, Gian Francesco (* Venice, 18 Mar. 1882; † Treviso, 1 Aug. 1973). Italian composer and musicologist. Although his work is uneven, and he was less influential than Casella or Pizzetti, he was the most original and inventive Italian composer of his generation. One of Italy's most sought-after teachers in the first half of the twentieth century, Malipiero developed a style based initially on his intimate knowledge of earlier Italian composers such as Vivaldi and Monteverdi (many of whose works he edited for performance), of Gregorian chant, and of Italian folksong. Unlike his friend Casella, he did not feel drawn to neoclassicism, preferring instead the new avenues opened up by Debussy; nor did he turn his back entirely on the nineteenth century, despite his avowed distaste of what he regarded as the excesses of German music. Transparency of texture, together with melodic and instrumental inventiveness, characterize much of his music. His vast output includes also a number of works for the theater, including three *Commedie Goldoniane*, *Pantea* (1919), the gigantic trilogy *L'Orfeide* (1920-5) and *Torneo Notturno* (1929).

Martin, Frank (* Geneva, 15 Sept. 1890; † Naarden, 21 Nov. 1974). Swiss composer. He had no formal musical training, and lived in Zürich, Rome, Paris and, latterly, Amsterdam. He evolved a highly personal idiom, influenced initially by Romantic music, although he was subsequently attracted by the works of Debussy. However, a performance of Bach's *St Matthew Passion* heard in his youth was the single most important musical influence, and he himself composed several quasi-liturgical works, including a Requiem written as

late as 1971-2, as well as a secular cantata, *Le Vin herbé* (1938-41).

Simplicity of expression and directness of communication concerned Frank Martin throughout his career, and for all that his mature style is characterized by unconventional modulations and extreme chromaticism, his scores are remarkable for the vibrancy of their textures. It was an instrumental work, the *Petit symphonie concertante* of 1945, which brought him fame. An impressive list of works includes the fine Violin Concerto, the Concerto for seven wind instruments, percussion and strings, and a quantity of chamber and vocal music. The piano does not figure prominently among his compositions, the *Eight Preludes* of 1948, the two concertos and the *Ballade* being the only pieces highlighting the instrument.

Martinů, Bohuslav (* Polička, East Bohemia, 8 Dec. 1890; † Liestal, Switzerland, 28 Aug. 1959). Czech composer. He spent some years as a violinist in the Czech Philharmonic Orchestra, then lived for seventeen years in Paris before taking up residence in the USA, a ten-year stay which led to the composition of a number of large-scale works. A restless exile, he always planned to return to his homeland, but never took up the appointments offered him in Prague. He returned to Europe in 1951 and spent his last years in Switzerland.

Martinů acknowledged the prime influences on the development of his style to be Moravian folksong, the Italian *concerto grosso*, the Elizabethan madrigal and French music, particularly Debussy; and the traditional Classical procedures of sonata form held little interest for him. An 'advanced' (although ultimately tonal) idiom and motoric, driving rhythms are characteristic, as are the exuberance and tunefulness which mark out his idiom from much twentieth-century music. He was one of the most prolific composers of the century. Early works up to and including his Paris sojourn show him responding to the jazz influences of the period; probably best-known is *La Revue de cuisine* originally written as a ballet.

The works of his maturity include a large number of concertos, and the piano features prominently in many orchestral pieces, notably the concerto for two string orchestras, piano and timpani, and the *Toccata e due canzoni*, one of his most arresting and entertaining compositions. Outstanding among his hundred or so works for piano solo are the *Fantasie a toccata* and the Sonata of 1954, while the opera *Julietta* (1936-7), subtitled 'La Clef des songes,' which hovers between reality and a dream-world, is central to his work for the theater, which also includes ballets. Chamber and choral music also form a significant part of his output.

Medtner, Nikolai Karlovich (* Moscow, 5 Jan. 1880; † London, 13 Nov. 1951). Russian composer and pianist. Medtner's German descent and Russian environment produced a striking mixture in his personality. He graduated from the Moscow Conservatory in 1900 with a gold medal for piano playing, but as a composer he was virtually self-taught, though much encouraged by Taneyev. Apart from chamber music and about a hundred songs – among which are some of the finest written in the twentieth century – Medtner's compositions are entirely for piano, influenced by Schumann, in the early works especially, and Brahms.

Menotti, Gian Carlo (* Cadegliano, 7 July 1911). American composer of Italian birth. He had already written two operas when he entered the Milan Conservatory at the age of thirteen. In 1928 he began studies at the Curtis Institute of Music in Philadelphia, where a close friendship with fellow-student Samuel Barber began. In 1936 came his first great success, the opera *Amelia goes to the Ball*. *The Consul* (1950) is regarded as one of his best achievements – the direct, tuneful idiom deriving from Menotti's admiration for the great nineteenth-century Italian opera composers and Musorgsky.

Several more operas, and a madrigal-ballet appeared between 1951 and 1971, the most successful being the television opera *Amahl and the Night Visitors*. *The Saint of Bleecker Street* (1954) received a number of awards, but

later operas were less favorably received. From 1958 Menotti was director of the Spoleto Festival. Other works include two church operas, two more one-act operas for children, a song-cycle, and chamber and orchestral music, including a Triple Concerto, concertos for violin and for piano (one each), and a symphony.

Messiaen, Oliver (* Avignon, 10 Dec. 1908). French composer and organist. *See pp.267-272.*

Milhaud, Darius (* Aix-en-Provence, 4 Sept. 1892; † Geneva, 22 June 1974). French composer. He initially studied violin at the Paris Conservatoire but eventually decided that he ought to devote himself to composition. He was soon drawn to polytonality, which was one of the most distinctive features of his music. In 1916 he went to Brazil as secretary to Paul Claudel – then French minister – and on his return in 1918 he was taken into the circle surrounding Cocteau, and so became one of 'Les Six.' The opera *La Brébis égarée* (1910-15) caused a riot when it was mounted at the Opéra Comique in 1923. The year before, he had visited America and fallen under the influence of jazz. He visited America again in 1923 and returned there during World War II, retaining a teaching post at Mills College, Oakland, California until 1971. He was also professor of composition at the Paris Conservatoire. His numbered works reached op.441, although they are of widely ranging character and quality. His most personal contribution was probably his use of bitonality, with which he often produced some of his best compositions and most personal expression.

Nancarrow, Conlon (* Texarkana, Arkansas, 27 Oct. 1912). Mexican composer born in America. Nancarrow studied first at the Cincinnati Conservatory (1929-32) and then privately in Boston with Slonimsky, Piston and Sessions (1933-6). He fought in the Spanish Civil War in 1937, then returned to Mexico in 1940, taking Mexican citizenship in 1956. His *Thirty-Seven Studies for Player Piano* (1950-68) indicate his main field of interest, and are a particularly important contribution to the literature of the instrument.

Nielsen, Carl (* Sortelung, nr. Nørre Lyndelse on Funen, 9 June 1865; † Copenhagen, 3 Oct. 1931). Danish composer. Nielsen entered the Copenhagen Conservatory in 1884, enrolling as a student of violin and composition; in 1889 he joined the orchestra of the Royal Opera and in 1908 succeeded Svendsen as conductor. For all its Romantic origins, Nielsen's music belongs quite firmly to the twentieth century, his predilection for polytonality

and an abrasive dissonance imparting an aggressive quality to his six symphonies, which are his greatest achievement. Other orchestral works include concertos for violin, for flute and for clarinet, while his earliest published work, the *Little Suite* for strings is an attractive, Romantic piece, though not typical of his mature style. Apart from some piano music and songs, Nielsen wrote a number of choral works, and a quantity of chamber music, including the engaging Wind Quintet in which he portrays the characters of the players for whom it was composed. His experience in the opera orchestra contributed to his sense of the theater, evident in numerous pieces of incidental music for various plays, and, above all, in his comic opera *Maskarade*, which achieved enormous popularity in his native Denmark.

Nono, Luigi (* Venice, 29 Jan. 1924). Italian composer. He studied composition with Malipiero and also graduated in law, then pursued his musical studies with Maderna and Scherchen. *Variazioni canoniche*, a twelve-tone work, put him in the forefront of Italian music, and the first performance of *Il canto sospeso* ('The Broken Song') in 1956 brought him international recognition. Scored for three solo singers, chorus and orchestra, its text is based on letters of young Resistance fighters, victims of the Nazis. Using the characteristic avant-garde technique of fragmentation, words and syllables split between voices, within a framework based on rhythmical, numerical as well as notational series, Nono achieves a moving account of human suffering. The electronic production of sound

became an important feature of his music, as in *Intolleranza 1960*, an anti-capitalist, multi-media event (Venice, 1961, later revised). From 1964 Nono also worked actively in the dissemination of political ideas, allied to discussion of his music, among workers and trades unions, justifying his use of avant-garde methods to underline his anti-establishment commitment. Later electronic works are the *Musiche per Manzu* (1969), *Y entonces comprendio* (1969-70), *Für Paul Dessau* (1974), *Notturni-albe* (1974), while a non-electronic work is *Ein Gespenst geht um in der Welt* (1971), for soprano, chorus and orchestra. Between 1972 and 1975 he worked on a stage work *Al gran sole carico d'amore*.

Novák, Vítězslav (* Kamenice, 5 Dec. 1870; † Skuteč, 18 July 1949). Czech composer and teacher. Novák first studied law and philosophy at the University of Prague, but after lessons in composition with Dvořák turned to music. His course completed, he became celebrated as a teacher of composition, and at the age of thirty-nine was appointed professor at the Prague Conservatory. Mendelssohn, Grieg and Schumann were his early models; later, Brahms and, of course, Dvořák dominated his musical thought.

Novák's compositions may be divided into three periods: the first includes the G minor Piano Trio, the overture *The Corsair*, his F major *Serenade* for chamber orchestra and a group of small piano pieces. There followed a nationalist phase, with Novák exploring Slovak folk music and writing works under its influence. This nationalist element, together with his ardent Romanticism, led to a phase in which programmatic music predominates: symphonic poems, song-cycles and piano music. Between 1915 and 1934 Novák was concerned principally with writing operas and dramatic works for chorus and orchestra. Late chamber works include the D minor Piano Trio and the Third String Quartet.

Orff, Carl (* Munich, 10 July 1895; † Munich, 29 Mar. 1982). German composer and educationist. After studies in Munich, he became well known for his teaching methods, co-ordinating music, dance and gymnastic training, and encouraging amateurs and children in creative music-making, improvisation and performance. This approach is embodied in his *Schulwerk*. His style was shaped by diverse influences – his interest in pre-Classical musical styles and Gregorian modes, his admiration for Brecht and the folk music of Africa – especially with regard to the theater, for which he composed most of his music. *Carmina Burana* (1937) sets humorous, frequently bawdy, low Latin and German texts to pungent, percussive Stravinsky-like rhythms, with the minimum of contrapuntal and harmonic distraction. *Der Mond* (1939) and *Die Kluge* (1943), on mythical, fairy-tale subjects, pursued Orff's ideal of anti-Romantic operatic form. *Catulli carmina* is a sequel to *Carmina Burana*, and nearly ten years later, in 1951 Orff completed the third part of the trilogy, his cantata *Trionfo di Afrodite*. This 'concerto scenico' employs an archaic, ritualistic approach, using Latin and Greek texts, and harking back to sixteenth-century Italian musical forms. In 1949 Orff made a setting of Sophocles' tragedy *Antigone*, in which a largely percussion-based orchestra provides a backcloth to events on stage; in 1957 he composed a musical play *Comoedia de Christi resurrectione*, and two years later another work from Sophocles, *Oedipus der Tyrann*, this trilogy being completed with *Prometheus* (1966). His last large-scale work was *De temporum fine comoedia* (1973), a kind of musical apocalypse.

Palmgren, Selim (* Björneborn [now Pori], 16 Feb. 1878; † Helsinki, 13 Dec. 1951). Finnish composer, pianist and conductor. He was a pupil of Wegelius, teacher also of Sibelius; after attending the Helsinki Conservatory, his studies continued in Berlin, where Busoni was his piano teacher. After some years as a conductor he devoted himself to composition and the piano, touring Europe and America, teaching composition for a time at the Eastman School of Music. Palmgren composed a good deal of piano music (five concertos and numerous smaller pieces), an opera, choral music, and various orchestral works, among them the suite *From Finland*, but he is best known for his many dramatic and lyrical songs.

Panufnik, Andrzej (* Warsaw, 24 Sept. 1914). Polish composer, pianist and conductor, naturalized British subject. By the beginning of World War II Panufnik had established himself as a composer of some repute in his native Poland; the war years, however, were spent in obscurity, composing and undertaking clandestine concert work with a fellow-

composer and pianist, Lutoslawski. Most of his compositions written before 1944 were destroyed in the fighting. With the end of the war Panufnik embarked on a busy conducting and composing career, receiving orchestral commissions and numerous honors from the Polish Government. However, the artistic pressures under the Communist régime eventually induced Panufnik to settle in Britain, and in 1961 he became a British citizen. Much in demand as a conductor of some of the world's leading orchestras, he directed the City of Birmingham orchestra from 1957 to 1959, thereafter, however, devoting himself mainly to composition. His most notable works from this period are a series of symphonies, in which his feeling for architectural, symmetrical proportions replaces traditional Classical forms. Other compositions include the choral *Universal Prayer* (1968-9), *Autumn Music* (1970) and a series of concertante works.

Partch, Harry (* Oakland, Cal., 24 June 1901; † San Diego, Cal., 3 Sept. 1974). American composer, instrument-maker and performer. Partch was mostly self-taught, and his researches into tuning persuaded him to reject conventional Western traditions and invent not only his own system with a forty-three note scale, but the instruments required to propagate it. He then formed and trained his own group, Gate 5 Ensemble, to perform his works on the instruments he had invented.

Penderecki, Krzysztof (* Debica, 23 Nov. 1933). Polish composer. He was only twenty-six when he carried off all three prizes in a national competition for Polish composers. A year later came the *Threnody* (Hiroshima) for 52 strings, then in 1965 the *St Luke Passion*, which brought him international recognition. *Threnody* demonstrates Penderecki's extensive knowledge of string technique, based on his early training as a violinist. With *Emanations* and *Strophe* he had shown remarkable grasp of serial and aleatoric processes, while *From the Psalms of David* reveals his predilection for choral writing and commitment to religious subjects. The dissonant, polyphonic writing incorporates sound effects such as whispers and shouts, while *Dimensions of Time and Silence* carries unorthodox vocal techniques even further; *Polymorphia* (1961), exploiting the idea of sound clusters in conjunction with unorthodox playing techniques, produces a welter of string sound. Penderecki studied and incorporated electronic techniques but eventually discarded them, although his use of quarter-tone clusters, pitchless notes, fragmented sounds, and effects such as slow *glissandi*, approximate at times to electronic compositional methods. Other works include two Symphonies (1973 and 1980), a Violin Concerto (1972), a Partita for harpsichord and mixed ensemble and a virtuoso Sonata for cello and orchestra.

Petrassi, Goffredo (* Zagarolo, nr. Palestrina, 16 July 1904). Italian composer and teacher. After Dallapiccola he is the most important and influential Italian musician of his generation. Petrassi developed in his music a strongly neoclassical idiom, colored in later years by twelve tone writing. The orchestral *Partita* of 1932, based on three baroque forms, established Petrassi as one of Italy's most promising composers between the wars. A predilection for classical forms emerges in the eight concertos for orchestra, the first of which dates from 1931, the last from 1972. The slight tendency to academicism in his instrumental music is offset by the lyrical adagio of no.1, by the graceful Second Concerto, and the rare Bartókian elements of no.4. The Fifth is even more intense, quoting as it does from Petrassi's own *Coro di morti*, a setting of words by Leopardi for male chorus, three pianos, brass, double-basses and percussion. Serialist techniques appear in the Third Concerto (1952), which explores the intrinsic character of each instrument. By the Fifth Concerto dodecaphony had been fully absorbed into his idiom. The Seventh Concerto (1961-2) is a collective virtuoso display piece.

Pfitzner, Hans (* Moscow, 5 May, 1869; † Salzburg, 22 May 1949). German composer and conductor. *See Volume III.*

Pierné, Gabriel (* Metz, 16 Aug. 1863; † Ploujean, Finistère, 17 July 1937). French composer and conductor. César Franck and Massenet were among the figures who guided Pierné's studies; in 1890 he succeeded Franck as organist at Sainte-Clotilde. He conducted at the Concerts Colonne for nearly thirty years, and composed prolifically. Two distinct idioms reflect the twin influences on his career: to Franck we may attribute the serious character of some works, while the light operas would appear to owe something to Massenet. Pierné also wrote for the ballet and

incidental music for plays. His principal orchestral works are *Fantaisie-ballet* and *Poème symphonique*, both for piano and orchestra, a piano concerto and a concert piece for harp. Among his chamber music are the Violin Sonata, the Piano Quintet and Piano Trio, and the Cello Sonata. Pierné also wrote a quantity of piano music, some pieces for organ, and more than fifty songs.

Piston, Walter (* Rockland, Maine, 20 Jan. 1894; † Belmont, Mass., 12 Nov. 1976). American composer and teacher. Piston taught himself the violin and piano. He worked briefly as an architectural draftsman and played the violin in theater orchestras and dance bands. After studying at Harvard, he went to Paris for lessons with Nadia Boulanger and Paul Dukas. The author of one of the most widely-used text-books on harmony, Piston was not only a renowned teacher, numbering Carter and Bernstein among his pupils, but also a prolific composer.

He had little interest in the development of a specifically American style, and his idiom is strongly neoclassical, influenced initially by Stravinsky and Roussel, with a high regard for Classical forms and a fondness for fugues and counterpoint. His compositions include eight symphonies, two violin concertos, a viola concerto, a concerto for two pianos, and a concerto for clarinet. Piston wrote no operas and little vocal music, but a quantity of chamber music includes several string quartets, a piano quintet, a string sextet, and a number of pieces for wind and strings. The colorful score of his ballet suite *The Incredible Flutist* (1938) is one of his most popular works.

Poulenc, Francis (* Paris, 7 Jan. 1899; † Paris, 30 Jan. 1963). French composer and pianist. Poulenc received his first piano lessons from his mother and then, at the age of sixteen, from Ricardo Viñes. In 1917 and 1918 he made the acquaintance of Auric, Honegger, Milhaud and Satie. During his military service (1918-21) he continued composing, but realized that he lacked the neccessary foundation. He tried Paul Vidal and Ravel as teachers before settling on Koechlin (1921-4). During that time he also sought out Schoenberg in Vienna, Casella in Italy, and became a member of 'Les Six.' Diaghilev's production of *Les Biches* (1924) established Poulenc's reputation, but it was more than ten years before he reached a new peak with his *Litanies de la Vierge Noire* (1936). By this time he had also established a working relationship with the singer Pierre Bernac. He remained in France during World War II, and in 1947 had a great success with his first opera, *Les Mamelles de Tirésias*. In 1948 Poulenc and Bernac made the first of several visits to the USA.

In the earlier part of Poulenc's career critics tended to underestimate his significance as a composer, largely because of the simplicity and directness of his music. In the post-war period, however, his stature began to grow with his output – piano music, chamber music, orchestral music, operas, ballets and incidental music as well as film scores, church music and songs. It was in the last domain – *mélodie* – that Poulenc made his greatest contribution.

Prokofiev, Sergei (* Sontsovka, Ukraine, 23 Apr. 1891; † Nikolina Gora, nr. Moscow, 5 Mar. 1953). Russian composer. *See pp.223-6.*

Rachmaninov, Sergei (* Semyonovo, 1 Apr. 1873; † Los Angeles, 28 Mar. 1943). Russian composer and pianist. *See pp.83-93.*

Ravel, Maurice (* Ciboure, Pyrénées-Atlantiques, 7 Mar. 1875; † Paris, 28 Dec. 1937). French composer. *See pp.59-73.*

Reich, Steve (* New York, 3 Oct. 1936). American composer. Studied philosophy at Cornell University (1953-7), then composition at the Juilliard School (1958-61) and Mills College (1962-3) with Milhaud and Berio. He also made a study of African drumming. In 1966 he founded the group Steve Reich and Musicians, performing himself on keyboard instruments and percussion. Only ensembles of which he is a member may perform his music, which is especially concerned with canon in extended or elaborated form, with emphasis on the subtleties of rhythm. His works are often constructed from a single chord or phrase, and he also experiments with multiples of the same instruments, either live (*Four Organs*, 1970) or live and recorded (*Violin Phase*, 1967).

Respighi, Ottorino (* Bologna, 9 July 1879; † Rome, 18 Apr. 1936). Italian composer. At the age of twenty-one Respighi became principal viola of the opera orchestra in St Petersburg, where he pursued his composition studies under Rimsky-Korsakov. For the next few years he was active in solo and chamber music work, but after lessons with Max Bruch in Berlin he turned whole-heartedly to composition. His earliest compositions (including two operas) established his reputation, and in 1913 he was appointed professor of composition at the Accademia di S. Cecilia in Rome, where he spent the rest of his life. Melodic, finely wrought and imaginatively orchestrated, Respighi's music shows the influence of Rimsky-Korsakov and Richard Strauss and of the modal writing of an earlier age. His transcriptions and arrangements include orchestral versions of some of Bach's Preludes and Fugues and the C minor Passacaglia, as well as ballet music (*La Boutique fantasque*) from the music of Rossini; he also made free adaptations of Monteverdi's *Orfeo* and other baroque works. He is best remembered for his impressionist orchestral scores, *Fontane di Roma*, *Pini di Roma* and *Trittico botticelliano*. Popular, too, are the two sets of *Antiche arie e danze per liuto* arranged for orchestra.

Riley, Terry (* Colfax, Cal., 24 June 1935). American composer and performer. He studied composition at Berkeley, then moved to New York and Paris (1962-4), where he worked in French Radio recording studios and began to experiment with extended repetition of short phrases, tape loops and layers of recorded sound. Since 1970 he has devoted much of his time to the study and performance of Indian music. Improvisation is also an important element in his work.

Ropartz, Joseph Guy (* Guingamp, Côtes-du-Nord, 15 June 1864; † Lanloup, Côtes-du-Nord, 22 Nov. 1955). French composer and conductor. Ropartz was twenty-one when he entered the Paris Conservatoire, studying with Massenet and later with Franck. His works show the strong influence of Franck, both in their purity of expression and in their formal, often cyclic structures. Another influence was the landscape and music of his native Brittany, evident not only in the chamber music but also in his opera, *Le Pays*, and his orchestral music, which includes five symphonies and several symphonic poems.

Roussel, Albert (* Tourcoing, Nord, 5 Apr. 1869; † Royan, Charente-Maritime, 23 Aug. 1937). French composer. *See pp.74-7.*

Rubbra, Edmund (* Northampton, 23 May 1901; † Chalfont, Bucks., 14 Feb. 1986). English composer, pianist, teacher and writer. He studied composition at the Royal College of Music with Cyril Scott and Holst, and from 1947 to 1968 lectured in music at Oxford University; from 1961 he also taught composition at the Guildhall School of Music in London. Rubbra was a leading exponent of English symphonic writing in the middle of the twentieth century – his eleventh symphony is op.153 – as well as composing a great deal of chamber, vocal and choral music.

Ruggles, Carl [Charles] (* East Marion, Mass., 11 Mar. 1876; † Bennington, Vermont, 24 Oct. 1971). American composer. He studied music at Harvard and in the 1920s and 1930s was associated with Ives, Varèse and Cowell, sharing their aim of searching for a new spirit in music. Unlike them, however, he composed music that was atonal and polyphonic.

Notable among many unfinished and unpublished works are his opera *The Sunken Bell* (*c.*1912-23), largely destroyed; his largest composition, *Sun-treader* (1926-31) for orchestra; *Evocations* for piano (1935-43, revised 1954); and *Organum* for orchestra (1944-7).

Satie, Erik (* Honfleur, 17 May 1866; † Paris, 1 July 1925). French composer. *See pp.77-9.*

Schaeffer, Pierre (* Nancy, 14 Aug. 1910). French composer, theorist, writer and teacher. He began his working life as a telecommunications engineer in Strasbourg in 1934 and two years later became a technician for French Radio. In 1941 he founded 'Jeune France,' an association for those concerned with music, theater and the visual arts. In 1942 he was involved in setting up the Studio d'Essai which was both the center for the Resistance within French Radio and also the birthplace of *musique concrète.* It was Schaeffer's tape recording of 1948 that inaugurated the medium. In 1968 he was appointed associate professor at the Paris Conservatoire to teach electronic composition – recognition of his early perception of the importance of electronic techniques.

Schmitt, Florent (* Blamont, Meurthe-et-Moselle, 28 Sept. 1870; † Neuilly-sur-Seine, Paris, 17 Aug. 1958). French composer.

A pupil of Massenet and Fauré, Schmitt won the Prix de Rome in 1900. After travels in Europe and Turkey he returned to Paris, writing prolifically for the stage (ballets and incidental music, but no opera), orchestra (symphonic poems and two symphonies, the second completed in the year of his death), chorus and voice (songs with orchestra and with piano), and for the piano numerous pieces on a smaller scale.

Schmitt is remembered chiefly for the powerful Piano Quintet (1908), written in cyclic form and the *Lied et scherzo* for wind ensemble. Of his works on a grand scale, the most notable are his monumental setting of Psalm XLVII and *La tragédie de Salomé,* written in 1907 for the dancer Loïe Fuller.

Schoenberg, Arnold (* Vienna, 13 Sept. 1874; † Los Angeles, 13 July 1951). Austrian composer and teacher. *See pp.187-205.*

Schreker, Franz (* Monaco, 23 Mar. 1878; † Berlin, 21 Mar. 1934). Austrian composer, dramatist and teacher. He studied with Fuchs in Vienna, where he later founded the Philharmonic Chorus – giving the first performance of Schoenberg's *Gurrelieder* in 1913 – and became professor at the Academy (1912). For ten years his operas enjoyed enormous success, but after his move to Berlin (1920), where he became a distinguished director of the Musikhochschule, his more refined style led to a decline in popularity. He composed choral music and songs, as well as orchestral and chamber music, but his principal works were his operas, for which he wrote his own libretti. These favored erotic, Freudian subjects, and musically used his own system of 'sound-tints,' evident in his luxuriant and subtle orchestration; the most interesting are *Der ferne Klang* (1902-12) and *Die Gezeichneten* (1913-18), but their production complexities have prevented almost any revivals.

Sessions, Roger (* Brooklyn, N.Y., 28 Dec. 1896; † Princeton, N.J., 16 Mar. 1985). American composer, theorist and teacher. Educated at Harvard and Yale, Sessions lived in Italy and Germany for some years before returning to America in 1933 and becoming a renowned teacher of composition. He was himself a student of Bloch. After an early tendency toward neoclassicism he turned to dodecaphony, his first major work in this idiom being a sonata for solo violin. After that time he added six symphonies to the two already composed in 1927 and 1946, other important orchestral works being the Piano Concerto, the *Divertimento* (1959) and the *Rhapsody* (1970). Music involving voices includes *The Idyll of Theocritus*, *Psalm CXL*, a Mass for male voices and organ, a cantata *When Lilacs last in the Dooryard Bloom'd*, *Three Choruses on Biblical Texts*, and two operas. His chamber music evinces the same austerity and intellectual complexity of musical argument.

Séverac, Déodat de (* Saint-Félix-de-Caraman, Haute-Garonne, 20 July 1872; † Céret, Pyrénées-Orientales, 24 Mar. 1921). French composer. Séverac received his main musical training at the Schola Cantorum under Magnard and d'Indy. Nature and the landscape of his native Languedoc were the prime inspirations for his music, which is frequently modal in character and belongs very much to the French impressionist school. His piano music, which together with his songs makes up the bulk of his published works, abounds in bell-like effects, the sounds of rivers and waterfalls, and of chanting. His orchestral music includes two symphonic poems, *Nymphes au crepuscule* and *Les Grenouilles qui demandent un roi*, and a suite, *Didon et Énée*, and his chamber music includes a piano quintet. He also composed some operatic, incidental, church and organ music.

Shostakovich, Dmitri (* St Petersburg, 25 Sept. 1906; † Moscow, 9 Aug. 1975). Russian composer. *See pp.226-233.*

Sibelius, Jean (* Hämeenlinna, 8 Dec. 1865; † Järvenpää, 20 Sept. 1957). Finnish composer. *See pp.95-105.*

Skalkottas, Nikolaos (* Khalkis, Evvoia, 21 Mar. 1904; † Athens, 20 Sept. 1949). Greek composer and violinist. He studied with Jarnach (1925-7) and then Schoenberg (1927-31), and he also took some lessons with Weill (1928-9). Although in his youth he had been hailed as one of Schoenberg's most promising pupils, the art of composition, indeed, having supplanted his studies as a talented violinist destined for a solo career, from 1933 to 1945 he earned his living as an orchestral violinist in his native Athens, composing many works but publishing nothing.

Twelve-tone techniques dominate his main compositions, which include three piano concertos, a violin concerto, two symphonic suites and the overture *Ulysses* (in reality a one-movement symphony for large orchestra). Hindemith is recalled in the conciseness of his style, and Stravinsky in the acerbity of rhythm that lends wit to music which can be both warm and eloquent. Atonality rather than strict serialism is found in some pieces. The folk music of Greece, too, made its mark, as in the colorful *Five Greek Dances* for strings. Throughout his compositions Skalkottas shows his intimate working knowledge of instruments – complex and difficult though his music frequently is, the demands made on players are based on first-hand experience of the techniques of playing.

Skriabin, Alexander (* Moscow, 6 Jan. 1872; † Moscow, 27 Apr. 1951). Russian composer and pianist. He studied the piano with Konyns and Zverev, and Taneyev supervised his musical education at the Moscow Conservatory, which he attended in 1888-91. He had already started composing, with Chopin the dominating influence, and he continued to compose prolifically, mainly for the piano, in the succeeding years, during which he made a number of concert tours. In 1897 he joined the staff of the Conservatory, but from 1905 to 1911, when for much of the time he was traveling in western Europe, he was supported as a composer by grants from his publishers, first Belyayev, then, after his death, Koussevitzky. Of the numerous piano works from his early career, the 24 Preludes, op.11, have long been regarded as essential items in the pianist's repertoire.

Skriabin's pursuit of theosophical mysticism came to permeate every aspect of his musical philosophy and activities. He envisaged a total synthesis of the arts, dominated by music, combining to serve the Perfect Rite, an overtly erotic philosophy of cosmic union, with Skriabin himself as the musical Messiah preparing the way for the last great Act of Fulfillment. This new doctrine was first publicly proclaimed in 1903 in his Third Symphony, or *Divine Poem*, and further revealed in the *Poem of Ecstasy* (1907), both of which show Skriabin's adventurous harmonic experiments. His last orchestral work was *Prometheus, the Poem of Fire* (1910), which calls for a huge orchestra with a large percussion section and parts for chorus and light- or color-organ.

Smyth, Dame Ethel (* London, 22 Apr. 1858; † Woking, Surrey, 9 May 1944). English composer. *See Volume III.*

Stenhammar, Wilhelm (* Stockholm, 7 Feb. 1871; † Stockholm, 20 Nov. 1927). Swedish composer, pianist and conductor. Stenhammar became something of a national hero with his patriotic compositions, and he was also well known in Sweden as a conductor, making his début at the age of twenty-six with his own overture *Excelsior!* Operas and incidental music to plays formed an important part of his output. The second of his two symphonies and the orchestral Serenade achieved popularity in Sweden, while the last three of his six string quartets show him moving away from Viennese influence to a more personal idiom.

Stockhausen, Karlheinz (* Burg Mödrath, nr. Cologne, 22 Aug. 1928). German composer. *See pp.281-9.*

Strauss, Richard (* Munich, 11 June 1864; † Garmisch, 8 Sept. 1949). German composer. *See Volume III.*

Stravinsky, Igor (* Oranienbaum, nr. St Petersburg, 17 June 1882; † New York, 6 Apr. 1971). Russian composer. *See pp.167-181.*

Suk, Josef (* Křečovice, 4 Jan. 1874; † Benešov, nr. Prague, 29 May 1935). Czech composer and violinist. Suk was a founder-member of the Bohemian, or Czech, String Quartet; during his studies at the Prague Conservatory

he also became an excellent pianist, and took lessons in composition with Dvořák. In 1922 Suk became professor of composition at the Conservatory. Outstanding among his first compositions is the lyrical, sensuous *Serenade*, op.6, for strings.

Moods of brooding introspectiveness returned with the deaths of Dvořák in 1904 and of Suk's wife Otilie (Dvořák's daughter) the following year. Suk's grief found expression in the Second Symphony (1906), and there followed masterpieces such as *A Summer's Tale* (a symphonic poem) and his tender piano pieces *O matince* (About Mother), written for his son in 1907.

With his Second String Quartet (1911) Suk developed a strikingly advanced style, notable for its involved polyphony. The triumph over his grief came with *Zrani* (The Ripening), a symphonic poem dating from 1917, on nature and life, again expressed in his most 'advanced' idiom. He also wrote incidental music, works for violin and choral compositions.

Szymanowski, Karol (* Tymoszówka, Ukraine, 6 Oct. 1882; † Lausanne, 29 Mar. 1937). Polish composer. Although not always accepted as such in his native country, Szymanowski considered himself a national composer. Early musical models were Chopin and Skriabin, followed by Wagner and Strauss; then, acquaintance with the music of Debussy and Ravel, and subsequently Stravinsky, transformed his approach to composition. At the age of thirty-nine the final ingredient was added – the folk music of Poland.

Szymanowski composed three symphonies, song-cycles, and much piano music, including studies, mazurkas and three sonatas. His violin music, often written for his friend Paul Kochanski, includes two concertos as well as several works for violin and piano, the best known being *La Fontaine d'Aréthuse*, the first of the three *Myths*, op.30. There are also two surviving operas and several choral works, notably the oratorio *Stabat Mater* (1929), in which Szymanowski simplified his usual colorful, Romantic style and individual harmonic idiom to great effect.

Tailleferre, Germaine (* Parc-St-Maur, nr. Paris, 19 Apr. 1892; † Paris, 6 Nov. 1983). French composer. Against her parents' wishes she entered the Paris Conservatoire (1904), where she met Auric, Honegger and Milhaud, who introduced her to Satie. When 'Les Six' emerged in 1920, she was one of the group. She experimented with polytonality, and serialism as late as 1958 with her Clarinet Sonata, but never forgot Fauré and Ravel, whose music she admired and with whom she studied orchestration.

Thomson, Virgil (* Kansas City, Missouri, 25 Nov. 1896). American composer and critic. He studied with Nadia Boulanger and worked as a conductor in the USA and in Europe. He held various teaching appointments in America and was a brilliant critic. His chief contribution as a composer has been to the development of American musical theater. His *Four Saints in Three Acts* (1928) is one of the most highly-regarded American operas, along with *The Mother of us All* (1947), both with libretti by Gertrude Stein. Other important works include ballets, the *Missa pro Defunctis*, and film scores, notably *The Plow that Broke the Plains* (1936), *The River* (1937) and *Louisiana Story* (1948). Orchestral compositions include two symphonies, three concertos, (for cello, flute, and harp respectively), while there is an extensive list of vocal, choral and instrumental music, much of this for the piano, including a notable series of musical portraits.

Tippett, Sir Michael (* London, 2 Jan. 1905). English composer. *See pp.256-261.*

Tournemire, Charles (* Bordeaux, 22 Jan. 1870; † Arcachon, 4 Nov. 1939). French organist and composer. After studies with d'Indy, Tournemire became organist at Sainte-Clotilde, Paris, where Franck, then Pierné, had previously held the post. He gave organ recitals throughout Europe and became a professor at the Conservatoire. His compositions include two operas, choral music, eight symphonies and shorter pieces of orchestral program-music, chamber music with piano, and organ music, including a treatise on the art of organ playing.

Tudor, David (* Philadelphia, 20 Jan. 1926). American pianist and composer. He studied organ, piano and composition, and was organist at St Mark, Philadelphia (1938-43) and Swarthmore College (1944-8). He was associated with Cage, Feldman, Brown and Wolff, performing their piano works, and he gave the first American performance of Boulez's Second Sonata in New York in 1950. He composes and performs his own live electronic music, often combined with a visual program.

Turina, Joaquín (* Seville, 9 Dec. 1882; † Madrid, 14 Jan. 1949). Spanish composer, conductor and teacher. He took piano lessons with Enrique Rodriguez and made his début as a pianist in 1897. Encouraged by his success, he went to Madrid, where he met Falla and studied piano at the Conservatory with Trago. In 1905 he moved to Paris, studying with Moszkowski and with d'Indy at the Schola Cantorum. In 1914 he returned to Madrid, having a distinguished career as composer, conductor at the Teatro Real and teacher; in 1930 he became professor of composition at Madrid Conservatory. His works reflect strongly the rhythms and melodies of Spanish, and specifically Andalusian, popular music. Piano music constitutes the greater part of his output, though there are several songs and a considerable amount of chamber music, as well as stage and orchestral works.

Ussachevsky, Vladimir (* Hailar, Manchuria, 21 Oct. 1911). American composer of Russian birth. He went to America in 1931 and graduated from Pomona College in 1935. After further study and academic appointments, he became professor of music at Columbia University. In 1951, unaware of the *musique concrète* group in Paris, he made the earliest American experiments in the electronic medium. In 1959, with Babbitt, Sessions and Otto Luening he founded the Columbia-Princeton Electronic Music Center in New York.

Varèse, Edgard (* Paris, 22 Dec. 1883; † New York, 6 Nov. 1965). French–American composer. *See pp. 279-284.*

Vaughan Williams, Ralph (* Down Ampney, Glos., 12 Oct. 1872; † London, 26 Aug. 1958). English composer. *See pp.120-9.*

Villa-Lobos, Heitor (* Rio de Janeiro, 5 Mar. 1887; † Rio de Janeiro, 17 Nov. 1959). Brazilian composer. The composer of more than 700 works, Villa-Lobos has long been regarded as Brazil's most important musical figure. As a young man he received little orthodox musical instruction, acquiring his expertise in composition as a performer on cello and guitar. His idiom stems from an intimate knowledge of Brazilian folk music,

to which he devoted much research and energy. An enthusiastic and energetic administrator and pedagogue, he became, after four years in Paris, director of Brazil's National Music Academy. In 1932 he was put in charge of the country's musical education program: an important part of his *oeuvre* consists of music, mainly piano music, for children. Central to his output are the dozen or so pieces he called 'choros,' for various instrumental combinations, for solo piano, or for voices and instruments. Brazilian percussion instruments appear frequently in his compositions, most of which have little in common with mainstream European music, although the nine *Bachianas brasileiras* derive inspiration from the music of Bach, re-created in a Brazilian idiom.

His works include five symphonies, many symphonic poems and smaller orchestral pieces, ballets, operas, a large quantity of chamber music (including seventeen string quartets) and vocal music.

Walton, Sir William (* Oldham, Lancs., 29 Mar. 1902; † Ischia, 8 May 1983). English composer. *See pp.251-6.*

Webern, Anton (* Vienna, 3 Dec. 1883; † Mittersill, 15 Sept. 1945). Austrian composer. *See pp.188-204.*

Weill, Kurt (* Dessau, 2 Mar. 1900; † New York, 3 Apr. 1950). German composer, American citizen from 1943. He grew up under the influence of German Romanticism, but three years' study with Busoni led him to bold musical experiments, refined his style and taught him the value of economical expression. Early works include the Concerto for violin and windband, which veers between jazz, popular music and neoclassicism. In 1927 he met the playwright Bertolt Brecht, and their collaboration led to a number of popular operas, including *Die Dreigroschenoper* (1928) and *Aufstieg und Fall der Stadt Mahagonny* (1930). Weill's operas combine dialogue with orchestral interludes and short, cabaret-style songs.

Fleeing from the Nazis in 1935, Weill settled in America, where he composed film music and musicals, producing a number of highly praised scores, such as *Street Scene*, before his sudden death.

Weinberger, Jaromír (* Prague, 8 Jan. 1896; † St Petersburg, Florida, 8 Aug. 1967). Czech–American composer. Studies in his native Prague were followed by lessons with Reger in Berlin. He achieved fame with his first opera, *Schwanda the Bagpiper* (1927), its use of Bohemian folk-tunes, colorfully orchestrated, contributing to its international popularity. In 1939 Weinberger settled in the USA, his main works written there being *Song of the High Seas*, *The Lincoln Symphony*, *Czech Rhapsody* and *The Bird's Opera*. Compositions for solo instruments include pieces for organ and a harpsichord sonata.

Wellesz, Egon (* Vienna, 21 Oct. 1885; † Oxford, 9 Nov. 1974). Austrian composer, musicologist and teacher. He was drawn into the orbit of the Second Viennese School, becoming a pupil of Schoenberg and his first biographer, and a close friend of Webern. He made special contributions to the study of baroque opera and Byzantine music and hymnography, and maintained an interest in the music of Debussy, Ravel and 'Les Six,' and Bartók. He formed a friendship with Hugo von Hofmannsthal, who provided the libretto for the opera *Alkestis* and the scenario for the ballet *Achilles auf Skyros*. Other operas are based on diverse subjects, from Goethe, Euripides, and Aztec mythology.

Wellesz wrote prolifically in a style which makes individual use of twelve-tone techniques. His orchestral music includes nine symphonies, composed between 1945 and 1971, and a Violin Concerto. In 1938 he moved to England, becoming a respected and influential teacher.

Williamson, Malcolm (* Sydney, 21 Nov. 1931). Australian composer, pianist and organist. He came to London in 1950 to continue his studies, primarily with Elizabeth Lutyens. He has composed prolifically in most musical forms and admits to considerable use of serialism, though his idiom is predominantly lyrical. He made an intensive study of Messiaen's music, learning the organ in order to play his works for the instrument, and the instrument continues to be an important factor in his work as a composer.
Concerned with communication through music, Williamson has written a number of pieces which involve audiences with performers as well as operas for children; more recently he has been engaged in experimental music therapy. His works include symphonies, concertos and quasi-ceremonial works, as well as chamber music, ballets and operas.

Wolf-Ferrari, Ermanno (* Venice, 12 Jan. 1876; † Venice, 21 Jan. 1948). Italian composer. The operas *Susanna's Secret*, *The Jewels of the Madonna* and *School for Fathers* are the works by which Wolf-Ferrari is remembered. He wrote eleven more operas, and his other works, notable for their neoclassical style, consist mainly of chamber music, such as the two piano trios, the two violin sonatas, and a piano quintet, as well as pieces for cello and for organ. There are also a 'Chamber' Symphony and a Violin Concerto.

Xenakis, Iannis (* Braila, 29 May, 1922). French composer of Greek parentage and Rumanian birth. He entered the Athens Polytechnic with the intention of becoming an engineer, but war broke out and Greece was invaded. Secretary to the Resistance groups in the Polytechnic, he lost the sight of one eye. He arrived in Paris in 1947 and took French nationality. There Xenakis met Honegger and Milhaud and received encouragement and advice from Messiaen and Scherchen. He also met the architect Le Corbusier, who, after asking him to undertake some engineering calculations, took him into closer collaboration in his architectural practice. Xenakis sees no cleavage between the theories of music and architecture; even those pieces most directly concerned with problems of sound are permeated by his obsession with space.

Variety and musical progress derive from violent contrasts in dynamics, pitch and note-lengths. His principal compositions include *Metastasis* (1953-4), for 61 instruments each playing a different part, which explores string sonorities, especially glissandi and tremolo; *Eonta* (1963-4), a concerto for piano and brass; and *Terretektorh* (1965-6) and *Nomos gamma* (1969), which attempt to break down the barriers between artists and audience. He also composed incidental music for Seneca's *Medea* (1967), scored for male voices and orchestral instruments using the extreme range of their registers, and *Le Polytope de Montréal*, a kind of audio-visual, *son-et-lumière* presentation for the 1967 Expo. More recent works include electronic scores, works for piano and for percussion, while some of the vocal or choral works, such as *Nekuïa* (1980), are more warmly lyrical than his earlier compositions.

Zemlinsky, Alexander von (* Vienna, 14 Oct. 1871; † Larchmont, N.Y., 15 Mar. 1942). Austrian composer and conductor. He studied at the Vienna Conservatory from 1887 to 1892. In 1893 he joined the Wiener Tonkünstlerverein, where he attracted the attention of Brahms, who recommended his Clarinet Trio, op.3, for publication. The following year he met Schoenberg (who married his sister), and together they founded a society for the promotion of new-music concerts in Vienna. He was active as a conductor of opera in Prague, where he premièred Schoenberg's *Erwartung*, and in Berlin, and as a teacher, before moving to the USA in 1938.

While Schoenberg moved on from the expanded tonality of the late Romantic idiom, developing his twelve-note theory of composition, Zemlinsky remained firmly rooted in the tradition of Brahms, Mahler and Strauss and in the music of Schoenberg's own early period. His works include orchestral and chamber music, songs, piano music, ballets and several operas, including the masterly *Der Kreidekreis* (1933).

Zimmermann, Bernd Alois (* Bliesheim, nr. Cologne, 20 Mar. 1918; † Gross-Königsdorf, nr. Cologne, 10 Aug. 1970). German composer. From 1958 until his death he taught composition at the Cologne Musikhochschule and directed the department of radio, film and stage music. His own music is highly personal and is basically atonal, with quotations from many varied sources often playing a vital role; it includes orchestral, vocal and instrumental works, latterly incorporating electronic sounds and jazz. His opera *Die Soldaten* (1958-60, revised 1963-4) is considered the most important from a German composer since Berg.

CUMULATIVE INDEX

Works are normally listed under composers; institutions are listed under place. Figures in **bold** type refer to principal discussion of a composer and his work; figures in *italics* refer to subjects or authors of illustrations.

PICTURE CREDITS

The producers and publishers wish to thank the following institutions, collectors and photographers who have made illustrations available: Acquavella Gallery, New York (52); Archives Théodore Stravinsky, Geneva – François Martin (172ab, 181b); Art Institute of Chicago (30a); Arts Council of Great Britain (98a, 99, 102, 103b, 123a); Ateneum, Helsinki Barber Institute of Fine Arts, The University of Birmingham (75a); Bibliothèque de l'Arsenal, Paris (170c); Bibliothèque de l'Opéra (3, 70bc, 74ab, 78b, 79a); Bibliothèque Nationale (9, 20ab, 22, 23a, 24ab, 25, 28, 29bc, 30bcd, 32abd, 33ef, 37b, 38a, 41bc, 43b, 44, 45b, 46a, 48bc, 51a, 56c, 57c, 58, 60, 61c, 63, 64ab, 65ab, 65b, 66, 68b, 72b, 73a, 5b, 76ab, 77ab, 93ab, 173ac, 184c, 224ab, 225, 227a, 241a, 306b, 308bd, 310c, 311c, 315a); British Library (11b, 135b, 143a); British Museum (57b, 61a, 69b, 87ab, 115b, 118b, 126a, 162cd, 163c); Busch-Reisinger Museum, Harvard University, Cambridge, Mass. (215, 298b); Cau Ferrat, Sitges (183d); City Art Gallery, Manchester (115a); The Cleveland Museum of Art, gift of Mrs Louise M. Dunn in memory of Henry G. Keller (239b); Dance Museum, Rolf de Maré collection, Stockholm (15b, 81a); Deutsches Theater Museum, Munich (220b); Editio Musica, Budapest (10b, 144, 145a, 147, 148, 149bc); Elgar Foundation (112, 113ab, 116ab, 117a, 118a); Embassy of Finland, London (96b, 104abc); Fischer Fine Art Ltd. (195, 202ab); Galerie der Stadt, Stuttgart (198a); Galleria Nazionale de Arte Moderna, Rome (182a); Harvard Theater Collection (170b); Helsinki University Library © Breitkopf & Härtel, Wiesbaden and Kalevalaseura, Helsinki (98c); Historisches Museum der Stadt Wien – courtesy the estate of Arnold Schoenberg (203); Paul Hindemith Institute, Frankfurt-am-Main (216ab, 219); Hungarian National Gallery, Budapest – Alfred Schiller/Corvina (146b); Jane Voorhees Zimmerli Art Museum, Rutgers State University, New Brunswick, N.J. (43a); Leeds City Art Gallery (123a); Library of Congress, Washington, D.C. (90ab); Moravské Museum v Brno (130, 133ab, 136b, 137, 140ab, 141b, 143b); Munch Museum, Oslo – Munchforlaget A/S (17b, 53a); Musée Carnavalet (31d); Musée d'Albi (31d); Musée de Pontoise (23b); Musée des Arts Décoratifs, Paris (26b, 67a); Musée des Beaux-Arts, Dijon (38b); Musée du Jeu de Paume (46b); Musée du Louvre (26a, 27); Musée Municipale, Saint-Germain-en-Laye (34, 37a); Musée Nationale d'Art Moderne, Centre Georges Pompidou, Paris (14a, 51c, 67b, 163d); Museu d'Art Modern, Barcelona (10a, 54bc); Museum of Modern Art, New York – collection Gian Carlo Menotti (176a); Museum Ludwig, Cologne (214); Národní muzeum v Praze – Theater section (135a, 138ab, 139abc, 141b, 142; National Film Archive, Stills Library, London (81b, 163e); National Portrait Gallery, London, (122b, 138); -- courtesy Mrs E. Ayrton (254a); New York Public Library (156b, 179b, 240b, 241b, 243b, 280a, 296b, 304b, 313d, 316a); Northwestern University Library, Special Collections Department, Evanston, Illinois (14b); Novello & Co. Ltd., (305d); Oesterreichische Nationalbibliothek – Musiksammlung (194bcd, 201b); Oeffentliche Kunstsammlung, Basel (11a); Opernhaus, Zürich – Covent Garden Archives, Royal Opera House (198b); Orfeó Català, Barcelona (54a, 55ce); Peters Edition Ltd., London, (304a); Philadelphia Museum of Art (278); Royal Ballet School, Richmond, Surrey – courtesy the Royal Ballet Benevolent Fund (254b); Royal College of Music (117b, 124, 125c, 184b, 304c, 306c, 308c, 310b, 311a); The St Louis Art Museum, Missouri (243a); Arnold Schoenberg Institute, University of Southern California, Los Angeles – courtesy the estate of Arnold Schoenberg (186, 189ac, 190ab, 192a, 196b, 200, 204ab, 205ab); Sibeliusmuseum, Turku (16, 96a, 97, 98b, 100a, 101); Society for Cultural Relations with the USSR, London (86ab, 226a, 231ab, 232b, 233); Staatsgalerie, Stuttgart (150); Städtische Galerie in Lenbachhaus, Munich, © Cosmopress, Geneva (191); Stravinsky–Diaghilev Foundation (169a, 170b, 172, 173b, 174b, 177a); Tate Gallery, London (114, 122a, 126b); University of Turku, donation from the painter 1924 (103a); Victoria and Albert Museum (259a); – Houston Rogers (257a); Wadsworth Atheneum, Hartford, Ct. (6, 62b, 174a, 175ab, 183ac); Walker Art Gallery, Liverpool (119); The Walters Art Gallery, Baltimore, Maryland (47a); Yale University Music Library, New Haven, Ct. (234, 236ab, 237ac); – courtesy Associated Music Publishers, New York (237b); courtesy Aivi and Pirkko Gallen-Kallela (94, 99, 103ab); courtesy the Britten Estate, Aldeburgh (260b); courtesy the trustees of Sir John Soane's Museum – Godfrey New Photographics Ltd (178b); © David Hockney 1975 – Petersburg Press (247b); courtesy James Seawright (298a, 299a); Casella collection, Rome (183b); Parmenia Migel Ekstrom collection, New York (47b, 53b, 68a, 170a, 176b, 177b); Sir Peter Pears collection (259); © John Piper (127); Marilyn McCully collection (55a); private collection (73b); private collection, Budapest – Attila Vécsy (206); private collections, New York (202a, 226b); private collection, Switzerland (171ab, 275); Mrs Ursula Vaughan Williams collection (17a, 120ab, 121, 123b, 125ab, 128ab, 129); Richard S. Zeisler collection, New York (166, 178a); Gerald S. Ackerman (243b); Agence de Presse Photographique Bernand (154b, 161, 199a, 274a, 289a, 294, 302, 303bc); Agence Explorer – Fiéret (153b); Agence Top (226, 270, 272a, 274b, 302a); Bryan and Cherry Alexander (153a); Arxiu MAS (10a, 54b); Atlantic Recording Corporation and Star/Rights Co. (291c); Erich Auerbach (149a, 157b, 159a, 180, 181a, 185b, 250, 253a, 255a, 262a, 264a, 265ab, 271a, 283, 303c, 307c, 308a, 309ab, 310ad, 317c); Australian Information Service – Neil Murray (152); BBC Hulton Picture Library (106); Clive Barda (242, 258a, 276a, 305ab, 307a, 312bc); © Reverend John Barnaby (125a); Bildarchiv Preussischer Kulturbesitz, Berlin (West) (82, 93c, 136a, 306d, 318c); Boosey & Hawkes Music Publishers Ltd., London (88a, 244ab, 245a, 260a, 306a, 309c, 315b); E. Boubat (266, 270, 272a, 281); © BBC (247a, 262b); W. J. Brunell (128a); CBS Records (282); J. P.Charbonnier (274b); J. W. Chester/Edition Wilhelm Hansen Ltd., London (56a, 314a); Jochen Clauss – Storypress (248b); Colorphoto Hinz (11a); Columbia–Princeton Electronic Music Center (297, 299b); A. C. Cooper (226a); Culver Pictures (135c); Mike Davis Studios Ltd. – Jesse Davis (163e); Dolmetsch Musical Instruments (184b); Zoë Dominic (185a, 248c, 249a, 253b, 257b); Alphonse Le Duc Editeur, Paris (269); Editions du Seuil, Paris (61b); Editions Salabert, Paris (163c); EMI Records Ltd (109, 293c); Mike Evans (258b); Ralph Fassey (155, 272c, 286b, 287, 288, 300b, 318b); Fred Fehl (241b); Bryan Ferry, Antony Price, Neil Kirk, Sally Feldman and Cream (291b); Fisa (55bd); Giraudon (170c), 218b); © Gloucester Journal (128a); © G. D. Hackett, New York (100b, 132b, 141a, 145b, 156a, 157a, 184a, 192c, 199b, 208ab, 209ab, 211b, 212, 213abc, 239a, 245b, 301, 313c); Hans Hammarskjöld – Tiofoto, Stockholm (103c, 249b); Harlingue-Viollet 32c, 33c); Olga Hilmerová (135a, 138ab, 139abc); Hopecraft Photographers (110); Illustration/Sygma (21b); © Interfoto MTI, Budapest (146a); Istituto Geografico de Agostini, Milan (142); IRCAM – J. P. Armand (277); – Gérard Lyon (276b); – Serge Korniloff (300c); Max Jones (162ab, 163ab, 164acdef, 165abcdf); (Jarmo Koskinen (103a); Lauros-Giraudon (18, 23b, 26a, 27, 31d, 46b); Siegfried Lauterwasser, Überlingen, Bodensee (246ab); Lebanese Tourist Office, London (154a); Jean-Pierre Leloir (159b, 160b, 273, 300a, 313a); Serge Lido (280b); Roland Liot (37a); Malvisi Archive (73b); © Angus McBean (129); MC Productions and The Apple (290b); Colette Masson, Paris (246c); F. A. Mella (182a, 183b, 289b, 296c); André Meyer collection, Paris – Ziolo (29a, 31ac); Gjon Mili – Time Inc. (179a); Lee Miller (240b); Sheila More, Paris (138); J. F. Munro (305c); National Film Archive, Stills Library (228c, 252b, 255b, 261b); Novosti Press Agency, London (62a, 84c, 85, 88b, 89ab, 169b, 222, 229, 232ac); Lennart Olson – Tiofoto (285e); Otava Publishing, Helsinki (94); C. R. Peters Corporation (296b); Philips Photo Department, Eindhoven (284, 285ab); Rainsville Archive (8ab, 15a, 33d, 37c, 40, 41a, 42, 45ac, 50, 51b, 56bd, 65a, 69a, 70a, 71, 78a, 79b, 80b, 84ab, 90ab, 91, 132a, 194a, 227b, 230, 249cd, 307b, 314d); David Redfern (158ab, 292c); David Redfern Photography – David Ellis (290cd); – Max Redfern (291d); – Andrew Putler (291a); Rex Features Ltd. (290a, 292ab, 293b); L. Rousseau (303a); Editions Salabert, Paris, (316c); Scala (39, 182b); G. Schirmer Music Publishers, London (240a); B. Schott's Söhne, Mainz (217a, 220a, 252a, 312d, 314b); – Carl Bauer (218a);– Rudolf Betz (220b); – Eduard Renner (221); – Hanne Zapp (217b); Service de la Recherche de l'O.R.T.F. – Michel Lioret (296a); Siemens A.G., Karlsruhe (286a); Sotheby's, London (240c, 257b); Spectrum Colour Library (247c, 292d); Ullstein Bilderdienst (248a); Universal Edition A.G., Vienna (188, 189b, 193, 196a, 197, 201a); Universal Edition (London) Ltd. (160a, 305c, 313b, 314c, 317ab, 318a); VAAP, Moscow (228b); Roger-Viollet (12abc, 13, 33a, 36, 57a, 72a, 80a, 182c, 192b, 224b, 228a, 311b, 312a, 316b); Virgin Records Ltd. (293a); Weidenfeld Publishers Ltd (224c); Mark Westwood (292b); Reg Wilson (246d); Madeline Winkler-Betzendahl, Stuttgart (271b); Derrick Witty (259a); Worcester City Council (110); courtesy the Herbert Press Ltd. and Hamish Hamilton Ltd. (259ab, 261a, 263).